Music in the
20th CENTURY

MUSIC IN THE
20th CENTURY

from Debussy
through Stravinsky

———— ◆ ————

WILLIAM W. AUSTIN
PROFESSOR OF MUSIC, CORNELL UNIVERSITY

———— ◆ ————

LONDON: J. M. DENT & SONS LTD.

PRINTED IN THE UNITED STATES OF AMERICA

for

J. M. DENT & SONS LTD.

Aldine House · Bedford Street · London
First Published in the United States of America, 1966
First published in Great Britain, 1966

for

DONALD JAY GROUT

Unknown realms have opened up to the art of music: it has not yet by any means traversed them; at first it lingered on the edge, trembling with emotion at the sight of these unexplored treasures. In more recent years, it has taken a few steps further and discovered horizons still more luminous. . . .

The higher forms of art, like those of science and of all thought, are a privilege. This privilege will never be abolished: it is becoming more exclusive. But it is no question of birth or money. Even those who are born poor may acquire it by virtue of their intelligence, and they may be consoled by it. In all groups of society, in all countries, beyond all borders and beyond the seas, the purest music of today recruits unknown friends. In this sense, the only true sense, music may be called universal. And this power is more surely than ever guaranteed to music by its recent progress.

Louis Laloy,
Debussy (1909)

Contents

"THE ART OF MUSIC . . . HAS TAKEN A FEW STEPS FURTHER"

"IN THIS SENSE . . . UNIVERSAL"

List of Plates

Preface

ANYONE INTERESTED in the music of Schoenberg, Bartók, and
Stravinsky can use this book. The achievements of these three composers, together with the collective achievements of jazz, form the
center of our subject. Around this center, our horizons extend to the 20th-
century work of Debussy and his contemporaries all over the world, and
to the young and middle-aged composers whose fame is growing in the
1960s. Readers who would prefer to subordinate our central concerns to
something near one or another horizon will readily agree to disagree with
each other at least as much as they disagree with the present author. On
the contrary, most readers who are prepared to focus attention on Schoenberg *or* Bartók *or* Stravinsky will share some interest in all the three composers, and may be pleased to partake in a growing consensus affirming their
importance. Some, to be sure, might like to add a fourth or fifth name to
the three. But again, they will recognize that each additional name would
repel from the consensus more participants than it would attract. Likewise,
to place at the center, with Schoenberg, Bartók, and Stravinsky, not another individual but another style—jazz—risks repelling some. But there
is room to hope that this recognition of jazz may rather make evident an
extended and strengthened consensus. If most readers interested in Schoenberg, Bartók, and Stravinsky are only slightly interested in jazz, they may
still be supposed willing to entertain the possibility that some jazz deserves
their continuing study too, or at least to indulge the author's hope even if
his evidence leaves them unconverted. And if his hope is realized, they will
sooner or later agree that jazz belongs at the center, that Armstrong, Ellington, Parker, and the rest together deserve the kind of attention given to each
of the greatest three composers individually.

Intelligent study of any music, as many jazz fans demonstrate better than
many devotees of Beethoven's symphonies do, balances the accumulation of
facts and interpretations with continuous practice in making music, and
continuous, repeated, attentive, discriminating listening. Because of this,
some admirers of Beethoven who look for a book to help them understand
20th-century music look in vain. A book cannot possibly provide the desir-

able balance. But whoever is genuinely interested in Schoenberg, Bartók, or Stravinsky must have begun to provide it for himself, and must be able to provide it further, to the extent that time permits. A book can save time if we use it to guide our practical study and listening.

No one finds time enough to come as close to Beethoven or to Stravinsky as he comes to his wife or child. Amateur concert-goers and record collectors, cultivating music only on the margin of their main responsibilities, may take comfort in considering the limitations of every sort of professional musician. A musicologist specializing in Stravinsky may come closer to him than the musicologist working on a perspective view of Stravinsky's era, but the perspective view of Bartók may enlarge and deepen or perhaps upset the Stravinsky man's ideas. A pianist or singer or conductor comes closer to his own repertory than a mere listener, but he envies the listener's freedom to explore a wider range. A student composer comes close to the masters in a special way. And a good teacher is the best student: he needs to be. The interests of all these specialists need not conflict with each other, nor need they constitute any barrier to intelligent amateurs.

The kind of study that can be guided by this book is motivated by an interest more urgent and more persistent than merely tolerating or enjoying some of the music of Bartók when it happens to turn up, something more than playing a piece of Schoenberg with competence and with pride in the idea of contemporaneity, something more than recognizing the several styles of Stravinsky in their historical order and context and speaking about them with glib reverence or irreverence. Real interest, like thirst or hunger, means seeking out the music, in notation or recorded performance or both, so as to return to it over a period of years, to discriminate with delicacy among different performances, to accumulate a repertory of an important and congenial composer's main works in various forms and media, and to relate each new experience to a gradually growing and deepening sense of the work as a whole.

How rare is this kind of thirst for music? How much rarer for Schoenberg than for Bach or Mozart or Beethoven or Tchaikovsky? No one knows. Most of us who share such a thirst for Bach wish it were more widely shared than it seems to be in fact. We are apt to speak as though everyone concerned with music at all either shares our kind of interest or at least recognizes its value. But in fact most performers, amateur and professional, do not. Most subscribers to opera and concert series surely do not. Only a tiny fraction of these groups that supported the musical life of the 19th century and still support its continuation in the 20th have shown the kind of interest that Schoenberg, Bartók, Stravinsky, and good jazz need. No wonder, then, that Schoenberg makes slow progress toward repertory status. But in the middle of the 20th century, on the contrary, a good many record collectors do share our kind of interest and gratify it to some extent. Their number is growing all over the world, and there is no limit in sight to their potential development in numbers, in diversity, in contemporaneity, and in depth of understanding. Likewise among professional musicians, whose total number in proportion to the number of listeners continually declines, there may be a growing proportion who share our interest, for the conditions of 20th-century musical life demand that musicians be connoisseurs, not servile producers of a staple commodity. However rare and personal the connoisseur's thirst may be, we share it widely enough to warrant coordinating our efforts to satisfy it.

With respect to Debussy, some readers may be surprised at his prominence on our horizon, and at the emphasis given here to his influence on Schoenberg, Bartók, Stravinsky, and many younger composers, for in some ways they seem more remote from Debussy than from Bach or Beethoven. But more informed readers will share the author's confidence that knowledge won in recent years will suffice to extend and strengthen the consensus in the direction of Debussy. From Debussy's own point of view, as we shall observe, the deep interest of a few listeners is more important than acceptance in the public repertory.

In the opposite direction, toward the composers coming into international prominence after the middle of the century, there is of course no one figure corresponding to Debussy. Many readers doubtless share the author's urgent concern for the music of John Cage, Benjamin Britten, Milton Babbitt, Pierre Boulez, Hans Werner Henze, and a dozen more composers now middle-aged, not to name here any really young composer. They should note in advance that this book offers guidance to their work only indirectly. It mentions some of them frequently in connection with older composers. It includes an evaluation of many books and articles about them in the annotated bibliography. But a limit has been set, not quite arbitrarily, at the year 1910: the styles of composers born in 1910 or later are not discussed at length in the text, with the exception of Charlie Parker, who died in 1955. For it is characteristic of our time that most serious composers in their forties and fifties, however famous and influential, are not yet so accessible to a scholarly survey as some earlier generations were at a corresponding age. Further, the evidence of the preceding generation indicates that we are probably overlooking two or three middle-aged composers who will prove to be as important as those now famous, and that we shall soon wish to reinterpret the achievements of several in the light of their works not yet written. We need more and better criticism of Cage, Britten, and the rest—daring, fresh responses as well as cautious, patient scrutiny. This book includes such men only as representatives of continuing lines of stylistic development, or as especially perceptive commentators on the works of their elders.

What is most pertinent here is the fact that our various judgments of Cage, Britten, Babbitt, and Boulez depend very much on our knowledge and understanding of Schoenberg, Bartók, and Stravinsky. When we disagree about the newest music, we are likely to find great difficulty in even understanding each other's arguments, because some of us take for granted what others ignore, and too often we refer by the same label to quite different ranges of experience. As we come to share a long experience of the music of Schoenberg, Bartók, and Stravinsky, in relation to our shared experience of Bach, Mozart, and Debussy, and as we clarify our ways of discussing this experience, we shall be ready to argue more effectively about their successors. We need not expect to agree. But we may hope to avoid talking at cross-purposes when we can appeal to common understanding.

If our interest leads us particularly toward Boulez, Jean Barraqué, Karlheinz Stockhausen, Luciano Berio, Mel Powell, and other "post-Webernites," then of course we need some common understanding of the work of Anton Webern, pupil of Schoenberg, contemporary of Bartók and Stravinsky, whose influence began to spread only after World War II. To contribute to this particular common understanding is one of the principal tasks that a historian today can undertake.

Webern rose to fame as Paul Hindemith stepped down. Hindemith had often in the 1930s and '40s been ranked with Schoenberg, Bartók, and Stravinsky as one of the central, indispensable composers. In some quarters today he is dismissed abruptly. Our perspective view permits us to study both Webern and Hindemith with sympathy, and to anticipate a continuing fluctuation between the attitudes they represent. The claim of Boulez that Webern is "the only threshold" remains to be proved, while on the contrary it is not far-fetched to see some resemblances between Boulez and Hindemith. Without a fair consideration and criticism of Hindemith's whole career, we are in danger of further confusing our arguments when we refer hastily to one or another aspect of it. Hindemith's work, moreover, is too good and too extensive to permit his name to sink into oblivion, no matter how severely some of us may criticize his mistakes or reject the attitude he represents.

Along with Hindemith and Webern, a third representative figure is proposed in this book: Sergei Prokofiev. The grounds for emphasizing Prokofiev are different from those in the cases of Hindemith and Webern, but no less firm. Prokofiev's music is unquestionably known and loved by more musicians than Hindemith's or Webern's—by musicians, not to speak of listeners. Moreover, some of Prokofiev is probably better known than Hindemith's or Webern's music even to the young composers whose attitudes and aims are closer to the latter's. Yet the richness and strength of

Prokofiev are seldom acknowledged and more seldom fully explored except by partisans antagonistic to Webern. To present a balanced treatment of Prokofiev in the perspective of his greatest contemporaries is a novel undertaking, another of the most interesting tasks for a historian today.

Between the generation of Hindemith and Prokofiev and the generation of Cage and Britten, no two or three composers have yet stood forth among the dozens of interesting ones, to win international recognition and respect comparable to that of their elders. It is possible, to be sure, to identify five leading composers now about sixty years old, who constitute a representative group corresponding in some ways to the representative three, Webern, Hindemith, and Prokofiev: this group comprises Dallapiccola, Shostakovich, Messiaen, Carter, and Fortner. To consider each of them at some length, in relation to their predecessors and their pupils, is yet another novel and important task for a historian. Yet in the historian's perspective these five cannot claim so much attention as their elders do, nor do they fundamentally affect the pattern seen in the work of these elders.

It is not possible to do justice to Cage or Stockhausen within the framework provided by Webern, Hindemith, and Prokofiev. If their work is as important as their admirers believe—whether to the art of music or rather to new ways of living—then they will require each a new chapter, or, better, a new book.

If Britten's work is as important as *his* admirers believe, then Cage and Stockhausen are at best marginal ephemera, and furthermore Webern, Hindemith, and Prokofiev may all be skipped over, to proceed directly from Schoenberg, Bartók, and Stravinsky to Britten. The present writer is deliciously tormented by a vacillating judgment of this question. Every new work of Britten's is exciting, partly because this question stays alive.

Brief and cautious treatment of the composers as mature as Cage and Britten does not mean that the book is written from the point of view of, say, 1950. So far as possible for a single author, our survey incorporates studies of the most recently available works of Stravinsky and of other composers born between 1860 and 1910 and the most recent results of artistic performance and scholarship. It assembles for the first time the findings of many specialists on the major figures discussed and offers, by comparison with other comprehensive books of reference, surprising facts and ideas about a host of other good composers, including Fauré, Janáček, Elgar, Mahler, Strauss, Sibelius, Busoni, Satie, Koechlin, Roussel, Scriabin, Vaughan Williams, Reger, Rachmaninov, Ives, Falla, Bloch, Malipiero, Kodály, Casella, Griffes, Berg, Varèse, Villa-Lobos, Martin, Honegger, Milhaud, Pijper, Piston, Orff, Thomson, Sessions, Cowell, Gershwin, Poulenc, Weill, Copland, Pepping, Blacher, Finzi, Distler, and Alain. On all these composers, the author's views have been modified within the past decade by the discoveries and interpretations of specialists, both scholars and performers, together with his own continuing practice at the piano.

The knowledge assembled here is not definitive. Further discoveries and reinterpretations may be expected to modify continually what we know about the past, however recent or remote. Indeed, one of the chief values of assembling our knowledge concerning a subject such as ours is to stimulate further special research and criticism. Even at the center of our subject our ignorance is glaring on some questions of fact, and on questions of opinion our disputes boil up continually. This book presents such questions openly, and even emphasizes some of them, citing arguments of opposed positions in the hope of provoking better answers. Moreover, the author's own judgments are interwoven with the presentation of fact and accepted opinion, in the confidence that readers can make the distinction for themselves and recall, when need be, the author's disclaimer of omniscience.

If this book proves fit to serve as a handbook—that is, a fair summary of scholarly knowledge of the subject and a guide to the literature, comparable to the books of Gustave Reese and Manfred Bukofzer in the Norton series— it will not completely supersede earlier attempts to satisfy the same need. The volume on *Moderne Musik* by Hans Mersmann, in Bücken's great handbook of musicology (1927), remains valuable in many ways; the more time passes the more amazing are Mersmann's prompt perceptiveness, inclusiveness, and balance. The present work, if it dared to rival Mersmann, would have to do for some genius younger than Henze what Mersmann did for Hindemith, in the handbook and elsewhere. All of Mersmann's writings are irreplaceable documents and delights; the handbook is a model as well. For the benefit not only of this model, but also of wonderful conversations and correspondence, and of his reading of my chapter on Hindemith, I am greatly indebted to Professor Mersmann. Among the many later German surveys, that by Karl Wörner (1954) is outstanding for its comprehensiveness, accuracy, and documentation, though compared with Mersmann it is more concise and less penetrating; I have used it continually and I look forward to new editions of it. The volume by Paul Collaer (1955, 2nd ed. 1958, English transl. 1961) complements Wörner's with its emphasis on France, its first-hand but judicious evaluations, and its humane perspective, while coming closer than most other authors to Wörner's professional standards of scholarship. To M. Collaer I am grateful not only for this beautiful book, but also for specific help on Satie and Milhaud, and again for conversations that contributed indirectly to the development of my understanding and judgment. Though my book includes much that is omitted by Mersmann, Wörner, and Collaer, my ability to make use of new material depends to a considerable extent on them—far more than is evident from my particular references to them. And as I have benefited by comparing them with each other, I recommend that my readers compare me with one or two of them.

It is a pleasure to acknowledge the generous help of many friends and colleagues who like Professor Mersmann and M. Collaer have discussed my work and have read parts of this book in manuscript. My teacher Walter Piston at Harvard, who long ago showed me how to analyze scores in his classes, helped me in the early stages of planning and read several of the first chapters. My colleagues at Cornell, D. J. Grout, John Kirkpatrick, Robert Palmer, Karel Husa, and Harold Samuel, have all contributed richly. Professor Robert A. Hall, Jr., has given me the benefit of his knowledge of English music. Professor Arthur Mendel, Princeton University, checked and improved the chapter on Hindemith. Mr. Malcolm Brown, Indiana University, and M. Pierre Souvtchinsky, Paris, gave invaluable advice on Prokofiev. Mr. Hans Moldenhauer, University of Washington, and Professor H. H. Eggebrecht, University of Freiburg im Breisgau, helped to refine my ideas on Webern. Professor R. S. Beckwith, University of Buffalo, suggested improvements of style and substance throughout most of the book. Professor P. H. Lang, Columbia University, and Mr. Nathan Broder have read drafts of the whole book and contributed many extremely helpful suggestions. Mr. David Hamilton guided my last revisions, helping especially to organize the notes and bibliography. For the index I had the enthusiastic help of my family, Elizabeth, Ann, and Margery Austin. The shortcomings that remain in spite of all this help are my own.

A fellowship from the Guggenheim Foundation and lesser grants from the Faculty Research Committee at Cornell have been indispensable aids to my work.

Acknowledgments

Permission to reprint text or music examples is gratefully acknowledged, as follows:

Béla Bartók, *Allegro barbaro,* © 1918 by Universal Edition, renewed 1956. Copyright and renewal assigned to Boosey and Hawkes Inc. for the U. S. A. only. Reprinted by permission. *Dirge No. 2,* © copyright MCMXLV by Music Corporation of America (Leeds Division), 322 West 48th Street, New York 36, N. Y. Used by permission. All rights reserved. First String Quartet, reprinted by permission of Boosey and Hawkes Inc., sole agents for "Kultura" (Hungarian Trading Company) for the U. S. A. *Improvisation,* Op. 20, No. 7, © 1922 by Universal Edition; renewed 1949. Copyright and renewal assigned to Boosey and Hawkes Inc. Reprinted by permission. Sixth String Quartet, © 1941 by Hawkes & Son (London), Ltd. Reprinted by permission of Boosey and Hawkes Inc. Tune 41, from *Music for Children,* © 1946 by Boosey and Hawkes Inc. Reprinted by permission.

Claude Debussy, *Ballade de Villon à s'amye,* permission for reprint granted by Durand et Cie., owners; Elkan-Vogel Company, Philadelphia, agents. *Prelude to the Afternoon of a Faun; Syrinx,* permission for reprint granted by Editions Jean Jobert, Paris, copyright owner, and Elkan-Vogel, Inc., Philadelphia, Pa., agents.

Gabriel Fauré, *Chanson,* Op. 94, reproduction authorized by Heugel et Cie., Paris, publishers and copyright owners of *La Chanson,* Opus 94, music by Gabriel Fauré, poem by Henri de Regnier.

Paul Hindemith, Madrigal, *Strength Fathers Form,* copyright 1958 by Schott & Co., Ltd., London; quoted by permission of the copyright owner and Associated Music Publishers, Inc., New York. *A Composer's World,* reprinted by permission of the publishers from Paul Hindemith, *A Composer's World,* Cambridge, Mass.: Harvard University Press, copyright, 1952, by the President and Fellows of Harvard College.

Leoš Janáček, *They Chattered like Swallows,* © 1925 by Hudebni Matice, Praha. Copyright renewed 1953. Reprinted by permission of Boosey and Hawkes Inc., agents.

Olivier Messiaen, *Les Corps glorieux,* by permission of Alphonse Leduc & Co., 175 rue Saint-Honoré, Paris Ier, owners and publishers; copyright 1942.

Ferdinand Morton, *Jelly Roll Blues,* copyright 1915 Melrose Music Corp. Copyright renewed and assigned to Melrose Music Corp. Used by permission of the publisher.

Maurice Ravel, *Pavane de la belle au bois dormant,* permission for reprint granted by Durand et Cie., Paris, copyright owner, and Elkan-Vogel Co., Inc., Philadelphia, agents.

Erik Satie, *Morceaux en forme de poire,* © 1911 by Rouart LeRolle & Cie. By permission of Editions Salabert, Paris. All rights reserved.

Arnold Schoenberg, *Mima'amaḳim*, Op. 50b, © copyright MCMLIII by Israeli Music Publications Limited, Tel Aviv. Used by permission. *Little Piano Piece*, Op. 19, No. 6; *The Sick Moon,* from *Pierrot Lunaire;* Suite, Op. 25, reprinted by permission of Mrs. Arnold Schoenberg. *Orchestra Piece*, Op. 16, No. 2, reprinted with permission of C. F. Peters, 373 Park Avenue South, New York, N. Y. 10016.

Jean Sibelius, *Mélisande*, with permission of the original publisher, Robert Lienau, Berlin-Lichterfelde.

Igor Stravinsky, Arrangement of *Song of the Volga Boatmen*, reprinted by permission of J. & W. Chester, Ltd., copyright owner. *Fisherman's Song*, from *The Nightingale*, © 1961 by Boosey and Hawkes Inc. Reprinted by permission. Lullaby from *The Rake's Progress*, © 1949, 1950, 1951 by Boosey and Hawkes Inc. Used by permission. *Poetics of Music*, reprinted by permission of the publishers from Igor Stravinsky, *Poetics of Music*, Cambridge, Mass.: Harvard University Press, copyright, 1947, by the President and Fellows of Harvard College. *The Rite of Spring*, © 1921 by Edition Russe de Musique. Copyright assigned to Boosey and Hawkes Inc., 1947. Reprinted by permission. *A Sermon, a Narrative, and a Prayer*, © 1961 by Boosey & Company Ltd. Reprinted by permission of Boosey and Hawkes Inc. *Symphonies of Winds*, © 1926 by Edition Russe de Musique. Copyright assigned to Boosey and Hawkes Inc. Revised version © 1952 by Boosey and Hawkes Inc. Reprinted by permission. Symphony in Three Movements, copyright 1946 by Schott & Co., Ltd., London. Quoted by permission of the copyright owner and Associated Music Publishers, Inc., New York.

Edgard Varèse, *Déserts,* copyright 1959 by G. Ricordi & Co., New York. All rights reserved.

Anton Webern, Orchestration of Ricercar from Bach *Musical Offering,* copyright 1935, renewed 1963 by Universal Edition A.G., Vienna. Used by permission. Piece for Orchestra, Op. 10, No. 4, copyright 1923, renewed 1951 by Universal Edition A.G., Vienna. Used by permission. Symphony, Op. 21, copyright 1929, renewed 1956 by Universal Edition A.G., Vienna. Used by permission.

———————————◆◆———————————

The kind assistance of the following in obtaining pictorial illustrations is acknowledged with thanks: Dr. Percy M. Young, for the photograph of Elgar with his father; Mrs. John Sloan, for her husband's portrait of Varèse; Durand et Cie. for the title page of Debussy's *Children's Corner* (permission for reproduction granted by Durand et Cie., Paris, copyright owners; Elkan-Vogel Co., Inc., Philadelphia, agents); and J. M. Dent & Sons Ltd., for the photograph of Nielsen, from their publication, *Carl Nielsen: Symphonist,* by Robert Simpson.

Music in the

20th CENTURY

CHAPTER I

The Adventure and Achievement
of Debussy
(1862-1918)

OF ALL the musicians who ever lived, Claude Debussy was one of the most original and most adventurous; at the same time, un- like many original adventurers, he was a consummate master within the limits of his exquisite style. For every sort of voice and instrument he made music that diverged radically from the common practice of his predecessors—Bach to Brahms, or Rameau to Rimsky-Korsakov—and his music won a permanent place in the repertory of every kind of performer and performing group. His achievement is unique.

The seductive influence of Debussy's style spread quickly throughout the Western world. It freed his compatriots in France from their obsession with Beethoven and Wagner, and enabled France to replace Germany and Austria, at least temporarily, as the center of attraction for musicians in England, America, Russia, and the other distant regions of our civilization. Whole generations of Spanish musicians thanked Debussy for showing them the way to their own music. Austria and Germany accepted Debussy as they had accepted only Chopin of all foreign composers in the 19th century. Even in Italy, the perennial center of song, Debussy's lure was stronger than that of any foreign composer since Italians like Palestrina and Marenzio had mastered the secrets of the Netherlanders, Josquin, Willaert, and Rore.

Debussy's influence spread not only geographically, but also socially, into nearly every kind of music making: into church and school and ballroom as well as theater and concert hall and home. Not that his own compositions were much used in all these places, but rather that his ways of thinking, in melodies and chords and tone colors, were contagious. Without necessarily

I

knowing the name of Debussy or the sound even of his *Clair de lune*, everyone who grows up hearing and making music in the Western world in the 20th century learns to imagine, dimly or vividly, sounds and sequences of sounds like those that Debussy imagined for the first time.

Debussy's music may prove to be the last to exercise such a thoroughly pervasive influence. In the first half of the 20th century nothing matched it, though there was no lack of bold adventure and impressive achievement. The change that Debussy set in motion throughout his musical culture may be the last that can occur throughout it, for this change was part of the culture's disintegration. Perhaps it was also part of the slow preparation for the worldwide culture or sharing of cultures that we can only hope for, not yet foresee.

Debussy opened up the music of Western Europe to the music of the rest of the world. He absorbed a profound influence from the Indonesian gamelan and occasionally he made use of Afro-American ragtime. What he learned from these exotic musics helped him to loosen European conventions, and to promote a further free give-and-take, not only of influence but of values, among people sensitive to music all over the world.

He established no new conventions. He founded no school. He disowned the Debussystes, and declined to prophesy the future of music. His work, in spite of its vast influence, is modest, slender, and personal. It cannot rank with that of Bach or Mozart or Wagner in quantity or scope. Debussy's mastery was no easy fluency, although his friends knew him as a marvelous improviser. Because he was both so bold in his undertakings and so fastidious in his finishings, he abandoned more projects than he achieved. When his life was cut short at fifty-six (1918) he left undone all but one of the many operas he had dreamed of. His one completed opera, the setting of Maeterlinck's play *Pelléas et Mélisande*, can give a misleading notion of his whole adventure and achievement unless it is considered along with a fair selection of the various smaller works both earlier and later. Indeed, some consideration of the abandoned projects as well is desirable to establish a true understanding of his character and style, and thus of his enormous significance in the music of the 20th century.

The first performance of *Pelléas* (1902) marked the beginning of Debussy's vast influence. The success of *Pelléas* furthered the dissemination of his earlier masterpieces, *The Afternoon of a Faun* (1892–94) and the *Nocturnes* (1890) for orchestra, the string quartet (1893), the songs on poems by Bourget, Banville, Baudelaire, Verlaine, Louÿs, and Debussy himself, and such piano pieces as *Clair de lune* (1890). This list was enough to establish him as a major composer, and to arouse expectations of a life work on a grand scale.

The expectations were not fulfilled, and what Debussy did in the 20th century had to wait for half the century to pass before many people could appreciate more than a few marvelous piano pieces such as six or eight of the twenty-four preludes. The 20th-century works were all by-products of abandoned large projects.

———•—•———

From 1902 to 1907 Debussy's chief project was an opera based on Edgar Allan Poe's grotesque satire *The Devil in the Belfry*, which he knew in the translation by Baudelaire. Debussy planned for the devil to whistle rather than sing; he planned a chorus composed of many interwoven parts for the individual burghers, vrouwen, and urchins. From about 1890 onward he had been obsessed with another Poe story, the symbolic, introspective, "arabesque" tale of horror *The Fall of the House of Usher*. He worked on this almost steadily from 1908 to 1910, and again for some months in 1912. In the fall of 1916 he completed the libretto and sent it to his publisher, and then abandoned his musical sketches. At various times he mentioned several other interesting large projects to correspondents and interviewers: a version of *Tristan* based on that of Bédier, a *Romeo and Juliet, As You Like It, Orpheus, Amphion, Dionysos, No-ya-ti* or the *Palace of Silence*, and a musically continuous, coherent *St. Sebastian*. But these were vague dreams, whereas the two Poe tales absorbed an immense amount of Debussy's energy. In 1909 he wrote to his friend and principal publisher Jacques Durand: "I have got into the way of thinking of nothing else but *Roderick Usher* and *The Devil in the Belfry*. . . . I fall asleep with them, and I awake either to the gloomy sadness of the former or the sneers of the latter." The manager of the Metropolitan Opera in New York, Giulio Gatti-Casazza, paid to secure the first performances of the Poe operas, even though Debussy protested that he could not promise them for any date whatever. In 1925 Gatti-Casazza recalled conversations dating from 1908 onward, in which Debussy had told him: "Edgar Poe possessed the most original fantasy among the literatures of all lands: he found a note absolutely new and different. . . . [But] I must tell you that what increases in me is not geniality but uncertainty and laziness." Debussy's self-reproach of laziness, taken somewhat seriously by his biographer Léon Vallas and others, is belied by the perfection and originality of nearly all his finished work—that of his last years as well as that of the 1890s—and even by the amount of it, when we regard everything but *Pelléas* as a by-product. He was never really lazy. He was always uncertain. He could work fast: he transferred *Pelléas* from vocal score to full orchestral score in one month, just before rehearsals began. He composed the extensive music for d'Annunzio's *St. Sebastian* in about four months, 1911. But he was habitually hesitant, slow to make his choices. He had worked a whole decade composing and revising *Pelléas,* playing and singing it for his friends, and complaining about his difficulties. Before *Pelléas* he had abandoned other large projects. A comedy by Théodore de Banville, *Diane au bois,* was his first large independent effort. He said of it in 1886: "I have, perhaps, undertaken a work beyond my capacity. Since no precedent exists, I find that I am obliged to invent new forms." A year later he temporarily gave up *Diane,* and produced some less ambitious pieces to satisfy the requirements of his Rome prize. In 1891–92, with *Diane* still in abeyance, his chief concern was *Rodrigue et Chimène,* a libretto prepared especially for him by Catulle Mendès. But when he discovered Maeterlinck's *Pelléas,* he cheerfully abandoned the hundred pages of vocal score that he had written for *Rodrigue.* Finally, and most interesting of all, the *Prelude to The Afternoon of a Faun,* his most famous piece, was rescued from an abandoned project of a dramatic realization of Mallarmé's famous poem, which had replaced the similar project of *Diane.* Thus Debussy's failure to finish his most ambitious 20th-century projects was no lapse or exhaustion of his genius. Rather, both early and late he consistently failed to achieve the large forms that would faithfully embody the boldest adventures of his imagination.

The successful achievement of *Pelléas* was as much an obstacle as a helpful precedent for the later projects. This is emphasized in a whole series of intimate letters. To André Messager in 1903 Debussy wrote:

It is too soon to say I am done with the *Devil.* The scenario is nearly finished; I have almost decided on the coloring of the music, but I still have many a sleepless night ahead. . . . As for those people who hope piously that I can never escape from *Pelléas,* they are quite mistaken. They must realize that if this were the case I should turn at once to growing pineapples, for I think it is altogether disastrous to repeat oneself.

A little later he reported to Messager that he was working, "but not as I should like—perhaps I was over-eager, or perhaps I was aiming too high. . . . The Claude Debussy who worked so joyfully at *Pelléas,* . . . I have not been able to recapture." In 1911 he gave Caplet a vivid account of his frustration: "Music no longer consoles me much.—I am not getting to the end of the two little dramas of Poe. For every measure that goes fairly freely, there are twenty that stifle under the weight of a single tradition whose lazy, hypocritical influence I detect in spite of my efforts. Note, it is little help that this tradition belongs to myself." The failure of these projects was not due to exhaustion or dissipation of energy, but to Debussy's insistence on both novelty and perfection.

Debussy's big projects were all operas. Although, like Beethoven, he wrote only one opera, he was more constantly concerned than Beethoven with projected operas, and quite unlike Beethoven he wrote no series of works to correspond with the nine symphonies, eighteen quartets, and thirty-two sonatas. Debussy's continued concern for opera has been ignored by his biographers, not to mention authors of appreciation texts, encyclopedia articles, and program notes. His own words may be partly to blame, for he said some harsh things about opera: "One would think that when music enters the Opéra it must don a uniform like a convict. It also assumes the pseudo-grandiose proportions of the edifice itself, taking its measure from the celebrated grand staircase, which, because of an error in perspective, or too much detail, really gives an ultimate impression of . . . meanness." Remarks like these on the institution of opera, on certain tired performances of *Pelléas,* and on the most famous operas by Gluck, Meyerbeer, Saint-Saëns, Puccini, Mascagni, and Charpentier, have led Vallas and others into the mistaken inference that Debussy disliked the very idea of theater music and withdrew his energy from it in fastidious disgust after *Pelléas*. It is more likely that his bitter criticisms reflect both the depth of his concern for opera and the loftiness of the ideal by which he measured it, the ideal that he realized once and strove for the rest of his life in vain.

In the sixteen years of his life after *Pelléas* he was tormented not only by the frustration of the Poe projects, but also by every other kind of personal trouble. First there was an ignominious domestic wrangle, which alienated nearly all his friends and exposed him to prolonged public humiliation. Victor Seroff's biography tells about this in lurid, exaggerated detail; Debussy's letters to his second wife, Emma Bardac, testify that he never regretted the wrangle and that he enjoyed many hours of "voluptuous tenderness." Then, along with his increasing fame, there was the great annoyance of journalistic misinterpretation, which set him at odds with d'Indy, Satie, and Ravel. And along with his climb from Bohemianism to a life of some luxury there was the nagging lack of money, which drove him to occasional journalism of his own and occasional public performances as pianist and conductor, which he found irksome. Finally there was a cancer, which incapacitated him for a year in 1914, required an operation at the end of 1915, and stopped his work long before it released him to death.

But despite disappointments and difficulties of all kinds, Debussy continued to achieve, as by-products, beautiful pieces of music, astonishingly varied, and prophetic of the music of two generations later. Without these pieces, the literature of 20th-century music would be far poorer, even though its history might still begin with Debussy because of the immense influence of what he did at the end of the 19th century. The finished work of 1902–1913 includes his largest orchestral composition, *La Mer* (*The Sea*), the three *Images* (*Pictures*) which outgrew their original conception as piano pieces and became orchestral, and finally the ballet, *Jeux* (*Games*); it includes for piano the treasury of pictures and preludes and the children's pantomime *La Boîte à joujoux* (*The Toybox*); the dances for harp and strings, and a few shorter pieces of chamber music; eight songs; and the incidental music for d'Annunzio's mystery-play, *Le Martyre de St.-Sébastien* (*The Martyrdom of St. Sebastian*).

———•—•———

In 1915 began the final surge of production: the sonata for cello, the sonata for flute, viola, and harp, the twelve studies for piano, the suite for two pianos, and a children's song. In the winter of 1916–17 Debussy completed his last composition, the violin sonata.

All these 20th-century pieces offer invaluable lessons to anyone who wants to perfect his musical taste or technique. Any single piece, studied closely, contributes to this perfecting; any selection that represents the various media displays the essentials of Debussy's style; but Debussy is one of the few composers whose whole work is relevant to the appreciation of each single piece. Late works illuminate the early ones, and early ones, in turn, when understood more thoroughly than before, point to meanings in the late ones that we have missed when considering them separately.

A brief consideration of two of Debussy's most hackneyed piano pieces can illustrate what is to be gained. The mere titles, *Clair de lune* (1890) and *Golliwog's Cakewalk* (1905), call to mind for most 20th-century music lovers some fragments of characteristic rhythm and harmony, and a train of associated thoughts and feelings. *Clair de lune,* ah, yes! "salon music," the sentimental bromide of moonlit atmosphere for a quiet romance with tears in the eyes; rhythms at first vague and hesitant then flowing smoothly to accompany an elusive but not at all disturbing melody; chords well spaced for the piano, sweet and succulent, different enough from Chopin to identify Debussy somehow, but obviously closer to Chopin than to Bartók or Stravinsky. On the other hand *Golliwog,* ah, yes! a cute encore piece, with a syncopated motif over a bouncy accompaniment, moving to a slam-bang quick ending, obviously closer to Gershwin or Shostakovich than to any more venerable master; maybe it indicates that Debussy lost his way in the 20th century, forgetting or inhibiting his own flavor of 19th-century Romanticism and not quite arriving at any new flavor of his own in our tough, sophisticated world.

Now both these little pieces belong to suites. Their distinct characters are enormously enhanced and clarified by their proper contexts, while either suite is varied enough to belie any simple view of Debussy's whole character or his stylistic development. *Clair de lune* is the third of four movements constituting the *Suite bergamasque*: the other three movements are livelier and harder to play, with problems to occupy the concert pianist and ample rewards for the best audience. The first piece is an elaborate prelude with an extraordinary form dominated by intense joyous feeling. The second is a quaint minuet that runs off toward melancholy and ends with an ironic *glissando*. The last is a *passepied,* tuneful, spiky, ingeniously developed, and ultimately serene. Serving as the quiet relief and moment of mystery within this suite, *Clair de lune* is exactly right, and its mystery can be awesome. Similarly, the *Golliwog* belongs to the *Children's Corner,* a whole gallery of toys, among which the Golliwog comes last because he is a funny old dear. His truculence is not so different, after all, from that of the Passepied, just as his predecessor in the suite, *The Little Shepherd,* is not so different from *Clair de lune.* To detach the two favorites from their contexts is not quite fair. To build an abstract notion of Debussy on the basis of such detached fragments is fatal. To hear the favorites in their proper contexts, to compare the earlier and later ones, to think of them against the background of the projected settings of Banville, Mallarmé, and Poe, rescues them from triviality. Small as they are, both these pieces are highly original and utterly perfect. They are less original, to be sure, than some other pieces of Debussy, but not unworthy of a major composer.

The details of Debussy's music all depend on their contexts. His technical innovations—his new freedom in using dissonant sounds, his use of peculiar scale-formations, his violation of traditional rules about counterpoint—all these were accepted in context by many listeners, while small-minded musicians isolated them, either to condemn or to praise them out of context, and to misrepresent Debussy's over-all intention. Adequate understanding of Debussy's techniques can arise only out of some intuitive sympathy with his intention, and this sympathy will ensure that the detailed techniques are referred to whole forms. The details are fascinating indeed, and a proper study of them can greatly enhance our sympathetic understanding of the whole forms, and our enjoyment. Here, to do justice to details in context without devoting a whole book to Debussy, we must choose first a short piece, not part of a suite, so as to look and listen all the way through; then, having agreed on a vocabulary, we can proceed to point to some details in other contexts.

———————

Most suitable for our purpose is the flute solo, composed in 1912 as incidental music for the scene of the death of Pan in a play by Gabriel Mourey, *Psyché.* The piece was published in 1927 with the title *Syrinx* (*Panpipes*). Flutists all know and love it, and although flutists seldom have occasion to play an unaccompanied solo in public, several of them have made beautiful recordings of this one, so that amateurs may readily become familiar with it. It can be played on other instruments, though the cool, tremulous quality of flute tone is an essential aspect of the idea. It can even be sung, if transposed to a suitable pitch (down a tritone, in our examples).

This little piece shows many features of Debussy's style in the least possible space. The importance of tone color is one. Another is the predominance of sheer melody over rhythm and harmony, which latter have great subtlety but no independent value whatever. The melody seems like a long cadenza, a rhapsodic improvisation. But not a note of it is random. It is almost as remote as plainsong from the tunes that animate dance measures and mark off the periods of a dance with strong cadences on a key-note; more than plainsong, its pure melody, uncontrolled by a text, makes an intelligible pattern. The first phrase presents two related but contrasting

EXAMPLE I.1   Debussy, *Syrinx*

ideas: the drooping wavy line of measure 1 and the little loop of m. 2. In the second phrase the first idea returns and grows, overleaping several catch

EXAMPLE I.2

breaths, to a soft, slow, high point, m. 8. The wavy idea returns again, an octave lower, softer, but faster, and grows now to a climax of sadness, m. 13, which dissolves in the low, slowing loops of mm. 14–15. Then the loop has

EXAMPLE I.3

its turn to grow into distinctive new phrases, which make the contrasting middle section of the piece. The last of these phrases leads smoothly to a return of the first tempo and the first idea, m. 26, followed as at first by the second idea, which is now stretched out to extreme poignance, with the

EXAMPLE I.4

highest and loudest note of the whole piece. The first idea returns for three more descents, and to complete the phrase the loop returns at low pitch, gradually slows, and finally loses itself in a complete whole-tone scale,

EXAMPLE I.5

drifting down to silence without anything like a conventional cadence. The whole shape does show the conventional pattern, A A′ B A″. But the units are asymmetrical: 8, 7, 10, 10 measures. And what might normally be the most conspicuous articulation, at m. 15, is the most smoothly connected. This is a crafty structure. It deserves the name that Debussy gave to the ornate melodies of Bach, as well as to his own first pieces for piano: arabesque.

The rhythm of the melody is as intricate and peculiar and intelligible as its contour. This rhythm tapped on a drum would be incoherent, unrecognizable; the underlying pulse tapped on a drum would show hardly two beats alike in duration. The opening two measures establish the slow, heavy pulse, and let it lapse. The first growing phrase confirms the pulse, only in order to override it. By now there is an enormous range of note-values: ♪, ♪, ♪, ♪, ♪., ♩, ♩ . The third phrase restores the pulse, quickened, then makes it elastic, restores it again and then introduces an important new value, ♪³ . The middle section is all *rubato,* but in spite of that it flows more urgently than the others, with fewer varieties of notes. The last phrase, beginning like the first, includes a real disruption of the pulse, and a slowing to immobility. The whole effect is languorous, yet nervous and supple. Debussy's rhythm never surges ahead long without a sighing interruption, and it never drifts far without at least a shudder.

His rhythm seems to fit his physique, as we can see it in the photographs of Gauthier's collection: in many of these he is seated, on a chair or on the ground, even though people stand around him; in many more he leans against a wall or a tree, or at least on a cane, or, in one, a bass clarinet. In these pictures, almost as regularly, he smokes a cigarette. The only characteristic gesture that his friends report is his sudden way of flicking off the ash.

The harmony of this piece, like its rhythm, is a dimension of the melody, not an accompanying part. According to the commonest technical use of the term, "harmony" is composed of chords, units of two or three notes heard simultaneously. In this sense, of course, *Syrinx* lacks harmony altogether, unless we are willing to consider imaginary, implied chords, or at least to hear part of the melody as a broken chord. But a broader meaning of the term is more convenient for technical use, as well as closer to its general, nontechnical meanings—agreement, coordination, coherence. In our sense, "harmony" is any coordination of pitch-relations, distinguished from, but interacting with, the organization of time-relations (rhythm), of loudness (dynamics), of tone-color, and of melodic motifs and contours. Thus harmony comprises not only chords but also scales and modes and keys and every other pattern of pitch-relations, no matter how awkward to name. In this broad sense harmony contributes as much as rhythm to the distinctive shape and flavor of Debussy's piece, and this piece illustrates Debussy's great harmonic daring, perhaps even more clearly than a piece full of rich chords.

The pitches of the first phrase are related in a hierarchy. One note, E in our version, is the most important because it is repeated and accented, and it begins and ends the phrase. But the configuration of the other notes prevents the E from sounding like a tonic: they do not point to it as a satisfactory resting-place for the last phrase of the piece. They are subordinate to it in a way that makes us expect to find it in turn subordinated to some other note in a later phrase. But again, our expectation does not point toward a particular note. It is a vague expectation that might be satisfied by any one of several sequels, such as these four alternate endings:

EXAMPLE I.6

Hypothetical answering phrases

The next most prominent note in the first phrase is the lowest note, G. Though short and unaccented, it is exposed by the leap down from the next lowest note, and by the wide leap up to all that follows it in the phrase, so that its pitch lingers in memory. The other notes, in order of importance, are the Bb, somewhat similarly exposed; the C and D, accented by serving as passing tones from E to Bb; the Eb's, F's, the high Gb, and finally the Db and B, which all serve to ornament the essential motion of the melody.

The note-sketch in Example I.7 continues this empirical sort of analysis through the middle section. To play this may help to clarify the more theoretical discussion that remains. And even apart from any theory these notes may help performers and listeners hear how harmony contributes to the expressive contrasts of the various phrases, how it links them together, and how it makes the end a completion without dispelling the ambiguity of our expectations. These are the purposes of Debussy's harmony. These purposes, better than any theory old or new, justify his departures from common practice.

EXAMPLE I.7   Outline of Debussy, *Syrinx*

The end is the whole-tone scale, the series of whole steps that fill the space of an octave with smooth continuity and symmetry, while avoiding the clearest, strongest intervals of the ordinary diatonic scale, the fourths and fifths. This unnatural scale is so characteristic a device of Debussy's style that whenever we think of it we think of him. No other composer has used it so often or so skillfully, although the Russians from Glinka to Tchai-kovsky all used it deliberately and effectively on special occasions. Debussy learned it from them, and proceeded to develop it further. Parodies of Debussy rely on the whole-tone scale to identify their subject. But Debussy himself never uses the scale in the way his parodists use it, as a pre-established fund of material for just any sort of melody and rhythm. He uses it sparingly, and differently in every instance. In some pieces he does not use it at all. In a very few, the prelude *Voiles* (*Sails* or *Veils*) and the picture *Cloches à travers les feuilles* (*Bells Through the Leaves*), he uses it through most of the piece. In *Syrinx* he holds it in reserve until the end. Here it serves, as nothing else could, to relax and at the same time to condense and preserve the ambiguous meaning of all the other harmony that has gone before. This unique, discreet use of the scale is more truly charac-teristic of Debussy than the mere fact that he uses it.

In other passages of *Syrinx* where the melody sweeps up or down an octave without a change of direction, there are always gaps in the scales. There is never a continuous, complete scale—diatonic, chromatic, or whole-tone—until the end. Most of these sweeping passages, measures 5–7, 10–12, 20–21, suggest a pentatonic scale, such as a pianist can play on the black

EXAMPLE I.8   Debussy, *Syrinx,* mm. 11-12 and 20-21

keys only. This is another of Debussy's favorite devices, as Constantin Brailoiu has shown in a fascinating, thorough study. But since the penta-tonic scale with its asymmetrical gaps is a pattern common to several styles, since it was used by Liszt and Wagner and constitutes the norm for many kinds of folksong throughout the world, it does not stand out to identify Debussy's music as does the comparatively arbitrary, mechanical, cerebral, abnormal whole-tone scale. In *Syrinx* the pentatonic scale appears only in the quick sweeping passages in the middle of phrases. It enables us to hear many notes as if at once, and to prolong in memory the important notes that began the phrase, with whatever expectations they aroused. The penta-tonic scale is not a starting point or a concluding point, but only an easy support for the middle of the phrase. This extraordinary way of using the pentatonic scale is once again more characteristic of Debussy than the mere fact that he uses it.

If we look for a scale underlying the first phrase, or the piece as a whole, we naturally think of chromatic scales, one or another of various scales, variously written and variously sung, that use all the notes of a keyboard, dividing an octave into twelve half-steps. Debussy uses the chromatic scale more freely than it was used in the common practice of the past. He follows the lead of Chopin, Liszt, Wagner, and Franck, all of whom occasionally accumulated so many chromatic deviations from the diatonic norm that their norm disappeared. But in *Syrinx* there is no such occasion. The chromaticism is always comprehensible as expressive inflection of diatonic motions. On the other hand Debussy does not wait for deviations to accumulate, but begins his music with its most chromatic moment, before establishing any norm.

Nevertheless a diatonic norm does lurk behind the first phrase, and behind the whole piece. The five chief notes of the first phrase belong to a diatonic scale, and the next phrase fills in the two notes that complete this scale, F and A. The same scale returns for the last phrase of the piece, but now when the two delayed notes appear they are part of the whole-tone scale, which includes only the lowest one of the original five notes, G. Meanwhile, in the middle section a different scale, diatonic and chromatic mixed, has underlined the thematic contrast, mm. 16–17, and another complete and pure diatonic scale has smoothed the transitions, mm. 11–15, 21–25. The prevailing chromaticism obscures the modulations from one diatonic scale to another but does not obliterate the contrast between them. (In transposing the piece to a singable range, we have incidentally made the diatonic scales more apparent to the eye. The notation of the piece as published adds to the obscurity inherent in the music. Because of this, Hellmut Seraphin argues that Debussy's lost manuscript may have been edited by Fleury.)

The diatonic scales of *Syrinx* are not major scales. The one in the middle section, mm. 16–17, is C minor; its chromatic ingredients conform fairly closely to common practice for the minor mode. The other scales are modal, in the vague sense of the word. That is, they are used in a way that leaves their fundamental note uncertain. They suggest, without definitely establishing any of them, the ancient diatonic modes common to plainchant and many kinds of folksong. (The first and most important scale of the piece suggests the Phrygian mode on A, the Aeolian on D, the Dorian on G, and the hypothetical Locrian on E. All these modes share with the ordinary major mode on F the same set of whole steps and half steps, the same pitch names though in a different order. The ordinary F minor, with its chromatic inflections of the sixth and seventh degrees, shares all but one of the same notes, the A.) The various modes, like the pentatonic scales, are regular resources of Debussy's style, just as important as the whole-tone scale. He rarely maintains a single mode for a whole phrase, never for a whole composition, as Beethoven did in the mystical "Prayer of Thanks on Recovery from Illness, in the Lydian Mode" of his Quartet, Op. 132, and as Berlioz, Liszt, and other 19th-century composers occasionally did for special, archaic effects. Debussy's modality is more like that of his favorite Russian, Mussorgsky, unselfconscious and fluctuating. Maurice Emmanuel quoted him as arguing with their teacher, Guiraud, about 1890: "Music is neither major nor minor, or rather, it is both at once. What keeps it fresh and supple is a continual fluctuating between major and minor thirds. . . . Mode is what the musician thinks of at a given moment; it is unstable."

Debussy's combination of modality and chromaticism is his own. Modality and chromaticism have been opposites in the history of Western music. From the mysterious beginnings of polyphony in the Middle Ages down to the Enlightened Age of Scarlatti, Rameau, and Bach, chromaticism gradually smoothed away the distinctive asymmetries of the diatonic modes, either reducing them to the major and minor which came to dominate common practice, or, more rarely, leading toward some freely chromatic style, as in the typical music of Gesualdo and Frescobaldi. But Debussy evades this opposition. He uses chromaticism and vague modality together, to create fresh, delicate tonal patterns such as that of *Syrinx*.

The tonal pattern of the piece as a whole has no single, unequivocal center. The last note is one of the principal notes, but to call it a tonic would be to invite dispute. The piece is not definitely in the key of G or any other key. The avoidance of definite key is its most radically novel feature. In this respect it is a rare extreme case, though not unique, in Debussy's whole work. Most of his pieces center on a tonic. Still, most of his pieces have some tonal ambiguity. Hardly ever in his music is tonality so neatly explicable as in the common practice of the past. He avoided what he called "those little affectations of over-precision in form and tonality that so encumber music." *Syrinx* represents Debussy's extreme attenuation of tonality, and it shows that this attenuation is not a merely negative aspect of the music, not a matter of reticence or incoherence or revolt, but rather a disciplined freedom to create unique tonal patterns, which along with rhythm and melody and tone-color give the music its shape and character. The fictional mouthpiece of Debussy's journalism, *M. Croche, Anti-dilettante,* says: "Discipline must be sought in freedom, not in formulas. . . . Music is an ensemble of diverse elements. You make them into a dance of abstractions! I prefer a few notes from an Egyptian shepherd's pipe, for he collaborates with the landscape and hears harmonies unknown to your textbooks."

Syrinx obviously resembles several other works of Debussy—*The Little Shepherd* from the suite for piano, *Children's Corner*; the *Épigraphes antiques,* originally for flutes and harps, later arranged for piano duet; the songs, *La Flûte de Pan* and *Le Faune*; and of course his most famous orchestral piece, the *Prelude to The Afternoon of a Faun,* of 1892–94, twenty years before *Syrinx.* A comparison of the *Faun* with *Syrinx* will educe some basic features of his stylistic development. Their similar moods are evoked by similar means: the sweet tones of the flute, the melodic arabesques, the languid but nervously fluctuating rhythms, the discreet whole-tone scales, pentatonic scales, free chromaticism, and vague modality. These are the devices of the style that we have observed so far. In the *Faun* as in *Syrinx* the way they are used is more important than the mere fact of their use. Some differences are obvious too: the greater length of the orchestral piece, its wealth of voluptuous sonorities—the full string choir, four horns, harps, antique cymbals, and the various woodwinds that occasionally take over the leading melody from the flute. Less obvious but reassuring to some listeners—to others all too obvious and hence, paradoxically, estranging—are these: the roughly A A' B A'' form, the E-major ending, and the set of primary chords in D♭ major that underline the lyrical middle section. The D♭ section is almost like an aria of Gounod or Massenet. (These two masters of 19th-century French opera had encouraged Debussy in his student days, and he was fondly loyal to them.) Because the *Faun* is so familiar, and makes some use of well-worn patterns, we are likely to underestimate its harmonic complexity and originality. Our close study of *Syrinx* prepares us to estimate the *Faun* more justly.

The harmonic dimension of the melody contributes to the shape of the *Faun,* while chords, though undeniably fascinating, are subordinate, enhancing the melody's ambiguity more than they point to its true direction. Thus the first chord appears only at the end of the long, swaying, expository phrase by the solo flute. The chord is a thrilling surprise. It is dissonant, in the technical sense of the word, but it is not harsh. Considered in abstraction from its color and its context, it is the same sort of mild, rich dissonance as the famous first chord of Wagner's *Tristan.*

EXAMPLE I.9   Wagner, Prelude to *Tristan und Isolde,* beginning

EXAMPLE I.10   Debussy, *Prelude to the Afternoon of a Faun,* beginning

Only a composer thoroughly familiar with the *Tristan* chord could have conceived the beginning of the *Faun*. Debussy heard *Tristan* as early as 1879; in 1895 his young friend Samazeuilh heard him sing, play, and analyze the last act of *Tristan* magnificently, as part of a course of weekly sessions on Wagner's whole work from *Tannhäuser* to *Parsifal*, held in the salon of a rich lady. But the concrete sound and the function of the chord in the *Faun* are quite different from the sound and function of the *Tristan* chord. The *Tristan* chord embodies the principal motif of the opera; its constituent notes belong to four distinct melodic lines straining against each other in a polyphonic texture; the four lines pull ahead to complete a phrase in the following chord. Debussy's chord, on the contrary, splashes over four octaves in the harp, and dissolves into another rich chord with new voicing and tone-color, while the main melody remains stationary, and is freely imitated by the French horn. The chords are repeated after a silent pause, and then fade away before the flute resumes. They are as it were in parentheses. They provoke a sensuous thrill, rather than an emotional tension. They leave the melody uncommitted to any key, free to suggest rapid and subtle shifts of emotion like those suggested by *Syrinx* rather than the long sustained development of *Tristan's* yearning. The melody does not really commit itself until it sinks down to the E on the last page of the score. In the first section it grows through four phrases to embrace with its first *forte* an important new motif, and to make its first cadence, on B. This articulation

EXAMPLE I.11 Debussy, *Prelude to the Afternoon of a Faun,* first cadence

corresponds to the one at measure 8 of *Syrinx*. After an animated interlude, the oboe takes up the melody, which grows again, through a very long, accelerating phrase, incorporating another new motif (Ex. I.12), rising to the octave above the starting-point, and leading into the relaxed middle section. The parallel with the corresponding section of *Syrinx* is close. The middle section's contrasting theme begins with downward leaps like those

EXAMPLE I.12 Debussy, *Prelude to the Afternoon of a Faun,* motifs in
    counterpoint

in the first theme, m. 3. The first note is the same pitch, though spelled
differently. Likewise the supporting bass D♭ is after all the opening C♯ of
the first theme, which has recurred throughout the first two sections with
ever-changing chordal backgrounds. Thus the middle section is not like the
trio of a march or minuet, but an organic continuation of the melody from
the first sections, which would be incomplete without it. The new theme
grows, through three overlapping phrases, by assimilating the two supplementary motifs that occurred in the growth of the first theme. The melody
never settles down to a cadence; even the last phrase moves on, taking what
has been the highest note of the section, B♭, up to fresh B♮. The recapitulation of the first theme differs from the exposition much more in the *Faun*
than *Syrinx.* The four phrases of melody are slower, and gradually descending, with fanciful detours. The first and second phrases set out from E and
E♭, and end in the air, on C and B. They are followed by short animated
interludes. The third phrase at last restores the theme to the pitch of the
beginning, but it goes on to bring back the supplementary motifs, and then
to lead into the fourth phrase. Here there is a final, poignant chromatic twist
for the motif of m. 3, which prepares the big cadence on E. In the coda,
the flute recalls its first note, and now this is accompanied by the *Tristan*
chord, which gently resolves at last into the tonic.

Most of the chords throughout the piece are as dissonant as the first one.
Ordinary, consonant triads, such as the final chord, are as rare as in the
music of Wagner and Franck, but there are still enough of them to maintain
the distinction between consonance and dissonance, and to feed our expectation that dissonance will ultimately be resolved to consonance. Among the
mild dissonances, full dominant-ninth chords, such as accompany the first
appearances of the two supplementary motifs, are more frequent than in
any music before Debussy. His taste for them is evident in his earliest songs
and piano pieces. Whereas Wagner and Franck usually reserve these five-
voiced chords for climaxes, Debussy makes the same chords sound bland.
His nonchalant use of them is in keeping with his adaptation of the
Tristan chord—sensuous rather than emotional, and hardly concerned with
polyphony. It is not that the chords have become routine and must give
way at climaxes to more tangy chords, but rather that Debussy wants less

emphatic climaxes and relies on his elaborate melody to make the climaxes he wants, so that he can use the ninth chords as calm background for almost any kind of motion by the melody. *Syrinx* has shown that chords are not indispensable to Debussy's style. The *Faun* shows the essential principle of their use: intermittent freedom from polyphony and constant subordination to the main melody. In his own words: "A chord in a structure of sound is like a stone in a building. Its true value depends on the place it occupies and the support it lends to the flexible curve of the melodic line."

The principle behind Debussy's use of chords shows up with extreme clarity in passages where a series of similar chords accompany a melody in parallel motion, one chord for each note of the melody, like a thickening of the melodic line. This procedure may be heard in *Pelléas* at the beginning of Act 3, Scene 2 (in the vault); in the first pages of *Le Martyre de St.- Sébastien*; in the *Danse sacrée* where the harp enters; or in the three pieces *Pour le piano,* or the *Pictures, Soirée dans Grenade* and *Et la Lune descend,* or the prelude, *Canope.* Debussy's parallel chords, especially parallel ninth chords, invite parody, like his whole-tone scale. Teachers at the Paris Conservatory around 1880 were already joking about Debussy's parallels, imitating them by the mixture-stops of an organ. But parodists usually overlook the fact that Debussy's chord-streams always parallel a bit of significant melody, to enhance some quality inherent in that melody. The chords are free from polyphony in order to serve melody.

The same principle is hidden but effective even in many passages where the chords seem to conform to the common practice of part-writing, with similar or contrary motion among some voices, and parallel motion only at the conventional intervals of thirds and sixths. The principle is betrayed by the unusual rhythmic pattern of the chords' root-movements—what Rameau called the fundamental bass. The rhythm of the roots follows the rhythm of the main melody, instead of making a slower, steadier counterpoint to it, as in common practice. Striking examples of this characteristic harmonic rhythm are the beginning of the Quartet, most of the short prelude *La Fille aux cheveux de lin,* and parts of the *Faun.*

On the contrary, some of Debussy's chords last for a whole phrase of melody. The peculiar fast motion of chords in some passages makes a sharp contrast with the slow motion in others—motion as slow as Wagner's or Bruckner's. Debussy lets none of his new procedures become habitual. Each of them is to be understood only in relation to whole forms and to the ideas embodied in the whole forms.

———•·•———

Debussy's principle is hard to learn. It is too vaguely general to be taught systematically, as the common practice of earlier composers has been quite successfully taught. In 1912 the composer René Lenormand (1846–1932) compiled a *Study of Modern Harmony,* which exhibited chords from the works of Debussy and other living Frenchmen, and tried to justify their departures from common practice as a systematic "evolution" of the musical vocabulary. Parallelism was the subject of Lenormand's first chapter, but Debussy's principle eluded him. When he asked for Debussy's judgment of his book, he received a characteristic reply:

It is all quite correct and almost mercilessly logical. . . . All these experiments, all these colors, plunge you eventually into a state of alarm from which you emerge with a question mark like a nail in your brain. Whether you meant it or not, your essay is a severe censure of modern harmony. There is something almost barbarous about your quotation of passages which, being necessarily detached from their context, can no longer justify their "curiousness." Think of all the inexpert hands that will utilize your study without discrimination, for the sole purpose of annihilating those charming butterflies which are already somewhat crumpled by your analysis.

On the other hand, when Louis Laloy (1874–1944), a subtler scholar than Lenormand, wrote an article in 1902 "On Two Chords" and their context in *Pelléas,* Debussy sent him an unsolicited note of thanks, which led to an intimate, lasting friendship and to Laloy's excellent book on Debussy. He was not impatient of analysis as such, but rather welcomed the kind of analysis that treated a composition as a living whole. In the crotchety words of *M. Croche,* he expressed his own ideal of criticism: "I try to see, through the works, the multiple movements that have engendered them, and whatever inner life they contain: is this not a different concern from the game of showing them off like monstrosities?" Debussy's ideal is relevant not only to his own music, but to any music, and especially to later music in which more startling techniques are likely to distract listeners from "whatever inner life" the works contain.

Many writers less conscientious than Lenormand have groped toward formulating Debussy's chordal principle, exaggerated it, and oversimplified it. Even after half a century there are a few who agree with the most pedantic of Debussy's teachers at the Conservatory, like Delibes, and the most superficial of his critics in the journals of the 1900s, like Saint-Saëns, Lalo, and Tiersot, regarding his practice as an anarchical, wanton attack on the eternal requirements of harmony. Other writers, more admiring if less precise, claim in program-notes and reference books that Debussy's chords are all disconnected and "nonfunctional"—that is, that they produce *only* immediate sensuous effects and contribute nothing to tonality. But in fact all his chords are connected through his melody, and there are always a few of them connected with each other in traditional polyphonic fashion to reinforce the melodic cadences of the tonality and form, thus articulating the composition. Debussy's freedom does not mean that he abandons or destroys the resources of the past.

For polyphony, while never inhibiting the use of chords, is still present, and important. Though the moments when our attention is divided between two or more melodic lines occur mostly when a single chord is providing a stable background, as in Ex. I.12, still there are some other moments, like Ex. I.11, when countermelodies move the chords as surely as they do in *Tristan* or a Brahms symphony or a Bach fugue. There are moments in the *Faun*, such as the next to the last appearance of the main theme, where the free counterpoint over a stable chord produces extremely dissonant combinations of seven or eight simultaneous notes. Such moments are rare in the *Faun*, but frequent in *La Mer* and *Jeux*. Debussy never starts from a contrapuntal combination of melodies, as other composers often do, and he never falls back on contrapuntal devices to substitute for the constant renewal of his main melody. But he does not disdain all counterpoint. His countermelodies are brief, rising out of chords and sinking back into chords. When their moments of interest are past, the voices that carry them are utterly lost in the chords. It is impossible to trace a subordinate line of melody through a whole piece. In most phrases it is impossible to trace a four-voiced framework from beginning to end, or to imagine a four-voiced background that would not change the musical sense of the phrase. This is a radical departure from the common practice of composers all the way back to the 16th century. Still it is not the end of polyphony.

There is abundant liveliness in the polyphony even when it is a chordal background with no countermelody to draw attention from the main melody. The chords are often broken, and often ornamented with figuration that perfectly fits the instruments, so as to facilitate their production of the desired tone colors and dynamic accents. When the instrumental medium is the full orchestra, as in Ex. I.13, the *Faun's* only *fortissimo,* this inconspicuous animation of the polyphony is especially complex and subtle. Polyphony and orchestration overlap. As may be seen in Walter Piston's textbook on orchestration, there is some overlapping in any well-written music for orchestra. In Debussy's music the overlap is much greater than in common practice. He adds to all the devices of Mozart, Weber, Berlioz, and Wagner the possibilities that he learned from the heterophonic music of the Far East, which he heard repeatedly and admired intensely at the Paris World Exhibition of 1889. (André Schaeffner suggests that he must have experimented with the Javanese gamelan that was acquired by the Conservatory museum in 1887.) In Ex. I.13 the first harp varies the flute parts in almost the same way that the smallest bells of a Javanese gamelan vary the slower basic melody.

In all the details we have examined, the *Faun* shows Debussy's combination of originality and refined craft—adventure and achievement matching each other, and both very great.

EXAMPLE I.13 Debussy, *Prelude to the Afternoon of a Faun*, orchestral polyphony

If, with vivid memories of the *Faun,* we listen again to *Syrinx,* we may hear more poignance, a more intense sweetness, in all its fluctuations of rhythm, dynamics, and tonality, than we heard before. If we are singing or playing the melody, we may find our tempo a shade more moderate, that is, slower than before, so that every note as long as a sixteenth has time to sound with a certain weight, without delaying the flow. We may swell the tone a shade louder where wedges call for a swell. Performed and heard in such a way, *Syrinx* suggests that Debussy's development in the interval of twenty years was like Beethoven's and most great artists', a matter of expressing himself more concisely; only if it is performed or heard in a perfunctory way can it suggest that what he had to say became less interesting.

The *Faun,* to be sure, affords some sort of pleasure to many perfunctory members of concert audiences and consumers of phonograph records, who either cannot or will not make the effort required for enjoyment of *Syrinx.* Probably *Syrinx* too, in its original scenic, dramatic context, charmed most of its comparatively small audience without their actively listening. But for a concert piece *Syrinx* is too restrained: it gratifies only those who closely follow—and to some extent anticipate—its melody. Likewise the richer beauty of the *Faun* is reserved for sensitive, responsive, anticipating listeners, and these are almost as scarce for the *Faun* as for *Syrinx.* Although most serious musicians and music lovers can produce on demand a recognizable approximation of the first phrase of the *Faun,* few but flutists and conductors can be relied on to remember its exact rhythmic values and its exact ordering of half steps and whole steps. Without a firm grasp of these, appreciation can only be superficial, and comparisons of Debussy's style with earlier and later styles can proceed only by slippery pictorial and literary analogies.

Debussy composed for the few sensitive, anticipating listeners, and he valued above all their sincere, spontaneous reactions. Unlike Beethoven and Wagner, he never addressed "all mankind." On the contrary, a letter to his friend the composer Chausson, 1893, proposed facetiously: "Instead of spreading art amongst the public, I would suggest founding a Society of Musical Esotericism." Twenty-one years later, in the face of the cataclysm of World War I, he felt, as he wrote to Durand, that all he could do seemed "miserably small," yet that his duty was to go on making the best music that he could. He always supposed that *Pelléas* and his other pieces for the theater would be enjoyed by a greater part of mankind than his songs or his purely instrumental music—by enough people, he hoped, to make him rich. But the *Faun* was addressed to connoisseurs of Mallarmé, an elite group. Debussy never expected it to become more famous than *Pelléas.* When Nijinsky made a ballet of the *Faun,* in 1912, Debussy was no more pleased than the censors: he found Nijinsky's movements too stiffly stylized for his supple rhythms; the censors found some of them too close to masturbation. If Debussy's music was to be abused in such a way, it was not his concern. Several of the preludes for piano, he told Mrs. Liebich, his first biographer, should be played only "entre quat'z yeux"—for a single listener. *Syrinx* he left as the private property of the flutist, Louis Fleury (1878–1925), who permitted its publication only after his death. Even *Pelléas* is no great popular success and contains no excerptible hits, although it is the only opera since Verdi to win both the whole-hearted respect of a scholarly critic like Joseph Kerman and the devotion of enough singers and opera lovers to keep it in the repertory of many companies. In *Pelléas* Maeterlinck presents a fundamental doctrine which Debussy's music fits as perfectly as it does the symbolic scenery and the frail, poetic character of Mélisande. This doctrine is to renounce all hope of commanding or resisting fate, or even comprehending it, and rather simply to accept the inexplicable beauty and loneliness and suffering of every living thing. Such a thought is obviously unfit to stir a massive audience. But Debussy enabled it to touch deeply whoever was ready for it. His other projected operas, we have seen, were to be as esoteric as *Pelléas,* though very different in mood. In short, Debussy's work as a whole is a style and a set of forms whose enjoyment is a special privilege, as Laloy expounded in the passage quoted in our preface. Truly to appreciate Debussy is perhaps one of the most exclusive privileges. Yet his works go on recruiting unknown friends from all parts of society, from all parts of the world.

The changing relations between composer and society in general can be understood only through knowledge of the experience and views of particular composers and particular listeners. Our recognition of Debussy's esotericism, together with the pervasive superficial influence of his style and the continuing recruitment of friends for his works, prepares us to consider the same issue as it affects Schoenberg, Stravinsky, Ives, Webern, Varèse, Prokofiev, Copland, Elliott Carter, and Charlie Parker.

CHAPTER II

Catchwords and Issues of 20th-Century Music

D EBUSSY'S STYLE is commonly labeled "impressionism." This is the first and foremost of many dubious catchwords of modern music, introduced by hurried journalists to pique the curiosity of hurried readers, and then preserved by compilers of reference books—encyclopedias and historical surveys—where their uncertain connotations are apt to mislead. In our present survey these words are used rarely and cautiously, never to summarize a style or to classify a composer's work. The whole list of them can be assembled with advantage to show at the same time some of their meanings, valid and invalid, and some of the range of Debussy's style and taste.

"Impressionism," like many of the terms to follow, was borrowed from the critics of painting. They had derived the word from the picture *Impression* by Claude Monet, an impression of the sun rising through mist over the Thames, first exhibited in 1874. They used it to label Monet's style, along with the styles of Manet, Renoir, and Degas, all roughly contemporary representatives of the great flowering of French art that both continued and contrasted with Delacroix's "romanticism" and Courbet's "realism," in opposition to the "classicism" that was approved and taught by the Académie des Beaux Arts in Paris and by academies elsewhere. Definitions of impressionism in painting naturally vary. They need not concern us here, except for their changing emotive connotations: at first, shock and disapproval by comparison with respectable academic painting; by 1900, patronizing acceptance and dismissal, by comparison with later more radical painting; and by 1950, stylishness, thanks to the "abstract impressionism" of several young Americans.

For many listeners Debussy's music has something in common with impressionist painting. To call his music "impressionistic" emphasizes this elusive common quality, and effectively connotes disapproval, or patronizing dismissal, or—more rarely—stylish enthusiasm.

Debussy himself disliked the term. He wrote to Durand in 1908, concerning his orchestral pictures: "I am trying to make something new—*realities, as it were: what imbeciles call 'impressionism.'*"

His taste in painting, which André Schaeffner has investigated closely, was somewhat different from that of the impressionist painters, or of the older composer Chabrier, who owned many Monets and Renoirs. Debussy did share their admiration for Japanese prints and for the luminous colors of Turner. But like his literary friends Mallarmé and Verlaine, Debussy found the expatriate American, James Whistler, the most appealing of contemporary painters. He liked Degas for his sense of movement. What he knew of Monet seemed to him repetitious, lacking in mystery. From Whistler Debussy reclaimed for music the title "Nocturnes," which Whistler had borrowed from Chopin. While some of the subjects of Debussy's "nocturnes," "pictures," "prints," and "sketches" might be fit subjects for Whistler or Monet—"clouds," "gardens in the rain," "reflections in the water," "the sunken cathedral," "fog"—others would be more appropriate for the rococo Watteau, or the classical Ingres or Puvis de Chavannes, or the post-impressionist Cézanne or the "syncretist" Gauguin. Moreover, there are many other compositions with no explicit pictorial association whatever.

Thus the label "impressionist" is misleading if taken to imply that Debussy deliberately sought a musical parallel for the techniques or moods of the impressionist painters. The momentous innovations of Cézanne— freedom for composition to distort perspective—and of Gauguin—freedom for color to serve expressive composition rather than representation—correspond to Debussy's innovations at least as well as Monet's freedom from linear clarity. It is misleading also if taken to mean that pictorial associations count for more in Debussy's music than in Couperin's or Bach's or Mozart's or Wagner's. The label is more subtly misleading if it merely lulls us into a narrow notion of Debussy's work, based on only a few pieces, perceived and remembered impressionistically.

Several writers, especially in Germany, have tried to establish a more precise definition of musical impressionism and to study in detail the differences as well as the similarities between musicians and painters, tracing their techniques to their fundamental attitudes and aspirations. These writers, among whom Werner Danckert is the most thorough and judicious, disagree with each other on details and on attitudes as well. They agree, however, that not all of Debussy is impressionistic.

Still, the term is oftenest used in a vague sense, simply to distinguish Debussy's style from earlier and later styles, rather than to distinguish any particular pieces or particular qualities within his style.

"Pointillism," the name for the technique of the painters Seurat and Signac, is often applied to Debussy's orchestration and to Webern's melodic style. Neither composer intended to suggest the analogy, but it is comparatively harmless.

———— • ————

"Symbolism" turns up less often than "impressionism" and "pointillism" in general discussions of music. But in any serious account of Debussy's attitudes and aspirations "symbolism" looms larger. Symbolism was a literary movement with a manifesto by the poet Jean Moréas (1886), to which Mallarmé, Verlaine, Rimbaud, and Maeterlinck adhered. The symbolists claimed Poe, Wagner, and Baudelaire as their chief precursors. They became in turn the recognized masters of leading 20th-century writers in many nations: Yeats, Joyce, Eliot, Pound, Stevens, George, Rilke, Lorca, Blok, Pasternak, Proust, Valéry, Claudel.

The connections between the symbolists and Debussy, traced with care by Edward Lockspeiser and other writers whose work Lockspeiser summarizes, were many and intimate. No other composer matched the poets so closely. He used their texts for songs and opera and instrumental preludes. He regularly attended Mallarmé's famous salon in the 1890s. His closest friend in this period was Pierre Louÿs (1870–1925), the poet of the *Chansons de Bilitis,* and a disciple of the symbolists. Another close and influential friend was Henri de Régnier (1864–1936), likewise a leading young symbolist. Still another good friend, the composer Dukas, shrewdly estimated that literary connections—these and some others—played a larger part in the formation of Debussy's style than any musical model. Other writers as important for Debussy as the symbolists, especially in his formative years, were Leconte de Lisle, Paul Bourget, Pierre Loti, Anatole France, and above all Théodore de Banville. Poe, as we have seen, was important to the end of Debussy's life. All these poets fortified his courage to deviate from common practice. They sharpened his sensitivity to unique forms. They recommended subtle suggestion as opposed to bald statement, and vivid sensuous imagery as opposed to diffuse emotion. Debussy did seek and find the musical equivalents of their verbal techniques. Especially in *Pelléas,* he gave musical embodiment to the attitudes they expressed in words, and there is good reason to regard *Pelléas* as the archetype of symbolism.

Yet "symbolism" is hardly a more adequate term than "impressionism" to sum up Debussy's whole style, which includes the making of "realities" as robust as *La Mer* and *Jeux* and the Study for octaves, or as transparent as *Children's Corner* and the Sonata for cello.

Both impressionism and symbolism radiated from France. More forcefully than any earlier movement since the grand classic age of Louis XIV, they displayed the French national character in the world of arts and letters. Debussy's music ranks with Cézanne's painting and Baudelaire's poetry, and even surpasses them, in the revival of French prestige. Because music and music teaching throughout Europe and America had been so dominated by Germans and Austrians, many musicians in France, like many in Russia and other countries, reacted by emphasizing all the more their national traits. Debussy testified in 1909: "Since those student days I have tried to slough off all I was taught. I have tried not to react against the influence of Wagner. I have simply given full play to my nature and temperament. Above all, I have tried to become French again." With a characteristic blend of pride and humility, he signed his late sonatas "Claude Debussy, *musicien français.*" His very last, unfinished composition was an Ode to France. In his criticism the most frequent and most impassioned theme was the past glory and future destiny of French national music. And he showed this concern not only in his explicit intentions, but also, to anyone looking for it, in his greatest achievements. His rhythms are like those of French speech and gesture. *Pelléas,* although it has no popular or patriotic theme, has been brilliantly analyzed by Donald Grout as "a focal point of French dramatic music, gathering up many essential national traits and giving them exceptionally clear and perfect expression, though colored by the individual genius of Debussy." He was at least as much a "nationalist" as he was an "impressionist" or "symbolist."

But "nationalism" in turn is too narrow a musical category for a composer whose work evoked such profound response from so many nations as Debussy's. And "nationalism" is too vague a principle to distinguish his style from earlier and later styles, or even from the contemporary would-be nationalist style of Guy Ropartz (1864–1955) and other composers of academic symphonies on French folksong themes. Debussy delighted in poking fun at them. When he himself used French folksong—in *Jardins sous la pluie (Gardens in the Rain)*, *Rondes de Printemps (Spring Rounds,* the third of the *Images* for orchestra), *La Boîte à joujoux (The Toybox)*, and the Cello Sonata—they were not themes for development, but allusions, like his Spanish and English allusions, or even, in *The Toybox,* his sly quotations of Verdi and Wagner, and in *En blanc et noir (In Black and White)* a Bach chorale.

On the other hand, "nationalism" is truly a current of thought connecting Debussy with predecessors like Weber, Chopin, Liszt, Mussorgsky, and Grieg, and with successors like Bartók, Stravinsky, Falla, Vaughan Williams, Szymanowski, Villa-Lobos, and Copland. Moreover, nationalism is a principle transcending all the arts. Like "technology" and "bureaucracy," "nationalism" names some of the most pervasive distinguishing features of life since the American and French Revolutions. The connections between any music and any such principle deserve attention if we want to see how music as a whole has changed in the 20th century. Viewed in broadest perspective, Debussy's Frenchness is epoch-making.

He had no wish to substitute French for German domination of the musical "world," for he was aware of a vastly larger world than that of his harmony teachers. He even doubted sometimes whether Germans could hope really to understand French music. He knew that no European could completely understand the various kinds of music produced by Asian countries newly accessible to Europe. He knew that some Far Eastern music was sophisticated, charming, and stimulating to his own creative imagination. His self-consciousness and daring to be himself and to be French resulted from his awareness that the German academic tradition simply could not comprehend the diversity of the world's music. Somewhat as, in political life, national independence of more and more groups and aggravation of their conflicts have been chief results of the gradually increasing intercommunication and economic interdependence of all the people in the world, so the spreading, accelerating interchange of music provoked a sharpening of national stylistic distinctions and rivalries. Debussy's nationalism shows this paradoxical situation more clearly than the better-known nationalism of 19th-century composers in Russia, Bohemia, and Scandinavia. For alongside his nationalism is his deep interest in several kinds of non-European music.

"Exoticism" is the common label for this interest. The word does not denote a coherent movement. It refers merely to any concern with extra-European cultures. Hence exoticism can be traced farther back in the history of the arts and sciences than the use of the word itself, a 19th-century coinage. But this interest became more intense and fruitful than ever before in the second half of the 19th century, as contacts of diverse cultures multiplied, thanks to European technology. Artists like Whistler, Gauguin, Whitman, Melville, Leconte de Lisle, Loti, France, and Debussy anticipated the attitude of systematic anthropologists like Franz Boas (1858–1942), of ethnomusicologists like Curt Sachs (1881–1958), and of the philosopher of *The Meeting of East and West,* F. S. C. Northrop. Debussy's exoticism is unmistakable in his "print" for piano, *Pagodes.* More subtle traces of it appear in the loose polyphonic or heterophonic texture of passages in nearly all his works, as represented by Ex. I.13 from the *Faun.* Furthermore, his uses of the whole-tone scale owe something to the Javanese *slendro* scale, which divides an octave into five nearly equal intervals, each a fraction larger than a whole tone. These important features of Debussy's style are more than exotic allusions, deeper far than Mozart's Turkish percussion, which corresponded to the *chinoiserie* of the Enlightenment, deeper than the various decorative Romantic orientalisms of Weber, Verdi, Lalo, Saint-Saëns, Borodin, and Rimsky-Korsakov, or even the Spanish color of Bizet and Chabrier. Debussy's exoticism broadened the main stream of Western harmony. His only significant precursor in this respect was Louis Albert Bourgault-Ducoudray (1840–1910), the composer who taught music history at the Conservatory. His successors, who are legion, owe much to his example. Thus it is surprising that a survey of musical exoticism like James Ringo's can omit to mention Debussy, or like Siegfried Borris's can equate Debussy with Strauss and Mahler in this respect. That his exoticism can be exaggerated as well as overlooked, however, is shown by Daniel Chennevière (better known as a composer by the adopted name Dane Rudhyar). His brief study proclaims that Debussy "introduced the Orient into music. With him classicism is dead forever." Debussy vastly deepened the mingling of East and West, but this need not be fatal to classicism.

Debussy has been regarded, by an early biographer, László Fábián, as a representative also of "expressionism," notably in *La Mer* and other works of about 1903–10. "Expressionism" floated unfixed in the jargon of art critics from the 1850s until Wilhelm Worringer, a scholar and esthetician, attached it to the style of Van Gogh, in opposition to "impressionism." Soon, however, other critics extended expressionism to include Gauguin and even Cézanne, with whom Debussy can be linked, as we have already seen. The word eventually came to be used in reference to any art, in any age, that distorts "real" images and avoids "ideal" norms of beauty for the sake of expressing the artist's feelings. In a narrower sense "expressionism" means the style of a group of young painters and sculptors who exhibited together in Germany during the decade just before World War I; Kandinsky was probably the greatest of them. These self-styled expressionists found literary allies in Strindberg, Wedekind, and several young German poets and dramatists. To both expressionist poetry and painting the composer Schoenberg contributed directly. Thus musical "expressionism" came to mean primarily the style of Schoenberg and his disciples. With this style Debussy had slight contact and little sympathy. Thus Fabian's attribution of "expressionism" to *La Mer* remains peculiar. Yet better exaggerate than miss entirely the contrast between this powerful work and the earlier, more impressionistic *Nocturnes,* or *Pelléas.* Further, Debussy's own words show that his thought moved toward expressionism in the broad sense. Whereas, in an interview in 1905, he urged composers not to "look for ideas within themselves when they should look around for them," in 1911 he reported to his old friend Godet about his slow progress on the Poe operas: "How much has to be discovered and then suppressed in order to arrive at the naked flesh of emotion!" The symbolism of Poe's *Usher* is very expressionistic, in the broad sense of the term. If Debussy had been able to complete his setting, Fabian's notion might have become generally accepted.

Occasionally Debussy's late work, especially *Jeux,* has been provocatively compared with other styles of painting—Rousseau's primitivism, Matisse's fauvism, Picasso's and Braque's cubism, Bonnard's intimism—and even with the later movement, surrealism, led by the poet André Breton. But none of these labels have stuck to Debussy or to any other musician.

Debussy had at least one contact with the movement-to-end-movements, "futurism." The poet Marinetti launched this movement in 1909. It attracted several painters, including Luigi Russolo (1885–1947), and, for about four years only, one composer, Francesco Balilla Pratella (1880–1955), pupil of Mascagni; Pratella contributed a single example of futurist music, using the whole-tone scale. Marinetti rewrote Pratella's manifesto, according to revelations of Claudio Marabini. In 1913 the painter Russolo invented the futurist "art of noises," which was to fulfill the tendency of composers "toward the most complex dissonances . . . by the supplementary use of noise and its substitution for musical sounds." This proposal naturally attracted attention. Debussy promptly commented in a review: "Will this [art] ever achieve the truly satisfying sonority of a foundry in operation? Let us wait and see, and refrain from ridicule." The art of noises, now called *"bruitisme,"* was introduced by Marinetti into the group of painters and poets that rallied in 1916 with the slogan "Dada," whence its fame reëchoed in histories and dictionaries. No composers were directly associated with Dada. The terms "futurism" and "Dadaism" have been loosely applied to composers as staid as Richard Strauss. They are seldom illuminating terms in talk about music.

———•—•———

All the "isms" we have considered, while theoretically opposed to each other, were complementary and successive phases of a more general tendency: to break loose from pedantic formula and commercial routine. If "romanticism" is the name for this general tendency, then clearly Debussy was romantic. But if "romanticism" connotes rather the shoddy formulas and routines that often in the 19th century merely replaced more subtle classic norms, then clearly Debussy was anti-romantic. "Romanticism" has so many more meanings than these two that it is a notorious source of misunderstandings. Debussy himself, as we might guess, was wary of the word's ambiguities, and used it skillfully in more than one sense. He praised Weber's *Oberon* for "this fiery abandon, these romantic rhythms," and mocked Berlioz for fixing "a romantic curl on old wigs." He recognized Wagner as the dominating figure of musical romanticism, and he discriminated scrupulously between the lasting power and beauty of passages like the prelude to Act III of *Parsifal* and the pernicious, ultimately passing influence of the *Ring's* too literal symbolism and its "too sumptuous grandeur, [which] defeats the legitimate desire to grasp its proportions." In the middle section of Debussy's famous piece for piano, *Golliwog's Cakewalk,* 1908, the opening motif of *Tristan* is quoted only to be ridiculed in a staccato comment. This is anti-romanticism at its most explicit.

Anti-romanticism roughly equals "classicism" or "neo-classicism." Debussy's relation to these terms was as ambivalent as his relation to romanticism. On the one hand, in keeping with his romantic rebellion, he told an interviewer in 1902 that he hated "classical development whose beauty is only technical and can interest only the highbrows." On the other hand, he wrote to Durand in 1915 that he was pleased with the proportions of his Cello Sonata "and the form, almost classical, in the good sense of the word." Many writers argue that Debussy progressed from the romanticism of the *Faun* and *Pelléas* to the classicism of the sonatas and studies. Some, like Laloy, consider *La Mer* the beginning of the classic phase. Others, like Fabian and Drew, postpone classicism to *Sebastian*, or later. Then there are critics like Carraud who call *Pelléas* "classical," referring to its revival of "the lucidity, the tact, the restraint, and the sense of proportion that characterize the classical composers . . . their charm and dignity of expression, their scorn of emphasis, exaggeration, and mere effect." And yet there are those like Rudhyar who insist, "With him, classicism is dead forever." Debussy himself, in reply to an interviewer's query in 1910 about "the rebirth of the classic ideal," propounded more questions than answers:

Where have we anything like common action, or general tendency? Once perhaps there were periods of discipline . . . but today! each one goes his way, tries to develop his own personality, if he has one, or to imitate his neighbor's and exaggerate it to the point of exasperation, and that is all. As for tomorrow, I do not know. Who can predict? Does the keen competition among artists portend the birth of a common ideal? Does it drive us to despair? Not at all. Music will be reborn. Let us work. Let each of us work according to his inspiration. The future will decide which works are classic.

"Neo-classicism" is what many writers call the style of Stravinsky from *Pulcinella* (1920) to *The Rake's Progress* (1951) to mark not so much its qualities of proportion and scorn of emphasis as its deliberate allusions to melodies, rhythms, and textures of older composers, especially those of the 18th century. "Neo-classicism" in this sense fits many other composers, from Strauss, Reger, Busoni, and Taneiev back through Brahms to Mendelssohn, even to the classic Mozart in exceptional pieces like his Handelian overture, K. 399. This neo-classicism too was shared by Debussy, especially in his piano music. The suite for piano duet (1889) has a minuet; the *Suite Bergamasque* (1890), as we have noted, has a minuet and a passepied; the suite *Pour le piano* (1896–1901) a sarabande and a toccata; the first set of pictures includes another sarabande as *Hommage à Rameau* (1905). There is a minuet again in the second sonata (1915). The fourth sonata, never written, was planned for oboe, horn, and harpsichord. Debussy expressed his strong liking for Rameau in several reviews and an unusually formal essay, published with the letters to Caplet. Throughout Debussy's prose a neo-classic strain is combined with the nationalist strain. (Gluck, he protests, does not deserve to be called classic.) And throughout his piano music there are ornaments and figurations like Couperin's and Rameau's. But his neo-classicism is not exclusively nationalist. In his hierarchy of values the supreme places are those of Bach and Mozart—Bach "in whom is all music," and Mozart, "my uncle." He might well have admired *Pulcinella* and the *Rake* as warmly as he did admire Stravinsky's *Firebird* and *Petrushka*.

But when the neo-classicism of the 1920s went "back to Bach," it emphasized or even exaggerated the least romantic features of Bach's style: the non-rubato, non-crescendo, and imitative counterpoint. Debussy naturally emphasized Bach's "adorable arabesques." He was forever opposed to whatever threatened to make music mechanical, bureaucratic, "dreary as a workshop." He was apprehensive about Stravinsky's "hard mechanism."

All these labels tempt us to hypostatize some vague but narrow notions of musical styles, which hinder us from noticing or remembering or enjoying music that we might enjoy if we could forget its label. Thus "expressionism" scares us away from whatever lucidity and humor there is in Schoenberg. "Neo-classicism" inhibits our feeling the poignance of Stravinsky. "Impressionism" beclouds both the radical novelty and the traditional strength of Debussy. (Likewise "total serialism" and "indeterminacy" delay our learning which of the composers tagged with these labels may be likely to hold our interest.)

The labels also tempt us to look for too simple relations among the styles—to see Debussy, Schoenberg, and Stravinsky as differing from each other more thoroughly than they do, and to see one superseding another in a straight line of historical development: impressionism, expressionism, neo-classicism. We know that the real relations among the styles must be far more complicated. We need to investigate such relations in order to deepen our understanding of any one of the styles. But this investigation is more hampered than helped by the terms we have surveyed.

The comparative investigation of styles can dispense with these "isms" altogether. Still better, it can relegate them to a subordinate place, and concentrate on the composers as complex persons, and on their compositions.

———•———

A composer's style and its development depend on the interplay of mysterious habits, intuitions, and choices. Any analysis of this interplay must be crude. But even a crude analysis of habits, intuitions, and choices may provide a better abstraction for comparisons between one style and another than labels like "impressionism" and "expressionism." The analyses that follow are metaphorical and suggestive, no more definitive than many other possible accounts. They are calculated to elucidate the great stylistic issues of 20th-century music while respecting the complex individuality of the great composers, beginning with Debussy.

Debussy learned three sets of musical habits. First, as a child singing and playing at the piano French folksongs, popular songs, salon music, and hits from current operas, he unconsciously formed habits that enabled him to improvise significant phrases. These habits he shared with not a few musicians. He did not think of them as habits but simply as spontaneous inclinations. When we refer to them as "spontaneous habits," our term does not conflict with other ways of identifying the same inclinations. Second, as a student, Debussy deliberately, easily, but reluctantly, learned from abstract exercises and from close study of a few masterpieces by Bach, Mozart, Beethoven, and 19th-century French composers, habits that enabled him to produce craftsmanlike large works with conventional tonality. These habits he despised as academic formulas, although he despised also composers like Berlioz whose mastery of them was incomplete. He rejected these habits because they conflicted with his spontaneous ones and with his more conscious ideals, which were shaped chiefly by literature. When we refer to "academic habits," we need not imply Debussy's distaste for them. Third, as a mature composer, once more unconsciously, he formed a few habits that enabled him to improvise passages of music recognizable as his own. Having formed these "personal habits," idiosyncrasies, mannerisms, he became conscious of them, despised them, and chafed at them. He wanted each new piece after *Pelléas* to make a new impression, as if of a new composer, newly inspired, chosen afresh.

Alongside his spontaneous habits he ranged all the possibilities that he learned from all the music of the world, especially Mussorgsky, Gregorian chant, Renaissance polyphony, Javanese gamelan music, and ragtime, to help him resist academic and personal habits. With all these possibilities at his disposal, and conscious habits blocked, he came to confront what Stravinsky later called "the abyss of freedom." Thereafter he complained often of a paralysis of the imagination. In 1909 he wrote to Caplet, "No, it is not neurosis, or hypochondria either. It is the sweet sickness of the notion of having to choose among all conceivable things." When he succeeded in making his inspired choices, he created unique and perfect forms. On the brink of the abyss of freedom he achieved much, though less than he hoped for.

The abyss is the freedom from all habits of musical thought, social and personal—a theoretical freedom to choose anything from the infinite realms of possible tonal and rhythmic relations among sounds. The realm of tonal relations, in which a singer of folksongs moves by habit without ever thinking of it, has preoccupied European composers. Their system of notation makes possible a control over the movements of their own and their performers' imaginations more extensive than musicians in other cultures ever dreamed of. Music notation does not comprehend the infinity of tonal relations, but it has been adequate and even stimulating for composers' explorations toward the abyss. For rhythmic relations it is less adequate, often hampering. Accordingly European composers, teachers, and theorists have somewhat neglected rhythmic relations, by comparison with the musicians of Africa and India, whose rhythmic habits may be more complicated than any European's calculations. Debussy's sweetly sickening multiplicity of possibilities still included relatively few rhythmic possibilities. His spontaneous rhythmic habits were strong, and his academic training had not upset these habits. It was his rejection of tonal habits and his acceptance of an unprecedented range of tonal possibilities that led him to the abyss.

The realm of possible tonal relations is infinite and also continuous. No finite composition can contain the whole realm. A composition may suggest its vast extent, or its continuity, or both. Or a composition may disregard these possibilities, maintaining its own coherence within a limited, habitual set of tonal relations, that is, a scale. Or a composition may seek coherence as a work of art through altogether different means, such as rhythm, while roving through an undefined part of the tonal realm. Or a composition may arbitrarily define a hitherto undefined set of relations and establish their coherence.

(The elementary units of tonal relations are intervals. A scale is a set of intervals. Most scales are traditional, abstracted from melodies, but some are calculated inventions.)

In Europe up to the Renaissance, and elsewhere as far as we know, composers chose one or another of the available, overlapping, habitual sets of relations (modes) for each composition, and rarely ventured beyond it. There is no indication that they tried to extend the conventional limits, or to reconcile two or more sets within one composition. Such matters concerned speculative theorists rather than practical composers.

In the Renaissance, however, some composers embarked on a great speculative enterprise, comparable to European science and European exploration of the globe. A good many composers, on occasions where the words they were setting provoked them, would deliberately reach out for new, distant tonal relations. At the end of the 16th century a few, like Gesualdo, became so addicted to this reaching out that they sometimes wandered aimlessly. Others, like Bull, occasionally tried to "integrate" the whole realm of all the overlapping conventional sets, which by now was vast enough to suggest the infinity of possibilities. Most, like Lassus and Palestrina, were satisfied with a tonal coherence less rigorous than that of a purely modal, unaccompanied melody, too loose to contribute much to the shaping of wordless instrumental music, but compatible with a perfect, highly sensitive shaping of vocal music.

In the Baroque period, 1600–1750, composers gradually created the new, complex conventions of "tonality" and modulation, whereby they could—and regularly did—establish the rational coherence of a tonal realm that was only slightly narrower than Gesualdo's. Any ventures beyond this large realm—through enharmonic modulation—were exceptional disturbances, suggesting the utter mystery of the infinite possibilities, within which the marvelous architecture of tonal compositions was one of the proudest achievements of human reason. Tonality was too complex a convention to become a spontaneous habit. It had to be learned by study. Teachers tried to make it an academic habit, but composers intelligent enough to learn it thoroughly were intelligent enough to explore beyond it.

Classic and Romantic composers accepted the convention of tonality as a starting point, as if it were given by Nature. They deliberately extended their reach out from it farther and farther, and with an intellectual virtuosity that matched their emotional intensity and was inseparable from it, for their outreachings, like Gesualdo's, used novel tonal relations to express strong emotions. Chopin and Fauré ventured farthest, or deepest, without losing their classic balance. Liszt, Wagner, and their successors achieved some magnificent feats, but at times they wandered aimlessly, either not knowing or not caring that they had failed to establish any coherence in the vast realm they traversed. Moreover, their habit of wandering corroded the sense of tonality, so that tonal coherence became a more difficult achievement than it had been even for the pioneers of tonality in the Baroque age.

Debussy's attitude toward tonal relations was as complex as the sense of tonality, but it was not a habit at all. He was sometimes content with some tonal realm narrower than Chopin's, but not often with the same realm. He was sometimes content to wander, but he did not succumb to the Wagnerian habit of wandering continually. He loved the plurality and diversity of conventions, and the open infinity of Nature. He was agnostic as to whether the infinite realm had any coherence or not. If some of his available sets of relations seemed discontinuous, very well—he could enjoy their discontinuity. He destroyed the European musicians' supposition that their favorite convention, the major scale, was peculiarly natural. But he was happy to use the major scale alongside other, older ones—the diatonic modes and the pentatonic scales. Also, he used and made famous the whole-tone scale, which was never a habit of anyone, but a construction, more narrowly limited and yet more suggestive of aimless wandering than any "natural" cultural growth, because it excluded the commonest intervals, perfect fifths and fourths, emphasized the tritone (diminished fifth or augmented fourth), and made its thirds and sixths all sound more or less like the uncommon, but not unrecognizable diminished fourths and augmented fifths respectively. Debussy felt no need to replace the old convention with any other, or to organize the relations among alternative conventions except for his personal purposes, different in each composition. He disdained all habits and distrusted all calculations. He liked coherence to be spontaneous, fresh, complete, modest, unemphatic, and free. He dared to hold his precarious footing on the brink of the abyss.

MacDowell, Rachmaninov, Strauss, Fauré, and other composers contemporary with Debussy glimpsed the abyss of tonal freedom, thanks partly to him. MacDowell and Rachmaninov never came near it in any published music, but both were aware of drawing back from a tempting adventure. MacDowell stopped listening to anyone else's music for fear of disrupting the delicate personal habits he depended on. Rachmaninov composed less and less. Strauss came close to the abyss and then turned back to reinforce his habits. Fauré clung firmly to his habits and leaned as far out as possible without snapping any of them.

On the contrary, Ives, Scriabin, Busoni, and Satie all plunged into the abyss. Busoni used this very metaphor in another context, writing to his pupil Egon Petri in 1905: "A man who has walked, jumped, or dived into the abyss is no more in awe of depths—that suits people who stay on the edge and dare not go down." The bold divers fished up various fragments of great interest. But none of them could achieve as perfect or ample or widely useful a work as their more prudent contemporaries. Certain habits clung to each of them, somewhat incongruous with their arbitrary choices. Their forms were seldom either craftsmanlike or inspired, though they all wrote inspired passages. Their achievements were not negligible, and their esoteric adventures remained exhilarating after half a century.

Meanwhile jazz transformed the popular music of European culture. It introduced rhythmic habits from Africa that eluded notation. It introduced new tone-colors. It left harmonic habits virtually unaffected. Debussy welcomed the beginning of this transformation.

Schoenberg formed his first set of habits through singing and playing the violin. In contrast to Debussy and all his contemporaries considered here, Schoenberg had no pianistic habit. He acquired his academic habits laboriously with little teaching, and along with these a profound knowledge of a wide range of German music from Bach to Mahler. Pursuing a course between Wagner and Brahms, Schoenberg developed his personal habits and approached the infinite abyss of freedom. When he encountered

Debussy, in 1907, he arrived at its edge. He too suffered occasional paralysis. He too achieved some inspired marvels on the brink. Unlike Debussy, he also accomplished astounding feats of speculative musical thought.

Looking back on his career in 1947, in a letter to the National Institute of Arts and Letters, Schoenberg made a characteristic grim joke of our metaphor:

I felt as if I had fallen into a sea of seething water, and since I could not swim or get out any other way, I flailed around as well as I could. I do not know what saved me, why I did not drown or become waterlogged. Perhaps my only merit was never to give up. . . . At least, I couldn't swim with the current. All I could do was to go against the current.

Schoenberg was fascinated equally by the infinite, ungraspable extent of the tonal realm and by its continuity, its absolute oneness. In nearly every composition he tried to suggest both. He was hardly interested at all in any alternative selection of intervals—he wanted complete, continual freedom for all. He became dissatisfied with his utmost reach outward from the limited, conventional realm. He felt impelled to reach further, and to move continuously, swiftly, by the largest possible strides. At the same time, he was not content to wander: he wanted to establish an adequate image of the coherence that he believed in so fiercely. For a long time he strove to relate his out-reachings to a single center, more strenuously than Debussy or Strauss or Scriabin did. But then he came to feel that the limits of tonality disturbed the continuity of his world-spanning strides. They were obstacles to the coherence that he might be able to suggest by some other means. He conceived the twelve-tone, equal-tempered scale as a representation of the infinity of tonal relations. By continually using all twelve tones and avoiding the definition of any habitual limited set, he could suggest the continuity of the infinite range of possible relations. He would trust his intuition to make his harmony cohere. Meanwhile, he would bolster the coherence of his music by every means other than harmony, in case his harmony was in fact as aimless as Gesualdo's or Reger's. He dismissed the question of enharmonic modulation. His conception of twelve tones as an "all" meant that every interval was slightly ambiguous, as in the whole-tone scale. Although in a piece by Schoenberg more different intervals were available than in a piece in the whole-tone scale, possibilities were many fewer than in a piece by Chopin or Wagner, where double sharps and double flats reach out to vast but measurable distances, in many but determinable directions from its tonal center. The perfect fifths and fourths (nearly perfect in equal temperament, and often quite perfect in the variable intonation of singers and players of orchestral instruments) resist enharmonic transvaluation; they stick out somewhat among the other intervals. Schoenberg guards against them by maintaining a thick texture full of the inherently ambiguous tritones and the minor seconds and major sevenths, which may easily be augmented primes and diminished octaves respectively. Thus his harmony does suggest the infinite totality, even though it is actually limited in a rather arbitrary and shifting manner.

Schoenberg's rhythms were as complicated and peculiar as his harmonies. The habits of march and waltz he never abandoned, but he overlaid them so thickly with rhythms of prose speech and personal gesture that the product was rhythmically newer than Debussy's.

After about five years of practice with his mature style, 1908–13, Schoenberg paused. When he began to publish compositions again, in 1923, he had constructed a sort of spaceship, the twelve-tone technique, to carry him out into the abyss, leaving behind some spontaneous habits and carrying along some academic ones. His technique was a device for limiting (not evading) choice, for preventing paralysis, and thus for maintaining the flow of intuition, on which he relied more devoutly than any other major composer. He wanted his achievement to be evaluated without regard to his technique. This was not yet possible in the decade after his death, for performances were still few, and most of these few were far from adequate. Meanwhile his technique, considered somewhat abstractly, became one of the chief facts of life for composers.

Stravinsky formed his first habits as a good amateur pianist with an extraordinarily wide-ranging and discriminating taste. He formed academic habits quickly but systematically as a private pupil of one of the greatest teachers, Rimsky-Korsakov, and on completing his studies in 1908 he discarded most of these habits. He was brought to the abyss of freedom through study of Debussy and through his own tendency "to search for sensation in all its freshness by discarding the warmed-over, the hackneyed, the specious." Stravinsky gave us the only ample account of the abyss, in his *Poetics of Music*. He credited Wagner with discovering it, and evading it by literary means, not musical. He identified the true protection from it: "a natural social discipline [that] imposed certain limiting conditions from without," as in the Middle Ages.

Stravinsky was in awe of the infinity of possibilities. The prospect of complete freedom paralyzed him: some sort of discipline, some sort of friction was necessary for any movement. He did not share Schoenberg's urge to invoke the totality of tonal relations any more than he shared the willingness of some composers to drift in it, or the reluctance of others to depart from the security of conventional tonality. He faced the infinity of temporal relations, as well as the infinity of tonal relations. He felt an obligation to discover concrete coherence among new, limited, but very large sets of relations. He regarded the undiscovered coherences of tone and time as objective, not subjective—in his terms, "ontological," not "psychological." He argued the desirability of fencing off the abyss by arbitrary restraints— scales and rhythmic patterns—self-imposed by each composer, and newly imposed with each new composition. His practice clarified his argument. Each new composition surprised his admirers, and showed that his freedom from one to the next was still unlimited, although the various restraints that he imposed on himself were chosen from procedures that had been habitual for some earlier composer or school, including in the 1950s the school of Schoenberg. His rhythmic discoveries were widely recognized as worthy of comparison with those of jazz. His shifting of tonal fences seemed to some observers hardly more adventurous than the prudent procedures of Strauss or Fauré, but for others they made possible the most monumental adventure and achievement in music since Debussy. Like Debussy, Stravinsky used multiple conventions, and achieved fresh coherence. In contrast to Debussy's illusion of ease, Stravinsky emphasized the achievement and its difficulty.

Bartók, on the brink of the abyss in 1905, reduced his habits to a minimum and then stretched his comprehension to a maximum. He saved the habits that he had just begun to cultivate, derived from East European folksongs, together with a few of the deepest ones he had acquired as an excellent professional pianist. His outward reach was greater than Fauré's or Stravinsky's. He maintained a precarious balance, in which he achieved marvels comparable to Debussy's and Schoenberg's. He leaned toward Schoenberg at times and corrected his balance by leaning toward Stravinsky. But his position was no mere compromise. He held in balance almost as much as Stravinsky and Schoenberg combined. His feat was more like a continuation of Debussy's fearful adventure, which he acknowledged as a model alongside Bach and Beethoven.

Bartók saw the infinite possibilities of harmony as neutral, indifferent to human purpose. He saw the various conventions as partial expressions of a common human need for balance. He sought to overcome the apparent discontinuities and conflicts among them by respecting their differences and organizing them in a hierarchy. He opened tonal conventions into each other, and reconciled them, with the pentatonic scales foremost, the diatonic modes surrounding them, the major-minor system and its chromatic extensions surrounding these, and enharmonic links opening all to the infinite further realm. Likewise he opened rhythmic conventions into each other, using both Romantic *rubato* and Stravinskian rigidity as variants of folk song and folk dance measures. His music is a play of overlapping forces fading gradually into infinity, rather than a binding together or an emphatic contrast of any limited set of elements.

After Schoenberg, Bartók, and Stravinsky, every serious composer was brought to the abyss as part of his academic training, which became less and less successful at instilling habits.

Prokofiev graduated from the St. Petersburg Conservatory in 1914, having easily reconciled his spontaneous habits as a piano virtuoso with some academic habits, provincial compared with Debussy's. As he explored the range of possibilities made public by Debussy, Reger, Scriabin, Schoenberg, and especially Stravinsky, he soon formed charming personal habits barely diverging from the social ones. He must have glimpsed the "abyss of freedom" but it was not in his character to linger there. He stepped back to a safe distance, without retreating all the way to common practice. He chose from the wide range of possibilities only enough to set his creative process in motion and to jog it from time to time. Occasionally he deliberately reinforced his native Russian habits, to prevent the ensemble of habits from becoming merely academic. His retreat from the abyss had motives both personal and social. Like Stravinsky he wanted to save himself from the paralysis that tortured Debussy. But also he wanted his work to serve his fellowmen—lay music lovers as well as fellow craftsmen. Possibly after 1933 he wanted it to serve the building of socialism in Russia and the preparation of a world-wide socialist peace. At any rate, he chose restraining principles unlike Stravinsky's and stuck to them, principles more conducive to making his music serve a larger audience. Moreover, he accepted "certain limiting conditions from without" imposed by the Soviet bureaucracy on behalf of a future "natural social discipline."

Something like Prokofiev's return from the lonely abyss, in various directions according to nationality and temperament, has been characteristic of many serious and highly gifted composers. Several of these, like Prokofiev, have not only communicated their own thoughts to their own communities, but have transmitted better than any poet or politician something of their national character to millions of people in other nations.

Hindemith graduated in 1917 from the Frankfurt Conservatory with habits derived from his playing the viola as a professional, and many other instruments as a brilliant amateur. There was no conflict between spontaneous and academic habits, which in Germany more than elsewhere overlap. His range of possibilities included some characteristic procedures of both Stravinsky and Schoenberg, and jazz. Hindemith was adventurous enough to gaze at the abyss of freedom, and vigorous enough to attempt to bridge it. He set out to develop personal habits of harmony that would suggest the totality of infinite possibilities by twelve notes, like Schoenberg, and respect the common element in all human conventions, like Bartók.

He hoped that these habits could become impersonal, academic for a future generation. Thus his stand, like Prokofiev's, had social as well as personal motives. It differed from Prokofiev's in its emphasis on craft and its demand that amateurs make music instead of consuming it passively. Hindemith left some room for unpredictable, inscrutable inspiration, but perhaps not room enough. He did not trust it to save him from the abyss. After he had brought his *Craft of Musical Composition* to the form of a book with exercises, 1939, his compositions confirmed the value of his craft for him, but excited less admiration than his earlier lucky finds. His craft was teachable; his pupils could imitate it more easily than they could imitate Debussy or Wagner or Bach, but they all rejected it sooner or later, to turn toward Schoenberg, Stravinsky, Bartók, or Webern, or to search out some other direction of their own.

Many other good composers envisioned something like Hindemith's ideal of a new convention comparable to tonality but much broader, if not inclusive of all infinity. No others made Hindemith's claim to have achieved the ideal, but many regarded their work as contributing to a communal achievement of it in the near future. This aspiration was no less noble, and no less naive, though perhaps more amiable than Hindemith's. The most inspired products of these composers too served many good purposes other than the advancement of a new conformity.

Webern engulfed his spontaneous habits as singer and pianist with an unprecedented erudition as well as immense craft. In 1906, a Doctor of Philosophy in musicology from the University of Vienna, he faced the abyss of freedom alongside Schoenberg, and began his career as composer. He formed his personal habits, very different from Schoenberg's, in the light of his different literary and religious orientation. Probably he suffered paralysis very often. He achieved a tiny work of extreme purity, which found almost no social resonance in his lifetime. Ten years after his death his work loomed as a major influence on Stravinsky's latest pieces and on young composers all over the world.

Prokofiev, Hindemith, and Webern represent the range of new styles after Schoenberg, Stravinsky, and Bartók. All six, together with Debussy, form a framework in which other contemporary styles can be approximately located.

CHAPTER III

Debussy's 20th-Century Music:
History in the service of
"recruiting unknown friends"

W IDENING CIRCLES of composers and listeners after the middle of the century, whose sympathies included Bartók and Webern, found Debussy's music, especially his late works, more important than ever. For example, Pierre Boulez, the most prominent young French composer of the 1950s, saw Debussy's late works as opening up a new conception of musical time, and of the "universe of music in general." Poulenc, Milhaud, Hindemith, and Stravinsky, who had seemed remote from Debussy in the 1930s, all acknowledged their abiding debts to him. An American composer, Allen Sapp, observed that *Pelléas* "presages our day, when we feel no longer the need for a tradition." Edward Lockspeiser drastically revised his concise book on Debussy, to pay tribute to the sustained inspiration and mastery of the late works; in his larger book, Lockspeiser showed Debussy as the initiator of a Freudian sense of music. Yet for most performers and audiences the late works were still awaiting discovery. Their ultimate historical importance, if never so great as that of *Pelléas* and the *Faun,* might yet approach a proper ratio with their intrinsic value.

The *Études* for piano (1915) are the least played of Debussy's piano music. But they are the best matched set of pieces he wrote. Together their range of mood and technique is immense, and every one of them is as rich as any of the more famous earlier pieces. They offer pianists hardly a moment that is not obviously difficult. They offer listeners no cues for daydreams. But they are no more "cerebral" or "neo-Classical" than the studies of Chopin, to whose memory Debussy's are dedicated. Pianists and listeners who master the difficulties of the studies are rewarded not only with the delight of the pieces themselves, but also with a deeper understanding of all

Debussy's earlier music. All his piano music needs, and the studies demand, a big piano with rich tone in the extreme registers, and a pianistic technique that controls the finest gradations of loudness throughout the range, so as to produce "opposed sonorities" rather than the warm, homogeneous blend, centering in the baritone range, that is typical of Brahms and his contemporaries. On the other hand, parallel chords must smoothly parallel the melody's rise and fall of loudness, with never a perfunctory treatment of their inner voices. The pedal must help sustain long notes and color short ones without destroying the carefully marked silences, staccatos, and *subito pianos*. A dry sound is seldom appropriate, but there is no place whatever for the blur that many pianists suppose warranted by "impressionism." The pianists Cortot, Dumesnil, Perrachio, Schmitz, Rosen, and Lee, writing about the study of Debussy, all emphasize the importance of his nuances. There are a few recordings of his own performances, made on player-piano rolls and later transferred to phonograph discs.

Singers, like pianists, have neglected the late works. Singers have better reasons than pianists for this neglect: there are fewer late songs than piano pieces, and many more early songs, which are worth singing again and again. But the early songs are best sung by singers who know the late ones too, just as the suite *Pour le piano* profits from the studies, and the *Faun* from *Syrinx*. Moreover, the best conductors, pianists, and other instrumentalists remember that Debussy was first of all a singer and composer of vocal music. His songs naturally demand perfect readings of the French texts, along with perfect musicianship. But while they benefit from a practiced diaphragm and a sweet, light vocal tone, the voice of an amateur singer who knows the words and music thoroughly will not mar them as badly as an ugly piano or a breathy flute mars Debussy's music, nor as badly as an amateurish voice mars Mozart. When Jane Bathori, who was the first singer of several of the late songs, wrote a brief guide to all of them, she emphasized absolute fidelity to the notes and the marks of expression. Maggie Teyte, who studied the songs and the role of Mélisande with Debussy, likewise testified in her memoirs to his "pedantic" precision and his "undercurrent of violence and terror." Teyte's recordings are among the greatest treasures of the whole catalogue of phonograph music.

The three ballades of the 15th-century poet François Villon, which Debussy set in 1910, are great poems, the most realistic that Debussy ever set, though not the most realistic that Villon wrote. Villon blended irony, passion, tenderness, and frivolity in a way that no other poet ever quite matched, a way that Verlaine, Maeterlinck, and d'Annunzio hardly dreamed of. Mozart could have found the right music for Villon if he had known him. Debussy's music is worthy of him. The end of the first ballade illustrates this wonderful blend. This passage illustrates also many of the technical details of Debussy's

EXAMPLE III.1   Debussy, *Ballade de Villon à s'amye,* conclusion

writing for piano and voice. The voice always has the center of attention. At times the accompaniment drops out for a line, but resumes on the last word, so as to maintain continuity. At the very end the accompaniment parallels the voice, with full triads. Elsewhere the accompaniment provides rich chords, and fragments of counterpoint, in a constantly changing texture. The voice's melody ranges just a little over an octave. Several of its phrases are rather like recitative, giving utmost clarity and ease to the words. But the refrain is a memorable melody, and the accompaniment, with its irregular, mostly slow-moving, often surprising changes of harmony, provides a kind of continuity that conventional recitative lacks. The refrain is purely modal—the Aeolian mode on F♯. Elsewhere both melody and accompaniment venture far from the tonal center, suggesting without clearly establishing rival centers; throughout the piece the cadences are all in F♯. Thus by the time a singer is familiar with the text and its form, the occasional augmented and diminished intervals are easier to find than they appear at first glance. The dynamic marks for the voice merely encourage the fluctuations implicit in the words, the rhythm, and the melodic contour. The marks for the piano are more profuse, and more needed, though they too, once they are meticulously observed, can be understood as derived from the central idea just as naturally as those of the voice. To observe some of the marks requires great care, no matter how familiar the piece: especially those of measures 36, 42–44, and 49. In all these instances a pianist must experiment with the pedals of each piano and the acoustics of each room in order to arrive at the realization of the right nuance.

The late chamber music, like the late songs and piano pieces, is less often played than the string quartet of 1893. The only reason for this is the comparatively rare media of performance that Debussy chose. In the repertory of cellists, Debussy's sonata surpasses all rivals since Brahms. The sonata for flute, viola, and harp is the last word in the vein of the *Faun* and *Syrinx,* with both the voluptuousness of the former and the austerity of the latter. The violin sonata is not quite so preëminent, but it is not nearly so disappointing as Debussy himself suggested in a letter to Godet: "I wrote this sonata only to get rid of it. . . . You who can read between the lines will see there traces of that Imp of the Perverse who drives us to choose the very idea that we should have rejected. This sonata is interesting from a documentary point of view, as an example of what a sick man can write during a war." When the piano part of this sonata is played by a man who knows the studies, and the violin part by a man who is not prejudiced against it, the music glows with health and peace. The rhapsody for clarinet, the rhapsody for saxophone, and the sight-reading exercise for clarinet, slight as they are, rank near the top of these instruments' slender repertories.

The ballet *Jeux* (1913) is Debussy's last, most difficult, and least performed piece for orchestra. Its scenario, by Nijinsky, is a landmark in the history of dancing. A man and two girls are looking for a lost tennis ball. They flirt, in every permutation of the trio. Then another tennis ball bounds on stage from the court, and the trio goes off into the woods. Nijinsky intended this as "a plastic vindication of the man of 1913," and of this man's treatment of personal relations as a kind of game. Debussy told Durand that the ending was "rather difficult to bring off, for the music has to make acceptable a rather *risqué* situation." Apart from the ballet, the music is difficult for performers to bring off, because of its intricate and constantly changing texture, built of short motifs that depend on rich chords, and also because of its fast rhythms, alternating several different waltzlike measures and syncopating against them. An analytical essay by Eimert suggests that in *Jeux* Debussy anticipated typical procedures of electronic music, not only in the motivic treatment of tambourine and cymbal but also in the mosaic-like form. Some recorded performances of *Jeux* are helpful introductions to this unique piece, but many live performances, with very many rehearsals, are needed to reveal its true shape, and to permit it to find its place in the history of music.

During the 1960s, performances by various orchestras that Pierre Boulez conducted by heart gave proof that *Jeux* was as sure and strong a master-piece as *La Mer,* and as profoundly original a landmark as its close con-temporaries *Pierrot Lunaire* and *The Rite of Spring.*

Because the true relation of Debussy's adventure to the adventures of other 20th-century composers has been obscured, his achievement has not yet been enjoyed as much as it might be. Whereas historical truth is worth pursuing for its own sake, its separate value is pale compared with the enjoyment of music. When history can serve to increase the enjoyment of music, then its intrinsic value is multiplied. Thus scholarly studies of Bach and Mozart, for example, have contributed enormously to some of the deepest delights that 20th-century men can know. So in a study of the new music of the 20th century, the greatest reward, and the greatest motive for uncovering the facts and organizing them in patterns of stylistic relationship, is an enhanced appreciation of music such as Debussy's.

Music history is like contrapuntal music. Its *cantus firmus* or central theme is some pattern of abstract styles, of technical and esthetic issues and tendencies, for which compositions provide the documentary evidence. But the theme allows attention to dwell from time to time on the compositions, which are also the more or less conscious motive for the study. Then there is an accompanying background, which shades off into all the history of men and women. History is concerned with musical activities of every kind, and with their relations to other activities, with the uses of music as well as its creation, with musical institutions and economic arrangements. All these matters are both interesting in themselves and relevant to our central theme.

Although the "exclusive privilege" of high art is won by intelligence, not birth or money, yet intelligence wins its privilege partly by understanding "groups of society," if only in order to escape their prejudices.

Patterns of social and economic change can be found to parallel the patterns of stylistic change. Economic changes surely condition the stylistic changes and, perhaps, in some sense, determine them. But the facts are so many, so varied, and so incompletely known that a conscientious historian must propose any pattern as a tentative hypothesis. Any pattern of parallel patterns is a mere speculation, not an explanation.

The immense peripheral background of music history can be kept in mind without commitment to any theoretical pattern. It can be drawn upon in relating the work of individual composers to their lives as individual and social men. Biographical facts can be selected and arranged to remind us continually of the immense dim background, and to show some of the concrete connections between a style and its immediate background, which any adequate theoretical pattern would have to fit. An emphasis on biography in this context has nothing to do with the old-fashioned myth that heroic acts are unconditioned, that composers create out of nothing. Within a biography there may well be reference to some abstract theory of social and economic tendencies, as well as to the concrete facts and to stylistic patterns. The biographical emphasis implies only that historians are no more free than their heroes from the limitations of human knowledge.

It should be needless to warn that our passing attention to biographies remains quite subordinate to our constant attention to the music itself. There may be students of Gershwin or Messiaen or Shostakovich, as there have been of Beethoven and Chopin, who try to connect particular works with particular emotional crises in the composers' lives, seeming to care more about the latter. But anyone interested in Debussy, Schoenberg, Bartók, and Stravinsky is on guard against this danger; what he must beware of is esthetic and historical generalization. Biography can be used with discrimination to combat the modern danger without courting the Romantic one.

Thus, in the background of Debussy's career let us note the unprecedented prosperity, freedom, and turbulence of musical life. The beginning of the 20th century was the most prosperous period in the history of music. The unfettered international capitalistic economy of Europe supported more full-time composers of serious music than any social organization before or since. It permitted far more musicians than it could support to compete for recognition in a market more extensive and complicated than the market for books or pictures. New music in old and new styles sped across national boundaries, almost around the world. It was published, sold, and performed in enormous quantities. The composers' rights were better and better protected by copyright laws, and by associations for their enforcement. At the same time performances of the 19th-century repertory were more and more frequent and profitable to star performers and their managers. Opera companies, symphony orchestras, military bands, church choirs, festival choruses, theater and dance ensembles, and institutions for musical education on many levels were expanding rapidly. The grandiose opera houses and concert halls built in the latter half of the 19th century in the world capitals were being copied in provincial cities. String quartets were beginning to make concert tours, like opera singers or virtuoso pianists. Wagner's sublime idea of the festivals at Bayreuth was beginning to be adopted elsewhere. The momentum generated in this period was so great that after World War I an immense amount of routine musical activity went on in the same direction, despite technological and social changes that hampered further growth, and despite changes of taste among an elite minority of musicians. The economic situation before the war stimulated Debussy and others to stretch their techniques and imaginations as far as possible, to take for granted the ultimate social value of their individual adventures, and to expect high rewards for their achievements. The war shocked them, and brought to their attention the profound, long-range upheaval in which the war was the first world-wide crisis.

The heyday of capitalism was not without many lingering traces of the older, aristocratic organization of society, in particular its patronage of music, which some rich bourgeois were ready to take over. Thus Debussy in his student days was supported, almost adopted, by the Vasnier family. In 1880–82 he was hired by Mme. von Meck, the "beloved friend" and patroness of Tchaikovsky, to tutor her children and play duets with them, while traveling all about Europe. When he won the Rome Prize (1884) Debussy won not only professional standing, but a distinct prestige among all cultivated Frenchmen, such as can hardly be imagined in a world more populous, more democratized, more publicized, more hurried and insecure. Of special importance to him and his work was the *entrée* the prize gave him to the circle of Mallarmé. Nothing like this would have been likely a generation earlier, before French men of letters had learned from Baudelaire to respect the claim of Beethoven and Wagner that composers were the greatest poets. Nor would it be likely a generation or two later, when so many beginning composers, with so many prizes, competed for attention that even their colleagues were ignorant of them. Debussy was born in the right decade.

For ordinary performing musicians, long freed from craft guilds and not yet protected by trade unions, the benefits of lingering aristocratic patronage and burgeoning middle-class prosperity were dubious. But this fact multiplied the benefits to composers. A successful opera composer, like Debussy, Strauss, or Puccini, was as remote from the men in the pit as an admiral from a sailor or a bank president from his clerk. He could demand of them uncounted hours of rehearsal at very low wages. An unrecognized composer, of course, might have to drudge on as performer or teacher, or give up music if he had to support a family.

European music was spreading over the world at an accelerating pace. Though not yet by radio or mass-produced phonograph records, music was transmitted by military bands, by missionary hymn singing, by concerts of world-traveling star performers, and by the network of educational institutions with their libraries of printed music.

The various musics of Africa and Asia, which Debussy and many other Europeans had heard for the first time at the Paris Exposition of 1889, were still, in an important sense, prehistoric, like the art of the dance. Literary histories existed, of course, in many Asian countries, and in some there were highly cultivated professional musical traditions, with theoretical treatises. But there were no archives of music, and no scholarly narratives of its development even in these traditions. In the various complex cultures of Africa, even literary records were lacking. And the "classical" Asian traditions almost completely neglected the folk music connected with their elaborate products and theories. The immense social and economic changes that were now overtaking Africa and Asia, in reaction to European conquest and infiltration, changed the old musical life along with everything else, in ways that can never be fully known. No doubt many precious musical ideas were lost beyond the possibility of recovery by any history.

A few pioneers, especially a group of psychologists in Germany and some anthropologists in the United States, were beginning to collect and study the music of the world. Their motive, in many cases, was to prove the universal validity of some abstract theory about scales or rhythms, or else to trace the "rise" of music from its origins to its supposed perfection in modern civilization. But their studies provided a foundation on which later scholars could work, disabused of such motives, partly by Debussy's loosening of Western polyphony and tonality, and also by the general trend of anthropological thought. Debussy's friend and biographer, Laloy, was among the first sophisticated students of Chinese music; his concerns with both kinds of music illuminated each other.

———•—

On the crowded, prosperous European scene at the turn of the century, Debussy and his contemporaries competed for recognition not only with each other, but also with many older composers. The oldest and grandest of all, though no longer active, was Verdi (1813–1901). In the generation of Verdi's pupils and Debussy's teachers, still vigorously productive, were Dvořák, Grieg, and Rimsky-Korsakov, all of whom died in their early sixties—1904, 1907, and 1908 respectively.

Closely contemporary with the three great nationalists were the two pillars of Victorian music, Sir John Stainer and Sir Arthur Sullivan, and the first academically respectable American composer, John Knowles Paine. In

Germany Karl Goldmark, Max Bruch, and Josef Rheinberger represented the solid center of the same tradition. All these men died soon after the turn of the century.

One composer who was past fifty in 1900, Gabriel Fauré, lived on beyond Debussy to nearly eighty. His distinctive style was still evolving. He was to contribute much to 20th-century music and his work must be described along with that of Debussy's contemporaries.

Many worthy veterans maintained their 19th-century styles up to the First World War, or even later. Along with Rimsky there were two other survivors of the Five, Balakirev and Cui, and Rimsky's oldest pupils, Liadov and Ippolitov-Ivanov. There was Tchaikovsky's pupil, the learned and witty master of counterpoint, Taneiev, and another important Russian, the choral composer and folksong arranger, Kastalsky. There was the pioneer of serious Spanish music and musicology, Pedrell, and the master of the popular *zarzuela*, Breton y Hernández. In England the two reformers Parry and Stanford paved the way for the great 20th-century revival there. In New England Foote and Chadwick broadened and deepened the tradition of Paine, and elsewhere in the United States Gilchrist, Gleason, and Kelley struggled to establish standards of serious music, while Sousa, Sankey, and Herbert represented various vital kinds of popular music. In Germany Humperdinck was the most eminent of many disciples of Wagner. In Italy Boito, Verdi's collaborator, kept his tradition alive. In France alongside Fauré there were Saint-Saëns, Massenet, Widor, Messager, Duparc, and d'Indy. Similarly eminent in their own countries were the Swiss Hans Huber, the Fleming Jan Blockx, the Norwegian Christian Sinding, and the Czech J. B. Foerster. There were many other composers comparable to these, whose fame was so restricted in time and place that their names would serve no purpose here. All these men were enjoying the professional prosperity to which the young aspired.

Besides the composers, there were such important veteran performers and teachers as the violinists Sarasate, Auer, Ševčík, and Ysaÿe, the pianist Leschetizky, the conductors Richter and Mottl, and scholars like Riemann and Pothier, all of whom lived well into the 20th century and contributed generously to its musical life, though they participated only indirectly in the development of its new musical styles. The increasing specialization of work within the field of music that these men represented, by comparison with the all-round musicians of the 18th century and earlier, was to proceed further in the 20th century. Performers, conductors, and scholars were not only to contribute alongside composers, but often to overshadow composers in the musical life of the new age.

Around 1900 dozens of able composers in their twenties or thirties began to be noticed and to strive for the kind of recognition that their elders had won. Richard Strauss was already securely established. Like him, many of this generation were to outlive Debussy, but most of them formed their styles and composed their chief works during his lifetime. A few exceptional figures born in the 1870s prolonged their formative developments after World War I: Koechlin, Roussel, Schoenberg, Vaughan Williams, and Ruggles. The rest may be grouped as Debussy's contemporaries.

As indicated in our survey of stylistic issues (Chapter II), some of the composers contemporary with Debussy departed more boldly than he did from the common practice of their elders, and others more nearly conformed. No one of them was at once so new and so successful as Debussy. No one of them exercised such profound and pervasive influence. No one of them needs, as Debussy does, to be studied thoroughly by every musician. A history concerned only with the great stylistic issues might neglect these composers, to proceed at once to Schoenberg. But a history that cares for concrete facts, for people, and for backgrounds—a history that lends itself to enhancing appreciation—will consider these composers one by one.

Among them at least twenty are familiar by name to every concert-goer and record-collector. Most musicians find among them one or two so congenial that a thorough study is as desirable as the study of greater composers. To be sure, most musicians find some of this group repugnant, or simply boring. The adventures of the bolder ones are likely to fascinate young composers and historians, while the achievements of the prudent are more likely to delight performers and listeners. On the other hand—what is more important—among the bold adventurers nearly every open-minded listener can find kindred spirits, while among the prudent achievers every musician can find valuable models of technical skill. It would be futile to specify just where the music of these men recruits its unknown friends.

Moreover, the careers and personalities of these men are as interesting as their works, and in studying them we learn more about the background they shared with Debussy, and the background they shaped for Schoenberg, Bartók, and Stravinsky.

Finally, there are available today many special studies of most of Debussy's contemporaries, correcting and enormously amplifying the information that circulated in histories written while they were still alive. The commonly accepted ideas about these composers are always fragmentary, often superficial, and occasionally quite mistaken. The special studies enable historians today to do justice to these composers. But sometimes such a special study of one man is seriously marred by ignorant prejudice against his rivals. The findings of the special studies, sifted and coordinated, make a new history.

The contrast between stylistic adventure and achievement shows up clearly in the Americans, MacDowell and Ives. These two were the only Americans before World War I who produced a body of concert music destined to command any considerable interest in Europe, although American popular music had begun to win an international audience somewhat earlier, and was steadily growing in importance. Thus their careers illuminate aspects of the world-wide social background of music, just as their works illustrate the stylistic issues. MacDowell's achievement was promptly and correctly greeted as slightly less than that of Grieg. Ives's adventures were belatedly and approximately revealed as comparable to the adventures of Schoenberg and Bartók.

CHAPTER IV

Contemporaries in America, Australia, Japan

EDWARD MacDOWELL (1861–1908) was the son of prosperous, art-loving New Yorkers, who in 1876 took their fifteen-year-old as an aspiring pianist to Paris. In 1877 he entered the Conservatory, where Debussy, eight months younger, was in his fourth year, about to make the decisive shift of his ambitions from performance to composition. MacDowell disliked the frivolous French. After a year he persuaded his family to send him on to Stuttgart and then Frankfurt. Here, gradually, he found his vocation as a composer, under the guidance of Joachim Raff (1822–82) and with the help of his American pupil Marian Nevins, who married him on condition that he would stop teaching and live for a few years on her small dowry. He proceeded to write a great deal of music, including two piano concertos. He returned to America (1888) and resumed teaching, first in Boston, and after 1896 at Columbia University in New York. His lectures at Columbia, later published as *Critical and Historical Essays,* indicated that he adhered to the taste he had learned from Raff: his great loves were Mendelssohn and Liszt. He was swayed by Wagner, but disapproved of the "intrusion of materialism" in his works. He respected Palestrina and Bach and Beethoven without knowing much of their music or understanding all he did know. He deplored Mozart's "empty concessions to technical display and commonplace, ear-catching melody." In short, he represented 19th-century idealism at its narrowest extreme. But he was not complacent.

In 1895 MacDowell met Hamlin Garland, whose realistic regional stories he thoroughly admired. When Garland gave him a crude performance of a Navajo song and dance, MacDowell confessed that his own music, even the "Indian" Suite, Op. 48, his last and best piece for orchestra, seemed in comparison "like milk and water." Garland recalled that MacDowell told him: "The weakness of our music is in its borrowing. I began by imitating the German composers. I am now on the way to being myself and as I am myself I will be Celtic-American rather than German-American or Afro-American." MacDowell's nationalism, thus sensibly qualified, was no rebellion. If he had lived long enough he might have achieved something as durable as Grieg or Dvořák. Just then (1892–95) Dvořák was in New York, composing his "American" works and stimulating young Americans to develop a national style. But MacDowell wisely recognized that a national style grows slowly. He concentrated on perfecting his personal manner.

Between 1893 and 1903 he composed the music in which he was most himself: eighteen songs, seven choruses, four sonatas and four sets of short character-pieces for piano—*Woodland Sketches,* Op. 51, *Sea Pieces,* Op. 55, *Fireside Tales,* Op. 61, and *New England Idylls,* Op. 62. A few of the short pieces became famous and hackneyed, particularly *To a Wild Rose* from the first set, and several other tender, dainty ones. Some of the more buoyant, lilting ones, like *Of Salamanders, Br'er Rabbit,* and *The Joy of Autumn,* and the somber, noble, clangorous ones like *To the Sea, To an Old White Pine,* and *In Deep Woods* remain favorites of all who know them.

The style of these pieces shows no fundamental divergence from common harmonic and rhythmic practice. MacDowell achieved his refined individual manner by narrowing his range of choices, rather than expanding it as Debussy did. His range was so narrow that his sonatas lacked the variety to warrant their length. "The continual richness in his harmonic texture," which Lawrence Gilman points to in his standard biography of MacDowell, makes every long piece cloying. This richness consists chiefly of seventh and ninth chords, connected by chromatic motion of the inner voices conforming to traditional rules but lacking contrapuntal interest. Even the bass line is undistinguished except when it carries the main melody. What is surprising in a pianist's music, the rich chords are seldom broken or otherwise decorated. In his playing, as described by his friend T. P. Currier, MacDowell emphasized and maintained the rich texture by "constant use of the 'half-pedal,' instead of the full pedal, which latter would have cut things out too clearly for him." The long pieces suffer too from the naive treatment of modulations, which occur often in sequences, hardly ever within a phrase. Finally, MacDowell's markings of tempo and dynamics, frequently changing and frequently at the extremes, are imprecise; performers must use great discretion to make tempo and dynamics contribute to maximum variety and unity. All reports of his playing mention its amazing extremes of thunderous power and fragile delicacy, just as the descriptions of his physique and personality emphasize both his athletic energy and his dreamy gaze.

In the short pieces MacDowell's narrowness is appropriate. The rich texture supports and colors the distinctive melodies. These are made up of short motifs, suggesting animated speech. They range over two or three octaves. They are full of diatonic appoggiaturas resolving into the chords. They develop and lead smoothly, in various interesting ways, to satisfying recapitulations. They seem spontaneous and sincere. Oscar Sonneck, in his fine study of MacDowell's revisions, notes that "he rarely changes his melodies—he changes them, if at all, for the purpose of a more typically MacDowellian harmonic zest and lucidity," whereas he seems to keep tinkering with the accompaniments for the sake of ever more "interestingly fluent motion of the middle voices."

The titles of the short pieces helped to make them famous and then helped equally to dissipate their fame. These titles and the attitudes they suggest, rather than any feature of the music itself, led Hans Albrecht and other scholars to class MacDowell as an impressionist. MacDowell's own notion of the relation between music and titles was naive. The novelist Upton Sinclair, who was an enthusiastic student in MacDowell's appreciation course at Columbia in 1899, told how "sometimes he would prepare unhappiness for himself by playing us this or that bit of his own music and expecting us to guess what it was about, and he would grope around for words, and find very jumbled and inadequate ones, and conclude with a gesture of despair." If extramusical associations are so important to his art, perhaps he is most justly represented by the songs, many of which are settings of his own verse. But in fact here too, as in the piano pieces, the purely musical charm is stronger than the interest of the objects that inspired MacDowell. Moreover, he argued that purely instrumental music was potentially loftier than song or music-drama, where "the necessity for the words drags it into the mud."

Toward the end of his short career, MacDowell, like Debussy, spent much of his enormous energy on an ill-fated mime-opera. This was inspired by Abbey's murals in the Boston Public Library depicting King Arthur and his knights. Sometime in 1902–03 while MacDowell was on sabbatical leave from Columbia, he destroyed all his sketches for this opera. He published no more music thereafter. What sort of adventure he drew back from we can only guess.

When he returned to Columbia he found his naively ambitious plans for music education thwarted. He resigned in indignation. Early in 1905, forty-three years old, he began to lose his mind, and in 1908 he died. His plucky widow lived until 1955, working tirelessly for the MacDowell Colony in New Hampshire, where successive generations of American composers, writers, painters, and sculptors benefitted from his and her idealism. Only after her death did the manuscript sketches and letters become accessible for study at the Library of Congress.

Charles Ives (1874–1954) grew up in Danbury, Connecticut, studied at Yale, and played the organ there and in New York City for a few years after he entered the insurance business (1898). Ives must have been acquainted with the music of MacDowell. Many of his own songs of the nineties resembled MacDowell's in their rich harmony and conventional rhythm. But he soon came to scorn MacDowell along with everything else that seemed to him merely "nice," genteel and shallow, though he never scorned popular music that showed vitality. By 1910 he was thoroughly committed to such rash adventures that everyone who knew him except his wife, Harmony Twitchell, considered him a crank. His adventures had begun in childhood, when his father, a bandmaster in the Civil War, spurred him to exercise his ear by playing melodies in two keys at once, to write phrases in the whole-tone scale, to speculate on quarter tones, and to observe and imitate strange effects of bells and echoes. When eventually Ives prospered in business, he published and distributed free (1919–22) samples of the work he had accumulated: the second sonata for piano, *Concord, Massachusetts, 1840–1860,* then a volume of *Essays Before a Sonata,* and last a volume of *114 Songs,* many of which were arrangements of pieces conceived for orchestra or chamber groups. In 1923 he composed three quarter-tone pieces for two pianos. Soon thereafter illness stopped his composing. By the time of his death just before his eightieth birthday, he was a legendary figure, inspiring and consoling many young Americans, though seldom exerting any musical influence. Henry Brant (b. 1913) was exceptional in finding Ives's work a real starting point for his own. Elliott Carter, who knew Ives and his music as early as 1924, in 1944 defined "his vision and challenge," and in 1960 reaffirmed his loyalty to the man and his critical regard for the music.

Very slowly Ives's music became accessible in print and on records. An enthusiastic biography by Sidney and Henry Cowell listed four symphonies and other large orchestral pieces, fifteen choral pieces, nearly two hundred songs, two quartets, four violin sonatas, and countless fragments. Though performances were still rare, recordings permitted anyone interested to share in the Cowells' enthusiasm. The *Concord Sonata,* hailed by critics at its first complete performance (1939) as the greatest American achievement in music, was still, twenty-five years later, the specialty of one brave pianist, John Kirkpatrick, but by now his recorded performance could be compared with several others. Kirkpatrick was cataloguing, collating, and editing the manuscripts at the Yale library. Until this work was completed and some fair proportion of the music could be known in performance, any account of Ives's development had to be sketchy. The best discussions, such as Bentley Layton's study of the 114 songs, were explicitly tentative.

Ives's adventures never aimed at finding a style or a perfect form. In his *Essays* he elaborated a dualistic theory of

what may be called reality, quality, spirit, or substance against the lower value of form, quantity, or manner . . . Substance in a human art-quality suggests the body of a conviction which has its birth in the spiritual consciousness, whose youth is nourished in the moral consciousness, and whose maturity as a result of all this growth is then represented in a mental image. This is appreciated by intuition, and somehow translated into expression—by "manner"—a process always less important than it seems . . . Manner breeds a cussed-cleverness—only to be clever—a satellite of super-industrialism.

Ives's application of his theory to Debussy showed its concrete meaning:

We might offer the suggestion that Debussy's content would have been worthier of his manner, if he had hoed corn or sold newspapers for a living, for in this way he might have gained a deeper vitality and a truer theme to sing at night and of a Sunday. Or we might say that what substance there is, is "too coherent" —it is too clearly expressed in the first thirty seconds. There you have the "whole fragment," a translucent syllogism, but then the reality, the spirit, the substance stops and the "form," the "perfume," the "manner," shimmer right along, as the soapsuds glisten after one has finished washing. Or we might say that his substance would have been worthier, if his adoration or contemplation of Nature, which is often a part of it, and which rises to great heights, as is felt for example in *La Mer,* had been more the quality of Thoreau's.

The composers whose "substance" satisfied Ives were few: Bach and Beethoven. Wagner he had loved and then outgrown:

This music had become cloying, the melodies threadbare—a sense of something commonplace—yes—of make-believe came. These feelings were fought against for association's sake, and because of gratitude for bygone pleasures—but the former beauty and nobility were not there, and in their place stood irritating intervals of descending fourths and fifths. Those once transcendent progressions, luxuriant suggestions of Debussy chords of the 9th, 11th, etc. were becoming slimy. An unearned exultation—a sentimentality deadening something within—hides around in the music. Wagner seems less and less to measure up to the substance and reality of César Franck, Brahms, d'Indy, or even Elgar (with all his tiresomeness); the wholesomeness, manliness, humility and deep spiritual, possibly religious feeling of these men seem missing and not made up for by his (Wagner's) manner and eloquence, even if greater than theirs (which is very doubtful).

Ives knew nothing of any composer later than Debussy during the years of his activity as a composer. He pursued his adventure with extraordinary independence. More than any other musician, writers like Thoreau, Emerson, and Ruskin represented the moral substance that concerned him.

His own music, when studied along with his trenchant, choppy prose, shows his substantial character, his Emersonian idealism and self-reliance.

Without the prose, unfortunately, much of the music fails to make any clear effect. For just as in the prose that we have sampled he uses commas and dashes to string together approximate epithets and subordinate clauses and even whole sentences, so in music, disdaining purely musical articulation, he heaps up motifs and chords, all pregnant with literary associations.

To guess what Ives is getting at in his sonatas and symphonies, it is essential to recognize the tunes he quoted, especially from popular church music, but also from dance music and military band music. It is desirable to know the texts and to sympathize with their meanings in the small towns and countryside of America. At the same time it is necessary to abandon all the inhibitions that are embodied in the strictly rational harmony and rhythm of these sources. Ives did not build a style on them. He rarely used them as themes for fugal or symphonic development. More often, like Debussy in his allusions, he quoted the simple melodies, or fragments of them, in a complex context, in order to comment on the life they represented. He wanted his music like his prose to connect this narrow, local life with the free play of infinite, universal ideas and feelings.

Thus he often arranged for two or more melodies to conflict in utterly unorthodox ways, creating polyharmonies and polyrhythms that simply had no unity short of the unity of the cosmos.

His own melodies are not memorable. His own rhythms are often sluggish, or jerky. His chords are mostly opaque blocks of six or more notes tightly spaced and doubled in octaves. He is unconcerned about performers' ease or gratification. In short, his command of musical materials is deficient. All this is mere "manner," and he knew that no manner whatever is quite adequate to the ideal "substance" of Bach and Beethoven. It is his boldness of imagined "substance" that compels admiration, and in some of his music a sympathetic listener finds unique delights, along with the moral challenge.

Soliloquy, or a study in sevenths and other things, published in 1933 with the date of composition 1907, exhibits Ives's fantastic congestion of bold ideas. The text is his own: "When a man is sitting before the fire on the hearth, he says 'Nature is a simple affair.' Then he looks out the window and sees a hailstorm, and he begins to think that 'Nature can't be so easily disposed of!'" The first sentence is to be "chanted or half spoken and somewhat drawling," adagio, almost a monotone, accompanied by a pattern of soft sustained chords, twice repeated. The second sentence is allegro, accelerando, forte, crescendo, with leaps and glides over major sevenths and minor ninths. The melody begins with a series of twelve different notes, and continues with two more series slightly defective. The accompaniment needs two or more players to reach its seven-note chords, all of which are constructed by piling up similar intervals, with no regard for contrapuntal parts. The accompaniment continues to repeat itself, retrograde, as the last measure (Ex. IV.1) repeats the next to last. The allegro is further organized by a

EXAMPLE IV.1   Ives, *Soliloquy,* climax

hail - storm,   and   he_____ be - gins to   think_____that

metrical pattern: 5, 6, 7, 8, 5, 5, 8, 7, 6, 5. Can this ingenious structure be heard, or imagined in sound? Ives rejected this question: "My God! What has sound got to do with music? . . . Why can't music go out in the same way it comes in to man, without having to crawl over a fence of sounds, thoraxes, catguts, wire, wood, and brass?"

A less prickly, though no less characteristic example is the song of 1908, *The Innate.* The bracketed motif hints at a familiar tune. After two more

EXAMPLE IV.2   Ives, *The Innate,* beginning

Voi - ces live in   every fin - ite be - ing, Of - ten

un - di - vined, near si - lence.   Hear them!   Hear__them in   you!   in____ oth - ers!

phrases the whole first phrase of the hymn *Nettleton*, by the American psalmodist John Wyeth (1770–1858), is clearly revealed in the voice part, but the accompaniment fades away to join the undefined, undivined voices.

Even though most of Ives's music may remain a soliloquy, overheard by few listeners, his precept and example of attentiveness to the "voices" in every finite being are an important contribution to a democratic musical culture. Whenever his extraordinary courage and self-reliance draw an admirer toward his humility before Nature and before the most ordinary music, then his work is proved worth while.

Among Americans contemporary with Ives and MacDowell, several maintained and transmitted a 19th-century tradition with more skill and amplitude than either of the heroes. These men's names give concrete meaning to our notion of tradition, even if we seldom revive their music; they indicate the complexity of the tradition as well as its dilution. Moreover, their music measures up well next to that of a Glazunov or Respighi or Franz Schmidt; occasional revivals mix patriotic piety with real pleasure. Ives's teacher at Yale, Horatio Parker (1863–1919), was good enough to command Ives's enduring respect. He composed songs, choruses, oratorios, operas, and organ music, all hard to distinguish from the works of his chief teachers, Chadwick at Yale and Rheinberger in Munich. The oratorio *Hora novissima* was Parker's most famous piece. Frederick Shepherd Converse (1871–1940) was another pupil of Chadwick and Rheinberger and also of Paine at Harvard, where he returned to teach. He composed symphonies, tone poems, chamber music, operas, oratorios, piano pieces, and songs—every form current. The orchestral tribute to *Flivver Ten Million* (1927) was outstanding in Converse's work. Daniel Gregory Mason (1873–1953) studied with Chadwick and d'Indy; he taught at Columbia. His several well-written books indicate that he felt a challenge to his habits and ideals, provoked by interests in nationalism and modernism; but he repressed these interests to defend what he regarded as musical orthodoxy, with his symphonies and chamber music as well as his criticism. This attitude makes him a suitable scapegoat for Gilbert Chase's survey of *America's Music*. But his overture *Chanticleer* (1928) may yet give Mason the last laugh. Edward Burlingame Hill (1872–1959) studied with Chadwick and Widor and taught at Harvard. His book on *Modern French Music* (1924) hails the French as conquerors (more than liberators) so that a proper Bostonian can maintain an attitude of dignified provincialism. His music, like his book, shows that he missed most of Debussy's significance; he best understood Chabrier, d'Indy, Roussel, and Ravel. Yet his understanding of Ravel's marvelous orchestration was as sophisticated as any Parisian's. John Alden Carpenter (1876–1951) was a pupil of Paine, Elgar, and the remarkable

German theorist in Chicago, Bernhard Ziehn (1845–1912). Carpenter learned something from Debussy and popular music, which he fitted into his essentially conservative habits. Like Ives, Carpenter was a successful business-man. His sensitive songs, including a cycle on poems by Tagore (1912) and a cycle of *Water Colors: Chinese Tone Poems* (1914), wear better than his later picturesque orchestral pieces, but these too are interesting, for in them Carpenter anticipates some of the traits of George Gershwin and Aaron Copland. Rubin Goldmark (1872–1936) was a New Yorker, nephew of Karl Goldmark, student in Vienna at both the Conservatory and University, and finally a student of Dvořák in New York. Goldmark composed all sorts of instrumental music. He transmitted the orthodox tradition to a group of distinguished pupils including Gershwin, Copland, Jacobi, Berezowsky, Wagenaar, Giannini, and Nordoff. Charles Martin Loeffler (1861–1935) grew up a violinist in France, Germany, and Russia. He came to America when he was twenty, played with the Boston Symphony Orchestra until he was forty, and then retired to full-time composition, having no family to support. More than any of the native Americans, Loeffler shared Debussy's interests in symbolist poetry, in new tone-colors, and in combinations of modality and chromaticism. His most famous piece, *A Pagan Poem,* was originally composed in 1901 for a remarkable chamber group: three trumpets approaching gradually from a distance to join seven winds, viola, bass, and piano. Henry Eichheim (1870–1942) was like Loeffler a violinist in the Boston Symphony Orchestra, who retired in his early forties to compose. But whereas Loeffler, already a cosmopolitan, became a recluse in Medfield, Massachusetts, Eichheim, a Chicagoan, became a traveler in the Orient, collecting instruments, studying the various musical systems, and producing a series of orchestral distillations: *Oriental Impressions* (1921), *Burma* (1927), *Java* (1929), *Japanese Nocturne* (1930), *Bali* (1933), *Korean Sketch* (1934). Eichheim more than any other composer of his generation took to heart Debussy's exoticism. A study of Eichheim's music is needed.

Three more Americans, less thorough masters of their craft, and less genteel in background, nevertheless contributed notably to the atmosphere of 20th-century music, to the aspirations of younger composers, and the attitudes of listeners. Henry Burleigh (1866–1949) was a popular singer who became the foremost composer among Dvořák's American pupils. His arrangements and adaptations of Negro songs, like *Deep River,* more nearly fulfilled Dvořák's vision of American music than did any folksong symphony or overture. Henry F. Gilbert (1868–1928) was a fiddler in theater orchestras whose taste outran his technique so far that he turned to various menial non-musical jobs, less distracting from composition, he believed, than menial music-making. He was MacDowell's first and most prominent pupil, an admirer of Charpentier, a convert to Dvořák's proposals, and an advocate of world-wide exchange of folksongs. His orchestral *Dance in the Place Congo* (1918) was the most nearly successful of many crude efforts to idealize Negro themes. There is a brilliant study of Gilbert, both sympathetic and discriminating, by Elliott Carter; Carter's respect may yet bring new friends to Gilbert. Arthur Farwell (1872–1951) discovered his interest in music after he had come to Boston from St. Paul, Minnesota, to study engineering. When he graduated from the Massachusetts Institute of Technology, he proceeded to Berlin and Paris for work with Humperdinck, Pfitzner, and Guilmant, omitting the development of any professional skill as a performer. By sheer intelligence and keen listening, he caught the spirit of revolt against German academicism and the connection between Debussy's nationalism and exoticism, which he was capable of analyzing even in *St. Sebastian*. He attempted to make similar connections for himself, first by using melodies of American Indians, later by experiments with various Oriental scales. His critical and philanthropic work, especially the Wa-wan Press for publication of serious American music, accomplished as much as his own compositions. All this diversified work won Farwell a prominent place in Chase's survey. Among his pupils was Roy Harris. The adventures of Burleigh, Gilbert, Farwell, and others had little direct influence on the music of Gershwin or Copland or most of their contemporaries. American culture had to renew in each generation its uneasy connection and contrast with that of Europe. But these precursors at least helped prepare American musicians to recognize what Gershwin and Copland achieved, after jazz had won its place as a truly new and American form of art. A recollection of their work, moreover, provides something of the perspective that is needed to consider the hundreds of American composers active at the middle of the century.

Probably the most solid and durable achievement by an American musician of this generation was that of Oscar George Theodore Sonneck (1873–1928). Born in New Jersey, he was educated entirely in Germany, as a thorough musician and musicologist. The few compositions that he published, songs on German texts, show that his gifts and his craft as a composer were equal to any other American's. It seems likely that he faced the "abyss of freedom" and decided not to dissipate his energy there, but instead to devote himself to scholarship and administration. His pioneering studies in the history and bibliography of American music are unequalled. He transformed the Music Division of the Library of Congress from a mere copyright depository to one of the greatest music libraries in the world, the natural place to preserve, when the time came, the manuscripts and other documents of Schoenberg, Rachmaninov, and other world-famous immigrants to America, as well as of MacDowell and a majority of younger American composers.

Finally, the American adventure fraught with greatest importance for world music was doubtless not that of any musician, but rather that of Isadora Duncan (1878–1927). Inspired by Whitman, Nietzsche, and ancient Greek art, she restored dancing to a place among the major arts, united it with the greatest 19th-century music, and stimulated the guardians of its most elaborate traditional form, ballet, to expand and deepen their work in preparation for some of the best music of the 20th century. Her influence was immense all over Europe, and especially fruitful in Russia just before the Russian ballet came to Paris. She was laughed at in America. On her last trip home she abandoned all hope for American art. She was enthusiastic about the Russian revolution, and did not live long enough to see her hopes for Soviet art disillusioned. Her achievement, like that of all dancers before the perfection of dance-notation and the sound-film, was evanescent. Her autobiography, though magnificent, is only tantalizing. But her adventure gives her a place among the most intelligently daring of Debussy's contemporaries.

———•—•———

The native music of American Indians was nearly lost. To most of the white population of America this was not music at all, but hideous "primitive" noise. In the United States the Indian population was so ruthlessly decimated, exploited, confined in reservations, Christianized and Americanized, that its music deteriorated and nearly disappeared before its remnants could be recorded and studied. When MacDowell, Farwell, and other young urban Americans thought of using Indian materials as a basis for a national style, they found them, just as Dvořák or Busoni did, in the books of the pioneer scholars, such as the indefatigable Frances Densmore (1867–1957).

In Mexico and some of the states of Central and South America, Indian culture persisted on a larger scale than in the United States, though not unharmed or unmixed with European and African influences. Only a few professional musicians in 1900 were awake to the interest of the native music.

At Buenos Aires and Rio de Janeiro Italian opera flourished throughout the 19th century. The most prominent composer in Latin America before Villa-Lobos, the Brazilian Carlos Gomes (1836–96), wrote operas in the Italian tradition and made his name known abroad with a few of their overtures. In Peru, where Spanish traditions were still alive, an Italian immigrant, Claudio Rebogliati (1843–1909), began the study and elaboration of Indian materials, which his successors were to continue.

Several Latin Americans of Debussy's generation undertook the struggle for musical independence, while still laboring to perfect the techniques of harmony, counterpoint, and orchestration. None of them achieved an international reputation. Authorities on South American music, like Gilbert

Chase and Kurt Pahlen, recognize as an outstanding and fairly representative figure the "father of Argentine music," Alberto Williams (1862–1952). He came home to Buenos Aires in 1889 from studies with Franck and others in Paris, founded a conservatory and publishing house, wrote theory and poetry as well as a vast amount of instrumental music, including nine programmatic symphonies, and welcomed impartially successive waves of European musical ideas and continuing aspirations for a native style. About 1910, according to Nicolas Slonimsky, Williams modified his Franckian style to incorporate whole-tone and pentatonic scales—the latter supposedly associated with the ancient music of the Incas.

Careers parallel to that of Williams were pursued in every corner of the globe where Europeans had settled. Alfred Hill (1870–1960) was the first prominent Australian composer. Born in Melbourne, trained in Leipzig, he lived for a few years in New Zealand, where his interest in native music was awakened. From 1916 on he was a leader of musical life at Sydney, and a prolific composer of works in all forms, using Maori themes.

———•·—·———

The influence of European thought and technology stimulated at least one remarkable achievement of Asian music—the songs of the great poet, Rabindranath Tagore (1861–1941). European music itself he rejected; it seemed to him devoid of spirituality. But European ideas set him free to combine several Indian traditions, classic and popular. With the help of his great-nephew, Dinendranath, he gave his songs permanent form, excluding the traditional freedom for improvisation. His musical achievement, studied so far by Trina Roy and Arnold Bake, will call for further careful investigation when musicologists have developed techniques for dealing with transcultural phenomena.

Shuji Izawa (1851–1917) was perhaps the first Asian musician to achieve distinction in the modern musical world. He returned to Tokyo in 1878 from studies at Harvard University, became secretary to the minister of education in the Meiji regime, and head of the society that soon developed into the National Academy of Music, with a staff of teachers mostly brought from Germany. While Izawa's work was chiefly an application of the Westernizing policy of the Meiji, he also began the collection of music for the *koto,* principal instrument of Japanese chamber music; koto music was the only one of various indigenous types, according to William Malm, in his survey of Japanese music, that proved capable in the first half of the 20th century of absorbing selected Western influences and continuing its own development.

Izawa brought the self-taught American Luther Whiting Mason (1828–96) to Japan in 1879 to help him write songbooks for the schools like those of Mason's *National Music Course*. By 1909, Suyeharu Togi reported, "every school in the empire, both elementary and secondary, came to have singing lessons as a regular course of study . . . The new and improved school songs almost entirely superseded the vulgar and indecent nursery songs formerly in vogue among the lower classes." Such are the ironies of nationalism. A provincial American, looking to Boston and thence to Leipzig and Vienna as the centers of the musical world, showed the Japanese what the Prussians themselves never thought of, the bureaucratic methods of compulsory music education. The program that Mason and Izawa established was carried on until World War II, when native songs were put into school books to supersede their synthetic ones for a while.

CHAPTER V

Contemporaries in Slavic Lands

SERGEI VASILIEVICH Rachmaninov (1873–1943) and Alexander Nikolaevich Scriabin (1871–1915) were pianists and classmates in composition at the Moscow Conservatory under Tchaikovsky's best pupil, Taneiev, and Rimsky's most precocious pupil, Arensky. Rachmaninov graduated at nineteen. His final exercise, the one-act opera *Aleko,* was produced the next year (1893). By this time he had completed his Op. 1, the first piano concerto, and Op. 3, five pieces for piano including the Prelude in C-sharp minor, which was to make him world-famous. But his career did not proceed so smoothly as it began. Its vicissitudes make a fascinating study, whether told in documentary style, as by the team of Bertensson and Leyda, or more journalistically, as by Victor Seroff. The relevance of these vicissitudes to the musical style can be vaguely felt, though it is hard to define.

While he eked out a living as a bored piano teacher, the young Rachmaninov composed his first tone-poem, inspired by Lermontov and Chekhov and dedicated to Rimsky, and his first symphony, based on Russian liturgical chants and dedicated to the beautiful Gypsy wife of a well-to-do friend. The first performances of these works were disappointing. Rachmaninov became morose. His habit of composing was blocked. About this time he joined an informal group of Wagner students, in which Scriabin was learning fast. The youngest member of the group, Leonid Sabaneiev, recalled: "Rachmaninov did not take part in the demonstrations; he sat in the corner in a rocking chair, with a huge orchestral score on his knees. From time to time we would hear, coming from his corner, some gloomy remark in his deep voice: 'A thousand pages more.' An hour later, more gloomily: 'Eight hundred eighty pages to go.'" In 1897 Rachmaninov became conductor for a new experimental opera company. Here he made a friend, the great basso, Feodor Chaliapin, who learned his greatest role, Boris Godunov, under Rachmaninov's direction; their friendship lasted all their lives. In 1900 the two young friends visited Tolstoy, whom they revered for his novel *Anna Karenina,* not for his more recent polemic, *What Is Art?* When he had heard them play and sing, Tolstoy demanded: "Is such music needed by anybody? . . . What is most needed by men—scholarly or folk music? . . . Beethoven is nonsense, Pushkin and Lermontov also!" Tolstoy's revolutionary ideas threw Rachmaninov into a lasting bafflement and despondency. His family, alarmed, sent him to an extraordinary psychiatrist who played the violin, loved chamber music, and specialized in treating alcoholism by hypnosis. His advice, over the next year, helped so much that in gratitude Rachmaninov dedicated to the doctor his second concerto (1901), which was quickly to become the most popular concerto since Tchaikovsky's. Rachmaninov now began to make enough money to live on from publications and performances in all the great cities of Europe. He married his cousin Natalia. Between 1902 and 1917 he composed two more short operas, two cantatas, including the setting of Poe's *Bells,* two choral services for the Russian Church, a third concerto, a second symphony, over forty piano pieces, and fifty songs.

In 1917, a few weeks after the October Revolution, Rachmaninov left Russia, never to return. He settled in the United States and became a virtuoso pianist, one of the most brilliant interpreters of the music of Liszt, and of all the Romantic concertos. In the last twenty-six years of his life all that he composed was five big works, including the fourth concerto, the third symphony, and the *Rhapsody on a Theme of Paganini*. There were no more original songs or short piano pieces. He told David Ewen in an interview, 1941:

A short piece for the piano has always given me much more pain, and has presented to me many more problems, than a symphony or concerto. Somehow, in writing for the orchestra, the variety of colors provided by the instruments brings me many different ideas and effects. But when I write a small piece for the piano, I am at the mercy of my thematic idea, which must be presented concisely and without digression.

His large instrumental works show the shortcomings of this lazy view of musical form, while the short works, whenever he succeeds in mastering the "many more problems," are his best. The liturgical pieces and the short piano pieces of 1910–17 show steady refinement of skill and taste, with virtually no change of style. While his melodic style has an elusive quality of its own, it remains as close to that of Tchaikovsky in late works as in early ones. There is no influence from any later music, even Scriabin's, which he liked, much less Debussy's or Stravinsky's, which he thought cerebral and insincere. But whereas the famous prelude and the second concerto contain phrases as thrilling as Tchaikovsky's, there are thrilling phrases and more in the last preludes and study-pictures for piano, the last songs, and the Vesper Service: these are sustained structures worthy of Mendelssohn or Chopin.

This growth of skill and taste within a familiar style was unusual in the 19th and 20th centuries. Most composers since Haydn, by contrast, have proceeded from one style to another, or through a whole series of styles. Rachmaninov's growth was more like that of a "pre-classical" artist. That such a growth was possible in the 20th century suggests that the tradition was not exhausted, as John Stuart Mill and other speculators feared it would be. But then the interruption of Rachmaninov's growth in 1897–1901 and its ending in 1917, at the age of forty-five, suggest how difficult a normal growth had become in an abnormal age.

Rachmaninov's manuscripts and letters left in Russia were gathered at the State Central Museum of Musical Culture, Moscow, and most of them were published after his death. There is another large archive in the Library of Congress.

Scriabin followed a course just opposite to Rachmaninov's. Setting off from the same point, he gradually modified his style until it was fascinatingly, radically different from common practice, while his craft became more and more mechanical and his taste more and more absurd.

Scriabin was twenty-one, fifteen months older than Rachmaninov, when they graduated at Moscow. He won a medal for his playing, but did not compete as a composer, partly because of disagreements with Arensky, who was stricter with his pupils than with himself. Scriabin never learned to read notes fluently. For five years after graduating he traveled in the West. He returned in 1897 to marry and to teach piano at the Conservatory. By 1903, having found generous patrons, he resumed traveling. In 1905 he left his wife and four children to live with a woman who shared his interests in Nietzsche, socialism, and theosophy. In 1906 his travels took him as far as the United States, but America was not friendly to his mistress. He returned occasionally to Russia, but his favorite domiciles were Brussels and various Swiss resorts. In 1915 he died of blood poisoning. He never got around to composing the ritual *Mystery* that he had talked about ever since 1903—it was to be performed by thousands of worshippers in a Tibetan Bayreuth and to result in the final "dematerialization" of the world. Rachmaninov was one of the musicians who came to the rescue of Scriabin's family, by playing benefit concerts of his music.

Throughout his life Scriabin composed mostly short piano pieces. Many of them are less than a minute long. For piano he also wrote sonatas, five of them at intervals up to 1907, then five more, 1911–13. For orchestra he wrote five symphonies, 1900–1910, of which the last three are known by

subtitles *Divine Poem, Poem of Ecstasy,* and *Prometheus, Poem of Fire.*
The titles of the early works—waltzes, mazurkas, preludes—acknowledge
the dominating influence of Chopin. The complete absence of chamber
music and almost complete absence of vocal music in Scriabin's list make
him a narrower specialist than Chopin or MacDowell. On the other hand,
from the accumulation of longer works toward the end of his life, from
the titles and programs of the orchestral works, and from the evidence of
his talk about the *Mystery,* it is apparent that Scriabin imagined himself
to be working on the scale of Wagner.

He is at his best in the least pretentious pieces of around 1903, such as
the *Albumleaf,* Op. 45, No. 1.

EXAMPLE V.1   Scriabin, *Albumleaf,* Op. 45, No. 1

Harmony is what gives this music its individuality. Seventh and ninth
chords prevail, and the first plain triad with root in the bass is the final
chord. Even this chord is a little obscured by the melody, which mixes
elements of major and minor modes in a characteristic way. Throughout
the piece the harmonic roots are clear, and their progressions are conven-

tional, but the melody and chords that rest on them are complex and ambiguous: no two listeners are likely to agree as to which notes are members of a chord and which are passing tones, appoggiaturas, cambiatas, and *échappés*. The melody is full of emphatic leaps. But these do not obscure tonality as much as Wagner's leaps do, because the melody carries on, across the leaps, two or more smooth chromatic lines, in a pseudo-polyphony like Bach's. The accompanying lines, of course, have no such interest as Bach's. In 1910, when the young conductor, publisher, and patron Koussevitzky produced three all-Bach concerts, Scriabin remarked that Bach was "entirely unnecessary."

The rhythm of the *Albumleaf* is also characteristic, though less interesting than the harmony. Its triplets, simple syncopations, and rubato resemble Schumann's or Liszt's more than Chopin's, though Schumann often ventured farther with such rhythmic devices. Scriabin's performance astonished listeners with its extremes of rubato: some listeners lost all sense of rhythmic organization, while others followed his gushing spontaneity and loved it. In a few instances Scriabin complicated the note-picture by using different meters for different voices, and in one instance, Op. 52, No. 1, he changed metrical signs nearly every measure: $\frac{3}{8} \frac{3}{4} \frac{2}{4} \frac{2}{2} \frac{2}{16} \frac{3}{4} \frac{2}{4} \frac{5}{16}$ etc. But this complication scarcely affected the sounding rhythm.

Fluctuations of loudness and tone color are coordinated very simply with the rhythm and the melodic contour, so that the alternating basic tensions and relaxations are all exaggerated, rather than counterpoised as they are in Bach or Beethoven or Debussy. Scriabin's playing was famous for its delicacy, sensuous allure, and nervous detail. His writing for the piano leaves much to the performer's discretion, but it can make satisfying effects in a wide range of loudness and tone-colors. The performer's choices are easier than in the music of MacDowell. For pianists who can reach a tenth, the spacing of the notes is very grateful.

When Rachmaninov played Scriabin, Scriabin's admirers protested that the performance was prosaic and hard, too fast for the detail, too cold in bringing out the harmonic logic. Scriabin himself said of Rachmaninov: "Everything he plays has the same lyric quality as his own music. In his 'sound' there is so much materialism, so much meat, . . . almost some kind of boiled ham." Rachmaninov's interpretation is approved by the Soviet authority, Danilevich, as correctly emphasizing the realistic strain in Scriabin and subordinating the decadent idealism and modernism that eventually led him astray.

The *Albumleaf* is more subtly formed than most of Scriabin's pieces. All too often he develops his two-measure inspiration by sheer repetition and sequence, but here he varies it and expands it convincingly. In larger works he follows the textbook model of sonata form, but his harmony lacks the driving logic that animates the successful forms of Tchaikovsky and Rachmaninov. In later works where harmony is more complex and peculiar, Scriabin deliberately simplifies the forms, maintaining rigorously the normal two- and four-measure symmetries and the literal recapitulations of longer sections. In the course of five minutes or more this has appalling results.

The harmony of the *Divine Poem* and some other works around 1903 includes the whole-tone scale, but always with a clear sense of a dominant chord, leading to eventual resolution in a tonic triad, though often passing through enharmonic metamorphoses on the way. Debussy's ways of using the whole-tone scale did not interest Scriabin. When he saw the score of *Pelléas,* he put it aside quickly, remarking that he disliked Debussy's "passivity."

The harmony of *Prometheus* and the five last sonatas avoids consonant chords altogether, abandons all reference to a major scale, and thoroughly mixes its dissonant chords with its twisting melodies. Scriabin intended to make "the melody a disintegrated harmony and the harmony a compacted melody." He chose one or two rich chords as the basic material for a whole piece. The famous *Prometheus* chord, for instance, reading from the bass upward, is C F# Bb E A D. Most of his "mystic" chords, like the *Prometheus* one, appear as stacks of fourths over the bass, in contrast to the traditional structure of thirds. But since at least one of the fourths is augmented and another diminished, the chord sounds like a dominant ninth just a little more ornamented than the ninths of the *Albumleaf,* with raised and lowered fifths that are enharmonically equivalent to minor thirteenths and raised elevenths respectively. The complexity of these chords is such that if they are inverted, then whichever note is in the bass sounds like a root, with the notes above it adjusting enharmonically. But because there is never a consonance, the enharmonic ambiguity is trivial. The bass often alternates between notes a tritone apart, so as to make the ambiguity of root and key constant and prominent, rather than dynamic and subtle.

Once more, the shortest pieces are the best, if least typical, among the late works. A few of them present spontaneous harmonic wanderings, unconfined by any synthetic chord or scale, yet more truly coherent in their brevity than the pieces that are so confined. Such is the Prelude, Op. 74, No. 4, very similar to the *Albumleaf* in its form and its wistful mood. Ambiguous synthetic chords are easier to discuss than the empirical coherence of this prelude.

The fascination of Scriabin's discussible techniques and of their gradual development in the course of his career led Eaglefield Hull and after him many other theorists and historians to overvalue Scriabin's sonatas and

EXAMPLE V.2 Scriabin, Prelude, Op. 74, No. 4

symphonies, and sometimes, incidentally, to belittle the mysterious charm of the short pieces. Hull called the *Albumleaf* "commonplace," and the Prelude "cacophonous." The Prelude made him wonder: "Has he passed beyond the possibilities of our musical system, or did his fine mental grip of things loosen?" Hull thought that the last sonatas were "a contribution to instrumental music worthy to rank with any of the great masters of the past—Bach, Mozart, Beethoven, Brahms, and Chopin." Boris Asafiev includes Op. 74 particularly along with the sonatas, as worthy to rank with Bach and Chopin. Other writers less familiar with the music have referred to it as typical of a general hypertrophy of chromaticism and decay of tonality, allegedly common to Debussy and Schoenberg. But in fact Scriabin's style is as remote from Debussy's or Schoenberg's as it is from Beethoven's or Rachmaninov's. Yet there is something typical of the times in Scriabin's concentration on harmonic novelty, as there is in his lurid solipsistic "philosophy" and personal conceit. Scriabin is a useful reference point in a picture of music history: more clearly than Wagner or anyone else, Scriabin embodies the straw man for anti-Romanticism. His decadent sort of romanticism provoked in the next generation a healthy emphasis on intelligence and craftsmanship. If sometimes the reaction went to the point of ascetic punishment of the senses and emotions, Scriabin and his ilk may be blamed as much as the rebels against them. Whenever, on the other hand, a rebel against romantic softness and sweetness, inspiration and expression, exalts some technique of calculating harmonies without troubling himself to master such traditional crafts as fluent sight-reading, counterpoint, and structural modulation, then he is an unwitting victim of Scriabin's worst influence.

———•—•———

One victim of Scriabin's influence who was intelligent enough to cure himself, and then generous enough to identify and adhere to Scriabin's true small achievement despite the bad influence, was the poet Boris Pasternak. As a boy Pasternak knew Scriabin personally and aimed to follow in his footsteps. His family, his teachers, and his hero all encouraged him. When he grew up, he came to realize that he, unlike Scriabin, would never be content to proceed without mastering the craft. He decided to give up music as a career, and to master the craft of language. For the delusion about music he blamed himself more than Scriabin; what he had to cure was his own

unpardonable adolescent arrogance, a half-educated person's disregard of everything that appears to him to be easily attainable and accessible. I despised everything uncreative, any kind of hack work, being conceited enough to imagine that I was a judge in these matters. In real life, I thought, everything must be a miracle, everything must be predestined from above, nothing must be deliberately designed or planned. . . . That was the negative side of Scriabin's influence, which in everything else became decisive for me. His egocentric nature was appropriate in his case. The seeds of his views, childishly misinterpreted, fell on favorable ground.

Pasternak's description of Scriabin's appearance is wonderfully vivid, and suggests something of the "inner correspondence" between his music and the way he lived.

He often went for walks with my father. . . . Sometimes I accompanied them. Having started to run, Scriabin loved to go on running and skipping, as though with his own momentum, just like a stone rebounding off the surface of the water, just as though had he run a little faster he would have become detached from the earth and sailed in the air. In general, he cultivated various forms of inspired lightness and unencumbered motion on the borderline of flight.

Looking back, Pasternak judges Scriabin's work with discriminating sympathy:

The flashing harmonies of his *Prometheus* and his last works seem to me only the evidence of his genius and not daily food for the soul. . . . In the studies of Op. 8 and the preludes of Op. 11, everything is already contemporary, everything is full of those inner correspondences, accessible to music, with the surrounding world, with the way in which people of those days lived, thought, felt, traveled, and dressed.

A Scriabin archive is maintained in his Moscow home. A collected edition of his works was begun in 1947.

———————

Russia, like the United States, had several composers more thoroughly competent and more prolific than its two most famous composers of the same age. Unlike the United States, Russia offered its composers facilities for prompt performance, publication, and intelligent criticism, as well as thorough training. Hence it is not surprising that dozens of Russians were able to achieve respectable work, and more than half a dozen made some lasting impression abroad. Alexander Tikhonovich Grechaninov (1864–1956) studied at both Moscow and St. Petersburg Conservatories. His pieces for *a cappella* chorus, and for chorus with instruments, including several large liturgical works, constitute his most distinctive achievement. Of his many songs and piano pieces, those for children are especially valuable. His symphonies and operas are less interesting, and his voluminous chamber music is really salon music, that is, innocuous, like that of his teacher, Arensky. The English expert on Russian music, Gerald Abraham, detects in a few of Grechaninov's works some influence from Debussy, Strauss, and Reger, absorbed into a style that is basically unchanging. Alexander Konstantinovich Glazunov (1865–1936), pupil of Rimsky, won high praise as a very young man with his symphonies, concertos, and ballets;

some of these were still played frequently in Russia after his death. Their
structure is monumental and dense, like Brahms; their orchestration is
rich, like Wagner, and brilliant, like Rimsky; their ultimate effect is smug.
As Glazunov grew older his orthodoxy became more rigid, and his works
appeared more slowly. He lost interest in the large orchestra, and now
preferred to write string quartets, piano sonatas, and organ fugues. Naturally his popularity waned, but he was still a prominent figure. Some
acquaintance with Glazunov is necessary for any thorough study of Stravinsky or Prokofiev, who rebelled against his academicism after learning a
great deal from it, or of his pupil Shostakovich, or other Soviet composers,
who emulated it while incorporating into it some elements of the rebels'
styles. Moreover, his symphonies cannot be altogether neglected by a conscientious admirer of Schoenberg, for Schoenberg recommended them to
his pupils as formal models. Nikolai Karlovich Medtner (1879–1951), after
completing the same studies as Rachmaninov and Scriabin, turned more
and more to the German heritage of his ancestors, literary and philosophical as well as musical. With unswerving idealism he held to his elaborate
pianistic style and strove to achieve forms like those of Beethoven's sonatas
and Schumann's songs. His short piano pieces, especially the *Skazky* (*Tales*)
are unanimously recommended as his best achievements. His own performance of much of his music was preserved on records. All three of these
upholders of academic habits emigrated from Russia—Grechaninov and
Medtner soon after the Revolution, Glazunov only after playing a large
part in the establishment of Soviet institutions. Glazunov died in France,
Grechaninov in the U.S., and Medtner in England. All remained Russian
in character.

Several more adventurous composers of the same generation broke their
habits and developed new styles, influenced partly by some aspect of the
music of Debussy. Vladimir Ivanovich Rebikov (1866–1920) rebelled as a
student, and never finished his course at the Moscow Conservatory. After
1900 he outdid Scriabin in his systematic, simplistic, and evidently sincere
modernism. In some works he used the whole-tone scale as a substitute for
the diatonic scale. In some he used parallelism throughout. He composed
"musico-psychographical dramas," in which, he said:

The music is merely a means of evoking feelings and moods in the listener . . .
There is no room for superfluous sounds; thus each note must be sounded together with a corresponding emotion of the performer. One must play and sing
with feeling. Only then will the sounds acquire the power of hypnotism . . . all
parts are to be performed in a sort of sound-speech, almost a natural speech.

These dramas, studied thoroughly by William Dale, anticipate many works
of the 1950s that claim to lead an "avant garde." On the other hand, Rebikov's piano music is recommended to amateur players by the English

teacher, Alec Rowley. Stravinsky in 1962 recalled his admiration for Rebikov's ballet, *Yëlka,* but did not inspire a revival of it. Sergei Nikiforovich Vassilenko (1872–1956) established a reputation with academic pieces of all sorts, and then, about 1906, turned away from his Moscow training. After experimenting with impressionism, he settled into a personal habit of expanding exotic melodies from Soviet Asia and elsewhere into conventional forms, the most satisfactory of which are suites of short pieces for chamber orchestra. Nikolai Nikolaevich Tcherepnin (1873–1945) likewise established a reputation as a follower of Rimsky, especially with his ballets. Then, somewhat cautiously and gradually, he expanded the range of his harmony and instrumentation to include recognizable reminiscences of Debussy and other French composers, in a manner rather like that of the Americans Loeffler and Hill. Reinhold Moritsovich Glière (1874–1956), prolific composer of instrumental works in all dimensions, is well described by Boris Asafiev as "an example of a composer whose task is to popularize ideas that once upon a time made their way with difficulty, but later justified themselves. At this point, Glière also accepts them, and exhibits them in a simplified manner (e.g., the Scriabinisms of Glière)." The biography of Glière by Igor Bélza, like most Soviet references, is more respectful. Glière's most famous work, the ballet *Red Poppy* (1927), exhibits only ideas that were already old in his student years but with timely extramusical associations and timeless musical verve. Yet another pupil of Rimsky, Alexander Afanasievich Spendiarov (1871–1928), became the "father of Armenian symphonic music," honored in the 1950s with a complete edition.

Scriabin, Rachmaninov, and their contemporaries provided together a richly varied scene for the emergence of Stravinsky and Prokofiev in the last years of the Czar.

Leoš Janáček (1854–1928) achieved national and international eminence surpassing that of all other Czech composers since Dvořák. This eminence was the reward of a long, hard, lonely adventure, which remained somewhat obscure even in the 1960s, after sympathetic attempts to elucidate it by Max Brod, the poet and literary critic, and by Jan Racek, Bohumír Štědroň, and other scholars working at the archive in Brno (Brünn), where Janáček had lived most of his life as a teacher. His most famous work was the opera, *Její pastorkyňa* (*Her Foster-Daughter*), composed 1894–1903, produced in Brno 1904, then produced in Prague, with revisions, 1916, and finally taken up in Germany and elsewhere in the 'twenties, with a new title, the name of the heroine, *Jenufa.* Most of the music that Janáček had written in the 19th century, including one earlier opera, *Šárka* (1887), remained unpublished. But *Jenufa* showed traces of his long journey, from imitations of Dvořák, through experience as a collector of folksongs in the provinces of Moravia, Lachia, and Wallachia, through an immersion in Russian music and literature, and through various theoretical speculations, to his own powerful yet delicate style. By the time *Jenufa* won recognition, Janáček had written mature works in various forms, including a series of distinctive choruses and some remarkable piano pieces. Then in his last decade he became more prolific than ever, and every new work was a masterpiece. Opera continued to be his chief concern, but the instrumental works were naturally more accessible than the operas to foreigners. Among these the Concertino for piano and chamber orchestra (1925), the Sinfonietta (1926), the wind sextet *Mládí* (*Youth,* 1924) and the two quartets (1924, 1928) were increasingly recognized, especially through recordings of the 1960s. A short piano piece cannot exhibit the full power of Janáček's style, but one such piece, *Štěbataly jak laštovičky* (*They Chattered like Swallows*), from the album *Po zarostlém chodníčku* (*Up the Overgrown Path,* 1901–08), has enough characteristic features to distinguish his style from any other.

EXAMPLE V.3   Janáček, *They Chattered like Swallows*

The main melody is composed entirely of two motifs, and one of these provides almost all the accompaniment as well. There is no rhythmic development of the motifs, such as we might expect from experience with 19th-century music. Neither is there any spinning-out of phrases based on them, as in Bach. The motifs are simply repeated, then modified by interesting harmonies, and repeated again. On first acquaintance the repetitions seem excessive, but as the piece becomes familiar they prove to be just right—skipping over any of them makes a gap in the form. Likewise, on first acquaintance the melodic units seem awkwardly truncated and the shifts of harmony seem arbitrary, but when the piece becomes familiar a long line holds each large section together, containing many of the little units within one breath. Ultimately the melodic energy even overrides the strong contrasts of rhythm and dynamics, and gives the whole piece a unity that could not be guaranteed merely by the motifs. In Janáček's notation, with nearly twice as many bar-lines as the transcription here, and with a key a half step lower, provoking frequent enharmonic changes of spelling (not of actual sound), the appearance of fragmentariness takes a long time to overcome. Our changes of notation give the reader a head start toward appreciation of the continuity.

Janáček's peculiar treatment of motifs is regarded by Racek and other students of his whole work as the chief characteristic of his style. According to Racek, motifs throughout his music are mostly derived from speech, and their repetition in phrases is freely derived from folksong. Janáček's own testimony tends to confirm this. His intensive study of folksong, especially Moravian and Slavonic, was partly guided by the philologist František Bartoš (1837–1906). Janáček provided an essay for the collection of songs edited by Bartoš in 1901, in which he argued that "folksongs originated from words." In 1905, he wrote in the magazine *Hlídka*:

The melodic curves of speech are an expression of the complete organism and of all phases of its spiritual activities. They demonstrate whether a man is stupid or intelligent, sleepy or awake, tired or alert. They tell us whether he is a child or an old man, whether it is morning or evening, light or darkness, heat or frost, and disclose whether a person is alone or in company. The art of dramatic writing is to compose a melodic curve which will, as if by magic, reveal immediately a human being in one definite phase of his existence.

He repeated and amplified this theory many times. In 1926 he stated it again, concisely and forcefully, in a letter to Jan Mikota:

After having studied the musical side of the language, I am certain that all melodic and rhythmical mysteries of music in general are to be explained solely from rhythmical and melodic points of view on the basis of the melodic curves of speech. No one can become an opera composer who has not studied living speech. I wish that this could be understood once and for all.

Janáček thus pushed to an extreme a notion that had been important for Mussorgsky and to some extent for many other composers. Janáček seems not to have borrowed the idea from anyone else, but to have arrived at it in this extreme form by himself.

His freedom of part writing too, his constantly adding and subtracting voices from the texture, probably derived, as Mussorgsky's similar practice did, from observation of folk polyphony. Janáček reported his observation with excitement, in another magazine, *Dalibor*, in 1905: "I have discovered something entirely new and peculiar in folk music. Perhaps the best name for it would be 'nocturne.' They are strange songs for more than one voice to which the people have given unusual harmonies. On my wanderings through the country I heard them in regions so far unexplored. I have no words to describe them." A special characteristic detail, possibly connected with the folk polyphony, is the frequent crossing of melody and accompaniment in the same register. Another is the free and frequent appearance of the fifth of a triad in the bass, marked in our example with an asterisk.

Janáček does not confine himself, however, to the chords and chord-progressions of folk singers or cymbalom players. His triads are often enriched with added sixths, as at the beginning of the Adagio. He uses many dominant sevenths and ninths, as in the final *meno mosso,* and augmented triads, as at the beginning and end of the first *meno mosso.* Each chord lasts long enough to support a motif. (In a large-scale piece one chord may last for several phrases.) The motion from one chord to the next is what connects the motif with its repetition. This motion is unpredictable, often made smooth by chromaticism. Janáček expounded his freedom of chord-progression and tried to support it by the acoustical and psychological theories of Helmholtz and Wundt, in his textbook *Úplná nauka o harmonii,* 1920. He protested all rules and habits of chord-progression, and urged students to listen to uncommon progressions carefully so as to find their precise expressive values. He wrote to his friend Ota Zítek in 1926: "One unusual chord can save a composition if the chord is a real bleeding knot of feeling." Janáček's compositions have many such chords. Surely his progressions depend more on his experiments at the piano and organ and his will to express feelings than on anything he heard in the music of Wagner or any other composer.

Janáček's free chromaticism never loses touch with a diatonic scale for long. Though the whole-tone scale is prominent in much of his music after 1905 when he encountered Debussy, it serves simply to fit the motifs over augmented chords. The same motifs return from the whole-tone to a diatonic scale without emphasizing the contrast. This procedure is utterly different from Debussy's—so much simpler that it may seem naive. But a listener no longer either attracted or repelled by the whole-tone scale can follow Janáček's expressive motifs and progressions through and beyond the scale with no difficulty. What matters to the form of a piece is the normal diatonic scale of the beginning and end.

Janáček's forms are various and loose. He cares nothing for classic and academic models. His quartets and sinfonietta have no sonata-form movement, and it is mere coincidence when his movements resemble rondos, as can be seen in *They Chattered like Swallows.* In the operas, of course, everything is subordinated to the drama, and since there are such contrasts of dramatic style and form among the operas, there are corresponding contrasts of musical form too. *Kát'a Kabanová* (1919–21) grips and pulls the listener from the beginning to end as surely as *Tristan,* though its chief unifying motif is merely an ominous set of eight notes on the kettledrums. *Fox Sharpears* (1921–23) is like a kaleidoscopic suite of folk-dances, brightened by wit and gentleness, and ending in a futile death. *The House of the Dead* (1927–28) is a series of grim episodes whose disconnectedness intensifies their Dostoievskyan misery.

Janáček's treatment of instruments is as unconventional as his forms. His writing for the piano includes many textures different from those of *They Chattered like Swallows,* but none with an obvious appeal to the pianist's fingers. The pieces under the impressionistic title *V Mlhach* (*In the Mists,* 1912) are the most varied and gratifying of his piano music. The predominance of high registers is characteristic. In the orchestra Janáček favors the wind instruments, and combines them in startling clear chords and counterpoints. The Sextet for winds is perhaps his most charming and most contrapuntal piece.

His choral music is recommended by all who know it as thoroughly idiomatic and as splendid text-setting. The *Slavonic Mass* (1926) is his greatest work of this sort, and the most suitable for performance outside Czechoslovakia. It is not a liturgical Mass, but a festive patriotic piece, comparable to the *Te Deum* of Berlioz.

In 1925, when Janáček was awarded an honorary degree, he replied to congratulations with a summing-up of his advice to the young:

> Grow out of your innermost selves.
> Never renounce your beliefs.
> Do not toil for recognition,
> But always do all you can.
> So that the field allotted to you
> May prosper.

His life and work reinforce this advice many times.

Two other pupils of Dvořák achieved distinction at home and some recognition abroad: Vítězslav Novák (1870–1949) and Josef Suk (1874–1935). Novák succeeded his teacher at the Prague Conservatory (1909) and presided there until the invading Germans removed him thirty years later. His stylistic development was ceaseless: after winning the praise of Brahms for his early expert and eclectic chamber music, piano pieces, and songs, he turned briefly toward Debussy and then toward Slovak folk materials to produce more characteristic works, culminating in a cycle of poems for piano, *Pan* (1910). From 1915 on Novák's main efforts were devoted to a series of comic national operas and ballets, but some of his finest achievements were symphonic poems, such as *De profundis* (1941). Suk was second violinist in the famous Bohemian Quartet (1882–1922) and then professor at the Prague Conservatory. His most successful work was a symphonic poem, *Zrání* (*Ripening,* 1913–18), and his most comprehensive and adventurous effort to realize his lofty ideal was a cantata, *Epilog* (1920–32).

Two pupils of the Wagnerian Zdeněk Fibich, active as conductors and composers of opera, won great success in Prague and deserved notice elsewhere. Karel Kovařovic (1862–1920) reflected the influence of Gounod, Massenet, and Debussy: Rudolph Quoika in 1958 called him "one of the best representatives of impressionism in Prague." His operas, *Psohlavci* (*The Dog Heads,* 1898) and *Na Starém bélidle* (*At the Old Laundry,* 1901) held a place in the repertory there. Otakar Ostrčil (1879–1935) adapted ideas from Mahler. His outstanding work was the symphonic variations *Stations of the Cross* (1928).

Other East European peoples had corresponding figures. Joseph Wihtol (1863–1948) was the foremost of the Latvian composers. He was a pupil of Rimsky and his successor at the St. Petersburg Conservatory, where he taught Prokofiev, among others. When Latvia became a nation (1918) Wihtol founded its conservatory and intensified his concern for native music and its use in concert forms. In 1944 he fled from the Soviets to end his days in Germany, but after his death Soviet Latvia honored his work. The most interesting Lithuanian of this generation was Mikalojus Konstantinas Čiurlionis (1875–1911). After studies at Warsaw, he composed a symphonic poem, *The Forest,* and after further studies in Leipzig his biggest musical work, *The Sea* (1904). With these pieces, according to the chief writer about them, Vladas Jakubénas, he succeeded in establishing a musical tradition for his nation. Meanwhile he had become a painter and a highly original explorer of the correspondences between visual and auditory images and forms, anticipating Kandinsky and numerous composers of the mid-20th century. One of his paintings, part of a cycle called "Sonata of the Pyramids," was bought by Igor Stravinsky in 1908; in 1961 Stravinsky remembered it as "powerful." Čiurlionis, in the last years of his brief life, was also a pioneer in the study of Lithuanian folksong. Jakubénas condemns his folksong arrangements, with one or two exceptions, but in view of his whole career and of its parallels in other nations, no single judgment of these arrangements can be accepted as final.

The career of Ignace Paderewski (1860–1941) was a unique high point in the history of music, an apotheosis of musical nationalism. Though the music he composed faded from memory while Janáček's grew brighter, none of their contemporaries nor any of the older giants, Grieg, Dvořák, Tchaikovsky, and Verdi, gave their nations so much as Paderewski. Not even the collaboration of Wagner and King Ludwig of Bavaria affected the lives of so many men to such a degree. Through his influence as a world-famous pianist, Paderewski raised an army, waged diplomacy, and won national freedom for a generation of his countrymen. After he had signed the Treaty of Versailles as first president of the Polish republic, he retired from politics and returned to his career as pianist. But once more in 1940, when Poland was overrun by Nazi Germany and the Soviet Union, Paderewski at eighty was ready to try again: he took office as president of the National Council and came to America, not as refugee but as representative. Here he died, still full of hope and courage.

As a composer Paderewski was prominent in Poland early in his twenties, the 1880s, with Chopinesque songs and dances and slight academic pieces, such as the Minuet in G, which later became a favorite of student pianists around the world. In 1884–85 he studied with Leschetizky. Then began his career as virtuoso. He continued to compose, in more and more serious forms. His works of the 20th century include a melodramatic opera *Manru* (1901), a piano sonata (1903), and finally a symphony (1907) subtitled "an epic poem of the Polish soul." With this work and its translation into political action, Paderewski completed his chief mission. He composed no more, but he played Chopin with ever-renewed devotion and diligence.

Leopold Godowsky (1870–1938) was a more prodigious pianist than Paderewski or Rachmaninov, if not so glorious. He is credited by Abram Chasins and others with extending the possibilities of piano technique to new extremes. Among his many compositions that exploit these possibilities to achieve solid musical satisfaction, the set of pieces called *Triakontameron* (1920) is especially notable. Godowsky left Poland as a child and lived mostly in America, while pursuing a thoroughly international career as virtuoso, teacher, and consultant—a career as peculiarly typical of 20th-century specialization as Paderewski's was of nationalism.

A greater contribution to the distinctive music of the 20th century than the pianists made was that of Wanda Landowska (1877–1960). Her achievement was to bring harpsichords out of museums and prove them to be concert instruments once more. Her career too was international, with periods of residence in Germany, France, and America. Though not a composer at all, she affected the thoughts of younger composers more deeply than any Polish musician since Chopin.

To envision together such diverse musicians as Landowska, Paderewski, Čiurlionis, and Novák is not easy. To see them in a panorama of their Slavic contemporaries, Janáček, Rachmaninov, and Scriabin, is harder. To put them in relation to Ives and MacDowell and Debussy is harder still. Yet this series of perspectives repays the effort, contributing to a sense of history that includes Bach, Mozart, Chopin, Tchaikovsky, Stravinsky, Prokofiev, and ourselves.

CHAPTER VI

Contemporaries in England and Northern Europe

OR THE CORONATION of Edward VII (1902), Sir Edward
Elgar (1857–1934) was commissioned to write an ode. At the suggestion of the king himself, the *Ode*, Op. 44, included Elgar's most
famous tune, which he had composed a year or so earlier as part of the
Pomp and Circumstance March, Op. 39, No. 1, now set to A. C. Benson's
text, "Land of Hope and Glory." Such a tune, said Elgar, comes only once
in a lifetime. In the same year Elgar's oratorio on Cardinal Newman's
Dream of Gerontius, Op. 38 (1900), was performed in Germany, and the
Enigma Variations, Op. 36 (1899), were winning their place in the repertories of orchestras all over the world. The high regard for Elgar evidenced
by these events was new. It was still far from universal. On the other hand
it was widely shared, and from that time on a similar high regard persisted
and spread, despite the continuance of opposition and condescension.

Elgar's life was never easy. He had struggled to reach the insecure
eminence that he enjoyed at forty-five. In the next seventeen years he
accumulated honors and produced his most ambitious works, but none of
these had the gratifying general success of *Pomp and Circumstance,*
Gerontius, and *Enigma,* or even of the earlier choral works, beloved by the
festival choirs of the English industrial towns. Then for the last fifteen
years of his life he brooded over big projects that he never finished, and
he finished only a few small pieces.

Elgar's music shows an individuality somewhat like MacDowell's and a
growth somewhat like Rachmaninov's, within the bounds of common
practice. Elgar grew up in Worcester, learning from his father how to run
a music shop and to play the piano, organ, and violin. He went on to the
bassoon, cello, and other instruments, and to conducting and arranging all
sorts of music for his choir in the Catholic church and for the instrumental
ensembles of his friends. He formed habits of musical thought with very

little academic guidance. His chief models were Handel, Rossini, Mendelssohn, and Schumann. The imitations that he wrote in his teens were short and amateurish. One of his first larger efforts was a Credo arranged by patching together sections of three Beethoven symphonies. When he began to compose large works on his own themes, he too often relied on a similar patchwork procedure. On the other hand, his wealth of practical experience enabled him to write for large orchestra more effectively than any academically trained Englishman, and to devise interesting new effects for large choruses. The distinguishing traits of Elgar's melodies—wide leaps and many sequences—are recognizable in sketches for a string quartet, 1879. Also firmly established in the earliest works are his love of noble march rhythms with off-beat accompaniments, and his reliance on what Bernard Herrmann calls "flexibility and nuances of tempo" . . . . "The tempo variations that arise in the course of an Elgar work are so subtle and elastic that they demand from the conductor and performer an almost complete infatuation with the music. For Elgar's music will not play by itself; merely to supervise it and give it professional routine playing will only serve to immobilize it." In his early twenties Elgar had his only advanced studies, under Adolphe Pollitzer, chief violinist of the Royal Academy. He heard first-rate performances of opera and symphony only when he visited London and Germany on holidays, mostly after his marriage at the age of thirty-one to his pupil Caroline Alice Roberts, thirty-eight, who helped him escape from provincial drudgery and strive to become a great composer. Thus he absorbed very late and very gradually the devices that appealed to him in selected pieces of Berlioz, Liszt, Wagner, Brahms, and Dvořák, with no sense of conflict among them. In particular he found that the principle of leitmotifs, which he studied in Wagner's *Parsifal*, reinforced his own "system," elaborated independently on the basis of Mendelssohn's *Elijah* and practiced in the cantatas that led up to *Gerontius*. He became a friend of Strauss and Fauré, whose music he respected without knowing much of it. Puccini was his favorite contemporary. Debussy he rejected, with the dictum that his music "lacked guts." He befriended younger Englishmen like Bantock, Ireland, Bax, Bliss, and Goossens, but he was indifferent to the revival of English folk song and Tudor polyphony and to the music of Holst and Vaughan Williams. In short, his taste remained that of the 1880s, the time when he was still unknown beyond Worcestershire.

Elgar showed his satisfaction as a mature man with his oldest musical ideas by revising and publishing as *The Wand of Youth,* Op. 1A and 1B (1907–08), two suites of pieces for a children's play that he had begun not later than 1871, and by using three of the pieces from these suites again as incidental music for another children's play, his biggest theatrical work, *The Starlight Express,* Op. 78 (1915). Again he used material from his early notebooks in the last pieces he finished, the *Severn Suite* for band, Op. 87 (1930), dedicated to his friend George Bernard Shaw, and the *Nursery Suite* for orchestra (1931), dedicated to the princesses Elizabeth and Margaret. Some admirers of his symphonies apologize for these light pieces as potboilers, but they need no apology. Some of them are Elgar's most attractive work. Their neat, unpretentious forms fit their gentle personal twisting of the common style.

The development that Elgar pursued, however, was an enrichment and increasing mastery of large forms. This development can be traced in the orchestral works that followed the *Enigma Variations,* each one more unified than the one before:

    1901   Op. 40 *Cockaigne* overture
    1901–1905 Op. 47 Introduction and Allegro for quartet and string
                  orchestra
    1899–1904 Op. 50 Overture *In the South* (*Alassio*)
    1907–1908 Op. 55 Symphony I, in A-flat
    1909–1910 Op. 61 Concerto for Violin
    1903–1910 Op. 63 Symphony II, in E-flat
    1902–1913 Op. 68 *Falstaff,* symphonic study
    1919   Op. 85 Concerto for Violoncello
and in the astonishing trilogy of chamber music:
    1918   Op. 82 Violin Sonata
                  Op. 83 String Quartet
    1919   Op. 84 Quintet for Piano and Strings
Tovey's *Essays* provide excellent analyses and appraisals of all these orchestral pieces including *Enigma,* except for the First Symphony. Tovey's preference for *Falstaff* is shared by many musicians who cannot share his indulgence for *Cockaigne.* In *Falstaff* a plenitude of delightful ideas compose a delightful, original order. Elgar divulged the details of his programmatic intent in an article on *Falstaff,* which Tovey collates with his own interpretation. The only important discrepancy concerns the ending: Elgar corrected Tovey's "Let him go to Arthur's bosom with a roll of muffled drums," "No: the drum roll is shrill; the man of stern reality has triumphed."

The Cello Concerto is even more admirably shaped, and it is not lacking in Falstaffian dreams and humor, but the orchestra's relatively muted brilliance, in deference to the soloist, makes it less immediately appealing. In this last major piece and in the chamber music that closely preceded it, Elgar tempered not only his love of full, exuberant sonority, but also his chromaticism. Chromatic passages are balanced and blended with modal and pentatonic passages in an individual manner, which warrants the surprising epithet that Hans Keller borrows from Schoenberg's famous essay on Brahms, "Elgar the progressive."

Moreover, this late manner reflects the "stern reality" whose triumph Elgar insisted on in *Falstaff*. Besides developing his mastery of large forms, Elgar underwent an obscure intellectual and religious change. The war affected him deeply, as letters published only long afterward, by Percy Young, reveal. Then, when his wife died in 1920, Elgar was inconsolable. He no longer practiced his Catholic faith. Sometime after 1913 he abandoned the oratorio that was to make a trilogy with *The Apostles,* Op. 49 (1903), and *The Kingdom,* Op. 51 (1906). The biggest project of his last years was an opera based on Ben Jonson's *The Devil is an Ass.*

In 1899 Frederick Delius (1862–1934) presented a concert of his vocal and instrumental music that startled musical London, appeased the skeptical father who was grudgingly supporting the thirty-six-year-old son, and enabled him to check some details of orchestration, for this was his first performance in England, and the fourth public performance anywhere of any of his work. Immediately thereafter Delius retired to Grez, a secluded village near Paris, where he lived the rest of his life, seldom hearing or thinking about any music but his own.

In 1900–1 he composed *A Village Romeo and Juliet,* his fifth and best opera, with its famous orchestral interlude, *The Walk to the Paradise Garden.* This is the earliest piece of Delius often played, and the piece praised above all later ones by sympathetic critics at the Delius Centennial Festival, 1962. Before World War I Delius went on to compose two more operas, a series of short pieces for orchestra, and a longer series of works for chorus with orchestra. In his last twenty years, despite a slowly oncoming paralysis and blindness, he added a few more pieces to these series, and also added shorter series of concertos and chamber music. The complete list of his works includes about fifty songs (mostly composed before 1900), a few unaccompanied choruses, a very few piano pieces, and one piece for harpsichord.

Delius won recognition in Germany during the first decade of the century, and was still admired there in the 1920's. He became generally known in England only after the conductor Thomas Beecham began to champion his music. From that time on Delius attracted a succession of fanatical admirers, including some of the best English musicians of the day, who ranked his *Mass of Life* (based on Nietzsche's *Zarathustra,* 1905) with Bach's Mass, his *Village Romeo* with Wagner's *Tristan,* and his harmonic daring with that of Debussy. He also attracted severe critics, and ultimately the critics persuaded most admirers that they had misjudged the breadth and depth of Delius. Philip Heseltine, author of the most abjectly admiring book on Delius, changed his mind soon after writing it, adopted a new name—Peter

Warlock—and as a composer struggled toward a goal opposed to Delius's. A later admirer, Eric Fenby, who lived with Delius in his last years and wrote out his last compositions at the blind man's dictation, came to distinguish more and more sharply between Delius's vast Nietzschean ambitions and his true achievement. Fenby agreed with most later critics that it was the slight, serene, admittedly shallow orchestral pieces that represented Delius's most distinctive and valuable achievement. Even these, in contrast to Elgar's most successful works, never serve to bind an English crowd together. Delius appeals rather to sensitive individuals who share, at least temporarily, his abhorrence of crowds. To be sure, his moods remind Englishmen of their countryside and of poets who have celebrated it, like Wordsworth and Housman. But natives of other countries can enjoy the moods of the cosmopolitan Delius with other associations or with none. Even when he uses an English folksong as theme for variations, he is less a national composer than Elgar, who quite rightly replied, when asked why he never used folksong: "I am folksong!" The achievement of Delius is a relatively slight and personal one.

Delius was, however, somewhat more adventurous than Elgar, if not so much so as either a thoroughly trained prize-winner like Debussy or a thoroughly uncompromising soliloquist like Ives. He ventured only a little beyond the bounds of common practice, and he was far from exhausting the possibilities within these bounds. Yet his little adventure was enough to give his music its distinctive sweet flavor. The adventure and the distinction are entirely in the realm of harmony.

Delius uses mild dissonance even more constantly than Debussy or MacDowell—chords of the seventh, ninth, and added sixth. But his chords are seldom so rich as Scriabin's. To accompany a simple melody he uses many different chords, as if inserting them between the few primary triads that support the melody and define its cadences. The cadencing chords are not obscured by the insertions. Many phrases reach their climax on the thoroughly clear and conventional chord I_4^6. The rich intervening chords are smoothly connected by chromatic motion of the inner voices, including more parallel motion than would be permissible in common practice. But the chromaticism rarely disturbs the diatonic norm, usually major, occasionally modal. And the parallelism never disturbs the relations between melody and bass. Parallelism in Delius is very different from parallelism in Debussy, which often has no connection with dissonance or chromaticism, and often deprives a melody of any independent bass. Delius uses dissonance, chromaticism, and parallelism together to make a smooth, luxuriant background, exactly as these devices are used after 1920 by Gershwin and Ellington, and after 1930 by most jazz pianists and arrangers of popular music.

Like MacDowell, Delius begins and ends most phrases in a single key.

When he does modulate, he overlaps phrases in sequence or he inserts a transitional passage between phrases of melody, just as he inserts the rich chords between the functional ones. The relation of one phrase to another is determined less by any feature of harmony than by the changing tempo, dynamics, and orchestration, all of which fluctuate very little within single phrases, serving like the harmony to make a smooth flow of feeling.

In slow movements Delius favors swaying barcarolle rhythms. In fast movements he likes a relaxed jig. His instrumental and choral sonorities are warm and glowing, whether soft or loud. But the effectiveness of both rhythm and sonority, and hence of the whole flow of feeling, depends very much on the insight and tact of the performers. Even Beecham complained about Delius's "indifference or ineptitude" in marking nuances. Likewise the choral conductor who knew Delius most thoroughly, Charles Kennedy Scott, testified:

He never had much to say about the performance of his music. He seemed content to leave it to others, provided he could trust their competence. A lack of executive ability probably accounted for this . . . Special sympathy is required in the performance of Delius' work. It will not give up its secret by rough and ready treatment. It is so sensitive and refined that the performer must have a like attitude, particularly as regards beauty of tone. If he is not a poet at heart, he had better leave Delius alone. Delius' music is above all a music of "distance," of background rather than foreground . . . It is the magic of colour, the stillness of far-off things, that entrance us; lively action, which must operate close at hand, scarcely enters.

Understanding of Delius's adventure may be made more precise, and perhaps some "special sympathy" for the Delian style may be aroused, by the romantic story of his youth, although many questions about it cannot be answered yet because no one but Beecham has had access to the manuscripts preserved by the Delius Trust.

The large, rich Delius family, immigrants to England from Germany, were among the chief patrons of music in the Yorkshire industrial town, Bradford. As a child Frederick improvised at the piano, studied the violin, fell in love with Chopin and Grieg, his life-long favorites; he scorned the Viennese classics, not to mention any English music or anything earlier than Haydn. When he was sixteen he gave up school, where he had excelled only at cricket. For the next five years his father tried to initiate him into the wool business, luring him with trips to France, Germany, Sweden, and Norway. Frederick learned to hate business and to love travel and Wagner. He and his father compromised temporarily on the project of growing oranges in Solano, Florida. Here for a year Frederick communed with Nature, admired the musical Negroes, resolved to become a composer, and briefly studied counterpoint with an organist from New York, Thomas F. Ward. In 1885 his brother relieved him of the orange grove. Frederick tried to support himself as a music teacher in Jacksonville, Florida, and then in Danville, Virginia. In Danville he made the only public appearance of his life as a performer, playing Mendelssohn's Violin Concerto. Now his father finally permitted him to become a music student, and he went at once to Leipzig. Here he learned more from knowing Sinding and Grieg, and from hearing Wagner, than from any true study with his official teachers, Reinecke and Jadassohn. In 1888 Delius moved to Paris and began composing operas. Among his friends in Paris were the Swedish dramatist Strindberg, the painter Gauguin, and the painter Jelka Rosen, who became his wife. About 1890 Delius discovered Nietzsche's *Zarathustra* and made it his gospel, to which he was faithful, unlike Scriabin, all his life. In 1893 a generous uncle paid for the first public performance of a piece by Delius. The next two performances came in 1897, then the London concert in 1899 that marked the turning-point of his career.

Some questions of particular interest that cannot be answered yet are just when and how much Delius learned about Debussy and other French composers. Percy Grainger testified that by 1907 Delius preferred Ravel to Debussy. He had hired Ravel, about 1902, to make the piano score of his French opera. But in the introductions of *Brigg Fair* (1907) and *Arabesk* (1910) the sounds of low flute, harp, and divided strings seem copied from Debussy's *Faun*. Did Delius find parallelism for himself in improvisation, as Arthur Hutchings supposes, or was this discovery stimulated by the similar practice of Chabrier and Ravel or the freer practice of Debussy and Satie? Answers to these questions would be valuable not only for better understanding of Delius himself, but also for a general picture of 20th-century music, for, just as Scriabin is the ideal target of anti-romanticism, so Delius, far more than Debussy, represents the narrow kind of impressionism that composers growing up around 1920 knew best and fought against. Debussy himself in 1901 heard some songs of Delius and described them in a review as, "very soft, very colorless songs, suitable for singing wealthy convalescents to sleep. . . . There is always a note clinging to a chord like a waterlily on a lake . . . or a little balloon blocked by the clouds." We can understand Debussy better to the extent that we know the distance between him and Delius. We can either enjoy or dismiss Delius himself without crediting him with any central historical significance.

———— •·•· ————

No other Englishman quite rivalled Delius's adventure or Elgar's grand and diversified achievement within the bounds of common practice, but several others achieved something worthy to be known abroad and enjoyed by posterity. Sir Arthur Somervell (1863–1937) wrote many songs, song-cycles, and sacred choral pieces. If the cycle on Tennyson's *Maud* is representative of these, they deserve a place in the repertory. Sir Charles Wood (1866–1926), already eminent in 1900 as a composer of oratorios, in later life concentrated on liturgical music. His *Passion According to St. Mark* (1921) shows his thorough craft and austere taste, by no means "Victorian" in the usual sense. Sir Henry Walford Davies (1869–1941) in his church music and other choral works, sacred and secular, likewise both refined and reinvigorated the central English heritage. Somervell, Wood, and Davies were all pupils of Parry and Stanford at the Royal College of Music, and all returned there to teach.

Sir Donald Francis Tovey (1875–1940) was another disciple of Parry. His superb essays, encyclopedia articles, and editions of the classics made him known to a wider public than did his compositions. Tovey was also (necessarily for his kind of scholarship) a profound pianist, conductor, and teacher, and a composer not to be dismissed as merely academic. His chamber music and concertos for piano and cello are noble pieces. His opera, *The Bride of Dionysus* (1929), is recommended by E. J. Dent as Tovey's most distinguished composition.

Less scholarly in manner than the Parry-Stanford group, perhaps more naive in their adherence to habits, were three composers of theater music. Dame Ethel Smyth (1858–1944), trained as a pianist in Germany, became a militant advocate of women's suffrage, and achieved the most memorable of her many compositions in a comic opera with a feminist moral, *The Boatswain's Mate* (1916). Sir Edward German (1862–1936), violinist, organist, and band-leader, became known, in the words of Fuller Maitland, "as the composer who carried on, as far as it could be carried on, the vogue of English light opera established by Sullivan." Norman O'Neill (1875–1934) was the oldest of a group of English students of Ivan Knorr in Frankfurt. As musical director of the Haymarket Theatre, London, he provided efficient incidental music for many plays. Roger Quilter (1877–1953) was another of the Knorr students. His songs constituted an irreplaceable monument of Edwardian gentility, by no means devoid of courage for adventure, but understating all that, rather.

Some other composers of the same generation pursued adventures more far-ranging than that of Delius if not so lucky in their outcome, adventures with an exemplary value for all the English-speaking world. Sir Granville Bantock (1868–1946) while still a pupil at the Royal Academy of Music, won his reputation with flamboyant cantatas and tone-poems with oriental programs. He persevered to set for soloists, chorus, and orchestra the whole of Fitzgerald's *Omar Khayyám* (1905–09). After he succeeded Elgar as professor at the University of Birmingham (1908) Bantock became increasingly interested in Celtic and Elizabethan poetry and music, in French and Russian music, and in the whole world's primitive music, folk music, and popular music (which he did not distinguish from each other). In later years he wrote less for large orchestra and more for unaccompanied chorus, wind bands, and chamber ensembles. These changes of interest are typical of the times, but in Bantock's case, as in many others, they are superficial. He never paused to examine his fundamental pre-Wagnerian habits, and no matter what the medium of performance or what the literary associations of his work, the rhythms are those of march and waltz, the harmonies are amateurish, and the sonorities are full. Josef Holbrooke (1878–1958) was a friend of Bantock and pupil of the same school. With very little recognition and very great assurance and energy he progressed from songs and chamber music through mammoth orchestral poems and choruses to a trilogy of operas on Celtic myths, *The Cauldron of Math* (1910–20). In his suite, *Les Hommages* (1900), whose four movements parody his four favorite masters, Wagner, Grieg, Dvořák, and Tchaikovsky, he betrays a superficial view of all of them. His energetic progress never brought him so far as he supposed from his earliest models, Sullivan, Rossini, and Spohr, though he used dissonance more continually, and though he regarded himself as a great innovator comparable to Debussy and Scriabin. He thought he had found that which we know Debussy sought: the musical equivalent of the tales and poems of Poe; at least ten of Holbrooke's large works are based on Poe. But the one piece that achieved any considerable popularity was the orchestral *Variations on "Three Blind Mice."* Havergal Brian (b. 1876) was a self-taught friend of Bantock and Elgar, who, like Holbrooke, doggedly completed vast and lofty works that were never performed, and only with *Three Blind Mice,* on which he wrote a *Fantastic Symphony* (1907), achieved any public success. The account of Brian's life by Reginald Nettel presents the clearest and most accurate analysis anywhere of a composer's development in relation to industrial society. To this should be added Robert Simpson's account of Brian's late works, down to the Twelfth Symphony (1957). Rutland Boughton (b. 1878) was a pupil of Stanford and Davies, protegé of Bantock, who developed a simplified style based on folk-like melody, as the vehicle for operas of Wagnerian scope. These he sang, conducted, and produced in provincial festivals that never quite grew to the level of Bayreuth. His earliest opera, *The Immortal Hour* (1914), became an enormous success in London in the 1920s, and some of his later works commanded the respect of Elgar, Vaughan Williams, and especially of George Bernard Shaw, who carried on a delightful correspondence with Boughton from 1905 until he died. Samuel Coleridge-Taylor (1875–1912) was inspired by Dvořák and by the Jubilee Singers of Fisk University to seek a style that would represent the African heritage of his father. His

African Suite for orchestra (1898) was a pioneer work, a more important historical landmark than the trilogy of cantatas about Hiawatha (1898–1900) which won more fame. Coleridge-Taylor's last and best major work was a violin concerto (1911). From the distance of half a century, the individual quality of all these pieces seems faded, but Coleridge-Taylor's brief career is nonetheless memorable.

———•—•—

Gustav Holst (1874–1934) was both more modest and more radical in his adventures than Delius, Bantock, Holbrooke, Brian, Boughton, and Coleridge-Taylor, but in the perspective of 1960 his work seems as close to theirs as to that of his good friend Vaughan Williams, with whom his name is usually linked. Holst too formed his first habits on pre-Wagnerian models, especially Sullivan. He owed to Grieg and Wagner his first stimulus toward harmonic adventure. He could neither break his habits nor fit them smoothly with his choices. In his most famous work, the orchestral suite *The Planets* (1915), his insistent odd meters of five and seven beats, his thick streams of parallel triads, and his opulent orchestration, influenced by Stravinsky, are incongruous with the conventional, symmetrical cadences of melody and harmony; the striking ostinato figures quickly become tiresome because they maintain a tonic harmony that belies their excitement. But Holst himself was dissatisfied with most of his music, and regarded all his larger pieces as experimental. He knew that *The Planets* in particular was crude compared with Wagner or Debussy or Stravinsky, but that he was closer to the line connecting these composers than Elgar or Delius or any other Englishman except Vaughan Williams. He knew, too, that greater than any composer in or near this line was Bach, whose Sanctus represented his supreme ideal, from the moment he first heard it in 1892. He hoped that his experiments might enable some Englishman after him to approach the ideal more nearly. Several of his own works approach it more nearly than *The Planets*.

It was typical of Holst that when, as a student of Stanford at the Royal College of Music, he was compelled by neuritis to abandon the piano and organ, he learned to play the trombone. For some years he played in the orchestra of the touring Carl Rosa opera company. It was typical too that his later career as a teacher included pioneering work in adult education and secondary education as well as the more usual teaching of composition.

When about 1900 Holst encountered oriental poetry and music he was not content with Fitzgerald translations or with coloristic orchestration as a means of evoking oriental associations. He learned Sanskrit and something of Indian music theory. His chief works from 1900 to 1912 are settings of texts that he himself translated from the *Rig Veda* and other Brahman scriptures. The most appealing of these is the thirty-minute chamber opera *Sāvitri* (1908), a wonderfully novel conception, unfortunately marred by some lapses into the sentimentality that Holst more and more abhorred.

The chief devices that identify Holst's music throughout his life, as his pupil Edmund Rubbra points out, are all prominent in the exotic works: 1) five- and seven-beat measures, 2) bass lines descending through an octave with ominous even motion, usually quarter notes, 3) enharmonic modulations produced by juxtaposing minor triads whose roots are a major third apart, 4) recitative revolving around a central pivot note, and 5) melodic cadences descending the Phrygian scale. In addition there are occasional uses of Indian scales, and contrapuntal combinations of melodies whose scales or modes differ from each other.

From 1906 to 1916 another interest occupied him: the English folksongs that had just been gathered and published by Cecil Sharp and his disciples. Holst arranged many of these songs effectively for unaccompanied chorus, for amateur string orchestras, and for bands. His arrangements are invariably more imaginative and faithful to the spirit of the tunes than Bantock's, but they are almost always weakened by momentary lapses into Bantock's easy kind of chromaticism. The culmination of Holst's concern with folksong was his ingenious one-act opera *At the Boar's Head* (1924). But the most lasting example was doubtless the Suite No. 1 for band (1909), which marked a new epoch in band literature and was rarely equalled by the many composers who imitated it.

Holst participated vigorously also in the nationalist and neo-classicist revival of English music from the 16th and 17th centuries. He copied Purcell's prosody, especially in recitatives. The pieces of his last decade, such as the *Fugal Concerto* (1924), the orchestral poem, *Egdon Heath* (1927), and the fine *Choral Fantasia* (1933), show the benefit of his study of Renaissance counterpoint.

In working toward a more authentic nationalism than that of Elgar or Delius, Holst and Vaughan Williams were assisted by the scholarly achievements of two contemporary musicians, Cecil Sharp (1859–1924) and Arnold Dolmetsch (1858–1940). Sharp was the first great collector of English folk tunes, founder of the English Folk Dance Society, and stimulator of the composers' national spirit. He found his richest treasury of materials in the Appalachian hill country of the United States, which he visited in 1916–18. Dolmetsch was the first great modern builder of viols, recorders, harpsichords, clavichords, and other old instruments, a performer on all of them and an editor and interpreter of their music. Though his book on interpretation is largely superseded by later scholarship, this later work rests partly on the foundations that he laid; Robert Donington, for example, both exemplifies the continuity and acknowledges it in an excellent book on

Dolmetsch. The recovery of the great heritage of ballads and dances, and of the works of Tallis, Byrd, Dowland, and Purcell, though part of a world-wide movement in music, almost sure to be achieved sooner or later, might have waited for another generation if Sharp and Dolmetsch had not undertaken their lonely adventures at the turn of the century. Their work more than any composer's restored England to a leading part in the concert of nations.

———•—

The most prominent new national voice in music at the beginning of the century was that of Finland. In 1900 Jean Sibelius (1865–1957) began his international career, as assistant conductor and featured composer with the Helsinki Symphony Orchestra on its tour of the European capitals. The orchestra under its regular conductor, Robert Kajanus, played Sibelius's First Symphony (1899) and his newly revised versions of three symphonic poems, *The Swan of Tuonela* (1893), *The Return of Lemminkaïnen* (1895), and *Finlandia* (1899). These works made his reputation as a master of orchestration with an individual style, and as the preëminent representative of a patriotic Finnish spirit.

His immediate success was so great that in 1901 he dared to retire from the Helsinki Conservatory, where he had taught composition and played violin in a faculty quartet. He was able to live thenceforth on royalties from his music, together with a pension awarded him by the Finnish government in 1897. In 1903 he and his wife, Aino Järnefelt, built a comfortable house in the country where they lived on into a legendary old age. Up until the First World War they often traveled, to England and America and all over the continent of Europe. In these years Sibelius's style of composition developed steadily in all forms and media. He participated in the modern movement, and proved himself not merely a "nationalist" but also something of an impressionist, neo-classicist, and expressionist as well. Among the memorable works he wrote between 1901 and 1914 are not only the symphonies—II (1902), III (1904–07), and IV (1911)—but also the superb Violin Concerto (1903), many pieces of incidental music for the theater, the distinctive string quartet *Voces intimae* (1909), two perfect pieces for string orchestra, *Canzonetta* and *Rakastava* (1911), several severe and concise pieces for piano, several songs, and several quite various tone-poems for orchestra.

After 1914 Sibelius swiftly became a lonely old man. In spite of honors and adulation from Finland, England, and America, he was somehow cut off or withdrawn from participation in new currents of musical thought. Most critics and historians relegated him to the 19th century. Even for his closest students and most faithful admirers he was an enigma. In three more symphonies and a final tone-poem, *Tapiola* (1925), he pursued his own stylistic development, with increasing deliberation and self-criticism. At the same time he poured forth a large number of short pieces—songs, choruses, piano music, and salon-chamber music—which embarrass his admirers. An eighth symphony was often mentioned in interviews, but never completed. In his last thirty years he produced nothing memorable.

The style of Sibelius diverges from common practice more thoroughly than the styles of most of his contemporaries, though never so radically as that of Debussy. Sibelius has characteristic devices of melody, rhythm, harmony, orchestration, and form, which balance and complement each other. Yet the ending of every piece affirms its tonality, and once the ending is known, the ambiguities of the beginning and middle disappear, and the uncommon progressions lose their disturbing quality; the unconventional, carefully calculated form falls apart so that it could be shortened or rearranged without damage; the novelty of the music, in short, wears off, whereas Debussy's novelty shows up more and more clearly the more his music is studied. What remains for admirers of Sibelius is a personal quality stronger than that of Elgar (whom he admired) and a mastery greater in scope and sureness. Sibelius is ranked by Tovey higher than Bruckner, by Cecil Gray as second only to Beethoven. He is ranked as an epigone of Grieg and Tchaikovsky only by critics like Salazar who have scarcely listened to him. Either extreme judgment seems foolish to anyone willing to study both Sibelius himself and a fair number of his contemporaries and successors.

Many of the distinguishing habits of Sibelius can be seen in a short piece from his incidental music to *Pelléas*. The character-sketch of Maeterlinck's heroine, *Mélisande at the Spinning Wheel,* portrays her in gloomier costume than the music that Debussy gave her in his opera. This sketch was published in a piano arrangement by Johannes Doebber, with no mention of Mélisande, but rather with the title *Evening on a Forest Lake,* as the first number of a group of *Sibeliana, Moods from the Land of a Thousand Lakes.* The music fits this title as well as its original one. To be sure, this title might serve for almost any piece of Sibelius.

The melody of *Mélisande* depends on its accompanying chords. The poignant effect of the melody comes from its frequent dissonance against the calm, semistatic, nocturnal harmony. In the original version, instrumentation contributes to this relationship and to the mood: English horn is accompanied by strings, as in the supreme showpiece for the English horn, *The Swan of Tuonela.* The melody pulls against the accompaniment in augmented fifths, minor sevenths, and finally major sevenths that might be diminished octaves. But in every case the melody resolves to ordinary triads or diminished seventh chords along the diatonic line of least resistance.

This is typical of Sibelius. In the Fourth and Fifth Symphonies there are somewhat stronger pulls of dissonance than here in *Mélisande,* but the resolutions are equally conventional. The augmented triad and the *Tristan* seventh chord are Sibelius's favorite harmonies, but he hardly ever exploits the possibilities of enharmonic transformation that endeared these chords

EXAMPLE VI.1   Sibelius, *Mélisande*

to Liszt, Wagner, and Debussy. The famous *Valse triste* is full of these rich chords, but its many modulating sequences are simple, so that the rich chords are tamed to the symmetry of the waltz.

In *Mélisande* the chords themselves are not so rich. Their tonal meaning is not obvious at first, but it soon proves to be a definite F minor. The swaying between two chords with undeveloped ambiguities, even more than the specific structure of the chords, is typical of Sibelius. This device appears in many pieces, including the Fourth and Fifth Symphonies. Elsewhere an outright static harmony, usually tonic, is apt to persist for minutes, kept alive by a *tremolando* or some more elaborate figuration.

Mélisande's accompaniment has no contrapuntal interest, but without accompaniment the melody would be too symmetrical and redundant for a folksong or a waltz. The melody slowly develops its one motif, expanding like a plant through a modest range, and breaking off in various drooping feminine endings, until finally it dissolves in a scale with a slow turn. (The melodic bits marked *x, y,* and *z* show a family resemblance to many Sibelius themes.) Motivic development is the most discussed feature of Sibelius's style. He achieved a consummate model of such development in constructing *Tapiola* from a single motif, and he displayed the same sort of development prominently in the Quartet and the later symphonies. He spoke of it, too, in a conversation with Mahler, which he reported to his biographer Ekman: "When our conversation touched on the essence of symphony, I said that I admired its severity of style and the profound logic that created an inner connection between all the motifs. This was the experience I had come to in composing. Mahler's opinion was just the reverse. 'No, a symphony must be a world. It must embrace everything.'" Sibelius's logic is convincing enough, but rather unsubtle in comparison with that of Brahms or Debussy. Their motifs pervade their accompaniments, whereas Sibelius's are usually confined to his leading melody.

Likewise, his occasional use of modal scales, mixed with mild chromaticism, though far freer and more interesting than the modality of Delius, is naive compared with that of Brahms or Debussy. In *Mélisande* there is only a slight modal touch, but it is characteristic: the return to the tonic after the dissolving scale makes a doleful Phrygian effect, which seems merely accidental, not an organic outcome of the melody or the basic harmony. In the Sixth Symphony the Dorian mode is a continual influence but still not a profound one.

The unashamed parallel thirds with the scale, and also the thick thirds with the bass, are features prominent throughout Sibelius's music. They rarely sound like the sweet thirds of Italian opera or of Brahms, because they are kept apart from any strong progressions of chords. In the Violin Concerto thirds and sixths are more conventionally sweet, but in the last two symphonies and *Tapiola,* where strong progressions are very rare, the thirds and sixths are more frequent.

The form of *Mélisande* is its most peculiar feature. In spite of all its repetition and square phrasing, it never recapitulates the beginning. The brief section of contrasting animation and modulation, mm. 25–30, falls back to the transitional phrase that preceded it, and this rises now to the climax of the piece, m. 36. Then the contrasting section is under way again, and falls back again, to the same transitional phrase, which now breaks off—the rest is recapitulation of fragments in arbitrary order, until the final cadence. Sibelius's larger forms likewise avoid recapitulating their beginnings, and many of them arrive at a resigned cadence after many fragmentary reminiscences.

All these habits of Sibelius are evident in the pieces that established his fame in 1900, particularly in the best one of them, *The Swan*. The formation of his style cannot be traced in detail, because he destroyed much of his earlier work and refused to allow publication of several early pieces that were preserved. The studies of Ekman, Ringbom, Abraham, Johnson, and other scholars cited by them suffice to trace the outline of his development. Possibly further details, in answer to questions raised by this outline, may yet be forthcoming.

By the age of ten, Sibelius had learned to play the piano enough to compose a piece called *Raindrops,* which has been published in Furuhjelm's biography. Soon he played the violin, and determined to become a virtuoso. Among family and friends—amateurs proud of their serious cosmopolitan culture—he became thoroughly familiar with classical chamber music, and devoted to Grieg and Tchaikovsky. By himself he studied composition, using Marx's textbook. The earliest work extant in manuscript is a trio (1882) and from the following decade there are a dozen more pieces of chamber music described by Ekman. The first published work was a song

(1888) but this was an exceptional effort for him at this time. There was no orchestral music until much later. His fundamental musical habits were formed through the medium of chamber music.

In 1885, when he was twenty, he persuaded his family to let him quit his studies at the University of Helsinki and enter the Academy of Music. The director of the Academy, Martin Wegelius (1846–1906), guided his development for four years. Then in 1889 he went to Berlin, for fugal exercises with Albert Becker (1834–1899) and in 1891 to Vienna, for orchestration with Robert Fuchs (1847–1927). Thus his academic habits became fairly secure. Throughout his studies he held somewhat aloof from the Wagnerian influence that he saw "taking possession of so many of my friends, both young and old." In Berlin he heard Wagner with pleasure and profit, but he gained still more from the performances of Beethoven sonatas by Bülow, and of Beethoven quartets by Joachim. In Vienna his sympathies went to Brahms and Johann Strauss and the great singer of Meyerbeer, Pauline Lucca. He wrote his first published songs, Op. 13, on texts by the Romantic Swedish poet, Runeberg (1804–77).

He became a selfconsciously Finnish composer thanks to the political atmosphere of the 1890s, and thanks particularly to the conductor Kajanus, whose compositions were intended to form a Finnish national style. Kajanus inspired him, by precept and example, to draw programs from the folklore that had been gathered by Eliat Lönnrot into a sort of epic, the *Kalevala* (1835–1849). Sibelius told Ekman: "The environment in which I had grown up was as far removed from the *Kalevala* as possible. My mother and my Swedish grandmother had loved poetry of a very different kind." Now when Sibelius turned to the *Kalevala,* he found the stimulus to produce works that Kajanus—and most Finnish music-lovers—were delighted to accept at once as national. His first effort was *Kullervo* (1892), a symphonic poem with chorus and solo voices (unpublished). He began an opera, but abandoned it when advised that the libretto, which he himself had prepared from an episode of the *Kalevala,* was too lyrical; its overture, however, became *The Swan of Tuonela.* If a manuscript survives of its original form, 1893, a comparison of this with the revision of 1900 might reveal many interesting details. The suite of incidental music to the pageant, *Karelia,* published as written in 1893, is recognizable Sibelius, but far less refined and less distinctive than *The Swan.*

The earliest settings of Finnish texts available for study so far are two songs, Op. 17, Nos. 6 and 7 (1898). Considering these, the singer Astra Desmond notes

. . . how the style is changed to suit the totally different rhythm of the language. Spoken Finnish has rather a level monotonous sound, except for a marked drop in pitch at the end of phrases. Being a very much inflected language the words tend to get very long in some of the cases and the frequency with which long vowels occur in unstressed syllables decreases the effect of the stress. So in the Finnish settings we find that many repeated notes followed by a short falling phrase are a marked feature of the melodic line.

The same feature marks some of the most memorable lines in the first two symphonies. But of course other melodic shapes are also common, and no particular melodic shape is so essential a feature of Sibelius's style as his devices of harmony and form.

Sibelius set Finnish texts more often for chorus than for solo voices. The rich colors of a four-part male chorus were especially congenial for him. But more congenial still were the colors of divided strings and full wind choirs. He probably transferred to his orchestral music most of the best ideas that were inspired by Finnish words and voices, as he did in the beautiful suite, *Rakastava* (*The Lover*).

Thanks again to Kajanus, who allowed Sibelius "to try the effects of combinations of sounds and generally to see how my new scores sounded in reality," he achieved by 1900 the mastery of his own kind of orchestration, a clearer kind than that of Strauss, but thicker than that of Rimsky-Korsakov. In subsequent years he was able to absorb rapidly some of Debussy's orchestral devices that could serve his own rhythmic and harmonic purposes. In the symphonic poems of 1913, *The Bard* and *Oceanides,* he ventured still farther, breaking his melodies into fragments for the sake of elaborate orchestral effects that Ringbom and others call impressionistic. On the other hand, in his symphonies, beginning with the Third (1907), he showed a neo-classical restraint and economy of orchestration, in keeping with his persistent interest in chamber music.

The Fourth Symphony (1911) is widely regarded as the culmination of his style. Unquestionably it shows Sibelius straining for the utmost harmonic novelty that he could cope with. Very probably it shows his reaction to Debussy's use of the whole-tone scale—a complicated reaction, not an obvious borrowing. In the opinion of Simon Parmet, able conductor and friend of Sibelius, the Fourth Symphony is a tragic failure to achieve Debussy's sort of freedom, and all of Sibelius's later works and silences may be partially explained by this failure. The principal theme of the Fourth emphasizes a raised fourth degree, in bitter conflict with the tonic. But the tonic wins, and accordingly the forms are concise and clear, while the moods are all dark, without relief. Sibelius himself told Ekman that the work "described experiences of an introspective, spiritual nature, arising from pondering over the most important problems of existence, life and death." A few months after completing his Fourth, Sibelius heard Bruckner's

Seventh and was moved to tears. "What a strangely profound spirit, formed by religiousness. And this profound religiousness we have abolished in our own country as something no longer in harmony with our time." Shortly after the beginning of the First World War he pursued his ponderings: "How much pathos there is in our time. We are approaching the foreseen religious era. But it is impossible to define a religion—least of all in words. But perhaps music is a mirror." The last three symphonies he called "professions of faith." In them he painstakingly affirmed the ineffable religiousness that he wished to recover, through forms of great originality and interest. Then in *Tapiola* (1925) he expressed, through a still more remarkable form, a mood of desolation. For Wilfrid Mellers and other recent critics *Tapiola* is the one masterpiece of Sibelius most likely to hold a place in the repertory of serious music. The fact that no comparable work came after *Tapiola* suggests that Sibelius was baffled by his own adventure.

———◆◆———

Carl Nielsen (1865–1931) after achieving in his thirties an even more heroic position in Denmark than that of Sibelius in Finland, went on learning and boldly adventuring to the end of his life. His operas *Saul and David* (1901) and *Maskarade* (1906) held the stage in Denmark. But his adventures held the interest of very few people. His most ambitious instrumental works, the six symphonies and three concertos and the late organ piece, *Commotio,* only began to be noticed abroad in the 1950s. As formal achievements they must still be ranked below the symphonies of Sibelius. Nevertheless, Nielsen deserves international recognition for the grace and strength of some of his smaller works, for the peculiar treatment of tonality in the large ones, and above all for the rare humane wisdom expressed in all of them as well as in a short book, *My Childhood* (1927), and a collection of articles, *Living Music* (1925), both published in translation in 1953.

His father was a house-painter and village fiddler and cornettist, extremely poor but respected for his crafts and his character. His mother sang folksongs with conviction. When Carl was eight or nine he began to help support the family by tending geese for a neighbor who was better off. He also worked, in school holidays, trimming bricks, gleaning fields, and helping with all sorts of farm chores. He learned enough music from his father and a village school teacher to compose a polka for the violin. With immense delight he joined an amateur orchestra and advanced step by step from triangle to first violin. At fourteen he left home to start his career in a military band. Here he learned all the brass instruments and wrote pieces for them. He found an old piano teacher who gave him informal lessons in a tavern, introducing him to Haydn, Mozart, and Beethoven, and finally, with careful preparation, to Bach. Soon he composed a string quartet and took it to Copenhagen. There, from 1884 to 1886 he studied under Gade, the disciple of Mendelssohn. He supported himself by playing in dance bands. In 1889, at twenty-four, he won a place as second violinist in the Royal Chapel Orchestra, where he stayed until 1905, quietly pursuing his development as a composer, with a steady stream of works in all media. On his first trip abroad, 1890–91, he met and married the sculptress Anne Marie Brodersen. On the same trip he had his first opportunities to see and hear the late operas of Wagner. He recorded his reaction in a diary, which is quoted by his biographer Meyer:

I admire Wagner . . . the greatest genius of our century. But I don't like his spoon-feeding the audience; each time a name is mentioned, even if the person has been dead and buried for many years, the *Leitmotiv* is served up. This I find highly naive, and it almost makes me laugh. I cannot see that Wagner is hard to understand. That is nonsense.

His antipathy toward Wagner grew, until in *Living Music* he condemned a typical theme from the *Ring* in terms like those of Ives:

. . . ugly and dated, the more since it was composed in all seriousness and in the grand manner . . . It is the taste, excessive and unwholesome, in Wagner's theme that is intolerable. The only cure for this sort of taste lies in studying the basic intervals. The glutted must be taught to regard a melodic third as a gift of God, a fourth as an experience, and a fifth as the supreme bliss. Reckless gorging undermines the health.

Nielsen's First Symphony (1892) is as mildly anti-Wagnerian as the quotation from the diary. His 20th-century works, like the passage from *Living Music,* show his increasingly radical antipathy to Wagner. The First Symphony displays Nielsen's peculiar mixture of modality and chromaticism, organized as a dramatic contest between rival tonal centers, here C major and G minor. But the first cantata, *Hymnus amoris* (1891–96), is more profoundly adventurous. Nielsen sketched the text, dealing with the aspects of love from childhood to an old age. Then he had a friend polish it and another friend translate it into Latin for setting. He explained:

. . . this language is monumental and lifts one away from too subjective and personal feelings, which would be out of place where a polyphonic choir gives expression to so universal a power as love; and also one can bear the text-repetitions more easily in Latin.

Here Nielsen anticipates Stravinsky's *Oedipus.* The music of *Hymnus amoris* shows a new concern with counterpoint, especially that of Palestrina, which is to be found again in many of Nielsen's 20th-century works.

Debussy at Pourville, 1905 (The Bettmann Archive)

Debussy at Luzancy, 1893, with *(left to right)* Mme. Ernest Chausson, Ernest Chausson, Raymond Boucheur (The Bettmann Archive)

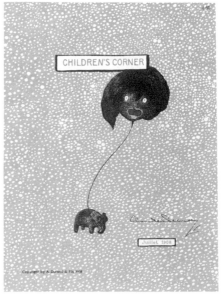

Title page of Debussy's *Children's Corner* (Durand et Cie., Paris)

PLATE 1

Debussy and Stravinsky (The Bettmann
Archive)

Stravinsky with Nijinsky as Petrushka
(The Bettmann Archive)

Hindemith and Stravinsky,
Santa Fe, 1961 (Tony Perry)

PLATE 2

Beginning in 1902 Nielsen collaborated with Thomas Laub, organist, antiquarian, and a reformer of Danish church music, to produce a vast repertory of hymns and school songs. This, above all, is what won him his place as the greatest Danish national composer. This work is reflected in the symphonies in a curious way: they carry on the idea of conflicting tonalities, sometimes to the point of horrendous dissonance, but when one key emerges triumphant (usually not the one suggested at the beginning) there are long, unashamed passages with the simplest triadic progressions, like a hymn, or static triadic harmony, like Bruckner's. The Fifth Symphony (1922) is reckoned by Nielsen's advocate, Robert Simpson, as the most sublime peak of his career. The Wind Quintet (1923), with its imaginative variations on a typical hymnlike theme, is said to be more popular in Denmark and surely merits a place in the international repertory. The late piano music exemplifies the same concerns on a becomingly smaller scale, especially the set of miniatures *For Young and Old* (1930). The final testament for organ, *Commotio* (1930), combines the characteristic harmony and counterpoint with a grand objectivity like that of the *Hymnus amoris*.

Contemporary with Nielsen and Sibelius in neighboring countries were lesser figures. The leading Swedish composers, Hugo Alfvén (1872–1960), Olof Wilhelm Peterson-Berger (1867–1942), and Wilhelm Stenhammar (1871–1927), variously and worthily carried forward the Wagnerian tradition established in Sweden by Andreas Hallen (1846–1925). Stenhammar turned in the latter part of his life more toward Brahms, and distinguished himself with a series of string quartets. Norway's national music, made famous abroad by Grieg and Sinding, was best maintained by Hjalmar Borgström (1864–1925).

In Belgium, Paul Gilson (1865–1942) ranked foremost as master of Flemish national opera, and second only to Franck as composer of orchestral music; his symphonic poem *De Zee* (*The Sea,* 1892) and his many later pieces for band deserved international recognition alongside Elgar, if not quite next to Strauss. His *Matrozenliederen en dansen* (*Sailors' Songs and Dances*) were regarded by his pupil Marcel Poot as the most original and most valuable of his works. Gilson's activity as teacher, his critical and theoretical writings, his journal, *La Revue musicale belge,* and his memoirs, reinforced his strong influence on the musical life of his country. An emigré from Belgium, Désiré Pâque (1867–1939), was among the lonely pioneers of "atonal" and "athematic" music; his own name for his distinctive procedure was "adjonction constante," that is, continual motivic addition. Albert Vander Linden, having studied Pâque's many unpublished works, judges them worthy of more attention than they have yet received. A middle way between Gilson and Pâque was that of Joseph Jongen (1873–1953), whose ample catalogue of church music and chamber music, in a style tinged with Debussyan harmonies, won respect and wide use.

A more distinctive representative of Belgium on the world-wide scene was the carilloneur Jef Denijn (1862–1941). According to Jacqueline Goguet, Denijn was the chief reformer of the ancient tradition of tower bells, and founder of an international school.

The most interesting composer of the Netherlands since Sweelinck was Alfons Diepenbrock (1862–1921). He was a classical scholar and school teacher, an amateur pianist, quartet player, and madrigal singer, who acquired mainly by independent study enough technique to compose some noble songs and choruses, and toward the end of his life a few pieces of orchestral music. Diepenbrock's chief interpreter, Eduard Reeser, describes his style as a synthesis of elements from Wagner and Palestrina, to which after 1909 are added elements from Debussy. Diepenbrock's collected essays testify to his intelligent nationalism and internationalism.

In German-speaking Switzerland, Hermann Suter (1870–1926) drew to a peak and a conclusion the mild national movement represented earlier by Huber. Suter's Symphony (1913) incorporates folksongs and dance rhythms, along with some Straussian traits, into a style basically similar to Brahms. In his oratorio setting of St. Francis's *Laudi* (1924) the same elements are joined by some suggestions of Gregorian melody and Bach-like counterpoint.

French-speaking Switzerland, slowly emerging through the 19th century from narrow Calvinist restrictions on the arts, was a mere province of a province of German music until Gustave Doret (1866–1943) and Émile Jaques-Dalcroze (1865–1950) turned to France for liberation. Doret went first from Lausanne to Berlin, where he studied with Joachim, and then to Paris, where Dubois and Massenet were his teachers. In operas, oratorios, songs, and some instrumental music, and also in his critical writings, he contributed much to the development of the following generation of Swiss composers. Jaques-Dalcroze, after studies with Delibes in Paris and with Fuchs and Bruckner in Vienna, traveled also in Algeria, and on the other hand studied the songs of his countrymen. He became famous abroad for his system of musical training with emphasis on bodily movement, "Eurhythmics." At home he was equally esteemed for his many songs and dances, festival cantatas, and patriotic operas. Doret and Dalcroze pointed ahead to Frank Martin.

CHAPTER VII

Contemporaries in Italy and Southern Europe

W HEN VERDI died, in 1901, Giacomo Puccini (1858–1924) was the most successful living composer. Income from his fourth opera, *La Bohème* (1896), and his fifth, *Tosca* (1900), made him rich. *La Bohème* won the affectionate and lasting admiration not only of the great singers of this Golden Age, like Enrico Caruso, and their enthusiastic admirers around the world, but also of so scholarly a musician as Anton Webern, who, according to the recollection of his friend Egon Wellesz, was deeply touched by the *pianissimo* ending of its first act. *La Bohème* was praised also by Debussy, in a conversation with Falla, as the most authentic and alluring picture of the life he had known in the artists' garrets of Paris. Puccini's harmony and orchestration in this work and even earlier owed as much to Wagner, Massenet, and Bruneau as to Verdi, whose *Aïda* had given him his first and foremost inspiration to compose, and whose *Traviata* was close in spirit to *La Bohème*. Puccini's counterpoint and forms, on the contrary, adhered to the simple rules he had learned under Amilcare Ponchielli at the Milan Conservatory, both now and later when his harmony and orchestration showed various 20th-century influences. Puccini's successful combinations of old and new elements constituted an adventure, however limited, worthy of recognition, and an achievement that commands respect even from disapproving critics.

Between *Bohème* and *Tosca* Puccini asked Maeterlinck for permission to set *Pelléas,* but Debussy had already secured this right—luckily for all concerned.

Tosca was and remained a greater hit than any setting of *Pelléas* could be. It was even more gratifying than *La Bohème* for leading singers and their fans. On the other hand, its pretensions as a tragedy on the grand scale never convinced discriminating listeners. Its powerful theatrical effects served no credible plot or characterization, although, to be sure, as Mosco

Carner has shown, Puccini's sincere belief in his subject and his ardent love for his heroine surpassed his belief in and love for anything in real life. The frequent use of climactic phrases—"perpetual pregnancy in the melody," as D. J. Grout calls it—never composes a satisfying melodic whole to compare with Verdi's arias. Rhythms are trite, mostly languorous, at the mercy of the singers' *rubato*. The harmony at the climax includes the Tristan chord in parallel motion and finally a long whole-tone scale, but these details are absorbed into conventional phrases, resting on strong harmonic progressions. The recurring *leitmotifs* assure an obvious sort of unity without development. The whole atmosphere reeks of sadism and masochism. "Love and hate are the same," says the villain Scarpia, and Puccini gives them the same kind of exasperated musical expression. The heroine claims special pity and privilege because she has "lived for art," but at last she is driven to deceit and violence to match her tormentor's. There are titillating references to politics and religion, without any statement whatever on these topics—the references serve only to enlarge the spectacular background of the melodrama. *Tosca* proved to be typical of Puccini's work in the 20th century, although each of his later operas had distinctive features worth study.

In his fifties and sixties, Puccini produced *Madama Butterfly* (1904), *La Fanciulla del West* (*The Girl of the Golden West,* 1910), *La Rondine* (*The Swallow,* 1917), *Il Trittico* (triptych of one-acters *Il Tabarro, Suor Angelica, Gianni Schicchi,* 1918), and *Turandot* (completed by Alfano, 1926). The first of these joined its predecessors as a favorite in the repertory. It treated with soft sentiment the timely theme of clashing cultures, not only in its plot but in its musical style. Puccini had now learned from Debussy that exotic scales and sonorities could be woven into sophisticated structures. Puccini's procedure, following Debussy's, is more thoroughgoing than earlier musical exoticism. Unlike Debussy, however, Puccini takes exotic pentatonic melodies outright as themes, and exploits the devices of ostinato, parallelism, and heterophony in a facile improviser's manner, through whole phrases. On the other hand, he continues to rely on the proven power of strong chord-progressions to achieve his emotional effects. The superficiality of Puccini's orientalism, compared with Debussy's, is shown in his subsequent works by their variety of sources and their similarity of shape and purpose: the Japanese color of *Butterfly* gives way to cowboy and Indian tunes for *Fanciulla,* and to Chinese melodies and sonorities for *Turandot,* but in both these cases the essential lines behind the colors are those of *Tosca,* just as the heroines are essentially the same character.

The Girl of the Golden West was commissioned for the Metropolitan Opera in New York. Its première (1910), with Caruso and Toscanini, was doubtless the supreme climax of American operatic life. Its success with the public, however, did not last. For audiences could not overlook the improbable plot and characters in an atmosphere that lacked the glamor of remoteness. Though every patient student of Puccini finds *Fanciulla* just as skillful and just as forceful in its symbolism as any of his other works, the skill and force only make obtrusive the absurdity of the whole idea.

In *La Rondine* Puccini tried to compete with Viennese operetta. Here he betrayed his deficiency in tunefulness. For all his "perpetual pregnancy in the melody," he could not compose a tune for the customers to whistle as they left the theater, or a waltz to dance to at the beer garden. Yet even in *Rondine* he showed his usual cleverness. Gianandrea Gavazzeni, composer and critic, would "give all of *Butterfly* for the delicious first act to *Rondine,* where Puccini, as if joking, succeeds in finding a narrative tone *à la* Maupassant." On the other hand, Puccini diluted the comedy with half-hearted tragic arias and love duets.

The *Triptych* Puccini intended to have performed as a whole, counting on the complementary effects of the grim realistic melodrama, the mystical all-female interlude, and the rousing, sly 18th-century comedy. Only the comedy was often performed. It came to be regarded by many critics as Puccini's most satisfying piece. But the public remembered chiefly its irrelevant lyrical aria.

The final work, *Turandot,* is in many ways the most interesting. It is based on a fine fantastic play by the 18th-century Italian, Gozzi, though Puccini and his librettists made some drastic changes. They added to the cast a tormented slave-girl, Liu, who is really the same character as Tosca and Butterfly. Her music is recognized by the opera's friends and foes as the best part of it, and the least adventurous. The setting permits Puccini to use various Chinese melodies, which he elaborates with sumptuous orchestration and occasional polychords in tribute to Stravinsky, whose early ballets Puccini studied and admired. But the complex tricks of *Turandot* are all in the service of drama that Puccini has reduced to lurid melodrama; they serve it effectively, to be sure, but they cannot redeem it, any more than they can convince anyone that Gozzi's cruel fantastic princess Turandot is redeemed in the end by Puccini's gratuitous kiss.

From some people Puccini provoked excessive reactions—a distaste for Verdi or for opera in general. Most Italian musicians of the following generation joined the musicologist Torrefranca in rejecting the whole tradition as an artificial, international one, and in trying to build a new national tradition on the rediscovered heritage of Palestrina, Monteverdi, Corelli, and Vivaldi. On the other hand, there is no doubt that Puccini's skill, combined with that of the singers, brought many new listeners and even subscribers to the opera houses of the Western world, so that he helped indirectly to make possible the revivals of Mozart, Rossini, and Bellini, as well as the survival and slow growth in influence of late Verdi and Debussy, and the various operatic experiments of younger men. It is likely, moreover, that the atmosphere of *Tosca* contributed something to Strauss's *Salome* (1905), Schoenberg's *Erwartung* (1909), Berg's *Lulu* (1937), and Britten's *Peter Grimes* (1945). Certainly *Tosca* was among the chief models for Menotti's *Consul* (1950) and Carlisle Floyd's *Susannah* (1955). Puccini's works and their direct and indirect influences were likely to persist as long as the institution of opera. While only naive or corrupt tastes could rank Puccini with Mozart, Verdi, and Wagner, ahead of Debussy or Stravinsky, nevertheless only a policy that despaired of opera altogether could afford to deny or neglect his kind of success.

———————•—•———————

At the opposite pole from Puccini is Ferruccio Busoni (1866–1924), one of the boldest, loneliest, most restless adventurers in music, whose exalted idealism would never allow him to compromise in the least for the sake of achieving success.

Busoni knew success well enough as child prodigy and as mature virtuoso of the piano, recognized by connoisseurs as the true successor to Liszt, with whom no Paderewski or Rachmaninov could seriously be compared. But his compositions were seldom played. As conductor he had an important influence too, introducing an élite audience in Berlin, 1902–1909, to a series of new works, including Debussy's *Faun* and *Nocturnes,* Fauré's *Pelléas,* and pieces by Elgar, Delius, Sibelius, Nielsen, and Bartók. As editor and arranger of the keyboard works of Bach and Liszt he was a controversial figure. And as author of scintillating essays, particularly the booklet, *Sketch of a New Aesthetic of Music* (1907), and an open letter, *Junge Klassizität* (*New Classicism,* 1920), he secured a prominent position in the German literature about new music. But this literature seldom did justice to him as a composer. Italian and English translations of the *Sketch* aroused less attention than the German original. His collected later writings waited to appear in Italian until 1941, when a group of composers including Luigi Dallapiccola began to hail him as their own ancestor. The first English translation of the later writings was published in 1957, although it was his English friend, the scholar E. J. Dent, who published in 1933 the best biography of Busoni.

His 20th-century compositions cannot yet be judged with any certainty. They are not readily available and not easily performed, and yet, as Dent says, ". . . we cannot hope to attain understanding of his vision until we have pursued it along his own track, sharing the successive experiences that each of his earlier works recorded." "Earlier works" here does not include those of the 19th century, for Busoni himself discarded everything before his Violin Sonata of 1899, and by 1912 he spoke condescendingly even of this. From 1900 to 1903 no new compositions appeared. After 1904, when he astonished Berlin by appearing without his beard and with a new concerto, every new piece has at least the interest of his unique, continuing adventure. The list is strange, with overlapping dates for the largest works—four operas—and cross-references to them from several smaller works—Dent speaks of these as "satellites."

One of the operas is *Turandot* (1917), based on the same play by Gozzi that served for Puccini's last work. But the contrast between Busoni and Puccini is sharper than ever in their ways of treating the same basic materials. Busoni condenses the play without changing its outline, and exhibits its supernatural fabulous character in a series of detached pieces of music, leaving the dramatic action and passion to be presented in spoken dialogue. Thus his work is ineffective, even amateurish, compared with Puccini's. Yet parts of the music are more stimulating than any of Puccini's. Busoni's operas, like his prose, suggest ideas that provoke meditation and promote the development of taste. His music does not aim to make drama, but "a rare half-religious and elevating ceremony." The operas other than *Turandot* are provocative and ineffective in different ways. *Die Brautwahl* (*The Bridal Choice,* 1906–1911) is based on a tale of E. T. A. Hoffmann in which a charming, irresponsible artist wins a beautiful girl away from a dull bureaucrat, with the help of two wizards—the action is an incoherent mixture of melodrama, fantasy, and farce, which the music cannot begin to pull together. *Arlecchino* (*Harlequin,* 1914–16) is another bewildering mixture of the same elements, plus fierce satire on conventional opera, on war, and on mediocre humanity, all compressed into a single, swift act, and presented with alternating use of German and Italian. *Doktor Faust* (completed by Philip Jarnach, 1910–25), based more on old German puppet plays than on Goethe's drama, and organized by an enigmatic Nietzschean interpretation of the legend, is by far the most elaborate and least effective of all. Busoni let Faust speak for him, as each of his heroes did, and he let Faust end by passing on his insatiable thirst to his infant son, saying, "I, wise fool, hesitator and waster, have accomplished nothing; all must be begun afresh." The adventure is more important than the accomplishment.

Busoni's strange adventure began in his childhood. Both parents were musicians. His mother was a pianist, half German, with a tendency toward scholarship; she taught him Schumann and Mendelssohn. His father was a virtuoso clarinettist, and a temperamental tyrant; he taught Ferruccio to subordinate mere notes to the melodic sweep of Rossini, Bellini, and Donizetti, and also to respect Bach. At the age of nine, already playing in public and composing copiously, Busoni chose Cherubini as the model most sympathetic to his tastes, admitting that Mozart and Beethoven might be greater. From 1879 to 1881 he pursued a concentrated course of study with

Wilhelm Mayer (1831–1898), which introduced him to the whole perspective of music history, equipped him with a mastery of Berliozian orchestration, and above all showed him how to appreciate Mozart and depreciate Wagner. As his travels continued, he absorbed the influence of Brahms, who took a sympathetic interest in his work, but Busoni was too Italian to become a disciple. In Helsinki, where Busoni served as piano teacher, 1888–1890, Sibelius's teacher Wegelius converted him to a serious interest in Liszt, which grew from then on. In 1894 he heard Verdi's new *Falstaff,* and this—not *Aïda* or even *Otello*—awakened his ambition to compose operas and to emphasize his Italian nationality. The Piano Concerto of 1904 shows the degree to which Busoni had absorbed all these influences.

One more influence, though slight and superficial, was indispensable for Busoni's further adventures: Debussy. In a letter to his wife, 1907, where he is summarizing the changes of his taste during the past two decades, he says, "I discovered for myself the latest Frenchmen; when they became popular too quickly for me, I dropped them." This discovery must have occurred before 1903, when Busoni conducted the first performance of the *Faun* in Berlin. Very likely his interest lasted little more than a year, for Debussy's piano music never appeared in his programs, and he revealed an oversimplified notion of Debussy's style when he tried, in an article for the magazine *Pan,* 1912, to contrast it with his own:

In this piece [*Lullaby-Elegy*] I first succeeded in striking a tone of my own and dissolving the form in feeling. All the stranger it was to read that my work was like Debussy's. This error I want to correct decisively. Debussy's art draws his personal feeling, strictly limited, out from his personality into the world: I strive to draw from the infinite that surrounds men, and to give back something shaped. Debussy's art means a limitation that strikes many letters out of the alphabet . . .; my aim is the enrichment, expansion, and extension of all means and methods of expression.

Debussy's music translates utterly different feelings and situations with formulae that sound alike; I try to find for each subject correspondingly different tones. Debussy's structures are parallel and homophonic; mine are intended to be polyphonic and "multiversal."

With Debussy we see the V_9 chord as harmonic foundation and the whole tone as principle of the melody, without any blending of the two; I try to avoid every system and to weld harmony and melody into indissoluble unity. He differentiates consonance and dissonance; I teach the denial of this difference. I try, intend, strive—not that I think I have already done it completely and comprehensively; for I feel myself a beginner, and Debussy is a finisher.

Each new influence appeared to Busoni by this time as a liberation from some confining rule or other, and his adventures were directed not to harmonizing influences but to winning ever greater freedom. The essential freedom of music is the guiding notion of his *New Aesthetic*. He pleads successively for freedom from rhythmic and formal conventions, freedom from programmatic interpretations, freedom for performers and transcribers from superstitious respect for notation, freedom for creators from the limitations of performing techniques, of instruments, and of our system of scales. Specifically he recommends scales that arrange half steps and whole steps in arbitrary ways; he says he knows 113 such scales, and offers eight samples. Further he proposes the division of our steps into third tones, and sixth tones. He recommends the dynamophone, the machine invented by Thaddeus Cahill in crude anticipation of the electronic music studio. "All efforts must aim at a new beginning." All should serve Nietzsche's dream of ". . . a super-European music, which can stand up under the brown sunsets of the wilderness, whose soul is akin to the palm, which is at home among great, beautiful, solitary beasts of prey and knows how to roam." Busoni confesses a doubt that this music can ever be attained. But he points a path ". . . up to the gate, to the bars that divide man from eternity—or that open to admit what is past. Beyond the gate true music sounds. No mere art of sounds. Perhaps to perceive it we must first depart the earth. Yet only for the roamer who has learned on his way to discard earthly fetters do the bars open." An epigraph for this *Sketch of a New Aesthetic* is thoroughly characteristic—"What do you seek? what do you expect? I know not; I want the unknown. What I know is unlimited. I want still more." This overweening ideal persisted through Busoni's later years, though questioned and qualified as we shall see. In 1920 he wrote in a letter to Selden-Goth:

Immateriality is the real essence of music. We are on the track of it. We wander through narrow underground corridors, at the end of which a strange, distant, phosphorescent light suggests a passage into a marvelous grotto. Once we have pressed our way into the vault of Nature's secret palace, then we can learn to let our soul soar out in speech and it will sound forth with melody ever more lofty and florid.

For an American reader, these ideas recall those of Ives. But Busoni modified his ideas in a way contrary to Ives. In his last year he dictated an essay on "The Essence of Music," in which he concluded:

Gradually I had to recognize, in following up my speculations, that our notion of the essence of music was still fragmentary and unclear . . . No genius can diminish the distance that separates us from the essence of music . . . Let us be profoundly grateful to the few elect, to whom it is granted at least, through their taste and form, insight and mastery, to make a miniature model of that sphere whence flow to them all beauty and power.

The *New Aesthetic,* viewed in the light of this last testament, had pleaded for an attempt to do something impossible. *Doktor Faust,* still unfinished, had been the mightiest attempt. But at last Busoni has recognized that more precious than any such attempt are the limited, finished "miniature models" of Bach and Mozart, perhaps something of Debussy, perhaps such modest pieces as Busoni's third and fourth sonatinas (1916, 1917).

Meanwhile Busoni's endless adventure predisposed him to sympathize with various contemporary, post-Debussy adventures. In 1909 he transcribed Schoenberg's Op. 11, No. 2. In 1911 he reviewed a Schoenberg matinée:

Is there to be a rebirth of sentimentalism? After hearing (playing and studying in ensemble) Arnold Schoenberg's piano pieces and songs, one might almost suppose so. Suppressed tears, sighs, gusts fluttering the branches of grief, rustling autumn leaves. Here and there a short cry of defiance or the fleeting appearance of morning sunshine. Interspersed a few Eulenspiegel tricks. . . . Naïveté in almost barbarous measure. And yet so much spontaneity, lucidity, and honor. . . .

But in a general article on new harmony, also 1911, he condemned Schoenberg's effort as "anarchy, an arbitrary juxtaposition and superposition of intervals according to whim and taste." Yet he gave no account of the difference between his "freedom" and Schoenberg's "anarchy."

In 1912, like Debussy, Busoni greeted the manifesto of the Futurists with a tolerant, skeptical smile. He noted that his *Sketch* had anticipated some of the Futurists' ideas. In 1917 the eminent conservative composer Hans Pfitzner published an article on "Futuristengefahr" (The Threat of the Futurists) in which he cited Busoni's *Sketch* as a leading Futurist document. Busoni promptly replied, denying any connection with the Futurists, defending his book, and protesting his reverence for form.

On a tour in America, 1910, Busoni met Arnold Dolmetsch and became a devotee of the harpsichord. He met a former pupil, Natalie Curtis, and took up her suggestion that he use American Indian melodies; they appeared in his *Indian Fantasy* for piano and orchestra (1912) and his *Indian Diary* (1914–16). Most important, he met Bernhard Ziehn, who showed him the "solution" to the unfinished final fugue of Bach's *Art of Fugue,* which Busoni proceeded to elaborate in his *Fantasia contrappuntistica,* for piano and orchestra (1910).

Finally in 1920 Busoni launched his slogan, "new classicism," which he defined broadly: "By 'new classicism' I understand the mastery, selection, and exploitation of all the achievements of past experiments, their incorporation in firm and lovely forms." He went on to prophesy three characteristics of the new classicism: unity of style throughout all genres, highly developed polyphony, and a spirit of serene objectivity. The slogan soon became popular, but Busoni's ideal was as remote as ever. He explained, in a letter to his son, 1922, "The crowd conceives classicism as something that harks back. . . . My idea (or, rather, feeling; personal need rather than constructed principle) is that the new classicism would mean a completion, in a double sense: completion as perfection and completion as ending, as conclusion of past attempts." He never claimed to have reached such a completion himself. It was his "personal need" to the end. He, like his Faust, passed on the need to his successors.

When Busoni heard Stravinsky's *Soldier's Tale* (1923) he was more enthusiastic in his praise than he was with any other contemporary music: "One had become a child again; one forgot music and literature; one was simply moved. *There's* something which achieved its aim! But let us take care not to imitate it! . . . *Toujours recommencer.*" Busoni's pupil Wladimir Vogel has suggested that Stravinsky's note of thanks after the performance of Busoni's *Five Pieces for the Cultivation of Polyphonic Playing on the Piano* just before the *Soldier* was an acknowledgment of indebtedness to Busoni for the neo-classic ideal. But Stravinsky's reconciliation of adventure and achievement was already under way when Busoni formulated his prophecy, and his growing concern with Bach was more with the concertos, sonatas, and suites than with Busoni's favorite toccatas and chorale preludes.

No other Italian composer contemporary with Debussy was so adventurous as Busoni or so frequently successful in achieving his aim as Puccini. Most of the others strove for success in opera, and several achieved it in isolated works—then failed to repeat it, even though their other works may have deserved it as much as those that kept their names alive. All these works stand in the shadows, not merely of Puccini, but of Wagner, Verdi, and Bizet. A list of them is desirable here as a reminder of their considerable place in 20th-century musical life, but their place in the history of styles is negligible.

1890 *Cavalleria rusticana*	Pietro Mascagni (1863–1945)
1892 *I Pagliacci*	Ruggiero Leoncavallo (1858–1919)
1896 *Andrea Chénier*	Umberto Giordano (1867–1948)
1902 *Adriana Lecouvreur*	Francesco Cilèa (1866–1950)
1904 *La Risurrezione*	Franco Alfano (1876–1954)
1909 *Il Segreto di Susanna*	Ermanno Wolf-Ferrari (1876–1948)
1913 *L'Amore dei tre re*	Italo Montemezzi (1875–1952)

In their later works these composers, except for the rather primitive Mascagni, tried to take advantage as Puccini had done of some of Debussy's discoveries, but none of them had any wish to abandon the habits they had grown up with in the 19th century, and they were unable to grasp the radical novelties of Debussy's harmony or the subtleties of his melody, rhythm, and form.

Three interesting Italians achieved some success in other genres. Enrico Bossi (1861–1925) was a fellow pupil with Puccini under Ponchielli. He became a virtuoso organist and eminent teacher. Bossi's outstanding large work is the oratorio *Canticum canticorum,* Op. 120 (1900). His later works indicate, however, a development that would repay close study, and they include many short pieces for piano, organ, and harmonium that offer immediate rewards to performer and listener. Among these are the *Satires* (1904), which exploit and deflate the "revolutionary" Debussyan devices of whole-tone scale, parallel ninths, parallel fifths, and simultaneous use of two keys. The St. Francis Triptych for organ (1923) and the ten pieces for harmonium (1920) incorporate the same devices into a smooth lyrical counterpoint that suggests Bossi's most distinguished pupil, Malipiero.

Don Lorenzo Perosi (1872–1956) was a central figure in the great 20th-century reform of Catholic church music. As musical director of the Sistine Chapel, 1898–1915, he gave advice to Pope Pius X, which led to the famous *Motu proprio* of 1903, whereby Gregorian chant, as interpreted by the monks of Solesmes, and the *a cappella* polyphony of Palestrina and Lassus were established as official models. In Perosi's own music these influences, together with Carissimi, Handel, Bach, and Liszt, serve chiefly to restrain an improvisatory fluency that is still based on such disapproved models as Rossini, Weber, and Schubert. The rhythms of march and waltz are very pallid here, but strong enough to determine the melodious phrases and their triadic harmony. Occasionally after 1904, when he began to hear of Debussy, Perosi used the whole-tone scale; he associated it with the idea of death, and harmonized it with triads in strong progressions, modulating rather incoherently. Matteo Glinski, who has made the most comprehensive study of Perosi's voluminous works, identifies as chief of them the series of seven oratorios on the life of Christ (1897–1900). His settings of the Mass and other liturgical compositions were widely performed all around the world, within the institution for which they were intended.

Better known to concertgoers than Bossi or Perosi was Ottorino Respighi (1879–1936), because of his opulent symphonic poems *The Fountains of Rome* (1914) and *The Pines of Rome* (1924), which Toscanini brought to life with wonderful precision and power. These pieces rely on the kind of melody that was as spontaneous for Respighi as for Puccini, together with the elaborate orchestration that he learned from a series of sources: his own experience as concert violinist and quartet player, his early lessons with the greatest Italian disciple of Wagner, Giuseppe Martucci (1856–1909), his later lessons with Rimsky-Korsakov and Max Bruch, and not least his study of the scores of Strauss, Debussy, and Puccini. He composed many other orchestral works, as well as operas, cantatas, songs, and chamber music. In the 1920s he tried to respond to changing tastes by using Gregorian modes and occasionally Gregorian themes, but the result, for instance in his Dorian quartet (1924), is almost like Perosi's style, an awkward constraint imposed on basically unchanged impulses to gushing melody and rich sonority.

Two Italian musicians of Debussy's generation played greater parts in the world's music-making than any contemporary composer, even Debussy himself. The immense fame of these two is relevant to any estimate of the historical significance of Puccini and Busoni, and still more of the younger composers like Casella and Malipiero. Enrico Caruso (1873–1921) was the most famous tenor in the whole history of opera. Arturo Toscanini (1867–1957) became the foremost conductor of the 20th century. He carried further the Wagnerian principle of subordinating singers and players to the conductor's will, and the second principle, which justified the first, of subordinating himself, the conductor, to the composer's will as manifested in the details of the score. His passionate insistence on "objectivity" was in harmony with many 20th-century trends. It was his great achievement to convey this ideal to a public almost as numerous and enthusiastic as Caruso's. The limitations of his repertory were narrow and even with these limits he often fell short of his ideal. Nevertheless, his work was such a prominent part of 20th-century musical life that no composer of serious music could escape its influence.

One Greek composer of Debussy's generation, though a pupil of Delibes in Paris, was content to devote himself mainly to Italian opera, with which he won some ephemeral international success. This was Spiro Samara (1861–1917). By contrast, Georgios Lambelet (1875–1945), who had studied in Naples, returned to Athens in 1901 proclaiming the need of a national style. He proceeded to lay foundations for one by collection and study of Greek folksongs, which up till then had been investigated only by Bourgault-Ducoudray. Lambelet's own compositions, mostly choral, had little success in competition with imported music, or even with Samara's provincial products.

"The father of modern Portuguese music" was José Vianna da Motta (1868–1948). He rebelled against Italian domination by submitting to that of Germany, where he had studied under Liszt in the 1880s. As a composer, though prolific, he was less successful than as a great pianist and teacher.

In Spain the most popular composer of Debussy's generation was Amadeo Vives (1871–1932), as little known abroad as the Greeks and Portuguese. After studies with the pioneer nationalist Pedrell, Vives produced his first works in his teacher's Wagnerian style, but then abandoned this ideal and made a successful career with over a hundred *zarzuela*-operettas, of which the most popular was *Maruxa* (1914).

Two Spanish composer-pianists, growing up under the domination of Italian opera, scorning the *zarzuela,* swayed by Liszt and Wagner, stimulated by Pedrell, and encouraged by Debussy, succeeded to some extent in establishing a new direction for Spanish music. They made it known abroad more favorably than it had been since Victoria worked in Rome. But their achievement was soon overshadowed by that of their young friend, Falla. These two intermediate figures were Isaac Albéniz (1860–1909) and Enrique Granados (1867–1916). Expert opinions differ on the value of their achievement, though agreeing that the best works of each are the suites of piano pieces, *Iberia* (1906–1909) and *Goyescas* (1909–1914), respectively.

Doubtless Manuel de Falla (1876–1946) was greater than Albéniz or Granados, but not so much greater, in a world perspective, as he appeared within the framework of Spanish music, or even in the view of Debussy. His achievement is slighter and only a little more adventurous than that of Rachmaninov or Puccini, slighter and only a little more solid than that of Respighi. The promised culmination of his career, a vast patriotic and religious oratorio, *Atlántida,* conceived in 1926, was found, when he died twenty years later, to have been barely begun; its completion was the work of his pupil, Ernesto Halffter. The critic Massimo Mila was not alone in regretting that Falla's last years were not devoted to more modest projects. Yet his finished work includes some unforgettable pieces, and some that continue to interest the most demanding musicians.

Falla's stylistic development was much like that of his older compatriots. The arias of Rossini, Bellini, and Donizetti were the probable sources of his spontaneous habits. His mother taught him to love and revere some of the piano music of Beethoven and Chopin. When he was seven he heard Haydn's setting of the *Seven Last Words of Christ* at the cathedral of Cadiz, for which it was composed; he remembered this as the greatest inspiration of his childhood. When he began to attend opera, he preferred Gounod and Saint-Saëns to the Italians, but his music testifies that he listened well to Verdi and his successors. He became a brilliant pianist, winning prizes at the Madrid conservatory. He despised the *zarzuelas,* including those he wrote himself in an effort to make enough money to go to Paris for further study. He was ignorant of folk music until he encountered Pedrell, who converted him and taught him, 1901–1904. Falla's first published piano pieces were dedicated to Albéniz; they are indistinguishable from his, to the ears of an American of a later generation. Falla's first opera, *La Vida breve (Life Cut Short,* 1905), went a step further, combining the *flamenco* dance rhythms and the ornamental modal melodies of the *cante jondo* with some simplified progressions of *Tristan* chords to fit an extremely simple, sentimental drama. Falla took his score of this opera to Paris, where it was eventually performed with some success. He stayed in Paris seven years, supporting himself as a pianist, learning informally from Debussy, Dukas, and Ravel, and dreaming of his next compositions.

Just before his return to Spain he made his settings of seven folksongs, with a fine economy worthy of Ravel, quite new for Falla. Then he produced his first ballet, *El Amor brujo* (*The Gypsy Lover's Ghost,* 1915), a loose collection of short episodes, including one that expanded a strong phrase of modal melody into a primitivistic showpiece, *The Ritual Fire-Dance.* His first and last concert piece for orchestra, *Nights in the Gardens of Spain* (1913–16), was more impressionistic—its orchestration closer to Debussy's *Nocturnes* than to his *Jeux.* (Falla first planned his *Nights* as "nocturnes" for piano.) Next came the first and last big piece for piano, *Fantasía bética* (1916–19), strangely deficient in melodic interest. And next the ballet, *Tricorne* (*Three-Cornered Hat,* 1913–19), produced by Diaghilev with expanded orchestration and sets by Picasso. Here melody abounds: the welcome humor of this work gave Falla reason to quote actual folk tunes, to borrow back from Domenico Scarlatti some 18th-century Spanish phrases, and to retrieve some of his own best youthful inspirations from the *zarzuela, La Casa de Tócame Roque.* The form as a whole is still utterly casual.

El Retablo de Maese Pedro (*Master Peter's Puppet Show,* 1919–23), Falla's last work for the theater, is perhaps his masterpiece. The unique, complex form of the action, with Don Quixote interrupting to comment on the puppets' episodes, justifies a profusion of contrasting musical ideas. Some of these ideas are derived from medieval and Renaissance music, which Falla studied assiduously just for this purpose, according to the careful critical study by Julio Jaenisch. Both the complexity and the archaism of the work make it disappointing to anyone still under the spell of *Amor brujo;* to other listeners the same features are fascinating.

The Harpsichord Concerto (1923–26), Falla's last completed extensive work, combines the refinement of *Master Peter* and the tunefulness of *Tricorne,* with a 16th-century folksong in the first movement, a noble canonic processional in the second, and ample reminders of Scarlatti in the *scherzando* finale. Although this work disappointed Landowska, to whom it was dedicated, it is a favorite of many younger musicians, including Gilbert Chase, who calls it "the most original, the most beautiful, and the most Spanish of all Falla's musical utterances."

The shorter pieces of the 1920s also have gratifying melody, novel sonority, and vital rhythms, though of course their forms are less remarkable than that of the concerto-sextet. Falla's distinctive and appealing personality is evident in each of them.

Falla's friend and disciple, Jaime Pahissa, helped him escape to Argentina in 1939, when he became disillusioned with the Franco regime in Spain. Pahissa describes Falla as a brilliant and indefatigable talker, a devout Catholic, and a great composer. In this estimate Pahissa is not alone. Santiago Kastner compares Falla favorably with Janáček, Sibelius, and Vaughan Williams. André Coeuroy's *Dictionnaire critique* maintains that "with Ravel, Bartók, Stravinsky, and Schoenberg, he dominated European music after the death of Debussy." But this must be dismissed as wishful thinking. By a strange coincidence, Soviet critics like Ivan Martynov also consider Falla a great composer, but their praise does not extend to his later "constructivist" works. Adolfo Salazar, who knows Falla's music thoroughly, refers to him often in the company of the great, but only in order to illustrate some generalization by a familiar, easy reference; if readers misinterpret his evaluation, neither Falla nor Salazar can be blamed.

As musician and man, if not on account of his several compositions, Pablo Casals (b. 1876) gave more to 20th-century music than Albéniz or Granados, probably more than Falla, perhaps more than Busoni or Puccini. He adapted violin techniques to the cello, as no one had done before; he made the unaccompanied suites of Bach accessible to millions; he personified the political conscience of music by refusing to give concerts in Fascist Spain or in any nation that assisted the Fascists; and he transmitted his wisdom, ripe but far from mellow, to a host of the best younger musicians in all parts of the world, as teacher, pianist, conductor, and ensemble player. That music-making of such intensity and delicacy as his could be infused with his democratic idealism was a precious encouragement to many more musicians in their strivings.

———— ◆ ————

CHAPTER VIII

Contemporaries in Austria-Hungary

THE PROFITS of Puccini were far surpassed by those of the operetta *Die lustige Witwe* (*The Merry Widow,* 1905) by Franz Lehár (1870–1948). This work smashed all records for public success: no other single product of a human mind had been transferred intact so swiftly to so many people as the *Merry Widow Waltz*. Fifty years later, to be sure, moving pictures, radio, and television enabled messages to reach more millions more swiftly than the *Widow,* but these media could not make a message memorable. The show ran in Vienna for over five hundred performances. Productions in every city of Europe and North and South America likewise broke theatrical records. By 1910 there had been about 18,000 performances in 431 theaters. Revivals were under way at once, and continued without a break for at least half a century. Moreover, the *Widow* was naturally a model for many later efforts in the field of popular music and perhaps exerted an influence on some "serious" works too: the noble heroine of *Rosenkavalier* (1911) is not dissimilar.

Lehár's supreme achievement embodied as much adventure as he ever attempted. His many later works ventured no farther, and achieved not quite such smashing success, although several of them came close to the mark set by the *Widow.* The waltzes from *Der Graf von Luxemburg* and *Zigeunerliebe* (both 1910) joined the *Widow's* in the center of the repertory of waltzes. Lehár's own favorites were *Endlich allein* (*Alone at Last,* 1914), *Das Land des Lächelns* (*The Land of Smiles,* 1929), and *Giuditta* (1934).

As the son of a military bandmaster, Lehár acquired his strong unconscious habits and the beginnings of his conscious craft from his father. Then, after thorough training at the Prague Conservatory, where Dvořák encouraged him, he followed in his father's footsteps to serve in the Imperial Army. Twice he quit his post to compose operas. When their reception was disappointing, he went back to his steady work, and in spare time worked on sonatas and symphonic poems. Meanwhile the marches and waltzes that he composed for his band with spontaneous ease were more and more successful. So he turned to the models of Franz Suppé, Jacques Offenbach, and Johann Strauss, and began to put waltzes and marches together into operettas. In comparison with the older models, Lehár's melodies were simpler and more symmetrical, while his orchestration was richer. In comparison with most contemporary followers of the same models, Lehár distinguished himself by spicing his harmony, rhythm, and orchestration with faint reminiscences of Slavic or Hungarian or popular Gypsy music, almost as Dvořák distinguished himself from rivals to the mantle of Brahms. These qualities made his first four operettas successful enough to free him from the military life. When the same qualities were joined with the *Widow's* especially neat, glamorous, timely libretto, by Viktor Leon and Leo Stein, the great hit was made. Vienna could enjoy its position as the world's musical capital for one more generation.

The sociological phenomenon of Lehár and his rivals for commercial success looms larger in the history of 20th-century music than the delights of the music itself. Lehár's success affects the meaning of Debussy's esotericism, and of all the later unpopular music of the century, including the varieties of jazz that transcended the commercial environment in which they arose.

———•••———

At the opposite pole from Lehár, Gustav Mahler (1860–1911) called himself an "eternal beginner." In a letter (1909) to his disciple, the conductor Bruno Walter, he described his adventure vividly:

I am and always remain the eternal beginner. And the little routine that I have acquired serves at most to increase my demands on myself. Thus, just as I should like to reëdit my scores every five years, so too, for conducting, I need to restudy a work every time. My only consolation is that actually in my course up till now I have never had to strike out in a new direction, but rather to keep going farther in the old. But in this going farther you get so far from all the well-worn paths that finally you have to blaze a trail, like the settlers in a new continent, by ax and spade. This is the reason for the passionate opposition that I meet in everything I undertake.

In the very last year of his life (1911) he wrote to another conductor, composer, and friend, Georg Göhler:

The Fifth had to be practically all rescored. It is inconceivable to me how I could make such beginners' mistakes again at that point. (Obviously the routine acquired in my first four symphonies had left me in the lurch here—since a quite new style demanded a quite new technique.)

The Tenth Symphony, left incomplete at Mahler's death, showed him again pressing beyond his immense technique toward some unprecedented ideal.

While Mahler was surely among the adventurers of his generation, he surpassed most of them in the quality and quantity of his achievements. He worked with frenzied speed in his summer vacations in the country between hectic seasons as conductor of opera and symphony. Especially after 1900 his works followed one another without a gap: Symphony V (1901–1902); *Kindertotenlieder (Songs of the Death of Children)* and *Five Rückert Songs* (1901–1904); Symphony VI (1903–1904); Symphony VII (1904–1905); Symphony VIII, with chorus, in two movements—*Veni creator spiritus* and the finale of *Faust* (1906–1907); *Das Lied von der Erde (Song of the Earth)*, a symphony in six movements, with tenor and alto solo (1908–1909); Symphony IX (or in Mahler's superstitious numbering, X, since *Das Lied von der Erde* was a symphony avoiding the fatal number IX; 1909–1910). Though always beginning afresh, Mahler also liked to finish a piece. He suffered "frightful birthpangs" to produce each one, and when it was finished he rejoiced. He played his latest work over and over on the piano for his wife, but never played unfinished work. When he conducted a piece of his own, he felt that all problems were solved, or dissolved. Unlike Busoni, or Ives, whose ideal of an infinite, cosmic music Mahler's ideal resembled, he had patience and persistence enough to bring his work to concrete reality. Unlike Ives or Delius or Scriabin, he cared about the finest nuances of loudness and tempo, and worked tirelessly to fix these details in his scores. A complete picture of his achievement still waited in 1965 for the publication of his final versions of the first seven symphonies, which Erwin Ratz had begun.

Great as Mahler's achievement may be, still it is less in total playing time and more specialized in forms and media than that of Debussy or of the man he recognized as his only worthy rival, Richard Strauss. In all his extant works there is no opera or chamber music; he wrestled with these forms to some extent in his 'teens and then destroyed his experiments when he found his way to song and symphony. There are no original keyboard pieces, though he won prizes at the Vienna Conservatory for piano playing, as well as for composition, and his first publication (1878) was his arrangement for piano of Bruckner's Third Symphony. His concentration on orchestral song and symphony throughout his mature years was necessary for him to achieve as much as he did against the pressure of time. This is part of the meaning of his phrase, "going farther in the same direction."

Alongside Strauss and other contemporaries, Mahler expanded the orchestra, going ahead to a historic climax in the direction already marked by Beethoven, Berlioz, and Wagner. The increasing number of winds is striking:

	Beethoven IX	*Tristan*	*Ring*	Mahler I	II	VIII
piccolo	1	(1)	(2 alter- nating with flutes)		(2)	2
flute	2	3	4	4	4	4
oboe	2	2	4	4	4	4
English horn		1	(1)	(1)	(1)	1
Eb clarinet	·			1	2	2
Bb or A cl.	2	2	3	3	3	3
bass cl.		1	(1)	(1)	(1)	1
bassoon	2	3	3	3	3	4
contrabassoon	1	1	1	1	1	1
horn	4	4	8	7+3 or more doubling	10	8
trumpet	2	3	3	4	6	4+4 offstage
bass trumpet		1	1	1	1	1
tenor trombone	2	3	3	3	4	4+3
bass trombone		1	1	1	1	1
tenor & baritone tuba		4	4	4	4	4
bass tuba	1	1	1	1	1	1

The purpose of this famous expansion was not a sheer increase of volume, but a greater variety of sound with more nearly continuous gradations. Like Berlioz, Mahler only occasionally required all his vast orchestra to play together, and his music was as often soft as loud. Its colors were continually shifting, blending or contrasting with each other, blending chords in perfect euphony or contrasting melodic lines in clear counterpoint, and fluctuating between blend and contrast to correspond with the fluctuation between chords and counterpoint.

When Mahler's orchestration is studied in its actual context of chords and counterpoint, and in the songs as well as the symphonies, his continuation of the expanding development of the 19th century seems less important than our mere list of instruments suggests. Indeed, an opposite tendency is noticeable. Egon Wellesz, in his survey of modern orchestration, calls it "an evolutionary tendency to replace the massive effect of the big orchestra with the thinner, more penetrating sound of solo instrumentation, in order thereby to make the web of themes and motives more clearly recognizable." Wellesz testifies, for instance, that Mahler's 1910 revision of his Fourth Symphony removed many doublings and achieved a marvelous new variety of thin sounds. He notes also that Mahler's use of trumpets is "in some respects an *economical* procedure," obtaining from one soloist effects like those that earlier composers would have obtained from a combination of several woodwinds with octave doublings. Another scholar, Mosco Carner, shows in fascinating detail how Mahler rescored Schumann's symphonies, lightening and clarifying their texture in many ways, to accord with his own ideal of economy. In this tendency toward economy and clarity, Mahler resembles Rimsky and Debussy more than Berlioz, Wagner, Bruckner, or Strauss, and like Debussy he partly anticipates the taste for chamber ensembles that was to become conspicuous with Schoenberg, Stravinsky, and Webern.

In another way Mahler's orchestration, even more than Debussy's, anticipated the taste of younger composers. The kind of sounds Mahler increased was more significant than the increase itself. Whereas the additions to the wind choirs made by Wagner and his contemporaries were mostly in the range of men's voices or lower, Mahler's additions were mostly in the range of women's voices or higher. His use of high-pitched sounds was frequent and characteristic, whereas he gave many rests to the horns and trombones, which had traditionally served as the orchestra's equivalent of the piano's sustaining pedal. Mahler's F trumpets and E-flat clarinets often scream with a wild passion that Wagner would have rejected as ugly. On one occasion, which Mahler described in a letter to his wife (1908), a trumpet player protested:

"I'd just like to know what's beautiful about blowing away at a trumpet stopped up to high C." This gave me an insight at once into the lot of man, who likewise cannot understand why he must endure being stopped to the piercing agony of his own existence, cannot see what it's for, and how his screech is to be attuned to the great harmony of the universal symphony of all creation. . . . I have, you see, been rehearsing the wind on its own—as in this vale of tears, where the consolation of the violins and double basses, which form the groundwork and anchor of all the other instruments, are as yet denied us.

Yet on the whole, Mahler's shrieking winds are more than balanced by the consoling strings and celestial harps. The general impression left by his works is of a rich fullness, not radically different from Wagner's.

In the percussion section of the orchestra Mahler exploited all the discoveries of Berlioz, Rimsky, and Debussy, and added a few. His Second Symphony makes wonderful use of big cast bells and of a pair of gongs with contrasting indefinite pitches. The Sixth uses cowbells and hammers on steel. The Seventh, Eighth, and the *Song of the Earth* use guitar or mandolin or both. The Eighth—nicknamed "symphony of a thousand"—also uses piano and xylophone, celesta and glockenspiel, organ and harmonium, delicately differentiated and astonishingly combined. Along with all these special effects, Mahler wrote for kettledrums and cymbals with consummate

skill and discretion. His treatment of percussion became a model for composers as diverse as Copland, Milhaud, Britten, and Shostakovich, as well as
for his great successors in Vienna, Schoenberg, Berg, and Webern.

---·•·---

The rhythmic patterns that Mahler emphasizes with his drums and bells
are not so novel as the sound-effects. Almost all his works are based on
march and waltz—sometimes the same tempo as Lehár's, but more often a
funeral march and a burlesqued *Ländler*. He often writes out the effect of
a retard or *tempo rubato,* as Brahms occasionally does. In addition, he over-
lays the basic patterns with melodic rhythms of some complexity, ranging
from very rapid scales and arpeggios to very long-drawn-out passing-tones
and appoggiaturas. In slow tempos, a triplet may take the place of two beats,
or two or four notes the place of three, and groups of five or seven are not
uncommon. Mahler's rhythms seldom suggest an easy swing. Rather they
are like his limping walk, as described by Walter: ". . . his foot-stamping,
hesitating, storming on again—all confirmed and strengthened the impression of someone possessed by a demon." The motions that his wife mentions
as typical of him are "wagging" and "fidgeting." But mixed with these
personal and conventional rhythms are others, like motions of wind and
water.

Mahler's harmony is more various, more distinctive, and more important
historically than his rhythm. It is nearly always based on the normal major
and minor scales, alternated or mixed with each other in such a way as to
maintain their traditional polar opposition and its traditional association—
major for hope and cheer, minor for pain and despair. Aside from this
Schubertian mixture of the modes, most passages in Mahler's music are
strikingly free of chromaticism. Many phrases rest on tonic pedal-points or
drones or ostinato figures, and many others proceed over slow progressions
of the basic diatonic triads. There is a tendency to avoid the most familiar
formula for cadences (V I) and to substitute modal progressions (V IV I,
and ii I). The most characteristic interval is the fourth; in the Seventh Symphony the fourths of a fanfare coalesce into a new chord, exaggerating
the similar effect in *Tristan*. The most typical dissonances are caused by
scalewise counterpoint over static harmony. To be sure, chromaticism appears
in other passages, with yearning effects like those of *Tristan,* or of the songs
of Mahler's friend and classmate, Hugo Wolf. But such passages in Mahler
never extend to the length of a movement, and there is nothing in Mahler
like Wagner's structural use of the *Tristan* chord, or the attenuated tonality
of Debussy. Mahler's Wagnerianism, as his most thorough biographer,
Donald Mitchell, has shown, is based more on *The Flying Dutchman,*
Tannhäuser, and *Lohengrin* than on Wagner's later works.

Tonality in Mahler's music is peculiar. Keys are related for him as they are in Schumann's cycles of songs or short piano pieces, to which Mahler's earliest works show many similarities. Modulations occur suddenly, at the joints of phrases, rather than within phrases. (In this respect, quite by coincidence, he resembles his contemporaries MacDowell and Delius.) Neither modulation nor return to the principal key makes any great contribution to Mahler's forms. His peculiar treatment of modulation is a moot point among experts: Dika Newlin and other writers following her call it "progressive tonality" in contrast to traditional "concentric tonality." Hans Tischler finds this term misleading, and prefers to emphasize what he calls Mahler's "dramatic key symbolism." The underlying issue in this debate is to define the connection between Mahler's practice and the later "atonal" practice of his devoted admirer, Schoenberg. Mahler himself never abandoned tonality; it is as strong a force in his last works as in his earliest. But it does not work in any of them as it does in Beethoven. Mahler's example was indeed one of the chief of many stimuli that led Schoenberg to his crisis in 1908. Mahler could not comprehend Schoenberg's Chamber Symphony (1906) or later works, though he strongly defended them against rioting audiences, and gave invaluable support to Schoenberg as a friend.

Mahler's tonality resembles Carl Nielsen's to some extent. But Nielsen is more literally dramatic, whereas Mahler is essentially lyric and free.

The harmony of *The Song of the Earth* is the most peculiar of all, and most convincing. For this setting of Hans Bethge's translation of Chinese lyrics, Mahler made ample use of pentatonic scales, and occasional use of a whole-tone scale, blending these smoothly into his diatonic and chromatic habits—so smoothly that their presence may easily be ignored; even though the main thematic material is pentatonic, there is nowhere any such obvious departure from Western norms as there is in Debussy or Puccini. The concluding "Farewell" of this masterpiece seems to dissolve melody and harmony, and rhythm too, into a tensionless interplay of the tones of the pentatonic scale, freely decorating the tonic C-major triad. This has suggested to some listeners a lingering farewell to Romanticism, or to Europe. Of course it also suggests, in keeping with the text, a farewell to life on earth.

Counterpoint is important throughout Mahler's works, and increasingly so in his 20th-century works. According to Walter, he studied Bach's *Art of Fugue* anew in 1900. Although his counterpoint is only rarely fugal, and almost never responsible for producing the progressions of chords, as Bach's does, yet the independence of melodic lines and the dissonant complications of their combinations are indeed more like the procedures in a Bach aria with instrumental obbligato than like those of most of Mahler's contemporaries. His increasing use of counterpoint is connected with his tendency to thinner, clearer orchestration. In 1909 he arranged and performed a suite of pieces by Bach. He conducted from the harpsichord and varied the harpsichord part at each performance. He wrote about this to his friend Paul Hammerschlag: "Quite surprising things resulted for me (and for the listeners). This dusty literature was illumined as if by a lightning stroke. It had a stronger effect (even coloristically) than any modern work." If he could have lived to learn from and take part in the further illumination of Bach's bright colors during the 1920s, his contribution would have been very great. To know that he took as much interest as he did in Bach helps some listeners to approach his last symphonies. And recognizing the importance of counterpoint throughout his work is prerequisite to any sound judgment of his historical position.

In most of his melodies, as in his rhythms and harmonies, Mahler relies on traditional associations. Many themes call to mind folksongs or popular songs of the cities (especially Gypsy songs) or hymns or bugle-calls or bird-calls. Then very frequently a theme is burlesqued with sudden modulations, exaggerated leaps, glides, and rhythmic fidgets, producing a bitter poignancy that is Mahler's most conspicuous distinguishing trait—one that strongly attracts or strongly repels, or both attracts and repels at once. Here again Mahler resembles Berlioz. The E-flat clarinet's distortion of the *idée fixe* in the last movement of Berlioz's *Fantastic Symphony* offers the classic model for Mahler's procedure. Mahler uses it habitually, perhaps compulsively, whereas the classicizing Berlioz reserved it for such special occasions. The parody procedure is the perfect embodiment of Mahler's Nietzschean egotism and Schopenhauerish self-pity. It bars him, as he himself knew, from the heights of Beethoven and Wagner.

———•·•———

In 1910 Mahler consulted his great compatriot and contemporary, the founder of psychoanalysis, Freud. Freud's notes on the interview include Mahler's account of his compulsion. His father was a barkeeper, ambitious to rise in the world. His mother was the crippled daughter of a genteel family, a martyr to her husband's brutality. On one occasion the bitter fighting of his parents drove the boy out of the house, where he encountered an organ-grinder playing *Ach! du lieber Augustin*. This juxtaposition of pathos and bathos, Mahler told Freud, came back to him at every moment of emotional tension, to twist his inspiration and prevent him from reaching his ideal as a composer.

At the same time, Mahler's self-conscious procedure sets him far above more ingenuous musical disciples of Nietzsche such as Delius and Scriabin. For many listeners Mahler's clashes of tragedy and vulgarity compel a sympathy stronger than any revulsion.

For Mahler the opposition of moods and of themes is the chief criterion of symphonic music. He advised the critic and would-be composer

Marschalk, in 1896: ". . . *Themes*—clear and *plastic,* so that they are distinctly recognizable in every transformation and further unfolding; then a working out, full of variety, and, above all, gripping because of the *development* of the inner idea and also because of the *genuine opposition* of the motifs placed in contrast to each other." Mahler successfully followed his own recipe. The opposition of his clear themes insures that listeners, once attracted, will be held to the end, even of a symphony more than an hour long. But this recipe shows in another dimension the distance between Mahler and Beethoven, whose means of holding attention are both more subtle and more powerful: organizations of harmony and rhythm that reveal the "inner idea," overruling all motivic contrasts and all fluctuations of loudness and orchestration. Mahler's symphonies lack Beethoven's kind of coherence, or Bruckner's or Elgar's or Sibelius's. For a sympathetic listener, such as T. W. Adorno, the forms of Mahler's symphonies are fascinating, and revealing. Yet even Adorno does not deny that Mahler's most satisfying works are the songs (including *The Song of the Earth*), where words provide an intelligible connection and limit for the opposing and developing melodies. Even though the voice sings only a strand in the orchestral web, the lines and stanzas of the verse form a basis for the music as a whole.

With his cycles of short songs, Mahler had achieved his own style and his utmost perfection of form before 1900, though in that year he was still refining details of orchestration in these works, exploiting the unrivalled knowledge that he accumulated as conductor in Vienna. In 1900 he took the Vienna Philharmonic to Paris, where he probably encountered Debussy's music for the first time. In 1901 he retired from conducting regular concerts, but continued in the opera; his productions of Mozart and Wagner were epoch-making. He restored the harpsichord for Mozart. He compelled the singers to consider the orchestra and the drama as a whole. He encouraged a transition from realistic stage sets to monumental symbolic sets. He tried to exclude all commercial motives from consideration. In pursuing these policies he naturally won ardent admirers and equally ardent enemies. The latter finally forced him to abandon Vienna, in 1907. The time he reigned there, however, was the most brilliant period of the Vienna opera, as well as of Mahler's life.

In 1907, already warned by doctors to moderate his feverish pace, he settled in New York, to conduct the Metropolitan Opera and then the Philharmonic Orchestra. He planned to retire from regular conducting when he reached the age of fifty, so as to devote himself wholly to composition. But his heart could not last. He died just short of fifty-one.

In 1902 Mahler married Alma Schindler, a fabulously beautiful and brilliant girl, who after his death pursued a spectacular passion with the painter Oscar Kokoschka, was married next to the architect Walter Gropius, and finally to the novelist Franz Werfel. Her memoirs and her edition of

Mahler's letters are foremost among the primary sources of information about him. Bruno Walter's "portrait" is the most persuasive presentation of the worshipful attitude found in many writings on Mahler. Walter lived to become first president of the International Gustav Mahler Society, founded in 1955, and to make marvelously faithful recordings of his superb, authentic performances of Mahler. Particularly when Walter found in Kathleen Ferrier the ideal singer for the *Kindertotenlieder* and *Das Lied von der Erde,* he made sure that Mahler's adventure and achievement would continue for a long time to exercise a powerful influence.

Mahler's achievement has been dismissed by many critics as something peculiarly Viennese, and hence, allegedly, unfit for international use. This judgment is unfair to Mahler, to Vienna, and to sensitive listeners around the world. Lehár, and earlier Johann Strauss, Schubert, Beethoven, and Mozart have amply proved that typical Viennese music appeals to millions of people everywhere. On the other hand, Mahler was recognized no more in Vienna than in Moscow or Amsterdam, and he hoped to find in America a "spiritual home" such as all Europe could not provide him. To be appreciated intensely and as a whole, his music requires, more than that of his compatriots just mentioned, some knowledge of and sympathy with his human character. Such knowledge and sympathy cannot be expected of many listeners, in Vienna or elsewhere, but it may be found in unexpected places—even in France, where the studies of Henri-Louis de La Grange promise great advances in the orderly and balanced appreciation of his achievement.

To an unknown correspondent who asked him for an explanation of his First Symphony (1894), Mahler gave some admirable advice:

Honored sir: Accept my heartiest thanks for your kind request. But it scarcely accords with my intentions, to confuse the public at a musical performance with technical musical commentaries; for as I see it this is all that happens when listeners are provided with a "program" and thus forced to look instead of listening!

To be sure, I consider it necessary that the motivic texture be clear for every listener. But do you really think that with a modern work the indication of a few themes is sufficient for this purpose? Acquaintance and experience of a musical work must be achieved by *thorough* study of it, and the more profound a work is, the harder the study, and the longer it takes. On the contrary, at a first performance the main thing is to submit to the work for better or worse, allowing the general, human, poetic aspect of it to have its effect. Then if it is appealing, study it thoroughly. How are you supposed to proceed when you make the acquaintance of a *man*, who is still deeper and better than his work? Where is the program? Here too the procedure is to cultivate his company eagerly, to look into him with alertness and sympathy! However, he is growing and changing, while the work remains the same. But comparisons always leave off somewhere!

From the crowd of young Viennese composers in the first decade of the century only a prophet could have picked Lehár and Mahler as outstanding. Among composers of operetta, Oscar Straus (1870–1954) and Leo Fall (1873–1925), closely imitating the *Widow,* achieved their respective hits, *The Waltz Dream* and *The Dollar Princess* (both 1907). Straus made his first, more modest successes in 1901–02, with skits and songs for the experimental Berlin cabaret founded by Ernst von Wolzogen, the *Überbrettl,* where Schoenberg was a lesser collaborator. The favorite Straus work in England and America was *The Chocolate Soldier* (1908), based on Shaw's play, *Arms and the Man.*

Among composers of "serious" music, Franz Schreker (1878–1934) and Franz Schmidt (1874–1939) produced music more congenial than Mahler's to some tastes—Schreker's to the more adventurous and Schmidt's to the more genteel. Schreker's opera *Der ferne Klang* (*The Distant Ringing,* 1912) was reduced to vocal score by the young Alban Berg; it provided a model for Berg's *Wozzeck* in its use of symphonic form for an act and of other instrumental forms for various scenes. Schreker's ballet based on Wilde's story of *The Birthday of the Infanta* (1908) was influential in its treatment of a chamber orchestra. Later, in Berlin, Schreker taught many younger composers, including Ernst Krenek. Hans Redlich, summarizing the extensive literature on Schreker, defines his transitional significance. The admirers of Schmidt, including two scholarly biographers, Andreas Liess and Hans Nemeth, recommend him as a worthy successor to Bruckner, unjustly treated by Mahler and others during his long service in the cello section of the opera orchestra. But the examples of Schmidt's music accessible outside Vienna, including the monumental apocalyptic oratorio *Das Buch mit sieben Siegeln* (*The Book of Seven Seals,* 1938), fail to justify the recommendation; it is easy to imagine that Mahler had good reasons for losing patience.

In Vienna as elsewhere musicians other than composers played increasingly important and varied roles in musical life. Three Viennese indirectly contributed more to composers of the later 20th century than either Lehár or Mahler, if not quite so much as Toscanini or Debussy.

Guido Adler (1855–1941) was the dean of musicology in his generation, editor of the *Denkmäler der Tonkunst in Österreich,* 1894–1938, and the *Handbuch der Musikgeschichte,* 1924, two enormous and fundamental compilations. In his teaching and his own writing he formulated the principles and techniques of "style criticism" in music. His summary article by that title remains the best exposition of the subject. In two books, *Der Stil in der Musik* (1912) and *Die Methode der Musikgeschichte* (1919), Adler tried to extend his principles to a systematic evolutionary philosophy, which mistakenly exalted the abstraction of style above all concrete values. For better and for worse, Adler's thought exercised a very wide influence. His pupils Anton Webern and Egon Wellesz introduced him to Schoenberg, who was glad to contribute to the *Denkmäler* some thoroughbass accompaniments to symphonies by the 18th-century composer Monn. Adler shared the admiration of these younger men for Mahler, and wrote a brief, notable tribute to him. Thus he initiated the alliance between university scholarship and the most esoteric contemporary composition, which was to become an important feature of musical life by the middle of the century, in sharp contrast with the notorious antagonism between Adler's predecessor at the University of Vienna, Hanslick, and his contemporaries Wagner, Liszt, and Strauss.

The theorist Heinrich Schenker (1868–1935) lived obscurely as a private teacher in contrast to Adler's academic glory. Moreover, Schenker published his theoretical writings in such an obscure, private, belligerent style that the dissemination of his insights was much delayed. But these insights, into the structure of musical masterpieces from Bach to Brahms, ultimately contributed to the development of musical thought as much as the classic treatises of Zarlino, Fux, and Rameau. By showing the detailed hierarchical relations of melody, harmony, and form, Schenker counteracted the tendency of the classic theorists to take melody for granted and to consider chords in mechanical abstraction. Thus his theory corresponded with Debussy's practice of subordinating chords to melodies, though this correspondence might have surprised Schenker. He insisted dogmatically that the practice of the masters from Bach to Brahms was the only good way to compose, and that clear tonality was the essential, natural, eternal basis of coherent musical thought. While condemning the pale imitators of the masters just as Debussy did, Schenker also condemned the great innovators of his time, as rebels against no mere tradition but the eternal law. Moreover he had little sympathy with music older than Bach's. To generalize his insights so as to apply them to Debussy and Stravinsky was a difficult and fascinating task, begun by some of Schenker's pupils, particularly Felix Salzer (who was a pupil of Adler, too), and carried on with great skill by Allen Forte and other younger men.

Fritz Kreisler (1875–1962) was the champion virtuoso of the violin, who transformed the ideals and habits of string players all over the world by his constant intense vibrato and who further transformed their repertory with his delicious encore-pieces—passed off for some thirty years as arrangements of neglected 18th-century masters but finally revealed as his own compositions. Kreisler's vibrato, and other idiomatic tricks that went with it, carried to an extreme a tendency noticeable in the preceding generation of virtuosos,

Sarasate, Auer, and Ysaÿe. His 18th-century hoaxes, on the other hand, partook of the newer, opposing, anti-romantic tendency, and advanced it as much as the work of Busoni or Reger or Satie. Kreisler's life as a world traveler was varied by periods of distinguished military service and of indolent amusement. In his easy use and enjoyment of a wide range of music he set forth an ideal of the art in society healthier than most composers'.

Dumetru Georgescu Kiriac (1866–1928) returned to Bucharest in 1900 from studies with d'Indy in Paris. He became the first Rumanian folklore scholar and a leader of the renewal of Orthodox church music. According to George Breazu, Kiriac determined the national style of Rumanian music, of which the greatest representative was the young George Enescu.

Hungary in 1900, despite the fame of its Gypsies and of Liszt's rhapsodies, and despite the efforts of some lesser 19th-century composers, was thoroughly provincial. The outstanding Hungarian composer of Debussy's generation, Ernő Dohnányi (1877–1960), completed his studies in Germany and began his career there as pianist and teacher, returning to Budapest only after World War I. His many compositions, in all forms, showed his mastery of Brahmsian academic skills. His *Variations on a Nursery Song* (1916) had more popular success than loftier works, of which the best was the Second Symphony (1957); his chamber music won and held admirers. After World War II, Dohnányi lived and taught in the United States, making for all who met him an astonishingly vital link with the 19th century, while Bartók and Kodály had brought Hungary to the forefront of 20th-century music.

---◆---

CHAPTER IX

Contemporaries in Germany

BOTH AS ADVENTURE and as achievement, the work of Richard
Strauss (1864–1949) was stupendous. In *Ein Heldenleben* (*A Hero's
Life,* 1899) he flaunted a self-esteem unmatched by anyone before or
after. And on the other hand, his achievement of excellence, sustained
almost steadily from the songs and chamber music of the early 1880s to
the songs and chamber music of the late 1940s, surpassed even Verdi's
record (from *Nabucco,* 1842, to *Falstaff,* 1893). Regarded as a whole,
Strauss's work was so bold, so good, so vast, and so complex that a short
account cannot do it justice. Still, measured as he sometimes measured himself and his contemporaries, by the standards of Mozart and Wagner,
Strauss is an epigone, a gleaner after the main harvest. And measured by
the standards of Debussy, which he tried in vain to understand, Strauss
falls short in both refinement and radical novelty. Therefore the study of
Strauss is only an optional part of a musician's curriculum, whereas the
study of Debussy is essential. But among the many optional studies, that of
Strauss is one of the most immense and most rewarding. The option to
study him appeals not only to the timid and nostalgic, but also to such
young devotees of Schoenberg as Robert Craft and Glenn Gould.

Strauss's effrontery in making himself the hero of his symphonic poem,
gaily quoting his own earlier works, and triumphantly battling his hostile
critics, was a scandalous offense to tastes that had accepted the heroism of
Beethoven and Wagner. It was enough to shock even Nietzscheans like
Delius and Scriabin, and the symphonic autobiographer Mahler. But
Strauss's estimate of himself was coolly realistic: he was indeed, at thirty-five,
tall, broadshouldered, slim, blond, a heroic world-figure such as Beethoven
and Wagner had become only toward the end of their lives, and such as
no contemporary composer could claim to be. His seven symphonic poems,
from *Aus Italien* (1887) to *Don Quixote* (1898), were established in the
repertories of orchestras around the world; they were recognized as a
culmination of the progressive development whose chief earlier representa-

tives had been Berlioz and Liszt, and which meanwhile had absorbed hundreds of more ephemeral efforts. Strauss had recently left his native Munich to become director of the opera at Berlin. As an extracurricular job there he founded the *Tonkünstlerorchester,* to present programs of the most advanced and ambitious new works. He was in demand everywhere as guest conductor. In 1904 he toured America, and incidentally roused bitter indignation in some quarters by accepting a huge fee for two concerts in Wanamaker's department store. He lent prestige, by writing a short preface, to a new collection of books on music, beginning in 1903, and to a periodical, *Morgen* (*Tomorrow*), beginning in 1907. He served as president of various composers' organizations, and helped reform copyright laws. In short he was, as Debussy recognized, a "dominating genius of the times." He was the only contemporary German whose work held Debussy's interest.

Ein Heldenleben was followed quickly by two more autobiographical compositions: the satirical one-act opera *Feuersnot* (*Fire Famine,* 1901) and the *Sinfonia domestica* (1903). Here Strauss redeemed his egotism, for some listeners if not for the public in general, by his unrivalled sense of humor. His true character, after all, was more like that of the prankish *Till Eulenspiegel* (1895) than that of the Nietzschean *Zarathustra* (1896) or even that of his first operatic protagonist, *Guntram* (1894), who had symbolized his youthful idealism and its disillusionment. In the *Domestic Symphony* Strauss turned his back on his critics and on every sort of social struggle, to celebrate the complicated, shifting, not quite exemplary but richly satisfying interrelations of his family: the six contrasting musical motifs portray three aspects of his own character, two aspects of his wife's, and finally the child around whom all contrasts are to be subordinated and harmonized. Contemporary audiences would have liked the piece better if Strauss had offered a stereotyped romantic portrait of his wife, Pauline de Ahna, who was in fact a jealous and demanding Wagnerian soprano, trained by Strauss for seven years before their marriage in 1894. (He portrayed her jealousy and ambition even more explicitly in the opera *Intermezzo,* 1924, but in 1944 he still called her his favorite singer of his own songs and a model *Hausfrau* and mother.) The *Domestic Symphony* failed to win the place it deserved in the opinions of Strauss himself and the present writer, as the last and best of the series of symphonic poems, partly because literal-minded, hero-worshipping audiences could not sympathize with its sophisticated humor, but more because too few conductors could master its complex counterpoint and virtuoso orchestration. Here and in the three famous operas to come, 1905–1911, Strauss reached his climax in orchestral magnitude and diversity, to be surpassed by Mahler only in his monstrous Eighth Symphony. Strauss augmented the winds as follows:

	Don Juan (1889)	Till (1895)	Domestica (1903)	Elektra (1909)
piccolo	1			
flute	3			
oboe	2	3		
Eng. hn.	1			
			oboe d'amore 1	heckelphone 1
		D cl. 2		Eb cl. 1
clarinet	2			Bb and A 4
		bass cl. 1		
			saxophone 4	basset horn 2
bn.	2	3		
contrabn.	1			
horn	4	8		
trumpet	3	6		
				bass tpt. 1
trombone	3			
				bass tbn. 1
tuba	1			

Incidentally, in 1905 Strauss codified his mastery of the large orchestra in a revision of the great treatise by Berlioz, which served from that time on as handbook for many arrangers and composers. On the other hand, in *Feuersnot* (1901) he had already begun to turn away from the full orchestral sound toward a more economical and soloistic kind of orchestration, which he improved in *Ariadne* (1912) and continued to vary the rest of his life, until he fully satisfied himself in his last opera, *Capriccio* (1942).

The *Domestic Symphony* represents a climax not only in orchestration but also in form: it is a continuous piece, based on the six themes that appear successively in a sonata-like exposition; their development incorporates a slow movement and a scherzo, and culminates, at the return of the tonic, in a triple fugue. This grand unity, first attempted in Schubert's *Wanderer Fantasy,* repeatedly approached by Liszt, almost achieved in Strauss's *Heldenleben,* he now tossed off as if it were no effort. None of the later comparable forms of Sibelius, Schoenberg, or Bartók accomplish this historic project with such nonchalance. Between the *Domestica* and *Capriccio* Strauss himself wrote no other work that was at once so long and so free of embarrassing slow sequences and awkward shifts from one section to another, although to be sure, every work of his contained long passages of marvelous continuity, and climaxes of overwhelming power.

For Strauss was not merely a follower of Berlioz and Liszt; their influence was indeed prerequisite for his symphonic poems, but it was an influence added in his twenties, at the persuasive insistence of his friend Alexander Ritter (1833–1896), to an uncommonly solid set of classical habits. Strauss's father was a brilliant horn player, violinist in a professional quartet, and

Charles Ives and his wife (The Bettmann Archive)

Edward MacDowell, the bust by C. Paul Jennewein in the Hall of Fame at New York University

PLATE 3

Sergei Rachmaninov, by Leonid Pasternak (The Bettmann Archive)

Edward Elgar with his father (Mrs. Elgar Blake)

Carl Nielsen

Giacomo Puccini, c. 1910 (Ricordi & Co., Milan)

PLATE 4

conductor of a good amateur orchestra, who commanded the respect of Wagner by his playing in the first performances of *Tristan, Meistersinger,* and *Parsifal,* even though he disapproved all Wagner's works after *Tann-häuser* and most other music since middle Beethoven. The father protected his precocious son from corrupting influences until he was sixteen, allowing him to develop his skills as pianist, violinist, and composer within the style of Mozart and early Beethoven, with only the choicest examples of Schubert, Weber, Mendelssohn, Schumann, and Brahms to represent modern variety. Richard finally won a trip to Bayreuth in 1882, as reward for graduating from the Gymnasium with distinction in all subjects except mathematics. To be sure, this paternal discipline roused the boy's enthusiasm for Wagner higher than any recommendation could have done; it also enabled him to study Wagner with a thoroughness matched by hardly anyone but Debussy, and to learn from Wagner what he needed without copying mere mannerisms or attitudes. Likewise, when he joined the 20th-century return to Mozart, Strauss did not merely embrace a new fashion, but rather confirmed his own deepest, most nearly spontaneous musical impulses. Meanwhile, his academic training was unconventionally rounded off by a year's apprenticeship with the great Wagnerian conductor Bülow, who dubbed him Richard II, and who taught him also to love, respect, and even envy his other namesake, Johann Strauss. Richard Strauss wrote in 1925: "I honor in Johann Strauss especially the spontaneity, the basic gift. In an age when everything around him had already turned more and more to the complicated and calculated, there appeared this natural talent with the ability to create from plenitude. He represents to me one of the last who had primary inspirations. Yes, the primary, the spontaneous, the primeval-melodic, that's it!" Finally, there were a few words of advice from Brahms, taken deeply to heart. Strauss reported them in his *Reflections and Recollections*: "Young man, take a good look at the Schubert dances, and try inventing simple, eight-measure melodies. . . . Your symphony contains too much thematic elaboration. There is no merit in this superimposing on one triad many themes differentiated only by rhythm." Hereafter Strauss made sure that his counterpoint was accompanied by moving chords. Yet he never noticed, apparently, that in the counterpoint of Bach, Wagner, and Brahms the bass melody both supported the moving harmony and participated in the motivic development. In Strauss's characteristic practice, harmony and counterpoint are not merely two aspects of the same musical thought, but two distinct elements, rather arbitrarily combined. It was typical of Strauss to accept Brahms's advice thus literally, and to hold fast to it even after he became convinced that he could make something more exciting, more Wagnerian, than either Johann Strauss or Brahms, something more vital for the culture of his own age and of the future than acceptable songs, dances, symphonies, and chamber music. It was typical of him too to acknowledge his great debt to Ritter in this respect. "I owe it to him that I discovered my dramatic vocation. Without his urging and collaboration I should scarcely have thought of writing an opera, in my abject awe of the gigantic work of Richard Wagner." Strauss began to become an opera composer when he began writing symphonic poems. These were, in a sense, for all their heroic size and success, mere substitutes or preparatory exercises for his operas. *Till Eulenspiegel* in particular became an orchestral piece only after a prolonged vain effort to make a one-act opera on the theme.

In 1903 Strauss gave a rare verbal expression of his idea of vocation and his claim to freedom:

Art is a product of culture. Its "mission" is not to lead an isolated existence for its own sake, in accordance with "laws" arbitrarily promulgated or designed for some momentary need and then later proclaimed as "eternal." Its natural mission is rather to bear witness to the culture of times and peoples . . . As with the development of the other arts, the history of music too shows a progress from the reproduction of indefinite or general, typical notions to the expression of a more and more definite, individual, and intimate circle of ideas. Since the inner process of this development is partly hidden under the shell of formalistic elements, some estheticians, who could grasp only the outer, formalistic parts while perceiving the essentials very dimly, if at all—myopic because of their lack of creativity—have been able for some time to spread confusion. Their doctrine was the dogma of infallible form; the living content of art was for them a book of seven seals. So in their myopia they claimed again and again that they could halt the natural development with their proud dictatorial command: "So far and no farther!" or could designate this or that epoch as the final highest flowering of all possible development. But the judgment of history passes by such a stand-pat esthetic, and proceeds to the order of the day.

Strauss's rejection of all restraining theory was like Debussy's. His appeal to history, however, was different. Again like Debussy, Strauss declined to be the leader of a "progressive party." No such party existed, he said after mature reflection. It was a mere slogan. Imitation of a progressive leader would be as futile as imitation of the past masters. Creation depended on free individuals. But again unlike Debussy, Strauss appealed from allegedly expert opinion to a broad public: "The main thing is the compelling contact between a creative genius and the mass who are ready for progress, far exceeding the limits of any possible party." The mass seemed for a few years to be compelled by Strauss's genius, and thus his sense of "mission" and of freedom were confirmed.

But in the course of his long life Strauss became disillusioned with the 20th-century public, which failed to show either the readiness for progress or the critical discrimination that the public of the late 19th-century had seemed to show. By 1933 Strauss decided that the progress of musical culture would have to wait for a reform of general education. Pupils in secondary schools should learn enough harmony and counterpoint to appreciate Bach and enough orchestration to understand Beethoven and Wagner. Until then the public would be misled and bewildered by programs, parties, slogans, and superficialities. Gradually Strauss came around to something like Debussy's policy of pleasing himself and an élite of unknown friends. He confided to Romain Rolland in 1925: "I am always expected to produce new ideas, great things. But I have the right, haven't I, to write the music that I like? I cannot endure the tragedy of this age. I want to make joy. I need it." In 1939 he instructed his last librettist, Clemens Krauss, to "put a bit to one side, please, the average theatergoer (though of course I do not despise him) . . . *Capriccio* is no piece for the public, at least not for a public of 1800 people per evening. Perhaps a morsel for cultural gourmets." At the same time Strauss recognized *Capriccio* as the "best possible completion of my theatrical life-work." The theme of *Capriccio* is the rivalry of a poet and a composer competing for a woman who loves each of them and their separate arts, but who loves most of all the product of their collaboration.

Strauss had another motive besides his urge for "compelling contact with the mass" that led him to concentrate on dramatic music. This he expressed in a letter to Rolland in 1905. Rolland had recommended that for the first performance in France of the *Domestic Symphony,* the literary program should be reduced to a minimum. Strauss concurred:

For me a poetic program is exclusively a pretext for the purely musical expression and development of my emotions, and not for a simple musical description of precise facts of life. For this would be quite contrary to the spirit of music. In order for music not to be lost in pure caprice and to drown in the infinite, it needs to be held within limits determining a form, and such limits are fixed by a program. Even for listeners, an analytical program should be no more than a sort of support. Let whoever is interested in it use it. Whoever really knows how to listen to music doubtless has no need for it.

The hazardous infinite that Strauss had to guard himself from, in terms of tonal and harmonic possibilities, was like a comfortable pool compared to the ocean envisaged by Debussy and Schoenberg. But the danger was the same—the danger of paralysis. The possibilities at Strauss's command were still surveyable and classifiable, but of course they were literally infinite, and having rejected all limiting theories he clung to the limits of a text to provide the basis for his choices. After *Capriccio* (1942) Strauss composed no more large works. For a series of beautiful, small, esoteric ones he found the necessary limits in the medium—unusual small ensembles of instruments, such as the twenty-three strings in *Metamorphoses* (1944) or the *Duet*

Concertino for clarinet and bassoon (1948). And finally, as his very last works, there came four songs (1949), the most intimate music he ever wrote.

———•———

Our sketch of Strauss's development has deliberately diverted attention from what seemed to many of his contemporaries the most startling and significant development of all, his turn from "expressionism" to "neo-classicism," from *Elektra* (1907–09) to *Rosenkavalier* (1909–11). This development loomed large to them partly because they could not see it in our long perspective, and partly because of their own acute interest in dissonance and modulation, which they supposed that Strauss shared more than he ever could. For him these devices were first and last mere technical means among others for the expression of "more and more definite, individual, and intimate ideas." He had no interest in the techniques for their own sake, and no need to expand technical resources. His dissonances, therefore, resolve to consonance in accordance with his habits, even when they are piled on thick and emphasized by rough rhythms and harsh orchestration. His modulations may be abrupt or dizzyingly swift for a few seconds, but his habit of tonality is never broken. Whenever Strauss shapes a piece so well that any cut or transposition of parts would damage the music, he does so by means of a chain of modulations returning to the tonic.

Harsh dissonances and dizzy modulations became prominent in Strauss's music as early as *Till Eulenspiegel* (1895). Here the *Tristan* chord is jammed into close position, blared by muted brasses, shrieked in an abnormally high register and growled in the depths, and trilled with a deliberately banal resolution—the chief one of many resolutions that Strauss found to supplement Wagner's various enharmonic transformations of the chord. All this contributes to *Till*'s antiromantic fun, just as does the mock-classic "rondo form" to which the subtitle calls attention. (Actually, as shown by Alfred Lorenz, the discoverer of Wagner's formal "secrets," the refrains and episodes characteristic of a rondo are to be found in the development section, but not in the big exposition and recapitulation that frame it.) Yet *Till*'s harmony on the whole, in contrast to *Tristan*'s, rests clearly on a major scale and pure primary triads. Some of the episodes are as conventional as Lehár. Both the obvious insolences and the basic complacency of *Till* are evident in the harmony of Strauss's other works up through the *Domestic Symphony*.

The one-act operas *Salome* (1905) and *Elektra* omit the complacency. They have no tuneful passages, and few simple triads. Their defiance of the public, no longer an autobiographical conceit, is now cynical, rather than courageous. Their protagonists are half-insane women, contriving murders and gloating over them. The poets, Oscar Wilde and Hugo von

Hofmannsthal respectively, brought these figures into close focus out of their ancient contexts, in order to scrutinize the ambiguity of the heritage of civilization. Strauss made them into monsters to transfix the public that had recently been thrilled by *Tosca* and *The Merry Widow*. With these new heroines he succeeded in reaching beyond the audience of his symphonic poems. (*Salome* was so successful that the publisher and first producer worked on *Elektra* page by page as Strauss composed it.) The monstrous fascination of his subjects induced this public to submit to Strauss's most difficult music, and to many moments of deliberate ugliness. For a listener to the music who overlooks the drama there are, to be sure, many beautiful passages, and the immense structures come close enough to their model, *Tristan,* to command admiration. But there are musically inexplicable flaws, jolts in the continuity, and on the other hand there is a lack of repose and of contrast that only the drama justifies. The thick counterpoint of motifs in rapid, jerky motion is almost unrelieved.

To perform this music accurately, Strauss saw by 1925, conductors must "treat it like Mendelssohn's elfin scherzos." When performers succumb to the temptation of rushing and shrieking, the dramatic effect is not really enhanced, but it is still powerful enough to make some listeners accept mere dramatic noise as all that Strauss intended. Singers and players may stray from each other as far as a fifth in pitch, or two measures in time, without becoming unduly conspicuous. Probably never before was music publicly performed and applauded in such a shambles: its example in this respect was followed all too often in performances of new music thereafter. As to whether an accurate Mendelssohnian performance was worth the strenuous efforts and restraints that it required, opinions still differed after half a century. But by then musicians could comprehend the scores sufficiently to recognize the traditional harmony amid the dissonance.

Besides using all the devices of Wagnerian harmony, with more speed and shrillness and concentration than ever before, Strauss used for the first time in *Salome* a few new ones. The opening motif of the opera and the main idea of the "Dance of Seven Veils" suggest an Oriental scale with raised fourth degree. The whole-tone scale, loud against a dissonant pedal-point, announces the entrance of King Herod. John the Baptist's ascent from his dungeon is accompanied by a theme suggesting a chord of fourths, though this suggestion is never explicitly developed. An unresolved poly-chord, D minor against B major, represents Herodias's exasperated demand that Herod order John to be quiet. This last bit of perversity Strauss referred to in 1942 as "bitonality," and apologized for it as "a unique experiment with a special material, but not recommended for imitation." His warning came too late. Strauss's "bitonality" was imitated as glibly as Debussy's whole-tone scale, and almost as widely. Strauss himself never again used this device, though there are many resolved polychords in his later works, as there are, to be sure, in earlier works of his and of many other composers, including Bach. Strauss left the exploration and extension of the device to such men as Ives, Busoni, Ravel, Bartók, Schoenberg, Stravinsky, and Milhaud; all of these but Ives were directly spurred by *Salome*.

The combination of new techniques—whole-tone scale, fourth chords, and unresolved dissonance—all suggest that Strauss had learned something from Debussy, though his use of the techniques is as different from Debussy's as the character of Salome is from that of Mélisande. More important than any technical borrowing is the basic idea of setting to music a work of avant-garde literature that was not written or even adapted for the purpose; in this respect too Strauss had learned from Debussy. But between the basic idea and the superficial techniques, in the realm of rhythm and melody and tonality and form Strauss had no patience to learn.

The poet of *Elektra,* Hugo von Hofmannsthal, had achieved fame in his twenties, before the turn of the century, as an "impressionist" comparable to Stefan George and Rainer Maria Rilke. Hofmannsthal had then abandoned lyrical poetry, maintaining his eminence with criticism. Now he seized on the connection with Strauss, and devoted most of his remaining years to their collaboration. Their correspondence, discussing works in progress in endless detail, makes as good reading as the works themselves. *Rosenkavalier* was Hofmannsthal's first proposal of a subject for Strauss to set to music. It became their most famous work, and in the opinion of many critics their best, though some preferred *Arabella* (1927–33) and the authors themselves were proudest of their most grandiose effort, *Die Frau ohne Schatten (The Woman without a Shadow,* 1911–17). *Rosenkavalier,* in the present writer's opinion, was also Strauss's most cynical, most rambling, and most repetitious work in proportion to its length.

The dissonance in *Rosenkavalier* is mostly soft and slow, with the familiar connotation of romantic yearning or else a playful coloristic thrill. There is no occasion for the violence of *Salome* and *Elektra*; on the contrary, there is ample opportunity for *gemütlich* diatonic consonances like those of *Till* and *Feuersnot.* Nevertheless, the prevailing texture of *Rosenkavalier* is just as elaborate in its counterpoint and modulations as that of *Elektra*—even more so in some passages, where Hofmannsthal has supplied farcical complications that exceed those of Mozart's librettist Da Ponte. The most distinctive and marvelous feature of *Rosenkavalier* is the final trio of soaring sopranos. The most memorable feature is its indulgence in many waltzes, friendly parodies of Johann Strauss. Although waltzes are anachronistic in the 18th-century setting of the opera (Hofmannsthal was inspired, like Stravinsky forty years later, by Hogarth's prints of a "Rake's Progress"), still they fit the atmosphere of gracious, luxurious Vienna more naturally than the similar waltzes fit into *Zarathustra, Salome,* and *Elektra.* Next to the waltzes, what maintains the opera as a favorite in the repertory is the central role, the Marschallin, for this beautiful, rich, young matron, easily bored and easily amused, is a sentimental cousin of *Salome* and *The Merry Widow.* She can be portrayed with conviction by almost any soprano; interpreted by Lotte Lehmann and directed by Max Reinhardt she became an irresistible seductress. H. L. Mencken justly commented: "*Salome* and *Elektra* have been prohibited by the police, at one time or another, all over the world. I believe that *Der Rosenkavalier* is still worse, though the police leave it unmolested. Compare its first act to the most libidinous jazz ever heard on Broadway. It is like comparing vodka to ginger pop. No woman who hears it is ever the same again." And this is relevant to a just estimate of Strauss's supposed change of style. Taking account of all the elements, technical, poetic, and social, the change from *Elektra* to *Rosenkavalier* may best be described as diversion, a sort of tacking along the long course toward *Capriccio,* rather than a retreat from expressionism or a victory for neo-classicism.

Of Strauss's late operas only *Arabella* had any lasting success with the public; none exercised any influence on contemporary composers. Reference books commonly asserted that "his inspiration flagged," taking literally what he himself may have said with some irony. But this complaint had been frequent since *Don Juan* (1889); it meant merely that someone was not interested enough to study the newer works. For those friends and conscientious critics like Romain Rolland and Gustave Samazeuilh, who knew the three famous operas thoroughly, each later one was a delightful surprise, and each in its way at least as good as any of the three. For Samazeuilh the supreme masterpiece and moral landmark was *Friedenstag* (*Day of Peace,* 1938). Each opera aroused controversy when revived after Strauss's death. Moreover, each one attracted a few admirers who ignored or disliked the famous three. The same is true of the ballets and still more of the late songs and chamber music. None of these works are mere routine, but none have either the obvious boldness of *Salome* or the more profoundly personal boldness of *Ein Heldenleben* and the *Domestic Symphony.*

Strauss's principal adventure was utterly different from Debussy's. Strauss's was an adventure in poetry and history and culture, rather than in harmony and melody and the sensuous correspondences in nature. In the end it was clear that Strauss had compromised his adventure to satisfy himself with marvelous achievements within the bounds of convention. He had relinquished the adventure gradually, beginning with the very first work in which he undertook it, *Guntram.* He achieved his greatest effect on other composers in *Salome,* before his retreat was apparent, and his greatest effect on the public in *Rosenkavalier,* where his retreat was easily detected and deplored by followers of fashion. He achieved his finest works for himself and unknown friends after most critics and most of the lagging public had ceased to pay attention.

Strauss's grandeur is attested by Müller von Asow's voluminous thematic catalogue of his works, the literature about them, and the phonograph records of them. No other 20th-century composer can be studied quite so thoroughly and so readily, thanks to the vast literature that Müller von Asow has sifted.

The adventure and achievement of Max Reger (1873–1916) were utterly paradoxical. Yielding without resistance to his spontaneous fluency and to the habits inculcated by his teacher, Hugo Riemann, he drifted into a strange adventure: he developed a style more distinctive than that of Strauss or any other contemporary German, and he anticipated some leading principles of Schoenberg, Hindemith, and Prokofiev. What he achieved in his short life occupies thirty-five thick volumes in the Collected Edition, and embraces all forms except opera; yet this achievement was less important than the adventure, for despite the persistent efforts of his admirers, none of his music won general acceptance in standard repertories, or even held the respect of a majority of competent critics. One of Reger's most persuasive advocates, Egon Wellesz, granting that his forms are defective, argues that he cannot be judged by any particular work, but only collectively by his whole output.

The principles that gave Reger's output a definite place in 20th-century music may be indicated by the slogan "back to Bach." He proclaimed his allegiance in answer to a questionnaire by the journal, *Die Musik,* in 1905: "Sebastian Bach is for me the beginning and end of all music, the solid foundation of *any true progress!* . . . a sure cure, not only for all those composers and musicians who are sick of 'indigestible Wagner,' but for all those 'contemporaries' who suffer from any sort of spinal atrophy. To be *'Bachisch'* means to be thoroughly German, intransigent." Not all Reger's music is so intransigent or so similar to Bach's as this statement would suggest. But many of his compositions, to be sure, are canons and fugues, and many more are so pervaded by counterpoint that his work as a whole stands out in contrast to that of all his contemporaries. Not only in his emphasis on counterpoint, but also in his frequent use of steady rapid motion, like that of some Bach toccatas and concertos, and his use of other Baroque patterns such as chorale prelude, passacaglia, and jig, Reger's practice confirmed his precept. Also like Bach, and like very few others, Reger wrote several pieces for the unusual media of unaccompanied violin and unaccompanied cello. In general he wrote more organ music and chamber music than orchestral music. Moreover, in contrast to the self-conscious originality and profundity of "tone-poets" like either Strauss or Debussy, Reger's whole output shows a craftsman's confidence, an unquestioning acceptance of established religion, and a delight in *musikantisches Musizieren,* ensemble music-making regardless of any audience or any posterity. Whether this confidence and delight resemble Bach's complex faith any more than the skeptical attitudes of Debussy and Strauss is a question for philosophers to debate, but it never troubled Reger, for his knowledge of Bach was by no means comprehensive or profound. (In 1903, according to his friend and pupil Karl Straube, Reger was acquainted only with Bach's organ works and the *Well-Tempered Clavier,* not with his vocal music or chamber music.) But an anti-Romantic attitude was inseparable from Reger's counterpoint, and his successors inherited counterpoint and attitude together. A recent biographer, Eberhard Otto, has summed up his significance in a carefully equivocal statement: "To the same degree that Reger succeeded in digesting Bach's substance—the polyphonic character, the unique tension and compression of harmony, and not least the solid religious foundation—to that degree he became the great teacher for the future." Schoenberg and Hindemith estimated "that degree" very highly. Schenker and Tovey estimated it as close to zero. But Tovey found a peculiar charm in Reger's style, to which all Classic or neo-Classic or neo-Baroque principles were irrelevant, and which he could appreciate without waiting to study quite all of Reger's enormous output.

Reger relied on Bach as a foundation, but not as a guarantee. More important was the "true progress" built on this foundation. In 1907, when his old teacher, Riemann, published an attack on the "progressive" tendency of Strauss, Reger hastened to affirm his own progressiveness just as vigorously as he had plumped for Bach. In answer to Riemann's reference to Brahms, Reger wrote:

What guarantees immortality to Brahms is by no means his attachment to old masters, but rather the fact that he was able to produce new undreamed-of spiritual moods, on the basis of his own individual spirit. Here is the basis of all immortality, not the mere attachment to old masters, which, by itself, stern history converts to a death sentence within a few decades.

Reger was confident that he too was producing new moods. He was not so patient as Brahms to study Bach; he simply used Bach as antidote to Wagner.

His conspicuous counterpoint was, in fact, dominated by a kind of harmony quite unlike Bach's. Even in Reger's many fugues, the chief interest lies in the swift chord-progressions, rather than in the interplay of melodies. Each voice in the texture, to be sure, claims attention from time to time; no voice is mere accompaniment. But each voice's melody is composed of short fragments; every melodic phrase is twisted at one or more points to fit the restless movement of harmonic roots; and no pair of melodies shows the independence and the dynamic balance that typify Bach's counterpoint.

The fast pace and the wide tonal range of chord progressions mark Reger's harmony, whether or not the texture is contrapuntal. This novel, nervous harmonic fidgeting is what Schenker disapproved, and what Tovey and other listeners found charming. The vocabulary of chord-structures and non-harmonic tones is not novel, nor even consistent. For many pieces Bach's vocabulary suffices; for others the richer vocabulary of Wagner and Hugo Wolf is drawn into the hurrying movement; in at least one piece, the *Romantic Suite* (1912), whole-tone scales contribute material. But these differences are superficial, compared with the peculiar harmonic movement.

Reger's chords range far from the tonal center of the phrase, but they are linked in strong progressions. Each phrase contains so many chords that the tonal center is hard to remember, and the effect of several such phrases together is quite disorienting, like the effect of occasional cadenzas in the music of Chopin and Liszt. It is unlike the stretching and straining of tonality in Wagner's dissonant polyphony, and unlike the attenuated tonality of Debussy. Reger explained his procedure as an extension (or rather a compression in time) of classical modulation, as analyzed by Riemann. He published a little treatise, *Beiträge zur Modulationslehre* (1903), to show the full scope of his wide-ranging chords, compressed into phrases with no pretense at melodic interest. Still, many listeners, like Schenker, cannot believe that Reger intended the effect that he produced; they condemn his music as obtuse. Others, supposing that it was the natural, honest product of his individual sensibility, find it valuable enough to compensate for some formal incoherence and other faults of taste.

Reger's music for organ, with gradual swellings from *pp* to *fff,* as well as frequent contrasts within a phrase, suggests that he depended on the constant use of the crescendo pedal. The surprising fact is that he rarely played the organ after he was sixteen years old. He approved a performance by Straube of one of his pieces with the whole dynamic scheme radically simplified. Reger's own indications of tempo according to the metronome are as unreliable as the dynamic marks. Hans Klotz, who edited the organ works for the Complete Edition, says the marks are mostly too high, sometimes twice as high as intended; Fritz Stein, compiler of the Reger thematic index, says that the slow tempos are almost always marked too slow.

Reger's interest in the orchestra began only after he was thirty, and reached a climax about three years before he died. His interest in the organ, on the contrary, lapsed from 1905 to 1913, and his interest in songs was also in abeyance during those years. Memories of the organ affected Reger's orchestration. He hardly ever contrasted melody with accompaniment, or one melody with another in counterpoint, but rather sought a homogeneous sound, based on full string parts, varied from time to time by the conventional choirs of the winds, and decorated frequently with harps. Whereas Mahler, the master of the big orchestra, made it sound like chamber music, Reger, who wrote over seventy works for chamber ensembles, kept improving the blend, brilliance, and weightiness of his orchestra, and his last big work, the Mozart variations (1914), has the most ponderous and dramatic quality.

When Reger varies another composer's theme, or uses a chorale as cantus firmus, the articulations of his thought can be followed easily enough. Wilfrid Mellers suggests that "Reger is most impressive when he is least in awe of Bach: in large-scale works like the lovely Mozart or Hiller variations in which . . . he has a lilting cantabile lyricism to give buoyancy to the chromatic texture." And these are the pieces most often performed. But in some of his other late works, like the *Romantic Suite,* the Fourth and Fifth Quartets, the Clarinet Quintet, the piano quintets, and the songs of Opp. 137 and 142, Reger lets his fantasy wander in what he calls "musical prose," intimating what Wellesz identifies as "a new principle of variation." He avoids symmetry and recapitulation. He does not maintain the identity of themes or even motifs. Characteristic intervals, recurring in various motifs, supply a kind of unity. These are the works that represent Reger's new moods most distinctively, and therefore anyone who is charmed by the variations or chorale preludes should proceed to these.

Dozens of other German composers in Strauss's generation achieved renown only within Germany and within their own lifetime. Their works neither penetrated abroad nor held a firm place in German repertories. Critics who have studied these works characterize and classify them by reference to Brahms, Strauss, Wagner, and Debussy; they do not lament the world's indifference so convincingly as do writers on Mahler and Reger, or writers on such national heroes as Elgar, Nielsen, Diepenbrock, and many more. The most eminent of the neglected German composers is Hans Pfitzner (1869–1949). His most nearly famous work is the opera *Palestrina* (1917), glorifying a stereotyped legend of the inspired and unappreciated composer, in a fashion that must have made Strauss laugh aloud. The conductor Felix Weingartner (1863–1942), although his many operas and other works in a Wagnerian style are unlikely to be revived, played a greater part in the music of his day than Pfitzner, and holds a more important place in world music history, through his recordings and his books on conducting. Along with Toscanini, Weingartner represented the age of the virtuoso conductor at its best.

An exceptional figure is Sigfrid Karg-Elert (1877–1933), whose music for organ and for small wind ensembles was better known in English-speaking countries than in Leipzig, where he spent most of his life. His stylistic adventure is as exceptional for a German as his achievement: beginning as a pianist, with imitations of Schumann and Liszt, Karg-Elert published as his first major effort an orchestral suite after Bizet (1902). In 1904 he happened to meet Grieg and to win his support; then, somehow evading the direct influence of Brahms and Wagner, he acquired a taste for Reger, Debussy, Scriabin, and even Schoenberg; but during his service in an infantry band (1915–1918) he reinforced his respect for simple music and to some extent "unlearned the exaggerated, overheated principles" that had attracted him. It was about 1904 that he began to write for the harmonium; not until 1908 did he turn to the organ, and he never held a post as organist, though he played successful recitals in England and America.

Among the most amazing adventures and most solid achievements of 20th-century music was the reform of organ building, in which neither Reger nor Karg-Elert took part. The movement was initiated by Albert Schweitzer (1875–1965), a small but significant aspect of his heroic career, closely related to his thought and action in the realms of philosophy, theology, and medicine. All his other valuable musical work, seen in the perspective of his life as a whole, was subordinate or peripheral to this reform, which in turn was a typical part of his humanitarian ethical mission.

The leading 19th-century organ-builders were French, for instance Aristide Cavaillé-Coll (1811–1899), whose instruments were ideally suited for the music of Franck and his successors. But such organs were exceptional. Modern technology and salesmanship at the end of the century, especially in Germany, were filling churches with new mass-produced organs that exalted the values of loudness, variety, imitation of orchestral instruments, convenience for the performer, and economy for the buyer. Schweitzer, almost alone in his time and place, recognized that older organs embodied higher values such as our whole civilization was neglecting: clarity, honesty, sensuous beauty, proportion, craftsmanship, and reverence for the greatest relevant work of the past—in this case the organ music of Bach. In 1906, while teaching philosophy and studying medicine at Strasbourg, he launched the movement "back to the polyphonic organs desired by Bach; away with the orchestral organs!" His booklet on *French and German Organ Building and Organ Playing* converted Guido Adler, who invited him to the Third Congress of the International Music Society at Vienna (1909) and there he led in the formulation of the first *International Regulations for Organ Building*. For many years thereafter, as lecturer and recitalist, visiting Europe and America on leave from his hospital in Africa, Schweitzer continued to disseminate his profound insight, while the further definition and the practical fulfillment of the reform were gradually carried through by specialists, with the collaboration of many other scholars and organists. From about 1920 Wilibald Gurlitt's studies of Praetorius (1571–1621) inspired an important new phase of the movement, which spread to America in the 1930s, to England in the '50s.

As an Alsatian who had studied in Paris with Widor and become a friend of Romain Rolland, Schweitzer was able to appreciate both French and German traditions, to mediate between them, and to envision a European tradition that would be greater than either of them alone. As a musician who had grown up in the age of Wagner and made frequent pilgrimages to Bayreuth, he was able to see the inadequacy of the "orchestral" organs to make more than a caricature of the music that was arranged and composed for them, though he spoke respectfully of Reger's works. As an ordained Lutheran preacher and outstanding theologian, he could think of Bach and of organs in a way accessible to few musicians. As a professional student of Kant and all the idealistic philosophers who succeeded him, Schweitzer could regard the organ movement as an aspect of the general idea that he was to express in *Civilization and Ethics*: "The insight will soon dawn that we must begin again where the 18th century left off. What lies between that time and ours is an interlude with rich and interesting moments, but after all only a fateful interlude."

Schweitzer's work as organizer of the Paris Bach Society, along with Widor and others, and his famous book on *J. S. Bach: Musician-Poet* (1905) drew attention to Bach's liturgical vocal music, which was less known than the fugues for keyboard. Schweitzer interpreted Bach's organ music in the light of the vocal music, correcting the common mistaken notion of Bach as a cerebral, unemotional disciplinarian, and somewhat exaggerating the resemblance between Bach's use of motifs and Wagner's. Later studies of Bach largely superseded Schweitzer's, but the later development of the organ movement richly confirmed his insight.

CHAPTER X

---◆---

Contemporaries in France

GABRIEL FAURÉ (1845–1924) was fifty-five at the turn of the century. Despite his white hair and his dignity as professor at the Paris Conservatory, he could bound up a flight of stairs like a boy. He was as nervous as a boy about his newest work, his biggest up till then, the open-air drama *Prometheus* (1900), even though several distinctive works of his forties were now recognized by French connoisseurs as minor classics, especially the Requiem (1887–88), the cycle of Verlaine songs, *La bonne chanson* (1891–92), and the incidental music for Maeterlinck's *Pelléas et Mélisande* (1898). In the 20th century the fame of these 19th-century works spread to somewhat larger circles, while Fauré went on slowly but steadily composing works still more distinctive and more severely classic. Before he died, at seventy-nine, such admirers as Charles Koechlin could seriously claim that he was the greatest French composer since Rameau, and the greatest composer of any nation since Wagner. In the year of his death, he was recommended to Americans by the young Aaron Copland as "the Brahms of France." These claims were based not so much on the earlier works as on the career as a whole, and especially on the last four song cycles, the last six pieces of chamber music, and the last nocturnes and barcarolles for piano, all of which remained far from popular in France and scarcely known at all elsewhere. The pianist who specialized in playing Fauré's early works, Marguerite Long, never learned to appreciate the late ones, perhaps because of her melodramatic personal rupture with Fauré the administrator.

Most of the characteristics of Fauré's late style can be seen in the *Chanson*, Op. 94 (1907), Ex. X.1. Negative traits are obvious at a glance. The melody never repeats itself, yet never makes any strong contrast. The accompaniment likewise has no two measures alike, yet it never abandons its simple, dry pattern. The tempo is neither fast nor slow, and yet not a mere moderato, but a combination of light bounding movement and serene flow. Evidently this is a style of extreme subtlety.

The harmony is full of dissonance, but not yearning or grinding or luxuriating or amusing; it seems to be casual, or perhaps embarrassed and evasive. Inverted seventh chords are held too short a time to make any strong effect (measures 6, 10, 16–17). Fauré often replaces a leading tone by the tonic to which it would have led, making at once an unresolved suspension and an anticipation, or a brief inner pedalpoint (mm. 12, 18, 26, 27, 28). This harmony demands the keenest attention. Some listeners find their effort rewarded by a delicious pleasure and a sense of depth, while some others find the effect distastefully shy and nervous. Debussy, in one of his cattiest reviews, described a young lady playing Fauré: "The 'Ballade' is almost as lovely as Mme. Hasselmans, the pianist. With a charming gesture she readjusted a shoulder strap which slipped down at every lively passage. Somehow an association of ideas was established in my mind between the charm of the afore-mentioned gesture and the music of Fauré." But no one who really listens to Fauré, well played or sung, finds his harmony merely bland, as it may appear to perfunctory performers and audiences.

The hidden delights of the harmony depend not so much on the chords individually as on their peculiar progressions and modulations. The pace of root progressions is extraordinarily varied, and seldom slow. Fauré and Reger are alike in this respect, and these two composers are unlike all their contemporaries. But Fauré differs from Reger in his balances of strong and weak progressions, whereas Reger's are preponderantly strong, by fifth; here Fauré is the more original. And Fauré's modulations, too, are like and unlike Reger's: he hardly ever stays simply in one key for as much as a phrase, but he uses chromatic progressions only sparingly, he blends related diatonic scales together by vague modality—especially favoring the raised fourth of the Lydian mode—and finally, he makes each phrase lead so smoothly into the next that the one key of the whole piece is supreme throughout. These characteristics lift his music, for listeners sensitive to them, far above that of Reger.

But chord progressions and modulations, in turn, are less important than the counterpoint of melody and bass, which gives rise to all the chords and makes any substitution a perceptible weakening or coarsening of the music. The bass line must be heard, not as a mere support for the vocal melody, but as a complementary melody itself. It contains an extraordinary amount of smooth stepwise motion in proportion to the decisive leaps that had been characteristic of bass lines ever since the late 15th century. Every skip and every change of direction in Fauré's basses is an expressive surprise, yet the line pulls inexorably to its traditional cadences. In all Fauré's music the bass makes rich contributions. In his piano playing the strength of the bass was notable. He might have shortened somewhat the labors of other pianists

EXAMPLE X.1   Fauré, *Chanson*, Op. 94

if he had marked his bass lines with slurs and dynamic signs, as we have done in our reduction of the song. To be sure, he might also have made things easier for pianists by doubling his bass with octaves, or by filling in the rests of the inner voices with a full texture. His earlier songs and piano pieces bloom more readily than this song with a rich, warm sonority. But he tended more and more to economize, to indicate his harmony rather than dwell on it, so as to keep his rhythms alert and his counterpoint singing, yet subordinate. When harmony, rhythm, and counterpoint are fully mastered by performers, the economical piano writing turns out to be quite warm enough, and invariably grateful for the instrument, though at first it may appear dry and abstract, as in the beginning of the last Nocturne, or even inept and harsh, as in the last Barcarolle.

Fauré's vocal melodies are similarly grateful for singers who master the whole music, and similarly more economical and thus more difficult as his style progresses. They are always too subtle to read safely. An innocent-looking skip of a third may be quite hard to sing in tune until the accompanying chords are familiar (mm. 8, 24, 25). But then a third or a fourth, or a mere step, may become as rich as the sixths and sevenths of a more effusive style. And the fitting of words and music always turns out at last to be perfect, though at first it may seem that an almost conventional symmetry has been imposed on the verse, with little regard for its own meter, not to mention its opportunities for dramatic declamation.

Fauré's writing for strings is similarly effective, with the Quartet, at the very end of his life, the most refined piece. His writing for orchestra, in the unique opera, *Pénélope* (1907–13), cannot be judged with certainty until it has been played more. Some writers have supposed that Fauré left the orchestration to an assistant. But his letters indicate that he did it himself, with pleasure though with haste. The conductor Inghelbrecht, loving the music and finding the orchestration ineffective, rescored it in 1949, but in 1957 he was still debating with himself which version to use.

Regardless of the medium, Fauré adhered to traditional four-part writing. He was concerned more with counterpoint than with the sonorous surface of the music, even though he seldom used imitation or other contrapuntal devices, and never made a turgid effect. His modest, vital counterpoint is equally remote from the self-satisfied fugues of Reger, from the variable loose texture of Debussy, from the brilliant density of Strauss, and from the otherworldly counterpoint of Mahler. Fauré's is closer than any of these to the counterpoint of Bach, especially that of Bach's sarabandes and slow arias, while at the same time it remains closer than most of the new styles to 19th-century models, including Mendelssohn, Schumann, Chopin, Gounod, and Fauré's teacher, Saint-Saëns. Fauré demonstrated his concern for counterpoint and his attitude toward tradition in the reforms that he instituted when he became director of the Conservatory in 1906. He created a new course in counterpoint, to be begun after a single year of harmony, and he required all students to study music history, under Bourgault-Ducoudray.

Fauré himself learned his craft not at the Conservatory but at the Niedermeyer school of religious and classical music, where he studied from the age of ten to twenty, and where he soon afterward returned to teach. He recalled his memories of the school with great affection in an article written at the end of his life. The Niedermeyer course was unusual, emphasizing, along with Bach and Mendelssohn and a few 16th-century works, the glories of plainsong and the problems of improvising chordal accompaniments for it that would respect its modes. Niedermeyer's book on accompanying will doubtless be a principal source for the comprehensive detailed study of Fauré's stylistic development that is yet to be carried out. For the habits instilled by Niedermeyer must have been reinforced in the course of Fauré's long service as church organist, ultimately at the Madeleine.

Saint-Saëns came to teach at the Niedermeyer school in 1860, when Fauré was fifteen. A lifetime friendship sprang up at once. Saint-Saëns introduced into his class the latest works of Schumann, Liszt, and Wagner, together with his own, which Fauré liked best of all. He continued to like them after he had developed his own style. In 1910 he wrote to his wife:

Wagner's polyphony, excessive though always quite justified, Debussy's *chiaroscuro*, and Massenet's writhings of ignoble passion are all that stir or grip the public today. While Saint-Saëns's clear and *loyal* music, to which I feel closest, leaves this same public cold.

And again in 1922, after the death of Saint-Saëns, Fauré published a eulogy of his master.

The magnetic power of Wagner drew Fauré to Cologne in 1878, to Munich in 1879, and to Bayreuth in 1896, although there is no evidence that Fauré studied Wagner's works as closely as Debussy or Strauss did. In *Prometheus* and *Pénélope* there are some superficial Wagnerisms that must have made the worldlier younger men smile. Fauré apologized to his wife for some of them. He feared that *Prometheus* was "an outrageous imitation of Wagner." In *Pénélope,* he explained, orchestral motifs were to make explicit to the audience what the characters hid from each other. "It is the Wagnerian system, but there is no better one . . . It is true that this devil of a man seems to have used up all the formulas." Worst of all, the motif of Penelope's anguish is a *Tristan* chord, loud, sustained, and richly doubled in octaves; it is a naive exaggeration, in contrast to Debussy's voluptuous, nonchalant use of the same chord, or Strauss's reckless, witty travesties of it. Fauré confessed that he was trying to bring to the writing of the opera "this ardor and this tenacity which have never been too easy for me," and that he did so not for his own sake, but for that of his wife, who evidently nagged him to produce big works for a big public, and accused him of frivolity or laziness when he worked on songs and piano pieces. After *Pénélope* he refused "to embark on any such adventure ever again!" In his last decade he left the wide world to Wagner, Debussy, and Massenet, or rather, to his pupil, Ravel, while he himself, within his own modest limits, achieved his impressive series of masterpieces.

Through the whole first half of the 20th century the tradition of César
Franck flourished vigorously in France, despite the untimely death of his
most distinguished pupil, Ernest Chausson (1855–1899). Though few of its
products were able to compete successfully on the international market, their
persistent quantity, their high quality of craft, and the idealism that they
represented were important factors in the world. In 1894 the tradition was
embodied in an institution, the Schola Cantorum, through the efforts of the
young choral conductor Charles Bordes (1863–1909) together with the old
organist Alexander Guilmant (1837–1911) and the composer-pedagogue
Vincent d'Indy (1851–1931). Contemporaries of Bordes, faithful as he was
to Franck and not subordinate to d'Indy, included Gabriel Pierné (1863–
1937), Guy Ropartz (1864–1955), Charles Tournemire (1870–1939), Louis
Vierne (1870–1937), and Dynam-Victor Fumet (1867–1949). Organists
everywhere keep alive the works of Tournemire and Vierne. Fumet we shall
encounter in connection with Satie. A host of slightly younger men upheld
Franck's tradition as they received it through d'Indy, who became director
of the Schola in 1900: among these, Albéric Magnard (1865–1914), Antoine
Mariotte (b. 1875), Déodat de Séverac (1873–1921), Joseph Canteloube
(1879–1957), Gustave Samazeuilh (b. 1877), and Jean Cras (1879–1932)
each produced at least one work to make his name known abroad, along
with many others that are recommended by René Dumesnil and other
writers who know them as worthy of cultivation. But these writers agree
that none of them can rival the preëminent pupil of the Schola, Albert
Roussel (1869–1937). Roussel's stylistic development, leading far from
Franck and d'Indy, will concern us in Chapter XXII.

The best-known and perhaps the finest realization of the conservative
ideal of d'Indy was achieved by Paul Dukas (1865–1935) in the symphonic
poem based on Goethe's ballad, *The Sorcerer's Apprentice* (1897). Dukas
was a classmate, friend, and supporter of Debussy, a close friend of d'Indy
and his circle, a superb critic, whose collected articles have lasting value, and
a teacher whose benign influence can be found in the work of such diverse
pupils as Olivier Messiaen and Walter Piston. Dukas followed his one
world-famous piece with four grand achievements, and four gemlike miniatures. There were two of each for piano—the Sonata (1900) and the
Variations on a Theme of Rameau (1902), the *Prelude on the Name of
Haydn* (1909) and the *Lament of the Faun,* in memory of Debussy (1920).
There was a single opera, *Ariane and Bluebeard* (Maeterlinck, 1897–1907),
and a ballet, *The Peri.* There was a charming villanella for horn (1906) and
one song, a *Sonnet of Ronsard* (1924). The opera, *Ariane,* in which he
borrowed some devices from *Pelléas,* won him the esteem and friendship
of the poet Paul Valéry, and was the chief inspiration of the Catholic
existentialist philosopher, Gabriel Marcel. The production of *Ariane* by
Schoenberg's brother-in-law, Alexander von Zemlinsky, in Vienna (1908)

was important for the development of the whole Schoenberg school. But Dukas found his ideal more and more difficult to satisfy; at the end of his life he destroyed all his unfinished works, so that no one can hope to know what elements of adventure they may have embodied.

Alongside the erudite and lofty traditions of d'Indy and Dukas, a tradition of facile craftsmanship survived in Reynaldo Hahn (1874–1947), whose songs were sung around the world. Hahn's memoirs and his correspondence with Marcel Proust show that he adhered to tradition by choice, not from ignorance.

Erudition, idealism, taste, and a modest adventure were combined in the work of Maurice Emmanuel (1862–1938), favorite pupil of Bourgault-Ducoudray and his successor as professor of music history at the Conservatory. Emmanuel's many scholarly works won wider recognition than his compositions, but he regarded himself always as an artist first, whose scholarship was at the service of the art of music. Emmanuel's notion of polymodality may be found again in the music of his pupil Messiaen and other younger composers.

Abel Decaux (1868–1943) was an inconspicuous organist who somehow composed four piano pieces, *Clairs de lune* (1900, 1902, 1903, 1907), of such freakish originality that he was hailed posthumously, by Gisèle Brelet, as a "French Schoenberg." More knowledge of Decaux than Mlle. Brelet uncovered might someday win him a significant place in the history of styles.

Eight of the more venturesome musicians of this generation, led by their teacher Fauré and sympathizing with Debussy more than with d'Indy, formed the Société Indépendante Musicale in 1907. The greatest of these were Koechlin, who ventured farthest, and Ravel, who achieved the most; they will concern us later. Four of the others achieved works valued in France and deserving to be known abroad: Louis Aubert (b. 1877), André Caplet (1878–1925), Roger Ducasse (1873–1954), and Jean Huré (1877–1930). (Another of this group was the critic Émile Vuillermoz.) Still another independent pupil of Fauré was Florent Schmitt (1870–1958). His sympathies turned more to Chabrier and Richard Strauss than to Debussy, but his prolific output showed many varied influences. Piano duettists, wind players, and choral singers, looking for solid works to diversify their repertories, may be grateful to Schmitt. His lavish orchestral works represent his expansive personality better. His biographer, Yves Hucher, agrees with his French public in regarding the *Psalm* for chorus and orchestra (1906) as best of all.

It was a concert of the Société Indépendante Musicale in 1911, followed by articles in the S. I. M. Bulletin, that first brought acclaim to the most astonishing and controversial of Debussy's contemporaries, Erik Satie (1866–1925). For an ephemeral publisher's catalogue, in 1913 or 1914, Satie wrote a blurb, which has been translated by Rollo Myers in his book on Satie:

He is considered to be the strangest musician of our time. He classes himself among the "fantaisistes" who are, in his opinion, "highly respectable people." He often says to his friends: "Although born short-sighted I am long-sighted by inclination. . . . Shun pride: of all the evils from which we suffer this is the most constipating. Let those unhappy people whose sight does not see me blacken their tongues and burst their ears."

Such is the everyday conversation of M. Erik Satie. We must not forget that the Master is looked upon by very many of the "younger" school as the forerunner and apostle of the revolution now taking place in music; MM. Maurice Ravel, E. Vuillermoz, Robert Brussel, M. D. Calvocoressi, J. Écorcheville, Roland-Manuel, etc., have introduced him as such, and their affirmation is based on facts the accuracy of which is undisputed.

After having essayed the loftiest genres the eminent composer now presents some of his humoristic works. This is what he says about his humor: "My humor resembles that of Cromwell. I also owe much to Christopher Columbus, because the American spirit has occasionally tapped me on the shoulder and I have been delighted to feel its ironically glacial bite."

Two or three years earlier, before any prominent publisher had accepted either lofty or humorous works, Satie wrote to his faithful younger brother, Conrad:

In 1905 I set to work with d'Indy. I was tired of being reproached with an ignorance that I supposed I had, because competent persons pointed it out in my works. After three years of hard labor I received my diploma in counterpoint from the Schola Cantorum, signed by my excellent teacher, who is indeed the best and most learned man in the world. So there I was, in 1908, with a certificate at hand giving me the title of contrapuntist. Proud of my learning, I began to compose. My first work in this genre was a chorale and fugue for four hands. I have put up with many an insult in my wretched life, but never was I so scorned as now. What had I been doing with d'Indy? I had written earlier things of such profound charm. And now! What dull pretension! Whereupon the "young" organized an anti-d'Indy movement and performed the *Sarabandes*, the *Son of the Stars*, etc., works formerly considered the fruit of a great ignorance, mistakenly according to these "young." Such is life, old man. You can't win.

These two statements together—the flashing, biting irony in public and the wry bafflement in private—fairly indicate Satie's personality and his unique historical position.

The works of Satie's twenties that were made famous at a concert in 1911 by Ravel (1875–1937) and his friend the brilliant pianist Ricardo Viñes

(1875–1943) were all short piano pieces: 3 Sarabandes (1887), *3 Gymno-pédies* (athletic exercises of Greek youths, 1888), *3 Gnossiennes (Scenes from Gnossos,* 1890), and 3 Preludes from *Le Fils des étoiles—Wagnérie Kaldéenne (Son of the Stars—Chaldean Wagneresque,* 1891). Two of the *Gymnopédies,* arranged for orchestra by Debussy in 1895 and conducted by him a few weeks after Ravel's concert, became the most famous of all Satie's music. The works of his late forties and fifties, on the contrary, though promptly published, performed, praised, and criticized, never became established in any regular repertory. Thus many opinions about him are based more on gossip and glib generalization than on adequate knowledge of representative music. The complete list of his compositions is impressively long and varied; it can lead anyone who enjoys the *Gymnopédies* to both disconcerting surprises and further profound charms; the titles in themselves afford a unique entertainment, but not a safe basis for any judgment.

The final movement of Satie's first suite for piano duet (1903) exhibits many of his distinctive traits. A simple rhythmic pattern persists beyond

EXAMPLE X.2   Satie, *Morceaux en forme de poire,* beginning of Finale

the point of unintentional monotony to make a sort of hypnotic effect, yet without any dynamic emphasis. In the *Gymnopédies* and *Gnossiennes* (including the fourth *Gnossienne,* which makes a "sort of introduction" for this suite) this trait of rhythm is exaggerated to an immobility that seems either sublime or maddening. Moreover, the sets of *Gymnopédies* and *Gnossiennes* and also the *Repulsive Airs* and the *Mutilated Dances* of 1897 are not suites, but triple versions of a single rhythmic idea. In the 20th-century works, on the contrary, regardless of whether they come in groups of three, there is a contrast of rhythm from one piece to the next, and often there are abrupt contrasts within a piece. But always there is a recognizable peculiarity about Satie's rhythm. Even in the central piece of our suite, despite the lilt of a polka, the relief of frequent dynamic contrasts, and the utter symmetry of four-measure phrases, there is a characteristic strange obstinacy and abruptness. In the finale, as in most of Satie's music, the phrase lengths are as irregular as those of plainsong.

Melody, of course, is the most prominent and most fundamental element of Satie's music. The rhythm is simple in order to permit concentration on melody and it is peculiar because the melody is peculiar, "singing" as only the piano "sings," wandering over the twelve notes of the keyboard with blithe disregard of scales, yet often suggesting one or another diatonic mode. Its typical upward motions are quick and light, its downward motions slow and heavy. Its articulation is clear and natural. Its form, in such a short piece as this, is satisfying, though in a piece as long as the *Gymnopédies* one may be tempted to make cuts.

The accompanying chords enhance the harmonic peculiarity of the melody in a peculiar way. Most of the chords are common triads, but their connections are seldom common. Richer chords are interspersed among them with a gawky amateur's unconcern for part-writing or any other consistency. Occasionally the result is disappointing, as in the final cadence, mm. 21–22, but far more often, as in the eerie ostinato of the third phrase, mm. 13–18, or the unanalyzable modulations of the second, 8–12, Satie's intuition rivals that of such great explorers of unsystematic chord progressions as Monteverdi and Mussorgsky. By 1918, if not before, Satie formulated his harmonic principle, in a sketchbook quoted by Roger Shattuck:

To have a feeling for harmony is to have a feeling for melody. The serious examination of a melody will always constitute for the student an excellent exercise in harmony. A melody does not have *its harmony*, any more than a landscape has *its color*. The harmonic *situation* of a melody is infinite, for melody is only one means of expression in the whole realm of Expressions. Do not forget that the melody is the Idea, the contour just as much as it is the form and content of a work. Harmony is lighting, an exhibition of the object, its reflection. In composition the parts no longer follow "school" rules. "School" has a gymnastic purpose and no more; composition has an esthetic purpose in which taste alone plays a part.

This purely negative principle resembles Debussy's principle of subordinating chords to melodies, but it is still more radical. The resemblance is enough to account for some confusion among critics, but Satie deviates much farther than Debussy from the common practice of the past. Of the younger composers who have followed Satie's principle, only a few have made such lucky finds as he did. He himself, in the *Danses de travers* (1897) and in the *Nocturnes* (1919), was content with chords that cast a dull gray over his melodies.

Harmony contributes little or nothing to the form of our example. Tonality is not attenuated, as in Debussy, or confused, as in Reger, but simply neglected. Satie showed that a short piece could have a satisfactory form without unifying tonality. According to Shattuck, he speculated on a "super-atonal" system. But his negative principle provides no basis for a system, and his empirical practice shows no more concern to avoid tonality than to establish it.

Form is the great issue in the suite. Every writer on Satie tells the story: Debussy had observed a lack of form in Satie's earlier music, and in reply Satie brought him the

3
MORCEAUX
en forme de Poire
(à 4 mains)
avec une
Manière de commencement,
une prolongation du même,
& Un En Plus,
suivi d'une Redite.

Altogether seven pieces. *Poire* means not only "pear," but also, in slang, the dupe of a hoax. Is this music a hoax? or is Satie saying that he himself is a dupe? or Debussy? The "sort of introduction," which is the fourth *Gnossienne,* written in 1890, is longer than Piece I. The "prolongation" is a complete contrast to the *Gnossienne.* With all this hocus-pocus in mind, most listeners find amusing moments in the music itself, though some insist that the titles are the only joke and that in this suite, at least, Satie's expressive purpose is innocent and straightforward. Historians and critics are tempted to suppose that Satie meant to make Debussy a dupe. But the story connecting Debussy with this piece rests on no documentary evidence. So a conscientious historian must examine all the biographical evidence that might be relevant. It is regrettably fragmentary and fascinatingly complicated.

Satie's mother died when he was six, and his father sent him to live with his grandparents in his native town, Honfleur, opposite Le Havre at the mouth of the Seine. Here he began lessons with the village organist, Vinot, a disciple of Fauré's teacher, Niedermeyer. It is probable that Vinot trained him to harmonize plainsong before he had heard enough urban music to establish any habit of respecting the major scale and its leading tone. In 1878, at twelve, Satie rejoined his father in Paris. The next year the father married Eugénie Barnetsche, a neighborhood piano teacher and composer of pallid salon waltzes. Erik hated his stepmother and her music. But he submitted to attending concerts, and to enrolling in the Conservatory. He preferred to spend his time reading fiction and strolling through the city. He probably played and wrote harmony exercises without ever accepting his parents' plan to make him a musician. He began, however, to earn a living playing accompaniments in cabarets. Here he met Dynam-Victor

Fumet, the pupil of Franck who had lost his scholarship because of anarchist activities. Fumet's unpublished compositions, and especially his improvisations, according to the memoir of his son Stanislas Fumet, stimulated Satie to his first adventures in unresolved ninth chords, fourth chords, and other sorts of dissonance. (Both young men probably found a stimulus in Chabrier's chords of the 1880s, though Satie never showed a command of Chabrier's marvelous treatment of tonality, rhythm, and texture, to which his chords were subordinate.) Fumet's interest in alchemy, which finally resolved in conversion to the Catholicism of Léon Bloy, probably encouraged Satie in his eccentric literary and religious interests. Satie associated briefly with the cult of Joséphin Péladan, *Rose-Croix,* and that of Jules Bois, *Le Coeur,* and then, in 1895, he established his own "abbey of the church of Jesus the conductor." His music of the nineties was somehow connected with these religious concerns; the meager evidence so far available can be used to support various interpretations of the connection:

1) Satie was cynically joking in a ponderous way;
2) he was deeply committed to a fantastic ideal, which he abandoned by 1900;
3) he served a subtler ideal, to which he remained faithful while protecting it with a shell of irony;
4) he was uncertainly groping his lonely way amid conflicting ideals.

The last seems likeliest. In his memoir of 1924 he said: "Personally I am neither good nor bad. I oscillate, if I may say so. Also, I have never really done harm to anyone—nor good, moreover." His work in the cabarets enabled him to form some crude musical habits, but these could neither bind him nor help him when he wanted to write serious music, and until 1900 he seems to have kept his serious thoughts quite distinct from his experience with popular music. On the other hand, in 1889 he heard the exotic music at the Exposition, and at once added to his fund of possibilities for choice: the *Gnossiennes* (1890) use scales with augmented steps and non-scalar grace notes.

Satie and Debussy first met in 1891, at the cabaret *Auberge du clou.* They became friends at once. Debussy gave Satie a copy of his Baudelaire songs, 1892, with the inscription "For Erik Satie, gentle medieval musician, strayed into this century for the happiness of his very friendly Claude Debussy." They continued friends until Satie at last became famous. When Satie moved from Bohemian Montmartre to the working-class suburb Arcueil in 1898, he returned weekly to visit Debussy, to use his piano, and to drink his wine, perhaps sometimes too much. About 1900 Satie wrote to his brother: "If I did not have Debussy . . . I do not see how I should go about expressing my poor thought. . . . You ask for news of *Pelléas et Mélisande*; I shall tell you simply this—very *chic,* absolutely hair-raising." But by 1910 or 1911 the friendship became strained. Ravel's concert and Écorcheville's article about it, acclaimed Satie as "the forerunner and apostle of the revolution," in order to demonstrate what both Ravel and Debussy owed to Satie, to prove that Ravel was no mere imitator of Debussy. Satie reported: "One who is not happy is the good Claude. It's his own fault: if he had done earlier what Ravel has done, his position would be different . . . Why won't he leave me a tiny little place in his shadow?" Still in 1913 Debussy presented Satie as his *protegé* to Stravinsky, who liked him very much. In 1913, however, Debussy wrote an article on "The Forerunner, Wilhelm Rust," making the point that forerunners in general were overrated by the historians who studied them. In 1917, when Debussy failed to attend Satie's *Parade,* Satie sent him a letter, described by Laloy as "almost insulting." Debussy received it on his sickbed, tore it up, and murmured "Pardon!" Satie in turn repented, shortly before his own death seven years later, saying privately to Roger Desormière, "How I must have made Debussy suffer when he was sick!" But in a public lecture on Debussy, about 1922, he did not refuse credit for a certain decisive influence:

Debussy's esthetic is connected with symbolism in several of his works; it is impressionist in his work as a whole. Please forgive me—am I not a little the cause of this? So they say. Here is the explanation. When I first met him, he was all absorbed in Mussorgsky, was searching avidly for a path not easy to find. In this search I was far ahead of him: the prizes of Rome or other cities did not impede my progress, since I carry no such prize on my person or on my back, for I am a man of the race of Adam (of Paradise) who never carried off any prize—a lazy fellow, no doubt. I was just then writing the *Fils des étoiles*, on a text of Joséphin Péladan, and I explained to Debussy the need for a Frenchman to give up the Wagnerian adventure, which did not correspond to our natural aspirations. And I made him note that I was not at all anti-Wagner, but that we ought to have a music of our own—without sauerkraut, if possible. Why not use the means of representation introduced to us by Claude Monet, Cézanne, Toulouse-Lautrec, etc.? Why not transpose these means musically? Nothing simpler. Aren't these all expressions?

Just there was a point of departure for almost sure achievements, fruitful even . . . Who could show him examples? reveal discoveries? point out the field to be explored? supply him with tested observations? who? I don't want to answer: this no longer interests me.

This evasive "explanation" is a fundamental document, which does better justice to both Satie and Debussy than most accounts of their relations.

In the light of all this, our questions about the *Morceaux en forme de poire* seem heavy-footed. When we play them or listen to them again we can imagine the gnomelike Satie arriving from Arcueil with his umbrella, speaking a few words in his peculiarly soft but precise enunciation, presenting the manuscript to Debussy with stiff solemnity, then laughing out loud as Debussy puzzles over the discrepancy between title and content, and alternately grinning and wistfully yearning as together they play, for Debussy's happiness. We remember that Satie calls himself a *"fantaisiste."* No other label fits so well.

After the "pearshapes," the next outstanding work is *Sports et divertissements* (1914), published in two-color facsimile of Satie's elaborate calligraphy, along with colored drawings by Charles Martin. Satie's preface to this volume reinforces our conclusion above:

This publication is composed of two artistic elements: drawing and music. The drawing part consists of lines—animated lines; the musical part is represented by dots—black dots. These two parts put together—in one volume—make a whole: an album. I recommend that you turn its pages with a tolerant thumb and with a smile, for this is a work of fantasy. Let no one regard it otherwise.

For the "dried-up" and the "stultified" I have written a chorale, sober and suitable. This makes a sort of bitter prelude, a kind of introduction quite austere and unfrivolous. Into it I have put all I know about boredom. I dedicate this chorale to those who do not like me. And I withdraw.

E. S.

The fantasy of *Sports et divertissements* includes another element, not mentioned in the preface: commentaries amounting to prose poems, such as this one:

EXAMPLE X.3   Satie, *The Swing*

C'est mon cœur qui se balance ainsi.   Il n'a pas le vertige.
It is my heart that swings.   It doesn't get dizzy.

Comme il a de petits poids.   Voudra-t-il revenir dans ma poitrine?
What tiny feet it has!   Will it want to come back to my breast?

The poem is touching and memorable in itself. There is no obvious relation here between words and music, or between music and picture, while the relation between words and picture is unexpected. Yet the "tolerant reader" can surely sense an occult wholeness among them, with a fragile charm that could have been achieved in no other way. So fragile a charm is certainly not meant for an audience in a concert hall, but in the age of the phonograph it need not be restricted to pianists.

In many of the little pieces of this album, the unity of music, words, and pictures is tighter than in *The Swing*. Most of the pieces, short as they are, are composed of contrasting episodes, ranging over the whole keyboard, and arriving at an occasional outlandish polytonal effect between melody and accompaniment, to coincide with an outlandish joke in the commentary. Aside from the chorale, there is no evidence of the contrapuntal studies that Satie pursued with d'Indy and Roussel, 1905–1908, and even in the chorale, where the chromatic lower voices conform to traditional rules, the soprano melody is supreme and the chords enhance its peculiarity.

In 1914 the poet Jean Cocteau met Satie, as he recorded in 1938, in the company of Ravel and Viñes and their rich friends the Godebskis, who loved Satie but made fun of him. Cocteau commissioned the five *Grimaces* for his projected version of *A Midsummer Night's Dream*. Then, in 1915, Cocteau conceived the idea for the ballet *Parade,* which was to be Satie's first long work and his chief work for orchestra. Cocteau, the precocious poet who had collaborated with Reynaldo Hahn to provide the Diaghilev ballet *Dieu bleu,* and had hoped to work with Stravinsky, envisioned a new kind of musical theater that would meet the famous challenge of Diaghilev, "Surprise me!" Cocteau's plans somewhat puzzled Satie, as he confided in a letter to the painter Valentine Hugo, but when Picasso joined the team everything worked out. *Parade* surprised Diaghilev to his satisfaction, and was produced in 1917, complete with a manifesto of "the new spirit" by Guillaume Apollinaire, a riot among the audience, and subsequent hijinks surpassing all other scandals of this scandalous age. According to the memoir of the painter Gabriel Fournier, Satie was insulted by the review of a dull critic, and replied with a postcard:

> Sir and Dear Friend,
> You are only an arse, but an arse without music.
> Signed, Erik Satie.

The critic sued. At the trial Cocteau was seized and mauled by the police for shouting the word that Satie had written. Satie was given a suspended sentence to eight days in jail. Within a year, Cocteau wrote a pamphlet of dazzling aphorisms and paradoxes, *Le Coq et l'arlequin* (*Cock and Harlequin*), to explain and propagate the ideal of *Parade*—an unrealized ideal of what contemporary theater ought to be. Cocteau's interpretation of Satie in accordance with this ideal, quoted or misquoted, with or without acknowledgment, became more famous than *Parade* or any other work of the composer. To break the spell of Debussy is Cocteau's chief purpose; he does not hesitate to treat Ravel as a mere Debussyste and to set Satie in opposition to both his old friends. He exalts Satie not only as a great forerunner, but as a greater destroyer.

Now, while Debussy delicately spreads his feminine grace, strolling with Stéphane Mallarmé in the Garden of the Infanta, Satie continues on his little classic path. He arrives here today, young among the young, at last finding his place, after twenty years of modest work. . . .

Satie teaches the greatest boldness for our time: be simple. Hasn't he proved that he could refine more than anyone? Now he levels out, he disengages, he strips the rhythm. Is this again the music to which, as Nietzsche said, "the spirit dances," after the music "in which the spirit bathes"? Neither music to bathe in, nor music to dance to: MUSIC TO WALK ON. . . . Enough of clouds, of waves, of aquariums, of Ondines, and of odors of the night; we need a music on the ground, A MUSIC OF EVERYDAY. Enough of hammocks, garlands, gondolas! I want a music built for me where I live as in a house. . . . The opposition that Erik Satie makes consists in a return to simplicity. After all, it is the only possible opposition in an age of extreme refinement. . . .

Never any magic, any recapitulations, any leering caresses, any feverishness, any dampness. Satie never stirs up the mud. His is the poetry of childhood, recaptured by a technician. . . . Satie's orchestra gives all its grace without pedals. It is a village choir spiked with a dream. It opens a gate to the young musicians who are a bit tired of the lovely impressionist polyphony. Hear him depart from a fugue and return to it with classic liberty.

"I have composed a background," said Satie modestly, "for certain noises that Cocteau deems indispensable for defining the atmosphere of his characters." Satie exaggerates, but in fact noises played a big part in *Parade*. Mechanical obstacles (lack of compressed air, among others) have deprived us of these "trompe-l'oreille" effects—dynamo, Morse code apparatus, sirens, steam engine, airplane motor—which I used as painters use "trompe-l'oeil"—newspaper, cornice, imitation wood. We could barely make the typewriters audible.

Cocteau followed up this momentous pamphlet in 1920 with a series of broadsheets on poster-paper, called *Le Coq*. In one of these sheets Satie defined his own position:

I never attack Debussy. Only the Debussystes annoy me. There is no Satie school. *Satisme* could not possibly exist. I should be found in opposition to it. . . . Let us thank Cocteau for helping us get rid of the habits of the latest impressionist music, tiresomely provincial and pedantic.

The difference between Satie and Cocteau deserves emphasis, because their collaboration received more emphasis than it deserved. But it is only fair to add Cocteau's comment from a lecture of 1923, *On an Order considered as an Anarchy,* published together with *Cock and Harlequin* in the book *Rappel à l'ordre*: "After the *Cock and Harlequin* we ran the risk of being taken seriously, which is the beginning of death."

Cocteau's version of Satie offended Stravinsky and wounded Ravel more than Ravel and Écorcheville's version of 1911 had wounded Debussy. Ravel and Satie were friends no longer. In 1920, when Ravel declined the Legion of Honor, Satie noted equivocally, in the *Coq,* "all his music accepts it." By 1928, when Ravel lectured in Texas, he had turned some of Cocteau's ideas to his own purposes; he formulated a judgment of Satie's whole career that became the conventional judgment of all but a few enthusiasts:

His was the inventor's mind *par excellence.* . . . Simply and ingeniously Satie pointed the way, but as soon as another musician took to the trail he had indicated, Satie would immediately change his own orientation and without hesitating open up still another path to new friends of experiment. . . . While he himself may, perhaps, never have wrought out of his own discoveries a single complete work of art, nevertheless we have today many such works which might not have come into existence if Satie had never lived.

From Ravel's point of view, this is a calm and even generous judgment. But it can no longer satisfy us when we have felt at first hand the unique charm of Satie's fantasy, irreplaceable by anyone else's more extensive work.

In 1957 the young critic David Drew heard in *Parade* something deeper than either Cocteau or Ravel had found:

Parade is a masterpiece, one of the rare triumphs of modern French art. If the dangerous disassociation of imaginative and technical content may be permitted, I would say that imaginatively *Parade* is the equal of anything in Debussy and superior to anything in Ravel. Although the work is almost entirely neglected or misunderstood, I believe that it has classic status, and that in years to come it will be as unthinkable to omit it from a survey of twentieth-century music as today it would be to omit *Le Sacre du Printemps* or *Pierrot Lunaire.* . . . The music of *Parade* . . . is unsocial, disengaged, objective,—in fact, the product of a spiritual exile that is almost pathological in nature. . . . It is certain that Satie himself was unaware of the powerful message he was conveying in *Parade.*

Responses as enthusiastic as that of Drew have been evoked by Satie from many men older than Drew but younger than Ravel: Darius Milhaud, Georges Auric, Henri Sauguet, Virgil Thomson, Wilfrid Mellers, and John Cage among composers and keen critics, and also Jacques Maritain, the neo-Thomist philosopher, who knew Satie in his last years and who wrote in 1943:

Magic . . . is the gift of an order exterior or superior to art. Wagner lived only for magic. . . . The case of Satie is the reverse. Through the passion of probity, he detests, he excommunicates in himself all possible magic, he ferociously cleanses his work of it. Repressed, magic then disguises itself in the queer taste for mystification that disarms the enterprises of mystery, and that protects the ironic snows of a virgin music.

But between the temperate judgment of Ravel and the snows of Maritain there is room for us to appreciate that *Parade* achieves what Satie intended: an appropriate atmospheric background for an interesting ballet, with a continuity too loose and arbitrary to make a piece for the permanent concert repertory, yet with a consistency and symmetry that makes it superior to the *Morceaux en forme de poire* or *Sports et divertissements* as a suite for the quiet delight of a tolerant listener. The three dances are happily contrasted with each other, not so violently contrasted as the movements of the earlier suites. The march makes good use of pentatonic and whole-tone scales. The American Girl's dance is ragtime, with sliding trombones, rather like Debussy's *Golliwog's Cakewalk*. The Acrobats' number is a waltz with polytonal effects like those of Stravinsky's *Petrushka*. The central ragtime and the beginning and end of the whole work are solidly in C major. Many other keys appear briefly, serving only as contrasts to C, without any hierarchical relation. If there is a novel disengagement of music and society here, it is Cocteau's achievement rather than Satie's, for the latter has come closer to conformity with live tradition in *Parade* than in any other work.

Satie's portrait of *Socrates* (1917–20) is a marvelous achievement, and because the atmosphere that the text requires is more solemn than that of *Parade* it has won the admiration of some musicians, like Alfred Cortot, whose tolerance for magical hoaxes and acrobatics is limited. Moreover, for Myers, who knows and sympathizes with all of Satie, *Socrates* is the best of all. He grants that the coolness and rarity of this atmosphere can appeal to no vast number of listeners, but estimates that the number is more likely to increase than to dwindle. If Cocteau's influence, irrelevant to *Socrates,* can be moderated, Satie might even find a wholly new group of admirers through this work.

The last two ballets and the other works following *Socrates* represent slightly new adventures. The atmosphere of *Relâche* (*No Show,* 1924) brought Satie and his collaborators Francis Picabia and Marcel Duchamp to the verge of Dadaism and surrealism, as Cocteau's noises had connected him tenuously with futurism. Picasso's *Mercure* (also 1924) connected him with a brittle sort of neo-Classicism. But no doctrine could really fit his fantasy.

Though Satie had said in 1920 "there is no Satie school," several young composers, who could profit from friendship with him and Cocteau, gave

Gustav Mahler, by Rodin
(The Bettmann Archive)

Heinrich Schenker
(Felix Salzer)

Richard Strauss at Weimar,
c. 1890 (The Bettmann Ar-
chive)

PLATE 5

Ricardo Viñes *(left)* and Maurice Ravel (The Bettmann Archive)

Gabriel Fauré and Mrs. Patrick Campbell, by John Singer Sargent

Drawings of Erik Satie, by himself

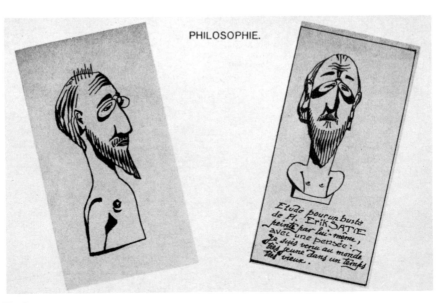

PHILOSOPHIE.

PLATE 6

him the affectionate title of "le bon maître." In connection with them his name became more prominent than his music. The critic Henri Collet in 1920 wrote an article on "The Russian Five, The French Six, and M. Erik Satie," rather arbitrarily grouping together Germaine Tailleferre (b. 1892), Louis Durey (b. 1888), Georges Auric (b. 1899), Darius Milhaud (b. 1892), Arthur Honegger (1892–1955), and Francis Poulenc (1899–1963). In 1923 Milhaud arranged for Satie to sponsor the débuts of another group, who adopted the slogan *L'École d'Arcueil*: Henri Cliquet-Pleyel (b. 1894), Roger Desormière (b. 1898), Maxime Jacob (b. 1906), and Henri Sauguet (b. 1901). Yet Satie persisted in preferring the company of poets, painters, and children to that of most musicians. The notoriety of his last years, though great enough to be useful to others, was not enough to relieve his poverty. He died at fifty-nine, a lonely man in a public hospital. The painter Valentine Hugo, visiting him there a few days before his death, was reminded of the farewell of *Socrates,* which he had set to such peculiar music.

———•—

Maurice Ravel (1875–1937) won a unique kind of success: almost every piece he published took a place in the concert repertory of the appropriate performers, and he provided something for every kind. In no other list of works, from any composer of any epoch, is such a large proportion of the music familiar to such a large number of music-lovers. Record collections can contain the complete works, all brilliantly performed; for many of them several performances are available, all adequate or better. Only the *Pavane for a dead Infanta* (1899) and the *Bolero* (1928) are often played badly. In addition, there are Ravel's orchestral transcriptions of most of his piano pieces, and his magnificent transcription of Mussorgsky's *Pictures at an Exhibition,* all likewise favorites of performers and listeners. This achievement forestalls criticism. For once, history can scarcely hope to contribute to appreciation. Yet even here, some complacent evaluations may be questioned—a style that is taken for granted may be exhibited as variable and complex, and the least familiar works may be recommended both to listeners who have heard *Daphnis and Chloë* (1909–12) too often and to those who cannot hear it often enough. Moreover, a careful account of Ravel's style and its development can help us define the similarities and differences among the many contemporary styles, and the links connecting them with earlier and later styles.

The first piece of the *Mother Goose* suite (1908) is a *Pavane de la belle au bois dormant* (*Sleeping Beauty*). Less hackneyed than the earlier *Pavane pour une infante,* which Ravel himself condemned by 1913 as defective in form and lacking in adventure, this pavane is no less tuneful and touching.

EXAMPLE X.4 Ravel, *Pavane de la belle au bois dormant*

The lyrical tune, like many more of Ravel's melodies, is straightforward, robust in comparison with Debussy's arabesques or Satie's mosaics or Puccini's broken sobs or Strauss's strainings and twistings. While Ravel's melodies have an elusive quality that makes them his, they are on the whole more like the best melodies of the 19th century than most contemporary melodies. They are also more like folksong, though always with a few sophisticated details that set them apart, such as the smooth transition here in m. 12. Most of all, they resemble the tunes of Massenet, Delibes, Bizet, Chabrier, and even Henry Ghys, arranger of the favorite salon-piece, *Amaryllis—Air Louis XIII*. Ghys was Ravel's first teacher, 1882–1887. His next teacher was a pupil of Delibes, Charles-René; he remembered Ravel's first compositions as spontaneous and interesting. Chabrier was the one of this generation that Ravel always acknowledged as his chief model.

The melody of our pavane, however, unlike these sources of Ravel's spontaneous habits, is modal. The whole step below the tonic occurs in every measure, and at the cadences it takes the place that would normally be occupied by the leading tone. Pervasive modality is almost as important a feature of Ravel's style as lyricism itself, and the two traits are closely related. Ravel probably learned to appreciate the various modes in the exotic music at the Exposition of 1889, which he heard with great interest, in the company of his classmate at the Conservatory, Viñes. In *Mother Goose* there is a fine imitation of the Javanese gamelan, *The Empress of the Pagodas*. The modal melodies of Borodin, Mussorgsky, and Rimsky-Korsakov undoubtedly influenced Ravel; he and Viñes studied and played their works throughout the 'nineties, and in the next decade they chose the first theme of Borodin's Second Symphony as the rallying signal of their group of friends, the "Apaches." Another likely influence in this direction was Satie; early in the 'nineties Ravel and Viñes got to know him through Ravel's father, an engineer and inventor who loved the cabarets. Ravel himself pointed to the influence of Satie on his unpublished *Ballade de la reine morte d'aimer* (1893) and on the waltz of *Beauty and the Beast* in the *Mother Goose* suite, which he called "a fourth *Gymnopédie*." But Satie never stuck to a single mode, as Ravel did in the Pavane. And when Satie turned to the major, in *Parade* for instance, he left the modes behind, whereas Ravel, in the finale of *Mother Goose, The Fairy Garden,* gives a characteristic modal tinge to his melody by emphasizing the third and sixth degrees of the major scale more than its normally strongest degrees, the tonic and dominant.

The pavane's melody is strictly diatonic, but the accompaniment has some discreet touches of chromaticism. This too is typical of Ravel; though there are passages in his music where chromaticism plays a greater part, on the whole he uses it as Borodin and the other Russians did, or Grieg, whose influence has been emphasized in Bruyr's fine study of Ravel.

Conspicuously absent from Ravel's music is the whole-tone scale, so closely associated with Debussy. In 1899 Ravel composed an orchestral overture, performed once and never published, for a projected opera, *Schéhérazade*. He told his first biographer, Roland-Manuel, that the overture was "badly constructed and crammed with whole-tone scales. There were so many of them in it, in fact, that I had enough of them for life." His avoidance of this radically untraditional yet all too fashionable device was thoroughly characteristic.

The basic chords underlying Ravel's music are common triads, but these chords are sometimes represented by empty fifths or simple octaves, and sometimes, on the other hand, obscured by counterpoint that makes rich sevenths and ninths, so that there is seldom any dwelling on the sound of a triad, and even the momentary explicit sounding of one is remarkably rare.

The frequency of the most dissonant intervals—major sevenths and minor ninths—is higher than in any earlier style. Ravel's new level of dissonance made his music interesting to Schoenberg, Webern, and Berg. Even in such a short, quiet piece as the pavane, these tangy sounds, marked with asterisks, prevail over the sweet thirds and sixths. In longer and more complex works the dissonance is often thicker. In some, chords of the eleventh and thirteenth are prominent, that is, structures carrying further the principle that points from triads to sevenths and ninths. But these towering stacks of thirds can always be explained alternatively as the outcome of counterpoint based on the traditional chords. They are not so essential to Ravel's style as they seemed to some contemporary theorists. More important is the prevalence of dissonant non-harmonic tones and non-dominant seventh and ninth chords, which we can observe in the pavane. For this trait Ravel probably owes something to his last teacher, Fauré, who was cultivating it in his own music of those years (1897–1905), as we have seen. But whereas Fauré produced dissonance with long, modulating phrases and *cantabile* bass lines, Ravel produced it more often with subtle movements of inner voices over simple, conventional basses, while varying the sonority from phrase to phrase by telling changes of register.

Ravel's chord progressions are mostly strong, satisfying the expectations that his modality and dissonance threaten to defeat. Here again he is close to Chabrier and to his own spontaneous 19th-century habits. This is the feature of his style that makes his music accessible to a wide audience, adaptable and easily imitated for commercial purposes, and tiresome to some restless 20th-century listeners. Ravel's harmonic rhythm has no originality. His originality is to combine with traditional harmonic rhythm an amazing amount of novel sonority and significant melody. The clearest illustration of this aspect of his style is of course the *Bolero*: a long, intricate, partly modal melody that sounds like a mere tune because of its rudimentary accompanying chords—tonic and dominant—this melody is repeated nine times with virtuoso variations of orchestration. The pavane illustrates the principle with typical modesty.

The pavane further illustrates an ingenious formal device that Ravel used many times: exploiting the loose relation of melody and harmony to make a recapitulation that is melodically literal and harmonically new, yet in accordance with academic convention. The melody in measures 13–16 is exactly that of 1–4, but the subdominant chord, replacing the original tonic, gives it a new poignance and enhances the total form. This device is almost a Ravel formula; it is applied effectively on a large scale in the Quartet (1902–03) and the Sonatina (1905).

Ravel's forms are nearly always clear and conventional. He adhered to the abstract textbook model of sonata form even in *Jeux d'eau* (1901), where his chief concern was to evoke a vivid picture by means of splashing sonorities. In several later works he copied a particular classic model: in the slow movement of the Concerto in G (1928–31) his model was Mozart's Clarinet Quintet.

Ravel's rhythm in general is traditional, like his harmonic rhythm and his forms, but not lacking in vigor or variety. Dances are suggested by most of his music, though he did not dance himself. He was a tiny man, "like a jockey," according to the memoir of Viñes, with narrow shoulders, and a big head, which he held very straight. When he got up from the piano he would straighten his elegant tie. Viñes contrasts Ravel's primness with Debussy's lounging attitudes. He goes on to compare Debussy, Satie, and Ravel as gourmets. Debussy ate delicately, savoring each detail of a meal. Satie loved sweets and put so much sugar in his coffee that it became a syrup. Ravel craved spices; he could devour an astonishing quantity of pickles and mustard. So his music absorbs the rhythms of pavane and habañera, waltz and bolero without upsetting its regular pace.

Counterpoint in Ravel's music is smooth and unobtrusive. On the rare occasions when there is reason for more conspicuous counterpoint, as in *Beauty and the Beast,* Ravel provides amply. In the pavane the subordinate lines are more than routine filling-in of a background, but they are not vitally interesting. With admirable economy they create shifting sonorities.

The precision and variety of the sonorities, and the ease with which competent performers can "bring off" Ravel's music, set it apart from that of most of his contemporaries. To be sure, *Mother Goose* is written for children to play, whereas most of his music is written for virtuosos, but when there are technical difficulties there is no question how to overcome them—simply by a bit more of traditional competence. The *Miroirs* (1905) and *Gaspard de la nuit* (1908) show off the utmost technical skill of a pianist in the tradition of Liszt. The Quartet (1902–03) and the Trio (1914) give string players corresponding tasks. And Ravel's orchestration, based on that of Rimsky, Strauss, and Debussy, gives every player a workout, while the conductor can bask in the glorious sounds. By comparison with Ravel's perfect finish, Debussy's music is almost as problematic as that of Ives.

It was inevitable, but unfortunate and unfair, that Ravel should be tagged as a Debussyste. The differences between their styles, as shown above, are more important than the obvious similarities. Yet coincidences seemed to put Ravel again and again in the shadow of Debussy. A chronological chart, better than a discursive account, can show all that is so far publicly known of these coincidences (see following page).

	Debussy's works	Ravel's works	Contacts between them
1893	*Faun*, Quartet		
1898		*Habañera* for piano (unpublished but incorporated in the *Rapsodie espagnole* 1907)	D. borrowed a MS copy and lost it.
1899	*Nocturnes*		
1901	*Lindaraja* (resembled *Habañera*, published posth.)	*Jeux d'eau*	
1902	*Pelléas*	*Shéhérazade* songs	R. and the "Apaches" attended every performance of *Pelléas*.
1903	*D'un cahier* (resembles *Habañera*)	Quartet	D. praised R.'s Quartet
1904	Dances for harp (commissioned by Erard)		
1905		Introduction and Allegro for harp (commissioned by Erard)	
	Images	*Miroirs*	
1907	*Ibéria*	*Rapsodie espagnole*	R. was quoted by Jules Renard, in his journal, as calling D. a "back number." R.'s alleged dependence on D. became a *cause célèbre* in the press, as amply recorded in Seroff's *Ravel*.
1908	choral *chansons*		
1909			R. arranged *Nocturnes* for pf.
1910			R. arranged *Faun*.
1911			R. played first public performance of D.'s *D'un cahier*.
1912	*Faun* danced by Nijinsky ten days before *Daphnis*		R. told Roland-Manuel: "It's probably better for us, after all, to be on frigid terms for illogical reasons."
1913	Mallarmé songs	Mallarmé songs	R. wrote an article praising D.'s *Images*.
1914		choral *chansons* Trio	
1915	sonatas		
1920		Duo in memory of D.	R. orchestrated D.'s *Sarabande*.

Ravel summed up his whole relation with Debussy in a document neglected by his biographers: the lecture on "Contemporary Music" that he delivered at the Rice Institute, Houston, Texas, in 1928:

For Debussy, the musician and the man, I have had profound admiration, but by nature I am different from Debussy, and while I consider that Debussy may not have been altogether alien to my personal inheritance, I should identify also with the earlier phases of my evolution Gabriel Fauré, Emmanuel Chabrier, and Erik Satie. The aesthetic of Edgar Allan Poe, your great American, has been of singular importance to me, and also the immaterial poetry of Mallarmé—unbounded visions, yet precise in design, enclosed in a mystery of sombre abstractions—an art where all the elements are so intimately bound up together that one cannot analyze, but only sense, its effect. Nevertheless, I believe that I myself have always followed a direction opposite to that of Debussy's symbolism. . . . It has been claimed with some insistence that the earlier appearance of my *Jeux d'eau* possibly influenced Debussy in the writing of his *Jardins sous la pluie*, while a coincidence, even more striking, has been suggested in the case of my *Habañera*; but comments of this sort I must leave to others. It could very well be, however, that conceptions, apparently similar in character, should mature in the consciousness of two different composers at almost the same time without implying direct influence of either one upon the other.

But to personal friends in his last years, including Jacques Février, Ravel expressed a wish "to die listening to the *Prélude à l'après-midi d'un faune,* which seemed to him the most perfect, the most moving work."

One more coincidence has been left out of account by Ravel and his biographers as well: just as Debussy's finished work after *Pelléas* was all the by-product of vain efforts to compose new operas, so Ravel's finished work from 1905 to 1917 was subordinate in his mind to an ill-fated project for an opera based on the play by Gerhart Hauptmann, *Die versunkene Glocke (La Cloche engloutie, The Sunken Bell)*. Even the largest of his finished works do not show the full range of his style and sensibility as he hoped to show it. The witty one-act opera, *L'Heure espagnole* (1907), was tossed off in a hurry. The sumptuous ballet, *Daphnis,* was accurately aimed to exploit the leaps of Nijinsky and the virtuosity of Diaghilev's orchestra. The big opera was to combine the stylized naturalism of the former with the ecstatic romanticism of the latter, and this combination Ravel never achieved. He approached it in smaller works: in *Noël des jouets (The Toys' Christmas,* 1905) and the songs to Jules Renard's prose satires, *Histoires naturelles* (1906), romantic lyricism is undercut by little shocks of realistic description, with an ultimate effect of desperate nostalgia. But whereas our imagination of Debussy's *Devil in the Belfry* can help us better understand the music he did write, because it enables us to think of his work as a whole, our imagination of the *Sunken Bell* contributes only a glimpse into Ravel's obscure personality; his works may be understood and enjoyed one at a time.

———•——••——

Among the least widely known of Ravel's works are the three songs of Mallarmé, set for soprano with two flutes, two clarinets, string quartet, and piano. These were written under the acknowledged but distant influence of Schoenberg's *Pierrot Lunaire,* at the time of Ravel's closest friendship and collaboration with Stravinsky (1913). In the opinion of Stravinsky, these songs are Ravel's most adventurous works, and therefore his most valuable.

When World War I began, Ravel was not quite forty, and his only family was his mother. He persisted in volunteering for service of any kind, and was finally accepted as a truck driver. In 1916, during a long wait for repairs to his truck, he wrote in a letter to his godmother, quoted by Seroff: "I have never been brave. But there it is, I'm eager to have adventures. It has such a fascination that it becomes a necessity. What will I do, what will many others do, when the war is over?" Even before the war was over he felt different. In letters of 1917 he complained:

An immense weariness that has come over me stops me from writing. Yesterday I became forty-two years old. It seems to me as though I am seventy. Only a year ago—think of it!—I was leaving for the front. I was preoccupied with curiosity, a desire for an adventure . . . I believe that I will never do another thing. I feel that I am finished.

And later that year Ravel confessed to Claude Delvincourt:

I have failed in my life . . . I am not one of the great composers. All the great have produced enormously. There is everything in their work: the best and the worst, but there is always quantity. But I have written relatively very little . . . and at that, I did it with a great deal of difficulty. I did my work slowly, drop by drop . . . and now I can not do any more and it does not give me any pleasure.

For a long time he undertook no further adventure like the *Sunken Bell,* and he never quite regained his confidence and composure. Yet in his desperation he went on composing wonderfully various and perfect pieces.

The tribute to Couperin (1917) is a marvelous union of old and new. *La Valse* (completed 1920) is the most vehemently moving work Ravel ever wrote. The Sonata for violin and cello (1920–22) "marks a turning point in my evolution . . . The reduction to essentials is carried to extremes." As if to give the lie to Cocteau's strictures on Impressionism, Ravel showed here a mastery of spiky counterpoint surpassing that of any young anti-Impressionist, and dedicated the first movement to the memory of Debussy. And then, in sharp contrast, the two-act opera, *L'Enfant et les sortilèges* (*The Child's Magic Dream*, Colette, 1917–25), is his sweetest, tenderest work; all the naughtiness of the spoiled child (who might be Ravel himself, according to both Roland-Manuel and Seroff) is forgiven in the choral peroration on maternal kindness. The concertos, incorporating "blue" notes and slow fox-trot rhythms, and the wonderful late songs are all by-products of another grandiose project—an oratorio about Joan of Arc. But this project never got far; Ravel's health deteriorated slowly and horribly during his last decade. In a manner that no doctor could explain, he lost his ability to write, to play, to remember music. At last a brain surgeon tried to find a cure, and Ravel never recovered from the operation.

Fauré, Debussy, Satie, and Ravel do not constitute a school. There is no trait shared by all four composers that distinguishes them from their predecessors or from their contemporaries in other countries. Although various techniques and attitudes are shared by one pair or another of the four, these cannot be seen in any pattern that would help us appreciate their work or identify an overriding tendency of the times. The actual connections among them, as disentangled here, prove that each composer was a unique, complex individual. It happened that only in France did so many of this stature live and work side by side in the early 20th century. Yet Debussy was the only one of them whose adventure and achievement were indispensable for 20th-century music everywhere. His worldwide influence, and the much lesser influence of his countrymen, was not like Wagner's, with a program for the future claiming to supersede the past, and a standard of judgment to be applied in all places and situations, but rather an invitation to freedom and an array of diverse models of "discipline within freedom."

CHAPTER XI

The Emergence of Jazz, to About 1923

JAZZ IS astonishingly new. It is music of the 20th century in sharp contrast to all earlier music. It is also, as we shall see, profoundly continuous with older music; its continuity with the past may be more important than its obvious novelty. But the novelty is not merely superficial. Jazz is a new musical style in a new social background.

Jazz is recognized by its new sounds. A fragment lasting no more than a second is enough for us to identify the broad stylistic category, to distinguish it from all earlier music.

Jazz fits new ways of life. It leads the rich to mimic the gestures of the poor, as far as they can, and not any picturesque peasants but the shuffling or swaggering workers of the poorest proletarian caste in the cities.

Jazz is an American product with a world market. It represents a fusion of West African and European musical habits, together with individual intuitions and choices, proliferating in many stylistic subdivisions. It disseminates bits of the European musical tradition to people in Asia and Africa who may have little interest in European music itself, but who may prefer an easy Western music to their ancestral heritage. And to many people in Europe jazz brings their most vital musical experience. Europe has produced no comparable product, no new style of popular music, though its old popular styles are not yet exhausted, and its new unpopular styles are of course far more elaborate and more comprehensive than jazz. Incidentally, musicians and critics in France were the first to appreciate the seriousness of good jazz. Hugues Panassié and Robert Goffin showed American intellectuals how to study its history; André Hodeir showed how to analyze its structure.

The novelty of jazz is almost matched by the novelty of the three most outstanding European styles since Debussy: those of Schoenberg, Bartók, and Stravinsky. But their sounds are not quite so new—they are mostly produced by instruments designed in the 19th century or earlier, with performing techniques that have hardly advanced beyond those of Debussy's generation.

Their functions are not quite so new—the special concerts, festivals, and broadcasts of contemporary music, the critical, theoretical, and historical discussion of it, and the teaching of it are offshoots or subdivisions of continuing 19th-century institutions. Finally, Europe is still the center of the unpopular "new music," although all three of its greatest composers took refuge in America from the horror of Hitler. The new European styles, however, are like jazz to the extent that they make a sharper break with the past than any previous novelty in the history of music.

Viewed from the standpoint of jazz, the music of Debussy and all his contemporaries, including Lehár and popular music of the period in general, merges together. Studied as closely as we have studied them here, every one of these composers differs from every other as much as he differs from the leading composers of the previous generation—Wagner, Verdi, Brahms, Johann Strauss. Both kinds of difference are great. Yet all these differences pale in comparison with jazz, or with Schoenberg, Bartók, and Stravinsky. The older styles, merged together, all seem sweet, smooth, distant, and romantic. Despite their variety they all share prevailing qualities of languorous rhythm and rich sonority, as opposed to the typical rough sounds and movements of the new styles.

From the standpoint of jazz, the music of Schoenberg, Bartók, and Stravinsky may be baffling, but it is often attractive, somehow sympathetic. Its admirers share with admirers of jazz a rather aggressive attitude toward "nice," comfortable music.

The new styles also, to be sure, are both alike and different. The differences among them, when scrutinized with sympathy, prove to be more important than any similarity. The novelty of Schoenberg's harmony, for example, is more radical than any novelty of jazz. The great range of Bartók's interests hardly touches jazz, and makes all jazz seem small by comparison. With Stravinsky jazz has a more obvious relevance, but only in some of his works, and only some aspects of these. But the similarity, however superficial, is important in a broad historical perspective.

The contrast is remarkably sudden. Just before World War I all four new styles emerged, independently and simultaneously. 1911 is the year of Bartók's *Allegro barbaro,* Stravinsky's *Petrushka,* and the first appearance of New Orleans jazz in New York; Schoenberg's *Pierrot Lunaire* was composed and performed in 1912, and in this year blues were published for the first time. Such a sharp chronological line, cutting across geographical and social continuities, is rare in the history of music.

The great dividing line is more emphatic because premature death claimed three composers who might have absorbed some of the novel elements: Mahler (1911), Reger (1916), and Debussy (1918). Now what had been novel in their work, what indeed in some ways anticipated the future, was submerged in the contrast between their romantic distance and the anti-romantic immediacy of Stravinsky and jazz.

The contrast has often been described in metaphors well worn from political talk. Schoenberg, in 1908, wrote in a program note, "I may confess to having broken off the bonds of a bygone aesthetic." Bartók, looking back in 1920, began his discussion of "The Influence of Folk Music": "At the beginning of the 20th century there was a turning point in the history of modern music. The excesses of late romanticism began to be unbearable. There were some composers who felt that this road would lead to a shoreless abyss, and that there was no other way out but a complete break with the 19th century." Bartók never committed himself to a "complete break," but he indicated sympathy for the feeling that one was necessary.

Stravinsky's friend and collaborator, the Swiss poet Ramuz, connected the "revolt" of jazz with that of Stravinsky: "Jazz was a true revolt of certain needs of music. And what I love to distinguish in the music of Stravinsky was a revolt of the same nature though in a quite different form, that is, made in the name of music as a whole against a certain kind of music, in the name of the material of music (in the full sense) against what was only an impoverishment of it."

In their contexts here, these figures of speech—"complete break with the 19th century" and "revolt"—naturally express approval of the new styles.

Similar metaphors were used more often with a contrary purpose: to lump together the new kinds of music as reprehensible freaks or portents of anarchy. The Nazi government of Germany, clinging to Strauss and Lehár, condemned all four new styles as part of the threat of cultural Bolshevism. The Politburo of the U.S.S.R. condemned them all as part of the foredoomed bourgeois decadence. And of course the salesmen of the capitalistic democratic world, paying for music to attract the attention of masses of prospective customers or to provide a soothing background in restaurants and waiting rooms, rejected all the new styles, including authentic jazz, as esoteric and offensive.

To defend the new styles, their advocates in the 1920s shifted the emphasis from their novelty to their achievement, their essential order, and even their vital continuity with the past; but this did not diminish the novelty. Listeners unready for the novel adventure could not appreciate the achievement or the historical continuity. And even sympathetic listeners, ready to try, often found difficulty in assimilating the new styles.

From the time of their simultaneous emergence the new styles developed side by side, maintaining their independence from each other and from the still vigorous older styles. Various newer styles appeared, but none of these was so important—that is, both so new and so widely valued—as jazz, Schoenberg, Bartók, and Stravinsky. Thus no later date marked a period in the history of music comparable to the date of their emergence just before World War I.

Because the development of jazz styles coincided with the development of Schoenberg, Bartók, and Stravinsky, and also because the best pieces of jazz, like any first-rate product of a cultivated art, require and repay study for their own sake, our consideration of jazz lies near the center of the present book. Other reasons support these two. The fact that both Schoenberg and Stravinsky occasionally found in jazz an inspiration or a bit of raw material is a supporting reason; this fact by itself, however, would not oblige us to pay attention to the findings of specialists on jazz or to investigate many sub-classes of the field. The long list of other "serious" composers who exploited some type or aspect of jazz in some of their works will detain us even more briefly, although such a list is the chief pretext for a token paragraph or two about jazz in many books; what Ravel, Berg, Milhaud, Hindemith, Copland, Weill, Seiber, Burian, Schuman, Shapero, Schuller, Henze, and the rest have done with jazz does add to its interest for certain listeners, but what Armstrong, Ellington, and Parker have done with and within jazz is more interesting to many listeners, not merely more agreeable but more moving and more memorable. Finally, the inconspicuous influence of jazz in the works of composers who have absorbed it and forgotten it—Frank Martin, Michael Tippett, and Elliott Carter, for example—may strengthen our interest. But our main reasons for attempting to coordinate jazz with Schoenberg, Bartók, and Stravinsky are the independent value of jazz itself and the coincidence of the four new styles in history.

———•·•———

Jazz is a style created by obscure American musicians, predominantly Negro. There can be no single outstanding composer in this style, because, first, an essential part of it is the responsibility of performers to improvise, that is to compose as much as they can while playing in reference to a nucleus of traditional harmony that they call a piece of music, and because, moreover, they improvise in ensembles, not merely as soloists. Jazz musicians do not play each others' compositions faithfully, as concert performers in the European tradition have tried to do, with increasing success. (Solo improvisation was still important in the European tradition in the 19th century, but improvisation in ensembles was discontinued in the 18th.) Jazz improvisation rather resembles many Asian and African traditions, in which the spontaneous give-and-take between drummers and melody players is prominent. But the given framework of a jazz improvisation is unlike that of any non-European music: it is a framework of chord progressions, defining a structure of a few phrases, like the theme of a set of variations in the European tradition. And when two or more improvised melodies are combined in counterpoint—not merely two or more variants of a single melody—this too is unprecedented outside Europe. Jazz musicians recognize the individual authorship of their traditional themes. They recognize also individual styles of performance, copy them, and parody them. But in a jazz performance each performer-composer must try to improve on the style he has learned. To play through the framework in its simplest form, or through a melody in its written form, is not jazz; what jazz musicians write down is not precise enough to enable the most expert of them to reconstruct what another means unless he has first heard it performed. If they were to refine their notation, the intricate rhythms would be impossible to read, and the labor of decoding them would be even greater than the labor of writing them. Thus in spite of its fairly wide appeal and wider influence, jazz maintains its distinct existence among musicians in close personal contact with each other. This style is embodied in the work of a group of men competing and collaborating, without respect for written authority.

Because jazz lacks a supreme master and written masterpieces, the study of jazz differs from the study of concert music. The chief documents of its history are the performances on phonograph records, which were very rare before 1923, and nonexistent before 1917. How the style arose and what it was really like before many examples of it were recorded we can never know as surely and thoroughly as we might wish. Hence legends are rife, and opinions differ. Opinions and even legends based on personal recollections are invaluable, although of course they need to be critically compared with each other and with all other evidence.

A uniquely ample exposition of such opinions was recorded for the Archive of American Folksong at the Library of Congress in 1938 by the jazz pianist, composer, and conductor Ferdinand Morton (1885–1942). Selections from this recording, including both talk and music, were issued to the public, and a superb book was based on it, *Mr. Jelly Roll,* by Alan Lomax. (Morton's nickname was a favorite phallic symbol.) Morton claims that he invented jazz in New Orleans in 1902. This boast is denied by all other participants in the development. But Morton's detailed recollections of the music sound authentic in his performances, and even if his share in the invention of jazz was slight, his mastery of it was great, and his contribution to jazz history was the greatest that any individual has made. Moreover, according to Lomax's interpretation, formulated after extensive checking by interviews with many other participants, Morton was typical of the group of inventors. He personally represented a clashing and merging of two castes that provided the conditions necessary for the rise of jazz. Morton was a proud descendant of French-speaking Creoles, in close contact with the white masters and professional men of Southern society, with French opera and Spanish dance music. He worked as a musician with many darker, illiterate Negroes, who brought into the cities a crude but lively and distinctive heritage from the plantations, with remnants of their varied heritages from West Africa. While some other writers have dismissed Lomax's interpretation along with Jelly Roll's exaggerated claim, they have not refuted it by evidence or argument. The whole history of jazz is viewed by the anthropologist and ethnomusicologist Alan Merriam as a process of "acculturation." This tends to support Lomax's account of the origins, and Morton's representativeness.

Morton published a version of his *Jelly Roll Blues* in Chicago in 1915, when he was thirty years old. He had probably played something like this version since his precocious New Orleans heyday in 1905. Lomax was told by the pianist James P. Johnson (b. 1891), teacher of Duke Ellington, that he heard Morton play *Jelly Roll* in New York in 1911. Morton made phonograph records of it in 1924 and 1938, as well as a version for his band, "The Red Hot Peppers," in 1926. It is a representative piece, not the greatest of its kind, but perhaps distinguished as the first of its kind to be written down and published. Morton recollected his motives and difficulties in accomplishing this:

In all my band work, I always wrote out the arrangements in advance. When it was a New Orleans man, that wasn't so much trouble, because those boys knew a lot of my breaks; but in traveling from place to place I found other musicians had to be taught. So around 1912 I began to write down this peculiar form of mathematics and harmonics that was strange to all the world . . . *Jelly Roll Blues* became so popular with the people of Chicago that I decided to name it in honor of the Windy City. I was the only one at the time that could play this tune, *The Chicago Blues*. In fact, I had a hard time trying to find anyone who could take it down. I went to Henri Klickman . . . but he didn't know enough. So, finally, I wrote the score out myself. Dave Payton and several more said what I had put down was "wrong," but, when I said, "Correct me then," they couldn't do it. We argued for days and days, but they couldn't find no holes in my tune.

The title "Blues" refers to the pattern of three four-measure phrases with their essential root-progressions: I, IV I, V I. This pattern is the common framework of most of the traditional music called blues, though the same name serves also for unaccompanied rural folksongs with a three-line stanza, vaguely distinguished from spirituals and work-songs by their wry mood. According to a study of *The Country Blues* by Samuel Charters, the distinctive pattern arose only about 1910, though related songs were collected as early as 1867 by Lucy Garrison, and doubtless originated earlier in the 19th century.

The stanza pattern may be repeated, with variations, any number of times. Jelly Roll's blues, as printed in 1915, comprises a four-measure introduction, three variations, a four-measure interlude modulating to the subdominant as if for a trio, and two more variations. (Only the introduction and the first two variations are reproduced here.) In the 1938 performance each variation is repeated, and more follow, in most of which Morton sings. Thus not only the melodic detail of the piece but its form as a whole is variable.

EXAMPLE XI.1   Morton, *Jelly Roll Blues,* beginning

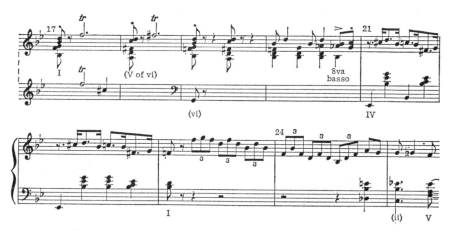

In this respect jazz resembles the variations on popular songs composed for keyboard at the end of the 16th century by Byrd, Bull, Sweelinck, and Frescobaldi, more than the cumulative variations of Beethoven and Brahms. A specific 16th-century pattern, the *passamezzo moderno,* has been proposed by Otto Gombosi as the ancestor of blues, but no continuous connection has been traced.

It is characteristic of blues that the main melody has short phrases, separated by pauses, long enough for an answering countermelody, as in the antiphonal and responsive choruses of tribal ceremony in Africa and elsewhere. The placing of the melodic phrases in relation to the beats and the chord-progressions is remarkably free, in contrast to any European pattern of melody and accompaniment. This freedom of phrasing, more than particular details of rhythm, is typical of good jazz improvisation.

Besides the pattern of phrases and roots, blues has its characteristic "blue notes." The C♯, appoggiatura to the D, in the first phrase, and the D♭, seventh of the subdominant harmony in the second phrase, imitate the glides and "dirty" intonations of the vocal style. For a singer, these would not be distinct notes as on the piano, but rather an expressive coloring—or discoloring—of the normal major third. The blue treatment is applied to the seventh of the scale in many blues, though not in the *Jelly Roll.* Similar treatment of the fourth is typical of spirituals. These elusive pitches are expressive, not accidental, as the singers prove by their solid true intonation of the tonic note and the diatonic fifth. The blue notes do not constitute a special scale or mode in the usual sense of those terms, because the pitches are variable over a range wider than some of the steps of the scale. Blue notes are expressive *because* they are elusive.

Further harmonic details characteristic of jazz are the placid-sounding added sixth in tonic chords and the mild chromatic passing, auxiliary, and "substitute" chords that decorate the simple pattern enough to make it obscure to a listener who is not already familiar with it or one whose attention wanders. In the 1938 performance Morton includes many more decorative notes than he wrote down in 1915, and he varies them slightly in repeating his stanzas. Some of these variants are indicated by the small notes in our composite version, which is still incomplete. But naturally all the harmonic variety of jazz is primitive in comparison with the harmony of Debussy or Strauss. The main interest of the music is not its harmony but its rhythm, tone-color, and counterpoint. Harmony is the indispensable nucleus of convention that makes possible the spontaneous and complex play of rhythm. Morton explained, in terms that Debussy would have approved:

About harmony, my theory is never to discard [or, discord?] the melody. Always have a melody going some kind of way against a background of perfect harmony with plenty of riffs—meaning figures. A riff is something that gives an orchestra a great background and is the main idea in playing jazz. . . . Now the riff is what we call a foundation, like something that you walk on. It's standard.

Jazz need not be limited to such "standard" chords and figures as Morton's but all good jazz adheres to his theory of the predominance of melody, supported by the foundation of figured chords.

The rhythmic notation of jazz, as we have noted and as its friends never tire of explaining, is an approximation. If the notes are played literally the music lacks the essential bounce or "swing" that we feel in an authentic performance. This is true to some degree, of course, of any music, even that of a composer as fastidious as Debussy. It is true to a high degree of the music of Bach and his contemporaries. Good 20th-century performers know better than did the best performers around 1900, though not yet so well as the best performers around 1730, how to interpret Bach's notation. With jazz still more than with Bach, the notation of rhythm is inadequate.

Nevertheless the notes show much. They show the beat, in quarter notes, emphasized (not invariably) by the "um-pah" accompaniment, which is played with a percussive staccato touch. In his performance Morton taps his foot to keep the beat sounding loud and sharp throughout. The beat holds the tempo steady, with absolutely no slackening for the end of a phrase or even of a variation. Actually the beat pushes the tempo just enough so that by the end of eight "choruses" it is measurably faster than it was at the beginning, although there is no more feeling of an accelerando than of a retard. Then, suddenly, in the performance, Morton shifts to a new, slower tempo, and the beat begins to push this in the same manner. The imperceptible push to the accompanying beat is characteristic of jazz. Either its omission or its exaggeration, which Morton deplored, can destroy the "swing." Also characteristic is the possibility of various tempos: a given tune does not have a set tempo, but rather its tempo is one of the many elements at the performer's discretion.

Along with the beat, the notes show the grouping of beats in duple meter, which is an invariable trait of jazz. The strong and weak beats are not differentiated by loudness, nor by a sense of weight. A conductor beats them all down. They may be distinguished by sonority, as here in the "um-pah" passages. With these and some other passages there is a tendency for strong beats to be staccato and weak beats somewhat sustained, but the opposite is possible too, as is uniform staccato.

The melodic motion that subdivides the beats rarely has an even flow. The normal subdivision appears in the notes as a dotted pattern of long and short. An exceptional passage of flowing triplets occurs at the end of the second phrase of the second chorus, and this is not part of an essential melodic phrase, but rather an ornamental flourish filling in a "break" in the accompanying harmony. Morton was especially fond of "breaks." The normal subdivision into long and short is hardly ever played by Morton, or by any authentic jazz musician, in the ratio 3:1, as it would be by conscientious performers of "classical" music since the late 18th century. Rather, depending on the tempo, the ratio may be 2:1 (fairly fast) or 3:2 or 5:2 or 4:1, like the dotted patterns of the Baroque period. In any case the ratio is likely to be not calculated but directly felt in relation to the beat as a whole, so that it increases the prominence of the beat and helps to maintain its equality of weight and its steady push on the tempo.

The normal subdivision of beats into long and short melodic notes is never maintained through a whole phrase. It gives way at least once, and in some phrases several times, to syncopation, that is, to an unexpected, off-beat accent, or the dropping out of an expected accent. Often, as in measures 20 and 24 of the *Jelly Roll Blues,* a syncopated note or chord comes sooner than expected, and lasts into the beat where it would normally have fallen. The "offbeat," "sooner-than-expected" notes are written as if they divided the beat into even halves. But they are played, as Winthrop Sargeant has pointed out, in accordance with the variable, uncalculated, unequal subdivision that has been established as normal. If they are all played literally, they sound stiff, out of the style. Far better omit the syncopation, as Morton does in mm. 4, 11, and 12. On the other hand, if an even subdivision is used rarely enough to be a surprise, as in m. 20, it fits the style.

The word "syncopation" is associated with jazz by many listeners ignorant of its meaning in any other context. They use the word to refer to the unequal subdivision of the beat into long and short notes, even if every beat is accented and every accent falls on a beat. In the usage of traditional music theory this is not syncopation: syncopation means only the unexpected accent and the absence of expected accent. Jazz involves this kind of syncopation too, as we have seen, but the naive use of the term points to the important fact that jazz combines syncopation with the unequal subdivisions of the beat. Syncopation alone, in the narrower sense of the word, is not enough to make jazz. The combination, obscured by the notation, is what makes the rhythm of jazz so elusive for performers who have not absorbed the tradition by ear. (The uneven subdivisions might possibly be regarded as syncopation, in the classical sense, against a theoretical, unheard, regular subdivision of the beat. But only in late developments of jazz, where very fast melodic motion is used in very slow tempo, are such theoretical sub-divisions imagined by the musicians.)

One more kind of syncopation is present in Morton's blues: the conflict between a temporary triple meter and the persistent duple, which is some-times called "cross rhythm," "polyrythm," or better "polymeter." This occurs unmistakably in measures 7–8, and possibly also in m. 20, with the differ-ence that here the triple meter is composed of beats only half the length of the persistent beat. The interpretation of m. 20 is debatable since only two notes, repeated only once, are not enough to define the triple meter for some listeners. In any case, polymeter is not so essential to jazz as the kind of syncopation described above.

Polymeter is the chief characteristic of the older style of piano music, ragtime. Ragtime, like jazz, as its historian Rudi Blesh has shown, was the product of Negro musicians, playing for Negro audiences, especially in cities along the Missouri, Mississippi, and Ohio Rivers, from about 1890 to 1915. It differed from jazz, as the critic Guy Waterman has shown, in its greater reliance on written notes and in its form-schemes, ABCD and ABACD. Morton explained: "Ragtime is a certain type of syncopation and only certain tunes can be played in that idea. But jazz is a style that can be applied to any type of tune. I started using the word in 1902 to show people the difference between jazz and ragtime." Both Blesh and Waterman recommend the revival of the music of the best representative of ragtime, Scott Joplin (1868–1917), but Waterman grants that "no ragtime composer crammed such towering musical logic into his work as did the purportedly uncomplicated Jelly Roll Morton."

Morton represents the fusion of ragtime, the rhythmic piano style, with blues, the improvisatory folksong style. Both are necessary parts of jazz. Improvisation permits the "cramming in" of more syncopation, and the free phrasing gives "logic" to an unprecedented amount of syncopation.

The rhythm of jazz fits a style of bodily movement—not only of dancing but of walking—characteristic of many American Negroes. The shift of weight from one leg to the other is obvious, decisive, heavy, like the beat of jazz. The weight rests securely on one leg and then on the other, rather than bouncing as in a march or gliding as in a waltz. Hardly ever do the two legs share the weight, as in marching or waltzing they often do and still more often appear to do. While one leg carries the weight, the other hangs loose, free to tap or shake before the next shift. Likewise the arms are loose, and the torso itself is flexible, as if sitting comfortably on the hips, rather than suspended from the chest as in the classic positions of ballet and military drill. The utter relaxation of many muscles corresponds to the freedom of melodic motion subdividing the beat. To the syncopations correspond all sorts of shrugs, flicks, and twists of the body that seem independent of the main shifts of weight. Anyone whose ideal of movement is exemplified in march and waltz is likely to see and hear the jazz movement as a shiftless slouching and shuffling or as sexually provocative and repulsive. On the other hand, anyone who finds the tense, straight torso of march and waltz an uncomfortable affectation is likely to welcome the jazz movement as simply natural and true. To alternate between the two is difficult. To compromise between them is to lose the sense of both, but this is what much popular music does, swinging just enough to titillate a decorous lady without insulting her, and syncopating just enough to send a teen-age group into ecstasy without straining the intelligence. Whether jazz expresses moods of cheerful vivacity or naked pain and hunger, whether it symbolizes compliance with mechanical routine or impulsive, anarchical protest, its characteristic gesture distinguishes it from other styles that may be used to express or symbolize the same moods and attitudes.

The fusion of blues and ragtime depended partly on a third influence, that of instrumental bands. These imitated both blues and ragtime, along with the music of the popular military and concert bands and every other kind of music that the bandsmen heard. Moreover, they made counterpoint a normal and conspicuous feature of jazz, if not an indispensable one for its best and most distinctive manifestations. This fusion of styles may have occurred first in the home-made "skiffle" bands, consisting of Harmonica, kazoo, tub (substitute for bass viol, or for a West African earthbow), and bones (percussion). Such bands were studied by Russell Roth in the 1950s, and recordings of them even found an audience, but their contribution to jazz was surely less than that of pianists, singers, and players of factory-made band instruments. Yet it is possible that jazz clarinet playing, for example, owes something to the kazoo. It is probable that jazz drumming owes much to the predominance and variety of drums, clappers, and other percussion instruments in amateur performance. And it is certain that jazz piano playing owes much to the loose counterpoint of bands. According to Morton, "no jazz piano player can really play good jazz unless they try to give an imitation of a band." Morton himself occasionally played trombone or drums instead of piano. In his performance at the piano he seems to have had these instruments especially in mind. The bass at m. 11 suggests a trombone taking the lead with its glides. The overlapping of melodies to make counterpoint is suggested in the final variations of Morton's recorded performance; this was too much for him to write out.

The sheer sound of a jazz band—its peculiar tone-color—is as important a feature of the style as syncopation or counterpoint, more important and more novel than blue harmony or polyrhythm. The instruments favored in the legendary period might include trumpet, cornet, trombone, tuba, clarinet, and occasionally flute and piccolo, all supported by the "rhythm section" of piano, mandolin, guitar, banjo, plucked bass viol, and various drums. The typical sound required a minimum group of trumpet, trombone, and clarinet, blowing over the foundation of banjo and drums. The absence of saxophones is noteworthy. Several of the most famous band leaders were trumpeters: the barber Buddy Bolden, the truckdriver Bunk Johnson, the butler Joe "King" Oliver, the Creole professional musician Freddie Keppard, and the still more respectable trouper with traveling minstrel-shows, W. C. Handy, who came to be known as "father of the blues." Growing up among them in New Orleans was Louis Armstrong (b. 1900), destined to personify jazz for all the world in its later, classic, "hot" phase. Armstrong's recollections of his childhood, though ineptly edited, provide a vivid picture of the rivalry of these trumpeters and their bands. *Shining Trumpets* is the apt title of Rudi Blesh's history, which emphasizes the contribution of the darkest, poorest men and their African heritage. Blesh's emphasis has been supported by Alfons Dauer with many transcriptions from recordings of African music and later New Orleans music. On the other hand, Barry Ulanov, Leonard Feather, and others have attacked the "New Orleans myth" with some evidence of parallel, independent developments in Negro communities along the Eastern seaboard, and H. O. Brunn has chronicled the activities of bands of white men in New Orleans as if the Negroes had had little to do with it. Lomax's account, subordinated to his biography of Morton, is the most credible. In any case, bands in general and trumpeters in particular extended the range of expression characteristic of the folksong blues and the piano ragtime, made counterpoint an important feature of the style, and developed the new tone-colors that carried the rhythm of jazz through the world.

More than anything in the tunes, more than any optional ragtime rhythm or blues harmony, and more, of course, than counterpoint, it was the new sound of the jazz bands that changed popular music most drastically.

Trumpets and clarinets began to displace the strings for playing dance music. As the fox-trot displaced the waltz in the ballrooms of the world, the brasses and reeds and battery of percussion came along to establish a new norm of sound. All through the 19th century trumpets and drums meant primarily marching. They were introduced to evoke a martial atmosphere in the midst of the dancing or singing or merely neutral strings of the orchestra. But in the 20th century trumpets and drums dance and sing, and they often provide a neutral background, while the strings are rejected, or used for special effects, and in general subordinated. The most remarkable novelties of jazz, in the perspective of the whole history of music, are its development of improvised counterpoint, for a few unknown friends, and its transformation of the norm of musical sound, for everyone.

———•—•———

Through the 19th century, from *Jump Jim Crow* (1830) through *Old Folks at Home* (1852) to the cakewalks of the 1890s, entertainers had imitated and popularized Negro songs and dances. But these were "specialty numbers" or "novelties" in the practice and trade of popular music as a whole, not affecting the norms of waltz and march and polka. Thus Debussy and Satie adopted ragtime alongside the older popular styles. But the influence of full-fledged jazz, especially the influence of its instrumental colors, very quickly came to pervade American popular music. Indeed, in the loose usage of many people, "jazz" means all sorts of American dance music from about 1911 on.

In 1911 a song by Irving Berlin (b. 1888), *Alexander's Ragtime Band,* spread a vague notion of the new style throughout the realm of American popular music. The main motif of this tune is an imitation of the blue third, detached from any melodic continuity. It lends itself readily to the ragtime rhythmic treatment. The tune itself is not jazz if Berlin's notes are played respectfully. But it is adaptable material for jazz, as are many of Berlin's later tunes and those of his successors on Broadway. In 1919 George Gershwin composed his first hit tune, *Swanee*. Like all his later music, it is faintly but noticeably tinged with syncopation.

In 1917 the name "jazz" became fixed to the new style. The "Original Dixieland Jazz Band," a group of young white men from New Orleans, led by Dominic James LaRocca (b. 1889), played for dancing in New York, and made the first phonograph records of jazz. Brunn's account of their adventure, based on many interviews and on the documents later deposited in the Archive of New Orleans Jazz at Tulane University, fails to substantiate LaRocca's claim to have been the greatest pioneer of the style, but contributes a desirable supplement to the accounts of the Negro heroes. Reconstructions by Don Fowler of the "ODJB" recorded performances prove that this band had a vital swing and admirable counterpoint, though less than Morton's "Red Hot Peppers" a few years later. By the time Morton's band and Oliver's were recorded, LaRocca had retired from music. He paid little attention to it until the popular revival and imitation of the Dixieland style in the late 1940s.

By 1920 there were jazz dance bands everywhere. The saxophone was added to the New Orleans instruments—often three saxophones to play full chords in close position. Their thick color dominated what Scott Fitzgerald meant by jazz, though their color was not absorbed into contrapuntal jazz until the 1930s. Paul Whiteman (b. 1890) augmented his hotel orchestra, without cutting out the strings, to produce the "symphonic jazz" that gave Gershwin a medium for his most ambitious ideas. Fitzgerald's good friend Edmund Wilson commented on Whiteman that in spite of the new elements "we should enjoy the music more if we were eating and talking while we listened to it." Whiteman's archives, at Williams College, await study.

The central tradition of jazz continued to develop mostly in Negro ghettos. Representatives and connoisseurs of the real jazz deplore the loose use of the term to include Berlin, Gershwin, and Whiteman, as they deplore these hybrid styles, despite the vitality they have shown. To them jazz is a distinct class of music, claiming attention like concert music, but differing from both concert music and utilitarian entertainment music in its inspired improvisation. But no style guarantees inspiration. The boldest Negro jazz players had little opportunity to pursue their ideas; to pursue the profession of music at all they had to compromise variously with commercial demands as much as the white men who exploited their inventions with greater commercial success. That a few of them were able to survive and persist in their adventure was amazing.

Nineteen hundred and seventeen marked the end of the glorious New Orleans period. Orders from the Navy closed the Storyville district, where prostitution had been permitted by the law since 1896. Now the clandestine houses that opened up in various parts of the city dispensed with lavish musical entertainment. Many of the jazz players who stayed in New Orleans put away their horns and devoted themselves to their regular menial jobs. Morton and others emigrated northward. Morton could never establish himself in a regular musical career. He earned more as a pool player than as musician, and this was only one of many dubious activities.

Chicago became the chief center for Morton and some of his collaborators in the 'twenties. Here a new group of young white men learned from the Negroes and helped to develop the central tradition until it could come to the surface again in the 'thirties and make a new, deeper impact on popular music.

In New York City there was some sort of jazz before 1920, but its nature is even harder to guess at than that of the New Orleans product, for New York chronicles are neglected in most surveys of the subject, and the special study by Charters and Kunstadt, as well as the memoirs of Tom Fletcher, and the conversations of James P. Johnson, recorded by Tom Davin, lack perspective. Among various events that arouse curiosity are a concert in 1910, described by Natalie Curtis Burlin, featuring a band of a hundred and twenty-five players, including several pianists and a big section of guitarists and banjoists, as well as a complement of bowed strings and winds; and a tour in 1919 by the "American Syncopated Orchestra" under the direction of Will Marion Cook (1869–1944), former pupil of Joachim and Dvořák, and later coach to Duke Ellington. In 1918 the Negro Lieut. James Reese Europe, of the machine-gun battalion of the 15th Regiment, U. S. A., was ordered to recruit a band. (He was already somewhat famous as accompanist of the dancers, Irene and Vernon Castle; Mrs. Castle McLaughlin later credited Europe with the invention of the foxtrot in 1913.) He told an interviewer that he got his reed players from Puerto Rico and the rest from all over the country; from New York he took only one man, his solo cornettist, because most of the New York musicians were too prosperous to be lured by the Army. Europe's band made a stir in Paris. Its rhythmic style eluded efforts by European bandsmen to imitate it. Europe and his men were not impressed by European music, except for something Russian, which reminded them somehow of their "Negro music."

Among Negroes in the smaller cities and the countryside of the South, a new church sprang up during the first decades of the century: the Church of God, or Holiness, or Sanctified Church. This denomination more than any other admitted instrumental ensembles and elaborate dancing as part of its ritual. Its contribution to the future of both folksong and jazz, according to John W. Work, was great. At the same time an increasing amount of secular entertainment for Negro audiences throughout the country was provided under the auspices of another new institution, the Theater Owner's Booking Agency, which sponsored along with its vaudeville teams the dynasty of blues singers, including "Ma" Rainey (1886–1939) and her protegée Bessie Smith (c. 1900–1937). In 1923 the classic blues of these singers, accompanied by young instrumentalists like Armstrong and Fletcher Henderson, began to circulate on phonograph records, segregated by the manufacturers as "race records" for Negro listeners. Reissued in the 1950s for unknown friends everywhere, these records proved to be the first durable achievements in the new style.

CHAPTER XII

Schoenberg to the Twelve-Tone Technique (1922)

T THE SAME moment that jazz emerged from New Orleans and elsewhere in America to transform the popular music of the world, the far more radically new music of Arnold Schoenberg (1874–1951) from Vienna, the foremost center of the European tradition, began to exercise a far more astonishing effect on the leaders of serious music. Only a few musicians performed any music by Schoenberg. Fewer still performed it often enough, or even heard it often enough, to lodge its melodies securely in their memories, or to recognize a wrong note played in a prominent position, much less in the middle of a chord. Almost none became acquainted with all his works, or even a representative sample. But most conscientious musicians studied one or another of his scores, listened to recordings when they became available, and read some of his words. Many more musicians and friends of music found whatever Schoenberg they heard, or heard of, an unforgettable, inescapable incitement to long thoughts about the radical new principles that he proposed and applied. Disagreeing about the meanings and values of these principles, everyone concerned had to agree that Schoenberg somehow contributed as much as any one man to the musical culture of the 20th century, and that his contribution was indispensable to a 20th-century picture of the whole history of European music. His eminence and his radical novelty were recognized by critics throughout the world before World War I. After World War II, just before Schoenberg died at the age of seventy-six, his name, more than ever, and more than any other, stood out, and stood for crucial issues. His work began to influence the habits of musical thought of millions of people who still could not quote a phrase or a single chord of his own music. To understand the issues and the amazing influence, it is desirable to explore the music and the character of the man; perhaps these are even more interesting for their own sake.

Schoenberg was not happy about his unique position in the world of music. He wrote the conductor Hans Rosbaud in 1947:

The understanding of my music still suffers from the fact that musicians regard me not as a normal, perfectly ordinary composer, who presents his more or less satisfactory, more or less novel themes and melodies in a not too inadequate musical language—but as a modern, dissonant, twelve-tone experimentalist. There is nothing I wish for more earnestly (if I wish for anything else at all) than to be regarded as a superior sort of Tchaikovsky—for goodness' sake, a little superior, but that is all. Or at the very most, that my melodies should be known and whistled.

No treatment of his ideas can do them justice while ignoring this earnest wish. Though no acceptance nor rejection nor evasion of his ideas is enough to make the wish come true, a respect for the wish is part of any fair exposition of the ideas.

Of all his mature compositions, *Pierrot Lunaire* (*Moonstruck Pierrot*, 1912), which first established his international fame, was for a long time the one most often performed, and by touring groups in the most widespread cities, though not to the largest audiences, since its medium was so unusual and so delicate: reciter, accompanied by an ensemble of five instrumentalists, playing eight different instruments. For some years *Pierrot* was the only example of Schoenberg's mature style available on phonograph records. By 1965 six different performances had been recorded, offering a valuable opportunity for comparison. The allure of the music was acknowledged by Ravel and Stravinsky and many other musicians. But still *Pierrot* was not known or understood in the way that the music of Ravel and Stravinsky was. Erwin Stein, pianist and pupil of Schoenberg, who prepared and conducted several performances of *Pierrot,* testified that the performers were unwilling to dispense with his conducting, and that when they tried to do so the vocalist always lost grip on the rhythm. Schoenberg himself, in a note for the first recording of *Pierrot,* wrote that his pupils Rudolf Kolisch and Eduard Steuermann, and his friend Erika Stiedry-Wagner, who had all performed the cycle many times, held two hundred rehearsals with the three new players to prepare the recording. The great singer Maggie Teyte studied *Pierrot* intensely, with the help of experts, and finally gave it up as incomprehensible. The conductor Alois Melichar reported that the first clarinetist in the Berlin Opera orchestra had played twenty rehearsals of *Pierrot* before anyone noticed that he was supposed to shift from a B♭ to an A clarinet from time to time. All this testimony encourages a skeptical view of most glib references to *Pierrot* and its significance.

On the other hand, the testimony of Louis Fleury, the flutist of Debussy's *Syrinx,* promises rich rewards to anyone who studies *Pierrot* thoroughly. Fleury played it under the direction of both Milhaud and Schoenberg, on tours, 1922–24. He and his colleagues found delight in overcoming the difficulties, none of which they could attribute to faulty calculation by the composer. Fleury also enjoyed observing the reactions of various audiences, and the ability of Schoenberg to command their respect, both by his music and by his presence. Fleury's description is vivid: "a small man, always in motion, with piercing and roving eyes and mobile lips. . . . He is no great conductor, no virtuoso of the baton, but his leading is exact and authentic." And finally, in the 1960s, Pierre Boulez, after conducting many performances of *Pierrot,* found it continually rewarding, theatrically effective, intellectually stimulating and altogether convincing, despite certain "insoluble problems" for the vocalist.

The cycle is a setting of twenty-one lyrics, three groups of seven each, all in rondel form, by the minor Belgian symbolist, Albert Giraud (1860–1929), in the unrhymed German translation by Otto Erich Hartleben (1860–1905). The poet's shocking, abrupt shifts between romantic and sordid imagery and his self-conscious references to the torment and ecstasy of poets may remind Americans of Dowson or Pound. There is no coherent narrative or argument, and no evident design in the sequence of the poems—only contrasts of mood, mostly united by references to the moon and the pantomime characters Pierrot, Columbine, and Cassander. If this poetry is to be set to music at all, it needs something radically novel. A setting of four of the poems by Abel Decaux, composed 1900–07, is described by André Schaeffner in 1950 as "atonal," though very little like Schoenberg's setting.

Schoenberg's setting is appropriately novel, and it matches both the contrasts and the unifying elements of the poems. It intensifies the contrasts by giving each piece its own tempo and by varying the instrumentation. Of the five players, one or more keeps silent in most of the songs. All join in for only four measures in Part I, two songs in Part II, and four in Part III. Moreover, each of these tutti passages is different, for three of the players alternate instruments: flute with piccolo (piccolo in chamber music!), clarinet with bass clarinet, and violin with viola, so that together with the cello and piano they make a fresh sonority for every piece. But these contrasts, and others, are less prominent than the uniformities of unresolved dissonance and contrapuntal texture, the prevailing use of staccato touch in the piano part, and above all the uniform novelty of the vocal melody, the recitation or *Sprechstimme* (speaking voice).

Except for a few scattered notes, the vocalist must not sing, must not sustain a steady pitch, not chant. She must not simply speak, either. Rather she must recreate the composer's speech-melody, observing his detailed indications of rhythm, dynamics, and gliding pitch-inflection, and adding no interpretation of the poetry on her own initiative. In a few places she is to whisper: the note-heads may be replaced by small circles, or left out altogether, or left in their normal shape with a cross on the stem of the note as elsewhere in this music, but the clearest indication of whispering is the additional instruction *tonlos*. According to Stein, Schoenberg did not intend to fix absolute pitches or even melodic intervals, but he did want the relations of pitches and intervals scrupulously observed. Thus if the last line of *The Sick Moon* goes too low for the reciter's voice, it might properly be performed as shown in Ex. XII.1 with the mark "X." The actual deviations of four of the recorded performances are indicated with the singers' names. All of them fail to preserve the relative sizes of intervals or the pitch-relation between non-successive intervals.

In *Prayer to Pierrot*, No. 9, by exception, a footnote calls for the reciter to "indicate" the pitches. The written rhythms, as well as the pitches, often make impossible any merely natural declamation. In many passages the notes are too long to permit a normal gliding on the vowels from one syllable to the next, and Schoenberg does not want the consonants anticipated. Especially noticeable are the long syllables that end sentences. They seem to call for a slow wail, unheard of in normal speech, but very apt for this poetry.

Sprechstimme is not peculiar to *Pierrot Lunaire,* but the way it works in *Pierrot* is peculiar to Schoenberg. He was the first composer to exploit the effect so extensively. The various precedents for it all differ somewhat. Free recitation with instrumental accompaniment, known as "melodrama," had

EXAMPLE XII.1   Schoenberg, *The Sick Moon,* from *Pierrot Lunaire*

bannt   mich,   wie fremde Melo - die._____
pierce   me,   like music from a - far._____

An un - still - ba - rem
Your un - quench - a - ble

Lie - bes - leid   stirbst   du   an Sehn - sucht,   tief er - stickt,   du
long - ings will   burst   forth   to kill you,   stran - gle you,   you

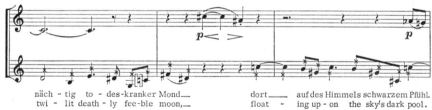

näch - tig to - des - kranker Mond___   dort___ auf des Himmels schwarzem Pfühl.
twi - lit death - ly fee - ble moon,___   float - ing up - on the sky's dark pool.

Den Lieb - sten, der im Sin - nen - rausch___
A lov - er   on his way in haste___

a long tradition, from Rousseau to Richard Strauss, but *Sprechstimme* is not so free. Singers have long used speech as a special device, bursting momentarily from the confines of the musical scale, while preserving the rhythm and direction of pitch indicated by the composer. Wilhelmine Schröder-Devrient, a favorite soprano of Beethoven and Wagner, was famous for her outbursts of speech at climactic moments. So was Chaliapin. Composers have invited the effect, particularly when they set "ha-ha" or "alas" to a descending scale or arpeggio, or a scream on a very high note. Moreover the whole tradition of recitative (in German, *Sprechgesang,* speech-song) invites intermittent vague glides. But Schoenberg does not reserve *Sprechstimme* for exceptional situations. Without leaving his reciter free, he makes gliding the norm throughout a composition. There are closer precedents: some young children, excellent mimics of speech-intonation but not yet masters of any musical scales or intervals, produce *Sprechstimme* in all their attempts to sing, without the inducement of any especially emotional text; instrumentalists and conductors often resort to the same device when they use their scratchy voices to indicate a rapid instrumental figuration; scanners of scores as complicated as Wagner's and Debussy's sometimes imagine, provisionally, a whole polyphonic texture, in tempo, with vivid tone-colors, but with quite indistinct pitches. All these ordinary practices are examples of *Sprechstimme,* closer to Schoenberg's usage than the exceptional exaggerations of recitative, or the dirty intonations of jazz. But Schoenberg's expressive exploitation of *Sprechstimme* makes a big difference. Another possible precedent is Humperdinck's children's opera, *Königskinder,* in its original version (1897). Most of the vocal parts here are to be performed in some manner between speech and song, but a manner that preserves or at least approximates the frequent unisons of voice and instrumental accompaniment, whether this is a lonely flute or full orchestra. Humperdinck substitutes x's for note-heads, as Schoenberg does in some of his later works. In 1910 Humperdinck revised *Königskinder,* abandoning his experiment in favor of normal song. He did not invent new melodies for the words he had already set, though he made some interesting improvements in detail. The revised form was more successful than the melodramatic form. Schoenberg, on the contrary, though often dissatisfied with a particular performance, never thought of abandoning *Sprechstimme.* And his instrumental parts give the speaker no help in locating the pitches.

Schoenberg first used *Sprechstimme* in a short section of his oratorio *Gurrelieder* (1900). He used it again in *Die glückliche Hand.* After *Pierrot* it became a normal feature of his style, applied to various kinds of texts. In his biggest work, the opera *Moses und Aron* (1930–32), the part of Moses, the true, tormented prophet, is in *Sprechstimme,* while that of Aaron, the seductive interpreter and compromising demagogue, is sung. This indicates a close relation between *Sprechstimme* and Schoenberg's other innovations, and indeed a close relation to his deepest purposes. Finally there are two compositions on English texts, the *Ode to Napoleon* (1942) and *A Survivor from Warsaw* (1947). In *Moses* and these last works the notation of the reciter's part dispenses with the staff, using instead a single line, as in a

Jelly Roll Morton (Culver Pictures)

Duke Ellington (Fred Plaut)

PLATE 7

Schoenberg, self-portrait, 1910 (The Bettmann Archive)

Anton Webern (The Bettmann Archive)

George Gershwin with his portrait of Schoenberg (D. G. Hackett from The Bettmann Archive)

PLATE 8

bass-drum part, but with the notes sometimes on the line, sometimes more or less above or below, and sometimes paradoxically qualified by accidentals.

More composers after Schoenberg than before him have written parts for recitation with their music, but not many have used *Sprechstimme,* and none have used it quite as he did. More commonly, the pitches are left entirely to the discretion of the performer. Schoenberg's pupil, Berg, refines on his teacher's notation to indicate many gradations between singing and speaking, and he calls on each performer to make use of the whole gamut. Another pupil, Webern, who wrote many songs and choruses, never used *Sprechstimme.* Its use as a norm is peculiar to Schoenberg himself.

In the instrumental parts of *Pierrot* and other mature works of Schoenberg, many passages resemble *Sprechstimme* in their elusive, wailing character. Some parts of the flute accompaniment in *The Sick Moon* exhibit this character: the flurries of sixteenth notes especially; the written intervals cannot be heard distinctly at such speed. Later in the cycle, as an epilogue to *Beheading,* No. 13, the clarinet presents a condensed version of the whole vocal line of *The Sick Moon,* subordinate to the flute's recapitulation of its melody; here the intervals can be heard, but they recall the speech melody in which they were not heard. In *Speck of Moonshine,* No. 18, the instruments and voice are in canon. In *Old Fragrance,* No. 21, the piano occasionally doubles the voice. Further, the instruments are often made to glide; in *Red Mass,* No. 6, the cello must glide from a plucked note, a novel effect that Bartók later exploited. Often the strings play at the bridge, or with the wood of the bow, mixing their written pitches with indeterminate expressive squeaks. To be sure, there are many other occasions when the instrumental pitches are distinct, but there are more instances of indistinctness than in any earlier music.

Not only the pitches of the *Sprechstimme,* but also Schoenberg's profuse notation of its dynamic nuances and articulation are hard to interpret. In *The Sick Moon,* measures 15–16, the flute is to begin *pppp,* and then become much softer. What can this mean? What does *f* mean on the low note at the end of m. 14, or *p* on the high note in m. 22? Is Stiedry-Wagner correct in letting the crescendo wedges of measures 6 and 8 supersede the written downward direction of the melody? Is the *ppp* for the voice in force from m. 15 all the way to m. 24, so that the *p* here means a little louder, or is a *mp* to be taken for granted in m. 19 or m. 22, so that m. 24 becomes softer? In m. 4 what is the sum of the slur, tenuto, staccato, and dynamic wedge modifying the flute's notes? In the preceding song, as mentioned above, the cello glides from plucked notes: what is the sense of the crescendo wedges that accompany these glides? In the vocal part of No. 7 again, m. 14, the slur and crescendo connecting two syllables are surprising, but they suggest an effective treatment of the part, until in mm. 24 and 25 the same combination of signs appears with short, unaccented syllables, to suggest what? In No. 3, m. 8, the same signs connect a whispered syllable with a spoken one! In No. 7, m. 16, the slur overriding the three consonants and the comma is another puzzle.

Some rhythmic problems are just as difficult, and perhaps more serious. In measure 14 of *The Sick Moon* how can the speaker fit the seven phonemes of the word *stirbst* into an eighth note's value? In the whole phrase beginning m. 12 how communicate to listeners the very apt expressive syncopation, when the flute's interlude has already quite obscured the metrical pulse needed to syncopate against? This problem of syncopation is urgent in No. 5, *Valse de Chopin,* and No. 19, *Serenade* in slow waltz tempo, with rubato as well as syncopation. In a few numbers Schoenberg uses the bar-lines for the mere convenience of the reader, with no significance to the rhythmic life of the music. This is a procedure he mentions in his *Harmonielehre.* But it surely does not apply to all his music, and particularly not to his waltzes. How can a performer decide where the bar-lines signify accents and where not? How can a listener grasp the rhythms without following the score?

Schoenberg's music is all full of difficulties like these. Too many students overlook them in their eagerness to find and evaluate the abstract rules governing Schoenberg's harmony, his use and disuse of scales and chords. Although it is his harmony that constitutes his great radical novelty, patient study of rhythm and dynamics, in relation to the words and their formal organization, is a prerequisite to appreciation of this concrete music. Moreover, this kind of study is possible for listeners untrained in harmony; perhaps they can appreciate the music more readily than those whose training has instilled too many irrelevant habits.

In his *Harmonielehre* (1911) Schoenberg noted: "Among laymen I have found people whose organs of apprehension were much more delicate than those of most professionals. And I know for sure that there are musicians who are more receptive to painting than many painters, and painters who are more receptive to music than most musicians." On the other hand, Schoenberg wrote to Marya Freund, when she had reported embarrassment before the audience at *Madonna, Red Mass,* and *Crosses,* in the course of reciting *Pierrot* (1922):

I never thought of such a possibility until now, and in all my life nothing has been more remote from my intentions, since never in my life was I anti-religious, or even unreligious. Apparently I have conceived these poems throughout much more naively than most people. I am still not quite uncertain [*sic*] whether this is so completely unjustified. In any case, I am not responsible for what people want to read into the text. If they were musical they would not bother about the text. They would whistle the melodies instead. But today's musical public under-stands the text at most, while it is absolutely deaf to music—no success in the world can persuade me otherwise.

To whistle the melodies, some grasp of their harmony is required. It is very hard to achieve.

The *Harmonielehre,* published a year before *Pierrot,* is a doctrine, a teaching, confined to matters of craft; it explicitly disclaims theory or system. The teaching of the craft, however, is continually intermingled with reminders of the richness and mystery of esthetic experience, and with speculations about creative and historical processes. For understanding Schoenberg these reminders and speculations, omitted from the published translation of the book, are its most valuable parts. A few of them make an especially valuable prelude to an exposition of his harmonic procedures.

We have progressed so far today as to make no more distinction between con-sonance and dissonance, or at most the distinction that we prefer to use con-sonances less, which is possibly only a reaction against the preceding epochs of consonance—perhaps an exaggeration. But to draw from this the conclusion that consonances are forbidden, because they no longer appear in the work of this or that composer, would lead to errors like our predecessors' rule against direct fifths. For my part I could calmly say to a pupil—but only because and as long as I know no better—that any chord and any progression is possible. Yet even today I feel that here too there are certain conditions determining whether I use this or that dissonance. We have too little perspective on the events of our own day to be able to recognize their laws. Too many non-essential things press into the fore-ground, obscuring the essential. If I stand in the midst of a mountain meadow, I see every stalk of grass. It is futile for me to search there for the path to the mountaintop. If I stand a little way off, the stalks of grass disappear and I prob-ably see the path instead. I suspect that the path, this very path, will somehow logically connect with the part already traversed. I believe that in the harmony we very modern composers use the same laws will ultimately be recognized as in the harmony of the old masters, only correspondingly extended, more generally con-ceived. Hence it seems to me of great importance to conserve the knowledge of the old masters. Precisely from that knowledge will be shown, I hope, the correct-ness of the path on which we are seeking our way. . . . Let the student then quietly proceed along the path taken by historical development. If he is studying harmony only from interest in works of art, if he wishes through it merely to gain better understanding of masterpieces, it does not matter whether he uses modern or unmodern exercises. . . . If he is a composer, let him wait patiently to go where his natural development impels him. Let him not wish to write things that one can take responsibility for only with the achievement of a mature per-sonality—things that artists have written almost in spite of themselves, obeying the compulsion of their development.

. . . I believe that a further development of harmonic doctrine is not to be expected at present. Modern music, using chords of six and more notes, seems to be at a stage corresponding to the first stage of polyphonic music. Accordingly a criterion for the juxtaposition of chords might be found through a procedure similar to that of figured bass, rather than an explanation of their function through methods of tracing them back to roots. For it appears, and probably will appear more and more clearly, that we are turning toward a new epoch of polyphonic style, and as in the earlier epochs the simultaneous sounds will be the result of voice-leading: justification only by melody. . . . In composing I decide only in accordance with feeling, with a feeling for form. This tells me what I must write; everything else is excluded. Every chord that I set down corresponds to an urge of my need for expression, and also perhaps to an urge of an ineluctable but unconscious logic in the harmonic construction. I am firmly convinced that logic exists even here, at least to the same degree as in the realms of harmony already constructed. I can adduce as proof of it my experience that corrections of an inspiration based on external, formal considerations, to which the alert consciousness is only too often inclined, have usually ruined the inspiration. That indicates to me that the inspiration was obligatory, that the harmonies that appear there are part of the inspiration, of which nothing must be changed. . . . For the progressions of such chords the chromatic scale can apparently be made responsible. The chord-progression seems to be ruled by a tendency to produce in the second chord tones that were lacking in the first, which are mostly those a half step higher or lower. But the voices seldom proceed by minor seconds. Then too I have noticed that doublings of a tone, octaves, seldom occur. This is perhaps to be explained by the fact that the doubled tone would acquire a preponderance over the others and thus would become a sort of root, which it hardly ought to be; but perhaps also from an instinctive disinclination (possibly exaggerated) to recall, even faintly, earlier familiar chords. The same explanation is suggested by the circumstances that the simple chords of earlier harmony do not readily appear in this environment. But I think this has another reason. I think they would have too cold, dry, inexpressive an effect.

With due allowance for all the qualifying thoughts so amply set forth, and with an expectation of returning to them, we may at last put in simpler terms the rules of harmony that can be abstracted from the music characteristic of the mature Schoenberg, including all but the last song of *Pierrot Lunaire*. (These rules will continue in force after the development of the twelve-tone technique.) These rules are few and purely negative, unlike his own tentative speculations in the *Harmonielehre*. They are more nearly what he had in mind in one of his "Aphorisms" of 1909: "My inclinations developed faster the moment I began to become clearly conscious of my disinclinations."

    1) Avoid octaves, whether as melodic leaps or as intervals between simultaneous notes.

2) Avoid major and minor triads and dominant seventh chords, either broken or sounding together without some other note.

3) When a melodic phrase exceeds an octave in range, avoid exposing equivalent pitches in both octaves. Rarely use phrases of smaller range.

4) Rarely use more than three notes in succession belonging to any one major scale. Never compose a whole phrase of notes from one major scale. After a series of notes from one major scale, avoid returning soon to the same scale.

That the rules as stated here apply to his music can be verified by anyone, no matter what his taste. These rules are inadequate, of course, to account alone for Schoenberg's choice of sounds. But so is his own talk about "obligatory inspiration," or any other account. The rules certainly do not pin down the "logic" that Schoenberg dimly felt. They do not even constitute a description of his harmony comparable to our descriptions of Debussy's harmony. They state, in neutral, technical terms, only some negative aspects of what anyone can hear. The logic of intuition transcends any technical rule. But technical command grows, as Schoenberg tells his students, by means of clear, limited rules, and furthermore, history can use these better than vague epithets as temporary substitutes for the highly desirable illuminating descriptions.

Most of our terms to describe harmony are liable to shift in meaning. Schoenberg was careful to define anew the terms "chromaticism," "dissonance," and "tonality"; his music impels us to question also "melody," "chord," "harmony," and "counterpoint." Finally it evokes a new term, "atonality." A new term with a precise or concrete denotation would be useful. But a new term for something both abstract and vague, quickly gathering emotive connotations, only complicates discourse. "Atonality" in most contexts is a complicating term. When it has a precise meaning, "atonality" means adherence to the four rules stated above. Its vaguer meanings depend on how we shift the meanings of "chromaticism," "dissonance," and "tonality."

Schoenberg emancipates the twelve notes of the chromatic scale from dependence on a diatonic norm. Each note is enharmonically ambiguous. Until now we have defined and felt chromatic notes and enharmonic ambiguities in relation to one or more diatonic scales. Even in the late works of Scriabin, where no diatonic scale appears, the ambiguous chords are related to two or three such scales, through their dominant character. When there is no such relation, "chromaticism" means something new. To say that *Tristan* or *Syrinx* or *Elektra* is very chromatic means that many notes deviate from the diatonic norms; to say that *Pierrot* is chromatic means that every note is as normal as every other. The difference is not a matter of degree, but a radical difference of meaning. To say that *Pierrot* is "more chromatic" than *Tristan* makes no sense, because the two kinds of chromaticism are not connected by more and less. Schoenberg proposed in the *Harmonielehre,* in a chapter added just before publication, the notion that the two kinds were connected historically: as Bach reduced the 12 x 7 possible diatonic modes to 12 x 2 major and minor modes, and as Wagner reduced these to 12 chromatic modes, so Schoenberg was reducing these to a single chromatic scale. In a special sense, then, his music is less chromatic than Wagner's. He no longer needs double sharps and double flats. His choice between single sharps and flats is more arbitrary than that of most composers. The interval comprising six degrees of the chromatic scale divides the octave evenly in two; it is no longer either augmented fourth or diminished fifth; it is not a balance of the two, but an independent thing. Looking at *The Sick Moon,* we see many augmented and diminished intervals. Listening we hear something new. We cannot guess which enharmonically equivalent spelling Schoenberg has used to write what he imagined, and we judge that his choice of spelling is irrelevant to the imagined sounds and their coherence. The best technical description of what we hear is simply the negative formula: avoidance of diatonic scales, octaves, and familiar chords. A more sympathetic description is "emancipated chromaticism."

Likewise Schoenberg emancipates dissonance from any reference to consonance. Up to now we have usually felt the effect of dissonance as an expectation of resolution in unison or a triad. In Debussy some exceptional dissonances are stable because of the melody they accompany. Even in late Scriabin, the continual sevenths and tritones point to possible triads. In *Pierrot,* on the other hand, we can no longer identify a non-chord tone. We can seldom distinguish between a progression from one chord to another and a movement of parts from one position to another within a single chord. Our expectation is only the vague one of something new. The *Harmonielehre* proclaims the "emancipation of dissonance," and suggests that the historic process of adding chords to the vocabulary has reached an end.

The emancipations of chromaticism and dissonance—or in other words the abnegations of diatonic and consonant norms—constitute Schoenberg's radical novelty.

———•—•———

He believed that his emancipations fulfilled historic tendencies. The increasing use of chromaticism and dissonance by Wagner and others led inevitably, he felt, to the goal of total emancipation. On the other hand, many able musicians and critics of his own time and later argue that

Schoenberg's abnegations are mistakes, if not crimes or signs of madness. The two opposite views do not exhaust the possibilities. Another view attributes continuity and value to Schoenberg's development, but denies the claim that it alone represents the main stream of music history. The abnegations may be one natural outcome of 19th-century tendencies without being the only one or the best one. Schoenberg's style may complement other styles in a long-range development toward something not yet imaginable. This view is implicit in the organization of our own survey. It is probable that Schoenberg himself would have preferred it for, as we have seen, he described his procedures only in complicated, carefully qualified terms, and cautioned students that his avoidances were perhaps exaggerations.

Schoenberg, like Ives, subordinated style to substance, and deprecated the importance of style. In his essay on "Style and Idea" (1933) he wrote:

Style is the quality of a work and is based on natural conditions, expressing him who produced it. . . . But he will never start from a preconceived image of a style; he will be ceaselessly occupied with doing justice to the idea. He is sure that, everything done which the idea demands, the external appearance will be adequate.

Accordingly, when his idea demanded something other than the emancipated style, he wrote such works as the Suite in G for string orchestra (1934), the Variations for Band (1943), and the "folksong" settings (1928–29, 1948). He included in the volume of essays on *Style and Idea* one called "On revient toujours" ("One always comes back"), defending such works:

A longing to return to the older style was always vigorous in me; and from time to time I had to yield to that urge. This is how and why I sometimes write tonal music. To me stylistic differences of this nature are not of a special importance. I do not know which of my compositions are better; I like them all, because I liked them when I wrote them.

Krenek and Leibowitz and other defenders of Schoenberg are not so tolerant. And too many opponents of his doctrine fail to credit him with this tolerance, or to listen to his music, regardless of doctrine, with tolerance and sympathy like his.

The final song of *Pierrot Lunaire* represents at least a glance backward to the old style, if not a real return. Its text calls forth the idea:

O old aroma of fabled times, again you charm my senses!
. . . A lucky wishing makes me happy for joys I have long despised. . . .

The first phrase of the song, unusually conjunct and limited in range, ends with a sustained E-major triad. The end of the piece is a low E octave. There are other references to the E-major scale. There are still deviations impossible to account for by the rules of common practice or by Debussy's vague principles, but the rules of the atonal style are equally useless here. It is a remarkable conclusion, noted with appreciation by Stuckenschmidt, Schoenberg's most judicious biographer, and ignored by many who profess devotion to the work.

For a revised edition of his *Harmonielehre* (1922), Schoenberg wrote a footnote, taking account of the label "atonal," which seemed to him absurd. He proposed a better label, if any label were needed—"pantonal," but he insisted that no label could substitute for a study of the facts.

In spite of Schoenberg's protest, and in spite of Berg's answer to the question "What is atonal?" (1930): "There is no more diabolical appellation than that word 'atonal,'" the word stuck as a label for Schoenberg's mature style.

The *Harmonielehre* treats tonality in connection with modulation; tonality is not an inalienable feature of tonal relations, but it is a prerequisite for modulation and thus the basis of all traditional forms except opera. Modulations, threatening the existence of tonality, only strengthen it in the long run if it persists. Tonality may be temporarily suspended (*schwebend*) between two or more centers. There are no limits to the power of extended (*erweitert*) tonality, though it is more easily threatened in regions remote from the central tone than in regions closely related by the circle of fifths. The most complicated chords and progressions may be used within a tonal cadence. But opera shows that another possibility is possible: waived (*aufgehoben*) tonality. Whether to waive tonality or to maintain it depends on the inspiration and choice of the composer.

If tonality enters the scene like an autocrat, with *a priori* faith in her firmness, then she will conquer. But she may be skeptical, may have recognized that everything described as the welfare of her subjects is only her own welfare, may have recognized how her rule is not quite necessary for the prosperity and growth of the whole. That she is admissible, but not indispensable. That her autocracy may indeed be a uniting bond, but that the dropping of this bond would favor the independent functioning of other bonds; that if the laws emanating from her, the laws of the autocrat, were waived, her former domain would not have to fall into indiscipline, but rather, automatically, following its own impulse, would give itself the laws that correspond to its nature; that not anarchy would ensue, but a new form of order. But she may add that this new order would soon look like the old, until it came to be just like it again. For this order is as ordained by God as the change that always leads back to it.

No later statement on tonality by Schoenberg modified this stand. In *Structural Functions of Harmony* (1946) a shorter statement echoed and epitomized the longer one: "My school, including such men as Alban Berg, Anton Webern, and others, does not aim at the establishment of a tonality, yet does not exclude it entirely. The procedure is based upon my theory of 'the emancipation of the dissonance.' " Whether tonality is established, extended, suspended, or waived in *The Sick Moon* may be left in doubt. What is important is that harmony here does not function in the service of the structure, to distinguish an exposition from a transition, or even a cadence from any other point. The structure is so short that the lack of harmonic function is not fatal. The words and their mere grammar give some shape to the little piece. Schoenberg recognized, explicitly in an essay of 1925, "Opinion or Knowledge," and again in the essay on "Composition with Twelve Tones," that his atonal style caused him to rely on brevity, extreme expressiveness, and words to insure his forms, deprived of any conscious control of the harmony. To compose long instrumental works he had to wait for the development of the twelve-tone technique, "which seemed fitted to replace those structural differentiations provided formerly by tonal harmonies."

Pierrot Lunaire exhibits some other devices contributing to form. *Night,* No. 8, for example, is subtitled "passacaglia." Its unifying ground can be heard in every measure; it consists of just three notes: E G Eb. But this is no typical passacaglia. Not only is the ground so unusually short, but also it is developed, beginning in measure 1, as Roland Tenschert points out, by transposition, inversion, and double diminution, so that it gives the piece not so much a form as an unprecedented motivic unity. Motivic development and contrapuntal treatment of motifs were favorite devices of Schoenberg no matter what his style. The "dropping of the bond of tonality" favored the independent functioning of this other bond.

Parody, No. 17, as already mentioned, is built of canons. With the piano accompanying, the viola leads off. Clarinet answers in inversion, two quick beats behind. In two more beats the voice answers the viola at the unison (or approximately so, depending on the reciter). After ten measures the piccolo interrupts. Then the voice takes the lead, with viola and clarinet following. In the third phrase, measures 16–21, the voice is answered by piccolo, while viola leads clarinet in an independent canon. In the fourth phrase, mm. 22–26, the voice is answered by clarinet, and viola by flute. Overlapping the voice's penultimate line, viola and clarinet begin their final phrase, and piano, followed by piccolo, prepare the voice's last line. These facts of imitation, once pointed out, or dug out by study of the score, can all be heard, and the balanced shape they present can be remembered and appreciated. What is harder to hear, if at all possible or desirable, is the harmonic relation of all these voices. It seems to be a case of "justification only by melody." And if the harmony is negligible, then the canons do not make polyphony in the traditional sense of this word, but rather a loosely woven texture that needs a new name. Brahms, Strauss, Mahler, and Reger could hardly have recognized this texture as related to their various kinds of counterpoint, although their examples doubtless encouraged Schoenberg to surpass them and "fulfill a tendency" in this respect just as he emancipated chromaticism and dissonance.

Still more complex are the canons of *Speck of Moonshine,* No. 18, which are repeated in retrograde motion, beginning in the middle of measure 10. Stuckenschmidt suggests that Schoenberg meant to represent Pierrot looking at his own back. But the retrograde motion can be appreciated only by a score-reader, unless listeners are affected subliminally by relations that they cannot perceive even with effort.

The complex, "contrapuntal" texture of Nos. 8, 17, and 18 is not typical of the whole cycle, but rather an extreme. *The Sick Moon* makes an obvious contrast. So does *A Pale Laundress,* No. 4, where the flute, clarinet, and muted violin play mostly in rhythmic unison, with continual crossing of ranges, always *ppp,* while the voice is to sound like accompaniment to them. Most of the songs stand between these contrasting extremes. In several passages Schoenberg marks the *Hauptstimme* (principal voice) or *I. Nebenstimme* (first subordinate voice) with distinctive signs ⌐ ⌐ directing that they are to be brought out, *espressivo,* while the other parts retire to form an accompanying background. In his later scores, beginning with Op. 22, Schoenberg refined this notation, using the signs ⊢⌐ and ⊣⌐ . Several friendly critics, including Krenek and Perle, sense a conflict between this texture of accompanied melodies and the free-and-equal treatment of dissonance and chromaticism. A texture in which every voice is equally important seems more appropriate to the atonal style. But Schoenberg and Berg felt no such conflict. They continued throughout their lives to compose melodies with accompaniments, and even in their most contrapuntal textures to mark one voice as *Hauptstimme.* Schoenberg's accompaniments, on the other hand, are richly varied, governed by no simple formula. He uses drones and regular ostinato figures less often than Debussy or Mahler, and very seldom for more than a single phrase. He varies the thickness of his texture, often sounding five or six notes together, and as often more as less, but rarely maintaining the same number through a whole phrase. Likewise two or three voices may move parallel, especially in fourth chords, but not often, and not for a whole phrase, as in Debussy and Satie. This continual varying of the texture is as characteristic as the complexity of texture in extreme movements.

Complexity and variety of texture, together with complexity and variety of rhythm and dynamics, outweigh Schoenberg's radical harmonic procedures in any consideration of his style as a whole. He seldom repeats a phrase without some variation. Even in a sequence he varies the motifs. Phrases are mostly unequal in length. They overlap each other or succeed each other with few pauses. Although the rondel form of the poems of *Pierrot* invites exact repetitions, recapitulations, and other symmetries, Schoenberg spurns any easy solution of his formal problem: every song is "through-composed," and every one in a different way. For listeners this means constant tension. It seems as if thoughts and feelings that the composer had experienced over long stretches of time were compressed to the utmost, to be experienced by the listener only after many rehearings. Alban Berg insists that this compression of rich variety is the only valid answer to the question "Why is Schoenberg's music so hard to understand?" Schoenberg himself concurred with Berg in a letter to James Fassett (1950).

Nearly all of Schoenberg's music, whether tonal or atonal, is hard to understand. *The Sick Moon* is not so hard as most of the early works, or the late works that mark a return to tonal harmony. The compression of complex variety, in texture and rhythm, bristles from beginning to end of his career.

———————

In Schoenberg's total output, the variety of forms and media is great. The preponderance of vocal music is striking. And within the class of instrumental ensembles, the preponderance of chamber music. This combination of interests—in chamber music and in vocal, even dramatic music—distinguishes Schoenberg from most composers since Mozart. Among his contemporaries only Fauré shares the combination of interests, and Fauré's output differs by including a steady stream of piano pieces, whereas Schoenberg's rather few piano pieces can be regarded as preliminary sketches for the music for voices and instruments together.

Schoenberg's unusual combination of interests appears at once in the one piece that is played more often than *Pierrot*, the early landmark, *Verklärte Nacht (Transfigured Night,* Op. 4, 1899), for it is a Straussian symphonic poem, closely following a text by Richard Dehmel, yet it is chamber music, a sextet for strings, full of contrapuntal delicacies and ingenuities. When arranged for string orchestra and used to accompany the ballet *Pillar of Fire,* this music convinced large audiences that Schoenberg was no fool or fraud. But to sense any coherence in the long form, listeners need to study the relation between musical themes and dramatic episodes, as specified in the program note that Schoenberg supplied for the recording of the original version. To grasp the admirable relations *among* themes and the resulting total form requires exhaustive study.

Poetry and chamber music combine again in a finer piece, the Second String Quartet (1907), where a soprano voice joins the instruments for the last two movements, as if it were a symphony by Mahler. And of course the combination is characteristic of *Pierrot*.

Schoenberg made many unusual combinations of thought and feeling. He never neglected either of them, though critics accused him alternately of neglecting each. He was neither a merely impulsive expressionist, nor a merely cerebral calculator. "Heart and brain" were equally important.

But the relation between heart and brain he never explained. And some listeners feel in his music that the relation is somehow queer. His biographer, Stuckenschmidt, emphasizes the contrast and combination, but leaves it unresolved: "The real problem of Schoenberg's music lies in its remarkable inner dualism. The most refined feeling for gradations of sound values is most strangely yoked with abstract braininess." If the intellectual interest of his work does not ultimately serve its expressive purpose, then no matter how strong the expressiveness may be, the intellectual side is pedantic. A satisfying harmony of thought and feeling, both so intense as they are in Schoenberg, must be a rare achievement.

Thought and feeling, strangely yoked, show up also in Schoenberg's paintings, which he exhibited in Vienna in 1910. His friend, the pioneer of non-objective painting, Wassily Kandinsky, contributed a wise comment on these paintings to the symposium published in honor of Schoenberg at this time (1912):

Schoenberg's pictures fall into two categories: on the one hand the portraits and landscapes painted directly from nature: on the other, heads imagined intuitively, which he calls "visions." The former Schoenberg himself designates as finger exercises, which he feels he needs, but which he does not particularly value, and which he does not like to exhibit. The others he paints (just as rarely as the first sort) to express emotions that find no musical form. These two categories are externally different. Internally they stem from one and the same soul, caused to vibrate in the one case by external Nature, and in the other by the nature within. . . . Schoenberg reproaches himself for "lack of technique." I should like to modify this reproach in accordance with the criterion given above: Schoenberg is mistaken—he is dissatisfied not with his painting technique, but with his inner wish, with his soul, demanding more of it than it can give today. This dissatisfaction I wish to every artist, at all times.

Kandinsky's technical and spiritual achievement, similar in many ways to the work of Schoenberg, proved when disseminated through the world to be harmonious. Schoenberg's thought and feeling continued to work separately, strangely yoked, for a later generation.

Schoenberg's father was a shopkeeper in Vienna. The family was never so prosperous as Freud's or Kafka's, but it occupied the same status in relation to the Austrian nobility, peasantry, and proletariat. Both mother and father loved poetry, painting, and especially music. They played and sang at home, and attended the opera as if it were the rite of a true, living religion. A younger brother became a professional singer. So did a cousin, Hans Nachod, whose few published memoirs offer precious glimpses of Schoenberg's youth. According to Schoenberg's own account of "My Evolution," he began at the age of eight to study the violin and to compose violin duets. Soon he branched out to viola and cello, teaching himself to play the classical repertory of chamber music and to compose Brahmsian pieces for his friends. He never became much of a pianist or singer. But he composed many songs, and dreamed of operas. He recalled, in a letter quoted by T. W. Adorno, that an early reading of a life of Mozart "stimulated me to write my compositions without resort to an instrument."

His father died when Arnold was fifteen. So there was no money to send him to university or conservatory. He went to work in a bank, and continued to educate himself, never deviating from the aim of becoming a composer. In 1894 he became a free pupil, and soon a close friend, of Alexander Zemlinsky (1872–1942). Zemlinsky, just graduated from the Vienna Conservatory, was embarking on his successful career as a conductor. Schoenberg wrote the libretto for Zemlinsky's opera, *Sarema* (1897), and made the piano reduction of the score.

Under Zemlinsky's guidance, Schoenberg imbibed the influence of Wagner. He heard each of Wagner's operas twenty or thirty times. His songs began to resemble Wolf and Strauss more than Brahms. Yet he never lost his love and respect for Brahms. He regarded his own mature music as a reconciliation of the styles of Brahms and Wagner.

In 1901 Schoenberg married Zemlinsky's sister, Mathilde, and moved to Berlin to work regularly as arranger and conductor of popular music, even composing several songs for the *Überbrettl* (super-cabaret). He met Strauss, who liked a sample page or two of Schoenberg's *Gurrelieder,* and proposed that Maeterlinck's *Pelléas* would make a good libretto for a Schoenberg opera. In 1903 Schoenberg returned to Vienna, to live with Zemlinsky and support himself by teaching harmony and composition privately: Wellesz, Webern, Stein, and Berg soon formed the nucleus of a group of devoted disciples.

Not yet acquainted with Debussy, Schoenberg used *Pelléas* as program for a vast symphonic poem, his Op. 5 (1903). The music is no mere matter of characters or atmosphere, like the incidental music of Fauré or Sibelius, but a musical narration of the whole drama; recognition of the references is prerequisite to understanding the episodes inserted among the sections of the vast sonata form. Berg's analytical guide, though quite uncritical, is a great help. But even with this help, the form may be a little incoherent. In a long letter protesting Zemlinsky's proposal to perform *Pelleas und Melisande* with a few cuts (1918), Schoenberg conceded:

You are right when you find the value of this work not in perfection of form . . .
If I had written more, I should not mind much if this work did not exist at all.
I cannot find it at all bad, though; I even find a lot of very good stuff in it, and
above all it has many a trait that points to my later development, almost more of
these than my first quartet.

The orchestration is full of virtuoso effects. In the eerie grotto episode,
trombones, *ppp,* slide through all positions. (New Orleans trombonists
would never recognize the sound.) The harmony has many remarkable
details, such as the opening sequence, in which the *Tristan* chord is a mild
resolution for sharper dissonances, or the unresolved raised fourth against
the tonic minor triad in the motif of the climax and conclusion. Six-voiced
whole-tone chords appear, though not suggesting the whole-tone scale. And
fourth chords occur, smoothly resolving to triads. Both these devices—the
whole-tone chords and the fourth chords—are cited in the *Harmonielehre*
as examples of the ambiguous, "roving" chords that threaten tonality, and
their treatment in *Pelleas* is used as evidence of the possibility that tonality
can be extended to include them. These details of conspicuous harmonic
novelty are not obstacles to understanding, or to the coherence of the form.
Indeed, they are interesting, not only as anticipations of Schoenberg's future
style, but also as some of the best, most expressive parts of this work. The
difficult passages are rather those displaying two or three contrasting motifs,
each rich in harmonic motion, each imitated in several contrapuntal voices,
and all accompanied by subordinate voices to provide resolutions of the
dissonances that the motifs leave hanging. Such passages are too turgid for
human perception, much less understanding or enjoyment. A further
difficulty of the work is the fact that the most memorable, beautiful melody
is the one intended to fit the jealous husband, Golaud, rather than the lovers.
Schoenberg's sympathy for Golaud seems to have spoiled his interpretation
of the drama as a whole.

"The climax of my first period," Schoenberg called his Chamber Symphony, Op. 9 (1906). It resembles *Pelleas und Melisande* in several ways;
the differences are a matter of degree. A symphonic scherzo and adagio are
inserted into the big sonata form more smoothly than the various episodes
of the drama, if still not so convincingly as the scenes of Strauss's *Domestic
Symphony* (1903). A fourth chord, arpeggiated by the horn, provides a
main theme; as a six-voiced chord it is sustained and insisted upon, though
finally resolving to a triad. Another main theme is composed largely of the
whole-tone scale, with augmented triads and altered seventh chords. The
central tonality, E major, is stretched to the utmost by these "roving" harmonies, but it is established all the more vehemently at the cadences. Not
harmony, but the dense counterpoint of themes and motifs is again the
main difficulty, for performers and listeners. Especially in the allegro sections,
the whole thick texture is made up of motifs; no subordinate voices resolve

the dissonances, and the resolutions provided by the motivic voices, leaping across each other in ranges of two octaves or more, can be appreciated only if the tempo is slowed down to a point where the melodies lose their passionate expression. At the proper tempo the players cannot hear enough to make the subtle adjustments of intonation that the harmony demands: an electronic performance might allow a few listeners to hear what Schoenberg presumably imagined. Schoenberg wrote to the conductor Pierre Ferroud (1922) asking him to rehearse each player of the Chamber Symphony individually. He insisted to another conductor, Paul von Klenau, that the piece "must be played precisely, since every note can be heard."

The instrumentation of the Chamber Symphony is unprecedented. It is not merely a reduced orchestra, but an ensemble of fifteen soloists, eight of them representing the Straussian woodwind choir, from piccolo and E♭ clarinet to contrabassoon; the two horns play enough to make up for the absent trumpets and trombones; and the string quintet, never suggesting an orchestral string section, shows off its most piercing high range, its harmonics and *col legno* effects, and its most percussive pizzicato. The average dynamic level is loud, and there are octave doublings of one or more melodies in many passages. Looking back from *Pierrot Lunaire,* these doublings seem more incongruous with the harmonic style than does the emphatic tonality. In comparison with *Pelleas,* the Chamber Symphony is distinguished more by its shrillness of sound than by its advanced harmony.

In 1907 Schoenberg became acquainted with the music of Debussy, as the present writer has shown in a special study (1962). Strauss conducted *The Afternoon of a Faun* in Vienna and Debussy's *Pelléas* was produced in Frankfurt the same year, in Munich and Berlin the following year. Schoenberg, in the *Harmonielehre,* says that he knew nothing of Debussy when he composed the Chamber Symphony, and that he came to know something about three or four years after composing his own *Pelleas.* His attitude is ambivalent. He notes Debussy's use of the whole-tone scale "as an impressionistic means of expression, almost as a tone-color," and his similar use of fourth chords:

In this sense every truly great artist is impressionist: the most delicate reaction to the slightest stimuli reveals to him the unheard-of, the new.

This is shown especially vividly with Debussy. His impressionism makes use of fourth chords with such great power that they seem inseparably connected with the new thing he has to say, and may fairly be claimed as his intellectual property, although it can be shown that similar things were written before and at the same time as his. Perhaps a contributing factor is that they express nature moods, for in any case it sounds as though Nature spoke thus. And clearly all other speech retires to make way for the speech of Nature . . . I was right when I instinctively guarded against the "back to Nature" movement, and when I marveled that a Debussy hoped to find Nature behind the pathways of art, on the parts of the path already traversed—in that hinterland of art, the meeting place of stragglers—that a Debussy did not feel that whoever wants to go toward Nature must go not backward but *forward*; on to Nature! If I had a motto, perhaps it could be this. But I believe there is something still loftier than Nature.

Schoenberg was impressed by Debussy's impressionism. He reacted against it by ceasing to use the whole-tone scale in any obvious manner. Further he was impelled partly by Debussy's example to push on to freedom from all rules and habits and at the same time to economize within a single piece—to choose among the possibilities and stick to a choice. But there is no indication that Schoenberg ever studied Debussy closely. There is some indication, in the essay on "Composition with Twelve Tones," that Schoenberg misunderstood Debussy's achievement:

Richard Wagner's harmony had promoted a change in the logic and constructive power of harmony. One of its consequences was the so-called *impressionistic* use of harmonies, especially practised by Debussy. His harmonies, without constructive meaning, often served the coloristic purpose of expressing moods and pictures. Moods and pictures, though extramusical, thus became constructive elements, incorporated in the musical functions; they produced a sort of emotional comprehensibility. In this way, tonality was already dethroned in practice, if not in theory.

If this too simple notion of Debussy's style was Schoenberg's belief in 1907, then he must have taken courage from it to proceed to his own atonal style. But in an article on "National Music" (1931) Schoenberg explicitly denied that any music outside the German tradition had influenced him; by now he was so sure of his own style that he deprecated Debussy's achievement:

While Debussy succeeded in stirring up the Latin and Slavic nations to fight against Wagner, he failed to free himself from Wagner. His most interesting discoveries are applicable only within the form and method of forming created by Wagner. In this connection it is undeniable that much of his harmony was also found in Germany independently of him. No wonder, for it consisted only of logical consequences of Wagnerian harmony, further steps along the path shown by the latter. . . . In my music, which arose on German soil uninfluenced from abroad, there is an art that most effectively opposes the Latin and Slavic struggle for hegemony. . . .

It should be needless to say that these reflections are irrelevant to an appreciation of Debussy. They are indications only of the challenge that Debussy's work posed for Schoenberg.

At about the same time that he discovered Debussy, Schoenberg discovered also Stefan George, a greater poet than several that Schoenberg found congenial. George was the most esoteric and controversial German poet of his time, transmitter of Mallarmé's symbolism, and prophet of a humanistic religion, which he announced as a veritable cult in his book of poems *The Seventh Ring* (1907). Schoenberg chose two of these poems for the extraordinary setting of a string quartet. They complement each other, though George did not juxtapose them.

Litanei (Supplication)

Deep is the sadness that surrounds me as I enter again,
Lord, into thy house. Long was the journey, weary are
flesh and bone, empty the coffers, full only the agony.
. . . From the depths of my heart arises a cry: kill
the longing, close up the wounds, relieve me of love,
and grant me thy peace.

Entrückung (Release)

I feel an air from other planets. . . .
I dissolve into tones, circling, wreathing . . .
yielding involuntarily to the great breathing. . . .
The earth shakes, white and soft as foam.
I climb across huge chasms.
I feel as if I were swimming beyond the farthest
clouds in a sea of crystalline brilliance.
I am only a flicker of the sacred fire.
I am only a mumbling of the sacred voice.

Schoenberg makes George's *Supplication* come as a climax of the long journey of his developing themes. They set out from a clear F-sharp minor, challenged by C major. They modulate more and more, with fourth chords and whole-tone scales. In the scherzo the chords move faster, and become obscured by the squeaking of bows at the bridge. There are moments of polytonality, and a quotation of the waltz that obsessed Mahler, "Ach! du lieber Augustin . . . alles ist weg!" ("Everything is used up!"). In the adagio, theme and variations, derived from the main theme of the first movement, wrenching chromaticism and dissonance express the ultimate cry from the depths. Then as an answer to this prayer comes the amazing finale, a release from tonality, into an unheard-of freedom where the tones swiftly circle, dissolve, and swim. Finally, when the voice has concluded, resigned to descend from the air of other planets, the instruments play a beautiful coda in F-sharp, successively resolving the remotest chords to pure triads in familiar relations with each other.

The whole quartet is simpler in rhythm and counterpoint than most of Schoenberg's music, but sufficiently varied to maintain interest. Compared with all the earlier works the quartet is the most concise and satisfying. It is perhaps the most perfectly finished work of Schoenberg's whole career. Adorno says that the work is an "echo of a crisis in personal life, whose sorrow, hardly ever mastered, first brought to Schoenberg's work its full weight."

The emancipated style first introduced in the finale of the quartet became the norm for whole compositions of the following year, the piano pieces Op. 11, and the George songs Op. 15. In these pieces major and minor triads and scales are avoided. Octaves still occur very often as doubling reinforcement of melodic lines, and occasionally as leaps in a line or as harmonic intervals approached by contrary motion of independent voices. Also phrases confined within a sixth or seventh are fairly frequent. The texture is sometimes congested and sometimes thin enough for beautiful effects.

Op. 16, *Five Orchestra Pieces* (1909), includes a perfect, unique tone-picture, the third piece, variously subtitled "Changing Chord," "Colors," and "Summer Morning by a Lake." This piece nearly realizes the amazing proposal that concludes the *Harmonielehre*, to make melody out of tone-color, without benefit of changing pitch: "*Klangfarbenmelodie!* What fine senses, to discriminate, and what highly developed intellect, to find delight in such subtle things! Who dares ask for theory here!" The first three measures of the piece are composed of smooth changes of color playing over a single, sustained chord.

EXAMPLE XII.2   Schoenberg, *Orchestra Piece*, Op. 16, No. 3, beginning

This is the essential idea of the whole piece. The voices move away from the chord, to be sure, by steps or half steps, maintaining such dissonant relations with each other as never to create a clear root-progression. Additional voices appear from time to time with sudden high flashes or low booms of contrast, but never breaking the continuity of the five principal voices. These articulate the form of the piece by their arrivals at transpositions of the original chord, as shown here:

Rehearsal no.		1	3	4		5	6			7	
Measure no.	1-3	9-13	19-21	25		30-32	38	39	40	41	43
Upper voice	A	G♯	B	C♯		A	B♭	A	G♯	B	A
Dynamics	*ppp*				*ppp* $<$ *mp* $>$ *ppp*						

In 1949 Schoenberg revised Op. 16 to dispense with the third oboe, the contrabass clarinet, the fifth and sixth horns, and the fourth trombone, so that a normal symphony orchestra could cope with it. He did not simplify at all the difficulties of intonation or rhythm.

The first two pieces of Op. 16 stand out among all Schoenberg's music because of their pedalpoints and ostinato figures; seldom before or after did he make so much use of this device. The last piece of the group, "The Obligatory Recitative," stands out as the earliest exemplification of the avoidance of octaves: here at last Schoenberg achieves the style that we have studied in *Pierrot*. But the style is not yet related to the ironic idea of *Pierrot*. On the contrary, Op. 16, for the few who knew it before *Pierrot*, seemed to correspond to impressionistic painting at least as nearly as did Debussy's music. Egon Wellesz, speculating in 1916 on "Schoenberg and beyond," elaborated this comparison at length. He also called Schoenberg "the last of the Romantics," and suggested that he was preparing the way for a new musical language incorporating influences of primitive music, folk music, and every sort of exoticism. With its openness to such a range of interpretations, Op. 16 was the likeliest of all of Schoenberg's works between *Verklärte Nacht* and the Variations for Orchestra to make its way some day to a wide circle of listeners.

Op. 17 (1909) is the half-hour drama with a single character, *Erwartung* (*Anxiety*). This work embodies the Expressionist spirit at supreme intensity. The text, prepared according to Schoenberg's suggestions by his friend Marie Pappenheim, surpasses Hofmannsthal and Strindberg in its intimate horror. The musical setting renounces every kind of repetition, so that the coherence of its immense variety depends entirely on the precise relation to the text. The work was first performed in 1924, and was revived more and more after 1950. Two recordings now allow its extraordinary power to be felt.

Op. 18 is a twenty-three-minute drama, *Die glückliche Hand* (*The Lucky Hand*, 1910–13). For this Schoenberg wrote his own scenario, combining four diverse scenes of grotesque horror and a quasi-religious doctrine more obscure than George's, perhaps more directly relevant both to music and to industrial society. To interpret it requires the special gifts of the sociologist-philosopher, Adorno. Without attempting to grasp it as a whole,

others may recognize, as does Stravinsky, qualities in this work that anticipate Boulez. A chorus in twelve parts, alternating singing and *Sprechstimme,* exhorts the anonymous hero:

> Trust reality! you keep trusting a dream.
> You keep attaching your longing to something insatiable. . . .
> You wretch! You have something transcendent within you,
> yet you keep longing for earthly happiness.

The wretched hero ends exactly as he began. The orchestral music of *Die
glückliche Hand* is simpler than that of *Erwartung,* more like that of the
Five Pieces, with short scenes loosely linked, many ostinato passages, and
more use of percussion than is usual for Schoenberg. The score indicates in
detail the changing colors of stage lights, to be synchronized with the music,
just as Scriabin's scores synchronize lights and music. The performance
of *Die glückliche Hand* in 1924 had no successor for many years. Yet in
1961 the young composer Luigi Nono cited *Die glückliche Hand* and Berg's
Lulu as the two greatest works of the century. Some acquaintance with this
work is surely desirable for anyone concerned with Schoenberg; anyone
who knows a little of it will never forget that Schoenberg's styles are
subordinate to his extraordinary ideas.

The *Six Little Piano Pieces,* Op. 19 (1911), are Schoenberg's most accessible music for performers. They are short, as short as Satie's miniatures
of the same year. Moreover, several of them, in slow tempo, are unusually
attenuated with rests. Yet within their few notes, or rather, perhaps, between
the notes, are concentrated feelings as intense as those of the grander music.
The last piece of the set, according to Wellesz, records Schoenberg's inspiration at the funeral of Mahler. Here a melody of just five notes, characteristically angular, stands out against bell-like fourth chords. The following
version of the piece, to make it easier to read, reduces note values, omits
half the bar-lines, and interprets the final fermata as filling out the long
measure. To clarify the very important dynamic contrasts, the marks have
been changed from *pppp* to *pp,* from *ppp* to *p,* from *pp* to *mp,* and from
p to *mf.*

EXAMPLE XII.3   Schoenberg, *Little Piano Piece,* Op. 19, No. 6

The extreme brevity, extreme softness, and extreme expressiveness of this piece are matched only by Webern. Schoenberg was closer to Webern at this stage of his development than at any other. He was searching for means to compose again on the scale of the Chamber Symphony and Second Quartet without sacrificing any of the intensity of his emancipated style. After a few more short works, including *Pierrot,* he pursued his search without completing any composition, until finally, in 1923, he arrived at the twelve-tone technique.

The search for technique was inseparable from the search for definition of spirit. The great unfinished oratorio, *Jacob's Ladder,* is regarded by Rufer, Stuckenschmidt, and others who have studied it as the key work of Schoenberg's entire career. In its fragments the first twelve-tone theme appears. In its libretto, published in 1917, the angel Gabriel and the "man with a mission" argue, interrupted by representatives of all sorts of people. The protagonist asks questions:

> Apparently I must enter into the midst of things,
> even though my word is never understood.
> Do they want it? does something urge me,
> because they resemble me, to enmesh myself with them?
> Am I the one who shows their hour and its expiration?
> who unites the whip and mirror, lyre and sword?
> who is their master and servant, teacher and fool at once?

Gabriel commands:

> Go! preach and suffer, be martyr and prophet!
> . . . When longing seizes you, rejoice,
> and do not ask for fulfillment;
> because your anticipation is directed to something indefinite,
> it does not deceive; longing is the recollection and divination
> of the superearthly condition.

The orchestra that Schoenberg planned, according to Winfried Zillig, was to multiply the mammoth forces of Strauss and Mahler: there were to be twenty flutes (ten doubling on piccolo), twenty oboes (ten English horn), twenty-four clarinets (six in E-flat, twelve B-flat, six bass), twenty bassoons (ten contrabassoons), twelve horns, ten trumpets, eight trombones, and four to six tubas. In addition four smaller orchestras would be needed offstage, and there would be a main chorus of seven hundred twenty, plus an offstage chorus as well. It is hardly surprising that Schoenberg found his vision unrealizable.

Meanwhile he had served briefly in the Austrian army, and had then begun to teach at the progressive school of Eugenie Schwarzwald. His pupils here included Hanns Eisler, Rudolf Kolisch, Erwin Ratz, Josef Rufer, Karl Rankl, Rudolf Serkin, Eduard Steuermann, Paul Pisk, Felix Greissle, and others. His older pupils, Stein, Berg, and Webern, together with the younger ones, formed in 1918 an organization "for the purpose of enabling Arnold Schoenberg to carry out his plan to give artists and music-lovers a real and exact knowledge of modern music." This was the *Verein für musikalische Privataufführungen* (Society for Private Musical Performances). A statement of aims, regulations, and achievements, by Berg, makes clear the complete discretionary authority of the perpetual president, Schoenberg. The Society's rules forbade applause, admission of non-members, advance announcement of programs, and public reporting of the meetings. All sorts of serious new music from all parts of Europe were played, with as many rehearsals as necessary to achieve good performance. The composers most often represented were Debussy and Reger. The Society flourished until it was disrupted by the inflation of 1921. It set an example to be followed by looser organizations of friends of music all over the world.

What Debussy had proposed as a joke, an institutionalized esotericism, Schoenberg took seriously. The "privilege of high art" was becoming more exclusive.

Schoenberg's Society was not limited to professionals, nor to the rich, nor to any other class. Anyone interested was welcome to apply to Schoenberg for membership, and Schoenberg could waive the dues for anyone who earned the privilege by intelligence. In this respect it was different from any previous esoteric society. And in this respect it represented the general social situation of new music, as Laloy had described it in 1909. After the institution was dissolved, the general situation continued, and Schoenberg's rules continued to apply.

CHAPTER XIII

Bartók to the Dance Suite *(1923)*

I N SCHOENBERG'S *Harmonielehre* and in the programs of his private
Society, the music of Béla Bartók (1881–1945) was accorded a place
alongside the most radical works of Schoenberg himself. Bartók throughout his life had no more success than Schoenberg in reaching a wide
audience. But immediately after his death appreciation of Bartók's music
began to spread. Its place soon became so great and so secure that it was
hard to recall how esoteric this music had seemed when new.

Bartók's name and his style are more familiar to some music-lovers of
the middle 20th century than those of Debussy or Wagner. Young performers now grow up on the forty-four Duos for violin, or the *Mikrokosmos*,
Bartók's six volumes of piano music, progressing from an absolute beginner's
problems to a virtuoso's. Three or four late concertos by Bartók have a
secure place in the repertory of orchestras all over the world. The *Music for
Strings, Percussion, and Celesta* is a textbook classic. All six string quartets
are played regularly, and their scherzo movements even serve as encores.
Bartók's less-known pieces are revived from time to time, more than any
of Schoenberg's except *Verklärte Nacht*. Thus Bartók's work contributes to
the continuity and solidarity of the world's multifarious musical culture: it
helps bridge gaps between old and new, between amateur and professional,
between conductor and routine player, between composer and scholar,
between the arts and sciences generally, between one nation and another,
one political ideology and another, one religion and another and none at all.
Its power to do this gives grounds for a hope that our culture can continue
to grow in the future, a hope that its ever widening gaps between ever
multiplying specialisms will not become unbridgeable. Bartók's biography
reminds us that the gaps are deep, and that the bridges represent incalculable
courage, constancy, humility, skill, and suffering.

Bartók's principal profession was that of pianist and piano teacher. In
1899, at the age of eighteen, he arrived in Budapest to begin his studies in
piano and composition at the Royal Academy of Music. His performance

at the piano was outstanding. He was sent to Paris in 1905 as Hungary's representative to compete for the Rubinstein prize; the prize went to one of the greatest pianists of the century, already established in his international career, Wilhelm Backhaus. In 1906 Bartók toured in Spain as accompanist of the prodigious violinist, Ferenc Vecsey. In 1907 he was appointed professor of piano at the Budapest Academy, a post he continued to hold until 1934. His pupil Andor Foldes has described his playing and his teaching as characterized by infinitely patient and rigorous attention to detail, in the service of extraordinarily intense and sustained feeling. He withheld nothing from the craft of performance, which was his profession.

Bartók's first and last teacher of composition was the pupil of Rheinberger and teacher of Dohnányi, Hans Koessler (1853–1926), who criticized his juvenile efforts so severely that from 1900 to 1902 Bartók did no independent composition. The titles of his works up to then suggest, along with the *Autobiography* (1921), that his spontaneous habits led to the waltz and polka written down for him at the age of nine by his mother, a widow and village school teacher with indomitable ambition; that then, aged twelve to fifteen, he had exchanged these for a few academic habits based on some study of harmony under Lázló Erkel, son of the opera composer Ferenc Erkel, and on independent acquaintance with the music of Brahms and with Dohnányi's Op. 1. Now in Budapest, both sets of habits were undermined, not only by Koessler's discouragement, but also by a first encounter with Wagner's *Ring, Tristan,* and *Meistersinger,* which Bartók studied enthusiastically but felt no desire to imitate.

Strauss's *Zarathustra,* heard in 1902, aroused greater enthusiasm. Bartók studied many Strauss scores, amazed his friends with his brilliant piano transcription of *Ein Heldenleben,* and published (1905) an appreciation of the *Domestic Symphony.* Better yet, he found Strauss a stimulus to renew his own efforts as composer. From 1902 to 1940 his fluency never slackened. But the fascination with Strauss soon wore off. In 1909, when he reviewed *Elektra,* he was severely critical.

Meanwhile, in 1900, he had met Koessler's private pupil, Zoltán Kodály, a student at the university, a year younger than Bartók. Along with Kodály Bartók was swept up in the nationalistic movement then pervading Hungarian literature and politics. He began to wear Hungarian costume, even when appearing on the stage. He scolded his mother for speaking German. He undertook a serious study of Liszt, saw through the "superficialities" that had repelled him earlier, and concluded that Liszt was more important than Wagner or Strauss for the future development of music in general.

Bartók first attracted public notice as a composer with his symphonic poem (1903) in honor of the hero of the revolution of 1848, Kossuth; an Austrian trumpeter refused to play Bartók's ugly distortion of Haydn's imperial hymn, but Hans Richter conducted the piece in Manchester, England, with considerable success.

About 1903 Bartók began to pay attention to popular Hungarian music, which he had formerly despised, as his teachers did. Kodály was a step ahead of him, writing a thesis on the subject at the university, completed in 1906, and a first article in the journal *Ethnographia* the year before. The two friends together published arrangements of *Twenty Hungarian Folksongs* (1906); they were chagrined to find later that one of these was a 19th-century popular song—only gradually did they learn to distinguish the oldest, most peculiar types of Hungarian music and to persuade the peasants to sing them for their cylinder phonograph. Bartók's first field-trip was a short one in 1906, near the home of his sister. In 1907 he won a grant to make a longer trip, to the Székely country in Transylvania, where he found a splendid repertory of pentatonic tunes. In 1908 he published in *Ethnographia* a report of his findings, the first of a continuous series of increasingly scholarly writings on folk music. By the end of his life he had recorded and transcribed about eight thousand tunes.

The nationalistic motive of his interest in folk music was soon superseded. In his total scholarly career the Hungarian materials have a smaller place than Rumanian, and there are also important studies of Slovak, Arabian, Turkish, and Serbo-Croatian music. In a letter to János Buşiţia (1909) Bartók points out that it is impossible to understand Hungarian music without comparing it with the music of neighboring peoples. Kodály, writing in 1950, says that Bartók felt a need for comparative study from the beginning. He began to collect Slovak songs in 1906, and learned the language. In 1908 he began on Rumanian songs, and learned that language very well. In 1931 he summed up his ideal in a letter to Octavian Beu: "My true guiding idea, which has possessed me completely, ever since I began to compose, is that of the brotherhood of peoples, of their brotherhood through and despite all war, all conflict. . . . That is why I do not repulse any influence, whether its source be Slovak, Rumanian, Arab, or some other; provided this source be pure, fresh, and healthy!" Toward the very end of his life Bartók told his friend Agatha Fassett that he had first grasped the significance of folk music in an amazing encounter with Arabian singers in North Africa, near Gibraltar, where he had gone alone, in 1906, after his concert tour with Vecsey. There, in a dingy inn, he had had the vision of a map that would show connections among many national songs, and he had resolved to work for the realization of this vision throughout his life. Bartók's nationalism was a necessary stage of his development but nationalism is an utterly wrong label for his work as a whole.

The effect of his folksong studies on his own composing was immediate, profound, and persistent. It was not to help him form another national style like that of Grieg or Janáček or Sibelius or Falla. Rather, paradoxically, he credited folk music with leading him to the adventure that commanded Schoenberg's respect and sympathy. Bartók wrote in his *Autobiography* (1921):

The study of all this peasant music had the decisive significance for me that it led me to the possibility of a complete emancipation from the exclusive rule of the traditional major-minor system. For the overwhelming proportion of the repertory of melodies, and the most valuable of them, adhere to the old church modes or the ancient Greek modes and certain still older modes (especially pentatonic), and moreover display extremely free and various rhythmic structures and changes of meter, both in *rubato* and in *tempo giusto* performance. Thus it was clear that the old scales, disused in our art-music, had by no means lost their vitality. Returning to their use, moreover, made possible novel harmonic combinations. This treatment of the diatonic scale led to liberation from the rigid major-minor scale, and finally to the completely free availability of every single note of our chromatic twelve-tone system.

Many Budapest musicians and music-lovers could recognize nothing Hungarian in the authentic folk music that interested Bartók and Kodály. It sounded oriental. And Bartók's compositions in the liberated style disappointed those who had liked *Kossuth*. These sounded almost French.

French influence, in fact, was another indispensable prerequisite for the development of Bartók's style. Kodály returned in 1907 from a year's work in Paris with Widor. He brought with him some of the music of Debussy. Bartók soon played the Preludes in public, as he continued to do throughout his life. He noted with astonished delight the importance of the pentatonic scale for Debussy, and connected this with Debussy's interest in the Russians and their folk music. He quickly mastered some of Debussy's devices of orchestration, and came to value, as Debussy did, a transparent texture whatever the medium. Very soon his distinctive style was mature.

In 1909 Bartók married a sixteen-year-old piano pupil, Marta Ziegler.

In 1910 the Waldbauer Quartet was organized, and played Bartók's most important work so far, the First Quartet.

In 1911 he and Kodály tried without success to organize a New Hungarian Music Society, to give orchestral concerts. When their effort was defeated, Bartók "retired" from public life, to pursue his teaching, composing, and scholarship. But in England, France, Germany, and Austria his work began to be valued more than it was at home. The short piano pieces won him a place among the foremost leaders of new music.

—————•—————

The big collection of Hungarian and Slovakian folksongs set *For Children at the Piano* (1908–09) is astonishingly mature work, marvelously varied in texture and rhythm, nearly always convincing in its integration of bold harmonies with basic, traditional ones. Rather than enriching the melodic forms with added detail, Bartók's accompaniments clarify and strengthen them with judiciously sparse rhythms and sonorities, and with slowly moving counterpoint. Ex. XIII.1 shows the forty-first Hungarian tune of this collection, which Bartók presents in seven stanzas.

EXAMPLE XIII.1   Bartók, Tune 41, from *Music for Children*

Bartók first presents this strong melody unaccompanied, loud, in the range below the bass clef. Then he plays it very softly, with doubling three octaves higher, and an accompaniment of just three notes, doubled two octaves apart, so that it is neither a bass nor a descant but the most delicate possible tonal interpretation. Bartók's three notes enhance the unity of the melody, its drooping curve, its ambiguity of tonal center (D or A?), and its rhythmically weak ending. The last note reveals a change of center from D to A, but where it happened is still obscure, and whether the F was ever a root or not is uncertain. At once, in the next stanza, this F becomes an important center, subordinate at first to the new bass note, B♭, but finally established as a tentative tonic. The clearer roots in this phrase make the contrapuntal dissonance more striking: the non-harmonic status of the melody's vital C♮ is astonishing, and beautifully expressive.

Now the accompaniment contradicts its B♭ with a surprising B♮. (Neither note has been specified by the melody.) But the chords with B♮'s merely pass on to a new position of the F chord, with A in the bass. The destination of the whole following stanza is this bass A, as root of its own chord. All the motion of the accompaniment, interrupting the little phrases of the melody, simply drifts down the diatonic scale to that destination. The three notes of stanza two are the essential notes here, but now their meaning is amplified. In the course of the drift poignant dissonance is matched by the gasping rhythm, but the very gasps are all subordinated to the long-range pull of the form.

Bartók is not content to enhance the unity within the melody, its drive from beginning to end. Now he shows how the song can drive steadily through three stanzas in one long exuberant crescendo and accelerando. He maintains the note A as a pedal, up to the final cadence, and with passing tones builds a simple harmonic intensification to justify the dynamic effect. Finally he adds a coda, as long as the tune, to repeat just once, but with great emphasis, his single strong root-progression, G to A.

The marvelous imagination, individuality, and ease in this little piece are obvious and delightful to a listener without benefit of a laborious description. But the description of such a piece is valuable—it provides the means for analyzing more complex compositions, whose coherence is not quite so obvious. Moreover it provides a precise reference for the terms that Bartók himself used in his discussion of "The Significance of Folk Music" (1931):

Many people think that harmonizing folksongs is a fairly easy task, or at any rate less difficult than composing with "original" themes. The composer, they think, is relieved in advance of part of his work: the invention of themes.

This view is quite false. To handle folksongs is one of the hardest tasks. I should go so far as to say that it is equally difficult, if not more so, to work with folksongs, as to compose a major original composition. One great difficulty is the heavy constraint of any pre-existing melody. Another is created by the special character of the folksong. It is necessary first to recognize this character, to feel it, and then in the setting to bring it out in relief and not to veil it.

In any case, setting folksongs requires just as much "happy inspiration," as they say, as any other work.

. . . They seem to suppose that a composer friendly to folksongs sits down at his desk to compose something; he racks his brain, without finding a single melodic inspiration; so he bestirs himself, picks up the nearest collection of folksongs, lifts one or two tunes and—a symphony comes into being at once, without the usual birth-pangs.

No! it is not so simple as that. The fatal mistake is to overestimate the importance of the *sujet*, the theme. These people forget the example of Shakespeare, who never invented the plot, the theme, for any of his plays . . .

Thematic material in music corresponds to the plot, the theme of a literary work. In music, as in literature or the visual arts, the origin of the theme to be elaborated is quite insignificant. What counts is how we elaborate it. In this "how" the artist reveals his skill, his power of shaping and expressing, his personality . . .

Sebastian Bach is properly regarded as the great consummating genius of the music of a hundred years and more before him. The material of his music consists of motifs, themes, and formulas that were mostly generally known in his time, or rather in the time of his predecessors. We find in Bach's music countless formulas that can be found as well in Frescobaldi and many other composers before Bach. Is this plagiarism? Not at all! Every artist has the right to sink roots in the art of the past. It is not only his right, but his duty. Why should we then not have the right to regard folk-art as such a rooting-ground?

The view that attributes such importance to the invention of themes arose only in the 19th century. This is a specifically Romantic view—the mania for individuality.

From all this it is clear that it need not be a sign of "impotence" and "lack of imagination" if the composer, instead of building on Brahms and Schumann, sinks the roots of his art in the soil of folk music.

There is another view, the reverse of the former: many think that it is sufficient for the blossoming of a national musical art to have something to do with folk art and to graft its formulas onto those of Western music.

This view shows the same weakness as those previously discussed.

Its representatives also stress the significance of themes, and neglect the importance of giving them form—the truly creative work. The test of strength of true talent is shaping form.

Thus we may say: folk music will have significance for art only when it can permeate and influence art-music through a shaping genius.

What Bartók means by "the special character of the folksong," "bringing it out in relief," and "shaping form," our example makes clear. His best music on original themes demonstrates the "permeating influence" that folk music wins through the work of a "shaping genius."

The extent to which folk music permeates Bartók's whole work can only be suggested here; a thorough study of this topic, such as John Downey's, is full of interest.

Among the *Bagatelles* for piano (1908) two of the most satisfying and original pieces are folksong settings, and two more have original melodies like folksongs. Some of the other *Bagatelles*, on the contrary, are more experimental and immature, first reactions to the contact with Debussy late in 1907. So are the *Burlesques* and *Sketches* of the following year or two. The forms of these pieces seem as arbitrarily established as those of Bartók's earlier Brahmsian, Straussian, and Lisztian music. The experiments with fourth chords, whole-tone scales, and polytonality are interesting because of their early date and also because of their thin textures, boldly exposing the experimental devices. But these pieces lack the satisfying shape that Bartók soon achieved in other works by coördinating these devices with diatonic or pentatonic melodies. The folksongs and pieces on folk-like themes have the most endearing and enduring qualities.

The Second Suite for orchestra, Op. 4 (1905–07), is especially interesting because, as Ivan Waldbauer has pointed out, its melody and rhythm depend on folksong, while the harmony is still Straussian, and the form consequently "veils the character" somewhat. Bartók returned to this piece in 1941, when he was unable to compose a new one; in arranging it for two pianos, he improved the form so enormously, by condensation and slight changes of texture, that he went on to revise the orchestral score accordingly. His "shaping genius" had fed meanwhile on the deep roots that he sank in the soil of folksong.

The *Allegro barbaro* (1911) is an epitome of Bartók's style, the earliest perfect original work, and the most widely known of his piano pieces outside the much later collection, *Mikrokosmos*. Its theme is not a folksong, but it resembles one in rhythm and phrasing. Its emphatic repeated notes are typical of Bartók's melodies from this time on (see Example XIII.2). The melody has been re-spelled here to show its complete and purely diatonic scale, with its pentatonic reference in the first two phrases. Half the barlines are omitted also, to show the symmetry of the phrases and the one

EXAMPLE XIII.2   Bartók, *Allegro barbaro*, tune

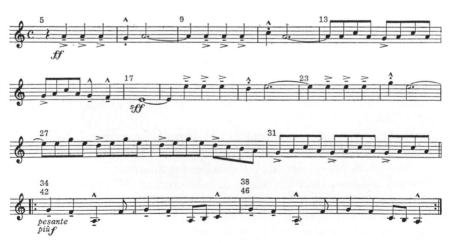

deviation from this symmetry, which tightens the link between the second and third phrases. (Measure numbers are those of the original notation.) Before considering the harmony, let us glance ahead at the extraordinary shape of the whole composition. The end of the exposition is marked by a fading of the accompaniment while the main melody rests. Then comes a long codetta, loud again, with four roughly equal phrases, and a longer fading away. At measure 101 the second half of the piece begins, with a subdued variation of the theme's first two phrases; a long developing digression, mm. 123–80; at last the recapitulation of the third phrase in a huge crescendo; and a final diminishing of the accompaniment. How this extraordinary shape is articulated by the harmony can be studied with the help of the following sketch, where white notes show the structural goals of consonance between bass and melody, and black notes show the motions that connect one such goal to the next, through counterpoint rich in cross-relations.

EXAMPLE XIII.3   Contrapuntal structure of Bartók, *Allegro barbaro*

The spelling here again, unlike Bartók's own, is designed to show the diatonic character of the melodic motions. It overemphasizes the polytonal independence of the two voices. What this picture shows as a cross-relation, C♮ against C♯, can be heard as such if the scheme is played softly, smoothly, not too slowly. On the contrary, when the music is played with all its "barbarous" percussive sonority, its doubled octaves, and its inner voice, chords are emphasized more than counterpoint: the intervals of the chords sound like harsh major sevenths, not diminished octaves; the C♮ is transformed into a B♯, as Bartók has written it. Of course Bartók's spelling makes queer melodic intervals: augmented seconds and diminished thirds, which can be heard only with effort. It is the double meaning of these notes that gives the music much of its excitement. What seems at first to be sonority or rhythm for its own sake is actually the proper clothing of the harmonic idea. Furthermore, the whole form belongs to this idea. In the codetta the ambiguities increase. The bass is momentarily distracted from its center to share some of the notes of the melody. But the bass wins out. The melody is distracted from its diatonic scale considerably more than the bass, and accepts the interpretation of its central A as third of the bass root. Then, with the beginning of the variation, a new bass brings a whole new set of relations. The eleven-note scale of the first part and the eleven-note scale of the second part have only one note in common.

EXAMPLE XIII.4

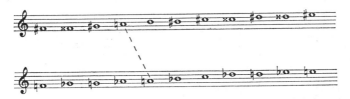

The new softness and tempo rubato fit this amazingly new harmonization. Then comes the development of motifs, with the bass restoring its tonic, veering to its subdominant, and proceeding through two more stages to the final phrase, a triumphant recapitulation. No music since Beethoven's has a form at once so original and so perfect. Bartók's use of harmony for the purpose of form is like Debussy's, but more insistent, more aggressive, setting in relief his more aggressive rhythms and melodies.

The harmony of this music cannot be described in a concise formula, nor understood by means of a label like "polytonality" or "extended tonality," although these may have some value simply to suggest the great difference between Bartók's harmony and the "atonal" harmony of Schoenberg, and if these terms are carefully used they can contribute to a good description, without attempting to summarize it. Bartók's harmony can be described just as rigorously as Beethoven's (which is not to say completely) in a patient, carefully qualified discourse using only traditional terms and musical notation. It cannot be abstracted from the form. Hence this analysis of *Allegro barbaro*, like the analysis of Debussy's *Syrinx*, can teach only a vague attitude to be applied in other pieces. Many pieces require the same

Scene from the League of Composers production of
Schoenberg's *Die glückliche Hand*. Stage design and costumes by Robert Edmond Jones

Stage design for Stravinsky's *Mavra*, by Leopold Survage
(Wadsworth Atheneum, Hartford)

PLATE 9

Prokofiev, caricatures by Sergei Eisenstein

Bartók *(right)* with Rudolph Kolisch, 1940 (The Bettmann Archive)

Edgard Varèse, by John Sloan (Kraushaar Galleries, New York)

PLATE 10

patience and care, although not every one is so complex as the *Allegro barbaro,* and not every one yields so much or so readily. For this piece itself, our analysis can promote a deep and precise appreciation.

The pounding rhythm and the harsh sonority that dominate this piece deserve a separate comment. They are what either attracts or repels attention and sympathy. They are the obvious and memorable novel features that identify Bartók's style in the minds of many listeners. For listeners who are repelled, no analysis of the harmony and form can make the music beautiful. For listeners who are attracted, the subtle harmony and form may have a chance to take effect in the course of many repeated hearings, without benefit of conscious analysis. Then, just as well as after analysis, the rhythm and sonority will be recognized as the fitting dress of the essential idea. As such, they are more thrilling than they can be at the first shocking encounter, but they no longer hold the center of attention. If the idea behind them were not so satisfying, this rhythm and sonority would soon become tiresome, even to the listeners who found them attractive to begin with. Since they are subordinate to the idea and the idea is what it is, these listeners can enjoy them more and more.

Another short piano piece shows enough contrast to the *Allegro barbaro* to warn us more forcibly against glib generalization of either its harmonic or its rhythmic features. The second *Dirge* (1910) has no clear root progression at all. Perhaps no single root or tonic is ever established. The first phrase is a folk-like melody, unaccompanied. Its boundary note, C♯, makes a strong claim to be tonic, but the central F♯ and the final D♯ challenge this claim. The second phrase repeats the first, with a C♯ pedalpoint, and a surprising new note for cadence, A♯.

EXAMPLE XIII.5   Bartók, *Dirge No. 2*

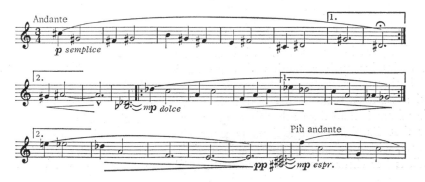

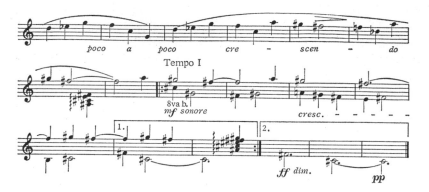

Then a double pedal accompanies the third and fourth phrases, which vary the first in an astonishing way, strengthening the new note (now spelled B♭) with its minor scale, but ending on a diminished triad, in utter irresolution. The next phrase is in bitter conflict with the diminished triad that persists beneath it. Also, it deviates still further from the model phrase: it no longer maintains the regular rhythm. But it ends with a resolution of its bitterest dissonances, F and A, in the mild one, F♯. Is this the root of a dominant seventh chord? The accompaniment at once incorporates this note, but now a new bass voice enters, to recapitulate, not quite exactly, the original pair of phrases, in a rich crescendo. At the very end the accompaniment fades away on a ninth chord, or is it a C♯ triad with added sixth and fourth?

The whole piece is a delicate, dream-like evocation of tonal expectations. When it is over, its fundamental immobility can be felt with a pang as sharp as the pangs of the most Romantic progressions. This kind of harmony is more obviously indebted to Debussy than that of the *Allegro barbaro*. Yet it is just as peculiar to Bartók. For Debussy's static harmonies are calm, and only his progressions evoke poignant feelings, whereas Bartók's harmony is continually disturbed by his growing melody. Bartók draws his melody and accompaniment farther apart in the dimension measured by the circle of fifths, so that his sharpest dissonances are sharper than any of Debussy's. But this difference is a matter of degree, not a radical new procedure like Schoenberg's. If the melody at its climax of tension resembles Schoenberg's melodies, this tension is later relatively relaxed, whereas Schoenberg maintains such a tension that no tensing—no intensifying—seems possible through melodic and harmonic means. Paradoxically we may even say that Bartók's maintenance of the diatonic norm enables him to range farther from it than does Schoenberg's once-and-for-all abnegation. We can show that Bartók is unquestionably more chromatic and dissonant than Debussy, without changing the meanings of these terms at all. To say that Bartók is less chromatic and dissonant than Schoenberg makes these terms vague and questionable. It would be better to say that Bartók is more chromatic and dissonant.

Despite their differences in atmosphere and technique, the *Dirge* and the *Allegro barbaro* belong together as expressions of the same fundamental personal attitude. They are similar in their reliance on diatonic folk-like melodies as points of departure. They share a concern with enharmonic ambiguities and a disdain of more familiar kinds of chromaticism. They both achieve novel kinds of order that are not apt to be repeated.

The elusive underlying unity we have suggested in the *Allegro barbaro* and the *Dirge*, Bartók himself indicates by putting together the contrasting short pieces of his Suite for piano, Op. 14 (1916). The opening Allegretto, like the *Allegro barbaro,* develops a dance-like tune with prominent repeated notes through a harmonic scheme that gradually builds a peculiarly functioning tonality. The closing movement, Sostenuto, resembles the *Dirges* in its mood, and in its soft, richly dissonant ending. The two middle movements, a scherzo-rondo, and an allegro-ostinato, are based on Arabian folksongs that Bartók had collected in North Africa in 1913. Thus the Suite embodies Bartók's ideal of internationalism.

The eighteen pieces for *The First Term at the Piano* are nearly all folklike, and nearly all delightful within their narrow range. The several groups of Rumanian songs and dances, including the Sonatina (1915) and also the fifteen Hungarian songs (1914–17) are deservedly popular, not only with pianists, but in various transcriptions as well.

———•·•———

Bartók's vocal music and his orchestral music up to the middle of his career are less widely known than the piano music. Several pieces remain unpublished. Those that are published show the same diverse elements and the same progressive integration of these around folk-like melodies. What might not be expected of a pianist, they show great sensitivity to the idiomatic peculiarities of the different media.

Bluebeard's Castle (1911) is Bartók's only opera. It is in one act, with two singing roles and a big orchestra. Its libretto, prepared with Bartók's collaboration by the radical poet Béla Balázs (1884–1948), provides not only a Kafkaesque atmosphere, but also a neatly articulated form, with mounting suspense: the young bride, Judith, persuades the brooding, gentle, tormented Prince Bluebeard to let her open, one by one, the seven doors of his dark, dank, bloody castle; when the seventh door reveals the three imprisoned wives of Bluebeard's morning, noon, and twilight, Judith must join them, to leave him alone in the hopeless night. The melodies are close to speech. Sometimes a phrase or two resembles the solemn sorts of Hungarian folksong. There is no sustained aria. The orchestral pictures of what the doors reveal are vivid and concise. To insure unity there is an orchestral motif associated with the dripping blood, a minor second, which develops in a climax of horrendous power, to be followed by a conclusion resigned to gloom. *Bluebeard* can be studied with profit, not only for its own sake, but also in order to transfer some of its associations of sound and mood to Bartók's most complex instrumental music, including his very last works.

The first ballet, *The Wooden Prince* (1916), lacks the concentration of the opera. Balázs provided the scenario, building again on a fairy tale. He included more varied moods than in the opera, but failed to weld them together convincingly. Bartók's orchestration shows his assimilation of a new influence—Stravinsky—particularly in the use of cornet and percussion. But in passages where the movements of the enchanted forest are matched by complex and novel sonorities, these do not make up for a lack of movement in harmony and melody. The more tuneful passages, though attractive separately, seem as disconnected as the plot.

Much better is the second ballet, *The Miraculous Mandarin* (1918–19; revised 1924, 1931). Its plot, by Menyhért Lengyel, was too lurid for the Hungarian censors throughout Bartók's lifetime; in the 1950s and '60s it began to win a place in ballet repertories all over the world. It is enormously exciting, as well as neatly shaped. The music, condensed to a more obvious neatness for concert uses, is among Bartók's most exciting compositions. The big orchestra displays all its virtuosity. There are no catchy tunes. The jagged melodies, however, propel the varied rhythms and sonorities through a development that makes sense apart from the scenario.

———•—•———

Bartók's string quartets surpass all his other music up to 1920 in complexity of form, variety of mood and melody, motivic development, and contrapuntal vitality. In all these respects they are endlessly fascinating. The Second Quartet (1917) is generally recognized as a masterpiece, perhaps the most beautiful music Bartók ever wrote. The First Quartet (1908) is slightly immature and diffuse only by comparison with the Second. It is still as satisfying as the quartets of Debussy, Ravel, or Schoenberg. The three movements make a huge cumulative effect:

I Lento, 4/4, ABA, attached without pause to
II 3/4, accelerando al Allegretto, alternating with Quieto; then Introduction (cadenza-like, Allegro and Meno vivo), attached to
III Allegro vivace, 4/4 sonata form, with fugal development (grazioso) and coda (agitato).

The final coda's statement of the principal theme is its first clear tonal exposition, the fulfillment of efforts that have been underway throughout the quartet.

EXAMPLE XIII.6   Bartók, First String Quartet, excerpts from coda

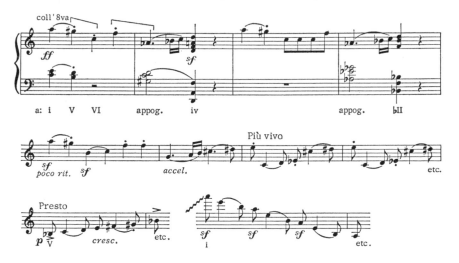

The enharmonic ambiguity of descending major sixth or diminished seventh has dominated the Lento, with its contrapuntal texture in which this interval is answered by a minor sixth or augmented fifth. No tonic note is firmly established in the first movement. A high A is the melodic goal of its first and last sections, but the beginning suggests F minor and A-flat minor as much as A, and the end, which is not an end but the beginning of the link to the Allegretto, more strongly suggests A-flat. The middle section is loaded with appoggiaturas, faintly recalling the principal theme. The end of the middle section has a fleeting reference to the fourths that are to dominate the final cadence, and the last section has the syncopated whole-tone scale leading into its A♭ chord. The Allegretto makes more obvious use of fourths and whole-tone scales, and connects the appoggiatura with the descending skip. It begins and ends with pauses on B major, but the key of B is never established as a functional center. Again the high A is important, but it is surpassed once by a high B. In the finale, near the end of the exposition, there is a soft, long-held, high C, to carry on the ascent from A to B in the Allegretto. The principal key is uncertain until the coda, but when it comes it explains as dominant the violin's hammered open E that began the exposition, development, and recapitulation, so that the whole movement, despite its length, can be recalled in one thought at least as easily as the first two movements. The sense of progress from the poignant uncertainty of the Lento to the barbaric strength of the Allegro depends partly on the harmonic relations described above. There is an immense wealth of harmonic detail, some of which is distracting—the middle section of the Lento, the quiet section of the Allegretto, and the cadenza-like introduction to the Allegro, all seem to hold back the over-all progress, but only slightly. By the end, these subordinate sections can be forgotten in the glow of the final affirmation. Kodály describes this quartet as "a sort of 'return to life' by a being who has gone to the brink of nothingness."

The Second Quartet has its affirmative, barbaric Allegro in the middle, centered so securely on its hammering D that all the percussive dissonance and freely wandering tritones fall into clear subordination. The slow movements at beginning and end are both in a vaguer A, with prominent augmented triads and fourth chords respectively. Thus once more we see that Bartók has established no new pattern, system, or routine. Rather he composes each of his forms freely, and each one is unique.

In the years of the Second Quartet and the second ballet, Bartók wrote also two of his richest works for piano solo: the Studies, Op. 18 (1918), and the *Improvisations on Hungarian Folksongs*, Op. 20 (1920). There are three studies, each one a fairly long piece, exploring only a few of the player's most advanced technical problems and only a limited range of harmony centered on a complex chord or polychord. Within such unusual limitations each study makes a convincing dynamic shape. Here for once Bartók avoids triads and diatonic scales, as Schoenberg does. Moreover he favors melodic leaps of sevenths and ninths. But he uses many octaves too, and unison passages, exact sequences, and long ostinatos, all of which are rare or absent in Schoenberg. And in each study the central harmony helps the forms cohere (as does the exceptional changing chord of Schoenberg's Op. 16, No. 3). The studies make no obvious reference to folk music. But its influence has led Bartók to their emancipated harmony, though he confines them to a relatively limited range of mood. The reappearance in later works of recognizable folk-like melody shows a still greater freedom and mastery.

Like Schoenberg, Bartók envisioned a fulfillment of the tendencies to increasing chromaticism and dissonance. In an article on "The Problem of New Music" (1920) he formulated his notion: "The ultimate goal of our strivings is indeed the unlimited and complete exploitation of all possible available tonal material. But of course certain connections of these (consonant) chords, particularly progressions suggesting the tonic-dominant relation, are utterly contrary to the music of today." He later won the freedom to use the tonic-dominant relation too, and to suggest this functional relation in progressions of dissonant chords. But first he demonstrated the possibility of a coherent order that included both diatonic melody and freely dissonant, chromatic harmony.

In the *Eight Improvisations* Bartók brings his wildest dissonances into the closest relation with his folksong roots. These pieces mark a culmination of his stylistic development. The melodies themselves are somewhat freely developed. Their settings are more than accompaniments. The relation between melody and harmony is approximately the same as in the *Allegro barbaro*, but here the melodies are simpler and the harmonies more complex.

The seventh *Improvisation* Bartók designated as his homage to Debussy. It was first published in the *Revue musicale* along with the tributes of Ravel, Satie, Falla, Stravinsky, and others. The melody is presented first with a tenuous, static, but symmetrically expanding harmony that suggests two diminished seventh chords, with no definition of a tonic. Stripped of ornaments, the symmetry of this accompaniment is evident.

EXAMPLE XIII.7   Bartók, *Improvisation,* Op. 20, No. 7, beginning

Then the harmony becomes restive, with auxiliary notes. But before there is any real progression, the tune returns, a fifth higher than before. While the tune continues, rhythmically compressed, the harmony moves down a half step, measure 17, and another half-step, m. 19. Finally in m. 20 it slides to a new structure, in bitter conflict with the melody. Now the restive auxiliary notes are resumed, with harsher dissonance than before. Then, in a smooth, four-voiced passage, there is further, indefinable, quasi-sequential motion of roots leading to the final recovery of the original harmony, tenuous again, accompanying a slow echo of the tune's last phrase (see Ex. XIII.8).

EXAMPLE XIII.8   Bartók, *Improvisation,* Op. 20, No. 7, end

Every note of this texture is clear, and every note is as expressive as the notes of a Bach fugue. The strength and tension that we have encountered in the *Allegro barbaro* and other Allegros are here fused with the grief of the *Dirge* and the quartet slow movements. This is surely as close as any composer comes to the goal of exploiting all available materials. And it is a perfect tribute to Debussy.

The two violin sonatas (1921, 1922) are Bartók's most difficult pieces. In the opinion of Pierre Boulez they are also his best. They show the style of the *Improvisations,* on the large scale of the quartets.

These sonatas were performed at the first and second annual International Festivals of contemporary music at Salzburg. Between the two festivals (1922) Bartók assisted E. J. Dent and others to organize the International Society for Contemporary Music on a permanent basis. The esoteric institution that Debussy had suggested and Schoenberg had first realized briefly was now firmly established. The ISCM was to persist as the chief institution for the promotion of the most serious new music. Many of Bartók's later works were first performed at its festivals.

In the *Dance Suite* for orchestra (1923), in contrast to the violin sonatas, Bartók speaks to a larger audience. This piece was composed for a festive occasion, the fiftieth anniversary of the merger of the cities Buda and Pest. Here triads have a place at last, alongside magnificent nine-layered fourth chords and horrendous polychords. Moreover, the sweetest possible sonorities of harp and soft strings have a place amid a profuse variety of shrill and percussive sounds. The sweet sounds recur in a "ritornello" that serves as tranquil interlude between the lively dances. The tunes are not actual folksongs, but very like folksongs, in their rhythm and phrasing. Bartók identified the origins of the first and fourth dances as Arabian, the second and third as Hungarian, and the last as Rumanian. A long finale develops themes from all the dances and intensifies their dissonances, in order finally to resolve them on the G that was the starting point and the stable central point of the ritornello. The form of the whole work is thus tighter than that of any ordinary suite, if looser than that of the quartets; it is as original and satisfying as that of the *Allegro barbaro,* and Bartók regarded it as a landmark in his career, pointing ahead to the numerous later instrumental works on a large scale.

In 1923 Bartók divorced his first wife and entrusted her and their child to the care of his sister, in order that he could marry a younger piano pupil, Ditta Pásztory.

In the same year, Bartók's first book-length publications of folk music appeared, and he was commissioned to write five articles for the unique *Dictionary of Modern Music and Musicians* edited by Eaglefield Hull.

Entering his forties now, Bartók had silvery white hair but no wrinkles on his handsome, delicate face. He was a small man, and his continual cigarettes gave the impression that he was nervous, but his voice was astonishingly deep, and the gaze of his black eyes was steady and intense. The "barbarous" violence of his music seemed at first incongruous with his almost ascetic appearance, but the voice and the gaze matched the spirit that this music revealed to its friends. Agatha Fassett, who knew him only when he was old and sick, tells how he once tried to teach her a Rumanian dance, overwhelming her protests that she could not dance at all. She had merely to stand still and forget all the "false modesty" of the middle classes, while he circled her, at first slowly, then faster and closer, until he was pushing her, harder and harder, stamping and shouting wildly. Afterward, having collapsed on the sofa, he recalled the people from whom he had learned this dance, their way of living, their faces when they sang at weddings and funerals; to preserve the significance of all this was much more than merely noting words and music from a book or phonograph record. He recalled especially one peasant woman, gawky, bony, drab, strong, who had represented for him the depth of human emotion, truth, and reality that was his ultimate concern.

CHAPTER XIV

Stravinsky to the Octet and The Wedding *(1923)*

FTER THE deaths of Bartók (1945) and Schoenberg (1951) no informed critic could doubt that Igor Feodorovich Stravinsky (b. 1882) was the greatest living composer. Once again every year or so he still astonished friends and enemies with a musical invention as new as any younger man's. Even before his great rivals had departed, the three ballets of his youth, *Firebird* (1910), *Petrushka* (1911), and *The Rite of Spring* (1912), had become irreplaceable classics of the symphonic repertory, the ballet repertory, and of textbooks in orchestration and conducting. The fame Stravinsky had won with those ballets enabled him to live as a professional composer, playing and conducting only his own music, writing and lecturing only rarely and on topics of his own choice, even though his later compositions were as esoteric as those of Schoenberg or Bartók, who had to teach regularly in order to be their own patrons. Stravinsky's influence on younger composers was great, but it was often superficial, and it met so much resistance and misunderstanding that he could scarcely be regarded as the musical leader of his age. Still, if such a heterogeneous age had to be represented by a single musician, then the unpredictable variety of Stravinsky's music together with its unfailing expert craftsmanship would make him the most likely representative figure. His versatility enabled him to compose fitting music for a jazz band or a liturgical choir, to use the twelve-tone technique when he became interested in it, and on the proper occasions to make arrangements for orchestra of a national anthem or *Happy Birthday to You*. Many musicians criticized his restless changes of style and the changing limitations that he imposed on himself; these were thought to be signs of some unacknowledged weakness. To close students and trusting admirers, on the other hand, the integrity and fidelity to truth that underlay Stravinsky's great versatility were equally great and amazing.

Stravinsky's life differed from the lives of the orphans, Bartók and

Schoenberg—a luckier life in many ways, though not without its own difficulties. His father, Feodor Stravinsky, was the outstanding bass singer at the major opera-house of St. Petersburg. (Even in 1956 the *Great Soviet Encyclopedia* gave equal space to Feodor Stravinsky and his son Igor.) The boy grew up amid Italian, French, and Russian opera, with professional standards of performance. Beginning at the age of nine, he learned to play the piano, to improvise, and to read through his father's library of piano-vocal scores. In his *Autobiography* (1935) he recalled his first experience of an orchestra: "Imagine my joy when for the first time I was taken to the theater where they were giving an opera with which as a pianist I was already familiar. It was *A Life for the Czar,* and it was then I heard an orchestra for the first time. And what an orchestra!—Glinka's! The impression was indelible. . . ." This impression Stravinsky remembered again in his *Conversations* (with Robert Craft, 1959) as "perhaps the greatest thrill of my life."

Neither the boy nor his family assumed that he would become a musician, though the possibility that he might had occurred to him even before he began his lessons. He was impatient with routine exercises in piano playing, as he was later in harmony. He was bored and lonely in school. An uncle introduced him to piano duet arrangements of Brahms's quartets and Wagner's *Ring,* and he studied them "fervently." A little later a friend introduced him to the works of Gounod, Bizet, Delibes, and Chabrier, in whom Stravinsky sensed an agreeable affinity to Tchaikovsky. In short, he became a very advanced connoisseur of music before he decided definitely on his vocation.

He studied law at the University of St. Petersburg, with the vague purpose of qualifying for the imperial bureaucracy. But he confessed in his *Memories and Commentaries* (1960) that he studied very little, and on one occasion was reduced to changing places with a friend for a final examination. At the University one of his best friends was the son of Rimsky-Korsakov. Soon he sought the composer's advice: he wanted to become a composer, but not to risk becoming a foolish one. After a cautious period of preparation, during which Stravinsky wrote his first large piece, a sonata for piano (no longer extant), Rimsky accepted him as a private apprentice. He submitted without reservation to the firm and comprehensive discipline that Rimsky offered. They worked together closely from 1903 until Rimsky's death in 1908. In the last years Stravinsky was at his teacher's house daily. In a sense Rimsky took the place of Stravinsky's father, who had died in 1902. The Symphony, Op. 1, written "under Rimsky's control," is naturally a more professional and less pretentious job than the early quartet by Schoenberg, or Bartók's symphonic poem, *Kossuth.* This earliest extant piece is at least as good as the mature works of Glazunov, which Stravinsky regarded as appropriate models. His career was decisively launched. Meanwhile he was graduated from the University and was married to his cousin Ekaterina Gavrilovna Nossenko.

From his first public work, Stravinsky proceeded with many surprising twists, but with no interruption and no prolonged brooding over a piece. If there were any unfinished works, Stravinsky never spoke of them. The dates he provided meticulously in his *Autobiography* and later volumes of reminiscences, and in the scores themselves. Several times Stravinsky returned to old works and revised their instrumentation or arranged quite new instrumentation; some of these revisions and arrangements merit special study, but others were undertaken from economic motives—Russian copyrights were not valid in the United States.

The first large independent work that Stravinsky undertook was the forty-five minute opera, *The Nightingale*. He had completed only the first of three acts when in 1909 he was unexpectedly commissioned to compose a ballet in a great hurry. The next four years were crammed with such excitement that the opera had to wait. When he finally took it up again, at the urging of the new Free Theater of Moscow, he feared that his style had changed too much to make a coherent work of it. But fortunately a sharp contrast was called for by the plot. This was based on Andersen's fairy tale about the Chinese Emperor's two nightingales—one a machine presented by the ambassador from Japan, and the other a miraculous real bird, whose guardians and interpreters were a cook and a poor fisherman. Stravinsky's style of 1913 was apt for the machine and the Chinese Court, which appeared only in Act II, while the fisherman's song and the nocturnal seaside forest atmosphere of Act I could remain in the style of 1909.

The fisherman's song is a folk-like melody. Stravinsky's colorful accompaniment, surpassing the models of his teacher, Rimsky, brings out the mystery and poignance and trustingness of this simple song (Ex. XIV.1). It is possible to find in the fisherman's song several characteristic traits of Stravinsky, though the song can be thoroughly enjoyed without noticing these. The rhythm of the melody, in spite of its slow tempo and its simple repeated patterns, has a breathless quality. Measure 3 seems almost a mistake, squeezing together two measures that would have made a symmetrical answer to the first two, with an equal number of syllables. This rhythmic quality is found in many Russian folksongs, in many melodies of Mussorgsky and some of Debussy, in not so many of Rimsky and almost none of Tchaikovsky, Rachmaninov, or Scriabin. Stravinsky's later rhythmic innovations often exaggerate this very quality.

The rapid irregular rhythms of the bird-like obbligato part are independent of the main melody. Typical of Stravinsky are the rapidity in slow

EXAMPLE XIV.1 Stravinsky, *Fisherman's Song,* from *The Nightingale,*
first stanza

tempo, the irregularity, and the independence. The staccato ostinato accompaniment is likewise independent, and likewise typical.

On close scrutiny the harmony is even more peculiar than the rhythm. Of the forty-three melodic intervals, twenty-one are thirds; twenty are steps, mostly subordinate to the thirds, and two are inconspicuous fourths. The predominance of thirds is extraordinary. Moreover, they make a structure whose tonality is not quite conventional, as can be seen in a reduction:

EXAMPLE XIV.2   Structure of Stravinsky, *Fisherman's Song*

Such a melodic structure lacks the variety and subtlety of Schoenberg's melodies. Its folk-like unity and freedom might have appealed to Bartók. But Stravinsky's ostinato accompaniment supplies chordal roots that Bartók would have rejected as unworthy of the melody. Stravinsky redeems them by placing the single progression, from V to I, just after the midpoint of the melody, rather than at the end, and by veiling this progression with the chromatic motion of the obbligato. This chromatic motion, to be sure, is part of his heritage from Glinka, Borodin, and Rimsky, but its use in connection with the irregular placing of the root progression is a typical twist of Stravinsky. The obbligato also contributes mild free dissonance throughout.

In a second stanza of the song, after a recitative-like interlude over rich ninth chords, *tremolando,* the obbligato is luxuriously duplicated a beat later and an octave higher, while the words proceed to the key idea of the opera:

> Across the sky moved the breath of God,
> and in his sea he caught a fish.
> He brought forth birds of all kinds,
> gave them a voice, did the breath of God.

At the end of Act I this variation returns for a third stanza, in which the fisherman's poetry soars off into the cosmos:

> Gave them a voice, did the breath of God,
> charmed with their voice the lands of the masters.
> Tears flowed from the eyes of wise men
> And the tears became stars in the sky.

At the end of Acts II and III, composed in 1913, there are new settings of the song for two more contrasting stanzas (shown in Example XIV.3). Dissonance is freer here than in the 1909 settings, but Stravinsky's use of his increased freedom is consistent with his use of the elements at his disposal earlier. The same may be said of the whole opera, though its intervening scenes contain richer dissonances.

EXAMPLE XIV.3 Stravinsky, *Fisherman's Song*, last stanzas

Stravinsky's collaborator in devising the libretto of *The Nightingale* was his good friend Stepan Mitusov, who was a leading figure in the vanguard of Russian symbolism. The two young men had met at Rimsky's house, in 1904 or earlier. Mitusov and his circle had acquainted Stravinsky with *Mir iskusstva* (*The World of Art*), the journal published by Sergei Diaghilev, and with the chamber music of Franck, d'Indy, Fauré, Dukas, Chabrier, and Debussy. These composers he admired, and he benefited from their influence to free himself gradually from that of Rimsky and Glazunov.

Debussy's Nocturne, *Nuages,* is the obvious model of the opening of *The Nightingale.* Rimsky had warned Stravinsky about Debussy in the famous words: "Better not listen to him; one runs the risk of getting accustomed to him and one would end by liking him." Stravinsky continued to listen, to like him, and to learn from him. In his *Memories* he quotes a diary entry acknowledging that he followed Debussy closely in Act I of *The Nightingale.* From 1910 to 1918 Stravinsky enjoyed the cordial friendship of Debussy. His summary judgment (1959) was: "The musicians of my generation and I myself owe the most to Debussy." This debt is most apparent in the Verlaine songs written in 1910; in 1911 Stravinsky paid homage by dedicating to Debussy his most adventurous work till then, the five-minute cantata, *Zvezdolikii* (*Celestial Visage,* text by Balmont, freely translated as *Le Roi des étoiles, The King of the Stars*), which Debussy acknowledged in a letter, published in Stravinsky's *Conversations*:

The music for *The King of the Stars* is still extraordinary. It is probably Plato's "harmony of the eternal spheres" (don't ask me which page!). And only on Sirius

or Aldebaran can I imagine a possible performance of this "cantata for worlds"!
As for our more modest planet, I dare say it will be flattened like a pancake to
hear this work.

I hope that you have completely regained health? You must, because music needs
you too much.

Debussy was almost right about the difficulty of the cantata; it waited until
1938 for a first performance. But in the light of Stravinsky's later music,
Zvezdolikii is prophetic. Its muted strings, harps, and celesta, its steady slow
tempo, and its chromaticism suit the mystical text. The contrast with the
famous ballets is extreme. Yet Stravinsky's individuality is recognizable
here, and if listeners had known this work as well as the ballets they would
have been prepared for the *Symphony of Psalms* (1930) and the *Canticum
sacrum* (1956).

In the piano studies (1908) that Stravinsky wrote as by-products of *The
Nightingale,* his model was Scriabin. But as he said in his *Memories and
Commentaries* (1960), "I could never love a bar of his bombastic music."
And this influence was not assimilated.

As for Rachmaninov, Stravinsky found nothing there to imitate even
fleetingly, though he often heard him play. Much later, in America, the
two composers exchanged polite greetings. According to Stravinsky in his
Conversations, "Rachmaninov's immortalizing totality was his scowl. He
was a six-and-a-half-foot-tall scowl."

In 1909, while Stravinsky was still working on the first act of *The
Nightingale,* Diaghilev was presenting in Paris the first season of Russian
ballet. The programs included Borodin's dances from *Prince Igor* and a
garland of Chopin dances entitled *Les Sylphides,* to which Stravinsky had
contributed orchestrations of the opening nocturne and the closing waltz.
The repertory in the next few years also included Rimsky's *Scheherazade*
and the Weber-Berlioz *Invitation to the Dance* transformed by Nijinsky into
Le Spectre de la Rose. All these works, with the rich choreography of the
young Fokine, represented a revolutionary contrast to the traditional 19th-
century ballets of Delibes and Tchaikovsky. They dazzled the public,
throwing into the shade all operas and concert music since *Salome,* if not
since *Pelléas* or even *Tristan.* Marcel Proust could describe the intensity of
interest in the Russian ballets only by comparison with the Dreyfus case.

Diaghilev and Fokine planned for 1910 a ballet on a larger scale, to be
based on the Russian folk tale of the *Firebird.* Music for this had been
commissioned from Liadov, but he was too slow. So in the fall of 1909
Stravinsky was called to the rescue. He was awed at his opportunity, and
not sure he could do the job in time. But he gladly put aside *The Night-*

ingale and all lesser projects. He worked night and day with Fokine, giving him the music as fast as it was sketched, section by section, and attending every rehearsal of the company and committee meetings of its directors. What resulted was a masterpiece that established Stravinsky at once, only twenty-eight years old, as a first-rate composer, in touch with the international audience of Debussy and Strauss. (At the première of *Firebird* Diaghilev presented Stravinsky to Debussy.) It was chiefly the splendor of *Firebird* and its sequels, *Petrushka* and *The Rite of Spring*, that maintained the burning interest of Diaghilev's seasons, and assured to Diaghilev a permanent place in the history of the arts.

Though *Firebird* is a loose sequence of seven short sections, it is unified by the ingenious use of an inconspicuous motif: the first four notes trace a pattern of intervals, enharmonically ambiguous, that recurs throughout the introduction, the firebird's dance, Kashchei's dance, the lullaby, and the finale. Looking back in 1960, Stravinsky jokingly suggested that this motivic work might be a precedent for his latest canonic and serial procedures. But it is closely connected with Rimsky's procedure in *The Golden Cock*. What is most remarkable about it, however, is Stravinsky's superior taste in handling his teacher's procedure; whereas Rimsky's repetitions are cloying, Stravinsky's only add to the delight of his contrasts of color and mood. Stravinsky's superior energy is evident in the infernal dance of Kashchei's subjects, full of syncopations and harsh sounds that clearly anticipate the *Rite*. The dancers at the first rehearsals, according to Diaghilev's *régisseur,* Sergei Grigoriev, found these rhythms new and difficult. Stravinsky hammered them out, at the piano, humming loudly.

Petrushka surpasses *Firebird* in both refinement and originality as much as *Firebird* surpasses *Scheherazade* or *The Golden Cock*. *Petrushka* is the one work that impressed the distinctive personality of Stravinsky on the largest public. It is also the most enduring masterpiece of Fokine, and was the most memorable dramatic role of Nijinsky. Debussy wrote Stravinsky about *Petrushka,* thanking him for a copy of the score:

There is in it a kind of sounding magic, a mysterious transformation of mechanical into human souls, by a spell whose invention seems to me, so far, to belong only to you. Finally there are orchestral guarantees that I have found elsewhere only in *Parsifal*. You will understand what I mean, I am sure. You will go much farther than *Petrushka*, certainly, but you can already be proud of what this work represents.

The brilliance and precision of the orchestration are indeed marvelous, but inseparable from the fresh rhythms and harmonies. The solo piano part, in its frequent parallel seventh chords on the white keys, and its germinal polychord of white against black—C major and F-sharp major—occupies the center of the work. But the whole orchestra, with shrill cornets and clarinets more conspicuous than those of Strauss and Mahler, provides much more than a background; as Wellesz notes in his book on modern instrumentation, Stravinsky stands out from his contemporaries because "the invention of his motifs proceeds from the instrument, so that every voice 'rings.' . . . It is striking how few agogic indications suffice for Stravinsky— in contrast to Mahler—to make his intentions clear."

The strong stomping and lifting beats of the rhythms, which seldom permit any rubato, and on the other hand the repeating and prolonging of dissonant harmonic complexes, which spread the few significant chord progressions over a long stretch of several phrases, help to account for the orchestral "magic." These harmonic and rhythmic features of the style make the music more satisfactory in piano reduction than *Parsifal* or *Pelléas*, but they also contribute to making every competent orchestral performance a thrilling one. Recordings conducted by Pierre Monteux, who led the première and then played *Petrushka* with orchestras all around the world throughout his life, are among the supreme musical performances of the century.

———— •—• ————

The third great ballet, *The Rite of Spring,* is the climax. Diaghilev referred to it as "the 20th century's Ninth Symphony." Though he probably understood little of it, he was delighted with its shocking effect on his audiences. Debussy, who read the piano duet version with Stravinsky before the first performance, declared that he was "stupefied," and then "haunted" as by "a beautiful nightmare." Many listeners on first hearing are "stupefied" and "haunted" by the wild, pounding rhythms and the great crescendos that break off at the top only in order to begin again. These fit perfectly the pictorial associations that Stravinsky himself described as his starting point, a sudden, surprising vision: "I saw in imagination a solemn pagan rite: sage elders, seated in a circle, watched a young girl dance herself to death. They were sacrificing her to propitiate the god of Spring." Roerich's scenery and costumes, and Nijinsky's perverse choreography are almost redundant, for the music itself can bring this vision to life. Many a paragraph of fervent admiration and poetic or historical interpretation of the *Rite* is made up of mere verbal variations on the theme of its overwhelming rhythm and loudness and its pictorial associations. With repeated listenings, however, these first impressions fade somewhat to make way for deeper impressions: the peculiar, rich chords or polychords fasten themselves on a listener's memory, along with fragments of the patterns of rhythm in which these chords are relentlessly repeated. There are seven outstanding chordal passages (Ex. XIV.4), the first of which, Stravinsky told Schaeffner, was the first and fundamental musical idea of the work. Its fundamental character and

EXAMPLE XIV.4   Stravinsky, *The Rite of Spring,* chords

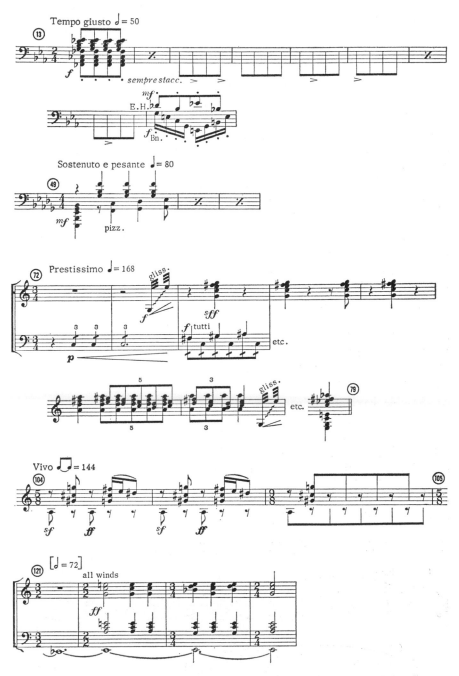

function, however, cannot be understood until many other features of the work have been studied.

The feature likely to become prominent next is the great variety of sounds produced by the big orchestra, not only the retching slides and flutters of horns and trombones in the climactic dances, but more especially the hushed but penetrating sounds of the two long, slow, introductory sections. The orchestration tends to keep the choirs distinct, with a minimum of overlapping or blending. Thus drums are prominent, but there are no harps, pianos, or celesta. Stravinsky emphasizes the percussive values of the winds and strings, but also he gives each choir occasion to sustain tone at a comfortable level of loudness. He includes solo passages for nearly every instrument, often in extreme ranges, and on the other hand his tutti passages are magnificently full and brilliant.

Gradually, as chords, rhythms, and orchestral effects become more familiar, melodies emerge in profusion. And as melodies come to the foreground, everything in the background becomes more meaningful. Most of the melodies are like fragments of folksong; they are enough alike to suggest that they are all part of one single song:

EXAMPLE XIV.5   Stravinsky, *The Rite of Spring*, melodies

Except for the tranquil song at rehearsal number 48, none of the melodies makes a complete phrase in itself. Most of them appear in the midst of long phrases controlled by an ostinato accompaniment; and they seem to contribute nothing to the movement of the accompaniment toward a cadence, yet the accompaniment prevents their reposing on a tonic. Indeed, if considered separately, each fragment of melody seems to be repeated with exasperating monotony, perversely blocked from achieving its goal. Yet when the melodies are considered together, a vague, slow cadential movement may be felt toward the tonic D. This movement is so powerful that the unusual restraints of ostinato rhythms and polychords are required to hold it in check.

Stravinsky's adaptation of folksong is very different from Bartók's. In the *Rite* one melody was taken from an anthology of Lithuanian folksong: this is the very first one, up to no. 1. Stravinsky adds to this symmetrical little tune a truncated chromatic phrase that utterly changes its significance. The chromatic phrase is developed in the introduction, and returns in the first and last dances; the folksong itself returns only at the end of the introduction, transposed, unaccompanied, forlorn. Likewise the later melodies, which might be folksongs or parts of folksongs, are not treated as themes, but rather are subordinated to the long-range melodic current moving toward D. Somewhat similarly, in *Firebird* and *Petrushka*, as the analyses of Edwin Evans show, the several identifiable folksongs fit into a form that is unified by other elements, not by anything belonging to them. In later works borrowed melodies are treated even more roughly. In the *Rite* Stravinsky's procedure is more surprising than elsewhere because there are so many distinguishable melodies and they are so fragmentary. But once this surprise is accepted and the continuity from one fragment to another is felt, however dimly, each of the melodies in the *Rite* is intensely expressive, and each is irreplaceable.

Stravinsky could always recall from early childhood hearing peasants sing, and seeing them and smelling them as they sang. He remembered his parents' disapproval when he all too successfully imitated one of their songs, with an accompaniment of farting noises produced by squeezing the right hand under the left arm-pit. He never studied folksong as Bartók did, but when he took a tune from a book he provided appropriate associations from his childhood memories. Stravinsky resorted to actual quotation only rarely, but the influence of folksong permeates much of his music as it does Bartók's, though his "shaping genius" is so different.

The listener who has discriminated this much in the *Rite* can enjoy it thoroughly without further analysis, and no further analysis is likely to contribute so much to his enjoyment as this elementary discrimination. Yet even before he has got this far, the listener may be tempted to study some details of rhythm.

For the *Rite* introduces a new kind of rhythm, as typical of the 20th century as the rhythm of jazz. This new rhythm appears first fleetingly in the "Mime of Abduction" (Ex. XIV.5, rehearsal no. 43) and the "Mime of the Two Cities" (no. 57), then persistently in the "Glorification" (Ex. XIV. 4, no. 104) and the recurring first section of the "Victim's Dance" (Ex. XIV.4, no. 142). This rhythm is made of units of time too short to be called beats, too short to be indicated individually by the conductor's hand or the dancer's foot. The units are written ♪ or ♪. They are quite strictly equal to each other. A pair of them forms a reasonably brisk beat, or three of them together form a moderate beat, still not slow. The two kinds of beats occur in no simple pattern, but so as to defy expectation, and their irregularity is insisted upon by strong staccato accents. This new rhythm of Stravinsky's can be distinguished from two opposite kinds of rhythm that somewhat resemble it: 1) the more flowing rhythms found occasionally in Mussorgsky, Debussy, Mahler, and many other composers, where moderate or slow beats are grouped in measures of unpredictably changing time signatures, and the beats are still felt as essentially similar; and on the other hand 2) the rhythms of various East European folk dances, occasionally transcribed or imitated by Rimsky-Korsakov and others, often exploited later by Bartók, where unequal successive beats are composed alternatively of two or three short, indivisible, equal units, but in a recurring pattern that shows up clearly enough in notation as a regular meter, though perhaps an unusual one. Stravinsky *combines* these two possibilities of rhythmic complication, to produce an effect of stumbling, of discontinuity, of unparalleled nervous tension. Moreover, Stravinsky combines another complication with these two: his beats are often marked by a thud in the accompaniment while the main melody has a gasp of silence, and then the motions of the melody occur as syncopated accents of the second or third unit within the beat. This syncopation is a more important characteristic of the rhythms of the "Glorification" and the "Victim's Dance" than the famous changes of time signature. Altogether, the changes, the syncopation, and the speed of the constant unit are enough to warrant Debussy's word, "stupefying."

The new rhythm of the *Rite* is as important as the rhythm of jazz because something like it appears in most of Stravinsky's later compositions and indeed in the music of a majority of serious composers after 1914.

The new rhythm is like that of jazz in its opposition to the fluctuating pulse-beat of the late Romantic period, in its jolting energy and its almost mechanical regularity. At the same time there is a great contrast between the rhythms of Stravinsky and of jazz. They achieve their similar effects by the entirely different means that we have described. In Stravinsky's opinion as reported by Robert Craft, jazz is not rhythmic at all: it is a combination of hypnotic regularity in the beat and indulgent rubato in the melodies, totally opposed to Stravinsky's sense of "ontological" time and human responsibility for conscious order. His interest in jazz centered on its sonorities rather than its rhythms.

Stravinsky expressed his characteristic rhythm vividly in his conducting, especially in the 1940s, when he had gained some experience as conductor and was still a youthful sleek man. He would lift his shoulders and chest, crouching forward until he seemed about to fall, or rather to pounce. His head was stretched far forward, chin up, and eyes piercing as if with steel. The motion of the stick might be a small one, but it made clear enough the precision and terrific force of his imagination.

The new rhythm of the "Glorification" and the "Victim's Dance" does not pervade the entire *Rite*. Other, more regular rhythms are equally striking, and have been almost as widely influential. The new rhythm, however, occupies a conspicuous place, at the climax, and the other rhythms may be felt as a preparation for it, and a final resolution of it.

The distinctive rhythm of the *Rite* is so new, so powerful, so hard to master, and so fascinating that it attracts the attention of students as an abstract problem unrelated to the melody and harmony of the music. Especially Olivier Messiaen's analysis of the rhythmic structure of the "Victim's Dance" had enormous value for his pupils, including Pierre Boulez and Jean Barraqué, both of whom published notes on it. Boulez went on to analyze the whole *Rite*, finding in the Introduction above all the kind of structure that won his highest praise. Some students have claimed that the *Rite* represents a sort of emancipation of rhythm, comparable to Schoenberg's emancipation of dissonance, and that rhythm works independently of melody and harmony in this music, or subordinates melody and harmony to its elemental power. This is a mistake. There is a value in analyzing the rhythm separately, to be sure, but to appreciate the *Rite* it is essential to restore the distinctive rhythm to its place and to see something of how it is actually coordinated with other elements to compose a unique form. The new and old rhythms together are in fact closely coordinated with the melodies and polychords. Just as in Bartók's *Allegro barbaro*, the rhythms and sonorities prove to be the fitting dress of a long-range, form-making harmonic tension. If the ostinato passages were merely static and disconnected from each other, as most analyses present them, they would soon lose their fascination; if the crescendos were not expressing a tension that was ultimately to be resolved, they would become embarrassing. If rhythm were actually independent, or supreme, the *Rite* could never have brought its distinctive kind of rhythm into the tradition of world music, but would have been merely an individual's experiment.

To identify the structural functions of Stravinsky's harmony is very difficult; to demonstrate them conclusively may be impossible—or may be the task of some future generation. Conventional harmonic analysis is not enough, even when its notions are extended to the utmost, as in the analysis of Bartók. Yet Stravinsky (up to such works as the *Movements* for piano and orchestra, 1960) does not approach the "atonal" style of Schoenberg. He himself seems to work intuitively and to care little about analysis. But he has provided a new metaphor that can be helpful in our groping efforts to follow his harmonic thought. His term is "polarity." As early as 1921 his friend the conductor Ernest Ansermet referred to harmonic "poles" in Stravinsky's music, and in 1939 Stravinsky himself (with the literary assistance of Roland-Manuel) expounded the idea, in his *Poetics of Music*:

We find ourselves confronted with a new logic of music that would have appeared unthinkable to the masters of the past. And this new logic has opened our eyes to riches whose existence we never suspected. Having reached this point, it is no less indispensable to obey, not new idols, but the eternal necessity of affirming the axis of our music and to recognize the existence of certain poles of attraction. Diatonic tonality is only one means of orienting music toward these poles. The function of tonality is completely subordinated to the force of attraction of the pole of sonority. All music is nothing more than a succession of impulses that converge toward a definite point of repose. This is as true of Gregorian chant as of a Bach fugue, as true of Brahms's music as of Debussy's.

. . . So our chief concern is not so much what is known as tonality as what one might term the polar attraction of sound, of an interval, or even of a complex of tones. The sounding tone constitutes in a way the essential axis of music. Musical form would be unimaginable in the absence of elements of attraction which make up every musical organism and which are bound up with its psychology. The articulations of musical discourse betray a hidden correlation between the *tempo* and the interplay of tones. All music being nothing but a succession of impulses and repose, it is easy to see that the drawing together and separation of poles of attraction in a way determine the respiration of music.

In view of the fact that our poles of attraction are no longer within the closed system which was the diatonic system, we can bring the poles together without being compelled to conform to the exigencies of tonality . . .

Composing, for me, is putting into an order a certain number of these sounds according to certain interval-relationships. This activity leads to a search for the center upon which the series of sounds involved in my undertaking should converge. Thus, if a center is given, I shall have to find a combination that converges upon it. If, on the other hand, an as yet unoriented combination has been found, I shall have to determine the center toward which it should lead. The discovery of this center suggests to me the solution of my problem. It is thus that I satisfy my very marked taste for such a kind of musical topography.

. . . Modality, tonality, polarity are merely provisional means that are passing by, and will even pass away. What survives every change of system is melody. The masters of the Middle Ages and of the Renaissance were no less concerned over melody than were Bach and Mozart. But my musical topography does not reserve a place for melody alone. It reserves for melody the same position that devolved upon it under the modal and diatonic systems . . .

A system of tonal or polar centers is given to us solely for the purpose of achieving a certain order, that is to say more definitively, form, the form in which the creative effort culminates.

This doctrine fits *The Rite of Spring*, in which Stravinsky has achieved a splendid form by putting the rich sounds into an order converging on the center D. Without conforming to the exigencies of tonality, he has brought together in his polychords poles of attraction that might have belonged to two or more different "closed systems" or diatonic scales and triadic chords. Thus the "poles" of the basic polychord (Ex. XIV.4, no. 13) are E♭ and F♭, opposed to each other yet connected by the "axis" of this complex sound, with its particular spacing and instrumentation and its rhythmic repetition. The successive drawing together and separation of these poles "determine the respiration of the music": they draw apart, somewhat relaxed, to the chord of E♭ minor with added major ninth, for the slow round-dance (no. 49); they draw together in various combinations, reaching a climax of tension and speed at the end of Part One (no. 79) and a supreme climax of surprise in the reversal of top and bottom poles, for the "Invocation of the Ancestors" (no. 121); another withdrawal marks the slow dance of the elders (no. 129) with its unique diminuendo, after which the chords function within the limits of the key of D with only slight extensions. The "correlation between the tempo and the interplay of tones" is more intricate than can be shown in these few articulating points, or even in the summary analysis of the form on p. 262, but this is enough to "betray the hidden correlation," if not to bring it entirely out of hiding. The lower case letters indicate minor chords or harmonies, the capitals major. Wedges show crescendos and the one diminuendo.

The form outlined here is no suite of detachable numbers, united by a motto chord or motif, as in *Petrushka* or *Firebird*. The *Rite* is a vast dynamic unit, as coherent as any symphonic allegro though unlike any earlier model of form. It provides no model for imitation, but rather, like the shorter works of Debussy and Bartók that have been analyzed here, it illustrates the vague general principle of form in which chords, however prominent, are subordinate to some sort of melodic motion converging toward a conclusion that both surprises and fulfills expectations. The meta-

PART ONE: The Kiss of the Earth

Introduction, slow		modal dominant a, tonic d, adumbrated and obscured
Dance of the adolescents	13	axis with opposing poles Eb₇/Fb
♩=112	16	fifth chord on Eb going to d
	18	Eb₇/Fb < Eb₇/C
	22	< c:IV₇ V₇ alternating <
Mime of abduction, faster 132	37	Eb₇/C₇/A₇/F#₇
	44	D/F⁵⁶
	46	Bb¹⁶ f♯⁶
Song, *tranquillo*	48	pentatonic Eb or Ab or f
Round dance, slow	49	eb₉ < Eb₇/A₇
Mime, faster 160	54	Eb₇/C¹⁶
Song, recapitulated	56	
Mime of two cities, faster 166	57	D⁶ < Eb₇/C₇
	64	Ab/d
Procession of the priest	67	<
The kiss, by the priest, slow	71	c/b
Dancing the earth to life, 168	72	< whole-tone scale to Eb/C⁶

PART TWO: The Great Sacrifice

Introduction, slow	79	d, decorated but firmly established
più mosso 60	89	e, etc.
secret mime of the girls	91	
più mosso 80	93	eb, etc.
tempo I 60	97	d, etc. <
[Mime of] glorifying the victim ♪=288	104	d:V₇ with high d# unresolved <
invocation of ancestors ♩=144	121	C₇/d pedal
Dance of the elders, slow	128	eb₉/d pedal >
Dance of the victim ♪=252	142	d: V₉ of iv <
shuddering episode ♪=126	149	iv i V of V, etc.
	165	D: iii V of vii <
tempo I	167	V₉ of iii <
maestoso ♩=126	174	V ostinato eb e bb a
tempo I	180	d: V₉ of iv <
maestoso	181	<
	184	iv <
tempo I	186	V < i

phor of polarity may offer no more than this vague principle, but it is valuable if it assists us to feel the principle at work.

The Rite of Spring never won the affection of all the admirers of *Firebird* and *Petrushka*. Its aggressive modernism was still potent when Walt Disney rearranged parts of it for his concert-cartoon film, *Fantasia* (1941), with pictures of erupting volcanoes and fighting dinosaurs.

On the other hand, the *Rite* was for some of its admirers the last great work of Stravinsky. All his later works in comparison seemed artificially constrained, calculated, dispassionate, frivolous, or ascetic to the point of inanity. Only a few moments in *The Wedding*, the Piano Concerto, the *Symphony of Psalms*, and the Symphony in Three Movements suggest moods comparable to those of the *Rite*, and each of these later works is obviously different throughout. The development that had led swiftly from *The Nightingale* to the *Rite* was not to stop there, when the composer was only thirty-two. His further development could be followed with sympathy by anyone who had penetrated very deeply into the earlier works. But listeners who were ecstatic about superficial aspects of the *Rite* were to be disappointed.

As the outstanding composer of Diaghilev's ballets, Stravinsky became a world figure. He met most of the celebrities of his age, and his relations with many of them were interesting. In 1912 he met Schoenberg and Webern. He heard Schoenberg's *Pierrot* and his *Five Pieces for Orchestra*, Op. 16. In his *Autobiography* he recalled his reaction to *Pierrot*: "I did not feel the slightest enthusiasm about the aesthetics of the work, which appeared to me to be a retrogression to the out-of-date Beardsley cult. But, on the other hand, I consider that the merits of the instrumentation are beyond dispute." In his later *Conversations* he amplified:

Diaghilev and I spoke German with Schoenberg, and he was friendly and warm, and I had the feeling that he was interested in my music, especially in *Petroushka*. It is difficult to recollect one's impressions at a distance of forty-five years, but this I remember very clearly: the instrumental substance of *Pierrot Lunaire* impressed me immensely. And by saying "instrumental" I mean not simply the instrumentation of this music but the whole contrapuntal and polyphonic structure of this brilliant instrumental masterpiece.

By the time of the *Conversations* (1959) Stravinsky had some acquaintance with most of Schoenberg's work, including unpublished materials, and he had a ready judgment of all:

We—and I mean the generation who are now saying "Webern and me"—must remember only the perfect works, the *Five Pieces for Orchestra* (except for which I could bear the loss of the first nineteen opus numbers), *Herzgewächse, Pierrot,* the *Serenade,* the *Variations* for orchestra, and, for its orchestra, the "Seraphita" song from op. 22. By these works Schoenberg is among the great composers.

Musicians will take their bearings from them for a great while to come. They constitute, together with a few works of not so many other composers, the true tradition.

In 1962 Stravinsky spoke about *Pierrot* again: "The real wealth of *Pierrot*, the leap of the whole musical imagination and the mastery of the new chromatic polyphony (*Pierrot* is not only the mind but also the solar plexus of early 20th century music) was beyond me as it was beyond all of us at that time."

Stravinsky's *Japanese Songs*, completed just after the *Rite*, are similar to *Pierrot* in their delicate instrumentation, and the last of these songs further resembles Schoenberg in its prominent melodic sevenths. But the differences between the two composers outweigh any similarities. The short phrases, abrupt rhythms, and repetitions all mark these songs as true Stravinsky. And no other work of his before the Septet (1952–53) is this close to Schoenberg. André Schaeffner in 1950 proved by meticulous checking of dates that the Schoenberg influence, if any, could have affected only the third *Japanese Song*, and only very superficially. Stravinsky and Schoenberg were in friendly correspondence in 1919; by 1925 they were estranged; their differing interests were widely regarded as irreconcilable until, after Schoenberg's death, Stravinsky proved otherwise.

In 1914 Stravinsky met Ernest Ansermet, the young Swiss professor of mathematics who had just become a conductor; through him Stravinsky soon met the poet C. F. Ramuz, with whom he was to collaborate for several years. Both Ansermet and Ramuz left priceless records of their association, Ansermet in scattered articles interpreting the intent of Stravinsky's music in the light of Maritain's Thomist philosophy, and Ramuz in a beautiful book of personal memoirs, representing Stravinsky as the ideal type of anti-idealist, at once primitive and civilized, sensual and spiritual, but never sentimental or idealistic. These two friends strengthened tendencies in Stravinsky's character that drew him away from Diaghilev, though Stravinsky's recommendation won Ansermet a job with the ballets. An important fresh influence was the sampling of jazz (in its printed form) that Ansermet brought back from America in 1916, and that Ramuz greeted enthusiastically as another manifestation of his ideal.

In 1917 Stravinsky met the Italian futurists; in their company he later recalled spending "some of the drollest hours of my life." One of them, the painter Balla, designed scenery for the ballet that used Stravinsky's early piece, *Fireworks*. Their leader, Marinetti, with their musical ally, Pratella, and their exponent of the "art of noises," Russolo, gave Stravinsky a demonstration of their invention. As he remembered the occasion in his *Conversations,* "I pretended to be enthusiastic . . . The Futurists were absurd, but

Paul Klee, *A Garden for Orpheus,* 1926 (Foto Kleinhempel, Hamburg)

PLATE 11

Aaron Copland, Virgil Thomson, Nadia Boulanger, Walter Piston, 1962 (Fred Plaut)

A committee meeting of the Soviet Composers Union, Moscow, 1946. *Left to right, seated:* Khatchaturian, Gadjibekov, Shostakovich, Glière, Prokofiev; *back row:* Shaporin, Kabalevsky, Dzerzhinsky, Koval, Muradeli

PLATE 12

sympathetically so, and they were infinitely less pretentious than some of the later movements that borrowed from them . . . The Futurists were not the airplanes they wanted to be but they were at any rate a pack of very nice, noisy Vespas." Among the other painters that Stravinsky remembered affectionately were Matisse, Derain, Delaunay, Léger, Chagall, Tchelitchev, and Picasso. He had met Picasso as early as 1910, and got to know him well in 1917, when Diaghilev made them a team to work on the ballet *Pulcinella*. Picasso's sketches of Stravinsky are justly famous; his drawings for the cover of *Ragtime* are marvelously apt; his stylistic development, through phases commonly called cubism and neo-Classicism, parallels the development of Stravinsky; and his work as a whole matches Stravinsky's in its variety, freedom, mastery, and influence on fashion.

In the decade after the *Rite*, Stravinsky composed many short pieces for small ensembles, and not one on so big a scale as that landmark, either in length or in medium of performance. No definitive account of his stylistic development is possible without a thorough knowledge of all these smaller works, among which several have been hailed as more profound or more consistent or more important historically than the *Rite*. But even the best surveys of his works, such as those by André Schaeffner (1931) and Eric White (1947), betray inadequate knowledge of some of these pieces, while more superficial accounts dismiss many of them as eccentric experiments whose chief value was to lead the composer on to his classic achievements of the later 1920s. Colin Mason, on the contrary, has proposed a reevaluation of the chamber music of the 'teens, in the light of Stravinsky's chamber music of the 1950s; according to Mason, Stravinsky anticipated Webern in some important ways. This view encourages performers to revive some of the pieces, especially the Three Pieces for string quartet (1914) and the quartet Concertino (1920); many performances are needed to warrant more than tentative judgments.

For most of the works of this decade, Russian texts constitute an obstacle to appreciation for foreigners. No translation overcomes this, not even the French translations of Ramuz, worked out with Stravinsky's help and with great poetic skill. In his *Conversations*, Stravinsky expressed abhorrence of translations in general, and cited a particular example from *Renard* (a "burlesque" for acrobats and singers, 1916–17):

An example of translation destroying text and music occurs in the latter part of my *Renard*. The passage I am referring to—I call it a *pribaoutki* [fn.: a kind of droll song, sometimes to nonsense syllables, sometimes in part spoken]—exploits a speed and an accentuation that are natural to Russian (each language has characteristic tempi which partly determine musical tempi and character). No translation of this passage can translate what I have done musically with the language. But there are many such instances in all of my Russian vocal music; I am so disturbed by them I prefer to hear those pieces in Russian or not at all.

The music of these works may yet bring forth more nearly adequate translations. And as the study of Russian in Western countries becomes more common, performances in the original will be more frequent. Meanwhile some knowledge of some of them is desirable for every student of Stravinsky.

The Wedding was the biggest work of the decade. It was begun in 1914. Just before the war, Stravinsky dashed from Switzerland to his home near St. Petersburg, and on to Kiev to obtain a copy of the recently published folk wedding rituals from the collection of Piotr Kireievsky (1808–56). From this book he chose and freely arranged texts to make a coherent cantata for chorus and solo quartet, which might accompany an unbroken series of short, ceremonial "choreographic scenes." Part One shows the preparations for a peasant wedding, first at the bride's house, then at the groom's, with ritually lamenting mothers and consoling friends, then the procession from the bride's house. Part Two is the feast at the "red table," with drinking and joking, in sight of the nuptial bed, which must be warmed up by a married couple. Finally the bride and groom retire, the door is closed, and the guests listen to the groom's solemn song to the bride. This text expresses Stravinsky's thought and character as *Die glückliche Hand* expresses Schoenberg's or *Bluebeard's Castle* Bartók's. Likewise it guarantees that anyone who is even slightly acquainted with it will not give too simple an interpretation to Stravinsky's famous declaration that "music is, by its very nature, essentially powerless to *express* anything at all." In its context in the *Autobiography*, this statement is a qualification of his account of how he delighted in the folk texts for *The Wedding*, their rich associations, and their musical sound. Though he does not say so, it is clear, to anyone acquainted with *The Wedding*, that his music fits the meanings of the words as well as their sounds—the deepest meanings, which no other music would fit so well. "Love" in these poems and this music is never *espressivo*. The poems and music are none the less expressive, in the ordinary broad sense of this word. Stravinsky explained in his *Expositions and Developments* that his "overpublicized bit about expression . . . did not deny musical expressivity," and he went on to avow that "one piece is superior to another *essentially* only in the quality of its feeling." *The Wedding* is great essentially in the quality of Stravinsky's love.

The composition of *The Wedding* was interrupted several times. The piano-vocal score was completed in 1917, and a score for an orchestra of about 150 players was begun, then a score using mechanical piano and harmonium, two cymbaloms, and percussion ensemble. Finally in 1921, when

Diaghilev was ready to prepare a stage production, Stravinsky decided to accompany the singers with four pianos and percussion. Their clangor is both brilliant and austere, unprecedented and exactly right for this extraordinary work.

Most descriptions of *The Wedding,* following the booklet by Viktor Beliaiev, emphasize the unity of its melodies, provided by a motif of a minor third and major second. More striking to some listeners is the release near the end of the work (beginning with the bride's solo at rehearsal no. 110) from melodies cramped in a narrow range to the broad "factory tune" that Stravinsky had learned from his friend Mitusov. This tune, he said, was the only one not of his own invention. It is also the only one that ranges over an octave, and the only one that the instruments play independently of the voices. The chorus concludes with it on blazing high B's just before the groom's final song. The unifying motif is not absent from this melody, but the motif does not account for its joyous fulfillment.

Each of the slighter stage works is peculiar. *Renard* is a repetitive fable of the fox, the cock, the cat, and the goat. It is to be sung, not acted, by four male singers, while clowns or acrobats mime it independently. The chamber orchestra includes seven winds, full battery of percussion, cimbalom, and strings.

L'Histoire du soldat (*The Soldier's Tale,* 1918) is a sort of Faustian travesty, adapted from Russian folk tales by Ramuz, to be spoken, with incidental music and dance, and with an important part for narrator, which occasionally overlaps the music. The moral of the work is stated against the background of a grand chorale: "You must not wish to add to what you have what you used to have. You cannot be at once what you are and what you used to be. You must learn to choose. There is no right to have everything; it is forbidden." The suite of musical pieces from this work, though formally puzzling, contains such marvels of melody, harmony, rhythm, and instrumentation that it became the most widely known work of Stravinsky between the *Rite* and the *Symphony of Psalms.* The tunes have no marked Russian character, but rather an international vulgarity, transfigured by a spirit that seems at first bitterly ironic, but more and more compassionate and affirmative. They include two marches, a fiddling dance, a tango, a waltz, and a ragtime. The ensemble represents an orchestra by a treble and a bass from each of its choirs: clarinet and bassoon, trumpet and trombone, violin and bass viol, together with all the drums one player can handle. The resemblance to a jazz band is not close, but the effect of clarity, brilliance, and economical variety is closer to jazz than to *Pierrot Lunaire.* The violin is kept in a low register, using many double stops and spiccato bowings; this treatment of the violin, the soldier's own instrument and his very soul, contributes as much as the whole ensemble to the special sound of the *Sol-*

dier. And at the end, for the devil's triumph, the melodic instruments drop out gradually while the drummer's part expands into a terrifying virtuoso solo. Here, far more than in the *Rite* or any other work, Stravinsky gives grounds for thinking of rhythm as independent of harmony. Throughout the *Soldier*'s dances there are amazing rhythmic jolts, in counterpoint against simple ostinato accompaniments, a modification of the new kind of rhythm characteristic of the *Rite*. Yet every listener remembers so many clear major scales and catchy tunes and familiar triads that this rhythm has not attracted so much study as it deserves.

Pulcinella (1919) was a commission from Diaghilev, who expected Stravinsky to arrange some pieces attributed to Pergolesi as Tommasini had arranged Scarlatti for *The Good-Humored Ladies*, and as Respighi was arranging Rossini for *The Magic Toyshop*. Stravinsky naturally did something different. He discovered and revealed to the fashionable world the astringent, healthy values of minor 18th-century music for 20th-century listeners. Without disturbing any of the borrowed melodies or rhythms or chord-progressions, and without adding any chromatic enrichment, he spiked the music with dissonant internal pedalpoints and with dry sonorities of a chamber orchestra, so gracefully that a suite and some separate numbers in various arrangements soon became repertory classics. Stravinsky's additions enhance the forward drive of his phrases and justify his repetitions; they are not arbitrary decoration but rather an enlivening and strengthening.

Mavra (one-act opera buffa, after Pushkin, 1921–22) was deliberately undertaken to define Stravinsky's esthetic position as opposed to Wagnerian music drama and the exclusive nationalism of Rimsky and Glazunov. Stravinsky claimed the legacy of the "Westernizing" Russians, Pushkin, Glinka, Dargomyzhsky, and Tchaikovsky. His treatment of the Russian text here is entirely different from that of *Renard, The Wedding*, and the shorter works; now he uses long, flowing phrases of melody, and triadic accompaniment. But the text is still an obstacle to appreciation, for its simple comedy seems dully artificial in translation, and it is difficult for singers or listeners to bring the characters to life. Here again there are musical delights that have made at least one aria a favorite. And again there is a special sonority: the orchestra is composed of twenty-four winds, nine strings, and kettledrums.

———————

In February 1917, when the short-lived Kerensky government took over from the Czar, Diaghilev called on Stravinsky for an orchestration of the *Song of the Volga Boatmen*, to replace the Czarist anthem at a gala performance. Stravinsky's arrangement, for winds and percussion, produced overnight, is a remarkable and characteristic piece. In it he discovered some

EXAMPLE XIV.6   Stravinsky, arrangement of *Song of the Volga Boatmen*

new diatonic consonances, as astonishing as his now customary dissonances. The full tonic chord occurs only in measures 3 and 9, and the spacing of its elements is peculiar, with a growling low third, and an octave gap in the middle range. There are empty fifths representing the tonic, mm. 12, 16, 20, and 28—since Debussy these have an almost normal sound, as they had before Monteverdi, but in Stravinsky's setting these pure consonances are almost incidental. The final chord is neither triad nor fifth, but an amazing single high-spaced sixth against the tonic octaves. The high note cannot possibly be the root of an inverted chord, yet its pale color is enough to make the chord as abnormal as any dissonance. There is no theoretical name for this chord. It is simply the final tonic chord of Stravinsky's *Boatmen*. It deserves to be famous, like the *Petrushka* chord and the *Rite of Spring* chord. Throughout the setting there are similar chords, not identical, but similar in their use of thirds and sixths, with unorthodox spacing, so as to contradict Rameau's principle of a fundamental bass. Stravinsky's chords are an outcome of the modal quality of the melody; they exaggerate this quality and fit the true shape of the melody as no other chords could. The melody defines its diatonic mode only in passing, mm. 14 and 18, but Stravinsky introduces the characteristic half step above the tonic in m. 1, and insists on its polar opposition to the tonic; the G could not be a tonic itself, but it contributes to the claim of D to be tonic, rather than F♯. In more conventional settings this claim of D, with the G assisting, is recognized by a modulation in the middle of the piece, mm. 13–20, usually involving a softening, sweetening of the texture, from which the return to the minor conclusion becomes pathetic. Stravinsky maintains a level tension through this dangerous section; by dynamics and by exceptional dissonances he guards against any relaxation here. He allows the D to persist in its claim in the final chord, so that it is not a chord of repose, but an epitome of the piece. The piece is his simplest epitome of his chief harmonic principle of polarity.

Stravinsky's contribution to the issue of the *Revue musicale* (1920) in memory of Debussy was a short chorale, conceived for winds but first written for piano. This became the nucleus and epilogue of the *Symphonies of Winds* (1921), one of Stravinsky's most poignantly beautiful masterpieces, with a form as original and convincing as that of the *Rite,* and as hard to define. The final chord, toward which the whole piece converges, is a quietly sustained, mildly dissonant one; the melody reposes on the very note that it held in various more dissonant, more questioning preceding chords, such as the first chord of the piece and the first chord of the chorale epilogue:

EXAMPLE XIV.7 Stravinsky, *Symphonies of Winds,* chords

etc.

Nowhere before the final chord is there an unquestionable tonic or a complete and unclouded major scale. The polar note D seems to attract all sorts of diatonic scale-fragments that it might belong to, major and minor and vaguely modal; these conflict with each other and are rejected, while the questioning chords keep returning. In the middle of the piece there is a relatively relaxed section of flowing two-voiced texture, like a pastorale, in which the melody draws toward an opposing pole of E major-minor, but the accompaniment continues to emphasize the D and to suggest G minor. Toward the end there is a dance-like section rising to a climax of loudness with the C scale in the bass against the dominant of D in chords above; after a *pianissimo* reminder of the chorale, the dance resumes in C, but then wanders to another polychordal situation A/E♭, after which the familiar questioning chord is relatively serene; this penultimate section is the only part of the piece with a broken-chord ostinato reminiscent of other Stravinsky works. All the fragments of melody are short and narrow-ranged, even more cramped than in the *Rite* or *The Wedding,* but once their coherence is felt, every one of them is as "pregnant" as the melodic fragments of Puccini, and the slow circling motion that connects them is worthy of Debussy.

At the same time that Stravinsky was completing *The Wedding,* he composed the Octet for winds, in which he used his polar harmony along with tunes full of major scales and triadic leaps comparable to those of the *Soldier,* to construct very different forms: a "sinfonia" or overture with slow introduction and brisk main section, a theme and variations, including a fugato, and a rondo finale with a coda that is like a jazz chorale. This is one of his most charming works, and one of his most contrapuntal. It was an outstanding success at the fourth festival of the International Society for Contemporary Music, 1926, but only after Stravinsky himself had introduced it at the Paris Opera House, inaugurating his career as conductor, and after it had appeared in another Paris concert devoted entirely to works of Stravinsky. The Octet soon came to be regarded widely as a model of 20th-century classicism, but none of the many works that imitated it could match its vitality and grace. Stravinsky himself did *not* regard it as a model. He never wrote another like it, but went on matching the surprise that it represented. His intention was never to define limits for anyone else, or for his own future activity, but always to choose the limits appropriate for himself at each stage of his life. At the stage of the Octet, after he had shown that folklore, jazz, popular marches, waltzes, and tangos, Pergolesi, and Glinka were all related to him and capable of renewal by his vital spirit, he was proceeding to renew the materials of Rameau or Haydn. He would proceed further at once, to Beethoven and Bach, then to Tchaikovsky, Verdi, Monteverdi, Rossini, Machaut, Webern, Gesualdo, Willaert, Tallis. Each new stage surprised people who wanted him to stand still. But his consistency was in his continual change. His constant renewal was his fidelity to tradition.

In his *Poetics of Music* (1939–40) Stravinsky presented his "dogmatic confessions" on such topics as tradition and academicism:

Tradition is entirely different from habit, even from an excellent habit, for habit is by definition an unconscious acquisition and tends to become mechanical, whereas tradition results from a conscious and deliberate acceptance. A real tradition is not the relic of a past irretrievably gone; it is a living force that animates and informs the present . . . A work is called academic when it is composed strictly according to the precepts of the conservatory. It follows that academicism considered as a scholastic exercise based on imitation is in itself something very useful and even indispensable to beginners who train themselves by studying models. It likewise follows that academicism should find no place outside the conservatory and that those who make an ideal of academicism when they have already completed their studies produce stiffly correct works that are bloodless and dry . . . We can make use of academic forms without running the risk of becoming academic ourselves . . . Now, I do not have a temperament suited to academicism; so I always use academic formulas knowingly and voluntarily. I use them quite as knowingly as I would use folklore. They are raw materials of my work.

In his *Memories* he added:

Whatever interests me, whatever I love, I wish to make my own. (I am probably describing a rare form of kleptomania) . . . Tradition is generic; it is not simply "handed down," fathers to sons, but undergoes a life process: it is born, grows, matures, declines, and is reborn, perhaps. These stages of growth and regrowth are always in contradiction to the stages of another concept or interpretation: true tradition lives in the contradiction.

Stravinsky's attitude toward tradition is like that formulated by T. S. Eliot in his essay on "Tradition and the Individual Talent" (1917), and more directly related to the whole "Tradition of Tradition" in French literary criticism, as admirably surveyed by Harry Levin. It is incidentally like that expressed by Wagner in *Die Meistersinger,* though in Stravinsky's opinion Wagner was the arch-destroyer of tradition. In fact, Stravinsky's attitude is by no means peculiar to him, but rather common to most major artists; only a few musicians are so self-conscious and explicit in stating it. Stravinsky's forceful statements, together with his music, contribute to the renewal of tradition that he praises.

The appearance of the Octet and *The Wedding* in the same year multiplied the surprise that either work would have produced alone. In an earlier epoch such works might have been separated by a generation, and they could hardly have been less than a generation removed from the *Rite*. But when a generation had grown up after them, and Stravinsky had continued to provide surprises for each decade, the works of 1923 could be seen as compatible with each other and with the *Rite,* all natural products of the genius of the age.

———— ◆ ————

CHAPTER XV

Jazz, Mainstream and Modern

T HE FOUR great new styles that emerged just before World War
I persisted up to World War II and beyond. Jazz, Schoenberg,
Bartók, and Stravinsky typified the period between the wars. Each
style remained distinct. Each continued to develop. Each expanded its
influence, though none was able to attract and hold the wide audiences that
Debussy, Strauss, Puccini, and Lehár had enjoyed, for older styles persisted
too, and the revival of still older ones became increasingly important in
musical life. Most of the serious composition by young men in the period
between the wars could be understood in relation to the three aging masters
of modern music or to the legendary jazz of New Orleans. However distinctive and however valuable the work of the younger generation might be,
none of it could rival the claim of the four great styles to be essential,
indispensable parts of a general musical education. What was produced in
these styles in the second quarter of the century confirmed the importance
that acute critics had attributed to them in the first.

The central tradition of jazz proved to be full of vigor and value. Its
possibilities for expansion and elaboration were unfolded, gradually at first,
then in a burst of novelty around 1940, and then again gradually, continually. Jazz influence on popular music, vague and superficial in the 1920s,
grew deeper in the 1930s and more pervasive in the 1950s. Its influence on
composers of "serious" music, including Schoenberg, Stravinsky, Hindemith,
Berg, Milhaud, Copland, Weill, and many more, was intermittent and
various, but altogether too frequent to be overlooked. More important was
the accumulation of performances within jazz itself that warranted serious
and repeated listening. Both the enduring interest of the best jazz and the
spread of its influence depended on phonograph records; experts studied
these with a scholarship as scrupulous as any paleography or documentary
research, guiding unknown friends all over the world to a critical appreciation of the central tradition.

The expansion and elaboration of jazz were accomplished by young men,
to be sure, rather than the originators of the style. "Jelly Roll" Morton and

his contemporaries were in some ways surpassed by the young Louis Armstrong, Edward "Duke" Ellington, Charlie Parker, and others, while the older men repeated themselves, or dropped out of the enterprise. But no one supreme individual rose out of this tradition; it remained essentially a collective enterprise, in which shifting relations of the individuals of various ages played essential parts, and the accomplishments of the young depended closely on their immediate native heritage. Young men won leading positions by technical proficiency within the established style—by playing louder, faster, with greater agility, with greater ease at extremes of high or low pitch, and with more precise ensemble in homorhythmic passages than their elders had done. Then they modified the style, by elaborating its kind of melody, harmony, rhythm, and tone-color, but without introducing any fundamental change. Their achievement was an expansion and elaboration, not to be compared with the obscure formation of the new style that had occurred at the beginning of the century.

A roster of outstanding jazz players, arranged according to their chief instruments and the dates of their birth, can serve to summarize many aspects of the history of jazz, and to provide a background for the stylistic analyses of a few examples. For connoisseurs of jazz each name on this list, and some others omitted from it, can call to mind personal tone-colors and peculiarities of melodic invention. The literature of jazz is largely a chronicle of the bands in which these men grouped and regrouped, to play together sometimes for a season, rarely longer, and in many instances only for a single recording session. Some of the finest performers, like Armstrong and Parker, made little effort to maintain a permanent group around them. The continuous groups of Ellington, Basie, and Lewis, conforming more nearly to patterns of both serious and commercial music-making, were exceptional in jazz, for the collaboration of individuals in the authentic jazz style could never be routine. It was a "discipline within freedom."

Our roster shows after each name the place where the man's musical career began or reached its fruition. New Orleans prevails at first, with a gradually increasing representation of New York. The Chicago group, from Beiderbecke (1903) to Goodman (1909), includes most of the non-Negro musicians who thoroughly devoted themselves to careers in jazz and made important contributions to its development. The Kansas City school, by contrast, is entirely Negro. Toward the end of the list appear indications of the "West Coast jazz" that challenged New York in the 1950s. It should be remembered, of course, that migrations from one center to another, by individuals and by groups, were common, and that new ideas were quickly disseminated throughout the jazz community by recordings, so that the places of origin indicate less marked divergencies than those indicated by Florence, Rome, and Venice in the music or painting of the Renaissance.

BIRTH	TRUMPET	TROMBONE	CLARINET	SAXOPHONE
1885	Joseph "King" Oliver, N.O., died 1938 (M. Williams)			
1886		Edward "Kid" Ory, N.O.		
1890				
1892			Johnny Dodds, N.O., d. 1940	
1895			Jimmy Noone, N.O., d. 1944	
1897			Sidney Bechet, N.O., d. 1961 (autob.)	
1898				
1899				
1900	Louis Armstrong, N.O. (autob., McCarthy, Goffin)	Jimmy Harrison, N.Y., d. 1931		Don Redman, N.Y.
1902				
1903	James "Bubber" Miley, N.Y., d. 1932 Leon "Bix" Beiderbecke, Chi., d. 1931 (Wareing, B. James)			
1904		Joseph "Sam" Nanton, N.Y., d. 1948		Coleman Hawkins, N.Y.
1905		Jack Teagarden, N.Y. (J. Smith) Tommy Dorsey, N.Y., d. 1956		
1906	Francis "Muggsy" Spanier, Chi.	J. C. Higginbotham, N.Y. Vic Dickenson, N.Y.	Leon "Barney" Bigard, N.O. Frank Teschemacher, Chi., d. 1932 Charles "Pee-wee" Russell, Chi.	Lawrence "Bud" Freeman, Chi. Johnny Hodges, N.Y.
1908	Henry "Red" Allen, N.O.			

BANJO/GUITAR	DRUMS	PIANO	BASS	BIRTH
		Ferdinand "Jelly Roll" Morton, N.O., d. 1941 (Lomax)		1885
				1886
John St. Cyr, N.O.				1890
			George "Pops" Foster, N.O.	1892
				1895
				1897
		Fletcher Henderson, N.Y., d. 1952		1898
		Edward "Duke" Ellington, N.Y. (Gammond)		1899
			Walter Page, K.C., d. 1957	1900
	Chick Webb, N.Y., d. 1939			1902
				1903
Eddie Condon, Chi. (autob.)		Thomas "Fats" Waller, N. Y., d. 1943 (C. Fox) William "Count" Basie, K.C. (Horricks)		1904
		Earl Hines, Chi. (Balliett)		1905
				1906
	Dave Tough, Chi., d. 1948		John Kirby, N.Y., d. 1952	1908

BIRTH	TRUMPET	TROMBONE	CLARINET	SAXOPHONE
(1908)	Max Kaminsky, Chi. (autob.)			
1909		Dickie Wells, N.Y.	Benny Goodman, Chi. (autob., Connor)	Lester Young, K.C., d. 1959
1910				Harry Carney, N.Y.
1911	Roy Eldridge, N.Y.			
1912				
1913			Woody Herman, N.Y.	
1914				
1915				
1917	John "Dizzy" Gillespie, N.Y. (M. James)			
1919				
1920				Charles Parker, K.C., d. 1955 (Harrison)
1921			Jimmy Giuffre, N.Y., Calif.	
1922				
1924		J. J. Johnson, N.Y.		Paul Desmond, Calif.
1925				
1926	Miles Davis, N.Y.			
1927				Lee Konitz, N.Y. Stan Getz, N.Y., Calif. Gerry Mulligan, Calif.
1928				
1929				Sonny Rollins, N.Y.
1930				Ornette Coleman
1932				

BANJO/GUITAR	DRUMS	PIANO	BASS	BIRTH
				(1908)
	William "Cozy" Cole, N.Y. Gene Krupa, Chi.			1909
Django Reinhardt, Paris, d. 1953 (Delauney)		Art Tatum, N.Y., d. 1956		1910
	Jonathan "Jo" Jones, K.C.			1911
		Teddy Wilson, N.Y.		1912
	Lionel Hampton, Chi., Calif.			1913
	Kenneth Clarke, N.Y.			1914
		Billy Strayhorn, N.Y.		1915
	Buddy Rich, N.Y.			1917
Charles Christian, N.Y., d. 1942 (Ellison)	Art Blakey, N.Y.	Lennie Tristano, Chi.		1919
		Thelonious Monk, N.Y. John Lewis, N.Y. David Brubeck, Calif.		1920
		Errol Garner, N.Y.	Jimmy Blanton, N.Y., d. 1942	1921
			Oscar Pettiford, N.Y. Charles Mingus, N.Y.	1922
	Louis Bellson, N.Y.	Earl "Bud" Powell, N.Y.		1924
	Max Roach, N.Y.			1925
				1926
				1927
		Horace Silver, N.Y.		1928
				1929
				1930
		Ray Charles		1932

Nevertheless, the fact that there is some slight peculiarity to Kansas City jazz and Chicago jazz, shared by little groups of masters, makes a striking contrast between jazz and most other arts of the 20th century, in which the very principles of regionalism and nationalism are international trends, and each new whim of a leader like Stravinsky or Picasso can be found reflected promptly, if dimly, by lonely individuals all around the world. The individual musicians who created jazz depended rather on their continual interaction in close-knit groups, imbedded in the rituals of their families and neighbors. Ralph Ellison, who played the trumpet in his boyhood alongside the guitarist Charles Christian in Oklahoma City, insists that much of the best jazz arose in obscure localities and never reached the commercial world of the great cities. Jazz shows its traditionalism in its local schools. The chronological overlapping of the schools, as they appear on our list, suggests their relations better than any brief consideration of them one after another.

Certain names on the list are followed by references in parentheses to the books by or about these men. Readers to whom many of the names are unfamiliar may safely assume that these parenthetical references distinguish the most prominent musicians.

Louis Armstrong links the New Orleans school of about 1915 with the Chicago school of the 1920s, the New York of the 'thirties, and the international jazz world of the 'fifties. In his own twenties and the 'twenties of the century, Armstrong left "King" Oliver's band to play and sing with various groups that permitted him a new freedom and a new kind of intricacy. His "Hot Five" made a series of recordings almost as satisfying as those of Morton's "Hot Peppers" or of Bessie Smith; Armstrong's records, despite occasional lapses of technique and taste, are more exciting than any others of the time, for they introduce new devices that point ahead to later developments of jazz, while at the same time they preserve the character of the legendary period.

Among the best of the Hot Five pieces is one called *Hotter than That,* published as a composition of Lillian Hardin, Armstrong's wife and pianist. The "hot" quality, however, is not in the conventional tune, but in the performance (1927), and especially in the parts of the performance in which Armstrong himself plays or sings. The tune and the ensemble, though essential to the musical whole, are subordinate to the virtuoso performance of the individual, which determines the unique form.

An introduction, played by the whole ensemble with trumpet as principal voice, consists of the last eight measures of the 32-measure tune. It leads immediately to the first "chorus," in which the trumpet is accompanied only by chords of the piano and guitar. Here Armstrong presents, as the basis for variations, a version of his wife's melody already loaded with as much syncopation as Morton or Oliver would have used for a climax after three or four choruses. Then Armstrong rests, giving the second chorus to Johnny Dodds, clarinet. Dodds's melody is conceived as a counterpoint to the basic tune, full of broken chords; it makes sense over the chordal accompaniment, in the absence of the tune, but its meaning is best appreciated by listeners who can imagine the tune in the background. For the third chorus Armstrong sings nonsense syllables, again varying the basic melody. Then in a static interlude of eight measures, he sings fragments, answered antiphonally by John St. Cyr, guitar. Then the trombone, "Kid" Ory, begins a solo, but halfway through this chorus the whole group joins, with trumpet dominating in an astonishing simplification of the main melody on straining high notes. A coda, for guitar, makes a beautiful surprise ending on a diminished seventh chord. The total form of this performance, like the "hot" rhythm, uses symmetrical convention as a foil for novel adventures. Yet the climax is the moment closest to tradition, when the whole ensemble joins in counterpoint.

Our example shows the five phrases corresponding to the last eight measures of the tune, in each of its variations.

A study of these few phrases can show not only the characteristic details of syncopation and phrasing, such as we have seen in simpler forms in Morton's *Jelly Roll Blues,* but also the sweeping progression of melody that gives Armstrong's performance as a whole its cumulative power. The bracketed motif with repeated notes is the outstanding idea of the introduction, where it brings a mild unexpected accent that welds the whole phrase together, as suggested by the metrical signs above the notes; the motif serves at once, slightly varied, to make the cadence. In the first full chorus, Armstrong shifts this motif very subtly, anticipating and consolidating it. In the vocal chorus he simplifies it, and then drastically changes the cadence in order to dovetail with the interlude, by way of the most expressive blue note in the whole piece. In the final chorus he brings the motif to a real development, starting four measures ahead, rising to the top note of the piece and overriding the caesura that had preceded the motif in each earlier chorus, so that the final, expected appearance of the motif is now late and the cadence is a quick blur of blue notes. A sympathetic listener can enjoy all this intricate melodic thought without benefit of verbal or graphic analysis, just as Armstrong composed it entirely in his imagination of sounds; but analysis can contribute to greater enjoyment, and it can open the way to new enjoyment for some music-lovers who have formerly allowed the melodic intricacy to be overshadowed by the harmonic and rhythmic simplicity of the accompaniment. The accompaniment supports this kind of melody, eggs it on, and gives it freedom. Such melodies seem to be

EXAMPLE XV.1   Armstrong, *Hotter than That,* variants of last phrase

invented only when the accompaniment is giving the right kind of support. Moreover, they probably grow out of the experience of contrapuntal music—Armstrong's single line often seems to be incorporating fragmentary antiphonal answers to its own leading ideas. But the one rich melody is now the proper focus of interest.

The harmonic relation between Armstrong's melody and the band's accompaniment is subtle. Whereas Dodds's melody is composed mainly of broken chords and simple ornaments, Armstrong's is more independent, more long-breathed, bolder in its dissonances—notably in the cross-relations marked by asterisks. Yet Armstrong's melody does harmonize convincingly, and its drive to the cadence is the Bach-like drive of a melody in counterpoint against a melodic bass. This harmonic subtlety is neglected in most accounts of Armstrong's style. It is what distinguishes him and his best colleagues from their routine imitators. It is also what points ahead most distinctly to the best work of younger men, like Charlie Parker.

———•———

Armstrong's expansion of the role of soloists was matched and balanced by Ellington's elaboration of the ensemble. Both these developments led jazz away from some of its folk-like qualities, toward a richness of form and expression comparable with the minor classics of European music. Both developments risked losing the folk-like honesty and intensity of jazz and reducing it to the average level of commercial entertainment. But Armstrong, Ellington, and a few others like them could afford to take this risk, relying on the devout honesty and strong intensity of their own characters to animate more elaborate kinds of music. Such musicians could not be content to limit the modifications they made in their tradition so narrowly as folksingers; their professional skills impelled them to develop the style. While Armstrong moved ahead to high notes, agile figures, intricate syncopations, and motivic developments, Ellington moved to rich chords, chromatic progressions, varied and sensuous colors, and delightful new organizations of contrasting colors. Both developments proceeded with reference to each other. Armstrong in his solos never departed altogether from the jazz ensemble, and Ellington in his arrangements never failed to leave room for the spontaneous contributions of individual players. Moreover, close harmony in an ensemble provided a background for more and more intricate melodies, while individual instrumental virtuosity made possible more and more elaborate ensembles. The complementary functioning of the two developments, viewed from a distance, can be seen to have preserved the essential balance of elements in jazz at the same time that the elements were transformed.

A song by Ellington supplied the name for the jazz style of the 1930s, "swing," just as Armstrong's favorite epithet, "hot," was used to distinguish the style that he represented in the 1920s.

The full title of Ellington's song has a profound truth and charm: "It don't mean a thing if it ain't got that swing." The word "swing," besides labelling a sub-class of jazz, denotes the relaxed vitality of jazz rhythm. Hodeir calls it "vital relaxation," and builds up a persuasive theory about its subtleties, which he contrasts with the more obvious "hot" tension created by loudness, high pitch, vibrato, blue notes, and rhythmic drive. He argues that the combination of "hot" performance and "swing" is the criterion of true jazz; they can be combined in varying proportions, but the complete absence of "swing" makes the music trivial, meaningless.

While swing, in Hodeir's sense of the word, characterizes Armstrong's music at all times, just as much as Ellington's, the word is commonly associated more with the "big band" that Ellington represents, in contrast to smaller groups like Armstrong's "Hot Five," characteristic of the earlier period.

A big band, in jazz, may consist of ten to twenty players. It must include three to six saxophones, playing frequently in chords with similar motion and identical rhythm. Clarinets are optional; one or more saxophone players may shift to clarinet from time to time, or there may be a clarinet soloist, but not a whole group of clarinets as in a military band. The jazz band is likely to include three or more trumpets used sometimes in the same manner as the saxophones, and it may include three or more trombones; the brass section must include at least two trumpets and one trombone, to balance the reeds. The "rhythm section" must include piano, bass, and percussion, and may be varied with guitar, banjo, and vibraphone. This ensemble is still a group of soloists, rather than a band or orchestra such as European music has known since Lully, with strings playing in unison. Unison effects for the big jazz band are exceptional; the sound of the tutti normally has at least two distinct strands of melody plus the percussive accompaniment. Moreover, the homorhythmic scoring is often subordinated in the course of a whole piece to a series of solos. On the whole, the saxophones' basic function is to provide a soft, sustained chordal background for the melodies of trumpet, clarinet, and trombone, regardless of whether these melodies are solos or thickened with chords. The most distinctive treatment of the band involves 1) four- and five-voiced chords, rather than plain triads, and 2) antiphony of the three melodic sections—reeds, trumpets, and trombones. In short, the big band is a harmonic enrichment of the antiphony of three soloists inherited from the New Orleans style.

Ellington's *Ko Ko* (1940) is a classic example of this treatment of the big band. A full score of just a few measures can give some indication of how the harmonic and coloristic enrichment affects melody and rhythm in this composition:

EXAMPLE XV.2 Ellington, *Ko Ko,* scoring

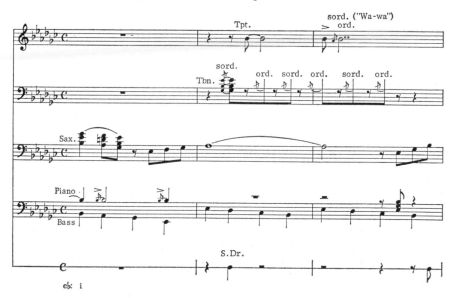

iv

The saxophone is the leading melody here, the cantus firmus. One chorus ends with the saxes in chords, and a new one begins with a solo. But this solo is a completely relaxed foundation for the accompaniment, which is more interesting by far. The trumpet answers each motif with another simple motif, syncopated and varied in color by manipulation of the mute. On top of this, the trombones play snarling chords, syncopated in a different way and also iridescent with mutes. Beneath the melodies and chords, the plucked bass notes are perfectly clear, maintaining the beat and the chord progressions. The drum is very discreet, but its contribution saves the bass part from monotony, and helps to define the four-measure rhythm. Best of all, the piano, with a single note, pushes the whole ensemble from one chorus to the next, and gives a fresh little push to each new attack of the sax. One can easily imagine Ellington at the piano, listening with delight to the perfect realization of what he has imagined.

Richard Boyer described the range of Ellington's procedures in composing for his band. Sometimes he would present them with a mere germinal idea, and preside with astonishing calm over their hectic collective improvisations during the course of two or three hours until they achieved something that satisfied him, to be written down more or less approximately. At the other extreme, he might write an elaborate "arrangement" that left only a little room for spontaneous variation. But in this case he was relying on his intimate knowledge of the players as individuals. Boyer reports his explanation:

You can't write music right unless you know how the man that'll play it plays poker. . . . You've got to write with certain men in mind. You write just for their abilities and natural tendencies and give them places where they do their best—certain entrances and exits and background stuff. . . . I know what sounds well on a trombone and I know what sounds well on a trumpet and they are not the same. I know what Tricky Sam can play on a trombone and I know what Lawrence Brown can play on a trombone and they are not the same, either. . . . I write for my band. For instance, I might think of a wonderful thing for an oboe, but I ain't got no oboe and it doesn't interest me. My band is my instrument.

The procedure in most cases lay between these extremes, so that most performances depended on a sketchy notation, some verbal agreements, and a few code-like signals, leaving considerable leeway for improvisation. Moreover, the sketches, agreements, and signals changed from year to year as the make-up of the band changed, so that every composition was fluid. In the 1950s Ellington began to send his sketchy scores to the Copyright Office in the Library of Congress, where they offered future scholars a treasury for study.

Ellington stood out among the masters of the big band for various reasons: his band included more fine soloists than any other; it benefited from an unusual degree of continuity and harmonious organization, so that each player in it could do his best within it; along with Fletcher Henderson's band, Ellington's was first to develop the style; its repertory centered on tunes of Ellington's own composition, alternating with more popular "ballads" and more traditional blues; its arrangements consistently showed a sense of both harmonic logic and harmonic adventure, rather than using the big sound for mere amplification of what a traditional small band could do as well; above all, it enabled Ellington to compose unprecedented little masterpieces like *Ko Ko* and *Concerto for Cootie*. To be sure, Ellington's work included some unsuccessful attempts at large programmatic forms, some embarrassingly cute moments, and even, occasionally, some imperfections of ensemble timing. Because of these faults, a few critics preferred the bands of Jimmy Lunceford and "Count" Basie, whose work was more reliable within only slightly narrower limits. But Ellington far surpassed these excellent conductors as a composer.

The big band style was the favorite dance music of the 1930s. Under the leadership of Benny Goodman, "king of swing," large audiences became acquainted with various kinds of jazz, and accepted for the first time the mixing of Negro and white performers. At the same time that sound-film, radio, and phonograph forced thousands of competent theater musicians to abandon their careers, the jazz community expanded and enjoyed more prosperity than ever before. The fashionable label, "swing," was naturally applied to a great deal of commercial music that displayed only superficial features of the style—especially its loudness and brassy tone-color, in contrast to the "sweet" dance music surviving from the 1920s. But the popularity of "swing" made possible the popularization of older authentic jazz and folk music, including that of self-accompanying blues singers like Huddie Ledbetter or "Leadbelly" (1885–1949) and Bill Broonzy (1893–1958), and the "boogie-woogie" piano blues of Meade Lux Lewis (b. 1905) and others. Finally the era of "swing" produced the revival of the New Orleans style, especially among white musicians, who properly adopted the label "Dixieland." Between these various revivals and the commercialized forms of "swing" the evolution of the central jazz tradition continued, both endangered and stimulated by the multiplicity of sub-styles that surrounded it.

Big bands provided the setting for an amazing development of the role of percussion in jazz. The virtuosity of a drummer like Gene Krupa, using a whole battery of drums and cymbals in assorted sizes, demanded solo passages in every program, and frequently rose out of the background to compete with the melodic instruments, though never ceasing to provide the steady basic beat, with its inspiring drive. Younger men, especially Kenny Clarke, began to reserve the drums entirely for quasi-melodic, offbeat effects, while relegating the regular beat to the cymbals, subdividing it, and even giving it a legato quality by the continual use of wire brushes. This style, further developed by Max Roach and others, became the most evident feature of "modern jazz" after World War II. Paradoxically, the modern drumming approached African drumming much more nearly than anything in the earlier jazz tradition. Around 1950 percussion instruments and elaborate rhythmic patterns from Latin American popular music were fashionable. Again, the modern drumming was incorporated into all sorts of small "combos," even mere trios of piano, bass, and drums, although it was most at home with big bands.

The development of the saxophones, less surprising, was equally important. Beginning in the 1920s, Coleman Hawkins revealed the potentials of the tenor sax as a solo instrument worthy to rival Armstrong's trumpet, or to stand out against the accompaniment of a big brass section. For these purposes the sax had to be played into the microphone, so that its sound was amplified enough to dominate the band. Hawkins and a few others were able to invent new varieties of tone color and to use them in melodies that justified this treatment of the instrument. In Ellington's band Johnny Hodges (alto sax) and Harry Carney (baritone) contributed more with their solos than any other players. Lester Young, after a wealth of experience on alto and baritone, as well as on drums, discovered a new "cool" style on the tenor sax, fully exploiting the microphone to permit a delicate tone, often without vibrato. He and his successors maintained the position of the sax as the instrument of most varied and intense expression in jazz. Small "combos" were led by saxophonists more often than by trumpeters, thus demonstrating the dependence of the "combos" not on the modest old-time bands, but rather on the big band of "swing."

The alto saxophonist, Charlie Parker, became the chief representative of the most adventurous jazz of the 1940s, whose label was "bop," from the nonsense syllable sung to some of his characteristic abrupt notes. Parker's genius is partly legendary, for he made rather few recordings and some of these were ruined by poor conditions or by his own bitter rejection of the role of entertainer. His fame and influence depend to some extent on this rejection, on the dismal suffering it involved him in, and on his early death. Yet recordings provide enough evidence of his genius to warrant the fame and influence too.

Parker recorded a version of the blues, entitled *Perhaps* (1948), with Miles Davis, John Lewis, Max Roach, and Curley Russell. Our example shows the melody of the first four choruses; it is preceded by a four-measure piano introduction on the dominant, and followed by two fine choruses by Davis, trumpet, and one by the piano, Lewis. The piece ends with an exact recapitulation of the first chorus, which Parker and Davis play both times in perfect unison. This basic melody, presumably taught by Parker to his colleagues, perhaps with the aid of notation, shows on an elementary level the chief features of his style: passages of flowing motion with frequent changes of direction and no obvious sequences; in contrast, abrupt beginnings and endings, with a feeling of impatience, self-consciousness, wry humor; brief emphasis on an occasional burst of dissonant, chromatic harmony, and no pausing to enjoy its resolution. These features are all intensified in the following three choruses, improvised by Parker. Each phrase is remarkable for the sheer number of notes at the fast tempo, and the longest, smoothest phrase comes in the last chorus. The flow of notes seems not merely syncopated against the cymbal's steady beat, but at times oblivious of the beat, freely redividing and subdividing whole measures. The entrance of each phrase suggests that its motion has already begun inaudibly and that its first sound, whether loud or soft, comes at top momentum. Phrase endings bring the motion to rest on chord tones (sometimes, to be sure, a seventh or ninth), avoiding the coincidence of chord progression, the familiar cadence. The very last phrase drifts down to the bottom of the register to make way for the entrance of the trumpet. Chromatic bursts occur inconspicuously within every phrase; their expressive value is always

EXAMPLE XV.3　Parker, *Perhaps,* theme and first solo

made clear by the fluctuation of loudness. At one point in each chorus, measure 8, there is a writhing of the harmony that resembles Bartók, whose music Parker claimed to admire. In the middle chorus this writhing produces a shuddering smear of pitch up to the crucial note, G♭. In Parker's last chorus he recapitulates his first variation, but now anticipates the G♭ and cuts it short. Though the principle of this improvisation is essentially the same as the principle of Armstrong's, or even Morton's, the personality or attitude expressed in Parker's melody and rhythm is as different as the detail—complicated, modern, speculative, anticlimactic. There is no virtuoso display of prowess: all the skill and imagination serve the nervous, volatile, personal feeling. The form of the whole performance differs accordingly. After his colleagues have made their satisfactory comments, Parker has no more to add, but concludes the work with a simple reprise and no coda. The first beat of m. 12 is simply the end, the best possible one. Parker liked to apply his style often to a harmonic framework richer than the blues, such as that of a tune by Berlin or Gershwin. He liked to play his long phrases at a tempo still faster than that of *Perhaps*. And he liked to dispense with the statement of any symmetrical point of departure, assuming that the "standard" tunes he used were so well known to the listeners for whom he played that their shapes could be recognized beneath any amount of harmonic decoration and despite any obscurity of overlapping melodic phrases. He found a few listeners capable of appreciating what he did, and ready to imitate him as far as possible. Naturally many listeners were lost in his maze and rejected it. Some were ready to applaud it without noticing when he made a mistake and played nonsensical dissonance, or when in his impatience he played a phrase that was deliberately trite. His music required for discriminating appreciation as thorough a specialized preparation as any "classical" style. He disapproved of the adaptations that his friend "Dizzy" Gillespie made in the new style to achieve some commercial popularity. He was unconcerned with the efforts of lesser men to exploit the style without mastering its harmonic foundations. He stood for jazz as a fine art, knowing that this meant exclusiveness.

Thus with "bop," jazz met the difficulties that had bewildered critics of new serious music ever since 1910. The best work was so complex in harmony and rhythm that it sounded at first incoherent, not only to laymen but to professionals very close to it. Good work could no longer be discriminated with any speed or certainty from incompetent work, and incompetent workers, in all good faith, took advantage of this situation to press their claims. Some narrow-minded professionals joined impatient laymen to condemn the whole style as a product of incompetence, if not of charlatanism or madness. At the same time some supporters of the new style preferred to interpret its political or poetical purity as depending on its incomprehensibility. The controversy had a momentary publicity value. But this was soon exhausted while the bewilderment went on. The jazz community had to learn to live with it, just as did people interested in other serious new music.

———•——

To the extent that provincial dance musicians and amateurs tried to follow the complex development of "bop," they succeeded in winning an indifferent acceptance at last for fabrics of sound and rhythm in which melody and harmony truly played little part. But this kind of noise could not long be popular for dancing. It provoked a reaction.

New commercial hybrids of various folk styles appeared on the scene. Many of these were ephemeral. Many were offensive to any discriminating lover of real folk music, urbane popular music, or jazz. But some of them had charm, a few had distinction, and altogether they changed the world's popular music in surprising ways.

The most remarkable new style, the most widely popular in the 1950s, and the most nearly related to jazz, was called "rock 'n' roll." It was rooted in blues and Negro church music. In utter contrast to "bop" it reverted to the most elementary formulas of jazz rhythm and triadic harmony; it favored melodies of narrow range and short phrase; it restored the bass drum to the heavy beat, louder than ever, and often so slow that the triple subdivision became explicit, even waltz-like. Here was a style that demanded a minimum of technical competence to provoke a maximum of hypnotic or stimulating effect on a susceptible audience. Yet this style also had room for subtleties, for variety of tone color and intricacy of melodic ornamentation. When represented by such an intense and imaginative musician as Ray Charles, "rock 'n' roll" deserved its popularity. Moreover, even in its crudest forms, the style had several interesting effects on fundamental musical habits, as Arnold Shaw has pointed out: it destroyed the thirty-two measure form, it explored odd-numbered patterns and rhythms, and further, through use of the old modes it weakened the position of the major mode as the norm of urban civilization. Debussy would have been delighted with these negative effects of "rock 'n' roll" as well as with the subtlety and spontaneity of Ray Charles.

"Rock 'n' roll," whether subtly imaginative or merely elemental, was not sweetened for commercial success. It represented more nakedly than any of its predecessors its source in the proletarian American Negroes' vast store of music and dance, and it was recognized as their product all around the world, by the mobs that welcomed it and the snobs that tried to escape it. Its wide acceptance helped to disseminate the more demanding kinds of jazz, which could then sustain interest longer than "rock 'n' roll" itself. Yet in itself it loomed as an immense social fact.

The central tradition persisted through the era of "rock 'n' roll" as it had before. The label "mainstream jazz" began to be used to distinguish the persisting forms from "bop," "cool," "Dixieland," and commercial hybrids. And branching off from the mainstream there were more and more experiments trickling toward the broader, older streams of concert music: several players toyed with flute, cello, and horn; David Brubeck, having studied composition with Darius Milhaud, made good use of polychords and polyrhythms without permanently losing the essential "swing"; Gunther Schuller (b. 1925) and others linked jazz with twelve-tone technique, Webernish instrumentation, and ambitious forms; the Modern Jazz Quartet proudly displayed canons and fugatos; Gil Evans (b. 1912) invented delightful new sounds for large orchestra. According to the jazz historian Marshall Stearns (1961), these experiments were tending to bring European "classical" music into a dominant position in the whole development of jazz. Yet Stearns recognized the balancing forces of the various revivals and of folk-like popular music, and the still distinct "mainstream."

That the "mainstream" was not only distinct but also moving was suggested by the appearance in 1958 of the young saxophonist Ornette Coleman, whose melodies were at once more bewilderingly complex than Parker's and more crudely intense than those of Ray Charles. Critics like Nat Hentoff and Virgil Thomson found Coleman's music beautiful and memorable.

The study of jazz expanded with the art. John Lewis established a summer school at Lenox, Massachusetts, which brought together many of the best players, students, critics, and historians, for fruitful exchanges. Some conservatories and universities established courses in jazz. "Dizzy" Gillespie appealed to the public schools to teach the appreciation of jazz. Lennie Tristano became the first professional specialist in jazz teaching, with his own school in New York. The vast bibliography of the subject was recorded by Alan Merriam and others. Encyclopedias of jazz—mainly biographical directories—were provided by Feather and Dauer. Comprehensive critical surveys, especially those of Finkelstein and Newton, enabled non-specialists to gain a perspective view of the samples of jazz within their experience.

With the help of such studies, unknown friends of jazz all around the world earned the privilege of enjoying this 20th-century music. In Japan, in Australia, in South Africa, in Sweden, everywhere there were ardent groups of jazz players, critics, collectors, and fans, setting themselves apart from the massive music business to cultivate their privilege. No other kind of music —no other kind of contemporary art whatever—had so many true and active friends as jazz.

CHAPTER XVI

Schoenberg to His Death
(1951)

WHILE JAZZ developed and spread through the world, Arnold Schoenberg carried forward the uncompromising new style that made most other music, old and new, seem like folklore. He created an imposing list of works in various forms and media, using various kinds and degrees of tonality and "atonality." From the privacy of his circle in Vienna he moved to Berlin (1926–33) as successor to Busoni in a position of high official honor and influence, which permitted him long, productive vacations in France and Spain; then, fleeing from the Nazis, he settled for a busy life of teaching in Los Angeles, California (1934–44), and here he continued to work, after he had officially retired, until his death at the age of seventy-six (1951). Only his closest disciples accorded him the recognition he craved as the greatest composer since Wagner. His style and his ideas never swayed fashion during his lifetime. Yet his challenging adventures could not be dismissed from the center of discussion of contemporary music.

Schoenberg's adoption of the twelve-tone technique in the 1920s provoked still more discussion than his radical "atonal" style, represented by *Pierrot Lunaire*. And this technique dominated fashions in the decade after his death. The gradual absorption of some sort of twelve-tone technique into various other styles, proceeding very slowly, almost secretly, in the 1930s, accelerating in the late 'forties and 'fifties, convinced more and more persons of Schoenberg's position as leader of 20th-century music.

The development of the twelve-tone technique was an important part of Schoenberg's achievement. He often insisted on the subordination of this part to his work as a whole. Yet he also recognized with some satisfaction the possibility and even, for composers, the desirability of studying the technique separately, as part of the common craft of manipulating musical materials. His first announcement of the technique, in private conversation with his pupil Josef Rufer, 1921, took the form: "I have discovered something that will assure supremacy for German music for the next hundred years." And in his classic lecture on "Composition with Twelve Tones" (1941) he predicted: "The time will come when the ability to draw thematic material from a basic set of twelve tones will be an unconditional prerequisite for obtaining admission to the composition class of a conservatory." By 1960 conservatories did not need to advertise such a prerequisite, for student composers were practicing the technique with eager interest, whether or not they listened to Schoenberg's music. Students of history, on the other hand, were increasingly aware that Schoenberg's technique could be understood adequately only by reference to his music.

To the historian and critic Paul Bekker, Schoenberg wrote in 1924: "I cannot be understood, and I content myself with respect." In 1939 he advised his friend, the great music educator Leo Kestenberg, to proceed cautiously in his efforts to make the music of Schoenberg known in Israel:

I should like to answer "gradually, step by step." In my music it has never been a matter of "style," but always of a content and its transmission, as precise as possible. Therefore my youthful works prepare for the understanding of my musical thoughts, and it is good to become acquainted with these before my manner of expression becomes so condensed as in my latest works. . . . And I believe that nothing of the third period [beginning 1923] should be presented earlier, since even for most "musicians" these offer hardly anything other than their style.

A decade after his death, the desirable gradual progress toward understanding Schoenberg's "content" was still difficult. Most musicians, still preoccupied with styles and techniques, now paid Schoenberg the highest respect, and not only composers were willing to study the late works rather closely just for the sake of the technique they exemplified.

In his lecture on the technique (1941) Schoenberg called it officially: "Method of Composing with Twelve Tones Which are Related Only with One Another. This method consists primarily of the constant and exclusive use of a set of twelve different tones . . . Mine is no system, but only a method, which means a *modus* of applying regularly a preconceived formula."

The most succinct example of the technique is the trio of the Minuet from the Suite for piano, Op. 25.

EXAMPLE XVI.1   Schoenberg, Trio, from Suite, Op. 25

A set of twelve different notes appears in the left hand part, measures 34–35. The right hand answers in canon by contrary motion, at the tritone; this is a "*modus* of applying a preconceived formula"—the right-hand part is a new "form" of the same "set," "series," or "row" (*Reihe*) that is to be used constantly and exclusively. The left hand continues with another form, the inversion starting from an octave above. The right hand answers with a simple transposition of the original form. We can readily understand what Schoenberg means by saying that "the basic set functions in the manner of a motive." It does so throughout the exposition of the little piece. The exposition is repeated exactly. Then, after two measures whose analysis is best postponed, comes a recapitulation, condensed and varied. The left hand plays twelve different notes that conform to the rhythm of the theme; they suggest also the pitch outline of the inverted form; they correspond to the retrograde order of the letter names in the transposed original form that was played by the right hand, mm. 37–38, except for the reversal of the notes C and A, which is whimsical, or ironical. The right hand answers this recapitulation with its inversion, at the unison, simplifying the pitch outline in the final measure, but maintaining the correspondence of letter names. Letter names, regardless of register, are the clues to many of the relations in the twelve-tone technique; "notes" or "tones," in Schoenberg's sense, are abstracted from register. Yet letter names are not the basic elements either, for enharmonic equivalents may be used whenever convenient. (Compare right hand m. 35 with left hand m. 36.) The elements are a new kind of abstraction, which Hermann Pfrogner aptly calls *Tonorte* (tone-places), and to which Michael Kassler has given a rigorous, mathematical definition as "note classes." By using the retrograde form of the series of letter names to approximate an inversion of the pitch contour, Schoenberg makes three measures, 41–43, serve as recapitulation of five measures, 34–39. This is the greatest novelty of the technique. The technique, then, is a means of condensing forms. This is not all it achieves, but this is characteristic.

Analysis is facilitated by a chart of letter names, which can be read up or down, right to left, or left to right. The "original row" appears at the top, left to right. Its inversion is at the left, top to bottom.

E	F	G	Db	/	Gb	Eb	Ab	D	/	B	C	A	Bb
Eb													A
Db													G
G													Db
D													Ab
F													B
C													F#
F#													C
A													Eb
Ab													D
Cb													F
Bb	Cb	Db	G	/	C	A	D	Ab	/	F	Gb	Eb	E

Transpositions, as required, appear parallel. Retrograde forms are simply read off backward. In Op. 25 Schoenberg uses the eight forms shown on our chart. For later works, where he uses more transpositions, all forty-eight forms can be shown in an equal area, by filling in the rest of the 144 spaces with the proper letter-names. For Op. 25 it is convenient to mark off the four-note groups; in other instances six-note groups will be more important. Finally, for Op. 25 it is interesting to note the cross-reference of the tritone Db G, occurring in all the forms; in the exposition of the trio these notes are always staccato, unemphasized, but in the Musette movement they are continually repeated to make a quasi-pedalpoint, in accordance with the tradition of such movements, and throughout the suite the constant association of these two notes provides an element of unity more readily perceptible than the various forms of the whole set.

Tracing the set in the Minuet and the other movements of the Suite, the analyst discovers that not every note, in the usual sense of the term, counts as a note in Schoenberg's sense, and that on the other hand a single note, in the usual sense, may count as two. Within one appearance of the set, any note may be repeated, and any pair of notes may be alternated as in a trill or tremolo; *the note*, in Schoenberg's sense, has been extended and ornamented with repercussions, but it is only one unit among the twelve. Contrariwise, no repercussion is needed to permit the counting of one suitably situated pitch as a member of two adjacent forms of the twelve-tone set. Both of these principles are illustrated in three measures from the Minuet.

EXAMPLE XVI.2   Schoenberg, Minuet, from Suite, Op. 25, midpoint

Though these principles are not exemplified in the trio, they are essential to Schoenberg's technique, and to a correct understanding of the very meaning of "note" and "set" in the description of the technique. Twelve-tone analysis of a texture of this sort brings out connections that can be heard in a good performance better than they can be seen in the notation, even with the guiding numerals; slight rhythmic changes in the notation can bring out the same connections, and thus can serve as a useful stage in the preparation of a good performance.

EXAMPLE XVI.3   Schoenberg, Minuet, from Suite, Op. 25, midpoint (rewritten for practice)

A few playings of this version make possible an enriched return to the original, with its repeated note(s) and its tied note(s).

A pianist who has learned from twelve-tone analysis to recognize this formal density in the little trio can make it perceptible to alert listeners, by subordinating the sixteenth notes and exaggerating the accents and swellings of the eighths. Further, with his grasp of the whole nine measures, he can emphasize a long-range melodic and harmonic motion, in which $B\flat$ and $E\flat$ alternately predominate over all other pitches. He cannot, on the contrary, make perceptible such a detail as the reversal of the A and C in measure 42. Would some ideal listener hear these notes as "wrong," violating the order of the set in which they appear, and then relish them especially because of their freedom? No; carefully controlled tests by the psychologist Robert Francès have shown that much more drastic deviations from a set pass undetected by experienced composers of twelve-tone music. If Schoenberg intended anything by this reversal, it could be only an ironic warning to analysts. Humbly then, let analysts persist.

When the second part of the trio is repeated, there is a new variant in the last measure, abandoning the canonic texture and leading toward the da capo repetition of the main Minuet. Here is another characteristic aspect of Schoenberg's flexible technique. This effect can be appreciated by anyone who listens repeatedly to the music.

In the murmuring episode between exposition and recapitulation, the two hands of the pianist maintain their canonic relation. Each hand has its twelve notes. Their order, however, is no more obviously like the rest of the trio than it is like the main Minuet. There is no trace of the rhythmic motifs of the theme. The "basic set" from which the theme was drawn is somewhat like a motif, but also it is an "order" abstracted from rhythmic values, like a scale. The episode is drawn from the abstract set, not from the theme. But this is not enough to account for the episode. The set is still more abstract. It is not a linear series, a row of notes in the literal sense; rows offer only a few forms, eight or forty-eight, out of an infinite number of possible "forms" of the set. In the episode, left-hand part of measures 39–40, the order is two-dimensional: 8 7   6 5
   12   11 10   9 1 2 3 4.
It mixes retrograde and original forms. It breaks the set into three groups of four notes each, and combines two of the groups in an ambiguous texture where two notes can arrive simultaneously but there are not two distinct voices. The analyst's task resembles cryptography. All the more fascinating! The solution here is not very hard to find; more puzzling problems arise in the main Minuet. Nor is it hard to find a reason for the mild puzzle here; the soft blurring of the texture is appropriate for just this moment in the form, while the vigorous recovery in m. 40 is a kind of retransition, teasing the listener toward the recapitulation.

For performer and listener, there is no need to disentangle the order from this blur; there may be some hope, but not much, of perceiving, remembering, and appreciating the mode of application of the basic set here—the most that is needed is to recognize a difference from the mode that prevails in the rest of the trio.

Nevertheless, our analysis demonstrates something important to the composer, something essential to the twelve-tone technique in general, for Schoenberg lays great emphasis on the principle that *"the two-or-more dimensional space in which musical ideas are presented is a unit."*

The elements of a musical idea are partly incorporated in the horizontal plane as successive sounds, and partly in the vertical plane as simultaneous sounds. . . . And this explains why . . . a basic set of twelve notes . . . can be used in either dimension, as a whole or in parts. . . . The unity of musical space demands an absolute and unitary perception. In this space, as in Swedenborg's heaven (described in Balzac's *Seraphita*), there is no absolute down, no right or left, forward or backward. Every musical configuration, every movement of tones has to be comprehended as a mutual relation of sounds, of oscillatory vibrations, appearing at different times and places.

Schoenberg's music is never lacking in some application of this principle. While some other composers may apply the preconceived twelve-tone formula like a stencil, mechanically copying notes from a written list like our chart, Schoenberg's modes of application are always varied, and always include textural blurs as well as motivic development. He too used lists of notes as an aid in composing, but he did not begin with such a list. Rather, he began with an "inspiration" of melody and accompaniment, and from this abstracted the series. (His starting-point for Op. 25 was the Intermezzo.)

Perhaps performer and listener might arrive at an appreciation of the over-all form of our trio, with its literal repetitions, without the benefit of any twelve-tone analysis. To many musicians, moreover, Schoenberg's combination of neat, traditional forms with his new twelve-tone technique seems incongruous.

But to Schoenberg the very purpose of the technique was "to replace those structural differentiations provided formerly by tonal harmonies." His free "atonal" style had hampered the composing of any long piece without a text; his wanting to compose such pieces was what motivated his search for the new technique. He believed not only that the basic set had a unifying effect, guaranteeing coherence, but also that the various "modes of application" distinguished expository, introductory, transitional, episodic, climactic, and concluding parts of a composition from one another. Therefore, if we are faithfully to analyze his technique we shall not merely identify the set again and again, but rather use the set to help us follow the forms.

In the thirty-three measures of the main Minuet in Op. 25, the basic set is applied twenty-six times, always with a blurred texture of two or more strands, occasionally as many as five. Nowhere does the set appear so clearly as in the trio. Thus, in its context the trio is an exceptionally simple, light piece, as trios are in the quartets and symphonies of Haydn. (It was composed in a day—Rufer's excerpts from Sketchbook V name the day, 3 March 1923—whereas the Minuet had required nine days.) The blurred mm. 39–40 are more characteristic of the movement as a whole than is the rest of the trio.

Moreover, in the entire Suite the Minuet is the gentlest, most lyrical movement, with the least variety of "modes of application" of the basic set. The set appears as a continuous theme only in the trio and in the first movement, Prelude, where it is accompanied by four-note groups that make surprising two-dimensional orders. The central movement, Intermezzo, preserves the original inspiration of the Suite, in which a broken chord makes an ostinato accompaniment for bits of melody. This inspiration dates back to July 25, 1921 (or even earlier, if Jan Maegaard has correctly interpreted unpublished materials). In February 1923, when Schoenberg completed his formulation of the twelve-tone set, he completed the piece and began three of the other movements to go with it. In the last movement, Jig, the variety is greatest; the texture sometimes thickens to six and seven notes, so that the set whirls through two or three of its forms within a single measure at fast tempo, and nearly congeals into a twelve-tone chord. The final phrase of the Jig illustrates a use of the set that is more typical of Schoenberg's technique throughout the Suite (and in later works too) than the simple trio where we began.

EXAMPLE XVI.4 Schoenberg, Jig, from Suite, Op. 25, end

The flourish just before the final phrase, like some other brief passages in the Jig, illustrates a sequential order of twelve notes that is quite free from the basic set, though still faithful to the characteristic tritone. This is an extreme degree of freedom, rarely encountered in Schoenberg's later works, where the sets seem to be chosen so as to give rise to similar formations more directly. The whole passage, and the whole Jig, unlike most 18th-century jigs, avoids imitative counterpoint. The trio's strict canons are unique in the Suite, balancing the Jig's extreme freedom.

Having sampled the range of "modes of application," from the canons of the light trio to the freedom and bravura of the Jig, we have an adequate idea of what Schoenberg's technique is. Shorter explanations are liable to misleading oversimplifications. Both shorter and longer accounts are frequently mingled with untenable statements about style. The technique is adaptable to many styles.

———•·•———

The twelve-tone technique does not affect the open question of "atonality." It is compatible with the "atonal" style, but also with other styles. Indeed, Winfried Zillig reports that Schoenberg looked forward to a future theory that would show tonality to be a special case of the twelve-tone technique. The connection with atonality that Schoenberg himself tried to make, in an exceptional passage of his lecture on the technique, is specious:

In my *Harmonielehre* (1911) I recommended the avoidance of octave doublings. To double is to emphasize, and an emphasized tone could be interpreted as a root, or even as a tonic; the consequences of such an interpretation must be avoided. Even a slight reminiscence of the former tonal harmony would be disturbing, because it would create false expectations of consequences and continuations. The use of a tonic is deceiving if it is not based on *all* the relationships of tonality.

The use of more than one set was excluded because in every following set one or more tones would have been repeated too soon. Again there would arise the danger of interpreting the repeated tone as a tonic. Besides, the effect of unity would be lessened.

The avoidance of octaves remained a cardinal principle of Schoenberg's style until 1942, when he modified it to permit big sonorities in the *Ode to Napoleon* and the Piano Concerto. To the end of his life the avoidance of octaves was an important consideration and operated in his choice of basic sets. But the avoidance of all emphasis he never attempted. And the avoidance of tonality was not often, if ever, his concern. (His argument here could be turned against the use of different *forms* of the set, for they bring some recurrences closer together than would the continual use of a single form.) No, his argument here is inconsistent with his practice and with the rest of his theory. It is worth attention chiefly for the purpose of correcting a widespread mistake. Both practice and theory call attention more frequently to the motivic and contrapuntal aspect of the technique than to its relation to tonality.

Likewise there is no necessary connection between the twelve-tone technique and the "emancipation of dissonance." The technique allows consonance. And in Schoenberg's Op. 25, though consonance is avoided, the dissonances are not so thick as in most of his music from Op. 11 to Op. 24.

A true connection between the twelve-tone technique and earlier trends in the harmony of Schoenberg and others is its "emancipated chromaticism." Though not every twelve-tone row avoids reference to diatonic scales, many do. Moreover the continual recurrence of all twelve notes, regardless of lingering references or emphases, unmistakably both defines and attains a goal—a terminus for the increasing use of chromatic notes. In this way, Schoenberg's adoption of the technique was a logical step in his stylistic development.

The development from free chromaticism to twelve-tone technique was not peculiar to Schoenberg, but closely paralleled or anticipated independently by Charles Ives (Ex. IV.1), by the young Viennese music teacher and theorist, Josef Matthias Hauer (1883–1959), the Russian emigrés, Yefim Golyshev (b. 1885) and Nicholas Obukhov (1892–1954), and the still younger scholar and experimenter from Cologne, Herbert Eimert (b. 1897). All these younger men, accepting the label of "atonality" that Schoenberg disliked, were more concerned with theoretical formulations of the new technique and with its significance for the future development of a common musical language than with its application to such forms and media as minuet and trio, sonata, cantata, and opera. Thus Hauer, according to Friedrich Wildgans, "designates himself not as a composer, but only as an instrument destined to follow the eternal laws of the cosmos and interpret them musically." His earliest publication (1912) was a piano piece, *Nomos* (*The Law*), in which his twelve-tone technique is adumbrated. His first public explanation of the law was an article on "Music of the Spheres" (June 1922). Here and in his later articles and books he condemns tonality, not merely as outworn but as utterly misguided. He proclaims the cosmic law of atonality, requiring the use of twelve-tone groups (not series). He recommends his *Zwölftonspiel* (game) as comparable to chess, or perhaps to solitaire or to mystical meditation, rather than a method of composing. His short compositions, as Karl Eschman shows, submit to habitual routines of rhythm and crude types of structure. Two letters from Schoenberg to Hauer, December 1923, indicate the great difference between the two, and the little realm where their interests overlap. In the light of these letters, it is impossible to agree with the contention of Egon Wellesz, advanced only after Schoenberg's death, that "Hauer's twelve-tone compositions showed him the way out of his own crisis." Rudolph Stephan, having surveyed Hauer's entire work, makes no judgment of its importance. Other authorities on Hauer's work, including Othmar Steinbauer and Walter Szmolyan, recommend it for its own sake, not for its historical importance. Nicholas Obukhov's series of twelve-tone chords, without doubling, were described and exemplified by Boris de Schloezer in 1921. Obukhov too ascribed "mystic meaning" to the equal treatment of the twelve tones. He devoted his life to the composition of one immense occult liturgy, *The Book of Life*. Schoenberg was probably unaware of him. More evidence on these matters will doubtless come to light in the future, but there is now enough to prove that Schoenberg, like the younger men, arrived at his own version of the new technique in the course of composing.

Once the technique was established, precedents for it could be observed in many earlier composers' works. Oliver Neighbour, for example, traces a development of chromaticism in the works of Bartók, Stravinsky, Debussy, and Scriabin, at the end of which Schoenberg "emerges . . . as the central figure." Gerald Abraham and others cite prominent twelve-tone themes in Liszt, Strauss, and Reger. Milhaud has found one in Mozart's *Don Giovanni*. The books on the technique by Leibowitz and Rufer, with many examples, emphasize the interaction of chromaticism and motivic development. Alan Walker and Hans Keller point to interesting serial techniques in Mozart and Beethoven. Peter Gradenwitz draws parallels with Near Eastern music, and Hermann Pfrogner with ancient Chinese theory. The value of all these comparisons is to prove that Schoenberg's technique is no arbitrary, unmusical trick, but rather a natural outcome of tendencies inherent in much music. Just as with the "emancipation of dissonance," study proves not that the twelve-tone technique is the only natural outcome, or the best one, but simply that it is one.

Finally, Schoenberg's disciples, Berg and Webern, shared in the development of the new technique. They had been his pupils before he composed *Pierrot Lunaire*, and by that time they had developed their own mature styles parallel to his. While he groped toward the twelve-tone technique, they were collaborating with him in the Society for Private Performances and they were steadily composing characteristic works in which many anticipations of the technique may be found. When Schoenberg discovered his new rules, Berg and Webern at once recognized the rules as relevant to their own practice, and they proceeded to develop them in their own ways. Roman Vlad's ample history of the twelve-tone technique shows the three composers' development together, stage by stage; each one is different at each stage. A letter from Schoenberg to Rudolf Kolisch, 1932, complains that Berg and Webern take the technique too seriously:

You have dug out the series of my string quartet correctly (except for a trifle: the second consequent phrase goes, sixth note C-sharp, seventh note G-sharp). That must have been a very great effort, and I do not think I should have mustered the patience for it. Do you think that it is useful to know this? I cannot really imagine it. According to my conviction, to be sure, it might be stimulating to a composer who is not yet well trained in the use of series—a clue to procedure, a mere craftsman's reference to the possibility of creating from series. But the esthetic qualities do not open up from this, or at most parallel to it. I cannot warn often enough against overvaluing these analyses, for they lead only to what I have always opposed: to recognition of how it is *done*; while I have always assisted people to recognize what it *is*! I have repeatedly tried to make this clear to Wiesengrund, and also to Berg and Webern. But they do not believe me. I cannot say it often enough: my works are twelve-tone *compositions*, not *twelve-tone* compositions. In this respect I am being confused again with Hauer, for whom composition is a matter of secondary importance.

Berg and Webern never disputed Schoenberg's emphasis, but they went on praising him for his great discovery and his great teaching. If his later compositions interested them less than his earlier ones, and less than their own adaptations of the new technique, still they never ceased to acknowledge his mastery and originality. For his part, Schoenberg never ceased to praise the genius of Berg and Webern, to help them in any way he could, and to address them as "dearest friends." The mutual devotion of all three composers, together with the variety and power of all their twelve-tone *compositions*, more than any theory of historic trends, obligate serious musicians to study the technique.

Schoenberg's Suite, Op. 25, and his other compositions of the 1920s display a new spirit, as well as a new technique. In the context of the German tradition their spirit is not so new as their technique, but since their technique sets them apart, many critics overlook their traditionalism. In the narrower context of Schoenberg's works, both earlier and later, the new traditional spirit of the 1920s is evident to anyone not obsessed by the technique. It is a playful spirit, confident, worldly, ironic, yet reverent toward the past. This is no longer the "expressionism" of Opp. 11–22, though it is not without some precedent in *Pierrot Lunaire*, especially No. 3, *The Dandy*, No. 12, *Gallows song*, and No. 16, *Vulgarity*. It is closer to Strauss and Reger and to Schoenberg's Chamber Symphony, Op. 9, than to the light moments of Mahler or Schoenberg's *Glückliche Hand*. It reflects an interlude of happiness and hope in Schoenberg's life, which was so laden with disappointments and disasters.

At the end of January 1923 Schoenberg visited Copenhagen, to conduct his Chamber Symphony. The Danish publisher, Hansen, arranged to publish the piano music and the serenade (Opp. 23–24) that he began to compose in 1920 and then put aside. Within a few days after his return to Vienna, he had won commissions for two similar works from Universal

Edition, where his *Harmonielehre* had recently been republished and his earlier works—the piano pieces, Opp. 11 and 19, the *Orchestra Pieces,* Op. 16, and *Pierrot,* Op. 21—were steadily building prestige if not profit. His delight in this new situation he expressed in a letter to Zemlinsky. Now he could cease teaching for a while, he would postpone indefinitely the great project of *Jacob's Ladder,* and follow his inspiration on a modest scale. He rapidly completed Opp. 23, 25, and 24, and without pause went on to Op. 26, the Wind Quintet. In the dancing rhythms of all these works his new cheerful mood is expressed—the movements of Opp. 23 and 25 that he had started earlier are the parts with more complicated, prose-like rhythms. The march that begins and ends Op. 24 is full of syncopations and ostinato figures comparable to jazz, or at least to Stravinsky's *Soldier's Tale.* The slow movement of Op. 26 has a calm, songful, long-breathed melody, such as Schoenberg had hardly attempted since Op. 10, and even this movement has a waltzing episode. The finale of Op. 26 is an exuberant rondo, with fugato, stretto, prominent whole-tone scales, climactic fourth chords, and a strong emphasis on the first and last note, E♭; it is like a vast expansion of the trio from Op. 25. The piece is as difficult for the winds as the Chamber Symphony, and hence performances are still too few and too rough to make possible a certain judgment of it, but its happy inspiration shines through even a fragmentary performance.

Schoenberg counts on his audience's knowing the classical repertory; as references in Opp. 24 and 25 to early 18th-century rhythms, forms, and moods are evident from the titles, so in Op. 26 the treatment of contrasting themes conforms to the "classical" rules of development and recapitulation that 19th-century theorists derived from the works of Beethoven. Schoenberg, like Riemann or Schenker or d'Indy, regards the classics as permanently valid norms, and his Quintet exemplifies them straightforwardly. Erwin Stein's essay on "Musical Thought: Beethoven and Schoenberg" (1927) offers an especially good exposition of Schoenberg's kind of neo-Classicism:

If music be sounding thought rather than sounding play, everything has to make sense, nothing must be a superfluous end in itself. Economy is the overriding requirement, concentration its result. A new principle arises: everything has to be thematic, nothing decorative. Filling-in parts . . . are banned by Schoenberg. What makes such strictness possible is the very mutability of motifs and themes which Beethoven initiated. . . . The depth of Beethoven's music consists in the depth of its motivic and other formal connections. Once we really grasp this fact, we know what music is "about," and where it has to try its luck in the future. . . . The time will come when we shall better understand how Schoenberg's "composition with twelve notes," too, derives—as a final consequence—from Beethoven.

The contrast with Stravinsky's "neo-Classic" Octet for winds is more important than the striking chronological coincidence. (Stravinsky finished the Octet in May 1923, when Schoenberg had just begun his Quintet; the Octet was first performed in October of the same year, and the Quintet in September 1924.) Stravinsky takes fragments of the classic heritage as points of departure for his peculiar polar harmony and his unique forms; Schoenberg brings his "emancipated dissonance" and chromaticism into themes and forms that resemble those of the classics. Stravinsky's immediate effect is that of a witty parody, but this wears off to reveal an intense poignance; Schoenberg's effect is that of amazing, unfathomable complexity, through which gradually emerge the intentions of joy and reverence. The two kinds of neo-Classicism arose as independently as the two kinds of revolutionary novelty that preceded them. Soon they seemed antagonistic. When Schoenberg took notice of Stravinsky's development, in his *Satires* of 1925, it was to deride the "little Modernsky" and his "wig just like Papa Bach." Schoenberg never listened for the Stravinsky poignance. Stravinsky, in turn, never studied Schoenberg until the older man died.

1924 was the year of many first performances—not only the new Op. 24 and Op. 26, but also the pre-war dramas, *Erwartung* and *Die glückliche Hand*. It was the year of Schoenberg's fiftieth birthday, celebrated by a special issue of the magazine *Anbruch*, with contributions by the leading Italian composers, Casella and Malipiero, as well as the Viennese group. Erwin Stein's article in this volume, "New Formal Principles," was the first public exposition of Schoenberg's twelve-tone technique. (It still serves as authoritative introduction.) In the same year, after a proper period of mourning for his first wife, who had died in October 1923, Schoenberg married Gertrud Kolisch, the sister of his pupil, friend, and interpreter, Rudolf Kolisch. For his new wife Schoenberg began a work more joyful than any other in his whole career—the Septet, Op. 29, with an overture (partly a waltz), a sort of foxtrot, a set of variations on *Aennchen von Tarau* (a popular song like *Die Lorelei*, by Silcher, c. 1840), and a jig-finale in which the song returns. Op. 29 was not finished until 1926, after Schoenberg had moved to his new post at the Prussian Academy of Arts, Berlin. Meanwhile in the fall of 1925 he had dashed off the series of choruses, Opp. 27 and 28.

A commission from Mrs. Elizabeth Sprague Coolidge (1864–1953), inaugurating her foundation at the Library of Congress, Washington, D.C., brought forth Schoenberg's Third String Quartet, Op. 30 (1927), another example of his Beethovenish thought.

His next two works reached out toward a wider audience. The Variations for orchestra, Op. 31, is the only one of Schoenberg's twelve-tone compositions included in Stravinsky's canon of the "true tradition." Adorno ranks it as *the* masterwork of modernism. Schoenberg's analytical comments on it in the essay on "Composition with Twelve Tones," and the more voluminous analysis by Leibowitz, in his *Introduction à la musique aux douze sons,* enable score-readers to trace the structure of this work; occasional performances permit the "sound," in Schoenberg's words, to be "the radiation of an intrinsic quality of ideas, powerful enough to penetrate the hull of the form." *Von Heute auf Morgen* (*From Today to Tomorrow*, Op. 32, 1929) is a one-act domestic comedy, like Strauss's *Intermezzo* (1924). Hans Keller emphasizes the importance of this work as clearly revealing the least recognized side of Schoenberg's character, and illuminating all the rest of both his character and his work. Its happy ending, with man and wife reconciled and humbled by their child, admirably offsets the misery of *Verklärte Nacht, Pelleas, Erwartung,* and *Glückliche Hand.* Its emphasis on *bel canto* singing likewise offsets the predominance of *Sprechstimme* in Schoenberg's works. Its use of saxophones brings it close to jazz, whose rhythms reappear here for the last time in Schoenberg's career. The "jazz age" was ended.

Three important later works, appearing at intervals amid Schoenberg's various output, continued the series of twelve-tone classics from the 1920s: the Fourth Quartet (1936), the Violin Concerto (1934–36), and the Piano Concerto (1942). These, together perhaps with Opp. 25–33, seemed likelier than *Pierrot Lunaire* or anything else since *Verklärte Nacht* to reach eventually some considerable part of the audience of Beethoven. Yet all these works were subordinate, for some listeners, as for Schoenberg himself, to another group: the religious works.

As early as 1926, with the drama *Der biblische Weg* (*The Biblical Path*), Schoenberg resumed the development of his religious thought, which he had postponed with *Jacob's Ladder* in 1922. (Even in 1924, joining the celebration of his 50th birthday, he referred to this oratorio as the major work under way, and to his current preoccupations as relatively minor.) In 1930–32 he devoted himself chiefly to the opera, *Moses und Aron*; thereafter he returned to this work intermittently, completing the text, which is his greatest literary achievement, and the music for two of the three acts, which surpasses even *Gurre-Lieder* as his most extensive musical composition. In *Moses,* the tangled theosophical ideas of *Jacob's Ladder* give way to something both clear and deep, orthodox and dramatic—the struggle to teach what transcends all perceiving and imagining. When *Moses* was finally performed, after Schoenberg's death, its drama won sympathy for its music from some listeners who had made no sense of his other works, and for others it cast new light on old favorites. The "unitary space" and the certain (even though imperceptible) unity of the twelve-tone technique seemed appropriate for the drama of man's union with the imperceptible God. Before the performance of *Moses,* Schoenberg's religion was manifested in two shorter works: a setting of the traditional text, *Kol Nidre,* Op. 39 (1938), and a short cantata, *A Survivor from Warsaw,* Op. 45 (1947). At the end of his life he was again working on original religious texts—the

Modern Psalms. The first of these he partly set to music; the point where he broke off, as Hans Keller has noted, is like the breaking-off point of *Moses,* a point of mystic transcendence. Such points are rare. Schoenberg's psalms include moments of doubt, bitter curses of his enemies, nationalistic pride in Israel, nostalgic musings on Jesus, and a theory of playful sex as the origin of evil. Only *Moses,* of all the religious works, sustains concentration on a central theme.

Another class of works was inaugurated in 1928 with the settings for unaccompanied chorus of three anonymous songs from the 15th and 16th centuries, labelled by the publisher, though not by Schoenberg himself, as folksongs. The settings might almost be mistaken for works of Reger or some lesser composer of his generation; they are too elaborate in their chromatic harmony and counterpoint to appeal to many amateur singers, yet too archaic to appeal to singers interested in Schoenberg's more characteristic works. In the 1930s and 1940s American publishers prompted the composition of several somewhat similar pieces, including the Suite for orchestra, the Variations for organ, the Variations for band, and another set of "folksongs," as well as the didactic *Models for Beginners in Composition.* Without any prompting, Schoenberg added to this list the Second Chamber Symphony. He defended such pieces as authentic "masterpieces," though of course not so important as his twelve-tone works; he never tired of repeating that differences of styles were negligible by comparison with the richness of ideas.

Two chamber works from the 1940s seem to resume a line of development from *Pierrot Lunaire* and the little piano pieces of Op. 19: the Trio, Op. 45, and the Phantasy for violin with piano accompaniment, Op. 47. Here special instrumental effects such as harmonics, double stops, *tremolando, glissando, col legno, sul ponticello* are used almost continuously, emancipated from reference to normal bowing and plucking just as dissonance is emancipated from consonance and the twelve-tone scale from the diatonic. Rhythm once more is extremely varied and prose-like. Motifs grow into novel athematic structures. Schoenberg told Thomas Mann and other friends that in the Trio he had "secreted" his experience of an almost fatal illness, with all the medical details, including hypodermic needle and male nurse. The Phantasy seems to need a programmatic explanation still more.

In the setting of Byron's defiant *Ode to Napoleon,* Op. 41, twelve-tone technique and Expressionistic devices combine with the nostalgia for triads and cadences. The combination seems forced and arbitrary to some sympathetic students of the *Ode.* Perhaps the combination was premature, for after separate further development of the various tendencies, Schoenberg combined them with amazing success.

All the variegated strands in Schoenberg's late works—neo-Classicism, religiosity, practicality, Expressionism, twelve-tone technique, Israeli nationalism, nostalgia for common chords and cadences, *Sprechstimme*—are woven together in his last completed work, the choral setting of Psalm 130,

EXAMPLE XVI.5 Schoenberg, *Mima'amaḳim* (*Out of the Depths*, Psalm 130), Op. 50b

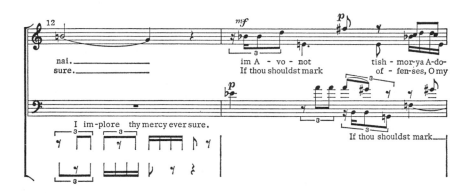

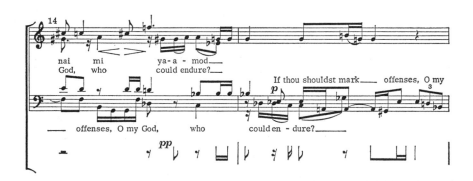

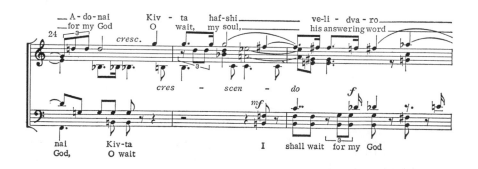

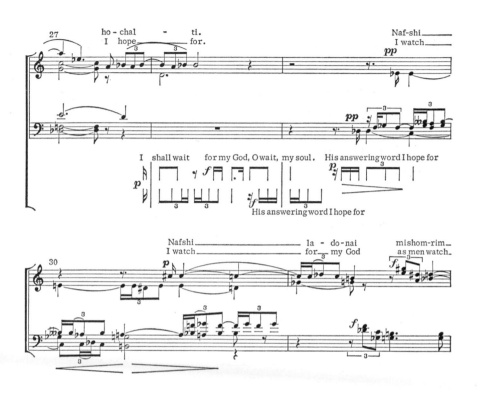

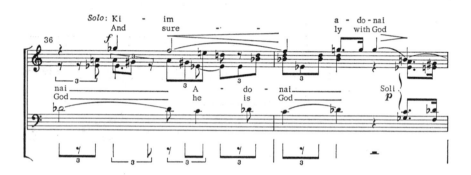

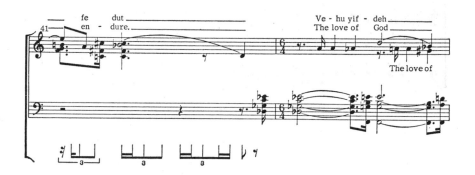

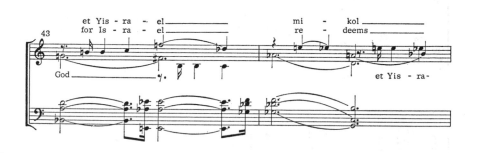

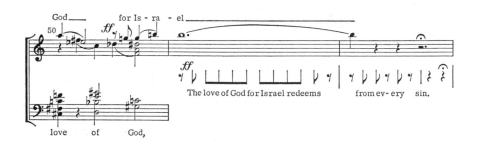

Mima'amaķim (Out of the Depths) Op. 50b. This piece was commissioned by Chemjo Vinaver, composer and choral conductor, for his excellent anthology of Jewish music. Schoenberg dedicated it to the Israeli nation. The version given here condenses the six choral parts and adds a translation of the text.

The spoken parts, "like a monotonous prayer murmured in a medium to low register," are wonderfully alternated with the sung parts, but for score-readers they can best be imagined at first as an accompaniment.

The twelve-tone set used in this composition is typical of Schoenberg's late choices; whereas in Op. 25 two notes were linked through several forms of the set, here six notes, and six pairs of notes, are so linked:

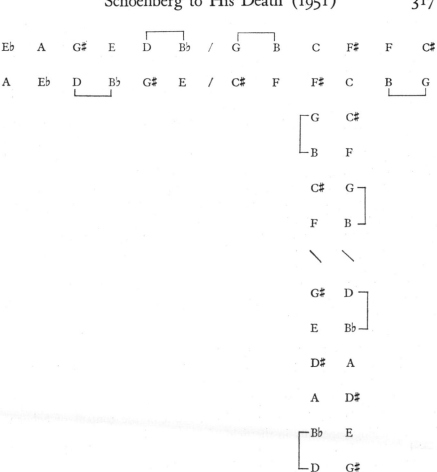

Both transpositions and inversions maintain the same division of the twelve notes into six-note subgroups (like Hauer's "tropes," or Richard Hill's "modes of the future," or what Milton Babbitt and other later theorists call "hexachords"). Within all the forms used, each pair of notes is maintained —our brackets show only two pairs as examples. These peculiar invariants of the set facilitate the smooth voice-leading in pairs, with frequent thirds and sixths, and the achievement of perceptible harmonic coherence throughout the piece.

The twelve-tone technique in itself does not altogether account for the smoothness and coherence of the composition, however; this is partly due to the restrictions of range, the repetitions of two- and three-note groups within a phrase, the very sparing use of major sevenths and larger intervals within a melody, and the great moderation in rhythmic patterns, admirably various but all naturally flowing with the steady pulse. Surely Schoenberg meant this psalm to be sung by amateur choirs of all sizes, and he restrained his style for their benefit. Vinaver had sent him a Chassidic melody for the text, and though he did not quote it, he was probably affected by its style. He wrote Vinaver, "I also profited from the liturgical motif you sent me, in writing approximately a similar expression."

Neither twelve-tone technique nor stylistic restraint accounts for the excellent treatment of choral speech. At the two most appropriate moments —the end of the opening exclamation, and the climax just before the final phrase—it is staccato shouting rather than murmuring. In the first phrase, the sustained tones last through the shouts; in the climax the shouts overwhelm the high soprano. Elsewhere the murmurs fade out and leave quiet singing to be heard clearly. And the entrances of the murmurs are marvelously varied in relation to the sung parts, sometimes seeming like extensions of these, and sometimes rather like muffled echoes from another realm. Altogether the combination of song and speech makes a setting of the text that intensifies its meaning more than either song or speech could do alone. This is Schoenberg's purpose, and all his skill and his extraordinary originality serve the purpose efficiently here.

In America Schoenberg taught many more students than in Europe. A colleague at the University of California at Los Angeles, Walter Rubsamen, reports that there were hundreds, among them several who distinguished themselves in one way or another, including Gerald Strang, Leon Kirchner, Earl Kim, John Cage, Dika Newlin, and Oscar Levant. Another pupil, Warren Langlie, provides an extensive account of the content of Schoenberg's teaching, especially in the field of counterpoint.

Schoenberg had more to teach than any one pupil could absorb. His teaching by no means stopped with his death, but rather expanded in range. Enjoyment of his work will always be "an exclusive privilege," but some knowledge of it is now indispensable to every serious musician. Its indirect effects will be incalculable for generations to come.

CHAPTER XVII

Bartók to His Death

(1945)

IN 1924 and 1925 Bartók was too busy to find much time for composing, for now his composing yielded precedence not only to his piano teaching and his folksong research and publication, but also to a strenuous schedule of concerts of his music all over Europe.

By 1926 he had adjusted to this new career. Moreover it inspired the kind of pieces he now wrote: the splendid Piano Sonata and First Piano Concerto, expanding the moods and techniques of his *Allegro barbaro* to a scale suitable for major works on concert programs; and two new groups of smaller pieces for piano, ranging over a wide assortment of moods and techniques. The suite *Out of Doors* evokes pictures as vivid as those of Debussy or Couperin, and one of its movements, *Night Music,* inaugurates a distinctive new genre of bird calls and insect noises in the dark, characteristic of Bartók from now on. The group of nine pieces includes the four *Dialogues* in austere two-part counterpoint, with many canons. It is possible in some of these works to draw parallels with contemporary trends in the music of Schoenberg and Stravinsky toward classic forms and contrapuntal rigor, and sometimes even with Stravinsky's renewed emphasis on major scales. On the other hand, it is possible to regard all Bartók's works of the 1920s, from the Violin Sonatas through the Fourth Quartet, as continuing his adventurous extensions of tonality and form, and leading to his own kind of neo-Classicism only later, toward 1940. In the 1920s he could absorb neo-Classic influences without turning back or turning aside or in any way diminishing his freedom.

In 1927, when his concert career took him to America, he composed a new landmark, the Third Quartet, outstanding among the six quartets as the shortest, most shocking in its shrill, Expressionistic sonorities, and most elusive in its continual variation of melodic motifs, mostly cramped within the range of a fourth, never issuing in a memorable tune. It is notable also for a new formal symmetry, embracing all movements in a continuous shape commonly compared with an arch or bridge or bow. This symmetry seems to arise out of the motivic counterpoint, with its symmetries of inversion, and the dissonant harmony, with its symmetrical fourth chords, diminished seventh chords, and bare tritones. From now on, through the *Music for Strings, Percussion, and Celesta* (1936), symmetry on a large scale is typical of Bartók. It is a vague principle, not a formula. It leaves room for non-symmetrical elements, such as references to sonata form, passages of melody and accompaniment, modal contrasts, and major triads. But all the elements are now organized in large forms more tightly than in such chain-like works as *Bluebeard* (1911), the *Mandarin* (1919), or the *Dance Suite* (1923), and more arbitrarily than in the last works, beginning with the Sixth Quartet (1939). Ernő Lendvai has made the best effort so far at systematic analysis of Bartók's large symmetries, based on study of all the major late works. According to Lendvai, Bartók gives formal functions to his harmony; roots related by minor third and tritone function interchangeably, so that the whole circle of twelve fifths is united in a single "axis" system, and tonic (C) dominant (G) subdominant (D) tonic (A) follow each other all the way round. Lendvai also finds the proportions of the "golden section," 3:5:8:13 . . ., recurring in every dimension of Bartók's late music. Though he does not cite the Third Quartet, this work fits his theories well. Yet their relevance to its intensity and integrity remains in doubt until they are digested by many musicians.

The Fourth Quartet (1928) represents the peak of Bartók's constructivism. Here, after the relaxation of the two delightful Rhapsodies, composed the same year, Bartók pushed symmetries and motivic tricks to their farthest extreme. Milton Babbitt, George Perle, and Allen Forte have discerned an approach to "serial" technique in the Fourth Quartet; like Schoenberg, Bartók seems to draw both melodies and chords from some kind of "basic shape," though Bartók's shape is more elusive than Schoenberg's rows. Colin Mason has shown in great detail the interaction of tonality, symmetry, and "latent serialism" in this work. Leo Treitler has concentrated on its harmonic procedures. Halsey Stevens, on the contrary, for whom the Fourth Quartet is perhaps "Bartók's greatest and most profound achievement," despairs of any harmonic analysis, and instead attributes its greatness to the motivic development and the obvious symmetry of the five movements. All these views, together with Lendvai's, offer some insight into the richness and unity of the work, though its richness is not exhausted by all of these views together, while its unity transcends their variety. A non-technical clue to the richness and unity of Bartók's thought and feeling, applicable ultimately to the quartets, may be found in his next composition, the cantata.

The *Cantata Profana* (1930) is Bartók's chief choral work, and his last big work that has any extramusical component. It is less than twenty minutes long, a continuous narrative. Bartók wrote the text himself, in Hungarian, basing it on Rumanian folklore. His regard for this text is indicated by the fact that many years later he made his own rhythmic English translation, which was finally published with his letters. Bartók's English is stiff, but it conveys the force of the tale more directly than a smooth translation:

> Once upon a time there
>   Was an aged man. He
>   Had nine handsome boys, they
>   Came to life through him. He
> Had not taught them any
>   Trade nor handicraft:
> Neither ploughing lands nor
>   Herding cows and hogs, nor
>   Rearing horses, oxen,
> Yet he has them taught to
>   Hunt in forests dark.
>
> Off they went to hunt in
>   Forests dark and wild.
> There they hunted till they
>   Found a brook, a bridge, and
>   Trace of wondrous deer.
> Those they traced, hunted,
>   So they've gotten lost and
>   Changed into stags.

With no pause over this marvel, the verses tell how the father goes into the forest seeking his sons. He encounters the stags, and prepares to shoot one. The stag calls out, "Dear father, do not shoot us, or we shall have to toss you on our antlers!" The father is not surprised or offended; he simply begs his sons to come home. The eldest son tells him to go back to their dear mother, leaving them forever. While the father asks again and again "Why?" the son explains:

> "We'll not go with you, for
>   Never shall our antlers
>   Enter gates and doors, but
>   Only woods and shrubs;
> Never shall our bodies
>   Wear a shirt and coat, but
>   Only foliage;
> Nevermore our feet shall
>   Walk on house's floor, but
>   Only on the sward;

Nevermore our mouth shall
Drink from cups and jugs but
From the clearest springs."

This extraordinary fable may be variously interpreted. Serge Moreux calls it a protest against the suppression of liberty by the Hungarian dictator, Horthy. Yet Moreux also suggests that Bartók and his friends thought of the Cantata as a sort of secular Passion. Szabolcsi reports that Bartók regarded it as his "most personal confession of faith." From a greater distance, thinking of Bartók in relation to music history, one can say that Bartók, like the sons of the old man, rejects the confining comforts of his parents' generation; he insists on freedom to roam the forests of musical possibilities, and on exclusive use of the clearest springs of musical thought; he helps men of the 20th century to cut through convention and to feel their unity with prehistoric hunters and with hunted animals, with the sounds of primitive music and the music of the night. Bartók's intention as revealed in this text is not nationalistic—whether the forest is in Hungary or Rumania or Africa or America makes no difference. Yet neither is his spirit individualistic; the eldest son speaks for the generation, and his voice falls back into the chorus, which sings its own experience and expectation. The same is true implicitly in all Bartók's works.

In the Second Piano Concerto (1931) and the Fifth Quartet (1934) and more often, of course, in the many wonderful shorter works contemporary with these, including *Mikrokosmos*, the "clear springs" of folk music bubble to the surface in folk-like tunes. Bartók's "shaping genius" still makes deliberate use of symmetry, but no longer insists on such motivic unity as in the Third and Fourth Quartets. The "shaping genius" seems more and more "permeated" by folk music, as Bartók explained in the article we have quoted (pp. 228–29) on "The Significance of Folk Music" (1931). These works of the 1930s appeal to some listeners who are not ready for the major compositions of the 1920s; but this does not mean that the later works are obvious or explicable in detail—only that their looser shapes are easier to grasp, as well as being in the long run more satisfying than the extremely tight ones. Jürgen Uhde, summing up Bartók's achievement in a tentative, personal interpretation, says:

Bartók's music, as a true expression of our time, in its melodic and harmonic aspect, is a "music of threatened order." This order remains generally audible; it does not evaporate into the inaudible, as happens sometimes, for instance, in twelve-tone music; but neither does it appear to be an enforced stability, such as can be noticed in many reactionary musical works. *Rather it stands fast.*

Not only in melody and harmony but also in rhythm does this music reveal its significance. The forces of primordial music appear in the realm of rhythm with perhaps the greatest purity. . . Since he brings the primordial forces of rhythm into relation with the intellectual power of long-range rhythm, i.e., form, there arises once more a sort of threatened order, which is altogether comparable with Bartók's melodic-harmonic order. . . Once more, in its rhythmic-formal relation, this music reflects a standing fast against a threat. Neither is form abandoned, nor does it arouse the false appearance of a harmonious balance of all forces. What is exciting and deeply significant in Bartók's form is just that it stands fast against the threatening explosive rhythmic force and the powerfully persistent expressive forces, stands fast just barely, but unerringly. . .

This music does not primarily echo, as much great music does, the perfection of cosmic order. It is not . . . a psalm and song of praise, but rather it comes much closer to the phrase of St. Paul about the "anxiously waiting creature"; yet it challenges us to stand fast and to hope.

This interpretation, backed by Uhde's perceptive observations and hints for performance of the *Mikrokosmos,* fits with the development of Bartók's practice, and with his attitude as suggested in the Cantata. It fits perhaps best of all the two masterpieces of the mid-1930s, the *Music for Strings, Percussion, and Celesta,* and the Sonata for Two Pianos and Percussion.

To use percussion instruments in a small ensemble is typical of the 20th century. To omit winds from the ensemble that includes percussion is Bartók's peculiar inspiration. Thus his melody and harmony can develop as they might in a quartet, with a uniform color, yet this uniformity can be relieved with the bright accents of the drums and xylophone, and sweetened by the gong and the delicate bells.

Bartók uses space as well as color—space more than color—to separate the contrapuntal lines in this music; the strings are divided into two antiphonal groups; the two pianos need to be heard in opposition, not simply blending together. This use of space is a Baroque device, new for Bartók in the Cantata, and new for modern chamber music in these pieces of Bartók. Though Bartók could not have foreseen the spreading of stereophonic record players, he provided for them some of their finest reasons for existence.

The differences between the two great works with percussion are as remarkable as the similarities. The *Music for Strings* is like a search, poignant and thorough; the Sonata for Two Pianos is like a celebration, festive, mysterious at times, playful often, and gloriously affirmative. The *Music for Strings* is tightly unified, like the Fourth Quartet, by a motif that grows from movement to movement, welding together every single note of the slow chromatic fugue, expanding into the necessary contrasts for a dance-like sonata allegro, breaking up into the characteristic fragments of an unusually long, complex, and exalted piece of "night music," and finally stretching and smoothing itself into modal scales for a furious presto rondo. (Robert Smith provides the most detailed account in English of these motivic connections; every book of program notes gives some account.) The Sonata for Two Pianos is quite unsymmetrical: a big sonata movement is casually followed by a short piece of "night music" and a short rondo-like sonata; each movement has its own themes and its own internal contrasts, far more than the *Music for Strings*. The Sonata has a wonderful new use of parallel thirds and sixths, which at the same time "threaten" tonality and enable tonality to "stand fast," on the white keys of C major.

The *Music for Strings* was dedicated to the Basel Chamber Orchestra and its director, Paul Sacher, who cultivated old and new music of all nations, while leaving the middle-aged music of the 19th century to others. Sacher's many commissions built a magnificent library for his orchestra; Bartók's first contribution was probably the finest. The Divertimento for Strings (1939) was another, lighter one, like an encore for warm friends. Meanwhile the Sonata for Two Pianos was a commission of the Basel section of the International Society for Contemporary Music—a more impersonal perform-ance, perhaps, than the pieces for Sacher. Bartók later arranged the Sonata as a concerto, with a colorful orchestral accompaniment, and he was sur-prised that the more peculiar original version was the more frequently performed. His specialities were addressed to the international, self-selecting élite that deserved them. After 1935 he wrote no more music especially for Hungarians. What he wrote was of course not merely for his Swiss or American patrons (the Fifth Quartet, Mrs. Coolidge; *Contrasts,* Benny Goodman) but rather for all the unknown friends so well represented by Sacher and the ISCM. He now had friends enough to keep him busy with new commissions while he gradually retired from teaching, and enough to support him when he fled to America, though not so many as to make him secure or at ease. His first years of exile, 1940–42, were bleak; his health failed and his composing stopped, but he played concerts and transcribed folksongs and recovered his strength to accept new commissions and fulfill them. In the last works he was to carry further the trend toward spon-taneous, casual forms with contrasting tuneful themes, begun in the Sonata for Two Pianos, as if he enjoyed a growing confidence in the marvelous power of music to reach and unite its listeners.

The Violin Concerto (1938) shows this growing confidence, not in its forms but rather in its exuberant virtuoso writing for the soloist, in its long sweeping crescendos for the orchestra, in its sequences, in its prominent triads and seventh chords and the strong progressions among these, and above all in the expansive, Romantic main melody of the first movement. At the same time, there are fascinating ingenious aspects of the work that recall the more severe pieces of the 1920s: the whole last movement is a variant of the first; the second theme in both movements is a rather awkward twelve-tone row, greeted with shrieks by the full orchestra and ugly blats by the brasses; the middle movement is a theme with six variations and a return. Informed opinions differ on how well the intellectual interest and the deeper values of this concerto are matched: Everett Helm thinks that despite the structural "tightness," there is somehow less continuity than in many of Bartók's looser works, and that perhaps "Bartók was for once so fascinated and occupied with questions of structure, variation and construction that he mistook the letter for the spirit." Wilhelm Twittenhoff, on the contrary, finds the concerto comparable to Beethoven in its dynamic synthesis of form and content or attitude. But while the question remains open, it is clear that the concerto represents no mere repetition, nor a diversion, nor a retrogression in Bartók's whole list of works; if it is to some extent a failure, this is because in his continuing adventure he here risked too much.

About the Sixth Quartet (1939) there is a firm consensus: here is a consummation of Bartók's music, a classic example. Helm calls it "the crowning glory of the quartets and the apotheosis of what has gone before . . . One of the most moving commentaries on our century so far." Here Bartók's marvelous ingenuity and discipline serve feeling with perfect efficiency, so that bitter anguish, sardonic wit, wild hysteria, and the most intimate desolation are transmuted into something serene, true, public, lasting. Bernard Wagenaar, who knew Bartók in America, testified: "During the last three or four years of his life he always carried upon his person scores of the later Beethoven quartets, and often pointed out to colleagues and associates great things to be found and enjoyed therein while strongly urging them to study those marvelous works again and again and again. . . . I think that in his last quartet he came very near his ideal." The list of tempos suggests the big contrasts and the cyclic unity of the movements:

> Mesto. Vivace—vivacissimo.
> Mesto. Marcia. Rubato, agitato. Tempo I.
> Mesto. Burletta, moderato. Andantino. Tempo I.
> Mesto.

EXAMPLE XVII.1   Bartók, Sixth String Quartet, beginning

The gloomy, searching mood, at first only introduction to a big sonata, gradually grows; the contrasting themes of the sonata are related to the *mesto* motifs, and the end of the sonata is a slowing, softening, and rising of pitch to return to the *mesto* mood. Then, to introduce the march, the *mesto* is led by cello, beginning a fourth lower than the original version, and accompanied by a muted countermelody played in eerie octaves; the sequence in the descending part of the *mesto* stretches out further, to bring the cello to a low C; the countermelody breaks off on an F#; very faintly, the second violin isolates the motif that will serve for the march. To introduce the *burletta*, the first violin takes the *mesto* melody to a new pitch, a step above the original; a sweet accompaniment in thirds, legato, suggests relaxation, but at measure seven a whole new phrase begins, with a rising sequence and an imitation of the melody, requiring a crescendo and an octave doubling of the melody, which continues through the last phrase, over a static tritone in the accompaniment. Finally, after the rather brutally joking movement, the *mesto* is expanded to four parts and to a chain of long phrases, with interpolated reminiscences and commentaries; the very last phrase finds the viola groping just as uncertainly as it did at the beginning of the quartet, with a few plucked notes for accompaniment, and then a final statement of the opening motif with soft parallel chords—not a tonal cadence, despite the fifths and triads, but an acceptance of the polar tension between G# and D. This acceptance of tension in a slow diminuendo seems more deeply satisfying than any strong, affirmative ending or any jolly final rondo could be: it makes the unity of the whole quartet more obvious and more significant than any symmetry; it is as if Bartók now recognizes, as World War II begins, the immensity and urgency of various threats to order, and still, quietly, modestly and proudly too, as long as he is allowed to live he "stands fast."

EXAMPLE XVII.2   Bartók, Sixth String Quartet, end

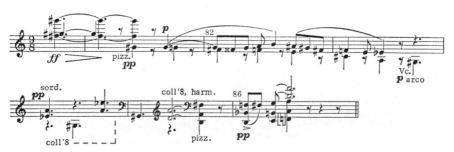

When the first phrase returns at the end, it is as rich and moving as any phrase by Strauss or Puccini, though it is made of nothing but steps and half steps. Unlike Puccini's often repeated phrases, Bartók's has been developed, extended, led to ever higher peaks of tonal strain. Unlike Strauss's developing phrases, Bartók's has never relied on chords and their progressions but rather, in counterpoint, has created chords and obscured them so that now their richness can be represented by the single line of plucked notes. The return is neither nostalgic nor triumphant. But it is a return of free human identity, the microcosm, not a dissolving into any macrocosm of nature or supernature such as Debussy and Mahler liked to suggest, nor submission to any limiting will, such as Stravinsky and Schoenberg preached. Bartók's tragic ending is closer to Aeschylus than any of these other composers could come.

The Sixth Quartet has a remarkable variety of rhythms. Some of them are familiar from Bartók's earlier works, like the pounding repeated notes of the *burletta,* the rhapsodic rubato that interrupts the march, and the folk-like swing of the second theme in the first movement, recalling especially the Cantata and the Sonata for Two Pianos. But in the course of the first movement there is a range of values, from shortest to longest note within a phrase, that is rare for Bartók or any other composer since Beethoven, together with a range of tempo, gradual rallentandi and accelerandi, and occasional abrupt contrasts, *pesante,* that is greater than Beethoven's and almost like Debussy's in *Jeux.* To use all these, and the stiff dotted rhythm of the march, surrounded by the smooth *mesto,* is an amazing feat of order.

The quartet has a variety of sounds, equally admirable. There is a new device, strumming a chord with rapid motion back and forth across the strings, as with a banjo. There are splendid new uses of glissando within a phrase of melody and by contrary motion within a chord progression. There is a glissando combined with trill. There are astonishing whole phrases in harmonics. There are phrases in double stops, making parallel triads against a countermelody, or five-voiced counterpoint. There are moments where one instrument is to play a quarter tone low, while another plays normal notes parallel, in a unique smear of sound. There are subtle exploitations of *bariolage.* There are contrasts of ordinary pizzicato with a strong snapping against the fingerboard. Yet all these idiomatic effects are subordinated to so many stretches of ordinary playing that listeners coming to this quartet from Bartók's preceding four think of it as comparatively mild. Of all the six quartets it is probably the most rewarding for amateur players to work on. Yet of course it challenges the utmost skill and taste any player can offer. The variety of sound is not used for its own sake, nor as a decorative surface, but rather in perfect fusion with the rhythms, melodies, and harmonies, as the embodiment of feeling in a precarious form.

Bartók's counterpoint likewise seems to attain a perfect balance in this work. There are easy gradations between unison and independent four-part writing. There are some dense homogeneous textures, contrasting with some extraordinary passages of opposing sonorities and rhythms. There are enough chords, placed at important enough points in the structure, to give an over-all impression that the quartet relies less on counterpoint for propulsion than the Third and Fourth Quartets, or the *Music for Strings*, or the Divertimento. Yet in a sense the Sixth Quartet is more profoundly contrapuntal than any of these, for none of its melodies is firmly supported by a chord, and its tonality and form in every movement depend on the interaction of melodies.

The splendors of the Sixth Quartet shine back on the earlier works, especially the Third and Fourth. These would be less interesting if they did not lead on to the Sixth. If some students prefer the Fourth to the Sixth, even this is partly because they can see the Fourth as turning-point in the long course of Bartók's development. The whole set of six makes a unique volume of first-rate 20th-century music, and the finest group of quartets since Beethoven. A seventh quartet was commissioned by the publisher Ralph Hawkes in 1944; Bartók left a few sketches for this when he died. Clearly the series of six was open to further, unimaginable development.

In his last two years Bartók completed one more piece of chamber music (the formidable Sonata for Violin Solo), one more song, and two great concertos. (Among many more projects he nearly finished one: he had done enough work on the Viola Concerto so that it could be completed by his young friend, Tibor Serly, who has written touching reports of how the labor was divided.) The Concerto for Orchestra swiftly became a repertory piece and a favorite of conductors, teachers, and recording engineers. Its popularity spoiled it for a few of Bartók's fans in the 1950s, but its subtle strength made it likely to survive their hasty dismissal. Bartók laid aside the Concerto for Viola in order to make time for the Third Piano Concerto, a parting tribute to his wife. This is the most refined and most lyrical of all Bartók's large works, a little like the Sixth Quartet in its serene but precarious balance of contrasting elements, yet utterly different in its firm tonality, its broad flow, and its tenderness. The appealing qualities of these concertos lured many listeners to begin their adventures with 20th-century music, and led others to a belated recognition of Bartók's stature and achievement.

In Hungary and in America, archives of Bartók's manuscripts and documents were established, and specialists began to publish the materials for a thorough knowledge of his work. János Demény undertook the most comprehensive biographical project. Halsey Stevens brought out the first scholarly survey. In England and Switzerland, where Bartók had been best appreciated during his life, writers like Colin Mason, John Weissmann, Kurt von Fischer, and Willi Reich contributed brilliant insights and connecting links. In the USSR Bartók's anti-fascism and his concern for folklore made him the one acceptable model of advanced Western music; his correspondence with the Russian folklorist Kolessa was published there. An Israeli scholar, Edith Gerson-Kiwi, made the best concise study of Bartók's scholarly work. In France the pioneer work of Serge Moreux was continued by several younger writers, most notably Pierre Citron. In Germany numerous theses were devoted to Bartók, and Walter Wiora better than anyone else showed his relation to the broadest and deepest currents of the general history of music, ranking him above Strauss and Debussy and all his contemporaries as the greatest master of the Western tradition since Bruckner, the greatest discoverer and appreciator of European folk music and its links with non-European music, and so the greatest guide to a desirable musical future for the world.

Bartók himself probably ranked Schoenberg and Stravinsky higher than Wiora does: he admired both of them, though not blindly, and his own development, however different, was somewhat affected by theirs. He certainly ranked Debussy higher than Wiora does, and recognized his own debt to Debussy long after he had so absorbed it that it could not be seen in any particular feature of his style. Like Debussy, Bartók never claimed to be a guide. Like Debussy he was capable of a healthy hatred of some music—Shostakovich's Seventh Symphony, for instance, which he jeers at in his Concerto for Orchestra. But Bartók never in his mature years wrote public criticism. If he thought about young composers at all, he expected them to go to the sources he had gone to; his way of working and living might be a model—not his own works, much less any rule or system derived from them.

Around 1950 many younger composers' music showed their acquaintance with Bartók and their admiration of him. Rarely did it show a penetrating understanding, and still more rarely a similar way of living and working. The Bartók vogue was superficial and ephemeral.

But after fashion had passed him by, Bartók's work remained, a large and living part of the musical culture of the world. From the wealth of his short pieces for piano and the Forty-four Violin Duets, students young enough to be his grandchildren were learning much, perhaps more than the generation between could learn from the quartets and concertos. More than Schoenberg or Stravinsky, Bartók left a source of possibly pervasive influence, unsystematic, open to every direction, rooted in the many-layered past, always fresh, energetic, precise, and personal.

CHAPTER XVIII

Stravinsky to The Rake's Progress

(1951)

S TRAVINSKY, in 1924, began a concert career as conductor and pianist, much busier and more lucrative than Bartók's or Schoenberg's, though still obscure compared with a Toscanini or Rachmaninov, and less than satisfying in the light of Stravinsky's early success. He provided himself with new pieces: the Piano Concerto, Piano Sonata, and Serenade in A. Each was a different kind of embodiment of the "traditionalist" policy that he had established in *The Soldier's Tale*, made firm in *Pulcinella,* deliberately proclaimed in *Mavra,* and epitomized in the Octet. But audiences and managers wanted to hear the early "revolutionary" ballets more than any of these strange new-old pieces, thus betraying their shallow understanding of the ballets, disappointing the composer, and perhaps inducing him to exaggerate his reactionary, counter-revolutionary stand. The new works, to be sure, won him fresh admiration from an élite larger than Schoenberg's close-knit circle or Bartók's international group of friends, and they gradually made their way almost as far as the audience that appreciated the *Rite*. But works like the Piano Concerto could never spread so far as *Firebird*. They presumed sophistication. They alluded not simply to Bach and Beethoven, but to separate traits of the classic styles. They treated these traits with such dry irony, such jerky stiffness, and such evident distortion that even a sympathetic listener needed several hearings to penetrate beneath the wit and skill to the glowing warmth of the melodies and the subtle continuity of the forms. All these works are often cited in discussions of 20th-century harmony or of neo-Classicism, but passages torn out of context do not fairly represent these pieces. Their melodies and forms need to be studied patiently, together, in the light of such precedents as the *Rite,* the *Volga Boatmen,* and the *Symphonies of Winds*. There may be more apparent triads in the pieces of 1923–25 than in the earlier ones, but many of these are like the special final chord of the *Boatmen,* not real functioning triads but rather peculiar consonances including non-harmonic tones. Similarly there may seem to be a restoration of tonality; the Serenade flaunts a letter-name in its title; but the converging tones do not exhibit the relations that define a key for Schenker or any other theorist. Finally, while diatonic scales are emphasized more than in the *Rite* (though no more than in *Petrushka*), chromaticism has an essential part to play in every movement, and in nearly every phrase. Once the works are known as wholes, they become amazingly rich, sweet, moving, unforgettable. They cannot be dismissed as derivations from *Pulcinella*.

In 1925, on his first trip to America, Stravinsky discussed his Concerto with James Francis Cooke. He allowed Cooke to publish his report as an essay by Stravinsky, "Chronological Progress in Musical Art." This essay, though superseded in some respects by later and more authentic expressions of Stravinsky's views, is precious evidence of their development, overlooked by most writers. Here Stravinsky promulgates his traditionalism with no metaphysics or psychology, but rather with what soon became a slogan: ". . . back to John Sebastian Bach, whose universal mind and enormous grasp upon musical art has never been transcended." At the same time, his traditionalism is modern and progressive: ". . . in my music, particularly in my concerto, I have endeavored to catch the note of our marvelous present, not the remote past. . . . America, with its gigantic growth, inspires me." Machines like the phonograph and player-piano delight him, and he counts on their progress to help restore the ideals of Bach.

When Stravinsky played his Concerto in New York, Edmund Wilson recognized its correspondence with the new formalism of T. S. Eliot. He spoke of Stravinsky's "peculiar cynicism, invigorating rather than dispiriting, which gives sharp edges to his music. He does not capitulate to the rhythms of the machines and attempt to imitate them: he opposes to them rhythms of his own, the rhythms of titanic dances. He owns a powerhouse himself and is in a different line of business. He is the artist, not as victim, but as master." Wilson confessed his own preference for *Petrushka*, but he could enjoy the sharper edges of the Concerto too.

Now Stravinsky returned to Diaghilev and his influential, fashionable audience. But not with a ballet. Rather, he proposed to Jean Cocteau an opera-oratorio, with Latin text, presenting the Oedipus story in terms at once monumental and modern. Cocteau, in pursuit of his unrealized ideal of modern theater ever since *Parade*, had collaborated with Honegger and Picasso on *Antigone*, which Stravinsky liked. Cocteau had ideas for Oedipus that later led to his play, *The Infernal Machine*. The Cocteau-Stravinsky *Oedipus Rex* was thus a consummately sophisticated work. It was epoch-making in both theater and music. Masks for the actors and a narrator in modern dress held the audience at a distance. The grandeur and the compassion of Stravinsky's style were here at last made explicit, with just the right qualifications of nervous irony and ultimate mystery. Stravinsky's marvelous way with words, hitherto known only in Russian, was now made accessible to every educated Westerner. His mastery of form was now extended to the span of an hour—his longest work up to the *Rake*. His interest in Italianate vocal melody, first unleashed in *Mavra*, was now splendidly combined with his declamatory choral writing, which dominated the work. If *Oedipus* failed to impress the Diaghilev audience, it was an immediate success with classicists from Berlin to Boston. After World War II it was revived more and more frequently everywhere.

Then at last (1927) Stravinsky was ready again for a ballet: *Apollo*. Mrs. Coolidge commissioned it for performance in Washington, D.C. Diaghilev produced it simultaneously in Paris, with ideally appropriate choreography by his new young ballet-master, George Balanchine. It is another landmark, as important as *Oedipus*, more intimate, and more delightful. Stravinsky and Balanchine restore to classic status the 19th-century tradition of ballet, with its white costumes, oblivious of both fashion and historical authenticity; its athletic virtuosity, conventionally moulded by a simple allegory; its symmetrical tableaux and patterns of movement; its string orchestra whose sensuousness is exaggerated by the expansion and subdivision of the cello section; its popular rhythms of waltz and polka. All the superficial features that had been farthest out of style, all that would be most shocking to the Diaghilev audience, were here taken seriously—with a saving pinch of irony—and made more noble than they had been for Delibes and Tchaikovsky. The music for the final apotheosis is as solemn as the end of *Oedipus*; the motto-chord (C F B D F$\sharp$), instead of resolving as in earlier scenes to C, goes to B minor, and all the frivolous and catty moments dissolve in a lasting impression of a truly superhuman balance.

The Fairy's Kiss, though longer than *Apollo* and in some other ways more adventurous, is a slighter work. It is easier for an unprejudiced listener to understand, but to such an expert and sympathetic critic as Lawrence Morton it is "the most problematic of Stravinsky's scores." It is a tribute to Tchaikovsky, taking themes from his songs and piano pieces as starting points for free developments. In his autobiography, Stravinsky refers to this work with great affection; he likes to conduct it "because in it I tried a style of writing and orchestration which was new to me, and was one by means of which the music could be appreciated at the first hearing." In his volume of *Expositions and Developments* he lists the sources in Tchaikovsky's works.

The Capriccio is to the Piano Concerto as the *Fairy's Kiss* is to *Apollo*—easier for listeners, though more complicated for the composer, and incidentally for the performers too. Stravinsky thinks of the Capriccio as a tribute to Weber.

The *Symphony of Psalms* (1930) surpasses all the works of the 1920s in one way or another. With its two pianos, augmented wind band, and only the lower strings, it recaptures the vibrant intensity of the *Wedding* and other earlier works. With its choir of boys and men it anticipates the austere spirituality of the Mass and other later works. And yet it is, like the *Fairy's Kiss* and the Capriccio, comparatively easy for an open-minded listener; its religion transcends race and creed, without denying either the composer's Russian Orthodoxy or his modern alienation. (He explains in his *Memories and Commentaries* that he had lapsed from the church in 1910, and returned to it in 1926.) The text comes from three psalms, making a dramatic sequence of prayer, testimony, and praise. The music matches this sequence with three movements, not to be interrupted: prelude, fugue, and symphonic allegro. The music not only enhances each part of the text, but also puts the prayer and the praise into a relation that Hans Mersmann expresses by an analogy: the Symphony is like a cathedral, with portal, nave, and choir. The following outline points to the formal and harmonic details that make audible this great structure.

I. Prayer—prelude—Ps. 39: 12-13 (Vulgate 38: 13-14)

	orchestral motifs, staccato		(e=)C: V
	then at rehearsal no. 2, legato, loud		I^6
Hear my prayer, O Lord		chant, altos	V_9
and my supplication.		continued, full chorus	
	interlude at 6-7, soft		V_7/I
Incline thine ears . . .		altos	
Do not keep silent.		outburst, as at 2	I^6
For I am a stranger . . .		gradual ascent	V_9
and a sojourner . . .			
O spare me,		outburst	I^6
Spare me, that I may recover strength,			V
before I go hence, and be no more.			

Without pause, a solo oboe begins the response to this mighty appeal, satisfying the dominant at last with a tonic in root position, but contradicting expectation at the same time with a minor third.

II. Testimony—fugue—Ps. 40: 1-3 (Vulgate 39: 2-4)

	orchestral exposition		c
I waited patiently for the Lord		choral exp.	e♭
and he inclined unto me and heard my cry.			
He brought me up out of an horrible pit,			
out of the miry clay.		orch. stretto overlaps	
He set my foot upon a rock		choral stretto, unacc.	
and established my goings.		diminuendo	
	orchestral stretto and canon		b♭ to c:V_9

And he hath put in my mouth	lyric extension	
a new song, a song to our Lord.	of subject	
Many shall see it and fear,		
and they shall trust in the Lord.	suddenly soft	E♭

The whole fugue represents no settled, separate unity, but an opposite pole to the prelude, and the grand converging motion that unites them takes place only in the last, biggest movement, with C major.

III. Praise—symphonic allegro—Ps. 150

Alleluia.	slow introd.	
Praise ye the Lord in His sanctuary		c to C
Praise Him in the firmament of his power.		
Praise ye the Lord.	fast, with orchestra	
Praise Him for His mighty acts.	dominating	
Praise Him according to His excellent greatness.		
Praise Him with the sound of the trumpet.		
Alleluia.	slow interlude	
Praise ye the Lord . . .	recapitulation	
Praise Him with the timbrel and the dance . . . and organs.	new lyric theme	D
Praise Him upon the loud cymbals.	soft, new chant	E♭
. . . high sounding cymbals.	still soft	
Let everything that hath breath praise the Lord.		
Alleluia.	slow conclusion	
Praise ye the Lord.		c to C

The first and last chords of the *Symphony of Psalms* are famous. The opening staccato blast, which recurs throughout the first movement, detached from its surroundings by silence, seems to be a perverse spacing of the E minor triad, with the minor third doubled in four octaves while the root and fifth appear only twice, at high and low extremes. But of course it is no mere perverse sonority, however isolated and insisted on. It is a structural "pole," in which the E is not a functioning root—much less a tonic—but rather like a non-harmonic tone in the chord whose root is the doubled G, dominant of C major. When the tonic C major finally arrives, in the last movement, its root is doubled in five octaves, its fifth is left to the natural overtones, and its decisive third appears just once, in the highest range. This spacing is as extraordinary as the spacing of the first chord, but with the opposite effect of super-clarity and consonance, thus resolving and justifying the first chord and all the horror of the miry clay.

It is characteristic of Stravinsky that he puts his most poignant, chromatic chord progressions at points where the words protect them from sentimentality: not "spare me," but "He set my foot upon a rock," and "Praise Him upon the cymbals of jubilation." To a listener alert to the paradox, these are sublime.

Similarly, it is characteristic of him to surround the excited dance-like praises of the finale with a solemn processional. Many listeners have complained that this music sounds more like lament than praise. But one who sustains his attention to embrace the relations of all three movements can feel the solemnity not as sorrowful, but rather as filled with genuine awe.

Not until the Symphony in Three Movements (1945) did Stravinsky again produce a work of such exaltation and such scope as the *Symphony of Psalms,* and the coherence of that work is more elusive.

———•••———

Meanwhile he wrote many pieces comparable to the Piano Concerto and *Apollo,* and many shorter pieces for various media of performance, no two of them alike in form or function, all alive with his individuality, and each profoundly rewarding to study. The severe little liturgical choruses, first composed to Russian texts and later fitted to Latin, pointed more surely than the *Symphony of Psalms* toward the Mass. The orchestral *Ode* and the *Elegy* for viola solo pointed farther ahead, to a series of gem-like memorial pieces in the 1950s. At the opposite extreme of moods, the Tango, the Polka, the Preludium, the *Russian Scherzo,* and the *Ebony Concerto* reinforced Stravinsky's connection with the world of jazz. The Norwegian suite, intended for a film, showed the style of Grieg to be as suitable as Pergolesi's for Stravinsky to transform. The themes were neither Grieg's nor Stravinsky's, but taken, according to his *Memories and Commentarie*s, from "a collection of Norwegian folk music my wife had found in a secondhand bookstore in Los Angeles." The two ballets, the absurd *Card Game* and the plotless *Scenes,* were wonderfully bright, neat, and pungent, without the shocks of *Apollo* or *Fairy's Kiss,* but replete with subtler surprises. The beautiful Violin Concerto, with its Bach-like arias, made a more notable and durable ballet, *Balustrade,* with scenery by Tchelitchev and choreography by Balanchine. The *Danses concertantes* for chamber orchestra also soon became a ballet. *Dumbarton Oaks,* conceived as a sequel to Bach's *Brandenburg Concertos,* and the graceful, limpid Sonata for Two Pianos awaited choreographers. *Persephone,* combining dance with speech and song, as in a loose garland draped over the classic forms of Gide's verse, awaited an adequate scenic performance, if that were possible, to make its many charms widely known. As Morton points out, this work has a French elegance and even a prettiness unusual for Stravinsky.

The Concerto for Two Pianos and the Symphony in C represent Stravinsky's most daring adventures in this period, his most austere intellectual exercises, and his most challenging achievements. They are highly contrapuntal structures, with many fugues and fugatos, on subjects that include hammering repeated notes. Their counterpoint, though relieved occasionally by dancing tunes with accompaniment, often develops into thick chromatic dissonance, so that the final harmonies in which the tones converge are still polychords rather than unison or triad. Their motivic work is worthy of Bartók, or of Beethoven. The tension that underlies their fabulous workmanship is enormous. Yet in performance all these works of the "neo-Classic" period 1930–45 can seem cold by comparison with the earlier and later Stravinsky.

The American violinist Samuel Dushkin worked with Stravinsky on his Violin Concerto, and then on the *Duo concertant* and the many arrangements, which they played together in concerts. Dushkin's memoir of their collaboration confirms the impression given by the music of this period, that it was the product of fantastic concentrated energy, infinite pains over detail, and astonishing persistence, but not of a system, and not without certain inexplicable intuitions accepted as gifts of God.

Stravinsky's most valued friend during the 1930s was the poet Paul Valéry, whose ideas on classic tradition had affected Stravinsky even before the two met in 1921. Valéry's *Art of Poetry* was the model for Stravinsky's *Poetics of Music*, written with the help of Roland-Manuel. In 1939 Stravinsky read the manuscript for Valéry, who approved it. Though the first listeners to Stravinsky's public reading of the lectures, like many readers later, were too shocked by the paradoxes and *bon mots* to recognize the architecture of the *Poetics*, this work nevertheless became established as a classic of musical literature, worthy of Valéry's sponsorship.

In 1939 Stravinsky came to America, to give his lectures at Harvard. In the same year his mother, his wife, and a daughter died of tuberculosis, in Paris. In the next year he married Vera Arturovna de Bosset Sudeikin, and brought her to America to settle in Hollywood. They became American citizens in 1945. Whether the move to America or the new wife or the ripeness of years were responsible, Stravinsky's fortunes began to improve from this time onward.

Léon Oleggini, in his book of 1952 on Stravinsky's esthetics, makes much of his Americanism:

Old Europe, committed to internal discords, international wars, and ineradicable prejudices, preserves a permanent divorce between tradition and progress. . . For a man so excited by new manifestations of truth and life as Stravinsky, Western civilization could not be the definitive position of his career. The incomprehension of certain Frenchmen was compensated for, to their shame, by the spontaneous acceptance that Stravinsky's music won in America, beginning with his visits there. Americans are apparently free from the pedantry, smugness, obfuscation, prejudice, and mania for abstraction characteristic of the European élite. Their spirit is not corrupted by centuries of argument and all sorts of fanaticism. They come to the world in the autonomy of their faculties, having so little history that they are apt to create it.

Oleggini exaggerates. The true marriage of tradition and progress is not easy anywhere. Stravinsky achieved it wherever he lived, and helped his unknown friends around the world to do so. After World War II he was again at home in Paris and Venice and Hamburg as much as ever, impartially guiding the élite of Europe and America by his example. In Madrid in 1955 he met the philosopher Ortega y Gasset, whose work he had long known; Stravinsky credits him, in his *Conversations*, with a unique European understanding of the United States.

A rare glimpse of Stravinsky's domestic personality is provided by Dagmar Godowsky, daughter of the composer, who in 1939, with what she admits was an absurd hope, schemed to become the second Mme. Stravinsky.

Igor was a black pearl. I took care of him. . . His worries became mine and he was worrying about everything—especially money. . . Still, with all his troubles, I.S. could be gay. When he laughed, one could see every tooth in his mouth. . . *La vie* was not *belle* for I.S. It really wasn't. Now that I saw him in Paris, I realized much. He was still searching for order in chaos. But he was very diplomatic and well-organized. . . His punctuality was inspired. . . I.S. had always been honest with me. My guile had been powerless with him.

Vignettes about Stravinsky's Hollywood life a few years later, by the composers Alexandre Tansman, Nicholas Nabokov, and others, give more evidence of his enormous energy, his malicious wit, his gusto, his honesty, and his toughness.

The Symphony in Three Movements (1945) is unique among all Stravinsky's works—the most comprehensive of all. It is very different from the Symphony in C. Within its vast scope it holds together ostinato crescendo passages reminiscent of the *Rite*, fugatos like those of the Concerto for Two Pianos, a delicate serenade, a brassy march, some shocking new instrumental combinations, and much more. The unity of these contrasting elements depends on no words or dance, or classic convention, but rather on the most elaborate "polar" harmony and its "hidden correlation" with tempos and sonorities. An outline, together with the chief motifs of the first movement, may guide listeners and score-readers to a sense of this obscure unity.

	rehearsal number	tones and chords of attraction
I Allegro		
exposition		
motto tirade	0 *ff*	c: V_9^{5b}
horn call	5 *p*	
syncopated chords over call-ostinato	7	g
motto tirade	19	c
motto chord over triad ostinato	22 *p*	
codetta	29	e
development	34 *p*	
halved note values	38 *mp*	G
piano concerto		
dance episode	50	D
renewed concerto	53	
preparation for return	60	
extreme contrasts		
recapitulation		
syncopated chords	88 *p*	G
concerto	97 *p*	
call	103 *f*	
motto	105 *ff*	g
	108	c
cadence	111 *p*	C
II Andante		
serenade, flute	112	D/d
harp concerto	118	F
cadence with trills	123	
più mosso—trio	125	
Tempo I	135	D/d
cadence	137	C
codetta	138	D/d=C:V
Interlude, connecting II and III	140	C: VofV V
III Con moto		
march, tutti	142 *f*	C/c
più presto, bassoons	148 *p*	
harp and piano together	152 *p*	Ab
motto chord, syncopated tirade	157 *f*	
motto in tremolo and tirade	163 *ff*	c: V_9
march in canon, bassoons	164 *p*	C (expected resolution)
tranquillo	168 *p*	
fugato, piano then harp	170 *mp*	
agitato	182 *p*	c: V
motto newly developed	185 *f*	Ab: ii
grand pause, then tutti	191 *f*	Db: V
motto chord, new cadence	194 *ff*	Db: I added 6 and 2

EXAMPLE XVIII.1   Stravinsky, Symphony in Three Movements, themes

The switch from C to D-flat at the end of the last movement is like the switch from C major to B minor in *Apollo*, but in the opposite direction: instead of solemnity, it suggests an amazing, relaxed, hopeful expansion, a new perspective on all that has passed, and a fullness of energy ready for a new beginning.

The Symphony in Three Movements, unique in itself, evoked from the composer a unique statement, qualifying in a new way his notorious contention that music expresses nothing. For the program book of the New York Philharmonic Orchestra at the première he wrote:

This Symphony has no program, nor is it a specific expression of any given occasion; it would be futile to seek these in my work. But during the process of creation in this our arduous time of sharp and shifting events, of despair and hope, of continual torments, of tension and, at last, cessation and relief, it may be that all these repercussions have left traces in this Symphony. It is not I to judge.

Many listeners who were still rejecting *Pulcinella*, the Serenade, and *Card Game*, found indeed a welcome seriousness and forthright passion in the new symphony. Others found in the symphony and the statement about it confirmation of their sense of depths in all Stravinsky, even the *Card Game*. Some found the reference to the final "cessation and relief" a kind of explanation of the harmonic structure.

The prominent parts for piano and harp merit special notice. In the first movement the piano leads the full orchestra in the "motto" and the syncopated chords, and then leads varied chamber-like combinations in the development of the horn call. (Tansman reports that Stravinsky began the work, in 1942, as a piano concerto.) In the slow movement the piano is silent; the harp, treated in a quite new way, more like the music of a Renaissance lute than like orchestral harp parts from Weber to Ravel, first accompanies solo winds, while the strings make a contrast, then leads wind duets and various other gentle ensembles, and finally joins the strings. Stravinsky revealed in 1962 that this movement was written originally for the scene in Franz Werfel's film version of *The Song of Bernadette* in which the Virgin appears to the heroine. In the finale both piano and harp are active, alternating their allegiance to the opposed winds and strings, leading the fugato. These sonorities contribute richly to the form of the symphony, even for listeners unable to follow the harmony.

In the last movement, at the beginning of the fast episode and again at the beginning of the tranquil fugato, Stravinsky introduces a new kind of texture: it is neither true polyphony of two voices nor heterophonic doubling of a melody with a variant, but rather an astounding melodic line of variable thickness, in which changing tone-color, dynamic accents, contrasts of staccato and legato, and uncanny rhythmic organization hold together a series of unisons and dissonances. On first hearing, it sounds as if two instruments were fumbling in an effort to play one melody in unison. One

EXAMPLE XVIII.2   Stravinsky, Symphony in Three Movements, finale

tries to identify the series of single notes that they might be aiming at. But no such conventional melody can be found. The dissonances are not mistakes, and not mere decoration, but essential bulges in the melodic line. Here is an invention worthy to rank with Stravinsky's rhythms and polar harmonies, destined to have great importance in his later works. It justifies his claim, in *Memories and Commentaries*, that 1945 marked the beginning of "a new period of exploration and revolution" corresponding to 1912.

Three comparatively modest but important works followed the symphony before Stravinsky came to his next great synthesis in the *Rake*. Each of the three is different; each contains hints of future developments away from the 18th- and 19th-century traits that prevail again in the *Rake*; each is perfect within its own limits; and each can be enjoyed separately, without concern for its place in Stravinsky's career. The Concerto in D, written for the strings of Paul Sacher's chamber orchestra at Basel, later made a gracious foil for Jerome Robbins's ballet *The Cage*. It combines continual chromaticism and continual clear predominance of a major scale in a sort of dogged concentration. Its middle movement, Arioso, has chord progressions conforming perfectly to the old rules of common practice, while every measure has distinctive features of rhythm and spacing. The rondo finale is like a perpetual-motion piece. *Orpheus*, written for Balanchine's New York City Ballet, is the most moving drama in all Stravinsky's works. Nearly all of it keeps to the range of loudness between *piano* and *mezzo forte*; near the end the full orchestra bursts out with a dissonant *fff*, as the Bacchantes tear Orpheus to pieces, but then, as Apollo transports Orpheus's lyre and his song toward heaven, soft horns and muted trumpet, accompanied by harp, make an otherworldly modal counterpoint that fades away on a serene dominant seventh chord. The presence of brasses and harp throughout *Orpheus* recalls Monteverdi's music for the same story; the climactic air of Orpheus in Hades recalls Gluck's setting; but these references are not essential to the expressiveness or the form of the music, whose discipline seems spontaneous and whose freedom seems unafraid. The Mass is a concise setting of the Ordinary, meant not for concert performance but for liturgical use. At times it suggests the homorhythmic passages of music by Machaut or Dufay, but again no historical reference is necessary for an unprejudiced listener who hears a choir of men and boys, supported by winds, pronounce the ritual words, to which Stravinsky's chords are all subordinated.

———•—•———

In his *Memories and Commentaries* Stravinsky records the origins of *The Rake's Progress*: "Hogarth's 'Rake's Progress' paintings, which I saw in 1947 on a chance visit to the Chicago Art Institute, immediately suggested a series of operatic scenes to me. I was, however, readily susceptible to such a suggestion, for I had wanted to compose an English-language opera ever since my arrival in the United States. I chose Auden on the recommendation of my good friend and neighbor Aldous Huxley . . ." Stravinsky's first letter to Auden sketched the final scene. Auden came to Hollywood. In ten days the two worked out their plot and a plan of arias, ensembles, and choruses, very close to the final libretto. The two were thoroughly congenial. Auden's worldliness, wit, and erudition delighted Stravinsky; his humility and Christian orthodoxy made him a fast friend. They attended together a performance of Mozart's *Così fan tutte*, which along with *Don Giovanni* was in many respects their model. Auden's letters show the stages of his progress in creating, with the aid of Chester Kallman, one of the finest librettos in the history of opera. Its symmetrical form unites elements of farce, melodrama, pastoral, myth, and moral lesson.

The *Rake* is not heroic. The central character, Tom Rakewell, juvenile tenor, is typified by his yawns. He means well, but he is impatient, lazy, gullible, and incurably hopeful. So he wishes for money (Act I, Scene i), for happiness (II, i), for his Utopian dream to come true (II, iii). Each wish is fulfilled by the volatile Nick Shadow. Each fulfillment brings boredom, absurdity, and dismay, until at the climax, in a graveyard, a year and a day from the beginning (III, ii), Nick is driving Tom to kill himself, and making a joke of it through a game of cards. At last Tom wishes for love and nothing else. He is saved. For Anne Trulove has been faithful to him throughout; her love is "sworn before heaven" and can "cheat hell of its prey." Nick descends to ice and flames. Still Tom must pay for his sins by madness. He thinks he is Adonis. In the final scene, Bedlam, just before his death, Anne joins him in a duet and then lulls him to sleep. She departs with Father Trulove; Tom wakes and dies; the chorus of madmen sings a lament. Then all the principals come before the curtain to point the moral to the audience: "For idle hearts and hands and minds The Devil finds A work to do, A work, dear Sir and Madam, For you and you."

The role of Tom is extremely difficult. Each of his arias shows a new de-

velopment of his passive character, and only the cavatina, "Love too frequently betrayed," is conventionally beautiful. Anne, on the contrary, has a
marvelously grateful part, ranging from a big aria and cabaletta (I, ii) to the
simple lullaby (III, iii), which is one of Stravinsky's most sublime melodies:

EXAMPLE XVIII.3   Stravinsky, Lullaby from *The Rake's Progress*

The parts of Nick Shadow and Baba, the bearded lady, are splendid comic
creations; their chief danger is that they may distract all the audience's attention and sympathy from Tom. Unless Tom holds the center, the variegated pieces of the opera fall apart.

With its richly allusive, witty, moralizing text, with its weak but
wonderful central character, and with its delicate scoring for chamber orchestra, the *Rake* demands an intimate theater, a good stage director, and
many rehearsals. Its elaborate scenes and costumes, and its requirements of
vocal range, agility, beauty and variety of tone, uncommon rhythmic precision, and Mozartean clarity in the orchestra put it beyond the range of
many small companies. In the decade after its composition it was produced

all around the world, but never with great success until Ingmar Bergman staged it in Stockholm. Colin Mason was not alone in judging that "on the stage it very nearly sinks under the weight of the theories that have gone into it." Yet Mason and other discerning critics still rank the *Rake* as "the greatest and most important neo-Classic work that has yet been produced."

The *Rake* was Stravinsky's last neo-Classic work. By now he was listening to the music of Webern, and preparing to embark on new adventures.

CHAPTER XIX

Webern

W HEN THE MUSIC of Anton Webern (1883–1945) began to be published during the 1920s, it attracted some attention by its extreme originality. (Only Op. 6 was printed earlier, at the composer's expense.) Webern was identified as a pupil of Schoenberg who surpassed his teacher by composing music almost entirely of sevenths and ninths and rests, in astonishingly short, mostly soft pieces. He seemed to be always on the verge of silence. Any page of his music at first glance, or any line quoted in a book or article, looked so fantastically strange that most of the pieces remained quite silent, unperformed. All the public performances of all Webern's music during his lifetime could be listed briefly; *most* of them took place at festivals of the ISCM, where noisier music overshadowed them. In surveys of contemporary music Webern could be dismissed as an extreme case, a maximum adventure and minimum achievement.

A decade after he died Webern was hailed by Stravinsky as "great composer" and "real hero," creator of "dazzling diamonds." Pierre Boulez called him "the one and only threshold." Indeed "post-Webernite" was a common label for Boulez and many of his contemporaries. His complete works were recorded by Robert Craft on four long-playing records. There were soon other recordings of several pieces for comparative study. Live performances of his instrumental music proved to be easier, and soon more common, than performances of Schoenberg's music. Hindemith conducted Webern's Symphony in 1962. Webern's achievement, though modest in extent, was now an inescapable part of the living tradition of music. D. J. Grout's *History of Western Music* devoted three pages to Webern. Ivan Martynov's survey for Soviet readers of foreign music in the 20th century, while warning them against Webern's influence, provided a musical example and thus ranked him above Berg, Satie, Puccini, and Poulenc as a factor in history. Moreover, Luigi Dallapiccola, recalling in 1958 his only meeting with Webern, in 1942, now understood Webern's insistence on his fidelity to "our great Austrian-German tradition . . . Schubert, Brahms, Wolf, Mahler, Schoenberg, Berg, and—Webern."

By 1960 Stravinsky, in his *Memories and Commentaries,* detected a reaction against Webern, but reaffirmed his "supreme importance." "He is the discoverer of a new distance between the musical object and ourselves, and therefore of a new measure of musical time." In 1962 an International Webern Festival was held in Seattle, where a collection of his manuscripts had been deposited in the Moldenhauer Archive at the University of Washington. Until James Beale and others had completed studies of these manuscripts, all accounts of Webern had to be provisional. Some elementary data were missing from the monograph by Walter Kolneder, the dissertation by McKenzie, and the authoritative articles by Craft and Wildgans, and on some points of fact these authors were not agreed. But enough was known to trace the course of Webern's development and some concrete connections between his achievement and the achievements of his contemporaries.

———•—•———

Both similarities and differences between Webern and Schoenberg appeared in all his works. Even his transcription of a Bach fugue (1935) was highly characteristic. Schoenberg, like Respighi and Stokowski and others, had arranged Bach's organ music for orchestra in such a way as often to suggest the sounds of organs, to differentiate the subject from the counterpoints, to set off big formal divisions, and to emphasize the grandeur of climaxes; Webern chose the six-part ricercar from the *Musical Offering,* which was not generally recognized as a keyboard piece, but rather was supposed to have been imagined by Bach in abstraction from any actual color. In arranging it, Webern varied the color and called for tempo rubato within every melodic phrase; his purpose, he explained to the conductor Scherchen, was "to reveal the *motivic* coherence" and "to indicate the way I feel the character of the piece."

EXAMPLE XIX.1   Webern, orchestration of Ricercar from Bach *Musical Offering,* subject

On first hearing, this procedure is shocking. Motifs stick out from the lines they belong to, whether these are subject or counterpoint; the "character" of the piece is infinitely poignant in its fluctuations, more explicitly Romantic than any Bach aria. But a listener soon discovers that the instrumentation also makes every note clear and significant; nothing is merely completing a chord; nothing is overwhelmed in the rich counterpoint; nothing is emphasized at the expense of its counterpoint. Moreover the unity of the whole piece is better served by Webern's continually shifting colors than it would be by contrasts more widely spaced. So the listener who accepts the sacrifice of obvious continuity within the subject is well repaid, and in the long run he may recover this continuity without giving up any of the new gains. As for big divisions of the whole form, Webern trusts Bach's notes to take care of these without any color contrast. The sounds of muted brass instruments predominate throughout. They are present from the beginning, and they penetrate the thickest counterpoint with wonderful effect. These sounds in themselves may shock listeners at first, since Bach never used them and since in the music of Debussy, Ravel, Mahler, jazz, and Stravinsky (before *Orpheus*) they are associated with moods that seem incongruous with a sober fugue subject. Webern strips away such associations from the muted brass sounds; he makes them serve in perfect equality with the several woodwinds and the strings. To associate the sounds and the fluctuation of sounds with Bach is an excellent preparation for listening to Webern's own *Klangfarbenmelodie*.

——— • ———

Webern's Five Pieces for Orchestra, Op. 10, show his extreme originality fully developed at the time of *Pierrot Lunaire* and *The Rite of Spring* (1912). He wrote the first of these pieces in 1911 and the others in 1913. His orchestra consists of seventeen players: one flute (doubling with piccolo), oboe, E-flat clarinet, clarinet (doubling with bass clarinet), horn, trumpet, trombone, drums, mandolin, guitar, celesta, harmonium, harp, one violin, viola, cello, and bass. The brasses are always muted. There is no tutti. There is no need for the markings of *Hauptstimme* and *Nebenstimme* introduced by Schoenberg, because, as in the Bach fugue, every note is made clear by the instrumentation, and the melodic motifs are brought out by continual sharp contrasts. Again as in the Bach, but more so here, performers and listeners have to learn to feel the continuity from one melodic fragment to the next. Thus in Op. 10, No. 4, the shortest of all, there is one continuous phrase made by the mandolin, trumpet, and trombone, and then an answer by the violin; as accompaniment, the harp's single chord diverges to viola and clarinet, then harp and celesta, overlapped by clarinet and mandolin. The pitchless snare drum marks the chief dividing point. Eight of the seventeen players remain silent. The emptiness of the range below middle C is

EXAMPLE XIX.2　Webern, Piece for Orchestra, Op. 10, No. 4

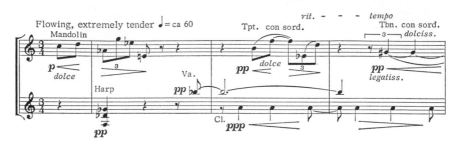

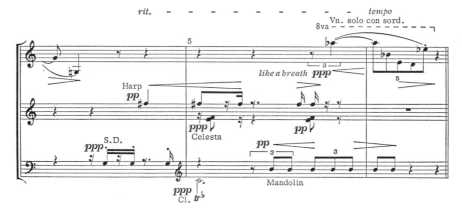

especially notable, and characteristic. The accompaniment, even after it is recognized as such, can never fade into a mere background, but rather becomes a counterpoint, crossing over the main melody into the high range, and incorporating instrumental colors previously heard in the main melody. This new relation of melody and accompaniment, undoubtedly an obstacle to immediate enjoyment, can become for the patient listener a means of the greatest enjoyment in nearly all Webern's mature music.

Webern exaggerates and unites, as it were, the "changing colors" of Schoenberg's Op. 16, No. 3 and the "wispy" quality of his little piano piece, Op. 19, No. 6. The combination is at first even more startling than either of Schoenberg's pieces; to many listeners it seems absurd; to others who claim more sophistication it is charming in its incomprehensibility, evoking day-dreams which these listeners would disapprove in listening to Debussy. But the most experienced listeners find that after repeated hearings Webern's music is not only significant but memorable, easier to anticipate than most of Schoenberg's and some of Debussy's. Its colors and its dynamics fit together. Moreover they fit perceptible patterns of rhythm and harmony.

In Op. 10, No. 4 there are two strong downbeats, mm. 1 and 5. The upbeats to these help to define them. The upbeat to measure 6 is a climax of richness in this context, followed by a very weak downbeat and a dissolution of the meter, along with the texture and color. All the other beats should be felt, and all the sounds heard against the silent beats. Webern's rhythms seldom recall march or dance. But a lifelike pulse beats in them always. It is a mistake to think that he evades time, or transforms time to space, or stops or reverses its flow. A conductor can help watching listeners feel the quiet pulse. Listeners to a recording do well to conduct the beats themselves. The slowness of the beats makes them easy to follow, once they are located. Then the varying subdivisions of the beats become peculiarly expressive, not merely vague evasions of the beats but precise motions within them. The triple subdivisions, with ties and rests, are as typical of Webern as flowing triplets against duplets are typical of Brahms. And Webern's reason for his triplets is like Brahms's reason: to enhance the contrapuntal independence of parts in a texture of melody and complex accompaniment. From Op. 3 through Op. 18 Webern uses triplets of this sort so often that no other subdivision of the beat can be regarded as normal; fairly often his triplets embrace two beats, as the quintuplet in m. 6 does here; sometimes a triplet straddles a bar-line (Op. 12, No. 1). When these rhythmic complications are combined with ritards and tempo rubato, as often happens, more practice is required than with Op. 10, No. 4 to hold on to the beats and appreciate their flow behind the spurts of motion and the apparently irrational, apparently isolated dabs of color. When the tempo is fast, the difficulty is great; but fast tempos occur seldom, and the great difficulties are not insuperable. Finally, when the rhythms involve words to be sung, they always fit the words splendidly—not only each syllable, but the lines of verse and the grammatical phrases and the entire form of the text. If it is not too far-fetched to think of Op. 10, No. 4 associated with words, the following may help some listeners to grasp the rhythm and melody (the upper line of our condensed score) and sing it to themselves: "What more marvelous thing than barely heard singing, far away from us!" Webern's rhythm explains his brevity. It is as if he had invented a way of experiencing time to correspond with what a microscope does for spatial perception. The fine detail of his rhythm, in turn, is justified by his brevity. He does not ask us to inspect a whole Mahler-like world through his microscope, but rather to discover how much of Mahler's world is present, hitherto unacknowledged, in every moment.

The melodic intervals, by now familiar, have a mysterious compelling order, however perverse from the point of view of any earlier style. Julien Falk has found an order that can be taught, with rules and exercises for composers who wish to imitate Webern: the major seventh (with diminished octave counted as equivalent) is his favorite interval—"the whole system rests on it." Next is minor ninth, almost as common, and then tritone, minor seventh, major ninth. Major seconds are rare, minor seconds very rare, in contrast to Schoenberg, Bartók, and Stravinsky. Other intervals are subordinated to the sevenths and ninths. In Op. 10, No. 4, Falk's observations fit. Though tritones actually outnumber the major sevenths in the melody, they are less conspicuous. The sevenths at the beginning and the ninths in measures 4 and 6 dominate. Moreover the accompaniment presents the same intervals harmonically, but with ninths at the beginning and sevenths at the end, combining with tritones. And *between* melody and accompaniment several more sevenths and ninths show up.

Besides the frequency of sevenths and ninths, their placing in the melody is characteristic. When these intervals occur in earlier styles—even in Webern's Opp. 1–4—the melodic leap is usually emphasized by rhythm, from weak to strong beat; then the leap is followed by stepwise motion, usually in the opposite direction. In Webern's mature style, on the contrary, sevenths and ninths may regularly occur off the beat and may be followed by rests, or by further leaps in the same direction. Thus their meaning is transformed. Their tension is nullified. They come to feel like thirds. Webern has lived through the Expressionistic wails of Mahler's Symphonies V–VIII, and all the way to the end of the *Song of the Earth*. This transformation corresponds approximately to what happened two or three centuries earlier with melodic sixths and octaves; in the style of Palestrina these intervals were the extremes of tension, but in the style of Bach they had come to resemble thirds. Webern's transformation of sevenths and ninths is very important. Until it is understood, his melodies appear to demand an impossible continuous high tension. But when the calmness of these intervals dawns on the performer, the beauty of the melodies can be heard at once.

There is a temptation to think of Webern's melodies as if they were lines for *Sprechstimme*, as if the big leaps were just anything except an octave. But this is as mistaken as to suppose that the leaps demand the traditional tension. Webern never uses *Sprechstimme*. His intervals are all clear and all essential. Nowhere is it possible to substitute a seventh for a ninth, or a minor seventh for a major seventh, any more than in Bach one could substitute a minor for a major sixth. Another mistaken effort to explain Webern's sevenths and ninths is to regard them as octave displacements of seconds. Seconds are elementary *moving* intervals of melody. Webern's sevenths and ninths are rather like members of broken chords, and his chords are ambiguous, wide-spaced, overlapping and slowly yielding to each other with never a clear chord progression. Webern is not distorting an essentially simple motion, but rather gliding with ease in the infinite realm of harmony.

The order of the melodies is more complicated and precise than a mere count of intervals shows. Henri Pousseur has suggested a way of beginning to analyze it, and a name for it—"organic chromaticism." He shows that each note is linked to both its chromatic neighbors, either by immediate major seventh or minor ninth in melody or accompaniment, or else by an "indirect" minor second progression that stretches through a motif and maintains the motion of the music.

The development of the twelve-tone technique naturally suggests another way of beginning to analyze Webern's chromaticism, even in pieces that antedate the formulation of the technique (1923). In Op. 10, No. 4 the first twelve notes are different; the last eleven notes are different; only five notes in between—from the trumpet's F through the trombone's G—are left unaccounted for, and these too can be seen as part of an eleven-note group— from the mandolin's E through the clarinet's C and D♭. Clearly Webern, like Schoenberg, was approximating the twelve-tone technique before he applied it methodically. Walter Kolneder cites ten instances of "twelve-tone fields" in Opp. 9–14. Hans Eggebrecht finds throughout this music a "non-serial twelve-tone method."

All these observations about the pitches of Webern's music still leave unexplained the coherence that can be felt when the pitches become familiar. Perhaps the main value of the observations is merely to break down prejudices that prevent us from feeling the inexplicable coherence. What is a melody? We cannot fully answer for the simplest folksong. Op. 10, No. 4 was once reprinted by Nicolas Slonimsky, in his series of articles for children, as an unusually simple illustration of how an orchestral score works, without comment about its style. Webern wrote to Slonimsky: "I am deeply touched that my music appears on the Children's Page. If only grown-ups were like children, free from prejudice against everything new!" Likewise, when his pupil Willi Reich planned a program of Webern's music in Basel in 1940, Webern wrote him: "As for your lecture: *nothing theoretical*! Rather say *how you like this music*! You will be believed and thereby achieve a favorable effect."

———— • ————

Webern was only a year younger than Stravinsky, two years younger than Bartók, nine years younger than his teacher Schoenberg, two years older than his friend and fellow-pupil, Berg. So he too grew up under the shadow of Wagner, and encountered Debussy only in his twenties. His earliest compositions, according to Moldenhauer, reflect the influence of Wagner and Wolf. The earliest one seen by Craft he calls "a naïve piece of Wagneriana." The present writer, having heard these works but not seen the scores, recognizes no more of Wagner than of Brahms. Webern grew up a member of the minor nobility, von Webern. His father was an engineer and administrator in the Austrian Imperial regime. By the time he graduated from the Gymnasium at Klagenfurt, at eighteen (1902), he had studied the piano, cello, and music theory, and was composing continually. He made a pilgrimage to Bayreuth. An entry from his journal, published by Wildgans, shows his keen and discriminating enthusiasm for the latest music of Strauss and Mahler. Now for four years he studied musicology under Guido Adler at the University of Vienna. In 1906 he won his doctoral degree with a thesis on Heinrich Isaac (c. 1450–1517) and an edition of Isaac's *Choralis Constantinus,* Part II, which Adler published in the *Denkmäler*. Meanwhile, in 1904, with his fellow student at the University Egon Wellesz, Webern had begun private lessons under Schoenberg. He composed a string quartet at the same time that Schoenberg was writing his First Quartet, Op. 7. Next he was inspired by the poetry of Richard Dehmel, which Schoenberg regarded as crucial to several stages of his own development.

Schoenberg's Chamber Symphony, Op. 9 (1906) made on Webern a "colossal impression." In his lectures of 1932, *Der Weg zur neuen Musik* (*The Path to the New Music*), Webern recalled his shock when Schoenberg returned from a vacation in the country with this score:

I immediately had the urge: "You too must do something like this!" Under the influence of the work I wrote a sonata movement the very next day. In this movement I came to the farthest bounds of tonality. . . We both felt that with this sonata movement I had brought about the emergence of a material for which the situation was not yet ready. I finished the movement—it was still tied to a key, but in a very remarkable way. Then I was going to write a variation movement, but had found a theme for variation that was really in no key. Schoenberg called Zemlinsky to help, and he settled the matter in the negative.

Now you have an insight into the struggle about this matter. There is no stopping. I wrote another quartet then, which was in C major—but only fleetingly. The key, the chosen fundamental, is invisible, as it were—"suspended tonality"!

Here Webern probably referred to his Quintet in C for piano and strings (1907). This piece is not so bold as the Schoenberg model, which Webern meanwhile arranged for piano and four instruments, but it is no less graceful or well formed. It stands comparison with Stravinsky's Symphony, Op. 1 (1907), or even with Bartók's First Quartet, completed the same year. But Webern never published this last student work. His Op. 1, Passacaglia (1908), is an expert piece for large orchestra and at the same time a very distinctive regeneration of the Baroque form that was to become fashionable in the 1920s. Craft points out typical stylistic features in the Passacaglia: 1) the economical technique of variation, rather than development, 2) the contrapuntal devices, including a retrograde inversion of a three-note motif in the theme itself, 3) the chromaticism, stretching the harmony rather far from the tonic D minor, even though this recurs regularly and is supported by ordinary cadences from the dominant, 4) the extensive use of triplets, 5) the transparency of instrumental writing, 6) the quietness of most of the music, and 7) the rests between the notes of the theme.

In 1907 Webern and Schoenberg discovered together the music of Debussy and the poetry of Stefan George. Webern began his songs, Op. 3, while Schoenberg composed the quartet, Op. 10, with the soprano *Supplication* and *Release*. Webern's Op. 2 (1908) is an unaccompanied chorus, as is Schoenberg's Op. 13 (1907), but the George text, with its brevity, "sweet trembling," and "quiet sadness," inspired Webern to a marvelous canonic piece, full of sweet thirds and sixths, hints of the whole-tone scale, and only the most delicate reference to a fundamental diatonic point of departure, G major.

In 1908 Webern finished his studies with Schoenberg and began his career as a conductor in theaters, summer resorts, and choral societies. Until 1910 his jobs kept him in or near Vienna, and he continued to see Schoenberg often. Schoenberg's first "emancipated," "atonal" pieces, Op. 11 for piano and the George songs of Op. 15 (1908–09), were understood at once by Webern. His own George songs, Opp. 3 and 4, were equally emancipated. He never returned to tonality thereafter. Schoenberg's orchestral pieces, Op. 16 (1909), were arranged for piano by Webern; the latter's pieces for big orchestra, Op. 6, came in the same year as Schoenberg's unpublished pieces for chamber orchestra (1910). Webern's Rilke songs with chamber orchestra, Op. 8, coincided approximately with Schoenberg's Maeterlinck song, Op. 20 (1911). Webern's most independent achievement of these years was Op. 5 (1909), the five movements for string quartet. The interaction of the two composers in these critical years promises to be a fascinating subject for more detailed studies than were possible before the publication of all the documents. It seems probable that Schoenberg's genius as teacher will be even more evident. He helped Webern quickly to acquire traditional craftsmanship and the freedom to discard the mere craftsman's restrictions. He encouraged Webern to develop personal habits that were unique.

In 1911 Webern moved to Danzig as theater conductor. Here he married Wilhelmine Mörtl. Soon they went to Berlin, then to Stettin. For the *Rheinische Musik- und Theaterzeitung* in 1912 Webern wrote an admirable and extensive account of Schoenberg's style, with eighteen musical examples; though little noticed, this article merited careful comparison with the contemporary and later accounts by Wellesz. Webern gave special praise to the brevity of Schoenberg's quartet, Op. 10, to the "athematic" structure of Op. 11, No. 3, and to the "infinite tenderness" of Op. 16, No. 2.

A letter of 1911 to Berg announces a Christmas present—the letters of

Kant, which Webern is studying and wants Berg to study too. He feels
something common to Kant and Beethoven, comparable to the influence of
Schopenhauer on Wagner, though not the same. He goes on to suggest
further parallels: "Strindberg and Mahler? Maeterlinck and Schoenberg?
Strindberg and Schoenberg! Emanations of God." He praises Kandinsky's
new book on *The Spiritual in Art,* and Mahler's new *Song of the Earth.*
Yet he is reading Goethe, along with Kant, "utterly enraptured."

In 1913 Webern wrote an allegorical play, *Tot (Dead),* which Moldenhauer describes as his "credo, a compound of very personal ideas and his
submission to a severe dogmatism." In the same year he composed the
Bagatelles for quartet, Op. 9, and the Pieces for chamber orchestra, Op. 10.

In 1915–16 he served as a volunteer in the Austrian army. He was dis-
charged on account of poor eyesight. Then he resumed his career as conductor, which earned him increasing prestige, though no prosperity, up to
Hitler's conquest of Austria (1938).

In the winter of 1917–18, and again for a month in 1920, he conducted
at the German theater in Prague. From 1918 to 1922 the Schoenberg Society
for Private Performance occupied much of his attention. For the season
1921–22 he also conducted the Vienna Schubert Society. From 1921 to 1926
he led the male chorus of the suburb Mödling, where he lived. From 1922
to 1933 he directed the Vienna Workers Symphony Concerts and conducted
the workers' chorus that took part in them—this is perhaps what Roberto
Gerhard refers to as his "lifelong association with the Austrian Socialist
party." From 1927 to 1933 he was conductor and musical adviser for the
Austrian radio. In 1929 he made his only extensive concert tour as guest
conductor; he revisited the B.B.C. in London several times, but otherwise
his public activity shrank back, in spite of his exertions. The details of this
record confirm the statement by Wildgans that Webern was "eminently
practical . . . not merely theoretical," as some of his admirers in the 1950s
pictured him. His concern for the concrete detail of music was more active
than Schoenberg's. And this, in turn, confirms the impression gained from
Webern's music, in contrast to Schoenberg's *Sprechstimme,* that every note
must be heard, remembered, anticipated, in tempo, with its exact duration,
color, and loudness, and of course its exact pitch.

A letter from Webern to Berg of 1919 reveals the combination of realism,
aspiration, and humility that pervaded his whole character:

I have been on the Hochschwab [mountain]. It was magnificent: because for me
this is no sport, no mere pleasure, but something quite different: search for the
highest, discovery of correspondences in nature for everything that serves me as a
model, everything that I should like to have in myself. And how fruitful this trip
was! These deep gorges with their mountain pines and their puzzling plants.
These above all are what touch me. But not because they are so "beautiful." Not

the beautiful landscape, not the beautiful flowers in the usual romantic sense move
me. My motif: the deep, fathomless, inexhaustible sense in all these, especially
these expressions of Nature. All Nature is precious to me, but what is expressed
"up there" is the most precious.

I should now like to press on to the purely real knowledge of all these phenomena. So I keep my Botany with me all the time and look for writings that
give me explanations of all that. This reality contains all marvels. Investigation,
observation of real Nature is for me the highest metaphysics, theosophy. I have
got acquainted with a plant "wintergreen." A little plant, rather like a May-bell,
not spectacular, hardly noticeable. But this smell like balsam. This smell! It contains for me everything of tenderness, movement, depth, purity.

The qualities of the wintergreen are also qualities of Webern's music. And
his scientific interest in plants prepares us for the assertion about science and
creativity in his lectures: "When one arrives at this correct conception of art,
there can be no more distinction between science and inspired creating. The
farther one presses, the more everything becomes identical, and at last one
has the impression of encountering no human work but rather a work of
Nature." Throughout the lectures Webern refers to Goethe's writings on
plants and on colors, the writings that inspired the "anthroposophy" of
Rudolph Steiner. He insists that music is "lawful Nature in relation to the
sense of hearing," as color is to sight, and that the coherence of a piece of
music is both organic and logical.

In 1926 Webern met the sculptor Josef Humplik and his wife Hildegarde
Jone, poet and painter. Frau Jone's poetry, mostly unpublished, supplied
the texts for all Webern's vocal works thereafter: a rare matching and
mutual stimulation of words and music, both dedicated to "lawful Nature."
The idea of an opera libretto was mentioned in one of Webern's letters to
Jone, but he never had time to undertake so big a task. Other letters to Jone
and Humplik, extending from 1926 to Webern's death, though published
only partially, reveal his feelings about every piece he was writing, and many
of his earlier works as well. They show his deep gratitude for every response
to his music, and his longing for a response sufficient to free his full time for
composing.

Beginning in 1929 Webern had a few private pupils in composition or
analysis of music. Among these were Frederick Dorian, Karl Amadeus
Hartmann, Humphrey Searle, Peter Stadlen, Leopold Spinner, and Willi
Reich, whose combined testimony, along with the letters, enables us to
picture Webern as a remarkable pianist, passionate singer, and faithful
friend, if not, perhaps, so talented or so systematic a teacher as he might
have wished. He confessed to Jone that teaching was a torment. Yet when
the time came that he had no more pupils, he was desperate for means of
existence.

From 1941 to the end of his life Webern did occasional editorial work for his publishers, Universal. For a month in 1944 he was drafted for air-raid warning duty. In 1945, two months after the armistice, Webern was killed by an American soldier. (A full account of the circumstances, compiled only in 1960 by Hans Moldenhauer, showed that neither Webern nor the soldier was to be blamed.) In the same year the first article by René Leibowitz appeared, marking the beginning of Webern's great influence. If he could have lived through his sixties, he would have known his life vindicated; he would perhaps have guided personally the development of many young composers. On the other hand, it may be that his death was a necessary condition for the final triumph of his work.

Over half of Webern's works are vocal. Though almost none of them were ever sung during his lifetime and none at all were sung often, he steadily devoted himself to song. During the decade 1915–25 he wrote no purely instrumental pieces, though all the songs of this decade, Op. 12 to Op. 19, have ensemble accompaniments unlike the earlier and later songs with piano. With Op. 17 (1924) he absorbed the new twelve-tone technique as a natural complement to the canonic procedure that he had developed in Opp. 15 and 16. The new device makes no conspicuous change in his forms or style. To understand Webern with any depth, study of the songs is essential. Indeed, as Robert Craft observes, "You will never get very much out of Webern until you undertake to sing it yourself: as soon as one gets the habit of singing the intervals one takes much greater pleasure in the music." It is worth the trouble to transpose them to the most comfortable range; then to study the texts, the rhythms, and the dynamics, so that no individual interval will be an isolated difficulty but every one will be part of a coherent melody. The Princeton conductor Thomas Hilbish has shown that a good high school chorus can sing the cantatas beautifully. Even the most difficult of the songs do not need big, operatic voices; they are difficult because they require agility in a wide range. A clear tone, with little or no vibrato, clear pronunciation of the text, and faithful observance of the dynamic marks bring the melodies to life.

The texts that Webern set are never amusing, frivolous, or satirical, and never grandiose, despairing, shocking, or vulgar. Most of them are difficult poems. Webern's choice from George emphasizes that poet's intimacy and his love of nature, rather than the heights and depths that Schoenberg found in him. Webern's later texts are devout, but no more conventionally so than the music. To anyone who can share Webern's intense devotion, the spirit of his music transfigures all its techniques. The music is subordinated to the ideas that the words make explicit.

The late instrumental works, however, are the ones that dazzled Stravinsky and younger composers in the 1950s. Each of them—indeed, each movement—is different in its rhythms, its shape, its treatment of twelve-tone technique and its innovations of texture. All are alike in being longer than Opp. 9 and 10, though still short by any other composer's standards. Webern wrote nothing on the grand scale of Schoenberg's Variations, but on the other hand none of his late works is so remote from classic models as Schoenberg's Trio and Phantasy. The late works are alike too in being easier to play, rhythmically, than Webern's Opp. 3–19, or any of Schoenberg's music, though no easier to read. They are alike, incidentally, in that all of them do, somehow, use twelve-tone technique; Webern adopted it once and for all, unlike Schoenberg, and maintained it without exceptions, unlike Berg; this firm commitment made him seem a surer guide. Boulez says that for Webern "the series became a many-valued mode of thought, and no longer only a technique," as it was for Schoenberg. This does not mean, however, that Webern thought of treating durations, rests, dynamics, and tone-colors according to a series, as Milton Babbitt (1945) and the "serialists" of the 1950s did. Rather, Webern's series of pitches fitted with his preoccupations, already established and ever developing, with the other aspects of his sounds. The late instrumental music has many fascinating technical aspects.

The Symphony, Op. 21 (1928) is in two movements: sonata-form and theme with seven variations. The little orchestra consists of clarinet and bass clarinet, two horns, harp, and strings without double basses. In the first movement, twelve-tone analysis reveals a strictly canonic network of four voices: the main melody and its accompanying melody are imitated by contrary motion, as can be seen in the analytical score (Example XIX.3). The series is such that its transposition by tritone is the same as its retrograde form. Therefore the set offers a total of only twenty-four different forms. (To read the inversions on our chart, follow the brackets connecting the vertical columns and read the last six letters from bottom to top.) The numbers on our chart are measure-numbers where a new series begins without overlap, at the beginning of exposition, development section, and recapitulation. (See p. 364.)

EXAMPLE XIX.3 Canonic structure of Webern, Symphony, Op. 21, first movement

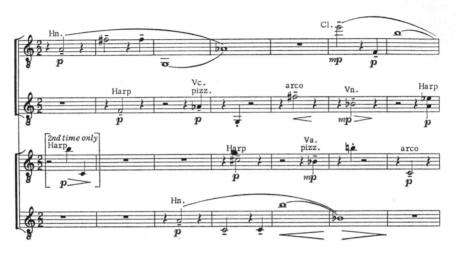

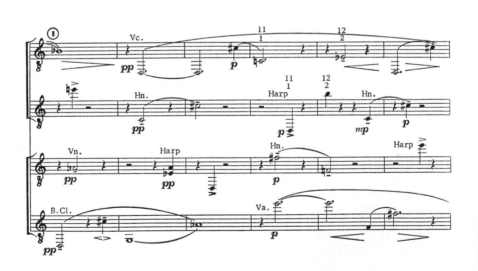

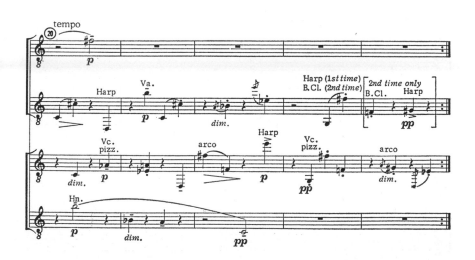

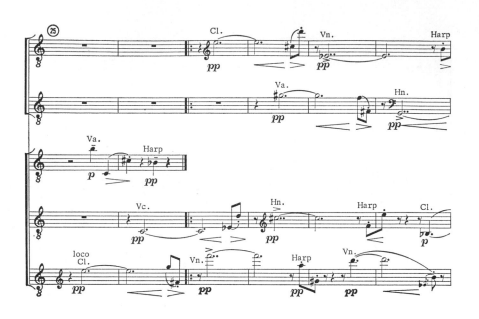

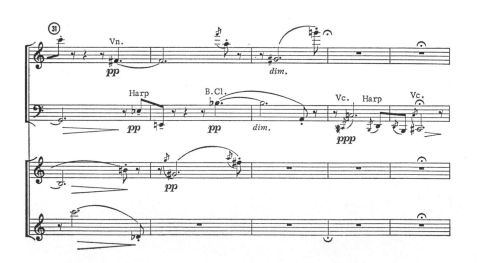

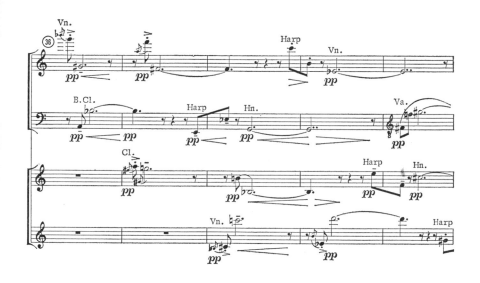

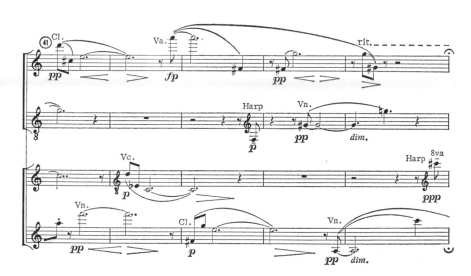

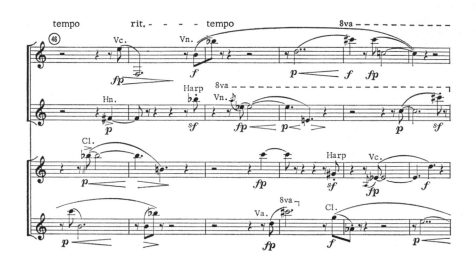

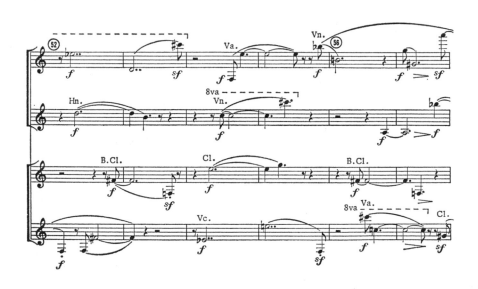

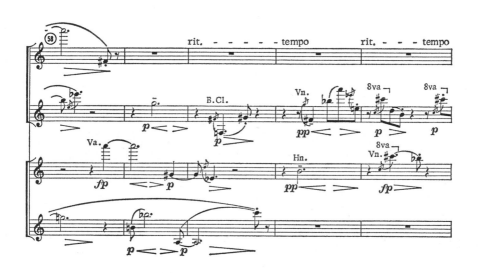

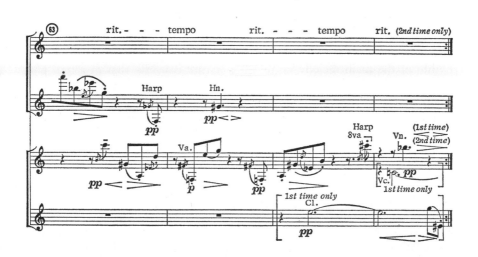

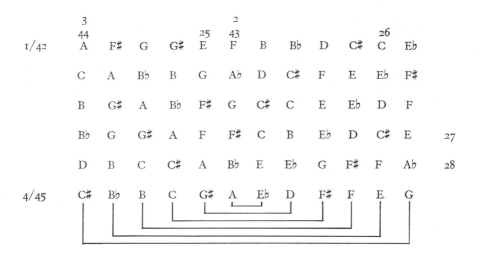

	3 44				25	2 43				26		
1/42	A	F♯	G	G♯	E	F	B	B♭	D	C♯	C	E♭
	C	A	B♭	B	G	A♭	D	C♯	F	E	E♭	F♯
	B	G♯	A	B♭	F♯	G	C♯	C	E	E♭	D	F
	B♭	G	G♯	A	F	F♯	C	B	E♭	D	C♯	E	27
	D	B	C	C♯	A	B♭	E	E♭	G	F♯	F	A♭	28
4/45	C♯	B♭	B	C	G♯	A	E♭	D	F♯	F	E	G

Elsewhere the first note of each group of twelve is also the eleventh (or less often the twelfth) note of a preceding group. The C in measure 11, for example, belongs to our top row, the next to last column; the E♭ in m. 12 is both E♭'s adjacent on the chart. The accompanying low D in m. 11 corresponds to two distant positions on the chart—first letter in the fifth row from the top, and next to the top letter in the seventh column from the left, which is completing the sixth column.

Within the development section, the accompanying voices imitate the rhythm of the main melody, so that the texture is nearly that of a four-part canon. Further, this section is subdivided at measure 34/35, and the latter half is a retrograde of the first half. The recapitulation is again looser, and the coda, from m. 61, is for only two voices. But to compensate, the recapitulation makes a climax of loudness, and the coda has faster movement. The complexities of the development are characteristically very soft.

Within the exposition there is something like a retrograde motion, beginning for the main melody in measure 12 and taking notes in groups of two or four. The effect is emphasized by the distribution of this line among the instruments, though it is obscured at the same time by the participation of the same instruments in other melodic lines. The ending of the exposition is a codetta for the accompanying voices, preparing for their extended coda at the end. The exposition, with quasi-retrograde and codetta, thus exhibits the imbalance that prevents it from being a complete piece in itself. Though it has no two contrasting themes, and nothing like modulation, it still resembles classical expositions by arousing the expectation of a longer section to follow.

In the recapitulation the main melody is so varied that it is not easy to recognize. The accompaniment is closer to the exposition. But the variation of the main melody, once it is recognized, can be appreciated as a magnificent one, with a sort of triumph in its enormous leaps, justifying the loudness.

Still better, the recapitulation varies and confirms the harmony of the exposition. Both sections use a limited group of notes, and the limitations are similar but different. In the exposition, the first note, A, is the center of the group of thirteen (Eb or D♯ appears in two octaves, as it must to maintain symmetry). In the recapitulation, the same A is prominent, but now all but one of the notes are higher, and prominent among them is an answering A, three octaves above the original one (Eb now appears in three octaves to maintain symmetry). The extreme A's resound in measures 56–60, almost like a cadence, though there is no hint of a triad with A as its root. Meanwhile, in the development section a greater variety of pitches has been heard, producing a sense of movement through stepwise relations that occur here and not elsewhere. The limitation of the notes in the exposition strikes the eye of everyone who glances at the score. In the recapitulation the limitation is less obvious, because of the frequent harmonics, notated lower than they sound. The symmetry of the pitches in the exposition is not hard to hear, because the range is the traditional choral range. The freshness of the notes in the development section is also striking—the very first note, and the extremes of high and low. In the recapitulation the symmetry is elusive, because the whole range is brilliantly lofty, and the harmonics, like whistles, may confuse our sense of which octave is which. But best of all and most difficult to hear, though by no means impossible, is the relation of the three sections, with their extraordinary harmonic procedure making a coherence and climax of form just as close to the sonata forms of Haydn as other composers' forms built out of traditional modulations.

EXAMPLE XIX.4 Harmonic structure of Webern, Symphony, Op. 21, first
    movement

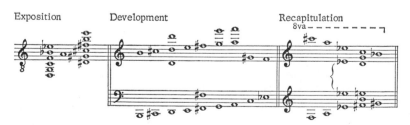

Webern stated in his lectures the formal ideal that is illustrated by this symphonic movement:

The style that Schoenberg and his school seek is a new saturation of the musical material in the horizontal and the vertical dimensions, a polyphony that formerly found its high points with the Netherlanders and with Bach, and then further with the Classics. Ever again the striving to derive as much as possible out of one principal thought. It must be said thus, for we are indeed writing the very forms of the classics—they are not at all used up.—Everything that they found by way of elaborate forms is found in new music too. It is not a matter of the reconquest or reawakening of the Netherlanders, but rather of a new filling out of their forms by way of the Classics; a synthesis of both these things. Also, it is naturally not a purely polyphonic thinking: it is both together.

So we want to insist: we do not depart from the forms of the Classics. What has come later was only modification, extension, abbreviation—but the forms have remained—even with Schoenberg! All of that has remained—but still something has changed: namely, the striving to establish coherence ever more densely, and thus to come back to polyphonic thinking.

He stated his view on harmony and its relation to form not quite so clearly, echoing Schoenberg's complicated thought on the subject:

The relation to a fundamental tone—tonality—has been lost. . . The relation to a fundamental tone had given those structures an essential foundation. It con-tributed to form, in a certain sense creating coherence.—This relation to a funda-mental tone was the essence of tonality.—Through all the events I have indicated, it now happened that this relation, at first, was no longer so necessary, and finally disappeared completely. A certain ambiguity of many chords had made it super-fluous. . . . The interpretation is also possible, by the way, that even with us a fundamental tone is still present—I definitely believe in this—but this no longer interested us in the course of the whole. . . Since there was no longer a funda-mental tone, or better, since events had come so far that the fundamental tone was no longer necessary, the need arose to *prevent* a tone from achieving preponder-ance. . . In the course of the twelve tones, then, none should be repeated. . . That really expresses the law: "Course of the twelve tones"—nothing more!—Now in this development remarkable things played a part, but they arose not theoretically but in accordance with hearing. . . Now you will understand how the style arose. Not only because we have lost tonality, but quite objectively from the standpoint of coherence. . . What is most important in twelve-tone composition is: the sub-stitute for tonality. . . Composition in twelve tones is no "substitute for tonality" but rather leads much farther. . . For the achievement of formal completeness tonality was supremely important. As if the light had gone out! so it seemed. (At least today we imagine it thus.) Then everything was in flux, uncertain, obscure —very exciting, so that there wasn't time to notice the loss.—Only when Schoen-berg promulgated the law were larger forms possible again. . . Here I can only stammer.—Everything is still in flux.—Even the old Netherlanders were not clearly conscious of the path. . . It is our faith that on this path genuine works of art can arise.—It remains for a later time to find the narrower regularities and connections that are present here and now in the works.—When one arrives at this correct conception of art, there can be no more distinction between science and inspired creating.

A genuine work like the symphony puts these "stammerings" in the proper light. Some of its regularities can now be described better than Webern himself managed to describe such matters, but it still leaves much for a later time.

An outline of the second movement can be followed without a score:

Theme	quiet	clarinet leads; harp and horn accompany
Var. I	livelier	strings only, in canon
II	very lively	cl. and b.cl.; hn., hp., pizz. strings accompany
III	moderate	all instruments sharing canonic parts
IV	very quiet	all, four parts, legato, triplets
V	very fast	strings tremolando, harp
VI	march-like	clarinets; horn accompanies
VII	broader	all, four parts
Coda	rit.	harp, strings

The theme divides in the middle of its sixth measure, with the last part a rhythmic retrograde of the first. Each variation has a similar structure, and perhaps the movement as a whole is similar too, with the fourth variation as the center—surely Variations II and VI correspond to each other, and the coda recalls more of the theme's melody than does any variation.

For twelve-tone counters there is a special detail in Variations II and VI: the horn alternates between two forms of the series. In II it plays F from row 3, E from column 5, again F and E, then D from row 3, G from column 5, again D and G, etc., maintaining a steady bouncing throughout the variation. In VI the horn takes its B♭ from column 7, B from row 3, and so on, making a free syncopated melody. The coda is a still freer mixture of columns 6 and 7.

The coda, with its grace notes and its relaxation of the rhythm, faintly recalls the first movement and so unites the whole symphony.

———•—•———

The Variations for Orchestra, Op. 30 (1940), is a bigger piece than the Symphony, in every dimension. Its orchestra has four woodwinds, four brasses, celesta, harp, timpani, and complete strings. Tuba and double bass take on new characters in this music. Its theme is twenty measures long, and contains contrasts of tempo and mood, though it is all unified by the four-note motif with which it begins, and which in turn shows two forms of a two-note motif. The six variations make a kind of "overture," as Webern explained to Reich. The theme serves as introduction;

Var. I, exposition of main idea, legato spurts of melody accompanied by repeated chords, staccato;
Var. II, transition, chords parallel;
Var. III, contrasting section, three-note groups;
Var. IV, recapitulation, varied by denser counterpoint;
Var. V, condensed recapitulation of introduction and contrast;
Var. VI, long coda, exposing the two-note motif.

The texture of the third variation is so thin that it is nearly like one un-accompanied melody. Then the counterpoint of the fourth variation makes shifting chords as gentle as Ravel's, and the rapidly changing textures of the coda unite all the earlier extremes. In his letter to Reich, Webern stammered some important hints about the harmony of this music:

What sort of *style* then? I believe a quite new one. Accurately following lawful Nature in its material, as the earlier forms that precede it follow tonality. Thus *building a tonality*, but one that uses differently the possibilities offered by the nature of tone. The difference rests on a system that makes "related to each other" (as Arnold expresses it) the twelve different tones customary up to now in Western music; but still without neglecting, on that account, (I wish to add, in explanation) the regularities as they are given in the nature of tone, that is, in the relation of overtones to a fundamental. To be sure, such neglect is really impossible, if we care any longer about expressing something in tones *in accordance with perception*! But surely no one will claim that we did not care about that.

The twelve-tone series of the Variations is such that its retrograde and inversion are the same, so that again there are only twenty-four forms. Moreover the series contains a five-note sequence, so that transpositions overlap. The whole set can be shown in a concise chart, to be read with a weaving motion, beginning from any letter in column 2, to the right, then down or from column 4 to the left, and then up. The arrows show two sample series. The concentration and curious simplicity of this set contrasts with Schoenberg's sets just as Webern's concentrated, transparent textures and small forms contrast with the textures and forms of Schoenberg.

The Concerto, Op. 24 (1934), is almost orchestral; the absence of a body of string tone is balanced by the presence of the piano as most important instrument, though not a virtuoso protagonist. Similarly, in the Quartet, Op. 22 (1930), piano and saxophone provide rich variety of colors. At the same time these pieces are somewhat easier to analyze than the Symphony and orchestral Variations; analyses of the Concerto by Leibowitz and Stockhausen became as famous in the 1950s as the music itself, and at least as

1	2	3	4	5
	A		Bb	
Db		C		B
	D		Eb	
Gb		F		E

G ———————→ Ab ———————⌐
⌐— B ———————— Bb ——————— A ◀—
⌐———→ C ———————— Db ———⌐
⌐— E ———————— Eb ——————— D ◀—
⌐——→ F ———————→ Gb

A	Ab	G
	Bb		B
D		Db		C
	Eb		E
G		Gb		F

Ab ◀———————— A ◀—⌐
⌐—→ C ———————— B ———————— Bb —⌐
⌐— Db ———————— D ◀—⌐
⌐→ F ———————— E ———————— Eb —⌐
⌐— Gb ◀———————— G

Bb	A	Ab
	B		C
Eb		D		Db
	E		F
Ab		G		Gb

influential on young composers. More disinterested and more helpful observations were provided by Colin Mason. The other pieces of chamber music have subtler variety, and greater delights for performers, if not for listeners. The String Quartet, Op. 28 (1938), is distinguished for its smooth rhythms and intensely lyrical melodies. The Trio, Op. 20 (1927), is outstanding among all the instrumental works for its density of counterpoint and complexity of syncopation. Adorno calls the Trio "probably the peak of his whole work." The Piano Variations, Op. 27 (1937), permit one player to master Webern's kinds of counterpoint; if the player's technique at the piano is only sufficient to observe the dynamic marks, he can learn to play the piece, half by heart, before he learns to read it in tempo, and to love it before he remembers all of it. To analyze its structure without playing it, or without singing some other richer music of Webern, is to miss its essence.

Webern's name was probably unknown to the religious philosopher Simone Weil (1909–43), and she surely never heard his music. But in her notebooks she wrote about music in a way that fits him especially:

Music gives a feeling of expectancy which the note that comes makes good and satisfies entirely, while being at the same time a complete surprise. This feeling is simply a reflection of the fullest possible attention wholly directed toward the Immediate. The function of the musician's art is solely to make possible this polarization of the attention. . . .

And elsewhere Simone Weil said again and again, "The Spirit is attention." Webern, like Weil, was extraordinarily capable of "polarizing" his full attention. His music performs the function of enabling the privileged listeners to do so too.

CHAPTER XX

Varèse, Orff, Messiaen, and Many Others

W EBERN'S ADVENTURE was unique. But his courage for adventure and his deplorable isolation were not uncommon. Ives persisted through more damaging isolation, as we have seen. After World War I, many other composers did so too, for even the leading serious composers—Schoenberg, Bartók, and Stravinsky—were unable to win anything like the status that Debussy, Strauss, and Puccini had enjoyed. A few of the loneliest adventurers who survived into the second half of the century began to receive some international recognition toward the end of their lives. Others were discovered posthumously. Others, very likely, remained for later generations to discover. Still others contributed, if only locally or ephemerally or even only negatively, to projects that would be carried further by younger men. The pioneers in all parts of the world were exploring unknown realms of music in various directions outward from all that was shared. The great diversity of these explorations was more characteristic of our age than any similarity to be found among contemporary styles, and perhaps more significant for the future than any one adventure in itself—even that of Webern.

An extreme case, beyond esotericism at the edge of solipsism, was Nikos Skalkottas (1904–49). He grew up in Athens, graduated from the conservatory there at sixteen (1920), and went to Berlin. He studied with Jarnach, Schoenberg, and Weill, and led a string quartet. According to his friend, John Papaioannou, he was publicly acclaimed by Schoenberg as the most talented of his pupils after Webern and Berg. About 1932 Skalkottas lost the support of his Greek patron. Then life in Germany became impossible because of the Nazis. He returned to Athens and earned a living as an orchestral violinist. "He felt," says Papaioannou, "that nobody in his country understood his aims. He never discussed serious music or his work, ever with his friends." When he died, the friends were amazed to learn that had composed over a hundred fifty works, mostly on a grand scale, and mostly using a personal version of the twelve-tone technique. A Skalkottas archive was formed, and the music began to be published; until this was further under way, no confident judgment of Skalkottas's importance could be made, though Hans Keller, on the basis of one concerto, hailed him as "original genius," and on somewhat more acquaintance ranked him on his own strange list of "greatest composers of the century": Schoenberg, Stravinsky, Shostakovitch, Britten, and Skalkottas.

A somewhat different solitude was that of Kaikhosru Sorabji (b. 1892), who forbade public performances of his music, though his publications up to 1930 had achieved some notoriety and also the respect of such a sober musician as Edmund Rubbra. His manuscripts, surveyed by T. W. Gervais, included four piano concertos, five sonatas, and a hundred studies, said to be all like the last published piece, *Opus clavicembalisticum*—that is, amazingly long, complex, serious, contrapuntal, and atonal in an original way. From his piano playing and his untutored study of Liszt, Busoni, Reger, and Debussy, Sorabji had developed his own habits. In the world where Stravinsky strove and schemed to reach an audience that was only a fraction of Puccini's, the place of Sorabji was minute and marginal. Yet he too was a characteristic part of this world.

Even more amazingly reticent as a composer was the famous pianist, Artur Schnabel (1882–1951). Specializing in the performance and teaching of the piano music of Beethoven, Schubert, and Brahms, he never played his own music or any contemporary music in public. He knew Schoenberg in Berlin after 1911, and under his influence repudiated all the compositions of his youth, but began to compose once more (1914) and continued, intermittently, until he died.

Carl Ruggles (b. 1876) resembled these younger men in the stylistic unity and distinction of his work, in its unremitting dissonance, chromaticism, and complex texture. He was naturally closer in spirit to his contemporary, fellow New Englander, and good friend in later life, Charles Ives. Ruggles achieved his style when Ives was falling silent. Ruggles renounced and destroyed all his earlier music, so that his development, from a few lessons with J. K. Paine around 1900, through some contact with the music of Debussy and Schoenberg, could only be guessed at. Though a generous patron enabled him to devote full time to composing and painting, his complete list of extant musical works is shorter than Webern's:

     1919   *Toys,* for voice and piano (text by Ruggles)
     1920   *Men and Angels* (rev. 1939), brasses
     1921–24   *Men and Mountains* (rev. 1936), orchestra; includes: *Lilacs,* strings

1925–26 *Portals,* strings
1927–32 *The Sun-Treader,* orchestra
1937–43 *Evocations* (ed. J. Kirkpatrick, rev. 1954, J.K.), piano
1945–49 *Organum* (arr. for piano, J.K.), orchestra
1958   *Exaltation,* hymn (unpubl., ed. J.K.)

Each of these short pieces illustrates the distinctive style and the steady straining for a vast, sublime, and mystical effect. Ruggles uses mostly legato melodies, full of tritones and sequences, free of all diatonic reference; he uses declamatory, unmetrical rhythms; a flux of loudness through a wide range; and thick colors with much octave doubling. He accompanies his melodies sometimes with a single voice in approximate canon; more often with one or two characterless lines and with sustainings of notes from the main melody that give an illusion of dense contrapuntal activity; between melody and accompaniment sevenths and ninths prevail, and any hint of a triad is exceptional. His endless revisions concern the rhythm, the accompaniment, the sustainings and the doublings. The excellent musicians who know Ruggles best esteem him very highly: Charles Seeger, Henry Cowell, Lou Harrison, John Kirkpatrick, and Peter Yates. But the present writer can only believe that these men's judgment is warped by their sympathy for the composer's character and his ideal. To this writer, Ruggles's letters to Kirkpatrick indicate extreme vagueness of musical imagination and narrowness of interests in the world, while his music seems the inspired groping of a dilettante ex-violinist. Still, every admirer of Ives should make up his own mind about Ruggles, comparing, as Yates suggests, "the breadth and versatility of Ives with that of Schoenberg, the purity of Ruggles with that of Webern."

More radically original than any of these composers was Edgard Varèse (1885–1965). Like his friend Ruggles, Varèse abandoned what he had done up to World War I, before his distinctive personal style was established; the early works were all lost. Unlike Ruggles, Varèse had been a prodigy and a Parisian. At twelve (1897) he had composed an opera after Jules Verne. At nineteen (1904) he had decided on a career in music rather than engineering; he continued all his life, however, to study science and technology, and his kind of music profited from this. He studied under d'Indy, Roussel, and Widor, but probably their skills never became habitual for him, for he detested the narrowness of d'Indy. Then (1909) he went to Berlin, where he was guided by Busoni toward unconditional freedom. He also knew and was encouraged by Debussy, Strauss, and Romain Rolland. Several large orchestral pieces that Varèse wrote in these years are said to have resembled works of Busoni and Debussy. Varèse founded and led choruses in both Paris and Berlin. He was alert to the discoveries of Stravinsky and Schoenberg. He was aware of the Futurists, but in 1916 he distinguished his own aims from theirs, and again in 1955 he denied any debt to them. He began an opera on Hofmannsthal's *Oedipus*. Then he served a year in the French army. Invalided out, he came to America (December 1915). Soon he took the lead in organizing concerts and international societies of new music. Again like Ruggles, Varèse won a certain limited fame with a short list of distinctive works. The dates given here are those supplied by Varèse himself in 1962:

1918–21   *Amériques,* orchestra of 132 players (revised 1928)
1921–22   *Offrandes,* soprano and chamber orchestra
1922–23   *Hyperprism,* winds and percussion
1923   *Octandre,* winds and bass
1924–25   *Intégrales,* winds and percussion
1927–28   *Arcana,* orchestra
1931   *Ionisation,* percussion and two sirens
1933–34   *Ecuatorial,* baritone, thereminvox, organ, brasses, percussion (rev. 1961, with Ondes Martenot replacing thereminvox)
1936   *Density 21.5,* (platinum) flute (rev. 1946)
1936   *Metal,* soprano and orchestra
1937   *Espace,* chorus and orchestra

After a gap of more than a decade, Varèse showed the relevance of his work to the concerns of younger men by adding:

1951–54   *Déserts,* winds and percussion, with interpolated tape-recordings of industrial noises
1957–58   *Poème électronique,* tape-recording, especially for the Philips Pavilion designed by Le Corbusier at the Brussels Exposition.
1960–61   *Nocturnal I* for soprano, chorus of basses, and orchestra

In 1965 Varèse was working on a piece begun in 1957, a setting of Henri Michaux's *Dans la nuit* for chorus, Ondes Martenot, winds, organ, and percussion.

The third instrumental section of *Déserts,* in condensed score, illustrates Varèse's style, on the verge of "electronic" music—indeed blending with the "organized sound" that precedes and follows this section.

EXAMPLE XX.1   Varèse, *Déserts*, third instrumental section

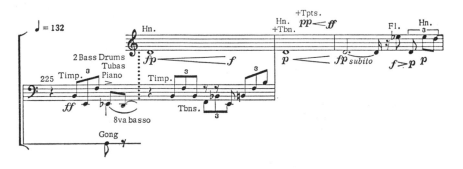

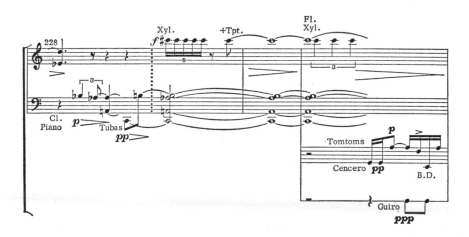

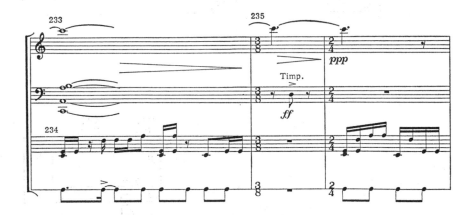

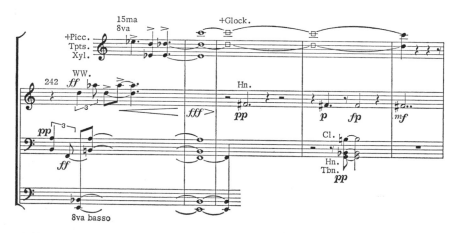

Varèse cared no more than Debussy for counterpoint. In this respect, especially, he differed from nearly all his contemporaries. On the other hand he did not subordinate chords and colors to melodic lines, as Debussy did. Rather, he subordinated both harmonic and melodic intervals to rhythm and sonority. Varèse used unresolved dissonance to produce new shrill sounds. These sounds, when organized in declamatory rhythms, immediately suggest his noble aspirations and his energy.

In 1940 Varèse wrote for the magazine *Commonweal* a defense of his work, disarming criticism: "I prefer to use the expression 'organized sound' and avoid the monotonous question: 'But is it music?' 'Organized sound' seems better to take in the dual aspect of music as an art-science, with all the recent laboratory discoveries which permit us to hope for the unconditional liberation of music, as well as covering, without dispute, my own music in progress and its requirements." In the 1950s Varèse was hailed as a foremost scout of the avant-garde, which now brought him strong reinforcements. Stravinsky told Craft, "there is nobility in his noise." Odile Vivier claimed for him a new motivic technique, not development or transformation, but *transmutation*; this seems an apt metaphor to describe the change of color by imperceptible degrees over a wide range, which electronic machinery made possible and which Varèse knew how to exploit, having imagined it years in advance.

Varèse was only intermittently active as a teacher, and his teaching was unsystematic, presupposing both mastery of traditional skills and eager imagination of future possibilities. But he was happy to share his ideas with anyone interested, and this was enough to inspire André Jolivet, Colin McPhee, John Cage, Lou Harrison, and other young composers who were already disposed to adventurous explorations. Moreover, a composer whose style turned out to be more conservative, William Grant Still, owed the discovery of his style partly to Varèse—"he taught me to express myself."

Among the names prominently associated with "electronic music" in musical journalism of the 1950s, one or more would eventually stand out from the rest as Varèse now stood out among older pioneers of "organized sound," of electronic instruments and mechanical noise-makers. In the 1920s, of course, Varèse's distinction was not so obvious; only Henry Cowell published a perceptive appreciation of Varèse then. A chronological list of landmarks in Varèse's realm has some surprising features. It includes the names of several prolific composers whose chief work is a valuable part of one or another quite different tradition, but who occasionally experimented with new ways of producing sounds; Varèse made experiment the foundation of all his work, and published only his distilled achievements. The list includes, on the other hand, inventors, some of whom did not compose at all, and most of whom composed pieces that caught attention only briefly; the music of Varèse gradually attracted more and more admirers, and became more interesting with every rehearing. Further, the list confirms what the career of Varèse suggests: that "neo-Classicism" is no adequate label for the period between the wars, and that there is no sharper break in the continuity of development at the end of that period than at the beginning. Finally, the list indicates the importance of Russia and America in this development, an importance at least equal to that of France and Germany.

1897 Thaddeus Cahill (1867–1934) patents "sounding staves."
1906 Cahill describes his Telharmonium.
1907 Busoni (1866–1924) in his *Entwurf* speculates on Cahill's inventions as means to "unconditional freedom."
1912 Henry Cowell (b. 1897) introduces "tone-clusters" in piano music, at the University of California.
1913 Luigi Russolo (1885–1947) presents the Futurist Art of Noises in concert at Milan.
1915 Lee de Forest (b. 1873) patents three-electrode vacuum tube and also electric apparatus for producing music.
    Francisco Ballila Pratella (1880–1955) in *L'Eroe* uses Russolo's *intuonarumore* to supplement orchestra.
1920 Emerson Whithorne (1884–1958) composes *The Aeroplane* for piano.
    Leon Theremin (b. 1896) exhibits Thereminvox in Moscow.
1921 Nicolas Obukhov (1892–1954) describes "crystal" and "ether" electronic instruments he designed.
1923 Andrei Pashchenko (b. 1883) in *Symphonic Mystery* uses Thereminvox.
1925 George Antheil (1900–59) in unfinished opera, *Mr. Bloom*, uses motors and amplifiers.
1926 Antheil's *Ballet mécanique,* with decor by F. Léger, is performed in Paris, later in New York, attracting attention to mechanical possibilities.
    Jörg Mager (1880–1939) exhibits Sphärophon, later also Elektrophon, Kaleidophon, and Partiturophon, with recommendations for new conceptions of composition.
1927 Theremin works in USA; returns to USSR 1938 and disappears.
    H. H. Stuckenschmidt (b. 1901), associate of Dada and of Antheil, in an essay symptomatic of widespread interest, hails "Machines, a vision of the future," as transforming the whole art of music.
    Paul Hindemith (1895–1963) composes for mechanical organ to accompany cartoon film *Felix the Cat.*

1928 Maurice Martenot (b. 1898) exhibits Ondes Martenot, in Paris.

Dimitri Levidis (1886–1951, in France 1910–39) writes Symphonic Poem for Ondes and Orchestra.

1929 Laurens Hammond (b. 1895) founds company for building electronic organs, later Solovox, Novachord, and other electronic instruments for popular use.

Ernst Toch (1887–1964), *Bunte Suite* for radio, combines chamber music, full orchestra, and "sound-effects."

Joseph Schillinger (1895–1943), *First Airphonic Suite* for Theremin with orchestra; also begins development of a mathematical method of composing, based on analysis of distinct "parameters."

1930 Georgii Rimsky-Korsakov (b. 1901) exhibits Emeriton, in Moscow.

Friedrich Trautwein (1888–1956) exhibits Trautonium, in Berlin.

Hindemith, Studies for three Trautoniums.

1931 Henry Cowell writes *Rhythmicana*, using Theremin's Rhythmicon, with orchestra.

Varèse, *Ionisation*.

1932 Darius Milhaud (b. 1892) in *L'Annonce faite à Marie* uses Ondes; first of many of his works to do so.

Telefunken firm begins mass production of Trautonium.

1934 Obukhov exhibits *Croix sonore*, chief instrument in his compositions.

1936 Harald Genzmer (b. 1909) writes Capriccio for Trautonium and winds.

Jacques Chailley (b. 1910) writes *Les Perses*, for Ondes, voice, and percussion.

André Jolivet (b. 1905) writes *Danse incantatoire*, for two Ondes.

1937 Carlos Chávez (b. 1899) in *Toward a New Music* prophesies elimination of performers as middlemen between composers and listeners, through sound film.

Olivier Messiaen (b. 1908) writes *Fêtes des belles eaux*, for six Ondes.

1940 Richard Strauss (1864–1949) in *Japanese Festival Music* uses Trautonium.

1942 John Cage (b. 1912), "For More New Sounds," advocates "experimental radio music" to carry forward efforts so far limited to percussion.

1944 Percy Grainger (1882–1961) and Burnett Cross patent experimental instrument for playing "free music."

Cage performs pieces for "prepared piano," substitute for percussion ensemble.

1945 Miklós Rózsa (b. 1907) in films *Spellbound* and *Lost Weekend* uses Theremin

1947 Martenot establishes classes for Ondes at the Paris Conservatory.

1948 Pierre Schaeffer (b. 1910) inaugurates "musique concrète" at Paris radio studio.

Jolivet, Concerto for Ondes and orchestra.

1949 Pierre Henry (b. 1927) with P. Schaeffer composes *Symphony for One Man*, chief work of "musique concrète."

Messiaen writes *Mode de valeurs et d'intensités*, for piano, key work in the evolution of Boulez and Stockhausen.

1950 Hohner firm, manufacturers of harmonicas, produce Electronium.

Varèse lectures in Darmstadt.

Pierre Boulez (b. 1925) writes quartet for Ondes, and distinguishes himself as performer of Ondes.

1951 Herbert Eimert (b. 1897) founds studio for "electronic music" at Cologne, with Werner Meyer-Eppler, physicist, Robert Beyer, composer, and others.

Cage, *Imaginary Landscape* for twenty-four radios, wedding an "aleatory" (chance) element to machinery.

1952 Oskar Sala (b. 1910) exhibits Mixtur-trautonium.

Otto Luening (b. 1900) performs *Low Speed*, composed by manipulations of magnetic tape.

Vladimir Ussachevsky (b. 1911, in USA since 1930) presents *Sonic Contours*, for tape and instruments.

Schaeffer, *Vers un musique concrète*, gives a full account of his work and aims.

Messiaen, *Timbres-durées*, for tape.

1953 Varèse, *Déserts*.

Sala, Concertino for Mixtur-trautonium and electric orchestra; *Concertante Variations*, for tape.

Luciano Berio (b. 1925) founds studio at Milan, where concerns of "musique concrète" and "electronic music" are reconciled and developed.

Karlheinz Stockhausen (b. 1928), *Electronic Study I*, with sine waves as exclusive basic material.

1954 International Congress on Music and Electroacoustics, at Gravesano, Switzerland, sponsored by UNESCO, reported in proceedings, and then pursued in periodical *Gravesaner Blätter*, with recordings.

Milhaud, *Étude poétique* for tape recorder.

Stockhausen, *Electronic Study II*, including non-stationary noises produced electronically.

Henk Badings (b. 1907), *Orestes*, incidental music on tape.

Ivan Vyshnegradsky (b. 1893), Study for electronic broadcast.

1955 Toshiro Mayuzumi (b. 1929) founds studio at Tokyo.

Eimert and Stockhausen edit *Die Reihe I: Elektronische Musik*.

Harry F. Olson and Herbert Belar exhibit RCA Synthesizer.

1956 Stockhausen, *Gesang der Jünglinge (Song of the Youths in the Fiery Furnace)*, outstanding example of "electro-acoustic" music, incorporating distorted vocal sounds.

Bruno Maderna (b. 1920), *Notturno*, for tape.

Giselher Klebe (b. 1920), *Interferenzen*, for tape.

Hermann Heiss (b. 1897), *Elektronische Komposition I*.

Ernst Krenek (b. 1900), *Spiritus intelligentiae sanctus*, for tape.

1957 Studios founded in Rome, Warsaw, Brussels, Delft, Tel Aviv.

1958 Varèse, *Poème électronique*.

Boulez, *Poésie pour pouvoir*, combining electronic and instrumental music.

Viktor K. Solomin, *Konstruirovanie elektromuzykal'nykh instrumentov*, indicates revival of Russian interest, at least in something like the Hammond organ.

1959 Studio founded at Toronto, Ontario.

RCA Synthesizer II established at the Columbia-Princeton Electronic Music Center.

Henri Sauguet (b. 1901), *Aspect sentimental*.

1960 Abraham Moles, *Les Musiques expérimentales*, and Fred K. Prieberg, *Musica ex machina*, provide comprehensive surveys of the field, one prescriptive and other journalistic.

1961 Milton Babbitt (b. 1916), *Vision and Prayer*.

1962 Studio at Yale, directed by Mel Powell.

New possibilities for the measurement and control of pitch, as well as of time and tone-color, were opened up by electronic technology. Scientific investigators like Fritz Winckel and Charles Shackford were beginning to shed floods of light on the microscopic intervals that actually occurred in all kinds of music without fully rational control. A number of composers were eager to exploit these possibilities too, though their concern was not so fashionable in the 1950s as the demand for "new sounds." Too often in the past, work with subtleties of pitch had led to dreary, inconclusive mathematical theorizing, clumsy keyboard instruments, and naïve compositions that won fleeting notice only by the supposed novelty of quarter tones. But the continual recurrence of this concern, its intensification in the 1920s, and its world-wide extent, as indicated in the following selective list, all suggested that its history would have increasing interest and value. It was surely plausible to imagine that the true fulfillment of the famous tendencies towards increasing chromaticism and dissonance would be neither twelve-tone technique nor organized sound, but rather a breakthrough to some new scale of pitches with more than twelve degrees in an octave. The list here is no more than a crude map of materials for the history of such strivings, for as yet the scattered materials had scarcely been assembled and compared, and the rival claims cancelled each other out in the judgment of most musicians. A complete history would of course trace speculations and experiments from antiquity down through the flurry of interest in the Renaissance. Our list begins in the middle 19th century, when the equal temperament of twelve pitches per octave seemed securely established.

1849   J.-F.-F.-E. Halévy (1799–1862), *Prométhée,* uses occasional quarter tones.
1863   Hermann von Helmholtz (1821–94), *Lehre von den Tonempfindungen* (*On the Sensations of Sound*), includes account of a harmonium with 31 tones per octave (tpo); considers 24 tpo and many others.
1864   Alexander John Ellis (1814–90) proposes the "cent" as unit of measuring intervals (1200 cents per octave).
1876   R. H. M. Bosanquet, *An Elementary Treatise on Musical Intervals and Temperament,* comprehensive survey, includes account of a harmonium with 53 tpo, exhibited in London.
1878   James Paul White exhibits "harmon" in Boston, 53 tpo. (Account by E. W. Tipple)
1890   Shohé Tanaka, *Studien im Gebiete der reinen Stimmung* (*Studies in the Field of Pure Intonation*) proposes 20 tpo, 70 tpo, etc.
1891   Carl Andreas Eitz (1848–1924), *Das mathematisch-reine Tonsystem* (*The Mathematically Pure Tone-System*) considers possibilities up to 104 tpo, and proposes solmization for 21 tpo; Eitz devoted his life to promoting this system in school music.
1898   John A. Foulds (1880–1939) composes a string quartet using some quarter tones.
1906   Richard H. Stein (1882–1942) publishes *Konzert-Stücke,* Op. 26, using quarter tones.
1907   Busoni (1866–1924), *Entwurf,* speculates on third tones and sixth tones.
1908   Jörg Mager (1880–1939) advocates systematic use of quarter tones.
       Percy Grainger (1882–1961) conceives "free music," emancipated from all scales.
1910   Arthur Lourié (b. 1892) composes quartet using some quarter tones, Moscow.
1911   Mager, quartet.
1912   G. Bender reports on "futurist" composers' "comatic" scale, 53 tpo.

1918 Ivan Vyshnegradsky (b. 1893) in Moscow composes pieces using quarter tones, and determines to devote his career to this field; after 1920 in Paris.

1919 Alois Hába (b. 1893) composes quartet in a quarter-tone system based on Czech folksong.

1922 Hába, *Die harmonischen Grundlagen des Vierteltonsystems* (*The Harmonic Foundations of the Quarter-Tone System*).

      Stein organizes International Congress of Quarter-Tone Composers, Berlin; Hába, Vyshnegradsky, and others attend and find little in common.

      T. O. Kornerup (1864–1938), *Musical Acoustics* (Copenhagen), advocates 19, 31, and 50 tpo.

      Eivind Groven (b. 1901), composer and scholar of Norwegian folksong, patents keyboard for a "natural scale."

1923 Hába establishes class in quarter-tone technique at Prague Conservatory.

      Georgii Rimsky-Korsakov (b. 1901) founds Leningrad Society for Quarter Tones.

      Charles Ives (1874–1954), Three Quarter-Tone Pieces for two pianos.

      Ernst Bloch (1880–1959), Piano Quintet, uses occasional conspicuous quarter tones in music of general interest.

1925 G. Rimsky-Korsakov, *Obosnovanie chetvertitonovoi muzykal'noi sistemy* (*Treatise on the Quarter-Tone Musical System*).

      Ives, *Some Quarter-Tone Impressions*, recalls his father's experiments of the 1880s, and opines: "Even in the limited and awkward way of working with quarter tones at present, transcendent things may be felt ahead—glimpses of thought and beauty."

      Alban Berg (1885–1935), Chamber Concerto, uses occasional "intermediate" tones, marvelous in context.

      Hans Barth (1897–1956) exhibits quarter-tone piano, New York.

1926 Julián Carrillo (b. 1875) exhibits in New York his "octavina," 48 tpo, and "arpa citera," 96 tpo; he claims to have composed with such intervals in Mexico since the 1890s.

1927 Hába, *Neue Harmonielehre des diatonischen, chromatischen, Viertel-, Drittel-, Sechstel-, und Zwölftel-Tonsystems.*

1928 Luigi Russolo (1885–1947) announces "enharmonic" machine capable of all intervals.

1930 Barth, Concerto for quarter-tone piano and orchestra.

1931 Jan Adam Maklakiewicz (1899–1954), *4 Japanese Songs*, with quarter tones, exceptional for him.

      Hába, *The Mother,* opera, climactic effort in quarter-tone system.

1932 Joseph Yasser (b. 1893), *A Theory of Evolving Tonality,* advocates 19 tpo.

1933 Anton Webern (1882–1945) has "no objection to the efforts with quarter tones and the like—there is only the question whether the time is ripe."

1935 Harry Partch (b. 1901) describes his "Ptolemy," reed organ with 43 tpo.

1937 Josip Slavenski (1896–1955) describes his "natural tone system" with 53 tpo.

1938 Olivier Messiaen (b. 1908), *2 Monotonies en quarts de ton,* for Ondes.

1939 Béla Bartók (1881–1945), Sixth Quartet, uses parallel quarter-tone ornaments.

1941 Arthur Fickénscher (1871–1954) describes his "polytone" at Charlottesville, Virginia, 60 tpo.

1946 Edoardo Cavallini, *Il Pluricromatismo nell' evoluzione musicale,* reports work of Emilio Scarani and Gioachino Russo, using 19 tpo, and pleads for agreement in notation.

1948 Andrzej Panufnik (b. 1914), *Berceuse*, uses 24 tpo.
1949 Carillo advises UNESCO that "this revolution in music, initiated by me, synthesizes in three essential points the whole future of music esthetics for many centuries to come."

Partch, *Genesis of a Music*, describes and defends his "monophony" using 43 tpo.

Mordecai Sandberg (b. 1897), *Ruth*, an oratorio, represents a fragment of his lifetime project of setting the Bible to music, with speech-like microtones.

Yvette Grimaud (b. 1922), *Chants à quarts de ton non tempérés*.
1950 Adriaan D. Fokker (b. 1887) installs organ at Haarlem with 31 tpo.

Lou Harrison (b. 1917) emerges from "laboratory" period to compose "strict" and "free" works specifying ratios for pure intervals.
1951 Pierre Boulez declares the "serial principle" adequate "to control a sound world with intervals more complex than semitones."

J. M. Barbour (b. 1897), *Tuning and Temperament, a Historical Survey*, provides a scholarly background for new studies, tending to dampen enthusiasm.
1958 Alain Daniélou (b. 1907), *Traité de musicologie comparée*, lists over 2000 possible tpo, with ratios, measurement in cents, and derivations.
1960 Stravinsky declares his eagerness for experiments in refinement of pitch.
1961 Joel Mandelbaum, *Multiple Division of the Octave, and the Tonal Resources of 19-Tone Temperament*, includes a critical survey and nine compositions demonstrating a wide range of stylistic possibilities.
1962 David Kraehenbuehl and Christopher Schmidt propose a new theory "on the development of musical systems."
1963 Myron Schaeffer discusses and demonstrates *Electronic Pitch Control*.

The label "experimental," justly rejected by Varèse, was accepted by John Cage, whose remarkable series of inventions loom large on our first list. Electronic and microtonal materials were welcome to Cage because he was a fearless explorer of all sounds and silences; he eventually found exploring more congenial than composing—rather than put things together, he gradually learned to let things happen, and rather than follow up and exploit any of his inventions he proceeded from each one to more and more astonishing discoveries, beyond the scope of our survey in this book, even though such pieces as the sonatas for prepared piano and especially some short songs showed that he was a composer too. On the way toward his rejection of composing, he popularized the idea of "indeterminacy" or "aleatory" music, in which the composer invites the collaboration of performers in deciding among alternatives. Various applications of this idea were found in the works of many composers of the 1960s otherwise remote from Cage. Aside from jazz (where also the division of responsibilities fluctuates) no other American musician exerted such influence abroad, or such influence on other arts, especially dance and painting. Cage's immediate disciples, Earle Brown and Morton Feldman (both b. 1926), Sylvano Bussotti (b. 1931) and Christian Wolff (b. 1934), along with the indispensable pianist David Tudor, participated in some of the most newsworthy musical events of the 1960s. The term "experimental" was convenient to designate a wide variety of music, including besides Cage's school Schaeffer's "musique concrète," all sorts of "electronic" music, and music somehow involving the use of computing machines. In this sense it was used for the titles of excellent studies by Abraham Moles, J. E. Marie, and Lejaren Hiller, and for a world congress of experimental music at Venice, 1961.

———·•·———

Not every adventure was aimed so far into the future as those of the experimentalists. Some adventures, indeed, though equally novel, seemed reactionary. Others aimed at comprehending several extremes rather than pushing a single one still further.

Three American composers, Wallingford Riegger, Vernon Duke, and Virgil Thomson, pursued remarkable adventures in versatility. They evaded the choice of a style by a sort of compartmentalized activity. They juggled styles without any attempt at synthesis. In a sense they carried forward Ives's disdain of style. Yet Ives's "substance," with its transcendental overtones, was not for them either. Each of them had his own distinctive personality and his own kind of humor. Indeed, to discuss them together is a deliberate joke. But not merely so. Juxtaposing them stresses the negative aspect of their work that gives them special historical significance. They personify the sheer diversity that distinguishes 20th-century music more than anything else.

Wallingford Riegger (1885–1961), like Ives and Varèse, enjoyed a widening—if not deepening—appreciation at the end of his life. Such excellent critics as Elliott Carter, Henry Cowell, Virgil Thomson, and Richard Goldman paid him tribute, and dissertations were written about him, the chief one by J. B. Schmoll. His unfailing modest charm and his quick, irreverent wit merited this attention as much as his music, which, if all of it was taken into account, revealed a baffled indecision and a nostalgia for his student years in Berlin, when *Till Eulenspiegel* had captured his wholehearted love as no later music could. Using numerous pseudonyms, Riegger earned a living with hundreds of conventional choral arrangements and teaching pieces. In his own name he wrote in more than one style. Some pieces like the *New Dance* (1935) and *Dance Rhythms* (1955), in which he at once yielded to his impersonal habits and tempered them with his wit, seemed to this writer likelier to survive than his pioneering American adaptation of the twelve-tone idea, *Dichotomy* (1932), or his third and fourth symphonies; these won prizes but the others won repeated performance.

"Vernon Duke" was originally the pseudonym adopted by Vladimir Dukelsky (b. 1903) at the suggestion of George Gershwin, for identifying his popular songs. "Dukelsky" meant the *real* composer, the sleek prodigy who had studied in Kiev under Glière, had shocked his teachers with borrowings from Debussy, had called himself a Futurist, but was shocked in turn and then captivated by Prokofiev. He had escaped from the Soviets by way of Constantinople. There he learned to prefer American popular music, especially Gershwin, to fake Gypsy songs, and he began to write and sell such tunes himself, ultimately including such a hit as *April in Paris*. In New York at eighteen (1921), he became a friend and admirer of Ruggles, Varèse, Riegger, and Szymanowski, and a close friend of Gershwin, who enabled him to go to Paris. At once, as if in a fairy tale, Diaghilev launched his career with the ballet *Zéphyr et Flore* (1925), and Prokofiev became his intimate and adviser. Both Duke and Dukelsky were too good to give up. Yet neither reached security in their "savage striving for success." Their achievements won high praise not only from Gershwin and Prokofiev but also from such expert and disinterested judges as Jerome Kern and Elliott Carter. In 1955, when the amphibious composer published his candid and colorful memoirs, *Passport to Paris*, he announced that Duke was his legal name in America and would serve for his next string quartet as well as his next Broadway show or Hollywood film score. The quartets, the symphonies, and the choruses all deserved serious attention and far more performances than they had yet received. In 1964 Duke assured himself a place in history by writing a bitter protest against the "deification of Stravinsky," to which Stravinsky replied with equally bitter contempt.

Virgil Thomson (b. 1896) told John Cage that soon after he determined to be a composer, in his mid-twenties, he envisioned the bulk of his music as "a large railway station, not particularly attractive, though details of it were interesting, but massive and full of variety, with many people going in and out of it." Cage, in 1960, studied the whole work with rare thoroughness, penetration, and sense of perspective. He prized its defiant variety, its unpretentiousness, and its comedy. He minimized such transient interesting details as the "surrealist collage" of some works, the agreeable local color and "neo-Romanticism" of others, and the ingenious adaptations of twelve-tone technique to polytonal harmony. But keeping in view the whole "railway station," he was not misled by the simplicistic triads and waltz rhythms, as were some critics, to classify Thomson as a moderate or reactionary stylist.

Thomson grew up in Kansas City, Missouri, where musical and literary life, despite their marginal concern to most of the population, were vigorous and varied enough to give a brilliant and energetic youth some freedom amid conflicting incipient habits, and some fondness for the habits despite their conflict. At twenty he was a good pianist, singer, organist, and journalist, without any instruction in composition or any fixed aim. His Missourian skepticism and self-confidence, reinforced by studies in the army, protected him from what he learned about music with E. B. Hill and others at Harvard (1919–23), with Rosario Scalero at the Juilliard School in New

York (1923–24), and with Nadia Boulanger at the new American school in Fontainebleau (1921–27). His pragmatic artistic policy took shape in friendly association with poets, including Cocteau, Joyce, and Pound, but especially Gertrude Stein and Georges Hugnet, and with painters, especially Christian Bérard and Maurice Grosser. This policy, together with his now brilliant skills, enabled him to compose variously, to write his sparkling book on *The State of Music,* and to become the most stimulating American journalist critic of the years 1940–54. Thomson's achievement as a whole is a memorable one. Though his "railway station" may serve no main lines of music history, young American musicians can learn from it as much as from any American music except jazz, while all around the world the "many people going in and out of it" continue to enjoy its occasional services.

In 1961 Thomson visited Japan for the world festival of music there. He reported with his usual penetration on "the need of East and West for each other," recognizing that among all the efforts to combine musics of distant cultures, most "are sterile, as hybrids so often are. What we are looking for is a strong cross-breed."

An attitude much like Thomson's found a persuasive representative in post-war Germany in Thomson's friend, Boris Blacher (b. 1903). His biographer, H. H. Stuckenschmidt, quoted from a talk by Blacher (1954):

A composer basically ought to write what gives him a kick. After all there are many kinds of music, easy and difficult to grasp, pure entertainment and pure experiment. There are some composers who follow only one path or another. That is basically a question of what fate decrees. But there are others as well—among whom I count myself—who compose now this way and now that, each as far as it gives them pleasure.

Blacher's ostensibly frivolous inconsistency of style allowed him to produce an enormous amount of music, including operas and ballets, to keep up to the minute with every fashion, from jazz to electronic music, and to become one of the most influential cosmopolitan teachers of composition in his time. He was especially famous for his use of systematically "variable meters," introduced in the *Ornamente* for piano (1950), and explained in a lecture the next year. But this device was only a striking and memorable tag, making his later scores recognizable at a glance; the various sounds of the music and the various underlying literary and social ideas were little affected.

Blacher's extreme versatility was fated, just as surely as the singlemindedness of a Webern. He grew up in China and Siberia, with English as his first language in school. He completed his studies in Berlin, and there worked as a bohemian arranger and theater composer, drawing inspiration from Stravinsky, Ravel, Milhaud, Hindemith, and the whole range of popular and folk music of the world. At times he sought roots in the folksongs of Estonia, the home of his grandparents, but he could make himself at home just as readily in America or Israel or Japan. It was easy to imagine him likewise at home on Mars.

Among Blacher's many pupils, Gottfried von Einem (b. 1918) was the most immediately successful.

Two of the pioneers in hybridization that Thomson might have had in mind in his report from Tokyo were the Netherlander Daniel Ruyneman (1886–1964) and the Canadian Colin McPhee (1901–64). Both of them, well acquainted with the music of Debussy, Schoenberg, and Stravinsky, were captivated by Indonesian music (Javanese and Balinese respectively), and their most interesting works were composed almost as translations from the Indonesian into European instrumental idioms. However slight the significance of these works themselves, Ruyneman and McPhee were likely to be remembered for their efforts in a field where they were sure to be followed.

Two more important composers in whose music certain oriental and primitive elements were deeper rooted than in Blacher's or Thomson's, Debussy's or Stravinsky's, were Carl Orff and Olivier Messiaen. These two were seldom considered in a single context, but they had more than one common trait.

———————•·•———————

The most amazingly radical composer of Germany since Wagner was commonly regarded as a conservative: Carl Orff (b. 1895). His drastic, simple style was obviously opposed to the complexity of Wagner, Strauss, Reger, Schoenberg, and his own exact contemporary, Hindemith. It was recognizably close to folksong, to some 19th-century popular song, and to the most accessible elements of Baroque, Renaissance, and medieval music. Hence his *Carmina burana* (songs from the 13th-century collection at the monastery Benediktbeuern, 1936) won world-wide praise from conservative critics and audiences, and corresponding scorn from the "advanced guard." His comic fairy-tale operas, *Der Mond* (*The Theft of the Moon,* 1938) and *Die Kluge* (*The Peasant's Clever Daughter,* 1942), though less successful abroad, held the stage throughout Germany more steadily than any other work since *Rosenkavalier.* But a little study of Orff's later music, his intentions, and his consistent development, shows that he does not fit a pigeonhole. Even *Carmina burana* has more in common with Debussy, Stravinsky, Bartók, and Varèse than with Lehár, Strauss, Pfitzner, or with Orff's rather conventionally eclectic friend, pupil, and rival, Werner Egk (b.

1901) or his younger pupil, Heinrich Sutermeister (b. 1910). Orff's work as a whole, up to 1965, contains nothing likely to repeat the success of the *Carmina burana,* but much that deserves study by both friends and enemies of that work.

Orff's biographer, Andreas Liess, reports that after the first performance of *Carmina burana* the composer told his publisher, "You can now delete all that I have written before and that you have unfortunately published. With the *Carmina burana* my 'collected works' begin." But then Orff rescued several of his earlier works with new versions. Further, as Liess points out, the very earliest juvenilia are highly characteristic, and each new undertaking is a natural stage in Orff's purification of style and concentration of purpose. As a child in Munich—brilliant and handsome son of an old military family—Orff studied piano, organ, and cello; he longed to study timpani as well; at home he sang, played duets and chamber music; he regularly attended concerts and operas. Before he finished Gymnasium he had his first songs published; still without any instruction in composing or even in harmony, he completed a huge Zarathustra cantata. Then he studied for one year at the conservatory, and encountered Debussy's *Pelléas,* which Liess identified as his "great orienting experience." A Japanese opera (1913) and a tone-poem, *Tanzende Faune (Dancing Faun,* 1914) testify to this. Liess mentions also the influence of Schoenberg's orchestral pieces, Op. 16, and the Chamber Symphony, Op. 9, which Orff arranged for piano duet.

From 1915 to 1917, and again, after brief service in the army, until 1919, Orff was active as conductor in theaters. In 1919–21 he was a full-time composer. But dissatisfied with his achievement, he paused to study for a year with the mystical recluse, Heinrich Kaminski (1886–1946), and to analyze music of Lassus, Palestrina, Gabrieli, and Monteverdi. He was not converted, however, to Kaminski's kind of polyphony. For at the same time he was fascinated by the new concert dances of Rudolph von Laban and Mary Wigman, which affected his gradually developing ideal of the role of music in the theater, of the theater in the modern world, and of the modern world in the perspective of all times and places. In 1924 he joined the dancer Dorothea Günther in founding a school, where he could work out the realization of this ideal.

Orff's *Music for Children* (1930–35, radically revised 1950–54) is a vast compendium, for use in nursery schools, kindergartens, and other groups. It begins with clapping and speaking, and progresses through the universal children's chant on a minor third to ensembles as elaborate as those of Orff's "grown-up" music. The simplest materials and forms are marvelously animated by means of specially designed instruments: xylophones, metallophones, and glockenspiels in several sizes, with removable parts to facilitate a slow, gradual expansion from three-note tunes and ostinato accompaniments to pentatonic, diatonic, and finally chromatic scales. With these basic instruments are often joined various drums and cymbals, further percussion instruments (but not toys), musical glasses, strummed guitar, and viola da gamba, to make magnificent sonorities, both bright and full. Occasionally recorders may join or replace voices. No instrument requiring professional skill is used. Yet the instrumentation is essential, never a matter of indifference, as in some of Hindemith's music for amateur fiddlers and tootlers. Orff's distinctive sounds, in the beautiful recorded performances by children, are complete, spontaneous, and never tiring. The rhythms, corresponding to these sounds, are mostly strongly metrical, without syncopation. March and waltz are rare. The elemental rhythms of strolling, skipping, running, swaying, and stamping prevail. Meters of five and seven beats, changing meters, and irregularities of phrasing occur as they do in folk music, where words or gestures evoke them, not out of impatience with the hypnotic familiarity of regular meters. The acceptance of regularity facilitates the grasping of long stretches of time in a rhythmic perception. If Webern has given us a sort of temporal microscope, Orff's rhythm is like a telescope. Dissonance, like rhythmic irregularity, occurs infrequently and without emphasis, as it did in some medieval music, before the rhythmic potency of dissonance had been explored. Thus the famous 13th-century English round, *Sumer is icumen in,* falls into place in Orff's work as no quaint curiosity, but as a part of the family. Harmony in general, as pointed out by both Wilhelm Keller and Ingeborg Kiekert in their analytical studies of Orff's style, is subordinate to "autonomous" melody, rhythm, and sonority. Even melody is secondary, in Kiekert's view; "rhythm and sonority are the dominating form-building elements . . . Out of words arises the variety of sounds, out of dance-movement arises the unifying power of rhythm, and so the sonorous variety coheres through the organizing rhythm."

Antigonae (1943–48) and *Oedipus* (1956–59) are Orff's most ambitious and most austere works. In the service of the Hölderlin texts, uncut, Orff makes the varied percussive sonorities and hypnotic rhythms, similar to those of the *Music for Children,* build unprecedented monumental forms. His expert choral writing provides additional variety. His solo vocal parts exploit a big range, and occasionally relieve the regular rhythm with elaborate rapid ornaments. But never do the melodies resemble traditional arias. Keller, Kiekert, and some other German critics regard these works as the most important operatic achievement since Strauss and Berg. Winfried Zillig thinks "Orff has succeeded in renewing, in an utterly personal way, the musical theater that ever since Wagner had stalled—even despite *Wozzeck*—in an apparent final phase." Everett Helm, pioneer commentator in English on Orff, hedges his judgment, but he too recognizes Orff's distinction and grandeur.

In 1961 at Salzburg a center was established for the worldwide propagation of Orff's school music. By now this work had been adapted (not merely translated) in eighteen foreign languages, including some of Asia and Africa. The English edition by Margaret Murray and an American (Canadian) one by Arnold Walter and Doreen Hall were rapidly winning attention.

The most independent and astonishing French composer between Debussy and Boulez was Olivier Messiaen (b. 1908). After World War II, as teacher of Boulez, Stockhausen, Luigi Nono, Karl Goeyvaerts, Bengt Hambræus, Makoto Shinohara, Maurice Le Roux, Samson François, Yvette Grimaud, Michel Fano, Serge Nigg, Bernard Flavigny, Marius Constant, Marcel Frémiot, Jean Barraqué, Gilbert Amy, Alexander Goehr, and many more, Messiaen exercised a great stimulating influence. His name became more widely known than his music, which was increasingly peculiar and hard to play, especially with respect to its rhythm.

On the other hand, listeners to any one piece of Messiaen—particularly the organ music of the 1930s, which was oftenest played—were likely to dismiss it as naïve or reactionary. Sometimes, like Orff, Messiaen was content to repeat an ostinato or a melodic fragment far beyond the limits that Stravinsky or Bartók would set. Often he luxuriated in triads, dominant sevenths, added sixths, and ninths, all closely spaced and thrust together with no concern for voice-leading. Moreover, his forms—chains of ten or more movements, many rondos with literal refrains, and loose ABA's with recapitulated rhapsodies—seemed mechanically connected with the titles, texts, and supplementary program notes, in which love, angels, and birds made a disconcerting "jumble of rainbows" (his own expression, in a sober book on his technique).

Photographs of Messiaen—always peering through his glasses, always wearing his collar open wide—suggested his strange combination of novel intellectual challenge and old-fashioned emotional indulgence.

For Messiaen himself, and for his most sympathetic and patient expositor, Antoine Goléa, there was no incongruity between his impressive erudition and his gushing expression. Technique served expression. Neither was an end in itself, but rather both together were part of a devout life. This life was hard and solitary. Even Goléa, revealing some of its most lurid, intimate torments, is first and last impressed with the solitude of Messiaen. The title of Messiaen's own book is significant, *The Technique of My Musical Language*. A language, in ordinary usage of the word, is shared by a group, larger or smaller as the case may be. "Musical language" commonly means shared habits, rather than a personal style. But Messiaen developed (and continued to develop) his own language. He does not propose that others use it. Neither does he claim exclusive right to any of its techniques. He offers an explanation for whoever cares to understand what he is expressing. As a teacher, he ingeniously analyzes the "languages" of Debussy, Stravinsky, and Schoenberg; he leaves each pupil free to develop a new "language" of his own. As an organist he improvises freely in his language. As a composer he humbly tries to tell the truth of his experience. The most discriminating critics of Messiaen, Claude Rostand and David Drew, recognize his integrity.

Messiaen has an incipient verbal language of his own, as well as his musical one, and his verbal innovations too serve his expression. In all his vocal music he uses his own texts. He regards himself as a surrealist poet, following the models of Breton, Éluard, Reverdy, and Hello. In *Harawi* (a cycle for soprano and piano, 1945) he mixes Peruvian words with French. In the title *Turangalîla* (symphony, 1946–48) he borrows and adapts a Sanskrit word. And in the *Cinq rechants* (madrigals for 12-part chorus, 1949) there are whole lines of pseudo-Sanskrit, confessedly invented. These three works together are a huge trilogy, which Goléa compares with *Tristan*. In them, through both words and music, Messiaen expresses more of himself than elsewhere, either before or after. A short excerpt from these works would be misleading, but their existence should be kept in mind as we examine the techniques and intentions of a simpler piece, more impersonal though no less characteristic.

This is the first movement (see Ex. XX.2) of the suite for organ, *Les Corps glorieux: Sept visions brèves de la vie des ressuscités (Radiant Bodies: Seven Short Visions of the Life of the Resurrected, 1939)*.

Unaccompanied melody is frequent in Messiaen's work. "Melody is the point of departure. May it remain sovereign!" Even more frequent than unaccompanied melody are phrases accompanied by a static rich chord, or by chords in almost parallel motion—chords in either case dependent on a single melody. What is rare is a chord progression motivated by melody or counterpoint. For the melodies loop around a center—here the D—without suggesting any such progression. Each phrase is complete in itself, and the loose chain of phrases is conventional. Repetitions unify the whole piece, but exaggerate the distinctness of parts. The melodic motion, fast or slow, is bodiless, beatless. Sometimes, as here, it vaguely suggests the flexible rhythm of plainsong, as chanted by the monks of Solesmes. But this suggestion is contradicted by several features of Messiaen's melodies: the use of single short notes between longer ones, the use of many short notes together after the danger of duple or triple grouping is past (measures 16, 18), and especially the leaps of augmented and diminished intervals on short notes. Altogether Messiaen's rhythm, if this term preserves its wealth of

EXAMPLE XX.2 Messiaen, *Les Corps glorieux,* first movement, excerpts

connotations, is extraordinarily weak. This very weakness allows him in his later music to explore temporal relations that give new meanings to the word "rhythm." The loose connection between melody and chords encourages him from the start to use a synthetic scale of eight tones within the octave, alternating whole steps and half steps. Messiaen calls this scale a "mode à transposition limitée"—a scale capable of transposition to a restricted number of points without duplicating by enharmonic equivalence—the whole-tone scale is thus restricted to a single transposition, the eight-tone scale to two; there are others, of less interest, though Messiaen uses all of them. In our example, mm. 1 and 2 and the variant of them in 12 and 13 illustrate Messiaen's favorite version of this scale. Most of mm. 5, 7, some of 11, and 18–19, illustrate a transposition of the scale. (To recognize this makes the melody more appealing.) Elsewhere the melody deviates into free chromaticism; Messiaen is no doctrinaire. This melody never hints at a diatonic scale, but in other pieces Messiaen freely mixes diatonic passages, and he sometimes uses the eight-tone scale so as to show its diatonic and polytonal affinities. The eight-tone scale often affects Messiaen's choice of chords. It provides a tritone for every note in the scale. Messiaen emphasizes the tritone not only by frequent use in both melodies and chords, but by beginning and ending phrases with this ambiguous interval. He claims that the interval can be heard in the overtone series, and that this justifies his use of it, descending, for a melodic cadence. Most composers who share Messiaen's Christian faith have revived the medieval horror of the tritone—*diabolus in musica*—and either avoid it as it was avoided in plainsong, or use it to depict sin. Messiaen means to depict here "the subtlety of radiant bodies . . . pure as the angels of God in the heavens." Without considering his language an outright code, we may learn from this intention something valuable for listening to his work in general, where tritones nearly always

Elliott Carter (Fred Plaut)

Dmitri Shostakovich

Luigi Dallapiccola *(left)* and Roger Sessions (Hy Reiter, BMI)

PLATE 13

Darius Milhaud (Fred Plaut)

Vaughan Williams *(center)* with R. L. Hull *(left)* and John Kirkpatrick at Cornell, 1954

Francis Poulenc accompanying Rose Plaut-Dercourt, c. 1960 (Fred Plaut)

PLATE 14

abound. His rhythmic and harmonic peculiarities together, associated with his devout intentions, constitute a coherent style that is worth learning to recognize.

Messiaen performed his complete organ music for a Ducretet-Thomson recording in 1956, at the Church of the Trinity in Paris, where he had played regularly for twenty-five years. Most of his piano music was recorded by his pupil, Yvonne Loriod, and even though few other pianists dared to play the later works, all of these, from the eight preludes (1928) through the *Vingt regards sur l'enfant Jésus* (*Twenty Gazes on the Child Jesus,* 1944) and the four studies in rhythm (1949–50) to the *Catalogue des oiseaux* (*List of Birds,* 1959), were likely to have historic importance.

Messiaen was the precocious child of two poets. His father, Pierre Messiaen, was to make a noted translation of Shakespeare, and the boy, at eight, read aloud all Shakespeare's works. His mother, Cécile Sauvage, had composed a book of verses to "The Soul in Bud" before he was born, and her book, he told Goléa, "surely influenced my character and my whole fate." From the age of five to ten, his home was in Grenoble. Later he often returned there for summers. He called himself "a Frenchman of the mountains, like Berlioz." Before he had any music lessons except his mother's, he played and sang the operas of Berlioz, Gluck, and Mozart; these shaped his most fundamental musical habits. At ten (1919), already committed to a musical career, he received as a gift from his harmony teacher, Jehan de Gebon, a copy of Debussy's *Pelléas.* "This present had such an influence on me that even now, nearly forty years later, I can analyze the whole score from memory for my pupils." At eleven he entered the Paris Conservatory, where he studied until he was nearly twenty-two (1930), winning a whole series of prizes. He acknowledged special debts to Jean Gallon (b. 1878) and Noël Gallon (b. 1891) for his command of harmony, to Maurice Emmanuel and Marcel Dupré for his knowledge of the literature of music, especially Greek scales and Indian rhythmic theories, and to Paul Dukas for the techniques of motivic development and orchestration and "the sense of artistic probity." His teachers introduced him to the early works of Ravel, Stravinsky, Schoenberg, and to some pieces of Berg, but he was apparently oblivious to most of the shrill music of the 1920s.

The banner of Berlioz, "Jeune France," served in 1936 to rally Messiaen and his fellow organist Daniel-Lesur (b. 1908) with two slightly older "outsiders," André Jolivet (b. 1905) and Yves Baudrier (b. 1906). Jolivet, advocate of magical primitive incantations, of the Ondes Martenot, of "every sort of music," broadened Messiaen's horizons, without uprooting his firm habits. Messiaen now began his teaching career at the École

Normale and the Schola Cantorum. He married Claire Delbos. He pursued his studies of the Scriptures and of birds.

In 1939, he served in the army. In 1940 he was captured and sent to a prison camp at Görlitz. Here he composed and then performed, with and for his fellow-prisoners, the *Quatuor pour la fin du temps* (*Quartet for the End of Time,* for violin, clarinet, cello, and piano, 1941). In this work his most famous rhythmic innovations first appear fully developed: 1) *valeurs ajoutées,* minimal units of time added to one or more members of a rhythmic group, thus modifying the whole group; Messiaen finds an analogy with the added-sixth chord, and in his *Technique* (1944) he attaches great value to this analogy; 2) *rythmes non-rétrogradables*; apologizing for the ugly term, Messiaen explains that it means patterns of rhythm ending in a retrograde version of their own beginnings, so that the retrograde of the whole is the same as the original; e.g. ♫ ♩ ♩. ♩ ♫ ; here Messiaen finds an analogy, still more remote, with his "limited" scales; in both devices he praises "the charm of impossibilities," logical limits to the freedom of choice. 3) *rythmes augmentés et diminués*—i.e. addition and subtraction of any fraction or multiple of the note values throughout a phrase; this is an extension of the traditional devices of augmentation and diminution of a fugue subject; but since Messiaen has already removed the regular beats that facilitate perception of rhythmic ratios, his procedure has a more dubious meaning.

In 1942 Messiaen was repatriated and became professor at the Conservatory.

In *Turangalîla* (1948) Messiaen introduced his most characteristic innovation, at once technical and pictorial, the principle of *trois personnages rythmiques* (three rhythmic *dramatis personæ*).

As on the stage . . . one of three [actors] acts . . . the second submits to the action of the first, and the third is immobile, passively attending to the action, so in the same way I use easily recognizable groups of durations. . . The active *personnage rythmique* is the one whose durations increase; the submitting *personnage rythmique* is the one whose durations decrease; the immobile *personnage rythmique* is the one whose durations do not change.

Active and submissive here seem the reverse of what might be expected, for decrease of duration means increase of movement. This paradox too is characteristic.

In the piano piece *Cantéyodjaya* (1948) and the four studies in rhythm for piano (1949–50) Messiaen made use of series of durations and dynamics analogous to Schoenberg's series of pitches. This procedure was eagerly adopted and extended by younger men, especially Karlheinz Stockhausen, and for a few years "total serialism" was much discussed. But for Messiaen himself the serial treatment of durations was only one of many possibilities to be explored and used for expressive purposes.

Still more surprising manipulations of durations characterize the later works. A treatise on rhythm was to culminate this development. But whether Messiaen's techniques really concerned rhythm, in the sense of perceptible ratios of motion, was a moot question. The present writer thought not.

The late works have a more obvious and endearing characteristic, their use of bird calls as exclusive melodic material. Messiaen made some helpful comments on this, which throw new light on his work as a whole:

In dark hours, when my futility is brutally apparent, when all musical languages —classic, exotic, ancient, modern, and ultramodern—seem to me reduced to the meritorious product of patient studies, while nothing behind the notes justifies so much work, what is there left but to rediscover the true forgotten face of music somewhere in the woods, in the fields, in the mountains, by the sea, among the birds?

There, for me, is the home of music. Free music, anonymous, improvised for pleasure, for greeting the rising sun, for luring a mate, for proclaiming your possession of a branch or a perch, for ending all dispute, dissension, rivalry, for using the surplus energy that bubbles up with love and joy, for filling time and space, for making generous and providential counterpoints with one's neighbors, for lulling fatigue and saying good-bye to some bit of life when night falls. . .

Earth occupies only a very little place in the universe, and birds occupy only a very little place on earth. So I am not going to take off into metaphysical considerations. But you will agree that if laughter is, alas, the peculiarity of man, then his artistic works are always somewhat like caricatures. In a tree there is a fantastic logic and a logical fantasy quite unknown to the most beautiful human palace. It is in a spirit of no confidence in myself, or I mean in the human race, that I have taken bird songs as model. If you want symbols, let us go on to say that the bird is the symbol of freedom. We walk, he flies. We make war, he sings. Among birds most fights are settled by tournaments of song. Finally, despite my deep admiration for the folklore of the world, I doubt that one can find in any human music, however inspired, melodies and rhythms that have the sovereign freedom of bird song.

This poetic, non-mystical attitude to the music of nature accords with the attitude of Debussy. It is easy to imagine that he might have joined in the laughter at Messiaen's *personnages* and at some of his music, but that he would have been pleased with the *Oiseaux exotiques* (for piano, winds, and percussion, 1956), as with Webern's Symphony, Varèse's *Poème*, Mandelbaum's 19-tone pieces, and Orff's *Music for Children*, all worthy continuations of his adventures. The variety of these continuations, more than their detailed resemblances to his works, indicates the depth of his influence.

CHAPTER XXI

Hindemith

W AS THE VARIETY of musical styles in the 20th century excessive? Was the solitude of so many able composers a symptom of some temporary rupture that could be repaired, some sickness that might be cured? Was the misunderstanding suffered by nearly every important composer avoidable? Was the lure of adventure less urgent than the need for a collective achievement that could restore order and reaffirm the continuity of musical culture?

Schoenberg, Bartók, and Stravinsky, each in his own way, especially after 1923, did reemphasize order and reaffirm continuity, yet without renouncing freedom, variety, and lonely adventure. Likewise Webern, Varèse, Orff, Messiaen, and others set their own kinds of technical and spiritual order and continuity against the chaos of each other's divergences. The resulting outlook for a student composer or a well-intentioned listener at mid-century was more bewildering than ever. The centrifugal development of styles that began before World War I could not be reversed. But many composers, critics, and friends of music thought this development should be stopped, or at least braked enough to make way for some sort of consolidation, not necessarily of style but of a common technique, a working language. "It is evident that we are now in a period of balance and organization: it was preceded by a period of somewhat destructive explorations, which abolished the tonal world and regular meter." This was the view, for example, of Pierre Boulez (1957) although he was still widely regarded as a grim new explorer, threatening more or less destruction in his turn. Similar views were expressed by many other men, and not a few devoted their lives to the search for "balance and organization."

The most eloquent, most energetic, most cheerful, and most nearly successful advocate and architect of a new common order between the wars, in the estimate of most observers, was Paul Hindemith (1895–1963). In his philosophical book, *A Composer's World* (1952), he deplored the "barbaric diversity of styles, total absence of some canon of beauty, . . . esoteric escape, on the part of many composers, from any responsibility towards society." The subtitle of this book was significant: *Horizons and Limitations*. His chief technical book, *Unterweisung im Tonsatz* (*The Craft of Musical Composition*, 1937), defined the limitations. Here he explained: "The new land had to be explored if it was to be conquered, and everyone who took part in this process knows that it was not without danger. The path to knowledge was neither straight nor smooth. Yet today I feel that the new domain lies clearly spread out before our eyes, that we have penetrated the secrets of its organization." He compared himself with Johann Fux (1660–1741), whose *Gradus ad Parnassum* had helped to preserve the contrapuntal craft of the Renaissance and Baroque periods from disappearing in the *galant* age of pretty tunes and tinkling accompaniments. Fux had doubted his power "to control the current of a gushing stream that has overflowed its banks, or to reconvert composers from their heretical way of writing." Hindemith screwed up his courage: "His 'gushing stream' seems to us, compared with the torrential flood of today, a mere overflowing mountain brook. Perhaps a single man's strength will not suffice today to dam the flood; perhaps what he attempts will not even be understood, much less valued. Yet the success of Fux's work shall be a good omen for mine." By 1952 it seemed evident that Hindemith had failed. His survey of the new domain was far from complete. His organization was irrelevant to the styles of most contemporary composers, and even the relation of his theory to his own practice, studied closely by Victor Landau and others, was problematic. Hindemith fell short of his noble aim, just as the adventurers of the generation before him—Ives, Mahler, Busoni, and Debussy himself—fell short of theirs. What Hindemith achieved nevertheless was vast and valuable. His work deserves to be studied apart from its history, for it includes many pieces that will long give delight to singers, players, and listeners, untroubled by historical considerations, and this delight is no mere pleasant pastime but an exercise of the spirit. Yet in historical perspective the value of the music is enhanced by the drama of Hindemith's honorable failure. It is this drama, together with the vast quantity of his music, that gives him a worldwide position of more importance than that of such older composers as Albert Roussel and Gian Francesco Malipiero or such contemporaries as Walter Piston, Roger Sessions, Willem Pijper, and Hilding Rosenberg, all of whom shared with him to some degree the desire to restore order.

At the outset of his career Hindemith was no conservative or consolidator, but a conspicuous radical—the boldest of his generation in Germany. A characteristic anecdote was told by an eye-witness, Max Rieple: in 1921 after the concert where Hindemith's Second Quartet aroused great excitement, Richard Strauss came up and addressed him in slurring Munich dialect: "Why d'you write this atonal stuff? You have talent!" To which Hindemith retorted in Frankfurterish, "Herr Professor, you make your music and I'll make mine."

The brash tone of Hindemith's reply can be recognized again in the little sketch of himself that he supplied for the *Neue Musikzeitung* (1922):

As violinist, violist, pianist, or percussionist I have "tilled" the following fields of music: all sorts of chamber music, movies, cafés, dance halls, operetta, jazz band, military band. Since 1916 I have been concertmaster of the Frankfurt opera orchestra. As composer I have written mostly pieces that I don't like: chamber music in the most various media, songs, piano things. Also three one-act operas, which will probably be the only ones, since with the perpetual inflation of the price of manuscript paper only small scores can be written. Analyses of my works I cannot give, because I do not know how to explain a piece of music in few words. (I'd rather write a new one in the time it takes.) Besides, I believe that for people with ears my stuff is really easy to grasp, and so an analysis is superfluous. For people without ears, too, such asses' bridges are no help.

Hindemith disclosed little more than this of how he had grown up in Frankfurt. His biographer, Heinrich Strobel, reported that he began violin lessons at the age of nine, and soon was composing in a steady stream. From 1909 to 1917 he attended the Hoch Conservatory, where thirty years earlier Edward MacDowell had studied under Raff. When Hindemith enrolled, the leading composer there, not mentioned by Strobel, was Ivan Knorr (1853–1916), who had lived and worked in Russia and then, in Frankfurt, had passed on his interests in exoticism and in Bach to Ernest Bloch, Percy Grainger, Cyril Scott, and other distinguished pupils. Knorr's successor was his pupil Bernhard Sekles (1872–1934), likewise noted for his use of exotic materials—Balkan and Chinese, according to Rudolf Louis—in otherwise unremarkable post-Wagnerian operas. Hindemith remembered Sekles in 1947 as "an ideal teacher." Another talented pupil of Sekles, Rudi Stephan (1887–1915), attracted attention during Hindemith's student years with his novel, abstract titles: Music for Seven Stringed Instruments (1912), Music for Orchestra (1913), and Music for Violin and Orchestra (1914). Perhaps equally important for Hindemith, as Klaus Holzmann suggests in a brief special study, was another teacher, Arnold Mendelssohn (1855–1933), who had turned away from opera and from romantic ideals to sober church music. He watched Hindemith's career with eager sympathy. Probably more congenial than any composer, however, was the violin teacher, Adolf Rebner (b. 1876), who gave Hindemith his place in the opera orchestra and took him into his touring string quartet as second violinist and later violist. The conductor at the opera was Ludwig Rottenberg (1864–1932); his influence on Hindemith, noted by Winfried Zillig, would be worth study. He had presented the first German performance of Debussy's *Pelléas*

(1907). During Hindemith's years as student and orchestral player, Rotten-berg produced the first performances anywhere of four successful operas by Schreker, two interesting ones by Busoni, the last one by Delius, the only one by Rudi Stephan, the most successful one by Wolfgang von Walter-shausen (1882–1954), and finally (1922) Bartók's *Bluebeard*, in the same season with Hindemith's three one-acters. Rottenberg's own songs and his single opera, a complete setting of Goethe's *Die Geschwister* (1915), won the praise of the excellent critic Paul Bekker. In 1924 Hindemith married Rottenberg's daughter Gertrude.

Meanwhile, in 1917–18, the twenty-two-year-old had served briefly in the army. One memorable experience he recounted, in a picture-book of 1955:

As a soldier in the First World War, I was a member of a string quartet that enabled the colonel of our regiment to forget the detested war. He was a great music lover and a connoisseur and devotee of French culture. No wonder, then, that his greatest wish was to hear Debussy's string quartet. We rehearsed the piece and played it in a private concert for him, with great feeling. When we had just finished the slow movement, the officer in charge of the news service burst into the room and announced that word of Debussy's death had just come over the radio. We did not go on to the finale. It was as if the breath had been knocked out of our playing. But here we felt for the first time that music is more than style, technique, and expression of personal feeling. Here music reached out over political boundaries, over national hatred and the horror of war. On no other occasion has it ever been so clearly revealed to me in which direction music should be developed.

The memory of Debussy's slow movement, fifteen years later, inspired the sublime opening measures of Hindemith's opera and symphony, *Mathis der Maler*, in which he too "reached out over political boundaries," through and beyond style and technique and personal feeling.

———— • ————

Hindemith's fame was achieved not so much at the Frankfurt opera house as at the little town of Donaueschingen, where Prince Max Egon of Fürstenburg subsidized a summer festival of chamber music by young Ger-man and Austrian composers, 1921–26. The first year Hindemith had to be coaxed to participate by the organizers, who had admired his first pub-lications. By the last year, when he was just thirty, he had finished a monu-mental opera that was performed all over Germany, *Cardillac*. But meanwhile he led the excitement at Donaueschingen. Thanks chiefly to his brilliance and energy, the festivals there attracted almost as much attention as those of the ISCM, in which he took part also. Thanks to the festivals, he could now give up his orchestra job and support himself through concert tours, playing viola either as soloist or in the quartet led by his Hungarian friend, Licco Amar (b. 1891). Soon all the anti-Romantic art-lovers of Germany hailed him as the authentic musical "type" of the Weimar Republic and its new, healthy, experimental spirit. Many looked to him as a welcome replacement for Strauss, a worthy rival and perhaps successor to Schoenberg and Stravinsky, with whom he was now in friendly association. Anti-modernists, of course, condemned him as a traitor to German culture, an upstart, an Expressionist, a degenerate; he provoked them further with a bit of jazz. Especially for Donaueschingen in 1922 he composed his *Chamber Music I* for small orchestra, with a frenetic finale labelled "1921," a travesty of a current hit of German popular music, with a raucous battery of percussion. The tender slow movement just before this finale made it all the more shocking. A more ambitious new work on the same program was *Die junge Magd* (*The Young Girl*), a tragic cycle of six poems by Trakl, with quiet accompaniment of flute, clarinet, and string quartet. But the jazzy afterpiece was what made headlines. For a souvenir to be played at home, Hindemith provided the piano suite *1922*; the impudent preface to its finale, "Ragtime," and the charming cartoon (by Hindemith) on the cover won this work also disproportionate attention in historical surveys and program notes.

In 1923 the chief new work revealed at Donaueschingen was the song cycle with piano accompaniment on Rilke's *Das Marienleben* (*The Life of Mary*). Here was a landmark in Hindemith's development, the earliest piece that he kept revising and finally (1948) issued in a new version when his explorations were complete. The special spirit of *Marienleben* is identified by Karl Wörner when he compares it to a woodcut by Ernst Barlach.

Among the many pieces of chamber music before *Cardillac*, outstanding ones are the lyrical third quartet, Op. 22 (1922), the brilliant *Kleine Kammermusik* for wind quintet, Op. 24, No. 2 (1922), and the profound first String Trio, Op. 34 (1924). Many more are interesting. Even the earliest published pieces are comparable to most of Reger or the earlier works of Strauss, and everything after Op. 21 is masterful. The sheer amount of music on the list of works, and the almost systematic provision of similar pieces for various media, are both characteristic of Hindemith, making a strong contrast with the lists of Schoenberg, Bartók, and Stravinsky—not to mention Webern, whose Bagatelles received their first performance at Donaueschingen, by the Amar Quartet. Hindemith composed so fluently, and regarded many of his products so casually, that there was no complete list, and few exact dates of composition were available.

In the eight years between the two big operas, *Cardillac* and *Mathis der Maler* (*Matthias the Painter*, 1932–35), Hindemith's copious production was more amazing than ever, especially since during these years he was the chief teacher of composition at the Berlin Hochschule für Musik, as well as a busy performer, an enthusiastic hiker in the country, and a beginning student of Latin.

While he continued to explore new instrumental combinations and new intricacies of harmony and counterpoint in such masterpieces as the viola concertos, Op. 36, No. 4 and Op. 48, he distinguished himself among other "advanced" composers by working strenuously for a *rapprochement* with the everyday musical life of students and amateurs. Even at Donaueschingen as early as 1925, *a cappella* choral music was added to chamber music; Hindemith's Op. 33 was the outstanding piece. In 1926 works for military band were called for; his Op. 41 was the greatest success. In the next years Hindemith took a leading part in larger festivals, at Baden-Baden and Berlin, with further contributions of *Gebrauchsmusik* (workaday music, literally use-music—i.e. music to satisfy the demand of a particular medium or occasion). So striking was this development that soon the term "Gebrauchsmusik" came to be a slogan attached to Hindemith's style, at least in most American discussions of his work. He complains with some bitterness, in *A Composer's World*, that "it has been impossible to kill this silly term and the unscrupulous classification that goes with it." His motive in writing for students and amateurs was not, as the term might suggest, crass commercialism. Neither was it to promote the ideology of the Youth Movement or any political party. The fact that Hindemith collaborated at one moment with the great Communist poet Brecht, once with the great nihilist Benn, once with the Bauhaus painter Schlemmer, and repeatedly with the cabaret satirist Schiffer, shows his impartiality. His motive was concern for music, and for the community of its friends. This concern was implicit in his earlier chamber music, and it grew more and more urgent, right down to the *Song of Hope* for UNESCO (1955), with audience participation in a final chorale. In *A Composer's World*, this concern is amply explained:

In former times the broad phalanx of those participating in music consisted predominantly of a vast middle field of amateurs: people who made music their hobby in the form of singing and playing but did not practice it professionally. At their right wing there was a relatively small number of professionals, and at the left an equally small number of mere listeners. . . The amateur . . . played in the orchestras together with the professional, he sang in the choirs, and for him all chamber music was written. Haydn's, Mozart's and Beethoven's quartets, even Brahms's chamber music counted mostly on the amateur. Today, with the number of participants . . . swollen from thousands to millions, their make-up has changed. . . If we assume that the former distribution of listeners, amateurs, and professionals was, expressed in per cent, about 5, 90, and 5, respectively, we can for our modern times take 95, 1, and 4 as a fair estimate. . . Once you join an amateur group, you are a member of a great fraternity, whose purpose is the most dignified one you can imagine: to inspire one another and unite in building up a creation that is greater than one individual's deeds. Amateurs of this kind, when listening to music, will not be the stupid receivers, the targets of virtuosity, the idle gourmands of which our audiences predominantly consist. . . The composer . . . would have to provide the music needed and appreciated by the amateur. . . He would have to search for a new technical and stylistic approach—a new human approach, too! Until through years of work and the concerted devotion of many like-minded musicians such technique and style are developed and many listeners have been converted, the work will frequently enough be similar to that of the boy at the dike. . . The composer, in addition to the mere technical practice of his craft, could be the helper and even the spiritual leader in a search for a more salubrious musical world: it should be his main objective to lift the consumer to a higher level by convincing him of the harm a constant yearning for entertainment produces; and as a means to this end the writing of suitable music for amateurs was recommended. Certainly, writing such music will not be the only means, but it will be the form in which the desire for replacing external brilliancy with genuine musical values finds its clearest expression. Once a writer's technique and style is organized in this direction, so that music which satisfies the amateur's wishes can be created, his approach to his entire work will inevitably undergo a radical change: the emphasis on moral aspects will now become recognizable also in his works written for the concertizing professional, and now he will talk with a different spirit to the general audience.

The number of performing amateurs that Hindemith reached was never so great as to turn back the momentous tide of change he described. Yet perhaps he saved the dike at the time of greatest danger, when radio and phonograph were only beginning to multiply the passive audience, and "new music" was still almost totally deprived of these media of reaching the millions. Ever since then, more and more amateurs could join him in the "great fraternity," and recognize in all his work his "moral emphasis."

Hindemith's "changing approach to his entire work" is shown in an exaggerated way by the difference between the two operas, *Cardillac* (1926) and *Mathis* (1934). There is an underlying similarity: in each case the protagonist is a great artist in conflict with authority and with a fickle mob. Cardillac is a monster, and his conflict is absurd. He wants to keep all his fabulous gold work for his own gloating delight; to do so he murders his customers. The brave young man who loves his daughter discovers that Cardillac is the murderer, is nearly killed himself by Cardillac, foils him, forgives him, shames him until he yields himself up to the mob, and then envies his transcendance of normal human powers and feelings. Mathis Grünewald, on the contrary, is a historical figure (1480–1530), whose paintings, neglected for four centuries, can be appreciated in the 20th as if they were contemporary. Hindemith makes him a fully credible personality, and sets the dramatic conflict within the hero's conscience. Mathis temporarily abandons painting to take part in the Peasants' Rebellion. Then he learns that this commitment, paradoxically, is a withdrawal from the people to whom he belongs, that his true duty is to use his distinctive powers, and to dedicate his art to God. Whereas in *Cardillac* the glittering, concerto-like music runs parallel to the rapid action, keeping at a distance and marking off sharply the contrasting scenes, with marvelous epic-dramatic effect, in *Mathis*, on the other hand, the warmth of complex feeling suffuses the music and unfortunately slows and obscures the action, so that the drama makes a better whole in imagination than in actual performance despite the symmetry of both action and music. The libretto of *Mathis*, Hindemith's own composition, is immensely rich and ideally coherent, even though it is impractical for the theater. Mathis identifies himself with St. Anthony, whose temptations he is to paint for the altar of St. Anthony's church at Isenheim. Obviously Hindemith identifies himself with Mathis, more closely than with the normal young man who envies Cardillac. When he revised *Cardillac* (1952) he wrote an entirely new libretto. *Mathis* needed no revision.

The prelude to *Mathis*, recurring in the middle of the opera, accompanies the painter's vision of the most famous panel in the Isenheim altar-piece, *The Concert of Angels*. Here Hindemith uses a phrase of a modal folk-song, *Es sungen drei Engel* (*Three Angels were Singing*), first in a slow introduction and then at the climax of contrapuntal developments of his own three themes—one for each angel. Mathis exclaims:

Lo! how a band of angels exchanges eternal paths for earthly ones! how each is absorbed in his mild duty! One is fiddling with a marvelously restrained arm; he cradles his bow tenderly, so that its delicate course may not be darkened by the roughness of the least shadow. Another with exalted gaze is stroking out of the strings his joy. A third angel seems to be transfixed by the distant ringing of his soul, and plays effortlessly. How ready he is at once to hear and to serve!

The music of *The Concert of Angels*, detached from the opera as first movement of the Mathis symphony, does not depend on this detailed association with words and pictures; it owes its fame among musicians partly to the fact that Hindemith gave a purely technical analysis of a phrase from it in his *Unterweisung*. But for anyone interested, the associations can enhance the coherence and intensity of the movement. Still more does this apply to the whole symphony, in which the slow movement corresponds not only to the Pietà of the altar-piece but also to two moving scenes at the end of the opera, and the finale is the Temptation not only of St. Anthony but of Mathis and Hindemith, with their triumphant resistance symbolized by plainchants, *Lauda Sion* and *Alleluia.*

The fame of *Mathis* was partly due to extraneous dramatic events. Performance of the opera was banned by the Nazis. They probably had not read the scene in which Lutheran books were burned by the Catholics at Mainz—a parallel to the Nazis' book-burning of 1933. Their main grounds for objection to Hindemith were rather the climax of his comic opera, *Neues vom Tage* (*News of the Day*), with the heroine in a bath, and his personal association with Jews. He was defended by the conductor Wilhelm Furtwängler, who played the *Mathis* symphony in 1934, amid horrendous tumult. But soon Hindemith was removed from his teaching post and encouraged to work mostly abroad. *Mathis* was produced in Switzerland in 1938, and Hindemith went there to live.

In Hindemith's career up to *Mathis* it is tempting to see a whole spiral of stylistic phases with distinct labels: his first publication, three pieces for cello and piano, Op. 8, and the First Quartet, Op. 10 (both 1918), represent his starting-point, "late Romanticism"; a violin sonata, Op. 11, No. 1, and some of the unpublished pieces, according to Strobel, show a brief transition through "Impressionism"; the one-act operas, Opp. 12 and 21 (1919 and 1921) are prime examples of "Expressionism"; the puppet play, *Nusch-Nuschi*, Op. 20, with its quotation from *Tristan* surrounded by obscenities, is the acme of "anti-Romanticism"; *Marienleben*, Op. 27, the Fourth Quartet, Op. 32, the chamber concertos, Op. 36, and *Cardillac*, Op. 39, are on the broad highway of "neo-Classicism" leading "back to Bach"; Opp. 43–45 and many works without numbers are *Gebrauchsmusik*; and *Mathis* completes the circle as "neo-Romanticism." If these labels are not allowed to obscure the independence and consistency of Hindemith's steady development, they are more appropriate here than when they serve to distinguish one composer's style from another's and to consign a whole life-work to a pigeonhole. But even in Hindemith's case the "isms" tend to oversimplify the complicated and subtle history that they summarize.

Hindemith's development in all its complexity and subtlety was followed and interpreted with amazing speed and skill by Hans Mersmann. His interpretation, soon adopted by many musicians and critics, associated the young Hindemith with the mature Stravinsky and Bartók. All three, Mersmann thought, were reorganizing the elements of music that had been broken apart in the chaotic transition period about 1905 to 1925. Their work was converging toward the achievement of a definitive 20th-century style, mature and balanced and comprehensive. Schoenberg, in this view, was honored for the decisive breakthrough from 19th-century style to the freedom prerequisite to a new style, but he seemed to be surpassed now by the younger composers.

Other critics, like Kurt Westphal, ranked Hindemith as the supreme culmination of the modern movement, the first achiever of a common stylistic goal.

Hindemith's own view of his development was different. For him, style, though conspicuous, was unessential. Even more than Schoenberg or Ives he subordinated style to idea and substance, for he distinguished more sharply than they did between style and technique. He emphasized technique, workmanship, humble anonymous craft, as the essential foundation of music. Style and personal expression grew out of technique, and all were properly subordinated to ideas. His development up to *Mathis* was not, then, so much the development of a style as the "changing approach" with its "moral emphasis," and simultaneously a growing technical command of the materials whose sheer abundance had overwhelmed the traditional technique and misled him and his contemporaries into technical flaws and stylistic "curlicues." He proposed now to share his technique with the world, for it seemed to him valid in all styles of all periods, rooted in Nature. His students, he thought, would be free to develop personal stylistic "amenities" of their own, though he hoped they would be more concerned with ideas.

Style, the crown and flower of technique, if bereft of invigorating imagination disintegrates into fashion. Routine and fashion—these are the worst snarls that can entangle the creative mind. . . Technique and style are obedient servants so long as they are kept under control. Once out of control they either totally dominate the process of constructing a piece, or they degenerate into routine and fashion. They are indispensable aids to our work; without their help we cannot produce any musical form. Yet, like many versatile but stupid attendants, they must be held in subservience if they are to give their best service; they must be treated with contempt. . . They must remain the humble slaves of superior ideas.

Thus his most important book, just after *Mathis*, is called *Unterweisung im Tonsatz*, instruction in the setting of tones, in techniques of melody, harmony, and counterpoint. It is not a complete guide to composition. It abstracts pitch relations from the "primary elements" of absolute pitch, intensity, and timbre; the mysterious, "primeval" element, rhythm; and all subtleties of style. But it is more comprehensive than traditional harmony and counterpoint, which took for granted that melodies were based on diatonic scales. With the third volume of the book, drafted in 1940 but left unpublished at Hindemith's death, the instruction embraces four-part writing. The new doctrine aims to provide a more general craft, including and reinterpreting the old disciplines, showing the disorder of some contemporary works and the arbitrary fashionableness of others.

Hindemith did not mince matters with vague insinuations. He attacked

Stravinsky and Schoenberg head-on. First he dissected the palpable but hitherto elusive weakness of a phrase by Eugène d'Albert (1864–1932). Then, politely but firmly, he showed that by his technical standards a phrase of Stravinsky was pitifully flimsy, and a phrase of Schoenberg grotesquely over-complicated. By implication he condemned many of his own early works, but he showed that in *Mathis*, where his personal style was unmistakable, he was wielding the same fundamental technique that underlay the styles of Machaut, Bach, Beethoven, and Wagner. This technique he expected to win welcome everywhere. It would not, to be sure, redeem a lack of creative ideas, but it would give composers true freedom to realize their visions, with their various personal styles.

Here was the summit of Hindemith's historic career; his descent was inevitable. His attack on Stravinsky and Schoenberg was the strongest they ever sustained, but it was vitiated by a fundamental mistake. Hindemith hardly considered or tried to consider the peculiar visions or ideas of these composers. He did not study their harmonic techniques as exemplified in whole compositions, or in relation to their rhythms and sonorities, much less in their gradual stylistic developments. By tearing fragments out of context he destroyed their function and value. His page of Stravinsky typifies only a few of the superficial "neo-Classic" tags of his style; it is an introduction to a splendidly coherent piece, which taken as a whole can be shown to satisfy Hindemith's rules well enough, though these help no more than 19th-century rules to grasp Stravinsky's distinctive power. The Schoenberg example comes from a development section that presupposes close attention to the simpler exposition; this piece as a whole has a technical coherence and ideal purpose to which most of Hindemith's rules are irrelevant, and in Schoenberg's work as a whole it is a minor production, like a sketch in comparison with his operas of the same period. Both these pieces, after a quarter of a century, continued to fascinate many kinds of musicians, while Hindemith's technique was generally rejected and his music taken for granted.

In his later music Hindemith's style, though undergoing some modifications, remained essentially the same. His technique was complete, in his view. It seemed less and less stylish. Accordingly, few musicians or music lovers penetrated to the profound ideas. Some accused Hindemith of allowing his technique—especially of fugue—to become a routine, but this accusation was rarely if ever founded on any detailed knowledge of his work. In his cycle of twelve fugues for piano, *Ludus tonalis*, the variety was as great as in Bach's forty-eight, *The Well-Tempered Clavier*. In Hindemith's other works the many fugal movements and fugatos were more various than

Haydn's or Brahms's. More discriminating critics, like Colin Mason, noted that Hindemith's concentration on harmonic techniques and grandiose ideas led him to scorn the sensuous refinements of spacing and instrumentation, and sometimes to neglect the vital element, rhythm. The metrical patterns of march, waltz, polka, and *siciliana* were more matters of habit than was the textural pattern of fugue.

More attention was paid to the revised versions of early works that Hindemith now brought out from time to time than to his new productions. Most judgments of the revisions were unfavorable. The present author's study of *Frau Musica* (1928, 1943) was an exception. With respect to *Cardillac* and *Marienleben* he agreed with Hans Mersmann, Rudolph Stephan, and Hans Werner Henze in preferring the original versions, if a choice must be made. Yet the opportunity to study both old and new versions was a precious gift to whoever wanted to share as much as possible of Hindemith's visions.

Although in the 1930s Hindemith's doctrine and music had an effect on many composers, especially in Germany and America, hardly any persisted in following him. It was rather easy to learn his technique, but difficult to use it in the service of any vision except his. The most notable of his pupils in Germany were Siegfried Borris (b. 1906), Harald Genzmer (b. 1909), Bernhard Heiden (b. 1910), and Franz Reizenstein (b. 1911), who emigrated to England. Heiden followed Hindemith to America. Among his pupils here were Howard Boatwright, Norman Dello Joio, Alvin Etler, Lukas Foss, Ulysses Kay, Easley Blackwood, Mel Powell, and Yehudi Wyner.

Beginning in Berlin, and increasingly thereafter, Hindemith devoted much time to the performance of medieval and Renaissance music. He repaired old instruments and had copies built. He himself played the viols and vielles, harps and lutes and theorboes, shawms and cornetts and recorders, and he inspired many students to go further with this work, notably Albert Fuller, George Hunter, and Paul Maynard. At Yale University, 1940–53, his Collegium Musicum was as important as his composition class: Boatwright suggests that it was even more so. Hindemith realized the ideal unity of old and new in a matchless manner.

Back in Switzerland in the 1950s and traveling all over the world—to South America, Japan, and again the United States—Hindemith became more and more a conductor, incorporating the heritage of the 19th century into his comprehensive musicianship. Unlike Stravinsky, who conducted only his own music, Hindemith conducted Beethoven and Bruckner. His own orchestral music, from the Symphony of 1940 onward, often recalled Bruckner's majestic sonorities; the most frequently played orchestral piece, the *Metamorphoses* (1943), took its melodies from Weber, elaborating them with great ingenuity; one of the most charming pieces, the Concerto for harp and winds (1949), used Mendelssohn's *Wedding March* as a cantus firmus throughout its finale. The series of sonatas, from the piano solos of 1936 to the tuba piece of 1955, had more in common with 19th-century models of lyricism and dramatic contrast than Hindemith's earlier, Baroque toccata-like works; the forms were various and imaginative, using fugues and passacaglias in ever new combinations with song and dance.

The biggest work after *Mathis* was an opera, *Die Harmonie der Welt* (*Cosmic Harmony,* 1950–57), about Johannes Kepler and his *Harmonices mundi.* This was even bigger and richer than *Mathis* in humane wisdom and splendid symbolism. It was not mystical, as is sometimes supposed. It was not diffuse, and not—to a well-prepared listener—tedious. But like *Mathis* it was, in the judgment of Briner, Pannain, and others, impractical for the theater. Hindemith's last opera was a more modest and more practical one, again full of interest and beauty, with text by Thornton Wilder, *The Long Christmas Dinner* (1961). His very last work was an unaccompanied Mass.

The best of the late works were the madrigals. Their texts, by Joseph Weinheber (b. 1892), fitted Hindemith to perfection, and enabled him to put his most refined technique at the service of various important ideas, in concentrated form. In the preface to the madrigals, he indicated their importance:

Since the demise of the Italian madrigal art and its somewhat later English afterglow in the 17th century, real madrigals have been written no more. In the development of styles of composition adapted to our modern techniques, there was no more place for such a quiet, inward art. Only the string quartet in its purest form as created by Haydn, Mozart, and Beethoven, even approaches the earlier ideal, but in my opinion the quartet never quite attained the uttermost balance of compositional virtuosity, ideal treatment of materials, and complete answering of the needs and abilities of the users, that characterized the Italian madrigal in its final period of splendor (Marenzio, Gesualdo, Monteverdi). The reason was that the attachment to thoroughly mechanized means of expression— musical instruments—though offering freer technical possibilities, no longer permits the most beautiful and natural source of sound, human voices singing together unaccompanied, to determine the organism of the work of art as boundary, spiritual reference, and goal-setter. Since our means of expression today—melodic, harmonic, and others—are no longer the same as then even for *a-cappella* song (although in this relatively narrow field of the technique of tone-setting, such revolutionary innovations are never possible, God be praised, as in the instrumental field), the attempt to recreate the madrigal art cannot be satisfied with the imitation of the earlier style, but the spirit of that style, its dignity and selfless attitude toward singer and hearer we may with all fervor seek to achieve again.

One of these fervent madrigals can illustrate Hindemith's splendid achievement. Its final quiet cadence, in this writer's opinion, attains the "uttermost balance" that Hindemith speaks of, and every note contributes towards it. The first quatrain of Weinheber's sonnet Hindemith makes an introductory fanfare, with solos against choral declamation on unchanging harmony. Then (measure 18) comes a magnificent long-breathed melody, with a light contrapuntal accompaniment, freely varying the number of voices above and below the melody; the first phrase fits one line of text; the second swells and spans two in a very characteristic way; the third and longest phrase, completing the quatrain, begins like the first and ends in a flowing melisma and a strong cadence on A (m. 44), but no pause. Now, for the sestet, there is a big contrast; a new, cramped melody, accompanied by detached chords, all ominously low and quiet, covers a three-line sentence. This melody is repeated with intensified color (mm. 54–64) while over it rises a new melody that gradually pushes the cramped one to the background; together they lead to a recapitulation. The last three lines of the poem fit the melody of the second quatrain, now in the top voice, accompanied by smooth full chords. The cadence is held off (mm. 90–91) and the last line of words is repeated, to extend the long phrase still further in breathless suspense, until the final shudder.

Mild dissonance prevails throughout. Major seconds and minor sevenths are present in almost every cross-section of the texture.

The sharper dissonances of major sevenths and minor ninths are used much less, and with care. They occur in measures 12–13, to differentiate the climactic phrase from the rest of the introduction, and in mm. 66, 68, 72, 74, 78, 80–81, 83–85, 88–89, 91, 93–95, to make a gradual fluctuating intensification of the final phrase.

The tritone is conspicuously absent from most harmonic cross-sections, but it appears with a wonderful chordal effect in measures 44–63, and then in counterpoint along with the sharp dissonances in mm. 74, 76, 83, 88–89, 93.

Hindemith's preference for mild dissonance is a trait of his personal style. His control of the "fluctuation" of dissonance is a detail of his technique, perfected by his systematic classification of all possible chords with respect to the intervals they contain, rather than a triadic norm. When this technical device is subordinated to such melodies as those of the madrigal, its value is incontestable. When other composers borrow either the technical device or the stylistic preference, without the melodies, Hindemith is not to blame.

Hindemith's melodic intervals show similar preferences and techniques, and much more. Steps and half steps are more frequent than skips; small skips are more common than big ones. The biggest is a minor seventh. Successive fourths in the same direction are used casually, measures 12, 43,

EXAMPLE XXI.1 Hindemith, Madrigal, *Strength Fathers Form*

have_____   to   bear our trou -   -   -   -
Wür   -   fel   sind ge - fal -   -   -   -

ble. Learn this from   cha - os:_____   I - ron hearts we
len. Des   Ab-grunds Weis-heit:_____   Un-er-schrock-nes

need   That dare sub - merge____ self,   dare____ . to____ suf - fer si - lent____
Herz,   Der Mut, zu   sink - en,   Mut____ zum__ To - des-schwei - gen__

____ to death,   so that____ the tower   may   rise re - wak - ing. Learn this from
____ Tut not,   da-mit____ der Turm   sich   neu er - he -· be. Des Ab - grunds

90, as if the broken fourth chord had a value corresponding to that of broken triads in the melodies of Haydn and Mozart. This is another brand-mark of Hindemith's style, indebted to but distinct from the thematic fourths of Schoenberg's Op. 9. Major sevenths and tritones are completely excluded as direct melodic progressions, and even among all the notes of a phrase these intervals are used with special care. Thus in mm. 26–29 the broken chord on F♯ is repeated, so that against it the bitter high F and G make a climax. In mm. 93–96 the emphasized E♭ is related to the tonic A through the B♭, and this relation is a balancing one for the different relation between the same notes in mm. 18–20.

While the melody as a whole exploits the chromatic scale, and in the middle section, measures 44–64, the chromatic basis is continually obvious, there are rarely two or more successive half steps. Cut apart into progressions of five or six notes, this kind of melody sounds diatonic, vaguely modal. In the introductory fanfare there is only a touch of chromaticism at the climax; this section begins as if its scale were pentatonic, and ends as if it were all a dominant in D♭ major. But according to Hindemith's theory such suggestions are merely incidental. Of course the chromatic scale contains the other scales. But its organization, he thinks, does not depend on them. The harmony of the introduction here is somewhat ambiguous, and by the end of the piece its meaning has become clear. There is no modulation in this piece; all the rich chords and all the twists of the melody submit to the single magnetic attraction of the A. Such twists as that at mm. 19–20, overriding enharmonic ambiguities, are the most characteristic details of Hindemith's melodies.

The bass voice has essentially the same kind of melody as the leading one, though duly subordinated by its slow rhythm. Here too chromaticism is basic, and quasi-modal fragments check the chromaticism from its tendency to shapeless sliding and confusion of tonality.

Inner voices, especially when they are buried in a thick texture, as in mm. 66–68, may submit to the shapeless chromatic tendency, but not for long.

Hindemith's restrained chromaticism is the essence of both his style and his technique. His explanation and defense of it in the *Unterweisung* includes much that is not touched on here. But our one example is enough to make clear its distinction from the styles of Stravinsky and Bartók, as well as Schoenberg and Webern. It is closer to Debussy's mixture of chromaticism and modality than to any of the famous contemporary styles. It is probably close also to Knorr, Rottenberg, Schreker, and other "transitional" figures. Yet Hindemith's rhythm and texture are so far from those of Debussy that the essential similarity remains hidden.

His texture is fundamentally contrapuntal. The interplay of melody and bass is continuous and vital. The bass is as independent and expressive as

Fauré's, and the harmonic range of the counterpoint is nearly as great as Bartók's, so that this is a new kind of counterpoint, utterly different from that of Strauss or Reger or any 19th-century composer, and different too from that of Bach, but closer to his than any other modern counterpoint.

The inner voices are not so contrapuntal as they may seem at first hearing. Parallel fifths and fourths are used freely, and direct fifths and fourths and octaves very freely. The inner voices fill in the chords, and they fill in rhythmic gaps with very small bits of significant melody; rarely does a third voice persist through a whole phrase with any melodic vitality, even when Hindemith writes fugues. In this respect his distance from Bach is still enormous. And in this respect once more we may detect, as does Albert Jakobik, a hidden debt to Debussy: the freedom to mix parallelism and homophony with polyphony enabled Hindemith to come closer to Bach than Reger.

Counterpoint in Hindemith's style, as in Schoenberg's, obscures harmonic progressions. In any cross-section of the texture except at a cadence it is difficult to distinguish the notes that belong to a chord from those that work as passing-tones, suspensions, auxiliaries, appoggiaturas, and *échappés*. Hindemith's theory admits this difficulty, but minimizes it. It constitutes a large ambiguity in his theory, a fatal defect, in the sympathetic view of a theorist like William Thomson. But this in itself is no objection to the music. When the form of a piece does not depend on modulation, obscurity of harmonic roots is no defect. On the other hand, Hindemith's theory leads him in some sonata movements to complicated tonal structures that for most listeners remain purely theoretical. In his revision of *Marienleben* he superimposed a systematic symbolism of tonalities that shocked and disaffected some of his warmest admirers. But such vagaries, fortunately, were irrelevant to the madrigals. The treatment of tonality in the whole set of twelve was so various, subtle, and convincing as to suggest that Hindemith had embarked on a fresh adventure.

In his sixties Hindemith's face and figure had acquired more sheer weight than conventional professorial dignity. His springy movements and his twinkling eyes were still those of the young practical musician, impatient of any solemn nonsense, always ready for a joke, delighting in hard work. Up to the end of his life he was capable of new adventures. And his record of immense achievement suggested that some day his noble failure would be forgotten while his manifold work would long nourish good musicians and active music lovers.

CHAPTER XXII

Further Steps in France, Italy, England

THE HERITAGE of craftsmanship and theoretical discipline that Hindemith tried to reform and restore to authority proved in fact to be not only more tangled and twisted than he thought, but also tougher and more flexible. While this heritage, to be sure, could impose no limits on young composers, its limits could be extended amazingly far, to include the shrill sounds and jerky rhythms characteristic of 20th-century music. The tradition was variously reinterpreted to make room in academic studies for Debussy, Ravel, and Stravinsky, and after Hindemith's effort at a thorough reform had failed, teachers proceeded slowly to digest the contributions of Bartók, Schoenberg, and Webern, and to dabble with jazz, all of which Hindemith had put beyond the pale. The heritage was weakened and frayed when stretched so far. It still invited reform. But it was surviving and penetrating into every corner of the world. It was far from sufficient by itself but it seemed still to be a necessary condition for the development of most young composers.

During the period between the two World Wars, alongside Hindemith, many composers developed personal styles that somehow balanced their elaborate academic techniques with their sensitive reactions to the profound innovations of Debussy and the more potent (if often superficial) stimuli of Schoenberg and Stravinsky.

Many musicians supposed that an impersonal evolutionary process would lead ultimately to a new common style. Their forecasts varied as to how long a process this might be and how much any one man's work could contribute to it. But as composers and teachers they contributed whatever they could toward the future balance that they imagined. That such musicians were to be found in every country, assuming responsibility for old and new institutions devoted to musical culture, made the idea of a converging evolution plausible.

From the point of view of a historian of styles, however, or that of a non-professional listener to music, the idea of convergence seemed illusory. There was no less variety among the achievements of Hindemith and other composers with similar hopes than among those of Stravinsky, Bartók, and Prokofiev, hardly less than those of Schoenberg and jazz. A just appreciation of Hindemith or Roussel or Sessions demanded more special study than Varèse or Orff or Messiaen (if not quite so much as Webern). No one of these composer's styles prepared for another as did the styles of Haydn, Mozart, Beethoven, and Schubert, or of Bach, Handel, Rameau, and Scarlatti. Each 20th-century style needed to be traced separately from its 19th-century roots. Many distinct styles could repay such parallel study for whoever was interested.

No one listener or historian could do full justice to all the hundred composers whose development in some sense paralleled Hindemith's. The historian at the service of other listeners would remind them that his unavoidable judgments are put forward as mere suggestions. He would base these judgments explicitly on comparisons with the major styles as he saw them, leaving to others the separate stylistic analyses of the parallel styles. In this way, a survey could best demonstrate the density of history, contributing once more to a growing appreciation of the major styles.

———•—•———

Albert Roussel (1869–1937) became the leading French exponent of a new classicism between the wars, in his fifties and sixties. He had a paradoxical advantage over such contemporaries as Dukas and Schmitt in the late start of his musical career. (He was a pupil of d'Indy, 1898–1907.) While his habits and tastes were like theirs, his were not yet so firmly established when they were shaken by Debussy's *Pelléas* and again by Stravinsky's *Rite*. After serving actively throughout the war (1914–18) Roussel was able to resume his personal development, absorbing what could help him from the new fashions, alongside the fresh inspirations he had found on a trip to India (1909). Moreover, his new works did not have to overcome the prejudices of listeners who would expect him merely to preserve an old style. Thus when he spoke in 1936 of a "need to reconstruct, to consolidate what remains standing and to codify the laws of a new equilibrium," his listeners thought of his Third Symphony (1930) and other recent compositions as meeting this need, achieving this new equilibrium.

Unlike Hindemith, however, Roussel did not claim to "codify the laws" himself, nor to apply any new laws in his teaching or in criticism of his contemporaries. His basic principles, expressed in a reply to questions by Louis Laloy in 1909 and maintained throughout his life, were vaguer and more generous:

A musician who limits his efforts to the more or less lucky imitation of the style and the procedures of a master brings nothing very interesting to music. A sin-

cere artist will be able to retain from *Pelléas* only a great example of independence and conscious liberation, rather than seeing in it a collection of harmonic
recipes. . . This is not to say that he will refuse to breathe the new air now blowing into the house in which the heavy odor of the Wagnerian heroes had weighed
down the atmosphere. But it is no reason, because we are breathing better, for us
all to lean over the same balcony; the house is vast and windows open on all the
horizons.

In 1919, Roussel wrote again on Debussy:

The influence of a Wagner or a Debussy can be fecund because it lifts the veils
from questions of a higher order, suggests to the mind reflections on the essence
of music, opens the path, through harmonic conquests achieved, to experiments
that are often fruitful. . . Composers . . . have submitted more or less to the impression of Debussy. To what extent have they departed from the path they
would have followed without this master's influence? Without examining each
case in particular, it seems that most have rediscovered, after a longer or shorter
period of hesitation, the direction toward which their own temperament led. They
have kept from the encounter only a sort of new harmonic inspiration, a more
decided independence from traditions, the taste for unknown sensation and the
thirst for rare sonorities. And also, one must recognize, a rather definite distaste
for grandiose subjects, long, pseudo-eloquent phrases, too obvious emotion. . . The
work of a great artist should be an example and not a model . . . a lesson valid
only by the suggestions that it awakens in an independent mind. What should be
learned from it is the limit where they stopped in their thrust toward new conquests, the possibility of going further ahead or of finding, on the right or left,
paths still unexplored, and finally, the truth that since art is continually evolving,
the artist who seeks within himself the secret of his art should never consider
the fashion and the taste of his epoch except from a point of view somehow
retrospective.

In a letter to Nadia Boulanger, 1924, Roussel proceeded to take a "retrospective" view of the current neo-Classicism:

In art as in life there is no stable state, but rather a succession of continual transformations, and when a form of art seems to become fixed before us, its disintegration has already begun. This natural reaction against existing tendencies
does not imply, of course, scorn or ignorance of the esthetic they represent, but it
is almost inevitably produced by the aversion of original artists for every formula
elevated to a system. . . External circumstances also contribute to help and to pre-
cipitate this reaction, and it seems likely that the recent cataclysm, for instance,
which we have witnessed, has had some influence on the present orientation of
the arts.

This orientation, as it affects music, is expressed by the return to clearer lines,
more emphatic accents, more precise rhythm, a style more horizontal than ver-

tical, a certain brutality sometimes in the means of expression, contrasting with the subtle elegance and the misty atmosphere of the preceding period, an attentive and sympathetic glance toward the robust frankness of Bach or Handel, in short, and in spite of appearances, a return to the classic tradition in a language freer and somewhat hesitant as yet. . .

For my part I have always considered the evolution of style an expansion, a generalization, within ever wider limits, of the sonorous play long familiar to our ears and our musical feeling.

Roussel's works are true to his principles. The same individual temperament is expressed in all of them—sensitive, subtle, cool, and sober even in moods of gaiety or passion. The same kind of "sonorous play" extends long-breathed rhythmic and melodic ideas into forms that command respect, beginning with the *Divertissement for piano and winds* (1906), while a continual expansion of distinctive harmonic and contrapuntal means is evident from the earliest to the latest works. Roussel's orchestration shows the slight influences of fashion, tending toward Debussy in *Le Festin de l'araignée* (*The Spider's Feast,* 1912) and toward Bach and toward Stravinsky in the Suite in F (1926), while his chamber music shows the persistent "thirst for rare sonorities." Other "external influences" are reflected especially in the vocal works; from Henri Régnier to James Joyce, Roussel's poems are well chosen, and give his settings an allure for a few listeners more potent than that of the better-known symphonies; his most ambitious work, the opera-ballet *Padmâvatî* (1918), is at the same time his most exotic and his most original. The "neo-Classic" ballet *Bacchus et Ariane* (1930) is the work of all Roussel's list that seems likeliest to hold a place in the repertory. Its many admirers, following the composer's principle rather than the ambiguous slogan, may find further delights throughout his works.

As teacher at the Schola Cantorum (1902–14) Roussel was concerned only with counterpoint; his lessons had limited value for such pupils as Satie and Varèse, or even the more congenial Paul Le Flem (b. 1881) and Petro Petridis (b. 1892). Later he gave lessons and advice in composition to Alexis Roland-Manuel (b. 1891), Knudåge Riisager (b. 1897), Bohuslav Martinů (1890–1959), Piotr Perkowski (b. 1901), Jean Martinon (b. 1910), and others, who had sought him out privately, and who went forward on paths just to the right and left of his. His example inspired still others.

Among the younger French composers who like Roussel pursued the familiar "sonorous play" within "ever wider limits," the best known abroad was Nadia Boulanger (b. 1887), because of her teaching. She ceased to compose when she lost her sister, Lili (1893–1918), the first woman to win the Prix de Rome. Her pupils, from all parts of the world, learned and then disseminated the ideals of Fauré, Debussy, Roussel, and Stravinsky—not a style or a procedure to be copied, but a constellation of liberating and stimulating examples. Her French pupils, including Jacques Chailley (b. 1910), Jean Françaix (b. 1912), and Michel Ciry (b. 1919), were specialists in diverse fields, rather than upholders of Boulanger's internationalism.

Eminent in France as transmitters of similar ideals and as composers in the traditional forms of symphony and chamber music were

Claude Delvincourt (1888–1954)
Henri Martelli (b. 1895)
Jean Rivier (b. 1896)
Raymond Loucheur (b. 1899)
Jean Cartan (1906–1932)
Pierre Capdevielle (b. 1906)
Tony Aubin (b. 1907)
Elsa Barraine (b. 1910)

Perhaps closer to Roussel as symphonist than any of these was the still younger Henri Dutilleux (b. 1916). Though none of these composers attracted so much attention as Milhaud or Messiaen, either to their own works or to their teaching, collectively they made Paris, more than any other city in the world, the center of the profession of musical composition.

The transplantation of the twelve-tone technique into French culture by the Viennese Alexander Spitzmüller (b. 1894) and the Polish-born pupil of Schoenberg and Webern, René Leibowitz (b. 1913), increased the strength of this culture for another generation: Leibowitz and his pupil Boulez proceeded to teach pupils from all parts of the world.

———————

The Italian composer who attracted most attention abroad in the years between the wars, Alfredo Casella (1883–1947), helped to shape what he identified as the "general aspiration toward a new order, which had the misfortune in the beginning to be called neo-Classicism." In his autobiography (1939) he described and discussed "this tendency" more amply than Stravinsky, Hindemith, or Roussel ever did. Moreover, Casella exhibited the tendency in his most famous compositions, including the eleven children's pieces for piano (1920), the ballet *La Giara (The Jar,* with Pirandello and Chirico, 1924), the *Scarlattiana* for piano and small orchestra, and the Serenade for five instruments (both 1926).

For Casella, as for Roussel, the commitment to a classic ideal was balanced, if not outweighed, by a recognition that "the struggle for the evolutionary continuity of art has not ceased today, as it never ceased in the past, and never will in the future." The most expert student of Casella's whole work, his friend Massimo Mila, emphasizes his continual adventure more than his achievement: "The Casellian quality *par excellence,* what unites all his styles (and no one is definitive, yet all are definitive at least in some works) is just this eagerness for novelty, this constant need to surpass himself, this barometric sensibility to the oscillations of contemporary taste." Casella was probably unique in his close exposure to these rapid oscillations.

His first teachers, his parents, instilled in him from infancy a knowledge and love of the German classics. He was a prodigious pianist, and his fundamental musical habits were determined by the keyboard solos and chamber music of Bach, Mozart, and Beethoven. The Italians that he knew best as a child were the Germanizing Sgambati and Martucci. The first opera he saw, at the age of eleven (1895), was Wagner's *Götterdämmerung,* conducted by Toscanini; he soon learned the score by heart. The next year, as a piano student at the Paris Conservatory, he greeted each new experience with enthusiasm. Soon he began to publish his piano reductions of orchestral works by Bruneau—symptomatic of the academic habits that stayed with him all his life. In 1898 came the most extraordinary experience, hearing the *Faun,* "like a fantastic world perceived for the first time." He met Debussy, with whom he later became a good friend and collaborator in two-piano music. He studied a little with Fauré, and decided to subordinate performance to composition; in 1909, alongside Fauré, Ravel, Falla, and others, he was active in the Société Musicale Indépendante. Meanwhile he had toured Europe, as accompanist of distinguished singers and as harpsichordist in a group, had studied the scores of Busoni and Strauss and Mahler, had made a successful orchestral version of Balakirev's *Islamey,* which had induced Stravinsky to seek him out in St. Petersburg (1907). Finally, in 1909 Marinetti's Futurist manifesto kindled his patriotism, since it showed that his native land could produce something to compete with the modernisms of the greater world. In the same year Casella made his "supreme decision to dedicate all my strength and activity to the achievement of a style of our own, which would be based on our great instrumental past but which would also be contemporary in its musical language."

As pianist, conductor, journalist, and organizer of concerts, still mainly in Paris until 1916, when he moved to Rome, Casella got to know both the *Rite of Spring* and *Pierrot Lunaire* more quickly and more deeply than anyone else knew both works. Their influences threatened to overwhelm his nationalism for some years. Looking back in 1939, though he felt independent of these influences, he still believed:

The "duel" between Stravinsky and Schoenberg is the synthesis of that whole period which began precisely in 1912 and cannot yet be said to have ended. . . Even if it appears today that the victory has been won by tonal music, this does not diminish the greatness of Schoenberg. Like very few other creators, he can say proudly that he has made music express that which it had never said before, and that he has enlarged the realm of fantasy to infinity. . . The *Rite of Spring* marks the end of Debussyan impressionism and immediately begins the age of constructivism, which denies every residue of linear imprecision. Confronting Schoenbergianism, it reaffirms in a sovereign manner the perennial reign of tonality, even though renewed with the new polytonal means.

By 1939, when Casella recorded this view, it was a common one. By 1947, when he died, the inadequacy of his view, for the purposes either of history or of a young composer's orientation, had become apparent. But he had felt within him, soon after 1912, the opposing attractions of the two most potent styles of his age, and his way of picturing them was true for him.

In a few works the influence of Schoenberg predominated: atonality helped Casella express his horror of war in the *Heroic Elegy* for orchestra (1916), and his tormented personal sentiments in the poem for piano, *A Notte alta* (*In Deep Night*, 1917). But then with peace, a happy marriage, growing fame, and vacations in the clear air of Tuscany, with the new works of Stravinsky—*Pulcinella*, the piano duets (one of which was dedicated to Casella), and the wind octet—with the commotion of Satie and Cocteau, and the arrival of jazz, Milhaud, Bartók, Hindemith, and the ISCM, Casella found his healthy mature balance, and produced the series of works already mentioned.

In his later years, without any such marked change of style, he expanded his interests to write three operas, as well as many concertos and chamber works, and finally a mass *Pro pace* (*For Peace*, 1944). The most successful of the late works was *Paganiniana*, divertimento for orchestra (1942). Besides these, Casella made many interesting transcriptions of pieces by Vivaldi, Clementi, and other Italian composers of the past. His series of excellent theoretical and critical writings culminated in a textbook on orchestration (1950).

Several times Casella's concert tours brought him to the United States. Once he remained in Boston to conduct a whole season of the "Pops" concerts. The patronage of Mrs. Coolidge was important in his career; his autobiography includes a charming vignette of her, as well as an enthusiastic tribute to the Library of Congress, where he found more old Italian music than in Italy.

At home Casella provoked some antagonism from Bossi, Respighi, and other less progressive musicians. His music was never played by Toscanini. Yet his enormous knowledge, energy, and generosity could not fail to have a large and beneficial effect on Italian musical life. He personified the new sense of tradition, at once national and international, progressive and restorative.

A conspicuous feature of Casella's mature style is what he himself, according to his pupil Roman Vlad, called "dissonant diatonicism": contrapuntal lines continually scrape against each other at the intervals of second and seventh, mostly without resolving to triads; yet for long stretches the motion of the lines is confined within a single diatonic scale, often C major or one of the old modes, using white keys only. This procedure Nicholas Slonimsky dubbed "pandiatonicism" and regarded as the typical harmonic feature of "neo-Classicism," without observing that it was more characteristic of Casella than of Stravinsky, and quite contrary to the practices of Hindemith and Roussel. Casella's diatonicism was indeed part of his deliberate reaction against Schoenberg. Encouraged, no doubt, by some passages in Stravinsky's Octet and subsequent works, Casella's procedure more nearly resembled that of the *Russian Dance* in *Petrushka*. In any case it was no principle of harmonic motion or structure, even for Casella, but rather like a temporary costume. It merits attention only long enough to clear away the prejudices it may arouse.

In the *Crucifixus* of his Mass (1944) Casella used a twelve-tone theme for a passacaglia. Vlad interprets this as evidence of Casella's recognition that the moment was at hand for a *rapprochement* with dodecaphony. Vlad himself had just at this time adopted the twelve-tone technique in his own compositions.

———•—•———

Casella's ideal of a new Italian classicism was shared by his friend and contemporary Gian Francesco Malipiero (b. 1882). But Malipiero was at the same time, as Guido Gatti pointed out, a romantic spirit. And after Casella had died Malipiero pursued fresh adventures alongside his pupils, including Bruno Maderna. His way of approaching the classic ideal was as different from Casella's as from the various classicisms of Busoni, Roussel, and Hindemith. The two friends differed in how they treated the old Italian masters: whereas Casella, coming to them in his forties, selected a few works, transcribed, arranged, rearranged, and parodied them, Malipiero, beginning at twenty, proceeded to make or supervise complete editions of Monteverdi and Vivaldi, not impeccable but essentially scholarly editions, which paved the way for these men's music to reach wider audiences than Casella or Malipiero himself could reach. The difference between the two was equally apparent in their attitudes toward Stravinsky: Malipiero first encountered both Casella and Stravinsky in 1913; he recognized the *Rite of Spring* as a masterpiece, and a useful model, but then he had no sympathy for Stravinsky's shift from Russian nationality and nationalism to Western elegance, and his judgment of Stravinsky's followers was severe; he wrote in 1942:

What "neo-Classicism" means is not easy to explain, but the descendents of *Petrushka* are a rather clear phenomenon, though strange. . . . [*Petrushka*] gen-

Design for Milhaud's *Creation of the World,* by Fernand Léger, 1922 (Collection, The Museum of Modern Art, New York, Gift of John Pratt)

Martha Graham in *Letter to the World,* music by Hunter Johnson, 1941 (Barbara Morgan)

PLATE 15

Stravinsky, bronze by Marino Marini (San Francisco Museum of Art, Gift of Mr. and Mrs. Walter A. Haas)

Stravinsky, Rome, 1954 (The Bettmann Archive)

PLATE 16

erated that musical spirit (also called sarcastic or ironic) that predominated for several years even in Italy. . . The descendents of *Petrushka* are born dead; hence all that is left of them is a faint memory.

Finally, the two friends stood in quite different relations to the tradition of Italian opera from Verdi to Puccini: although Casella grew up remote from all this, taking for granted the superiority of Wagner, he was pleased to win a word of encouragement from Puccini, and eventually he learned to value Verdi; Malipiero, on the contrary, had to struggle to shake off the habits he had acquired as a child from the operatic hits of the 1890s, habits eschewed by his teachers of violin and theory in Vienna (1898–99), his composition teacher in Venice and Bologna, Bossi (1900–04), and his favorite poet, d'Annunzio. Malipiero was never reconciled to the 19th century, nor entirely victorious in his struggle against it.

He repudiated most of the many compositions he wrote up to 1913. In some of these, nevertheless, such as the *Bizzarie* for piano (1908), his characteristic blend of slow-moving modal harmony and facile, declamatory melody was already clear and charming. His inventiveness in the realm of instrumentation appeared in the first work that he regarded as mature, *Impressioni del vero* (*Impressions of the True*, 1910), and continued to win admiration through the series of concertos, symphonies, and chamber music that he poured forth in the next fifty years. His style was especially suited, however, to choral music, which he began with the mystery, *San Francesco d'Assisi* (1922); he himself preferred of all his works the cantata on Vergil's *Aeneid* (1946). He wrote also many ambitious works for the stage; here especially he strove to renew the tradition of Monteverdi. Outstanding among these was the *Favola del figlio cambiato* (*Story of the Changeling,* Pirandello, 1934).

Malipiero in some of his late works, such as the series of Fantasies (1954), assimilated twelve-tone themes into his own style.

Alongside Casella and Malipiero in opposition to the decadence of Italian opera, more steadily active than either of them as a teacher, and to that extent a fellow-classicist, was Ildebrando Pizzetti (b. 1880). But here differences greatly outweigh similarities. Pizzetti's ideal was a purified opera, poetic and idealistic rather than melodramatic—like Verdi rightly understood. His instrumental works, songs, and choruses were subordinate to the operas. As for musical style, Pizzetti was content all his life with the materials and procedures he learned from his father and other teachers in his native Parma. He only screened out of the common style all spontaneous, dance-like tunes—vulgar in his estimation—so that what was left, despite the recognizable surge of Romantic feeling, was drier than any other sort of classicism.

Several younger Italian composers pursued classic ideals. Their fame was overshadowed before World War II by that of Casella and Malipiero, and afterward by that of Dallapiccola and Berio. But their works were recommended by the critics who knew them as no less valuable. Vito Frazzi (b. 1888) based a distinctive style on the use of what he called *scale alternate*, eight-tone scales alternating half steps and whole steps, like those of Messiaen. His pupil, Dallapiccola, wrote a valuable tribute to him. Mario Castelnuovo-Tedesco (b. 1895), a pupil of Pizzetti, wrote fluently in all forms; Roland von Weber recommended especially his songs. After 1939 he was a successful team-member in Hollywood, without compromising the idealism of his independent work. Vittorio Rieti (b. 1898), a pupil of Respighi, emigré to France and then to the United States, became one of the best disciples of Stravinsky; anyone capable of enjoying Stravinsky's concertos and chamber music can find delight also in Rieti's. Goffredo Petrassi (b. 1904) began his career under the influence of Casella and Hindemith; he widened his vocabulary to include the chromaticism that Casella had repressed, and to emphasize vocal music as much as instrumental. His "dramatic madrigal" *Coro di morti* (1941) and his unaccompanied choral setting of Lear's *Nonsense* (1950) were outstanding among his works. Roman Vlad traced in detail Petrassi's gradual approach to the twelve-tone techniques, and ranked him next to Dallapiccola, his exact contemporary.

Casella's friends in prosperous pre-1914 Paris included two young composers from other lands who, like Stravinsky, won such unusual early fame that their further achievements in the bitter post-war world suffered relative neglect. Thus George Enescu was remembered chiefly for his two *Rumanian Rhapsodies* (1901–02) and Joaquín Turina for his *Sevilla* suite for piano (1904) or his orchestral *Procesión del rocío* (*Procession of Our Lady*, 1913). Each of these composers went on to produce a body of work for various media of performance that deserved attention. Each developed his style independently, expanding his harmonic range without any "break with the past," and refining his treatment of classic forms.

George Enescu (1881–1955) was recognized in his native Rumania as the founder and outstanding master of a whole symphonic school, which flourished through several generations, down to Anatol Vieru (b. 1926), pupil of Khachaturian. By musicians all over the world Enescu was admired and loved for his teaching, his conducting, and his superb violin playing, especially of Bach. But he performed in public only in order to compose. Incidentally he was in private a good cellist and pianist as well. His training in composition was extraordinarily thorough, begun in Vienna under Robert Fuchs (1888–1894) and continued in Paris under Massenet,

Gedalge, and Fauré (1894–99). Naturally he knew Debussy and Ravel; he knew much of their music by heart, he recognized the novelty and perfection of their work within limits, but he felt more sympathy for Fauré, Dukas, Schmitt, and Honegger. Later he knew and appreciated Bartók and Roussel. Whatever he knew and thought of Schoenberg and Stravinsky he omitted to record in his beautiful *Souvenirs*, though Marc Pincherle testified that he played by heart at the piano episodes from *The Rite of Spring*; his late compositions make at least one listener guess that he assimilated something from each of his outstanding contemporaries without its disturbing his independent growth. These later works, whose chief resemblance to the famous *Rumanian Rhapsodies* was their perfection, included a noble opera, *Oedipus*, Op. 23 (1906–32), three piano sonatas, and eight elegant pieces of chamber music, likely eventually to find places in the permanent repertories of all serious performers.

Joaquín Turina (1882–1949) achieved something more modest and special. Federico Sopeña summed it up as "universalized Andalusianism." Turina's mature work called at least for rescue from the pigeonhole subordinate to that of Falla where it was thrust by many contemporary judges. Turina learned his craft under d'Indy (1905–14) more thoroughly than his famous older compatriot, and although his imagination was less powerful, it proved more fertile. In orchestration he submitted to the influences of Dukas, Debussy, Ravel, and finally Stravinsky, but these influences scarcely penetrated to his traditional harmony. Albéniz had persuaded him in 1907 that he had a duty toward Spanish rhythms, and he was faithful to them ever afterward. His orchestral masterpiece was the *Sevillian Symphony* (1920). His most ambitious work was the *Song to Seville* (1927). Alongside these he produced many songs and cycles of songs, chamber works with piano, and pieces for guitar, all of which delighted the performers and audiences who knew them.

Among younger composers in Spain, Joaquín Rodrigo (b. 1902) worthily continued the tradition of Turina; Gilbert Chase in his survey of Spanish music credited him with the most interesting work between Falla and Carlos Surinach (b. 1915).

———•——

Several English composers, like Enescu and Turina, achieved reputations before World War I that afterward failed to keep pace with their independently developing achievements. For one of these, Frank Bridge (1879–1941), the post-war period brought a drastic increase of dissonance and the deepening of an already specialized talent for chamber music. For others, such as Bax, Ireland, and Scott, the neo-Classic preferences for sonata forms and contrapuntal textures played a part in the development, while their independence from fashion was expressed partly by fidelity to Romantic rhythms and harmonies. Sir Arnold Bax (1883–1953) called himself a "brazen Romantic." His early Straussian symphonic poems based on the lyrics of Yeats, *The Garden of Fand* (1916) and *Tintagel* (1917), won him knighthood. His seven symphonies (1922–39) showed more refinement and no less vitality. John Ireland (1879–1962) was widely known for his Impressionistic piano pieces like *Island Spell* (1913), and for many sensitive songs; his texts in the 1920s were the bitter Housman and Hardy, and his piano style in the Sonatina (1927) was stripped to essentials; from 1930 onward he wrote a series of orchestral works, more robust than any earlier work and deserving of more performances.

Cyril Scott (b. 1879) concentrated at first on songs and descriptive pieces, especially for the piano. About 1920 he proceeded to opera, about 1935 to church music and children's music, and about 1945 to chamber music. All of this, in the judgment of Eric Blom and Michael Hurd, lacked variety. Samples were certainly less varied, less expert, and less vital than the music of Bridge, Bax, or Ireland. Yet Scott's name was better known than theirs abroad, for several reasons: he was the first Englishman, about 1903, to adopt from Debussy the obvious devices of whole-tone scale and parallel chord-streams; he became acquainted with Debussy, whose mild praise clung to his name even after his style had changed; he had been a pupil of Knorr in Frankfurt; he became and remained a good friend of Percy Grainger, a friend of Stefan George (who dedicated some poems to him), a poet himself, a wit, a thoroughgoing Theosophist, a provocative defender of Scriabin, Delius, Schoenberg, and Stravinsky; he abandoned the use of key signatures about 1909 and invented a new method for writing his vague rhythms. All this brought fame. What he did later, though no less valid for a later generation, was little noted when his early work had begun to wear thin. According to his own view, the early music had served a moral purpose and was quite properly forgotten; his new music would likewise serve its moral purpose when the time was ripe, and be superseded in turn. He despised classicism. His *Philosophy of Modernism* (1917) upheld a romanticism far from that of Arnold Bax. "What pedants call classicalism is nothing but that transformation *apparently* brought about when the dust of years settles on what was once a *romantic* masterpiece . . . In reality there are no rules, there are merely conventions." Yet Scott's romanticism was somehow restrained: "Futurism is an attempted elongation of romanticism carried to an illogical conclusion . . . The romanticist believes in newness *within* limits, the futurist believes in newness *without* limits." In a later book on *The Influence of Music on History and Morals* (1928, with various revisions during the next thirty years) Scott explained the moral purpose of both unlimited and limited newness:

We have been living in the Age of Destruction. . . . Ultra-discordant music has been used to destroy certain baneful thought-forms. . . It is now for Concord to rebuild. . . As we enter this new Age, we seek, primarily through the medium of *inspired* music, to diffuse the spirit of unification and brotherhood, and thus quicken the vibration of this planet.

The final sentence here, and his ideas in general, Scott said he had received by occult communications from a spirit once incarnated in Pythagoras. In his *Outline of Modern Occultism* (1935) he further explained 20th-century history as affected in its first quarter by "considerable occult activity," which had now withdrawn in preparation for a "flowering of occult forces" in the last quarter. Thus what others might call the reflection of neo-Classicism in Scott's late works fitted his personal history. The value of his explanation for a more general history was at least paradigmatic.

Bridge and Ireland, with their contemporary Vaughan Williams, all pupils of Stanford at the Royal College of Music, became respected teachers there. But there was no common English style. The generation of their pupils was as diverse as their own. Each of the English composers whose careers began between the wars sought his own dynamic and classic balance among the many traditions and innovations competing in the market of modern culture. Many succeeded:

> Gordon Jacob (b. 1895)
> Edmund Rubbra (b. 1901)
> Lennox Berkeley (b. 1903)
> Michael Tippett (b. 1905)
> Alan Rawsthorne (b. 1905)
> Howard Ferguson (b. 1908)
> William Wordsworth (b. 1908)

Each of these made a different limited selection of elements to weld into a personal style; each produced works that deeply touched a few of their contemporaries both at home and abroad; but by 1965 none of them had won such ardent champions as their more modestly limited contemporaries like Heseltine and Finzi, or their younger compatriot, Benjamin Britten (b. 1913). At least two of the older group, however, continued in the 1960s an admirable growth of power and refinement that might well win wider circles of friends: Berkeley's Second Symphony (1958) and his settings of poems by John Donne (1960, 1963) showed a marvelous intensification of his distinctive smooth style; Tippett's second opera, *King Priam* (1961), and his Concerto for Orchestra (1963) showed new warmth of melody, variety of sound, and grandeur of form along with the vital rhythms and the ethical purposes that were evident in the oratorio, *A Child of Our Time* (1944), and the earlier instrumental works.

Several distinguished refugees brought to England in the 1930s a variety of styles incorporating something from Schoenberg:

> Egon Wellesz (b. 1885)
> Roberto Gerhard (b. 1896)
> Karl Rankl (b. 1898)
> Mátyás Seiber (1905–1960)
> Leopold Spinner (b. 1906)
> Hans Keller (b. 1919)

By 1940 the twelve-tone technique was represented also by at least two native composers, Elisabeth Lutyens (b. 1906) and Humphrey Searle (b. 1915). By 1960 there were dozens of English "serialists," among whom the most prominent were

> Peter Racine Fricker (b. 1920)
> Iain Hamilton (b. 1922)
> Alexander Goehr (b. 1932)
> Peter Maxwell Davies (b. 1934)
> Richard Rodney Bennett (b. 1936).

In 1965 the critic Andrew Porter regretted that Fricker and Hamilton had already passed out of the spotlight; he regarded Goehr, Davies, and Bennett, along with four more young composers, as representing a "vital corpus of 'central' music," in between the left wing of Cornelius Cardew (b. 1936) and the right wing of Berkeley and Britten. The "central" tradition was strong and ever broader.

CHAPTER XXIII

Further Steps in the Soviet Union, America, Germany

IN THE USSR musical traditions proved capable of survival and some growth amid unprecedented changes in the social, economic, and political conditions that they depended on. During the 1920s a few Soviet musicians proposed to liquidate the traditions of symphony and chamber music as relics of bourgeois culture, and to devote all musical resources to developing a new proletarian tradition out of popular songs. A few others emphasized the analogy between the social revolution and the most radical innovations and experiments in music, such as microtones and electronic instruments. But more conservative ideas prevailed. Lenin's love for Beethoven helped. Most Soviet writers argued that the classical tradition was the rightful heritage of all mankind, and could best be upheld and extended by artists in a Socialist society. Stalin's nationalism modified the doctrine. Glinka, Tchaikovsky, and Rimsky were exalted next to Beethoven, above Wagner, Brahms, Debussy, and any contemporary unfriendly to Soviet Russia. These ideas promoted a continuity of musical tradition unusual in the 20th century.

Nikolai Yakovlevich Miaskovsky (1881–1950) achieved intermittently a stylistic balance whose center was the academic tradition he inherited from Rimsky, Liadov, Glazunov, and Glière, but which included often elements from Scriabin on one side and folksongs on another. He was no complacent epigone, but a sincere seeker for 20th-century counterparts to Beethoven's symphonies, with all their personal and social connotations. He sought persistently, accumulating twenty-seven symphonies, of which the twenty-first (1940) was the best known. His thirteen quartets, nine piano sonatas, and comparatively few other works were all subordinate to the symphonies. As teacher at the Moscow Conservatory from 1921 until his death, Miaskovsky was accorded almost continuous praise by colleagues and students and foreign sympathizers with Soviet ideology, such as Karl Laux. Moreover, he was praised for his personal qualities by several non-Soviet writers, including Nicolas Slonimsky and Andrei Olkhovsky. But on the contrary, in 1948 when General Zhdanov and other Party officials took notice of music, Miaskovsky along with his life-long friend Prokofiev was reprimanded for wasting his talents in arid formalism. And most Western musicians, even during World War II when Shostakovich became popular, found Miaskovsky too dull. Whether Shostakovich and other Russian composers of his generation actually studied Miaskovsky's scores and remembered them was dubitable, despite the biography by Alexei Ikonnikov, the catalogue by Viktor Vinogradov, and the collected edition of all his works.

Several pupils of Miaskovsky produced symphonies and chamber music during the 1920s and '30s that made their names known around the world and established their right to lead Russian musical institutions. But their later works disappointed the hopes that their early ones aroused. They seem to have decided that Miaskovsky's classic ideal should be subordinated to the more practical aim of providing usable new music for stage and screen, cantatas for festive occasions, and flashy concertos. The best of this group was the Armenian, Aram Ilich Khachaturian (b. 1903). Others were

> Mikhail Leonidovich Starokadomsky (1901–54)
> Vissarion Yakovlevich Shebalin (1902–63)
> Dmitri Borisovich Kabalevsky (b. 1904)
> Vano Ilich Muradeli (b. 1908)
> Sergei Alexevich Razorionov (b. 1909).

In Miaskovsky's generation there was also Maximilian Steinberg (1883–1946), pupil and son-in-law of Rimsky-Korsakov, who upheld the classic tradition at the Leningrad Conservatory. And in the next generation there were also Lev Konstantinovich Knipper (b. 1898) and Gavriil Nikolaevich Popov (b. 1904). Without the welcome of this group, Prokofiev might never have come home from abroad. Without them Russia could not have produced such great performers of the classics as the violinist David Oistrakh (b. 1908) and the pianist Sviatoslav Richter (b. 1914). Without them Dmitri Dmitrievich Shostakovich could not have become the representative Soviet artist and the only symphonist of the middle 20th century to succeed in reaching an audience like that of Debussy and Strauss.

Despite his fame, much of Shostakovich's music remained unpublished. And just because he was a heroic spokesman for his country, the facts about him and his music could hardly be disentangled from unverifiable statements, mostly emotive, about his relations with its government and official ideology. The principal facts, reported in an autobiographical sketch and in books by Martynov, Seroff, Danilevich, Sabinina, and others, are worth disentangling. Shostakovich was born at St. Petersburg in 1906. His mother was his first piano teacher; he imbibed her enthusiasm for the popular "Gypsy" songs of the day—just the reverse of Prokofiev, who had learned to scorn them. Shostakovich studied at the Gliasser school, and began to compose songs and piano pieces. At the age of thirteen (1919) he entered the conservatory. Glazunov encouraged him. Steinberg taught him theory and composition, while he continued to work at the piano under L. Nikolaiev; these studies constituted his first acquaintance with the classics. Shortly after he entered the conservatory his father died. The boy had to support himself playing the piano for movies. His work left him little time for general education, but he was lucky to find a friend in Ivan Sollertinsky (1902–44), who was then studying philosophy at the university, preparing to become a critic of drama and music. The friendship lasted even beyond Sollertinsky's early death: Shostakovich edited his collected writings (1956) and he never failed to pay tribute to Sollertinsky's liberating influence on his own development.

In 1923 the seventeen-year-old graduated as a pianist, playing Beethoven's Sonata, Op. 106. Two years later he graduated as composer, with the performance of his First Symphony, Op. 10, which immediately aroused worldwide interest. Now he was able to study on his own the music forbidden by Glazunov and Steinberg, including that of Mahler, Berg, Stravinsky, Prokofiev, Hindemith, Milhaud, and Krenek. He played piano recitals, and soon became musical director for various interesting dramatic groups: the Young Workers' Amateur Theater in Leningrad, the famous experimental Vakhtangov Theater in Moscow, the new world of sound films, and so on. This experience led up to the satirical opera *Nos* (*The Nose*, Gogol, Op. 15, 1927–28) and the ironic ballet *Zolotoi viek* (*Golden Age*, Op. 22, 1929), which confirmed his international reputation. Now he undertook a complex tragic opera, *Lady Macbeth of Mtsensk* (story by Leskov, Op. 20, 1930–32). The opera was performed in Leningrad in January 1934 and repeated there with success during the next two years. It played also in New York, Cleveland, London, Prague, Zurich, and elsewhere. Suddenly on January 26, 1936, the official newspaper *Pravda* condemned the opera as "A Mess Instead of Music." This was the first interpretation by the highest authorities of how the artistic policy of Socialist Realism was to be applied to music. The opera was withdrawn from performance. Shostakovich expressed gratitude for the criticism, and promised to reform his style.

Meanwhile he had married Nina Vasilievna Vasar and had begun to give full time to composing. Now in 1937 he became a professor at the Leningrad Conservatory. He withdrew his just completed Fourth Symphony, Op. 43, without any chance for it to become known abroad (until it appeared at last in 1962). He abandoned the musical theater except for films, for many years. He began to write string quartets.

His Fifth Symphony, Op. 47 (1937) was greeted as a model of Socialist Realism.

In 1941 Shostakovich served as volunteer air-raid watcher during the Nazi siege of Leningrad. He was then evacuated to Kuibyshev, where he wrote his Seventh Symphony, Op. 60, depicting the siege. This huge work, performed in July 1942 in New York by Toscanini, and thereafter played throughout the United Nations and broadcast by radio to audiences under enemy control, was a chief musical symbol of the Great Patriotic War. Its later revivals, however, were infrequent compared with performances of the Fifth.

In 1943 Shostakovich became professor at Moscow. In the same year his Eighth Symphony, Op. 65, disappointed expectations both at home and abroad. His Ninth, Op. 70 (1945), not only disappointed but shocked many listeners with its apparent frivolity. His Violin Concerto, Op. 99, and his cycle of Hebrew folksongs, Op. 79 (both 1947–48), were withheld from performance and publication until 1955.

In 1948 a conference of Soviet musicians was attended by General Zhdanov, representing the Politbureau, and a *Decree on Music* was issued by the Central Committee of the Party. Shostakovich, with Miaskovsky, Prokofiev, and other leaders, bore the blame for failure to apply the lessons of *Lady Macbeth*.

Despite this second, intensified rebuke, Shostakovich never lost his leading position. In 1949 he represented the USSR at the Conference for World Peace in New York. In 1953 there appeared his Tenth Symphony, Op. 93, praised at home and abroad. In 1954 he was named People's Artist of the USSR. On his fiftieth birthday (1956) he won the Order of Lenin. In the next year he became chairman of the Composers' Union, an office he still held in 1965.

His wife died in 1954, and his mother in 1955. The next year he married Margarita Andreievna Kainova.

In accordance with the general "thaw" in Soviet policies, the Central Committee of the Party passed a resolution on May 28, 1958, "On correcting errors in the evaluation of the operas . . ." reinterpreting the Decree of 1948.

Shostakovich's Symphonies Eleven to Thirteen bore interesting subtitles: Eleven, Op. 103 (1957), commemorated "1905," the year of the abortive revolution in which Rimsky had declared his liberalism; Twelve, Op. 112 (1961), celebrated "1917." Thirteen (1962) was not only a program-symphony, but a choral one, on poems by the young Yevgenii Yevtushenko, including his famous *Babyi Yar,* denouncing anti-Semitism; when Premier Khrushchev withdrew his support of Yevtushenko, Shostakovich's new symphony was also withdrawn.

Meanwhile in 1957 Shostakovich had returned at last to the theater, with a satirical operetta, *Cheriomushki-Moskva (Moscow-Levittown)*, Op. 105. He also revised *Lady Macbeth,* and eventually in 1962 it was produced once more, now named *Katerina Izmailova.*

During his long absence from the theater, Shostakovich had written numerous songs and choruses, less noted at the time than the symphonies, but gradually more appreciated, especially when sung by such an artist as Galina Vishnevskaya. Among these were the Pushkin songs, Op. 46 (1936, publ. 1943), songs on poems of Shakespeare, Raleigh, and Burns, Op. 62 (1942), the Hebrew folksongs, Op. 79 (1948), Lermontov songs, Op. 84, and Dolmatovsky songs, Op. 86 (both 1950), ten unaccompanied choruses, Op. 88 (1951), Pushkin monologues, Op. 91 (1953), more Dolmatovsky songs, Op. 98 (1955), and Spanish songs, Op. 100 (1956).

By now his string quartets had reached the number Eight, Op. 110 (1960). This work was a fascinating sort of autobiography, quoting themes from Shostakovich's works from the First Symphony on. The main motif of all movements was one borrowed from the scherzo and finale of the Tenth Symphony, made up of the notes D E♭ C B, in German usage D Es C H, that is, D. SCHostakowitsch.

Other memorable works of chamber music were the Piano Quintet, Op. 57 (1940), and the Second Trio, Op. 67 (1944).

These facts suffice to refute any simple interpretation of Shostakovich's ideological development. They are far from sufficient to provide a foundation for a convincing interpretation, but they are conducive to an open-minded sympathy with the music itself, with each new piece or newly revealed old piece.

The musical style of Shostakovich is remarkably consistent through all fluctuations of ideology, as well as in all different forms and media, and it is unmistakably his own despite various elements clearly derived from Bach, Liszt, Borodin, Tchaikovsky, Mussorgsky, Mahler, Taneiev, Stravinsky, Prokofiev, and so on. Among the traits characteristic of Shostakovich, A. Dolzhansky has identified a frequently appearing scale of eight notes—for example, E F G A♭ B C D E♭—which facilitates a blending of fragments from two or three adjacent diatonic scales—in this case E minor, F minor, E♭ major. In Shostakovich's melody and counterpoint, V. Kholopova notes the importance of complementary rhythms, of regular metrical accents, and of syncopated durations. In his treatment of traditional forms, particularly sonata, fugue, and passacaglia, Shostakovich displays ingenuity and freedom. But how all these detailed techniques serve his expressive purposes remains an open question.

A pupil of Shostakovich, Georgii Vasilievich Sviridov (b. 1915), was frequently mentioned by Soviet writers as the most promising younger symphonist. His *Oratorio pathétique* (1958) was a landmark of its period.

Other distinguished pupils were Nikolai Ivanovich Peiko (b. 1916) and Herman Hermanovich Galynin (b. 1922). Shostakovich's interest in symphony and quartet was shared also by such younger men as Moissei Vainberg (b. 1919) and Andrei Volkonsky (b. 1933), and by Vadim Salmanov (b. 1912), who succeeded Shostakovich at the Leningrad Conservatory.

In America there was little continuity between the 19th-century German tradition and the various classicisms of the 1920s and '30s, but these latter were spreading and flourishing vigorously in the 1950s and '60s. The achievements of Chadwick, Parker, and Converse, respectable enough by comparison with those of Glazunov, Liadov, and Glière, were forgotten or spurned by the generation that followed them. Most of the leading composers and teachers in the middle third of the century had studied either abroad—many with Boulanger—or else with Europeans who settled in America—first Bloch, then Schoenberg, Hindemith, Milhaud, Krenek, and others. But their students, even if they studied also with Messiaen or Boulez, maintained a continuity of interests, in contrast to the gap between earlier generations.

A few exceptional figures, nevertheless, are notable. Perhaps America's nearest equivalent to Miaskovsky was Arthur Shepherd (1880–1958). He was essentially loyal to the principles he learned in Boston from Goetschius and Chadwick (1892–97), yet his Westerner's spirit of adventure carried him through and beyond the naive nationalism of his friends Farwell and Gilbert, to share in the neo-Classic revival of counterpoint and chamber music. His pupil William S. Newman preferred his late works, such as the Piano Quintet (1940), to the symphonic *Horizons* (1927), where his use of cowboy tunes and a Mormon hymn brought him ephemeral world-wide attention. A younger pupil of Goetschius was Howard Hanson (b. 1896), director for many years of the Eastman School of Music in the University of Rochester, New York, and chivalrous champion of young composers on the national scene. Hanson won the first American Rome Prize (1921). During his three years abroad he explored and rejected neo-Classicism, and declared himself forever a Romantic. His opera *Merry Mount* (1933), his five symphonies (1923–55), and other works in all media showed the Romantic virtues of open mind and heart, but not enough intensity to keep them long alive, or to exercise a direct influence on younger composers. Leo Sowerby (b. 1895) was another winner of the first American Rome Prize, and a prolific composer in all forms and media. Sowerby's well-known pieces for organ and for chorus were less representative of his whole achievement, according to Burnet Tuthill, than some of his many unpublished works. Vittorio Giannini (b. 1903), teacher at the Juilliard School in New York, showed in his many compositions a superlative craftsmanship that always served to communicate a warmth of feeling far from academic, but not a distinctive style of his own.

Deeper intensity than Hanson's or Sowerby's, as well as greater sophistication in the currents of 20th-century taste, marked at least a dozen of the Americans whose training was partly with Bloch:

> Frederick Jacobi (1891–1952)
> Douglas Moore (b. 1893)
> Bernard Rogers (b. 1893)
> Roger Sessions (b. 1896)
> Leroy Robertson (b. 1896)
> Quincy Porter (b. 1897)
> Ernst Bacon (b. 1898)
> Herbert Elwell (b. 1898)
> Randall Thompson (b. 1899)
> Isadore Freed (1900–1960)
> Mark Brunswick (b. 1902)
> Theodore Chanler (1902–61)

Each of these men shaped a distinctive style, produced numerous works large and small, and as teachers helped transmit a greatly enriched heritage to the generation that followed them. All deserved more performances and more sustained critical attention than they had received by 1965. Moore's operas, Porter's quartets, Thompson's choruses, and Chanler's songs were valuable enough to attract friends around the world; systematic study would make them more valuable still.

The most widely respected member of this group—though none of his music was often played and not much of it was thoroughly known by his keenest admirers—was Sessions. "Traditionalism in the European sense," Sessions wrote in his *Reflections on the Music Life in the United States* (1956), "simply does not exist here." But "the 'great line of Western tradition' provides the most fertile source of nourishment also for American music . . . Schoenberg . . . intensified awareness of that 'great line.'" So did Sessions himself, more effectively than any other American composer of his time, though, as he acknowledged, many others made indispensable contributions. By 1956 he could smile at the "urbane, almost friendly argument between *diatonicism* and *chromaticism* . . . *neoclassicism* and the *twelve-tone* music."

He grew up in a family fond of music, played the piano, and at the age of thirteen decided to become a composer. Under the guidance of Edward Burlingame Hill at Harvard he became acquainted with new music at the same time that he practiced traditional crafts. World War I prevented his going to study with Ravel as he had hoped. Instead he went to Parker at

Yale. He began to teach. But it was not until Bloch appeared that he found guidance toward an intimate "knowledge of the real demands of composition." Finally he went to Europe in 1926. During the next years, while writing his first symphony and first piano sonata, he became acquainted with all that was going on in various advanced musical circles. In 1933, settled in America, he diagnosed the "crisis" of music in an important article. The crisis had begun before World War I; its chief symptom was the "confusion of tongues," and its cure would be a renewal of common principles. "The composer who is most truly of today, whatever his nationality or esthetic creed, is no longer seeking 'new possibilities' in the individualistic sense of the pre-war composers, but rather . . . submitting himself to the new *necessities* of his time." Disavowing the label "neo-Classicism," and dismissing as superficial the imitation of 18th-century devices, Sessions tried to define "the true classical tradition of the 17th, 18th, and early 19th centuries—the tradition which the Western world held in common under the leadership first of Italian and later of German music." He saw the necessity of the 20th century as "an experiencing anew of certain laws which are inherent in the nature of music itself."

In an essay on "New Vistas in Musical Education," Sessions went on to explain something of how he would meet the felt necessity. He differentiated not merely style and idea, as Ives and Schoenberg did, or common technique, personal style, and ethical vision, as Hindemith did, but four categories: technique, *métier,* style, and mannerism.

Technic, in any really profound sense, is the ability to sustain and develop an organic musical train of thought. Today it is too often confused with *métier,* which is the acquired knack of manipulating formulas. The former is the attribute of an active and creatively sensitized ear, the latter that of mere practice and knowledge.

Style, on the other hand, is the individual inflection which an individual, a nation, or an epoch, spontaneously and unconsciously gives to its music, and has, fundamentally, nothing to do with the conscious and carefully circumscribed choice of materials. . . But style in our day is too often confused with mannerism, a product of ultrarefinement and fundamental lack of creative force.

So Sessions would avoid mannerism, leave style to the unconscious limitations of his knowledge, employ the full range of conscious craft, and concentrate on the problem of "technic" in his "really profound sense," incorporating the development of intense thought. In all his works the vast range of his craft and the intensity of his thought are evident. These alone command both admiration and sympathy. For some listeners, to be sure, Sessions's unconcern with style is hard to share. For those capable of appreciating his technique, the music is deeply rewarding. And to observe the growth of this technique from one work to the next, up to the Fifth Symphony and the monumental opera, *Montezuma* (both 1964), is most rewarding of all.

Among the pupils of Sessions, at Princeton University and elsewhere, several became leading composer-teachers at the middle of the century:

Ross Lee Finney (b. 1906), pupil also of Hill, Berg, and others
Hugo Weisgall (b. 1912), pupil also of Scalero
Milton Babbitt (b. 1916)
Edward T. Cone (b. 1917)
Leon Kirchner (b. 1919), pupil also of Schoenberg
Earl Kim (b. 1920), pupil also of Schoenberg
Andrew Imbrie (b. 1921), pupil also of Boulanger
Don Martino (b. 1929)

Each of these men grappled independently with the kind of profound technical problem that concerned Sessions; their solutions merited separate and continuous study.

—————•—•—————

A contribution complementary to that of Sessions was made by another teacher-composer-critic, Henry Cowell (1897–1965). In contrast to Sessions's short list of weighty works, Cowell's catalogue, published by the American Composers Alliance in 1954, exceeded a thousand pieces. Up to 1962 there were fourteen symphonies and many series of lighter pieces. Cowell did not labor to develop a technique. Rather he happily indulged habits, some of them constant from his precocious childhood in California, others formed with amazing speed at his first contact with any new resource of craft or style. His knowledge was encyclopedic and his curiosity never sated. The "great line of Western tradition" was nowhere near enough for him. The neo-Classic consolidation of this tradition, including the contribution of Schoenberg, he saw as only a temporary stage on the way toward a grander synthesis that would "draw on those materials common to the music of all the peoples of the world, to build a new music particularly related to our own century." This ideal he set forth in 1933, with an essay "Towards Neo-Primitivism." Again in 1954, surveying "New Horizons in Music," he recognized that "the most successful conservative tendency at present and for the past few years is to integrate old and new musical means," but he urged that eventually "Western and Eastern arts must come together on an equal basis." Meanwhile he helped bring them together on any basis or none.

In his youth Cowell gave the name "tone-cluster" to his favorite device of playing several adjacent keys of the piano with his fist or palm or forearm. He never claimed to have invented the device, but his apt name for it made some people remember him chiefly as the "tone-cluster" man, especially after Bartók asked his permission to use it. Cowell liked also to reach inside a piano, circumventing the keyboard to produce unusual sounds from the strings. He left the systematic development of this idea to his pupil John Cage. With Leon Theremin, Cowell invented the Rhythmicon (1931), anticipating the electronic music of the 1950s. All these were only samples of Cowell's hospitality to every "new musical resource." He was no specialist, but an assembler and stimulator.

During the 1940s he wrote a series of eight *Hymns and Fuguing Tunes* for orchestra, gaily modernizing the inspirations of the neglected American psalmodist William Billings (1746–1800). This nationalistic neo-Classicism was as characteristic as his experimentalism. He found his most personal note in the use of Irish folklore, for instance in the *Irish Suite* for chamber orchestra (1929) and the *Celtic Set* for band (1942).

But the chief value of Cowell's work was cumulative—its loose combination of eager experiment, technical and cultural, with homely fun. In this respect he was more like Haydn, the founder of Viennese Classicism, than any 20th-century classicist, solemn or ironic. Moreover, as his friend and teacher Charles Seeger noted, in an essay full of wisdom, Cowell's work appealed more to a few curious musicians and musicologists than to audiences awaiting a "communication," which was not Cowell's concern at all.

If a classical composer is one who not only assembles but selects and assimilates a vast range of resources old and new, who not only sustains and develops but also restrains and finally conceals his complex processes of thought and feeling, all in order to create, as if spontaneously, a series of independent works that exemplify St. Thomas's criteria of beauty—order, clarity, and brilliance—then the 20th-century American classicist *par excellence* was Walter Piston (b. 1894). Piston was a cagy speaker and writer, mentioning only rarely and reluctantly the "elusive side of music," and never seeking to rally support for his views, but when pressed he defined his goal as "the perfect balance between expression and form." His achievement, in eight symphonies and many pieces of chamber music, was acknowledged by all who were acquainted with it as the closest approach by any American symphonist to this classic ideal. Though little known outside America, Piston deserved to rank with Dukas and Enescu, whose friendly counsel had supplemented his studies with Boulanger in Paris (1924–26). Many Americans and not a few musicians elsewhere benefited from his textbooks: Piston called special attention to "harmonic rhythm," the contribution of root-progressions to the rhythmic life of music, and this notion proved to have great value in several contexts. As teacher at Harvard University (1926–60) Piston guided the development of many expert composers, including

Arthur Berger (b. 1912), pupil also of Boulanger
Everett Helm (b. 1913), also Malipiero, Vaughan Williams
Irving Fine (1915–62), also Boulanger
Gordon Binkerd (b. 1916)
Ellis Kohs (b. 1916), also Wagenaar
Leonard Bernstein (b. 1918)
Harold Shapero (b. 1920), also Slonimsky, Krenek, Hindemith, Boulanger
Robert Moevs (b. 1920)
Robert Middleton (b. 1920)
Allen Sapp (b. 1922), also Copland, Boulanger
Daniel Pinkham (b. 1923), also Copland, Boulanger, Honegger
Noel Lee (b. 1924)
Billy Jim Layton (b. 1924).

Contemporaries of Piston, and like him pupils of Boulanger and teachers of younger Americans were Carl McKinley (b. 1895), Harrison Kerr (b. 1897), and Roy Harris (b. 1898). Harris was famous for his Americanism, especially in one stirring piece, the Third Symphony (1939), but in his own mature view (1961) he represented the classic line of Josquin, Palestrina, Bach, and Mozart, which had nearly been lost by the successors of Beethoven. His systematic reform of harmony was well explained by Robert Evett; the inspired melodies of his best works were not yet explicable. The foremost pupil of Harris was William Schuman (b. 1910).

American music for the first time, with the generation of Sessions and Piston, became a part of the Western tradition as a whole at its growing edge. In a sense mediating between the more striking and divergent Americans, Varèse, Ives, Ruggles, Cage on one side, and MacDowell, Copland, Gershwin, Menotti on the other, the broad main current was represented by the teachers grouped together here. Their leadership gave momentum to younger American composers who shared their concerns, regardless of whether they studied with these teachers or even studied their works as much as those of Schoenberg, Bartók, Stravinsky, and Hindemith. Thus, for example, three composers born in 1915, each in his own different way, similarly embodied the "grand line of Western tradition": Robert Palmer, George Perle, and Vincent Persichetti. Palmer, a pupil of Rogers, Porter, Harris, and Copland, had an earnestness like that of Sessions; Persichetti, pupil of Harris, had a keener ear, more encyclopedic knowledge, and more astonishing productivity than Cowell; Perle, pupil of Krenek, had a finesse like Piston's. Similar combinations of qualities could be found in the symphonies and chamber music of many more Americans in this period:

> Robert Sanders (b. 1906)
> John Verrall (b. 1908)
> Halsey Stevens (b. 1908)
> William Denny (b. 1910)
> Alvin Etler (b. 1913)
> Kent Kennan (b. 1913)
> Robert Kelly (b. 1916)
> Hall Overton (b. 1920)
> William Bergsma (b. 1921)
> Robert Kurka (1921–57)
> Ralph Shapey (b. 1921)
> Peter Mennin (b. 1923)

One composer seemed to combine Piston's mastery and grace, Cowell's scope and audacity, and Sessions's depth and grandeur. Moreover, he was a unique successor of Ives. By the age of fifty (1958) Elliott Carter stood at least equal to his foremost close contemporaries throughout the world—Dallapiccola (born 1904), Shostakovich (1906), Fortner (1907), and Messiaen (1908). Each new piece of his was a world event, not merely noted but eagerly anticipated by whoever wished to keep abreast of the times in serious music.

Carter was a neighbor of Ives in 1924–25. Ives's idealism he took to heart, but somehow he learned to match it with a 20th-century realism. He played the piano, and though he never thought of becoming a professional performer, he mastered the subtleties of such piano music as Fauré's. At Harvard he studied literature and philosophy. Not needing to earn a living, he proceeded unhurriedly to learn the crafts of composition and to let his own style mature. He studied briefly with Piston, Holst, and Boulanger, but mostly on his own. He taught briefly, not composition but rather "Music as a liberal art." He served in World War II. He won prizes with a series of modest works, ballets, songs, and choruses, which critics classed as competent and neo-classic; the individuality of their fluent harmony and rhythm and the rare vitality of their melody could be better appreciated after the first piano sonata (1946), where these qualities had developed to a striking degree and now permeated a magnificent big form. In each piece thereafter, Carter's development continued, by leaps so daring that an admirer like the present writer could only hope to understand after years of listening. Two string quartets (1951, 1959) were widely regarded as essential works of the literature, although their difficulty delayed their absorption into most repertories. In 1962 Stravinsky published a paragraph of detailed comment on Carter's Double Concerto for piano, harpsichord, and small orchestra; of all the American music he had heard, this was the piece that interested him most; he liked especially its "new-found good spirits"; finally, it was a masterpiece. This was an excessively rare tribute, not only to an American, but to any composer born between Berg and Boulez.

Carter's style, for all its erudition and novelty, was at the service of a substance that reached out for a wide audience. Richard Franko Goldman, surveying Carter's achievement, pointed especially to some innovations in the treatment of rhythm and tempo. But when Carter was asked to discuss these elements of his craft with a seminar at Princeton (1959) he warned against the danger of overemphasis on such things:

One technical fad after another has swept over 20th-century music as the music of each of its leading composers has come to be intimately known. Each fad lasted a few years, only to be discarded by the succeeding generation of composers, then by the music profession, and finally by certain parts of the interested public. . . Each of the trends of our recent past—primitivism, machinism, neo-Classicism, *Gebrauchsmusik*, the styles of Bartók and Berg, and now those of Schoenberg and Webern—has left and will leave in its trail numbers of really gifted composers whose music, skillful and effective as it is, is suffocated, at least for a time, by its similarity to other music of the same type. . . The tendency to fad has been greatly encouraged by the promulgation of systems, particularly harmonic systems. . . This kind of publicity can lead to a dead end even more quickly than the older fads derived from the actual sound of music. . .

Carter went on to talk more about the social predicament of a serious composer than about any separable technical problems. He pointed out that Americans still lacked opportunities for gaining practical experience in composing—that is, opportunities to hear their music, not just read through once but practiced by various performers and presented to various audiences. He found this lack of experience revealed in the "conventionality and timidity" of many American scores. And he found this situation all too typical of America. "We may be willing to accept the final, accomplished results of European training and experimental efforts but we cannot afford and are impatient with the step-by-step experience needed to produce them." The expansion of American music since the time of Ives seemed to Carter to complicate the difficulties for composers. "Today, even more than in his time, the division between the musician's professional code of ethics, his traditional standards of skill and imagination, established at another time and place, and the present standards of behavior respected, sanctioned, and rewarded by the society that surrounds us, is very pronounced." His reflections ended with no recommendation, but an unflinching emphasis on "how confused and desperate is the relation between the composer, the profession, publicity, and the musical public." For the student composers that Carter addressed here, the desperate honesty of these words was reinforced by the extraordinary gaze of his blue eyes and the characteristic forward thrust of his face as it lighted with a smile. In all his words, his acts, and his music, there was no bitterness, no complaint, no scorn or envy. Without ever losing sight of the "desperate" situation, Carter showed a way of working through it. What he once wrote of Fauré was true of him too: "warmth of feeling and loving kindness reveal themselves in every detail."

A close analogy may be seen between the work of Americans like Piston, Sessions, and Carter and that of their contemporaries in the Netherlands, Belgium, and Sweden, where earlier efforts to rival Grieg, Dvořák, and Tchaikovsky had been hampered by a relative scarcity of distinctive folk music. Now, however, was time to participate in the consolidation of the "great tradition." In each of these countries one or more leaders came forward to represent it in the ISCM, to interpret for it the work of Stravinsky and Hindemith, to reform its conservatories and establish serious musical programs in its radio studios, to guide and promote its young composers. As in America and elsewhere, these composers differed in more ways than they resembled each other. But the resemblance was important in historical perspective.

Willem Pijper (1894–1947) was the foremost composer-teacher-critic of the Netherlands. Pupil of Johan Wagenaar in Utrecht (1912–15), Pijper went on to study the music of Debussy and Mahler as guides to the creation of a Dutch style independent of Brahms and Wagner. In the opinion of the critic Fred Goldbeck, Pijper was closest to Debussy: "Pijper stands to Debussy as Webern to Schoenberg. Proceeding from the author of *Gigues* in his most concentrated and fantastic vein, he has carried unexpectedly far some of Debussy's virtualities." This comparison is useful but other comparisons are needed to balance it. Pijper himself, according to his pupil Karel Mengelberg (son of the conductor Willem Mengelberg), felt that his closest affinity was with Malipiero. His American admirer, Alexander Ringer, stresses his relation to the Netherlanders of the Renaissance and to the flourishing school of younger Dutch composers that he taught, among whom the most prominent were

      Guillaume Landré (b. 1905)
      Kees van Baaren (b. 1906)
      Henk Badings (b. 1907)
      Rudolf Escher (b. 1912)
      Hans Henkemans (b. 1913).

Pijper's influence was an initial stimulus, moreover, to the young Netherlander who most notably outgrew it, Ton de Leeuw (b. 1916). The catalogue of Pijper's works, by W. C. M. Kloppenburg, indicated that his three symphonies and two "symphonic dramas" would be the chief materials for a thorough study of his development; at the same time, the list included many pieces, such as the three sonatinas for piano and the Wind Quintet (1929), that might attract enterprising performers independently.

Pijper's favorite rhythm was the tango. His harmony often depended on the eight-tone scale of alternating steps and halfsteps, which he developed independently of Frazzi, Messiaen, and others. Some of his forms were distinguished by numerological constructions. The combination of these features gave his best music great distinction.

In Belgium, where no composer rose to such international fame as Pijper, there were many who reflected the trend to consolidate. The representative Flemish composer of the age was Arthur Meulemans (b. 1884), whose fourteen symphonies (1930–54) were matched by many works in all forms and media. Marcel Poot (b. 1901) and other pupils of Gilson rather cautiously assimilated some of Stravinsky's rhythms and dissonances into styles not essentially different from their teacher's, and forms as classical as Roussel's. Jean Absil (b. 1893) moved farther from Gilson, in the direction of Schoenberg; by 1960 he too could be recognized as representing a central tradition. Raymond Chevreuille (b. 1911) and Victor Legley (b. 1915) arrived at styles both more personal and more eclectic. If all these were overshadowed abroad by the surrealist André Souris (b. 1899) and his pupil Henri Pousseur (b. 1929), their work more adequately represented music in Belgium.

Five Swedish symphonists represented successive, distinct, yet overlapping types of neo-Classicism: Edvin Kallstenius (b. 1881) was trained at the Leipzig conservatory. Kurt Atterberg (b. 1887) studied in Berlin and admired Glazunov. Gösta Nystroem (b. 1890) studied with d'Indy in Paris and assimilated something from Debussy and Stravinsky. Hilding Rosenberg (b. 1892), after imitating Sibelius, went in 1920 to both Dresden and Paris; he studied especially the music of Schoenberg. Rosenberg's rugged quartets and concertos, profound operas and oratorios, won him respect as the preëminent Swedish guide to new music. Lars-Erik Larsson (b. 1908) studied with Berg and later admired Hindemith; with at least one piece, his *Pastorale Suite* for orchestra (1938), Larsson won the affection of many listeners. Three pupils of Rosenberg carried forward the international tradition in Sweden in the middle of the century: Karl-Birger Blomdahl (b. 1916), Sven-Eric Bäck (b. 1919), and Ingmar Lidholm (b. 1921). By now, to be sure, this tradition stemming from Rosenberg included a concern for the discoveries of Webern, and an intensified interest in medieval and Renaissance music, whereas the traditional ideals of Atterberg and Nystroem seemed remote, and the more fashionable neo-Classicism of Larsson reactionary. But all such contrasts paled in a larger perspective, such as that of a foreigner or even of some Swedish jazz musician; from their points of view the continuity of tradition was more evident than its variety.

In Latin America there were corresponding figures, participating in international currents of tradition and innovation with symphonies and chamber music, organizing institutions, and teaching the best talents of the next generation. The foremost Chilean composer was Domingo Santa Cruz (b. 1899). The foremost Mexican, as much more adventurous than the Chilean as his revolutionary government by comparison with the Chilean dictatorship, was Carlos Chávez (b. 1899). In Argentina the leaders were Juan José Castro (b. 1895), pupil of d'Indy, and Juan Carlos Paz (b. 1897), advocate of Schoenberg; their achievements were surpassed after World War II by Alberto Ginastera (b. 1916), the most polished of Latin Americans, not excepting the spectacular Brazilian, Villa-Lobos.

The international career of Ernst Krenek (b. 1900) illustrated vividly what Roussel called the "succession of continual transformations" characteristic of art and life, and what Mila attributed to Casella—a "barometric sensibility to the oscillations of contemporary taste." Krenek's constant concern was to see amid the chaos of competing tendencies the one direction that music ought to take. His work, more than any other composer's, displayed the spectrum of 20th-century tendencies as phases in a continuous process. For him, the idea of consolidating or balancing old and new elements governed only one brief phase. Before and after that phase he was more sympathetic toward Busoni's kind of new classic ideal; this he knew at first hand in Berlin, where he had followed his teacher Schreker from Vienna in 1920. Krenek continued something like Busoni's endless search for transcendent truth. What united all the phases for him was his ardent belief in the history of music as a unit, his sense that all but one direction must be wrong and that every goal was the point of a fresh departure, not only for individual efforts but for Music.

His most famous single work represented the brief phase of development that he soon judged to have been a reactionary mistake. This was an opera, *Jonny spielt auf* (*Johnny Strikes Up the Band*, 1927). Jonny, a Negro band leader from Alabama, steals the fiddle of Daniello, an oily virtuoso, who has stolen the mistress of the true protagonist, Max, a brooding intellectual opera composer. At the end Jonny and his jazz bestride the globe. With all too appropriate irony, the sensational success of *Jonny* became an obstacle to Krenek's earlier and later works.

His most important work, in his own estimation as he looked back in

1962, was another opera, *Karl V* (1930–33, first produced 1938). Here the Catholic Emperor and his confessor preach the union of freedom and historic responsibility. The music harnesses free rhythms and soaring curves of melody to the twelve-tone technique.

Besides these and many other operas, Krenek produced a steady stream of instrumental music, including five symphonies and seven quartets, and also a torrent of critical, historical, and theoretical writings. As a boy in Gymnasium at Vienna, he had drafted a historical novel. As a refugee starting a new life in America, he compiled voluminous memoirs, most of which were to be published only after his death; these would become invaluable documents for students of all 20th-century music, not only that of Krenek himself, since his international wanderings in the 1920s had brought him into intimate contact with many eminent musicians. A complete list of his published literary works, nowhere readily accessible, would require several pages. The selections from the memoirs (*Selbstdarstellung*, 1948) and the collections of essays, *Zur Sprache gebracht* (*Induced to Speak*, 1958) and *Gedanken unterwegs* (*Thoughts en Route*, 1959), whetted an appetite for more. The *Studies in Counterpoint Based on the Twelve-Tone Technique* (1940; German edition 1952) were also important for their relation to more music than Krenek's though not to that of Schoenberg, or even Berg and Webern, toward whom Krenek had become friendly when he returned to Vienna about 1930. Krenek's *Studies* directly influenced many composers who learned little about "the school of Schoenberg" until Leibowitz began to discuss it. All of Krenek's writings, naturally enough, including even the booklet on *Ockeghem* (1953), could best be understood in relation to his own music.

With his *Sestina* (1957) Krenek summed up "total serialism." With his *Spiritus intelligentiae* (1958) he embarked on electronic adventures. His search was unflagging. At the same time he continued to compose smaller works, such as the *Echoes from Vienna* for piano (1958), which resembled his earliest compositions. He was faithful to his ideal of comprehensive grand opera, with *Der goldene Bock* (*The Golden Ram*, based on Jeffers's *Medea*, 1964).

Whatever the fate of his works, Krenek had well fulfilled the ambition to help others become what he himself exemplified: "fervent, conscientious, and responsible carriers of the glorious traditions of Western music, the criteria of which are vitality and richness of imagination, lucidity of thought, complexity of organization, and eloquence in expressing universal human emotions."

Like Krenek and Hindemith, many other Europeans literally carried the "glorious tradition" to American conservatories and universities. Several of them composed symphonies and chamber music that might eventually hold a greater share of performers', listeners', and historians' attention than they were able to win from their contemporaries. Among these were

> Ernst Toch (1887–1964)
> Karol Rathaus (1895–1954)
> Alexander Tcherepnin (b. 1899)
> Nikolai Lopatnikov (b. 1903)
> Ingolf Dahl (b. 1912).

To mention two naturalized American symphonists who, by contrast, received adequate recognition during their lives—Nicolai Berezowsky (1900–53) and Richard Mohaupt (1904–57)—may give weight to the list of those who did not.

In Germany at the end of World War II conscientious musicians recognized a situation in some ways like that which had prevailed earlier elsewhere: their concerts, their publications, their educational system, their styles of composition had become provincial. They had been cut off from the advance of the "great tradition." Now their energies and resources were free to change the situation. This they did, with a speed as miraculous as that of the German economic recovery. They studied the music of Schoenberg, Bartók, Stravinsky, and Webern. They performed, published, recorded, and especially broadcast more new music than any other nation. They organized festivals, holiday study courses, and numerous critical journals. They produced new ideas in profusion, and new combinations of old and new. While veterans like Scherchen and Eimert and a prodigy like Stockhausen collaborated with Boulez and Nono to constitute a conspicuous international avant-garde or scouting party for the new ideas, a broad front of mature teacher-composers saw to the new combinations. Among these were a few who had taken part in the modern movements of the 1920s: Heinz Tiessen (b. 1887), Max Butting (b. 1888), Felix Petyrek (1892–1951), and Philipp Jarnach (b. 1892). More important were those who had begun their careers in the fields of church music and youth music but were now liberated to explore every field: Wilhelm Maler (b. 1903), Günther Raphael (b. 1903), Hans Brehme (1904–57), Karl Amadeus Hartmann (1905–63), and Wolfgang Fortner (b. 1907). Soon joining them was a still younger generation, among whom the most prominent were Helmut Degen (b. 1911), Jens Rohwer (b. 1914), Giselher Klebe (b. 1925), and especially Fortner's pupil Hans Werner Henze (b. 1926). Each of these made his unique contribution, meriting separate patient study. But by 1960, Fortner had distinguished himself as the most important, both as composer and teacher. Fortner, like Carter, knew and resisted the "hunger for new formulas." He had begun his career with works like the Concerto for organ and strings (1932) that resembled Hindemith. He had studied Hindemith's *Craft,* and preserved a high regard for it. But he had also studied musicology a bit, along with studies of composition and organ at Leipzig (1927–31). Gradually he came to the conclusion that in music, since the disruption of the 19th-century faith in progress, there could be no common style, and moreover no genuine craft. Instruction in composition, he argued, must incorporate a selective survey of history from Gregorian chant onward, and of the wide spectrum of contemporary styles. His students asked for rules, but he gave them something better.

The longing for order is common in the hearts of young people. The teacher is thus in a remarkable situation. In the desires of his students for order he is continually anticipated, continually surpassed. . . The teacher of such students must awake and develop in them quite other values, contrasting values, in order that they may not make their cabbalistic speculation into an end in itself, not replace music with the finding of rules. Thus if instruction in composition is given today, I think the point is to find the right balance for the relation between order and freedom, and to resolve this very tension by means of comprehensive historical acquaintance with music. We must study the past, if I may say so, in order not to imitate it.

. . . This comprehensive culture is necessary in order not to burden the young man with blinders, with prejudices. He should learn to recognize a work of art in the most various stylistic entanglements, to see its artistry; he should learn how in all these styles order and freedom lead to the actual work of art.

The actual works that demonstrated Fortner's own distinctive artistry appeared at the end of World War II: a symphony (1947), a cantata, *An den Nachgeborenen* (*To Posterity*, Brecht, 1948), and numerous pieces of chamber music. His "entanglement" with the styles of Stravinsky, Schoenberg, and Bartók was evident in these works. In 1950 came a ballet, *Weisse Rose* (*White Rose*), and seven elegies for piano, in which twelve-tone technique contributed to the further development of Fortner's style; there was not an abrupt conversion, like Krenek's, nor a mere sampling, like that of Piston or Bloch, nor a gradual approach such as was made by Stravinsky, Petrassi, and others, but an incorporation of the technique as one element of order to be balanced with an ever greater freedom. A climax of Fortner's growth was reached in the opera, *Bluthochzeit* (*Blood Wedding*, Lorca, 1953–57).

Around the middle of the century indications of a loosely consolidated tradition appeared in nearly every other country where professional music institutions existed. In Norway, a lonely Schoenbergian, Fartein Valen (1887–1952), was belatedly recognized as the chief local composer of the period. Valen's pupil Klaus Egge (b. 1906) and the more conservative Harald Saeverud (b. 1897) now maintained high standards in "polite rivalry." In Denmark the leading Nielsen pupil Jörg Bentzon (1897–1951) was overshadowed by his young cousin, Niels Viggo Bentzon (b. 1919), whose style showed influences of Hindemith and Schoenberg; other internationalists were Knudåge Riisager (b. 1897), Hermann David Koppel (b. 1908), Svend Erik Tarp (b. 1908), and Vagn Holmboe (b. 1909). In Finland the leading Sibelius pupil Leevi Madetoja (1887–1947) was succeeded by a pupil of Reger and Vassilenko, Aare Merikanto (1893–1958), the "pioneer of musical modernism in Finland." In Japan, though no younger man was yet so securely established as the Bruch pupil Kosaku Yamada (b. 1886), there were able representatives of more sophisticated European styles, such as the French-trained Tomojiro Ikenouchi (b. 1906), the German-trained Saburo Moroi (b. 1903), and his son Makoto Moroi (b. 1930). In Canada, where Healey Willan (b. 1880) and Claude Champagne (b. 1891) continued to uphold 19th-century traditions, the most sought-after teachers were John Weinzweig (b. 1913) and Jean Papineau-Couture (b. 1916), able representatives of the age of Stravinsky and Schoenberg.

Even in Austria the antagonisms of old and new gradually subsided. A pupil of Schoenberg, Berg, and Schmidt, Hanns Jelinek (b. 1901) began to lecture at the Conservatory on twelve-tone technique, and the chief of Schmidt's many pupils, Theodor Berger (b. 1903), made some use of the technique. Karl Schiske (b. 1916) and other younger men represented the new synthesis even more ably. While the most prominent Schoenbergian, Hans Erich Apostel (b. 1901), still lamented Viennese provincial conservatism, there were also representatives of the international avant-garde such as Friedrich Cerha (b. 1926).

Fortner and Carter and others like them faced the "abyss of freedom" without flinching. They recognized that the selection and balance of elements in every serious piece of music was a new achievement. No technical rules of procedure, no stylistic habit or preference, could now give composers, as Hindemith had hoped to do, a guarantee of competence or correctness. But the knowledge of as many techniques and styles as possible would help composers, they suggested, to make choices worthy of their professional tradition. Like Stravinsky, they recognized that "tradition is not simply 'handed down,' fathers to sons, but undergoes a life process," and that "true tradition lives in the contradiction."

CHAPTER XXIV

Prokofiev

IF THE QUESTION "which 20th-century composer best maintained and extended the classic tradition of symphony and concerto" were put to a world-wide sampling of orchestral musicians, concert ticket subscribers, and record collectors, the likeliest answer would be: Sergei Prokofiev (1891–1953). His name would surely turn up more often than that of Hindemith, and probably more often than that of Stravinsky, whose ballets are remembered before his symphonies, and whose traditionalism, where it is known at all, is known to be tricky, nourished on contradiction. Prokofiev's traditionalism seems self-evident. His achievement, in contributing to the standard symphonic repertory more new pieces than anyone else after World War I, is unquestionable.

Fascinating contradictions abound in connection with Prokofiev too. "Classic" and "traditional" have no simple single meanings for him. Their ambiguities call for unraveling, as far as possible.

He composed his *Classical Symphony*, Op. 25, when he was about twenty-five (1915–17), before the beginning of Hindemith's career, before the neo-Classicisms of Stravinsky, Schoenberg, Bartók, and Piston, but after Prokofiev had proved himself a rebel against both the academicism of Glazunov and the super-romantic ecstasies of Scriabin, and an admirer of the young poet Vladimir Mayakovsky (1893–1930), who combined Futurism and Bolshevism. (Prokofiev wrote an interesting report on the Italian Futurist noisemakers, whose work he heard in Rome, 1915.) At this moment the idea of his classical symphony was a joke—a bit of esoteric irony. But to cap the irony, his joke became a popular classic of 20th-century music. His six later, more serious symphonies were less successful, in varying degrees. His ten concertos, of which the third for piano was most popular, included some splendid pages, but nothing more distinctive than the *Classical Symphony*. His several later suites, which shared its popularity, did not represent quite the same tradition. Nor did any later work of his have so great an effect on other composers outside Russia.

Like Debussy's *Faun*, the *Classical Symphony* is played so much that many people suppose they know it without ever listening closely. If the

EXAMPLE XXIV.1a Prokofiev, Gavotte, from *Classical Symphony*: hypothetical version

EXAMPLE XXIV.1b Prokofiev, Gavotte: original version

tune of the Gavotte, third movement, were ironed out into a thoroughly innocent, traditional pattern, *blasé* listeners would never notice the missing
point, the twists of tonality that make it Prokofiev. It is possible even to
play the correct notes without feeling their gentle mockery of innocence.
These two versions are alike in rhythm and melodic contour. The melody's
big range and octave leaps are characteristic of Prokofiev, but in the first
version academic harmony makes them insipid. With Prokofiev's harmony
the melody comes alive. Now likewise if his harmonic scheme is abstracted
from the leaps and glides of the Gavotte, and heard instead as an academic
chorale, this too is pale, though a bit strained at the end, not unlike César
Franck.

EXAMPLE XXIV.2

Prokofiev's original stroke was to combine the rich harmony with the
rhythmic grace and vigor. Until he had forged the combination, these elements were quite incongruous. His melody gave them a fresh unity. Some
of Reger's melodies, which Prokofiev knew and admired from Reger's
visit to St. Petersburg in 1906, approached this combination, but Reger's
characteristic rhythms were more fluent, not so perky. When Prokofiev
discovered Ravel, about 1912, he recognized and admired a somewhat similar combination in his music, but Ravel's harmonies were more consistently
smooth progressions of rich chords. Prokofiev has deeper affinities with
these two composers than with most, but still only a rare measure of his
music could be confused with theirs.

Prokofiev's accompaniment participates in both harmonic and rhythmic
elements, free from academic rules of polyphony, yet supporting the tune

with vital melodic strands as well as chords. The chords themselves are mostly triads. The accompaniment is beautifully varied in spacing. Harsh thirds in a low range underline the melodic leaps. All this is true of almost any phrase by Prokofiev, though naturally not every phrase has such a catchy rhythm, and in many the triads are obscured by non-harmonic tones.

Prokofiev's melodies not only twist tonality; with their accompaniments they stretch tonality in a new way. To appreciate this requires more than sensitivity to detail; it involves rather long spans of time, beyond a single phrase, and it may be that some listeners who cannot name chords or modulations actually feel their long-range coherence and their stretching effect more acutely than some who pride themselves on a technical vocabulary and a readiness for atonal music. In Prokofiev's music every listener not numb to harmony feels the rich chord progressions as jolts in the rhythmic momentum. A listener who calls these jolts modulations, quickly reorienting his sense of tonality, may lose the momentum. Then when the cadence finally arrives, its return to the starting point may seem to him arbitrary. He may think that Prokofiev has been merely perverse in modulating so suddenly. He may speak of "side-slipping" when a jolt coincides with a parallel movement of chords. He may be well enough aware of Prokofiev's mockery, but miss its gentleness, and tire of it soon. If, on the other hand, a listener keeps his grasp on the melody all the way to its cadence, and hears the accompaniment in due subordination, then the final tonic is marvelously satisfying. To call the jolts along the way not modulations but rather abstruse relations to the single tonic, as shown in our analytical numerals, may help some listeners to subordinate them properly. But there is no harm in calling them modulations, provided their function is felt. In Prokofiev's best large works his melodic stretching of tonality spans many phrases, with sequential repetitions and even thematic contrasts. His modulations on a large scale are no different from the passing subordinate modulations within a phrase. His melodic unity, at its best, holds together whole movements.

Prokofiev's own analysis of the "basic lines" of his style, in a brief autobiography (1941), emphasized the "lyrical melodic line" as most important. He insisted that what others called the "grotesque" element was not distinct, but subordinate to melody, and not a constant element but an occasional "deviation," however frequent; he preferred to call it "scherzoishness," with several degrees—"fooling, laughter, mockery." The two together —lyricism and scherzoishness—he took credit for, as his personal traits. He left between the lines, as it were, an implication that his lyricism was equally personal when it tended toward a melancholy mood. Other distinct elements of his style—classic, innovating, and motoric—he traced to definite influences of his youth. "The classical line" he owed partly to his mother's devotion to Beethoven, Tchaikovsky, and Grieg, and her abhorrence of vulgar Gypsy songs, partly also to the enthusiasm for Haydn and Mozart instilled by his conducting teacher, Nikolai Tcherepnin, and partly to his lessons with Taneiev in counterpoint based on Bach. (The gavottes from Bach's Third Suite for orchestra and several suites for keyboard were models for Prokofiev's many gavottes; he imitated Haydn in the other movements of the *Classical Symphony*.) Both Tcherepnin and Taneiev had contributed much also to the "innovating trend," especially the search for new harmonies. The last "line," the least important, Prokofiev called the "toccata" or "motor" line, that is, the fondness for machine-like precision, speed, and regularity of motion; this derived from Schumann's famous toccata for piano, which Prokofiev had played with great success in his early recitals. (He was a prize-winning pianist, whereas his student compositions had won only qualified praise from Rimsky, Glière, Liadov, and Glazunov.) His analysis of these "lines"—classic, innovating, toccata, and lyric, deviating into mockery—was quoted with approval in most subsequent accounts of Prokofiev's style, though no two commentators agreed on how to relate his "lines" to the chronology of his works. An especially notable interpretation is that of Vladimir Fédorov, whose knowledge of the man and the music prevents him from oversimplification; but Fédorov does not apply his interpretation to any particular bit of music. In connection with our analysis of the Gavotte from the *Classical Symphony*, the most important of Prokofiev's generalizations take on concrete meaning.

Prokofiev relied on performers to appreciate his lyricism and help communicate it. Unfortunately, they can easily lose it in a tempo just slightly too fast or too slow—too fast for the harmonic jolts or too slow for the dancing rhythms. The right tempo is not to be calculated by metronome, but continuously felt as a balancing of the jolts and the momentum. There is a danger, moreover, of coarsening the rhythmic element by swells and accents just a bit too loud, staccatos too abrupt, and portamentos too crude. On the other hand there is some danger, especially in slow movements and contrapuntal passages, of losing the essential, simple, strong rhythmic element in a bland flow or machine-like regularity of equally stressed beats. Prokofiev is as hard to perform well as Mozart or Webern. Koussevitzky's performance of the *Classical Symphony* was a model of the right balance. If Koussevitzky had lived to play the Seventh, Prokofiev might have held the esteem of more sophisticated musicians than he did. A recorded performance of the Seventh by N. P. Anosov, conducting the Prague Philharmonic Orchestra, came closer to the ideal than its competitors.

———— • ————

The *Classical Symphony*, though typical of Prokofiev's technique and style, cannot represent his whole personality or his main aspirations. These may be suggested by a consideration of his dramatic works, which he naturally expected to reach greater audiences than his little joke. It is remarkable that Prokofiev, like Debussy, continually devoted his major efforts to opera, although his instrumental works won more attention from listeners, expert as well as amateur. The chief expert on Prokofiev, Israel Nestyev, notes many details to confirm the importance of the operas, but he never assembles these apart from the other works. A brief survey by Renate Jahn is valuable for doing just this. But Jahn, in turn, overlooks the fact that for Prokofiev ballets and films were substitutes for operas. He composed ballets and films on commission. He sought out his opera librettos and persisted in setting them despite every discouragement. Until all the mature operas can be seen on many stages, his achievement as a whole cannot be fairly measured. During his lifetime not one of the operas was a complete success, and several were not produced at all. The great popularity of the Suite from the comic film *Lieutenant Kizhe* (1934), the Cantata from the epic film *Alexander Nevsky* (1938–39), and the little fairy-tale personifying the instruments of the orchestra, *Petia i volk* (*Peter and the Wolf*, Op. 67, 1936), along with the early *Classical Symphony* and Third Piano Concerto, could not console him for the neglect of *Igrok* (Dostoievsky's *Gambler*, Op. 24, 1915–16, revised 1927), *Ognennyi angel* (*The Flaming Angel*, Op. 37, 1919–27), *Semyon Kotko* (Op. 81, 1939), and *Povest' o nastoiashchem cheloveke* (*The Story of a Real Man*, Op. 117, 1947–48). His most successful opera, and in Nestyev's judgment the best, was *The Duenna* (Sheridan, Op. 86, 1939–40, rev. 1943), the lightest of them, the most nearly like the *Classical Symphony*. The biggest one, representing his highest and broadest ambitions, was *Voina i mir* (*War and Peace*, Tolstoy, Op. 91, 1941–43, rev. 1946–52). Ten years after his death this was beginning to be known in Germany and America, and in Moscow it ran simultaneously in two theaters. There was a chance that Prokofiev would turn out to have been the greatest opera composer since Strauss and Debussy, or at least a strong rival to Berg and Britten.

Besides the sheer amount of operatic music, the overlapping dates and the revisions suggest something of Prokofiev's way of working. He was extremely diligent, fanatically neat and punctual, swift, yet patient. He often had many compositions under way at once. He apparently never abandoned a work unfinished. He was loath to let any finished work lie on the shelf unused.

The slightly diminished pace of his activity around 1930 reflects his very gradual, deliberate decision to settle in Russia, which he had left just after the Revolution, hoping to make his fortune in America. After 1927, while living mainly in France, he visited Russia regularly. When the Union of Soviet Composers was organized, subordinating ideological debates to a professional bureaucracy, he brought his family from Paris, about 1935. The next decade was his most productive time. In 1945, he suffered a serious accident. He never fully recovered his health. In spite of doctors' orders he went on working as hard as he could, and in the last years accomplished an amazing amount.

Jahn's survey of the operas traces a curve of development, from chains of simple tunes through continuous recitative to a balanced diversity of melodies. Nestyev quotes from the manuscript of the unpublished *Velikan* (*The Giant*, 1900), preserved in the State Archives at Moscow, a march-like "aria" with an ostinato accompaniment; he notes that even this childish work includes some traits of Prokofiev's later music—terrifying effects, sharp contrasts, and imitations of natural sounds; the rhythm of the march is characteristic too. Another unpublished work, *Pir vo vremia chumy* (*Feast in a Time of Plague*, 1903–09), written under Glière's guidance, was, according to Nestyev, "quite a professional work," with Italianate arias. According to Prokofiev himself, a scene for the *Feast* written later at the Conservatory shocked Liadov with its resemblance to Scriabin. *Maddalena* (Op. 13, 1911–13) had no arias at all. Its "harsh, tense recitative" was relieved only by a tuneful chorus of gondoliers offstage. *The Gambler* was "almost entirely conversational prose, without a single aria, chorus, or ensemble." Most of the vocal writing was extremely difficult because of the complex dissonant harmony, depicting the ugly characters, but the wise words of the Grandmother (*babulenka*) were set to fragments of folkish tunes. The continuity of the work depended more on the text than on Prokofiev's melodies, for whatever the character of these, their span was short. *Liubov' k trëm apel'sinam* (*The Love for Three Oranges*, Gozzi, Op. 33, 1917–19) had a march and scherzo that became famous concert pieces. In his autobiography Prokofiev recounted his unhappy adventures in Chicago, where Mary Garden produced this opera. "Taking the tastes of the American audience into account," he said, "I chose a simpler musical idiom than in the *Gambler*." Yet except for the march and scherzo and a few less memorable instrumental dances, his melodies were again fragments, entirely subordinate to the words. The comparative simplicity was in the lighter orchestration, suited to Gozzi's stylized comic fantasy, in contrast to the bitter realism of Dostoievsky. *The Flaming Angel* was serious and complicated again. Its Expressionistic mixture of medieval magic and lust brought forth new kinds of melody, never a simple tune but often a long modulating line amid surging orchestral counterpoint, that marked a great advance over the previous operas. Prokofiev meant the main role for Mary Garden, but her company disbanded and Prokofiev went off to Paris with his new wife, Lina Llubera. The *Angel* waited long. It never became widely known in Russia; Nestyev allowed it to stand for the nadir of Prokofiev's career, but he pointed out that Prokofiev drew valuable lessons from it. In the decade after his death, the *Angel* was performed in France and Germany with considerable success.

The first of his Soviet operas was a veristic melodrama. The hero, Semyon Kotko, "son of workers," is a Ukrainian soldier, just returned from fighting for the Revolution; he has to win his bride by foiling her father's antirevolutionary villainies. Nestyev praises the tuneful episodes, including folkish Ukrainian choruses, and especially the love duets, but he regrets their brevity, though he also admires the predominating declamatory passages. He suggests that the biggest "disappointment" of the opera is its finale—idyllic song instead of the heroism and patriotism that the drama might have permitted.

The Duenna, retreating from serious dramatic problems, marked a kind of advance with regard to the blossoming of long dance-like tunes, smoothly arising out of the declamatory melodies, or providing a contrapuntal continuity to support more fragmentary dialogue.

War and Peace in its final version, published in three volumes, has a similar smooth combination of many melodic types, and the tuneful types naturally range farther than ever before, with arias and ensembles that reveal romantic depths of character, and choruses that do justice to the epic background of the drama, without overshadowing the central figures and their action.

The *Real Man*, according to Jahn, has a similar wealth of melody concentrated in a tighter drama. The hero is a wounded flyer, who overcomes his handicap in order to fly again. In 1948, just after the Central Committee of the Communist Party had condemned Prokofiev's "formalist deviations and anti-democratic tendencies," the Union of Composers found this work unsuitable. But when, ten years later, the 1948 decree was reinterpreted, the *Real Man* was produced, and Prokofiev's admirers proposed it as a model of "Socialist realism" truly understood. It seemed likely to be a controversial work for many years to come. Meanwhile its principal tunes made a stirring concert march for band.

The decree of 1948 was directed specifically against an opera by Muradeli, *The Great Friendship*, which Premier Stalin had found offensive. The first complaint was that "it has not a single memorable melody or aria." The only other piece of music named in the decree was Shostakovich's *Lady Macbeth*; the famous criticism of this work in 1936 had not produced the desired reorientation of Soviet music. The "formalistic movement," represented by Shostakovich, Prokofiev, Khachaturian, Shebalin, Popov, Miaskovsky, "and others," had dominated composition and criticism. "Some composers" had "debased the lofty social role of music and narrowed its significance, limiting it to the gratification of the perverted tastes of esthetizing egocentrics, . . . one-sided cultivation of complex forms of instrumental wordless symphonic music, and a supercilious attitude toward such musical genres as opera, choral music, popular music for small orchestras, national instruments, vocal ensembles, etc." The Party leaders believed that "the Soviet people expect from their composers products of high quality in all forms, in opera, in symphonic music, in vocal art, in choral and dance music." It is probable that the members of the Central Committee were not acquainted with any of Prokofiev's operas.

The leading musician to interpret the 1948 decree was a composer, Tikhon Khrennikov (b. 1913), who replaced Khachaturian as secretary of the Composers' Union and who remained in office even after the policy changed. In 1948 Khrennikov specified several of Prokofiev's works as "formalistic." Some of these were the cantatas and other occasional pieces on political texts, chosen by Prokofiev himself, in an effort to satisfy the peculiar needs of Soviet institutions. Most of Khrennikov's references were to works of the 1920s, when Prokofiev was associated in Paris with the arch-formalists Diaghilev and Stravinsky. Others were the recent Sixth Symphony and Sixth Piano Sonata. The only recent opera was *War and Peace*, a work still in progress. There was no praise for any work of the "formalists." Presumably for Khrennikov even *Peter and the Wolf* was "garbage."

Prokofiev wrote a letter, to be read at the meeting of the Composers' Union, which his health forbade him to attend. He welcomed the decree. He acknowledged that "elements of formalism were peculiar to my music as long as fifteen or twenty years ago. Apparently the infection caught from contact with some Western ideas." He had tried to get rid of this infection and thought he had succeeded in *Nevsky, Zdravitsa* (*Toast to Stalin,* cantata, Op. 85, 1939), *Romeo* (ballet, Op. 64, 1934–36), and the Fifth Symphony (Op. 100, 1944). He would gladly reinforce 1) melody, 2) tonality, and 3) the predominance of aria over recitative in opera. To each of these three topics he devoted a paragraph.

I have never questioned the importance of melody. I love melody, and I regard it as the most important element in music. I have worked on the improvement of its quality in my compositions for many years. To find a melody instantly understandable even to the uninitiated listener, and at the same time an original one, is the most difficult task for a composer. Here he is beset by a great multitude of dangers: he may fall into the trivial or the banal, or into the rehashing of something already written by him. In this respect, composition of complex melodies is much easier. It may also happen that a composer, fussing over his melody for a long time, and revising it, unwittingly makes it over-refined and complicated, and departs from simplicity. Undoubtedly, I fell into this trap, too, in the process of my work. One must be particularly vigilant to make sure that the melody retains its simplicity without becoming cheap, saccharine, or imitative. It is easy to say, but not so easy to accomplish. All my efforts will be henceforth concentrated to make these words not only a recipe, but to carry them out in my subsequent works.

I must admit that I, too, have indulged in atonality, but I also must say that I have felt an attraction towards tonal music for a considerable time, after I clearly realized that the construction of a musical work tonally is like erecting a building on a solid foundation, while a construction without tonality is like building on sand. . .

I have been criticized for the predominance of recitative over cantilena. I like the theater as such, and I believe that a person who attends the opera has a right to expect not only auditory, but also visual impressions; or else he would go to a concert and not to the opera. But every action on the stage is closely associated with recitative; on the other hand, cantilena induces a certain immobility on the stage. I recall the painful experience of watching the action in some of Wagner's operas, when during a whole act, lasting nearly an hour, not a single person moved on the stage. This fear of immobility prevented me from dwelling on cantilena too long. In connection with the Resolution, I thought over this problem with great care, and came to the conclusion that every operatic libretto has elements demanding the use of the recitative, while other elements imperatively require a treatment in the arioso style. But there are also sections (and these sections take up considerable space, adding up perhaps to one-half of the entire opera) which the composer may treat as he wishes, either as a recitative or as an arioso. Let us consider, for example, the scene of Tatiana's letter from *Eugene Onegin*. . . This is the direction which I intend to take.

The development of Prokofiev's policy for opera as it proceeded throughout his life was compatible with the decree as he understood it. Whether his development was affected at all by the decree remains an open question. If at all, then to what extent, a more difficult question. And whether for better or worse, yet another. Most discussions of his music begin with an assumed answer to the last, but Prokofiev's own concluding words suggest a more subtle attitude: "I should like to express my gratitude to our Party for the precise directives of the Resolution, which will help me in my search of a musical language, accessible and natural to our people, worthy of our people and of our great country." The search was inevitably his own. His ultimate worth was to be measured in terms of the people, not of a Party directive, though he could receive this politely as a help in his search.

Prokofiev's three last dramatic works were true to the intention expressed in his letter. Here more profusely than ever he displayed melodies, varied in character, with tunes more prominent than recitative, and all united in complex tonal forms. The tunes can be made to sound trivial by a poor performance. But they deserve better. The two cantatas, *Zimnii kostér*

(*Winter Bonfire*, Op. 122, 1949) and *Na strazhe mira* (*On Guard for Peace,* Op. 124, 1950), amplified the concern for children that had inspired not only *Peter* but also many of Prokofiev's smaller works. These big cantatas were neglected in the West, chiefly because of political allusions in their texts; in Russia they won prizes, and Nestyev recommended them highly, though with apologies for their lingering complexities of harmony. The ballet *Skaz o kamennom tsvetke* (*Tale of the Stone Flower,* Op. 118, 1948–50) revealed Prokofiev's own personality more directly than any earlier work, for he and his second wife, Mira Mendelssohn, concocted the story out of several folkish tales by P. Bazhov. The protagonist is a potter, the only artist in all Prokofiev's works. He leaves his village, his wise old teacher, and his bride-to-be, to go in quest of the legendary stone flower, which will enable him to perfect his art. In the end, with magic help, he wins everything—he submits a perfect vase to the village fair, and dances happily with his bride. But he never comes to grips with the villainous overseer who in his absence has tormented and terrified the whole village and especially the heroine. The villain's defeat is magic too. It is connected with the hero's triumph only tenuously, through the mysterious god-like Mistress of the Copper Mountain, and through the fragile musical unity that Prokofiev gave to his ugly villain's music, his love music, and his folkish choral dances. Nestyev and other critics found the musical unity inadequate in performance, but perhaps a magical performance would someday make it convincing.

———•————

For at least one student of the scores, the *Stone Flower* is the most appealing of Prokofiev's ballets. The others, with their different strong and weak points, all merit continuing performance and study, but preferably in the light of the operas. The ballets do not show a consistent development. Rather, much more than the operas, they show Prokofiev's farthest strayings and sharpest turns of direction in his long search. The four that he wrote for Diaghilev lend support to Khrennikov's contention that Prokofiev squandered his native gifts to imitate Stravinsky's several styles. On the other hand, the two most successful ballets—*Romeo* and *Cinderella*—provide some evidence for the opposite view, that Prokofiev muffled his characteristic mockery to become a neo-Romantic, whether in response to Soviet policy or out of his own supposed mellowing. The ballets and operas together show that Prokofiev confronted the "abyss of freedom," but turned back without lingering at its edge.

Prokofiev and Stravinsky first met, according to Stravinsky's *Memories* (1960), in the winter of 1906–07, when both were pupils of Rimsky, the boy Prokofiev in an orchestration class at the Conservatory and Stravinsky in private. Stravinsky remembered: "His performance was remarkable—but I have always liked his music, hearing him play it—and the music had personality." Prokofiev was too busy discovering Reger, Debussy, and Scriabin to pay attention to the still unknown Stravinsky. But in 1914, he heard Koussevitzky play the *Rite*, and was swept away. That spring, when his mother offered him a trip abroad as graduation present, Prokofiev chose to go to London, where the Diaghilev ballet was on tour. Here he heard and saw *Firebird* and *Petrushka*. He played for Diaghilev, who appreciated the raw power of personality in such piano pieces as the Toccata, Op. 11. He hoped to interest Diaghilev in *The Gambler*. When Diaghilev rejected any idea of opera, Prokofiev was glad to agree to write a ballet like the *Rite*. His *Ala et Lolly* (*Scythian Suite*, Op. 20, 1914–15) was the result. It obviously resembles the *Rite* in its use of thick dissonant chords, played loud and staccato and repeated hypnotically in a quick tempo. There are some more subtle resemblances too, in orchestration. But the missing elements are most important: there is no syncopation, no trace of Stravinsky's characteristic new rhythm, and no structural use of the dissonant harmony. On the contrary, Prokofiev's rhythms are mere exaggerations of conventional ones, and his harshest chords are agglomerations of non-harmonic tones over a stable tonic; their thrill is momentary and does not bear many hearings. He uses fragments of melody as motifs, not as organic parts of a novel unity. He chokes off his own melodic gift for the sake of a superficial effect. The effect is powerful. As the achievement of a twenty-three-year-old whose only previous orchestral works had been the rather simple accompaniments of his first two concertos and three short student pieces in quite different styles, the *Scythian Suite* is admirable. But Diaghilev was not mistaken when, in 1915, he rejected the ballet as "not very interesting—*à la* Tcherepnin!" Prokofiev recognized in his autobiography that he had not understood the *Rite*. In 1915 he swallowed his disappointment, and accepted a new assignment from Diaghilev. He also established a personal friendship with Stravinsky, and wrote an enthusiastic review of Stravinsky's children's songs.

The next ballet, *Skazka pro shuta* (*Tale of the Buffoon*, or *Chout*, Op. 21, 1915, rev. 1920), is modelled on *Petrushka*, which allows for tunes. Thus it is a lesser strain for Prokofiev and accordingly a better piece than the *Scythian Suite*. A step backward into Stravinsky's past facilitated a step forward in Prokofiev's own development, even though he despised the folkish tunes and concentrated his attention on shrill orchestration and polychords, which he used as enriched dominants. When *The Buffoon* was finally produced in Paris, the unrelieved mockery of the music and the sadistic foolishness of the plot established Prokofiev's reputation as master of the "grotesque." *The Buffoon* includes, incidentally, a mock-fugue, an exception among Prokofiev's works. He never learned to appreciate the fugues of Stravinsky's Octet or Piano Concerto. *The Buffoon*'s fugue is a wild one, with voices entering a half step apart, and harmonies changing on each entry, from one enriched seventh chord to another.

Diaghilev's next assignment to Prokofiev, after a long interlude, was *Stal'noi skok* (*Leap of Steel*, or *Pas d'acier*, Op. 42, 1925), which purported to deal with life in the USSR. The music, according to Nestyev, was modelled on Stravinsky's *Wedding*. According to Prokofiev's autobiography, it marked a deliberate turn away from chromaticism to diatonicism, and a challenge to the frivolities of French taste. Nicolas Nabokov, who got to know Prokofiev at about this time, vividly describes his scorn for "that old crank Satie" and his "followers"; when Nabokov timidly protested that Debussy was different, Prokofiev rejected him too. "You know what Debussy is; . . . it's jelly . . . except perhaps it's very 'personal jelly' and the jelly-maker knows what he's doing." *Leap of Steel* was the opposite of jelly.

The last of the Diaghilev ballets was *Bludni syn* (*The Prodigal Son*, Op. 46, 1928–29), an austere yet lyrical treatment of the Gospel parable. Stravinsky's *Mavra* perhaps encouraged Prokofiev here to release his most straightforward lyricism. The dance of the Beautiful Maiden, as Nestyev observes, is the prototype of the music for Juliet, Cinderella, and Natasha Rostova. Furthermore, in its vacillating play between the keys of B minor and B-flat major, this piece anticipates several of the most important later instrumental works: the First Quartet, the *Pensées* (*Thoughts*) for piano, the Seventh and Eighth Sonatas for piano. All these pieces present an almost systematic, speculative mingling of the same two keys, in a personal melodic manner that transcends the division of chromatic and diatonic harmony.

Na Dnepre (*On the Dnieper*, or *Sur le Borysthène*, Op. 51, 1930) was composed for the Paris Opéra, and produced there without success. Prokofiev commented in his autobiography:

Considering that ten years elapsed before my early lyrical music was noticed, I presume this ballet's turn will come some day, too. I attribute the cool reception given to *Sur le Borysthène* to the fact that I was too preoccupied with the subject to pay sufficient attention to form. Originality of form is hardly less important for a composer than inner content. The great classics were also great innovators. True, the composer for whom originality takes precedence over content is working primarily against himself, for others will take his new ideas and clothe them with meaning, and they, not he, will be writing for posterity. But equally unfortunate is the composer who is afraid or incapable of originality, for whereas the creator of new harmonies is bound to be eventually acknowledged, the composer who has nothing new to offer will sooner or later be forgotten.

But Prokofiev's original thoughts about the Dnieper were no more welcome in Russia than in the West.

He had settled in Russia only a few months when he was commissioned to write his first full-length ballet, in classic ballet style, *Romeo and Juliet*. The choreographer Lavrovsky and the ballerina Ulanova have written about the difficult birth of this work, which they came to regard as the best ballet since Tchaikovsky. Prokofiev did not accept their suggestions so readily as he had accepted Diaghilev's. They found his music strange and cold at first, too lightly scored in many passages, and too brief in many scenes. They persuaded him to add both weight and length. His music inspired them to give up their idea of a happy ending. His powerful themes for the solo dances, Ulanova said, "literally dictated the pattern of the dance, making our task incomparably easier." The portrayal of Juliet, growing up from a mischievous girl to a tragic lover, as Ulanova finally realized Prokofiev's pattern, was one of the finest theatrical achievements of the age. Mercutio and Friar Laurence were perfect supporting figures. But Romeo himself was strained; anyone who knew the Romeo of Tchaikovsky's *Romeo* overture, or the Siegfried of Tchaikovsky's ballet *Swan Lake*, could not help sensing that Prokofiev had tried in vain to match their passion. Worse yet, the long, loud dances of the assembled courtiers and peasants were only theatrical instead of dramatic, and the tunes for these numbers were perfunctory. For one of them Prokofiev fell back on the gavotte from his *Classical Symphony*, extending it with slight variations and sheer repetition to nearly three times its original length.

Zolushka (*Cinderella*, Op. 87, 1940–44) is a natural sequel to *Romeo*, or rather to *Juliet*. The mean stepmother and the silly sisters make targets for Prokofiev's best mockery. He extends this to the whole court of the prince, and the girls from everywhere who try in vain to wear the glass slipper. One of these is introduced with the march from *The Love for Three Oranges*. The Courtiers dance a pavane, a passepied, a (new) gavotte, and a minuet. Cinderella and the prince have a chain of waltzes, satisfactorily close to the famous waltzes of Tchaikovsky's *Sleeping Beauty* and *Nutcracker*, grand enough to blot out memories of Cinderella's lowly beginnings and the horde of helpful fairies. Nestyev strains to interpret the fairies as symbols of Nature, and Cinderella as a realistic heroine of democracy, but Prokofiev's own comment on the work recognizes the drama as a dream, designed to "give the dancers ample opportunity to display their art."

If all Prokofiev's late music were as inflated as *Romeo* and *Cinderella*, or if anything after the 1948 decree were sweeter than the Cinderella waltzes, he would be a lesser composer, no matter how many listeners loved him. But in his mind the ballets were subordinate to the operas. And the last ballet, *Stone Flower*, was more serious than *Cinderella*, more complex and risky. And finally, there were also the sonatas and symphonies.

The changes of Prokofiev's interests in concert music counterbalance the changes in his ballets. Toward the end of World War I, as a deliberate relaxation from the strain of the *Scythian Suite* and *Buffoon*, he composed five of his most charming works—the First Violin Concerto, the *Classical Symphony*, the Third Piano Concerto, and the Third and Fourth Sonatas. During World War II, as if to compensate for *Cinderella*, he wrote five of his hardest, most solid works—the First Violin Sonata, Piano Sonatas 6, 7, and 8, and the Fifth Symphony. Whereas the *Scythian Suite* and *Cinderella* are worlds apart, these ten concert pieces are clearly parts of one world, which during the interval of two decades had developed, as might be expected, toward grander scope and concentrated complexity.

From the Toccata on to the Seventh Symphony, all these works exhibit the Prokofiev personality, with its four "basic lines" and more or less deviation into fooling, laughter, and mockery. Often the quick, laughing passages are subordinated to a melancholy lyricism; this is true of *Mimolët-nosti (Fugitive Visions*, for piano, Op. 22), the First Violin Concerto (Op. 19), the First Quartet (Op. 50), and the Ninth Piano Sonata (Op. 103); melancholy has the last word even in the pieces entitled *Sarcasms* (Op. 17). In some other works, such as the Second Quartet (on Kabardinian themes, Op. 92) and the Flute Sonata (also arranged for violin, Op. 94), laughter dominates, but it is a happy, healthy laughter. Cruel mockery like that of the *Buffoon* never dominates, but it too shows up in characteristic passages such as the finale of the Second Violin Concerto (Op. 63), the scherzo and finale of the Fifth Symphony, and the waltz of the Seventh. The climax of the "toccata line" is doubtless the finale of the Seventh Sonata (Op. 83), in steady 7/8 meter. The "classical line," if this means primarily reference to the traditional patterns of large instrumental forms—variations, sonata, and rondo—held Prokofiev's allegiance throughout his career, because he appreciated the flexibility of these forms. In his most chromatic pieces, such as the Second Symphony (Op. 40) and the first two sonatinas (Op. 54), the forms may be unsatisfactory; the melodies that span remote modulations cannot span an indefinite number of them, close together. But in the last symphonies and sonatas, all bigger in scope than either the *Classical Symphony* or the extremely chromatic pieces, the forms work. Thus the "classical line" is especially firm in the first movement of the Seventh Sonata, where the "innovating line" of dissonant harmony and tonal ambiguity is pushed to its furthest extreme, and cadencing chord progressions are veiled and long delayed. On the other hand, in the slow movement of the same sonata, the "innovating line" is evident in the unpredictable form, while the very commonest chord progressions, with smooth, sweet, chromatic ornaments, take a prominent place in the opening phrase. Diverse judgments of this phrase are useful touchstones to the attitudes of the judges.

For Nestyev this is "a beautiful singing theme" in contrast to the outer movements, where "boldness and stunning power" are "so exaggerated as to make it difficult for the listener to perceive any features of Soviet reality." For the American author of a preface to the sonatas, Irwin Freundlich, and the author of a thesis on them, D. L. Kinsey, the sweet phrase is a "reversion to an obsolete romanticism," marring what would otherwise be their favorite sonata. For Francis Poulenc, writing a swift survey of all Prokofiev's piano music, the same melody is "ah! marvelous . . . one of those melodies of which Prokofiev has the secret," and an essential part of the whole sonata. Every pianist who plays this sonata must judge for himself; every listener does well to inquire how far he and the composer are at the mercy of the performer.

Prokofiev was one of the great pianists of the age, one whose influence on other pianists was so great that Harold Schonberg calls him "the New Man of the century." Heinrich Neuhaus, who heard him often, from 1915 on to his death, wrote of his playing:

Energy, confidence, indomitable will, steel rhythm, powerful tone (sometimes even hard to bear in a small room), a peculiar "epic quality" that scrupulously avoided any sense of over-refinement or intimacy (there is none in his music either), yet withal a remarkable ability to convey true lyricism, poetry, sadness, reflection, an extraordinary human warmth, and feeling for nature . . . were the principal traits of his pianism. . . What was most valuable in Prokofiev's playing was his ability to convey the composer's thought process through the medium of his execution. How well coordinated everything was, how beautifully and naturally everything fell into place for the listener. So great was the spiritual and creative impact of his music that even Prokofiev's opponents who accused him of coldness and crudeness could not but be affected by it.

In performances that fall short of such an impact, the essence of Prokofiev's music is missing.

Prokofiev was described by his friend Vladimir Dukelsky as "looking like a cross between a Scandinavian minister and a soccer player . . . His lips were unusually thick . . . and they gave his face an oddly naughty look, rather like that of a boy about to embark on some punishable and therefore tempting prank." He was an expert chess player. He was never a theorist or teacher.

The slogans—"classicism," "romanticism," "formalism," "Socialist realism"—seem absurd when confronted with this strong personality and his vast, various work. His position in history cannot be honestly assessed in such terms. His joking use of the term "classical" for a title, and the special kind of humor in the music to which he gave the title, can be appreciated more and more as knowledge of his personality and work accumulates.

In the light of his whole career we can understand that when he wrote the *Classical Symphony*, Prokofiev was not only consciously retreating from the problems of Stravinsky, and mocking history by his retreat; he was also undertaking a fresh adventure made possible by the retreat, as he explained in his autobiography:

I spent the summer of 1917 in the country near Petrograd all alone, reading Kant and working a great deal. I deliberately did not take my piano with me, for I wished to try composing without it. Until this time I had always composed at the piano, but I noticed that thematic material composed without the piano was often better. At first it seems strange when transferred to the piano, but after one has played it a few times everything falls into place. I had been toying with the idea of writing a whole symphony without the piano. I believed that the orchestra would sound more natural. That is how the project for a symphony in the Haydn style came into being; I had learned a great deal about Haydn's technique from Tcherepnin, and hence felt myself on sufficiently familiar ground to venture forth on this difficult journey without the piano.

The paradox warrants underlining: *familiar ground* makes possible the *difficult venture*.

It seemed to me that had Haydn lived to our day he would have retained his own style while accepting something of the new at the same time. This was the kind of symphony I wanted to write: a symphony in the classical style. And when I saw that my idea was beginning to work, I called it the *Classical Symphony*: in the first place because that was simpler, and secondly, for the fun of it, to "tease the geese," and in the secret hope that I would prove to be right if the symphony really did turn out to be a piece of classical music.

. . . The first part of the *Classical Symphony*, the Gavotte, had likewise been written earlier, and later on, in 1916, I sketched the first and second movements. But a good deal of work still remained to be done when I returned to it in the summer of 1917. I crossed out the first version of the finale and wrote a completely new one, endeavoring, among other things, to avoid all minor chords.

The interplay of habit, intuition, and choice could hardly be more self-conscious. Pianistic habit was rejected, for the sake of free intuition of "better" themes. Academic habit was restored, yet a whimsical negative choice—to avoid minor chords—took precedence in one movement. A conscious motivating ambition, for fame and glory, was kept "secret," not allowed to control.

In all the later fluctuations of Prokofiev's style, habits and choices of similar sorts were involved in various sorts of interplay. He never made a once-and-for-all choice, as Webern and Hindemith did. He did not chafe against all habits, as Debussy did. He did not try to organize competing habits in a hierarchy, as Bartók did. He probably harbored many a "secret hope," whose fulfillment would be more magical than logical. Yet his intuition gave him no faith comparable to Schoenberg's or Stravinsky's. He made his choices quickly, without brooding, and he supposed that some of them were mistaken. He thought he was proved right by the popularity of certain works, but he did not choose to form habits based on these—rather he continued to hope that posterity would prove him right most of the time.

The Seventh Symphony was begun as a work for children, a choice in keeping with the strictures of Khrennikov. The work somewhat outgrew this intention, but to what extent is not clear. Nestyev reports that at the session of the Composers' Union following the first performance most speakers approved the "consummate beauty" of the music, but some objected to "the composer's ascribing to the Symphony a specific programmatic meaning associated with the theme of Soviet youth." For himself, Nestyev emphasizes the undeniable wealth of melody; he suggests some apt associations, but not a narrative or dramatic program. Shostakovich, Khachaturian, and Kabalevsky all refer to the Seventh as one of their favorites.

The symphony begins with a diatonic, legato, brooding melody for the strings, firmly establishing the fundamental minor key (C-sharp). As this melody begins to repeat itself, louder than before, it is interrupted by an animated idea from the oboe, as if from a child eager to play. The new idea moves the harmony through a series of surprising progressions to a minor dominant, where the brooding melody resumes, with the animated motion as accompaniment. Now there is a slight development of motifs. Soon this subsides, to make a soft flowing accompaniment for the next big theme. This is a great song of aspiration, firmly set in a major key (F) that is to hold for the rest of the exposition. This song suggests a grand scale. Its second phrase reaches the dominant. Now the first two phrases are repeated, louder. Can such exaltation go on for an answering pair of phrases? No. The tempo slackens, and an extraordinary new soft staccato melody, with bells, brings the exposition to its cadence. Short as it is, this melody imposes its fantastic character on the whole movement. The cadence is reinforced, after a fragmentary yearning motif from the clarinet, by a consoling motif of chords from the strings.

A development section begins quietly, with a curious compromise between the bell theme and the brooding theme. This grows and absorbs motifs from the aspiring theme, but soon sinks back. Harmonies change slowly through closely related keys. A new staccato melody for clarinet in low register prepares for the recapitulation.

The brooding theme is now stronger than before, but it never completes itself. Its development is shorter than in the exposition. With the transition to the aspiring theme there is a new counterpoint for the clarinet. The aspiring theme is now in the tonic major (D-flat), richer in sonority than before. But it gives way, just as in the exposition, to the puzzling bell theme, then the clarinet solo and the consoling chords of the strings. A short coda twists the brooding motif through a poignant series of chords to a cadence on the tonic major, but a final woodwind chord insists on the minor triad.

There is no mockery in this movement. But there is much more than innocence or mindless lyricism. The four main ideas, sharply contrasting in character, are set in a complicated relation of time and tonality; the relation is as original as it is traditional. To say that the music shows a child's evasion of adult fears and hopes, whether or not Prokofiev himself intended such a program, may give a hint of this wonderful relation.

The waltz movement begins and ends in the key that served as the main contrast in the first movement (F). None of the other keys touched on have clear structural significance. The changes of tempo in this movement provide an outline of its unique form.

(Rehearsal Number 18 is the beginning of the movement.)

18 Allegretto	37 Tempo I (Allegretto)	56 Tempo I
19 accel. & cresc.	38 accel.	61 Più animato
20 Allegro	39 Allegro	64 Più mosso
26 accel. & dimin.		
27 Più mosso		
28 accel.		
30 poco a poco meno mosso		
31 Più espressivo		

In the short allegretto section, strings introduce a sweet, gliding phrase; the clarinet answers; strings propose a sequel, and the full orchestra runs off the track. Yet this idea is the main idea of the movement. In the final section the full orchestra manages to complete it. Meanwhile a variety of things have happened twice, with variants. There is no grand *Cinderella* waltz here, but something more like a Beethoven scherzo, encompassing fragments of tunes that might be by Glinka and ferocious interludes that might be by Shostakovich. The whole could be only Prokofiev.

The slow movement is soft throughout, and steady. Its main melody has two phrases, loaded with expressive appoggiaturas. It is exposed, with varied repetitions and a codetta, all in the key (A-flat) that is dominant of the basic key of the symphony. Then comes a sort of trio section, mournful in character, beginning in the main key itself and passing through closely related minor keys to a surprising remote key (E), where the main idea returns, only to go quickly to the codetta, with another surprising harmony (C). Then the main idea begins once more, in the basic key of the symphony (D-flat), with the rich sonority of the first movement's aspiring theme. Halfway through, the sonority thins out to the soloistic texture characteristic of the exposition. At the last moment, unobtrusively, the key switches to the dominant (A-flat). In a short coda, slowing down, there are some new surprising chords, and the very last chord is disturbed by a seventh from the trumpet, accented and then left by skip.

The finale, a rondo-sonata movement, has a rollicking refrain like a polka, led by the strings, with many ingenious mild developments in which winds and bells take part, but never all together. As the exposition nears its end, the tempo slackens for a new chromatic theme, legato, espressivo. The woodwinds dissolve this in scale passages, which make a transition, with further slowing, to the central episode. This is a swaggering march, beginning in a key (C) opposed to the main key. Woodwinds introduce it quietly (the first time that winds have introduced a theme of such sustained importance). Strings join for the second phrase, which ends on the dominant. The whole is repeated, louder, with drums too. Then a still bigger, slightly varied repetition begins; in the middle this switches dramatically to the main key, and the full orchestra, *fortissimo*, ends on the dominant, where the tempo snaps back for a recapitulation. The march has never arrived at its own cadence; it seems destined to return for completion in a glorious optimistic coda.

The recapitulation proceeds, with minor but fascinating variants of the exposition. The slow, *espressivo* theme returns, and now a transition to the coda is made by the full orchestra, with rich chords. The coda is not the march, after all. Instead, the aspiring theme from the first movement restores the tonic. A repetition of this theme, with trumpet leading the tutti, twists the key at the climax toward the relative major (E) of the minor tonic. Here there is no cadence but a quick diminuendo. The strange bell-theme from the first movement restores the minor tonic, and then dissolves into an ostinato accompaniment for a series of short declamatory cadencing phrases, slower and slower, finally softer and softer, until everything fades away.

At the first performance the quiet ending was condemned. Prokofiev provided an "alternative," which is in fact an obviously inorganic addition: a hushed return of the polka refrain, rounded off by a few brisk tutti chords. Still no march, and no denial of the puzzling bells. But enough liveliness to persuade some listeners both in Russia and elsewhere that the whole symphony was happily subservient to the tastes of Stalin. Nestyev recognizes and prefers the "inexpressible charm" of the original ending. The "alternative" was discreetly shelved by Soviet conductors. It was played gleefully in America. But any informed listener who wished to do so could ignore it.

Only through the patient consideration of a whole piece such as the Seventh Symphony could Prokofiev's adventure be appreciated as well as his achievement, and his achievement evaluated as it deserved to be. Only in the whole form did the classical elements and the innovating elements, the lyricism and the rhythm, all have their full meaning. Only in the relation of the "alternative" to the whole symphony was Prokofiev's relation to 20th-century society adequately symbolized.

Outside the Soviet Union and its sphere of influence it was easy to ignore most of Prokofiev's music, including the Seventh Symphony. For Western musicians none of it could justly claim as much study as the music of Schoenberg, Bartók, and Stravinsky. But a little study was enough to show that it was not rightly to be classified with that of Glazunov or Khachaturian, much less with Lehár or Gershwin. In the decade after his death Prokofiev was gaining friends around the world, not losing them, and many of his friends, however different from each other their preferences and their interpretations, were finding more and more of his music to prize.

CHAPTER XXV

Composers Comparable to Prokofiev Born 1892 or Earlier

PROKOFIEV'S fond attachment to old habits of harmony and rhythm was shared not only by the many performers and listeners who loved his music, but also by a majority of contemporary composers, that is, by a greater number of remarkable creative musicians than had lived in any earlier century. The old habits, inevitably disturbed in the course of a composer's education when he encountered the music of Debussy and his successors, could still be incorporated into all sorts of new individual styles, and many of these, like Prokofiev's, could give immense delight and edification to performers, listeners, and still younger composers, despite the subordinate place assigned them by some historians. Koechlin, Vaughan Williams, Berg, Martin, Poulenc, Copland, Weill, Dallapiccola, Distler, and Alain are subordinate in roughly the same sense that Fauré, Janáček, Mahler, and Ravel are subordinate in their time; a swift history might pass them by without loss of continuity, but not without betraying the purpose to which history itself, in the view taken here, is properly subordinate.

The range of variety among the many relatively minor and relatively conservative styles of the 20th century is still great, as the names just listed may suggest. Many of these styles differ from Prokofiev's as much as from Schoenberg's. Several of them obviously incorporate something from Schoenberg along with some of the habits that he rejected. Many show a stronger attraction to Stravinsky than Prokofiev shows. Many show similarities to Bartók, especially in their relation to folk music. Many show some contagion from jazz. In the 1930s and 1940s some approached Hindemith; in the 1950s some were superficially affected by Webern. Their subordination to Prokofiev in our survey does not imply any influence from him, or even a similarity in any particular detail—only a vague similarity in attitude toward musical habits, which serves as a convenient means of distinguishing them from composers parallel to Hindemith. Further, it is convenient to treat first the composers born before Prokofiev or within the next year (1892) and then the younger ones, sweeping rapidly around the globe for each generation.

In affirming habits of musical thought, these composers affirmed also, with varying emphases, their concern for listeners and for the social institutions—church, theater, school, and nation—that enabled the musical profession to survive. In contrast to an adventurer like Varèse or a classicist like Piston (though not to Webern or Hindemith, Schoenberg or Stravinsky) these composers gave only part of their attention to instrumental music, preferring usually the participation of human voices and an attachment to words. Their social concerns ranged from mercenary to fanatically idealistic. But in any case they were not content with the ISCM or other new esoteric institutions, which seemed to them no more than laboratories for experiment. To be worthy of survival, the products of the musical profession, they believed, should somehow prove useful to laymen—to several thousands if not to several millions.

Church, theater, school, and nation, on the whole, provided little real demand for new music. Shaken by the vast, swift, baffling technological and social changes of the 20th century, these institutions clung to music of the late 19th century for an assurance of continuity. They accepted or even welcomed the revival of music from the 18th century and earlier periods. For new music they made room only by exception, and in new music they preferred old styles, modified as little as possible.

Thus the composers were frustrated in their hope of serving society. The total proportion of new music published and performed, in contrast to old music, was remarkably smaller than ever before. Of all new music used in churches, theaters, and schools (as also in concerts), the proportion that showed new styles was extremely small. None of the new styles of the 20th century became established as *the* musical style of a society, in the way that Strauss waltzes, Sousa marches, Sankey "gospel hymns," Sullivan operettas, Puccini operas, and Sibelius symphonies were established. Pale imitations of the models of these old styles found a readier market than even the mildest of new styles. Yet the imitations could not survive the test of continued use any better than the most esoteric experiments. And on the contrary, the best works in the new but conservative styles could eventually reach their scattered unknown friends, just as the works of Webern did. The phonograph could facilitate this process, even more than printing had long done for poetry and fiction.

Nearly every one of these composers, like Prokofiev, attracted some friends who ranked him higher than Schoenberg, Stravinsky, or Bartók (without knowing these men's work so well). Many of the minor masters revealed in their music, as they did in their lives, characters more amiable than those of their greatest contemporaries. To celebrate their work and to guide new friends to it is as important as to locate them in their historical context. At the same time, to indicate, for the benefit of their old friends and of others bewildered by the amount and variety of their work, some of its connections with the greatest achievements, both past and contemporary, is in keeping with their concern for public communities.

A famous artist, only incidentally a composer, who pondered his relation to the vast public with naive good sense, undistracted by the lore of history and esthetics, was Charles Chaplin (b. 1886). He won the public with his creation of the "Tramp," a fresh variant of the pantomime Pierrot, contemporary with the Pierrots of Schoenberg and Stravinsky. Around World War I Chaplin made a series of short films that were at once enormously popular and deeply respected by the most diverse critics; they remain among the finest achievements in the 20th century's distinctive medium of art and entertainment. The music for these films could be anything or nothing. Chaplin's efforts at composition were in those days only a private diversion and inspiration for him. When sound film was developed (1927) he studied composition in earnest, and thereafter provided the music for all his films. In addition he composed hundreds of pieces that remained unpublished in the files of Bourne, Inc., New York. His musical style, perfectly appropriate for the films, was an individual poetic shaping of elements from the styles popular in the English music halls where he grew up. When his musical craft sufficed for his purposes, he went on composing with no further musical development. Meanwhile, more sensibly than many real composers, he had formulated his answers to the great questions, "Can Art Be Popular?" and "Does the Public Know What It Wants?" Yes, he said, art can and even should be popular, but commerce can make shoddy substitutes temporarily more popular. People know what they truly want after it is available, not before. No formula does justice to their changing unsatisfied desires. An artist's changing personal taste will guide him to what the public wants of him more surely than any study of his own previous work or that of anyone else. If he neglects his own taste, either condescending to an audience or straining to impress his critics, he botches his work.

Few composers could be so sure of their own changing taste as Chaplin. Stravinsky, changing far more, protested his sureness so vehemently as to reinforce doubts of it that were aroused by the changes. Prokofiev, changing less, acknowledged more sensitivity to public reactions. Some composers were naturally affected more than Prokofiev.

One of the most prominent composers in the years between the wars, Arthur Honegger (1892–1955), defined his taste only by reference to the competing claims of public and critics. In his short, sad book, *I Am a Com-*

poser (1951), he testified: "My taste and my effort have always been to write music that would be accessible to the great mass of listeners, and yet sufficiently free of banality to interest the connoisseurs." This he succeeded in doing at the outset of his career with the dramatic oratorio, *Le Roi David* (*King David*, 1921). Again with *Jeanne d'Arc au bûcher* (*Joan of Arc at the Stake*, 1938), he won similar success, though here his effort was more obvious; listeners outside France were more fickle; and connoisseurs' judgments were divided. Within the smaller scope of the French theater, ballet, and motion picture, Honegger achieved many smaller successes, but no "great mass of listeners" followed his career, few performers installed his works in their regular repertories, and very few connoisseurs were keen enough to appreciate Honegger's distinctive flavor or his enormous range of technique and emotion. He found film music easy to compose, and opera most congenial. His five symphonies (1930–50) and three string quartets (1917, 1934, 1936) cost him more effort. For the piano he wrote some charming short pieces, including those of *Un Cahier romand* (*A Swiss Notebook*, 1923), but no sonata.

Honegger's style was essentially choral, whatever the medium. He played the violin only a little, the piano less. Singing was the basis of his habits. His vocal melodies fit the words marvelously, giving them a rhythm and intonation more like ordinary speech than Schoenberg's *Sprechstimme*. Accented syllables are often short, producing a kind of emphasis very surprising to listeners familiar with French singing. Honegger regarded his novel prosody as his most important technique. In the accompaniments, frequent ostinatos and a few strong chord progressions, conventionally coordinated with the melody, gave coherence and emphasis to long spans, while inner voices with chromatic passing tones, often in contrary motion, prepared the way for modulations that would link one passage to the next. Contrapuntal tricks were frequent, but somewhat arbitrarily imposed on the basic texture of melody and accompaniment.

Honegger's forms merited some special study. He had rebelled against the academic formalism of his teacher, d'Indy, without ever rejecting the atmosphere of Wagner and Franck that had inspired d'Indy. He was bored by recapitulations, even in the classics. He had no use for "tonal schemes" or any other scaffolding for forms except poetry. When he had no text, he relied on momentary intuition. The unique shapes of his orchestral and chamber music were always interesting; to some listeners they were deeply satisfying as well. At the end of his life Honegger acknowledged Prokofiev as his greatest contemporary; perhaps he would have done better to restudy the traditional forms and renew them as Prokofiev did.

If it is possible to imagine combining a wise, humble self-confidence steadier than Chaplin's with a craft and imagination more powerful than

Honegger's, this combination may characterize the little-known composer Charles Koechlin (1867–1950). At the end of his long, full life Koechlin wrote a profound essay on "Art, Freedom, and the Ivory Tower," in which he said: "I hold that there is no contradiction between the Ivory Tower on the one hand and on the other the deep utility of our art—its social role . . . We compose to manifest as well as possible our inner state. To do so we must have complete freedom." In accordance with this creed, Koechlin had exercised complete freedom in the use of every technical device that he learned from his teachers at the conservatory, including Fauré and Gedalge, from his contemporaries, including Debussy and Satie, and from his most important juniors, Schoenberg and Stravinsky. With what rare, penetrating sympathy he understood them is evident in his treatises on *Fauré, Debussy, Harmony, Orchestration,* and *The Evolution of Modern Harmony,* as well as in his compositions. He made all techniques serve to manifest his various expressive purposes, which were usually explicit in the titles, texts, and media of performance that he chose. On the other hand, he shunned publicity, leaving most of his works unpublished, on file at the Centre de Documentation de Musique Internationale, Paris. Many of the best works, according to the few Ivory Tower friends and critics who knew them, were even unperformed. Yet Koechlin's confidence in the ultimate social utility of his work as a whole was unshakable, and this confidence shines in the music, clearly addressed to ordinary listeners as well as professionals. The long catalogue of his works tantalized anyone who knew a few of them well. As to which of the big works for orchestra, or chorus and orchestra, were most important, each of several students had his own opinion. Jeanne Herscher-Clément, writing in 1936, recommended especially the *Hymne au soleil* (*Hymn to the Sun,* 1933), an outdoor festive piece, which later formed part of a vast *Symphony of Hymns.* W. H. Mellers, in his "plea for Koechlin" of 1942, picked *L'Abbaye* (*The Abbey,* 1899–1902, 1906–08) as "one of the few masterpieces of the 20th century." Hélène Jourdan-Morhange, in 1955, praised the *Seven Stars Symphony* (1933) and especially its finale, a portrait of Chaplin. Paul Collaer, in 1955, placed *La Course de printemps* (*The Race of Spring,* 1925–27), part of a huge cycle based on Kipling's *Jungle Book,* "among the most admirable works of music produced in the 20th century." For Pierre Renaudin, in 1958, the peak was *Le Buisson ardent* (*The Burning Bush,* 1938, 1945, based on Rolland's *Jean Christophe*). All agreed in lamenting the general neglect of these works.

The smaller works of Koechlin showed a striking change of interest around the critical year 1911. Up till then they were chiefly songs, but at that point, according to Renaudin, the forty-four-year-old composer felt ready to venture into "the hazardous field" of chamber music, which he cultivated steadily thereafter, along with other fields.

Koechlin's first string quartet (1911–13) revealed the distinctive style that was to be found in all the later published works. Long phrases of supple melody range over two octaves or more, proceeding mostly along diatonic scales, with a spontaneity very rare in the 20th century. The scales that these melodies start off with are usually familiar major scales, but sooner or later both modal and chromatic liberties are taken, so that the melodies seem to be expanding like some wild vine. Often there is at the start a drone-like accompaniment, and in general the chords are widely spaced, hardly connected by voice-leading, but from time to time there are swift changes of chords, among which those built on fourths are frequent. Moreover, the melodies branch out into freely imitative counterpoint, which often becomes elaborate and polytonal. The whole harmonic-contrapuntal technique is radically novel, yet somewhat bland. It makes no sense unless the melodies are performed with the utmost care for phrasing and for fluctuating dynamics—mostly in the range from *mp* to *pp*. The rhythms likewise are novel but unaggressive. Many of them are based on the patterns of jig or siciliana, but the melodies freely overrun the basic pattern with extra measures, half measures, beats, and half beats.

The prominent major scale, jig rhythm, and contrapuntal devices in Koechlin's music may be deceptive. At a glance, or a casual listening, these elements of his style have led some musicians to think of him as a minor "neo-Classicist." But Koechlin shuns the qualities that his contemporary Roussel approved in the classical reaction of the 1920s—precision, emphasis, robust or even brutal vigor. Koechlin, in 1926, deplored "The Return to Bach" as an anti-Debussy movement; he protested that Debussy was closer to the essence of Bach than his opponents, and warned that "the ceaseless search for movement and vigor, the love of rhythm *per se*, all this is a risky course for anyone who does not naturally possess this vigor. It has a basis in pride." In Koechlin's music there is no such pride. His jig rhythms often yield to rubato. His harmonies include the sweetest, clearest traditional chords. His dissonance is never for the sake of percussion or torment or satire, but rather for added sweetness or contrapuntal clarity.

Besides the quartets, a series of sonatinas and suites for various instruments embody Koechlin's remarkable late style. Beginning about 1935, he composed many unaccompanied melodies, some for flute, some for oboe, some for wordless voice. In 1947, at eighty, he ventured further into what he called "atonal, serial style," with a set of orchestral interludes that he intended to use along with portions of the *Seven Stars Symphony* for a projected ballet. He was as active and as generously interested in youth as ever. If he had lived to be ninety he would doubtless have contributed his wisdom to the development of electronic music.

Darius Milhaud (b. 1892), though twenty-five years younger than Koech-lin, was his good friend, a fellow pupil of Gedalge, and in many ways a similar composer. Koechlin dedicated to Milhaud, the young violinist from Aix-en-Provence, his viola sonata (1906–15) and Milhaud gave the first performance. In his autobiography, *Notes Without Music*, Milhaud tells how Koechlin visited him in Aix in 1914:

He arrived at L'Enclos swathed in a great shepherd's cloak, with half a water-melon under his arm. We talked together about music, discussing the *Sacre du Printemps* which we had hailed with such enthusiasm at its first performance a year before. We not only admired its violent rhythms, its harmonic discords and polytonality, all of which had been foreshadowed in *Petrushka*, but, on quite a different plane, the novelty of the work. In it the ballet was getting away from picturesque externals towards a dramatic and barbaric goal. Many musicians were quite unable to accept this rift with the past. Despite his admiration for Stravinsky, Debussy was anxious about the lines along which he was developing. Schmitt declared that 'all that was left to him was to tear up his music.' (What a pity he did not do so!) The younger generation, on the contrary, felt encouraged by this work, in spite of its profoundly Russian character, which kept it alien to our own aspirations.

Like Koechlin, Milhaud believed in using all sorts of techniques, old and new, to express all sorts of ideas and feelings. Eventually he surpassed Koechlin in sheer quantity of output and in variety of media. He shared Koechlin's devotion to the rhythms of jig and siciliana, and in addition he often adopted 18th-century forms with literal recapitulations. He shared Koechlin's interest in polytonality, which for him often meant accompany-ing a conventional expository phrase of melody with a progression of con-ventional chords, or parallel chords, only in contrasting keys, one of which would finally resolve into the other.

Unlike Koechlin, more nearly like Roussel, still more like Stravinsky (who was unquestionably for Milhaud the greatest composer of the cen-tury, and who delighted him above all when he renewed the lyric tradition with his comic opera, *Mavra*), Milhaud included among his favorite moods one that he indicated in his talks with Claude Rostand and in the tempo marks of many scores as "truculent." This mood he could share, moreover, with his life-long friend Honegger, and with their literary promoter, Jean Cocteau.

Thanks to Cocteau, Milhaud won a reputation for more truculence than he himself ever showed, beginning with his piano duet, *Le Bœuf sur le toit* (*Bull on the Roof*, 1919). This music was characteristic of him in many ways, while the circumstances of its composition and its fame, as he ex-plained them in his autobiography, were characteristic of his faulty public relations. Milhaud selected for this composition nearly two dozen delightful tunes from the popular dance music of Brazil, where he had worked during the war as cultural attaché in the French embassy, under the poet Paul Claudel. The catchy title was simply the title of one of the Brazilian tunes. Milhaud put them into an extraordinarily rigid, symmetrical rondo form, and spiced them with polytonal accompaniments. The form and the resulting mood of bittersweet nostalgia struck him as appropriate for accompanying any one of Chaplin's twenty-minute comedies. (Performers and hearers of the *Bull* would do well to bear in mind this association.) But Cocteau persuaded Milhaud to let him use the music for a new ballet; he then imposed on it, for all the world, his vivid associations, deliberately incongruous, farcical, topical, and cruel, repeating and exaggerating motifs from *Parade*. The *Bull* ballet was so successful in its day that a Paris bar was named for it. (Some program notes give the impression that the music is named for the bar.) Though the ballet was seldom revived, its moods were attached not only to this music, but even to Milhaud's personality and style as a whole. When David Drew correctly observed the bland innocence of the music, he protested that it was not shocking or witty, but "heavy-handed, boring, and confused . . . bad music." Drew had been misled by Cocteau's shock, and thus missed the sweetness and candor that actually made Milhaud's music live.

Besides the *Bull*, Milhaud and Cocteau collaborated on several other works, which invariably attracted attention and further distorted the common idea of Milhaud. His only ballet for Diaghilev was Cocteau's "monument to frivolity," *Le Train bleu* (*The Blue Express*, 1924). His most popular chamber opera was Cocteau's sardonic tale, *Le pauvre matelot* (*The Wretched Sailor*, 1926). The music of these pieces lacked the unfashionable grandeur of Milhaud's more ambitious works, and the quiet tenderness of his intimate masterpieces. These qualities, potentially appealing to a wider audience than Cocteau's, were long obscured by the truculence that was in fact no more than a foil for them.

Milhaud's generous, tolerant humanity and the musical style that fitted it were both mature before he met Cocteau, and consistently maintained long afterward. There was, he told Rostand, no evolution to be traced in his career, but rather a continuous outpouring along several parallel channels: opera, chamber music, symphony, concerto, chamber orchestral music, "divertissement," ballet, folkloristic music, and adaptations of "classics." Some consideration of all these "channels" is necessary for any fair estimate of Milhaud's historical importance.

Milhaud's grandeur showed up especially in his operas, and throughout the series of collaborations with Paul Claudel:

Protée (*Proteus*, incidental music 1913, rev. 1916, 1919)
L'Orestie d'Æschyle (*The Orestes Trilogy of Aeschylus*): *Agamemnon*, 1913; *Choéphores*, 1915; *Euménides*, 1916

L'Homme et son désir (*Man and His Desire*, ballet, 1917)
Christophe Colomb (grand opera, with film, 1928)
La Sagesse (*Wisdom*, cantata, 1930)
La Paix (*Peace*), Les deux cités (*Two Cities*), La Guerre (*War*) (all cantatas, 1930-35)
L'Annonce faite à Marie (*The Annunciation*, 1932)

Two more operas had librettos by Milhaud's cousin and wife, Madeleine: *Médée* (*Medea*, 1930) and *Bolivar* (1943). Two more were collaborations with Milhaud's oldest friend, the poet Armand Lunel: *Maximilien* (1932), about 19th-century Mexico, and *David* (1954), about ancient and modern Israel. All these big works repelled critics like Drew with their passages of opaque counterpoint on undistinguished melodies, their frequent ostinatos, and their streams of chords, while other critics greatly admired what D. J. Grout called "the completely impersonal, spectacular, monumental effect of this type of musical construction."

Several other operas and other vocal works, less grandiose, evoked a different kind of admiration. Thus Paul Collaer, surveying Milhaud's whole work up to 1947, finds the purest example in *Les Malheurs d'Orphée* (*The Woes of Orpheus*, 1921–24), and the present writer's favorite is *Esther de Carpentras* (1922–25). For both these, words were provided by Lunel. Both are modest chamber works, made up of very short numbers, all containing tuneful melodies. A similar refinement of Milhaud's style was represented by his setting of the Jewish Sacred Service (1947), which won the approval even of Drew.

In Milhaud's catalogue of eighteen quartets (1912–1951), thirteen symphonies (1940–65), and over twenty concertos (from 1926 on), his grandeur prevailed. In his many suites of short pieces, innocent tenderness and nostalgia alternated with gaiety, and among these were the most popular of all his works:

Saudades do Brasil (*Souvenirs of Brazil*, 1921) for piano
Suite provençale (1937) for orchestra
La Cheminée du roi René (*Roadside Scenes in Provence*, 1939) for wind quintet
Scaramouche (1939) for two pianos
La Muse ménagère (*The Household Muse*, 1944) for piano
Suite française (1945) for band.

At least one later suite can be recommended as deserving to rank with these: *Les Charmes de la vie* (*The Joys of Life*, after Watteau, 1957) for chamber orchestra. In a valuable survey of Milhaud's chamber music up to 1957, Colin Mason recommends especially the sonatinas for flute (1922), clarinet (1927), and oboe (1954) as deserving popularity.

How Milhaud formed his style he described very well to Rostand. He encountered the music of Debussy in 1905, when he was thirteen. He played Debussy's Quartet; then he studied the score of *Pelléas*, though he lacked the ability to play it at the piano or to analyze its chords and counterpoints. His earliest compositions show his admiration of Debussy, but the resemblances are superficial. When he decided in 1911 to abandon the violin for full-time study in composition, he resolved to "break the spell" of Debussy, although "my heart always remained faithful." He acknowledged the help he got toward this end from Koechlin and from the "French homespun" style of Albéric Magnard (1865–1915). Probably he was affected also by Richard Strauss, for he delighted in *Salome* and *Elektra* and still more in the brand-new *Rosenkavalier*, whose polytonal passages were more like Milhaud's than Koechlin's. All these influences encouraged him to indulge the habits of rhythm and melody that he had formed in childhood, while Debussy and Stravinsky provided what Milhaud took for a warrant to neglect the conventions of harmony that he had never thoroughly mastered. He set out to explore polytonal chords and contrapuntal textures in a systematic way that must have seemed to Koechlin delightfully naive; in his article on "Polytonality and Atonality" Milhaud concluded that these procedures, for all their fascination, were superficial, in contrast to melody "that comes from the heart." He preserved his naïveté and abjured the system, having added to his stock of habits a few serviceable rich chords, "more subtle in sweetness, more powerful in violence." From then on, he could compose with a fluency that was astonishing in the 20th-century. He could adapt various kinds of heartfelt melody—folksong and even jazz—to his style. He could, as it were, open the faucet wide and run it long for his grand works, and economize with brief spurts and gentle trickles for his modest ones. For all the variety of his works, there was, as he told Rostand, no stylistic development.

Milhaud's decorative polytonality, though encouraged by the example of Stravinsky, was utterly different from Stravinsky's "polar" tensions. In the 1920s the difference was too subtle for most observers, and Milhaud's ideas and practices won more prestige than they deserved. During the 1950s they won a more appropriate fame in connection with the jazz of his pupil, Dave Brubeck.

Milhaud's own interest in jazz was shortlived, but it inspired one of his undisputed masterpieces, *La Création du monde* (*The Creation of the World*, 1923). Cocteau aroused his curiosity, and on a visit to London in 1920 Milhaud seized an opportunity to hear repeatedly the band of Billy Arnold. Then in 1922, in Harlem, he was overwhelmed by the authentic music in many theaters and dance-halls. Back in Paris, he kept playing records that he had brought from New York. The occasion to make use of his new material was provided by a ballet, on which he collaborated with Fernand Léger and Blaise Cendrars. Here the "blue" thirds, the syncopations, and the sounds of saxophone and drums found a classic form. By 1926, when Milhaud next visited America, his interest in jazz was exhausted.

Milhaud's association with Satie, like the association of both composers with Cocteau, led to mistaken evaluations more often than to any accurate historical explanation. Milhaud was a good friend of Satie from 1918 until Satie died (1925). He loved Satie's *Socrate*, and still more his generous faith in the young. But Milhaud had little humor, and less fantasy. In 1921 the two collaborated to provide for an exhibit of paintings what they called "musique d'ameublement" (interior-decorating music). This was no publicity prank, but a serious prophecy of Muzak. Satie had the wry insight to propose the idea; Milhaud had the modest generosity to carry it out, whereas it offended the taste of the younger composers Poulenc and Auric as much as that of the public. Aside from this occasion, Milhaud's work showed nothing that could surely be attributed to Satie's influence, and Satie must have disapproved of many of Milhaud's persistent traits. Yet Milhaud appealed to the authority of Satie, rather than to any "grand line" of technical or stylistic tradition, when he thought about the future of music; he put his faith in youth—a boundless faith, for, he told Rostand, "Youth works with love, and what is done with love wins through in the end, sooner or later."

Two French contemporaries of Milhaud seemed, to their friends, to deserve as much attention as he did, though their works were far less known abroad: Jacques Ibert (1890–1962) and Georges Migot (b. 1891). Ibert's ballet, *Le Chevalier errant* (*Knight Errant*, completed in 1951) was the work that he regarded as "the synthesis of his favorite forms." Even more than his better-known early works, *Angélique* (opera, 1927) and *Escales* (*Ports of Call*, suite for orchestra, 1919), the late ballet showed superb craft and irresistible charm. Migot was more distinctive—a mystic whose techniques were inspired by Debussy. His outstanding works were oratorios, such as the *Passion* (1948).

Two slightly older composers, accepting the historic position against which Milhaud and Ibert rebelled—minor followers of Debussy—nevertheless achieved distinction: André Caplet (1878–1925) and Paul Le Flem (b. 1881). In the perspective of the 1960s these composers too were worthy of wider recognition.

Two more French composers represented more specialized interests: Marcel Dupré (b. 1886), and Louis Durey (b. 1888). Dupré was the preëminent organist and organ-composer of his generation, linking his masters Widor and Vierne with his pupils Langlais, Alain, and Messiaen. Durey was the oldest member of the famous group, *Les Six*, from which he withdrew officially in 1921; in the 1930s and on into the 1960s he was the leading French musician of Communist Front organizations.

Dupré was rivalled, as composer even more than as organist, by two contemporaries in neighboring countries: Paul de Maleingreau (Belgium, 1887–1956) and Hendrik Andriessen (Netherlands, b. 1892). Both of them were able to incorporate influences from Debussy and from popular music into a style whose sincere piety was a precious heritage. Later, more self-conscious seekers for a popular Catholic or Episcopal music seldom achieved so much. These men's works, on the contrary, were pale by comparison with Milhaud's *Sacred Service*, equally sincere and far more vigorous.

Milhaud lent vital encouragement to at least one older composer, as he did to many younger ones. He met Heitor Villa-Lobos (1887–1959) in 1915 in Brazil. Villa-Lobos was playing the cello for a living, as he had done ever since he was left an orphan at the age of twelve. He was also composing fantastic operas and symphonies, amalgamating popular tunes with snatches of the techniques of Puccini and Tchaikovsky. Once acquainted with the liberating examples of Debussy, Stravinsky, and Milhaud, Villa-Lobos quickly rose to be the most eminent composer of Latin America. Moreover, he attracted more attention in Europe than most North Americans; Messiaen, for instance, acknowledged an influence from him. But this eminence was not unchallenged.

The extent and variety of Villa-Lobos's two thousand works literally defied description. The lists compiled by Andrade Muricy and Carleton Sprague Smith aroused some skepticism; these compilers claimed no acquaintance with a large proportion of the works they listed, and especially with the most ambitious ones. Just after Villa-Lobos died, Carlos Maul accused him of unscrupulous plagiarism and misrepresentation, documenting his claims in a book. Much earlier (1943) Lisa Peppercorn discovered frequent rearrangements with new titles. If a complete critical list could ever be established, it would provide a basis for better judgment than any current one. All judgments agreed, however, in one point: that Villa-Lobos's work was extraordinarily uneven.

The untrammeled energy and great charm of such works as the Wind Quintet (1928) and the *Bachianas brasileiras* No. 5, for soprano and eight cellos (Aria 1938, and Dansa 1945) continually brought Villa-Lobos new friends. But the blaring thick sounds, loose forms, and *cliché* harmonies of some orchestral and piano pieces repelled those who, like the present writer, tried gingerly to penetrate further into his world. Perhaps, as C. S. Smith suggested, his greatest monument was the *Guia prático*, a series of music texts for the public schools of Brazil, to which he devoted much of his overflowing energy after 1935. Smith recommended also the songs and guitar pieces. On the other hand Vasco Mariz, a conscientious biographer, opined that in general the works for orchestra and piano were most important.

———— • • ————

Several North Americans born in the 1880s made habitual use of some sort of popular music as material for mildly novel styles in operas and concert works. Three of these achieved enough success, both at home and abroad, to keep their names alive, although their work was soon ignored just as thoroughly as that of such similar older composers as Farwell and Gilbert. Indeed the fleeting popularity of these men was an obstacle to serious consideration of their works. Perhaps scholars of a later generation would be ready for them. Each had his own favorite melodic source: Charles Wakefield Cadman (1881–1946) American Indian music; John Powell (1882–1963) Anglo-American ballads; and Louis Gruenberg (1884–1964) jazz. A more eclectic contemporary was Deems Taylor (b. 1885), whose operas were the most successful of any American's before Gian Carlo Menotti's (b. 1911), though less so than those of dozens of German contemporaries.

Meanwhile the popular business of "Tin Pan Alley" flourished on its nourishment from jazz, with leaders like Jerome Kern (1885–1945) and Irving Berlin (b. 1888).

Somewhat more distinctive and more durable than most other "serious" American music between Ives and Copland was that of Charles Tomlinson Griffes (1884–1920). The label associated with Griffes by whoever knew his name, for instance by Nicolas Slonimsky, was "foremost American composer in the impressionist genre." This was too simple to do him justice. A study of all his songs, by William Treat Upton, while arguing persuasively that a few of them were worthy of Ravel, pointed out that none were comparable to Debussy, several were close to Strauss and Busoni, and others were based on Japanese and Javanese materials supplied to Griffes by the singer Eva Gauthier. A thorough biography by Edward Maisel made clear the variety and complexity of his work. (Maisel's interpretation of Griffes's personality offended friends and patrons, but remained unrefuted.) Well trained as a pianist by the age of nineteen, Griffes went to Germany to become a virtuoso; he returned at twenty-three (1907) to support himself teaching school in his native region of New York State until he could establish himself as a composer. At thirty-five he had nearly succeeded. But influenza killed him just as he began to work at full speed. His most ambitious piece was a Piano Sonata (1919). Maisel elucidated the structural role in the sonata of a quasi-Oriental scale and an adaptation of Scriabin's harmony. For Maisel the Sonata was "the first major utterance in American music." Griffes showed both by his playing and by his comments an extraordinarily intelligent sympathy with Schoenberg and Stravinsky. Copland, Varèse, Prokofiev, and Milhaud were among the many who mourned his early death.

Ernest Bloch (1880–1959) brought to American music, as already noted, a new range of technique. A native of Switzerland, he was becoming internationally prominent when he settled here in 1917. He had learned from the examples of Debussy, Strauss, and Mussorgsky to transcend his thorough academic training in composition, under Jaques-Dalcroze and others, and in string playing under Ysaÿe. By 1912, Bloch had achieved a personal style, independent of the four great new styles that were emerging at the same time. Later, he was able to absorb from these new styles some of their technical tricks, without compromising any essentials of his own personality or his strong democratic idealism. He made the techniques serve his old-fashioned purposes of prophecy and exhortation, while he sacrificed only some luxuries that had been superfluous to him all along. Thus his *Concerto Grosso No. 1*, for piano and strings (1925), had his usual force and poignance, with an unusual spareness of texture and wariness of chromatics, doubtless in response to the famous economies of Stravinsky, Satie, and Hindemith. The Piano Quintet (1923) used quarter tones very effectively, in complete subordination to the tonally organized melody and the powerful conventional rhetoric. The Third String Quartet (1953) had Bloch's usual reassuring tonal structure, enhanced by unusual contrapuntal ingenuities that involve a twelve-tone series as the basis of its final passacaglia and fugue, reflecting a concern for some of the questions that obsessed Schoenberg.

In the same spirit, though not so successfully, Bloch tried on occasion to absorb other elements into his style; the symphonies *America* (1926) and *Helvetia* (1929) were potpourris of popular tunes that failed to blend. Their efforts to exhort an audience to patriotic fervor seemed accordingly strained. To make room for the special materials of these works, Bloch did sacrifice something essential to his style—the peculiar melodies and harmonies that he had associated with his Jewishness and with his ardent, lifelong interest in "the Jewish soul, the complex, glowing, agitated soul that I feel vibrating throughout the Bible." His most famous pieces are among those whose titles establish this association: *Schelomo*, rhapsody for cello and orchestra (1915); *Baal Shem—Three Pictures of Chassidic Life* for violin and piano (1923); and the *Sacred Service* (1934).

Joseph Achron (1886–1943) brought to America in 1925 a Jewish musical tradition quite different from Bloch's personal and prophetic one. Achron was born in Lithuania and grew up in Russia. As a prodigious violinist (one of Auer's best pupils) and a promising composer (pupil of Liadov) he was drawn into the Society for Jewish Folk Music, which flourished in

Moscow from 1908 to 1918 under the instigation of the critic Joel Engel (1868–1927), who later tried to establish it in Israel. According to Albert Weisser's book, *The Modern Renaissance of Jewish Music*, Achron was the best composer of the group, which included also

> Moses Milner (b. 1882)
> Lazare Saminsky (1882–1959)
> Alexander Krein (1883–1951)
> Mikhail Gnessin (1887–1957).

The group's ideal of a Yiddish operatic and symphonic style helped Achron define his own personality; at once he composed his most famous piece, a Hebrew Melody for violin and orchestra (1912). Thereafter he expanded and refined his style, incorporating something from Schoenberg and winning Schoenberg's rare praise; he anticipated characteristic developments of the best younger composers who settled in Israel.

Abraham Zevi Idelsohn (1882–1938) was the great pioneer scholar of Hebrew music. His operas and other compositions were negligible by comparison with those of Bloch and Achron, not to mention Schoenberg, but his ten-volume *Thesaurus of Hebrew-Oriental Melodies* (1914–32), his many writings on Jewish music in its complex historical relations with other kinds of music, and his teaching at Johannesburg, South Africa, at Jerusalem, at Cincinnati, Ohio, and elsewhere, did more than any composition to unite and advance the Jewish musical community.

———•———

A hard-won national style made Karol Szymanowski (1882–1937) the chief Polish composer since Chopin. Though his achievement as musician and patriot was pale beside that of Paderewski, nevertheless it was memorable, not only to younger Polish musicians but also to thousands of admirers around the world, especially to pianists who could play his mazurkas (1924–26), and violinists who could play his two concertos (1922, 1933). Szymanowski began his career under the influence of German models, including Strauss, but renounced his major works up to about 1910, when he absorbed the lessons of Debussy and Stravinsky, along with the allure of Scriabin. Then in the 1920s he began to use Polish folk materials, and his work became more and more powerful, economical, and profound. His *Stabat Mater* (1929) and other late vocal works, though little known outside Poland, supported the claim of admirers who ranked him near Bartók.

Zoltán Kodály (b. 1882) discovered and put to use the folk sources of his national style alongside his close friend Bartók, from 1906 onward. For Kodály, unlike Bartók, Hungarian nationalism remained a dominant motive, throughout all the drastic changes in his people's life. Finally under the Communists after World War II he was acknowledged as a hero, the greatest national representative of culture. He carried out a thorough and extremely promising reform of school music, based on the research that had culminated in his book *Folk Music of Hungary* (1937). Mary Helen Richards and others undertook to adapt Kodály's method for use in America, and it was influential in other countries too.

The quality of his compositions, in all media, was as steady as his character. From the Nine Piano Pieces (1909) and the Cello Sonata (1910) to the Symphony (1930–61) there was no stylistic development, but also no mere repetition of a formula. Three big choral works—*Psalmus Hungaricus* (1923), *Te Deum* (1936), and *Missa brevis* (1945)—gratified singers and audiences all over the world; many shorter choruses, together with some fine songs, school exercises, and folksong arrangements, supplemented these major works.

A younger colleague of Bartók and Kodály, László Lajtha (1892–1963), contributed richly to the collection and study of folklore, and also distinguished himself as composer of seven symphonies.

Kodály's final triumph must have surprised two of his contemporaries and compatriots who had won earlier success with more conservative styles: Leo Weiner (1885–1960), like Dohnányi, but more fastidious, used Hungarian folksong only as a flavoring for the Brahmsian style he had learned from Koessler; Imre Kálmán (1882–1953), another pupil of Koessler, became the preëminent composer of operetta after Lehár, exceptionally successful in absorbing some influence from American popular music without sacrificing the essential qualities of the tradition.

Most admirers of Lehár and Johann Strauss, whether or not they admitted Kálmán to their company, could only lament the replacement of "true" operetta in the 1920s by the spectacular musical shows of Robert Stolz (b. 1886) and Ralph Benatzky (1887–1951), in Vienna and Berlin, and the transplantation of this form to America by Rudolf Friml (b. 1879), Sigmund Romberg (1887–1951), and others. The most creditable post-war operettas were the more modest works of Maurice Yvain (1891–1965), never popular outside France and esteemed there only as ephemera.

One year younger than Szymanowski, Kodály, and Kálmán, the leader of national music in Greece was Manolis Kalomiris (b. 1883). Educated in Vienna and Kharkov, he was able in 1915 to fill the need for a national opera, with his *O Protomastoras* (*The Master Builder*, Nikos Kazantzakis). Outstanding among his many later works in all media was a one-act opera on Yeats's *Shadowy Waters* (1951).

———————

Ralph Vaughan Williams, toward the end of his long life (1874–1958), was revered as a personification of Englishry in music, comparable to Kodály, Szymanowski, and Bloch, perhaps to Sibelius and Janáček, perhaps even to Dvořák and Grieg. Yet English audiences never accepted Vaughan Williams quite as they did Elgar or Britten, while on the contrary some Americans rated his personal and universal worth high above theirs. For his concern was not originality or patriotism, but honesty and "musical citizenship." In the "Musical Autobiography" that he wrote for inclusion in Hubert Foss's study (1950), he argued: "Why should music be original? The object of art is to stretch out to the ultimate realities through the medium of beauty. The duty of the composer is to find the *mot juste*. It does not matter if this word has been said a thousand times before, as long as it is the right thing to say at that moment." And in his credo of 1912, republished by Foss, and paraphrased in his own book on *National Music* (1934), he wrote:

Art, like charity, should begin at home. If it is to be of any value it must grow out of the very life of [the composer] himself, the community in which he lives, the nation to which he belongs. . . Our composers are much too fond of going to concerts. There they hear the finished product. What the artist should be concerned with is the raw material. . . For instance, the lilt of the chorus at a music-hall joining in a popular song, the children dancing to a barrel organ, the rousing fervour of a Salvation army hymn. . . There are hardly any great composers, but there can be many sincere composers. There is nothing in the world worse than sham good music. There is no form of insincerity more subtle than that which is coupled with great earnestness of purpose and determination to do only the best and the highest.

Vaughan Williams was sincere. His works, large and small, did grow out of his life. Without any sham, they did stretch toward the ultimate realities; whether or not the big works attained the *mot juste*, they pointed the way for many listeners, while the smaller works often transported whole congregations of singers.

A selective list of Vaughan Williams's works indicates his advance from song to symphony—from a late, still hesitant beginning in his thirties through the exciting original work of his fifties to the steady grandeur of his eighties.

	Orchestra	*Voices*
1900		*Silent Noon* (D. G. Rossetti, song with piano)
1905		*Towards the Unknown Region* (Whitman, chorus and orch.)
1905, 07		*Songs of Travel* (R. L. Stevenson)
1906	*Norfolk Rhapsody*	*The English Hymnal* (ed. and contrib.)
1905–10		*Sea Symphony* (Whitman)
1909	Fantasia on a Theme of Tallis, for double string orch.	*On Wenlock Edge* (Housman, tenor with string quartet and piano)

1911		*Five Mystical Songs* (George Herbert, baritone, chorus, and orch.)
1914, rev. 1920	*London Symphony*	
1922	*Pastoral Symphony*	
1923		Mass in G minor (unacc. double chorus)
1925		*Flos campi* (viola, wordless chorus, chamber orch.)
		Songs of Praise (ed. and contrib.)
1928		*Oxford Book of Carols* (ed. with others)
1931	*Job*, a masque for dancing (based on Blake's illustrations)	
1931-35	Sym. IV, in F minor	
1943	Sym. V, in D	
1905-49		*The Pilgrim's Progress*, a morality (Bunyan)
1944-47	Sym. VI, in E minor	
1949-52	Sym. VII, *Antarctica*	
1954-56	Sym. VIII	
1957-58	Sym. IX	

Two turning-points in this list need special mention: the editing of the *English Hymnal,* which coincided with the discovery by Holst and Vaughan Williams of some of the folksongs to which Cecil Sharp was devoting himself; and the Fourth Symphony, in which Vaughan Williams astonished his admirers by taking up the challenge of shrill, harsh dissonance at the very moment when moderation was most fashionable, to frame a powerful tragic statement, perhaps a prophecy of World War II.

Folksong contributed something profound to Vaughan Williams's style, but something peculiar, not readily understood. His discovery of the dignity and vitality of his national heritage helped him define his own character and inspired him to make the most of techniques that were barely adequate for his ideal purposes. But he made no such extensive study of folksong as Bartók or Kodály. Elsie Payne has shown that in fact Vaughan Williams learned less from a folk style than from two particular melodies—*The Captain's Apprentice* and *Bushes and Briars*—which he transformed again and again. William Kimmel has pointed out the freely meandering quality of these transformations, their prominence as thematic material, and their suggestion of mysticism. Oliver Neighbour, in an extraordinary comprehensive balanced essay, has indicated how the whole forms of movements evolve from such melodic lines, "expanding as tunes cannot, yet retaining the same character," without the traditional motivic technique, and modulating without traditional tonal logic. Neighbour emphasizes also that "the highly personal quality of his use of mode and triad" has no necessary connection with folksong. Vaughan Williams himself, in *National Music,* said: "The knowledge of our folksongs did not so much discover for us something new, but uncovered for us something which had been hidden by foreign matter."

Vaughan Williams's sympathy with English music of the Renaissance, like his concern for folksong, was exaggerated by some of his admirers. Because he glorified a tune by Thomas Tallis and edited a volume of the works of Purcell he was supposed to have derived his style from theirs. But in fact he never became acquainted with much of this music, nor did he absorb it as Holst did. He never ceased to detest the harpsichord and the "Baroque" organ. His kind of counterpoint left room for many parallel progressions. His use of cross relations was not contrapuntal but chordal, often enharmonic or polytonal. John Bergsagel has shown that Vaughan Williams's nationalism on the whole was more a matter of poetry and of ineffable spirit than of any specific technique.

Before folksong or old English music in Vaughan Williams's development, and persisting to the end, were 19th-century norms of sonority and rhythm. As a child Vaughan Williams played the violin, loved Gounod, and recognized in Bach a lofty austerity. In the 1890s, studying under Parry and Stanford at the Royal College and at Cambridge, he floundered on the piano and organ, and despaired of imitating Brahms and Wagner. In 1897–98 he studied further in Berlin, under Bruch. Meanwhile (1895) he made friends with Holst, on whom he long relied for both technical advice and philosophical stimulus. Together the two discovered Debussy and freedom. Eventually (1908) Vaughan Williams went to Paris to learn orchestration from Ravel. Though he adopted Ravel's procedure of trying everything at the piano, he clung to his violinist's habit of melodic thought. And though he adopted melodic shapes from folksong he never tired of accompanying them with richly doubled triads. Moreover, all the familiar elements of his technique suited his sense of a mission. In *National Music* he explained:

Music is above all things the art of the common man. . . Music is above all others the art of the humble. . . What the ordinary man will expect from the composer is not cleverness, or persiflage, or an assumed vulgarity. . . he will want something that will open to him the "magic casements." . . . The art of music above all other arts is the expression of the soul of a nation . . . any community of people who are spiritually bound together by language, environment, history and common ideals and, above all, a continuity with the past.

Vaughan Williams exemplified what he preached.

Several English composers less famous than Vaughan Williams likewise exemplified his "common ideal." Two of his most promising disciples were victims of World War I: George Butterworth (1885–1916) and Ivor Gurney (1890–1937). Both wrote a few songs that kept their names alive.

Sir George Dyson (1883–1964) independently formed a somewhat similar style. His best-known work, the cantata based on Chaucer, *Canterbury Pilgrims* (1931), deserved the attention of all English-speaking singers and audiences. His autobiography revealed his extraordinary blend of zeal and detachment. Four English composers who came of age just before World War I found various compromises, rather like Honegger's, between the demands for novelty and continuity:

> Sir Arthur Bliss (b. 1891)
> Herbert Howells (b. 1892)
> Arthur Benjamin (1893–1960)
> Sir Eugene Goossens (1893–1962).

All were affected by Vaughan Williams to some degree. All surpassed him in facility, but fell short of his approach to the *mot juste*.

———•——

Joseph Haas (1879–1960) was the oldest of the composers who around 1920 developed a wilfully parochial German style—indeed in his case a Bavarian or Swabian style—based largely on folksong. Haas collaborated with Hindemith at Donaueschingen and Baden-Baden but never followed him to the ISCM. Their two sorts of anti-Romanticism overlapped only a little. By the end of his life Haas had achieved in his narrower sort not so much as Hindemith, to be sure, but a vast catalogue of songs, song cycles, male choruses, and piano pieces, and also several works in remarkably new large forms: folk oratorios and folk operas. He was a respected teacher, noted as much for his open-mindedness as for his sincere contentment and confidence within his own narrow limits. His biographer, Karl Laux, describes the development of his style. He began as a small-town school teacher, with amateurish efforts to imitate Strauss. Then he became a favorite pupil of Reger (1904–08) and diligently cultivated chamber music. But soon he showed a distinctive tendency toward clear textures and jolly diatonic tunes. Acquaintance with some music of Debussy, around 1915, helped him learn to vary the textures and support the tunes with chords occasionally freed from polyphony. (He was infected only briefly by the whole-tone scale, and never by any shyness of the authentic cadence or of the old-fashioned modulation to the dominant and back.) He then began to use folk tunes, perhaps attracted to them by the *Wandervogel* movement and the musical youth movement propagated by Fritz Jöde (b. 1887). The related liturgical movement inspired his *Deutsche Singmesse* (1924); from now on instrumental music was subordinate. A Haas Society, founded in 1949, tried to promote the study and performance of his works, but these could not interest the young musicians curious about Webern, even if, like

Karl Amadeus Hartmann, they had been pupils of Haas. Nor could they interest many people outside Germany. But a picture of 20th-century music that ignored them altogether, or classified them mistakenly as imitations of Strauss, Reger, and Pfitzner, would be unbalanced.

Among many younger composers who gained more prominence in Germany for their restrained vocal music than for their more adventurous instrumental music were Fidelio Finke (b. 1891) and Bruno Stürmer (1892–1958). They stood in relation to Haas somewhat as Bliss and Benjamin stood to Vaughan Williams.

An isolated figure in Germany, deeply revered by the few musicians who knew his work, was Heinrich Kaminski (1886–1946), son of the founder of the Old Catholic Church. He began the study of music only during his years at the University, and decided on a musical career when he was twenty-three (1909). He developed a personal style, for which he claimed as models Ockeghem, Bach, and Bruckner. The consummation of his work was the *Spiel vom König Aphelius* (*Play of King Aphelius*, 1946, for narrator, chorus and orchestra).

A Swiss pupil of Reger, Othmar Schoeck (1886–1957), won admiration abroad for his many songs, especially as sung by Dietrich Fischer-Dieskau.

Another fine specialist in song writing was the Finn, Yrjö Kilpinen (1892–1959). A catalogue of his printed works by Maire Pulkkinen lists over seven hundred settings of first-rate poems in many languages.

A specialist in songs and intimate piano pieces was the Catalan, Federico Mompou (b. 1893). Within his chosen limits he often achieved perfection.

Yuri Aleksandrovich Shaporin (b. 1889) was highly esteemed in Russia for his songs, his cantatas, and above all his opera, *Dekabristi* (*The Uprising of 1825*, composed 1925–53). After the death of Prokofiev, Shaporin was the dean of Soviet composers, representing in his modest, conciliatory personality as well as his work the ideal of the Russian musical community.

The most famous Czech composer after Janáček was Bohuslav Martinů (1890–1959). He became a fluent cosmopolite as well as a nostalgic patriot, chief representative of the neo-Classicist École de Paris in the years between the wars, then a Romantic American symphonist and pioneer in opera for television, finally an acknowledged leader among his compatriots, though he died an exile in Switzerland. His Sixth Symphony (1953) and his twelfth opera, *Recké pašije* (*The Greek Passion-Play*, Nikos Kazantzakis, 1955–58), were hailed by admirers like Ernest Ansermet as the most profoundly impressive works of their period. His chamber music was enjoyed by players everywhere. Yet some critics dismissed Martinů (on short acquaintance) as lacking either genuine style or memorable ideas. A sifting of his vast output was needed; Peter Evans and John Clapham began the task by distinguishing strong and weak points in the symphonies and concertos.

Among the strong points was the efficient treatment of the instruments, which allowed a professional orchestra to learn a piece with little rehearsal and produce effects as rich as any of Honegger's or Roussel's. Some of the weaknesses were literal repetition of long sections, frequent static harmonies, and superfluous passage-work. These qualities, both good and bad, doubtless reflected Martinů's long experience as an orchestral violinist, his early study of Strauss, his conversion to Debussy on hearing *La Mer* about 1910, and his hasty assimilation of jazz and of Stravinsky's rhythms. More important features of his music were the rhythms of Czech song and dance, the long melodic lines, and the humane attitudes that all these features served.

Ladislav Vycpálek (b. 1882) was esteemed in Czechoslovakia next to Martinů, for works in all forms, among which the *České Requiem* (1940) was at once most inclusive and most personal.

———•———

A grand-scale synthesis of old and new elements in the service of symphonic drama, such as was represented around 1950 by Martinů, Vaughan Williams, Honegger, Prokofiev, and younger men, had been achieved around 1920 by Alban Berg (1885–1935). Berg shared adventures with his teacher Schoenberg and his close friend Webern, but his work differed from theirs almost as Prokofiev's from Stravinsky's or Ravel's from Debussy's. Berg preserved snatches and phrases of diatonic melody, dance-like rhythms, triads and seventh chords and even occasional strong progressions of chords, amid an opulent flow of chromatic, syncopated, dissonant counterpoint. His wide range of style allowed him to quote from Wagner and Zemlinsky in his *Lyric Suite* for string quartet (1926), from Bach and folksong in his Violin Concerto (1935), and to make extensive use of jazz elements in *Der Wein* (Baudelaire, concert aria, 1929), and the unfinished opera *Lulu* (Wedekind, begun 1927). This obvious technical difference fitted Berg's relative youth, and his lasting youthfulness. His whole personality differed from the personalities of Schoenberg and Webern likewise: his lofty but delicate physique, his languorous asthmatic smile, his happy marriage to the beautiful singer Helene Nahowski. More important, his conservative eclecticism served his devotion to the theater, and made his biggest work, the opera *Wozzeck* (Büchner, 1914–23), not merely acceptable but overwhelming, shattering, world-shaking, to many listeners still baffled by Schoenberg and Webern.

Berg's conservatism and its value need not be exaggerated. He did not simply dilute or "humanize" Schoenberg's successive styles, though he did adopt procedures from the Chamber Symphony, from *Pierrot*, from *Erwartung*, from the Serenade, and from the Quintet. Rather he developed his own style around his own genius for lyric melody and dramatic form, to express his own sense of pathos, which was quite different from Schoenberg's theosophy and Webern's nature-religion. Incidentally, Berg anticipated the twelve-tone technique in his static accompaniment to the song, Op. 4, No. 3, in the Passacaglia, Op. 4, No. 5, and especially in the passacaglia of *Wozzeck*, Act I, scene 4; later he developed his own versions of the technique, radically different from either Schoenberg's or Webern's but no less ingenious or novel, incorporating new tonal relations of triads. Berg devoted his literary talents to explaining and defending the work of his teacher with whole-hearted enthusiasm. His voluminous correspondence with Schoenberg, Webern, and others, from which only fragments have been published, would some day be among the principal primary sources for a deeper understanding of the whole Viennese School. Moreover, in 1961 at Darmstadt Pierre Boulez predicted a growth of Berg's musical influence: "We are penetrating to the basic phenomenon of opposition that forms the foundation and key to his work; we are taking it as the occasion for an abstraction; and we can win from it useful points of departure for new solutions." Boulez noted the conservative aspect of Berg too, but he was sure that the essential novelty would emerge as more important.

Berg had just graduated from Gymnasium and begun to work in the civil service when he came to Schoenberg with his sheaf of songs (1904). He was a fair amateur pianist and a good choral singer, ignorant of Strauss and Mahler. Schoenberg described Berg's songs as "between Hugo Wolf and Brahms." He studied part-time for nearly two years; then, thanks to an inheritance, he studied full-time for five more years, stopping only when Schoenberg moved to Berlin (1911). Thus he acquired his knowledge of classical forms and contrapuntal techniques along with his knowledge of modern harmony. Fourth chords and whole-tone scales became habitual for him to the same degree as motivic development; indeed, his way of developing motifs depended on the use of these new harmonies, which could loosely connect and support whatever counterpoint eluded triadic logic. The whole-tone scale gave to some passages of the Sonata and a whole song, such as *Nacht,* from the seven *Early Songs* (1908), a more obvious relation to Debussy than any piece of Schoenberg or Webern had; yet Berg's sequences, his rubato, and his pervasive mood of yearning were more remote from Debussy than Schoenberg's orchestral picture of the changing colors, Op. 16, No. 3, or Webern's orchestral piece, Op. 10, No. 4.

Berg developed a somewhat deeper affinity with Debussy when in 1914— now himself a wretched orderly in the Austrian army—he turned to the problems of Wozzeck, a protagonist of ignorant, bewildered humanity under the oppression of stupid bureaucracy. (Schoenberg thought the subject unfit for music, and was amazed when the timid Berg proved him wrong.) Here the whole-tone scale and fourth chords served a different purpose, as Berg explained in his lecture on *Wozzeck* (1929):

The other result of my current investigations is the way I have met the need to provide folk-like tuneful elements, and thus the need to establish a relation within my opera between art-music and folk-music, something that in tonal music is quite taken for granted. It was not easy to distinguish these levels so clearly in this so-called atonal harmony. I believe I succeeded by filling out everything that extends musically into the folk-like sphere with an easily recognizable primitive quality that is adaptable even within atonal harmony. For example: preference for symmetrical construction of the periods and sentences, incorporation of harmonies in [parallel] thirds and especially in fourths, and indeed of melodies dominated by the whole-tone scale and the perfect fourth, whereas otherwise in the atonal music of the Viennese School diminished and augmented intervals prevail. Another such means of harmonically primitive music-making is so-called "poly-tonality." We find such a folk-like infusion in the military march (with its "wrong-note basses") and in Marie's lullaby (with its fourth chords).

In the same lecture, Berg denied that his powerful devices for depicting Wozzeck's drowning and the rise of the blood-red moon owed anything to Debussy: these "Impressionistic" passages were derived straight from Wagner (by way of Schoenberg's *Erwartung*) and they were coordinated with "a quite strict musical regularity." But on the other hand, Berg told Ansermet that the orchestral interludes of *Pelléas* had inspired the *Wozzeck* interludes, including the climactic epilogue, after Wozzeck's murder and suicide, before the final scene where his child takes up the role of ignorant butt for cruel children. This epilogue, Berg explained in his lecture, was "a confession of the author, stepping outside the dramatic events of the theater and appealing to the public as representing mankind." In the epilogue all the motifs associated with Wozzeck return, shaped into clear phrases in D minor. Then they grow through rich modulations to an over-whelming climax on a twelve-tone chord, which works clearly as a dominant preparing the recapitulation. Here is the essence and probably the summit of Berg's unique achievement.

An important and much discussed feature of *Wozzeck* is its construction in three acts, each of five quick scenes, with a traditional musical form for each scene. This construction owes nothing to Wagner, Debussy, or Schoen-berg. Berg got the idea from Schreker, perhaps reinforced by Busoni. He carried it to a logical extreme.

The works between the Sonata for piano, Op. 1 (1907–08), and *Wozzeck* included a Quartet, Op. 3 (1909–10, revised 1920), and Three Pieces for Orchestra, Op. 6 (1913–14). These began to win appreciation only after World War II; they needed many more performances to confirm the high estimate of their value by Stravinsky, Adorno, and other admirers.

The Chamber Concerto (1923–25), as Berg explained in his long and important dedicatory epistle to Schoenberg, was a virtuoso display of his composing skills and a romantic monument to the trinity Schoenberg,

Webern, and Berg. This work, like the earlier ones, and like *Lulu,* needed more performances to prove that its difficulties were worth mastering.

The *Lyric Suite* and the Violin Concerto, on the contrary, exercised wide influence in the 1930s, and were well established in the repertories of string players. These were difficult enough, but when played with thorough knowledge and love, as for instance by the Juilliard Quartet, they overwhelmed all sorts of listeners, just as *Wozzeck* did. All praise of the *Lyric Suite* was capped by that of Boulez, who declared in 1958 that it was "one of the greatest masterpieces that exist."

Two Viennese composers contemporary with Berg and Webern achieved distinctive styles of a milder kind. Joseph Marx (1882–1964) was best known for his songs, especially those written around 1910 under the influence of Debussy and Scriabin; the culmination of Marx's work, however, was in the quartets (1944, 1948). Egon Wellesz (b. 1885) was known less as composer than as biographer of his teacher, Schoenberg, and outstanding scholar of Byzantine music; but Wellesz's long list of compositions, including six operas and five symphonies, was interesting as a personal synthesis of features derived from Bruckner, Debussy, and perhaps Fux.

———— •—•— ————

Frank Martin (b. 1890) emerged as an international figure only at the age of fifty-five (1945) with his *Petite symphonie concertante* for harp, harpsichord, piano, and double string orchestra. He was now a more original composer than his Swiss compatriots Schoeck, Honegger, Bloch, and Burkhard. The predominance of chromaticism in his melodies, the occasional appearance of twelve-tone themes and ostinato patterns, together with the distinctive free forms, the fresh sonorities, the splendidly idiomatic writing for voices and all sorts of instruments, and the consistent mellow expressiveness of his music won for a moment the attention of many adventurous younger composers, including Roman Vlad and Karlheinz Stockhausen. But they did not learn his patience. The adventures of the young carried them past Martin before his work had time to reach an audience as wide as Berg's or Bartók's. And without the help of fashion his later works, continually more refined and powerful up through the Christmas oratorio, *Le Mystère de la nativité* (1960), would need many years to win the popularity they deserved. But just as Martin had worked patiently in obscurity until he was past fifty, so he could be patient with the perfunctory recognition granted him in his seventies.

Martin's fidelity to triads, to sequences, and to tonal functions represented something profoundly different from Honegger's compromise or Berg's synthesis, not to mention the sincere simplicity of Vaughan Williams. Martin recognized the opposite demands of originality and perfection, but not a valid conflict between public and connoisseurs or between primitive musicality and modern individuality. The tension of opposites that Martin recognized existed within himself as composer and also within every honest listener. This tension was heightened in the 20th century, he thought, partly because of our easy access to classic works, which made us discontented with any new work that was not both very different from them and very nearly perfect. The resolution of the tension was possible only through greatly extended independent studies together with a human grandeur or super-human grace not within reach of the will. Martin's triads, in their rich context, reflect a character that is extraordinarily patient, grave, gentle, hopeful, and faithful—not very passionate, not at all proud, but grand and gracious enough.

His long search for a stylistic solution he summed up in an article on his Violin Concerto (1952). His first biographer, Rudolf Klein, added a few details. Martin began as a mediocre pianist at sixteen (1906), writing in a conventional, impersonal style owing something to Franck, Strauss, and Mahler. For twenty years he proceeded to build up his technique within this styleless style, incorporating also something from Ravel, Falla, and Stravinsky. Then he studied and taught at the Jaques-Dalcroze Institute, and founded a trio in which he played sonatas of Bach and Debussy. It was only now that he absorbed the lessons of Debussy, especially of the last works, which he preferred to the earlier ones; on the basis of these lessons he explored jazz and the twelve-tone technique, choosing out of them only what enriched his sensibility. His first distinctive work was a suite for guitar (1933). His first fully mature one was the chamber oratorio, *Le Vin herbé* (the Tristan legend according to Bédier, 1934–41). From now on he composed more, and every work was unique and valuable. Perhaps most immediately accessible was the oratorio *Pseaumes* (*Psalms*, 1958). Most surprising was the setting of Molière's comedy, *M. de Pourceaugnac* (1960–63). Endlessly gratifying for a pianist were the Eight Preludes (1948).

Martin's literary and religious concerns he designated as "a second sort of technique" for the composer, and for the listener a possible avenue of approach, permitting a slow growth of the true understanding and love that depend not on words or concepts or moods but on memory of whole melodies, whole forms.

CHAPTER XXVI

Successors to Prokofiev

THE REVOLUTIONARY poet-dramatist Bertolt Brecht (1898–1956) gave good, conservative advice to his generation on the general problem of the arts and their audience:

There are many artists—and not the worst ones—who are determined in no case to make art only for . . . the little circle of initiates, who want to create for the whole people. That sounds democratic, but in my opinion it is not quite democratic. Democratic is to make the "little circle of connoisseurs" into a *big* circle of connoisseurs. For art needs knowledge. True as it is that every man is a potential artist and that man is the most artistic of all animals, it is also just as true that this potentiality can be developed and that it can also atrophy.

The importance of Brecht's plays and poems was much debated in the decade after he died. His contributions to music were not yet so widely recognized, but these were also apt to provoke much debate before their importance could be determined.

The young Brecht, a disillusioned veteran of World War I, made himself noticed in Berlin singing his ballads to his own simple tunes, accompanying himself on a banjo. For his first plays he composed incidental music. Then he collaborated with a series of professional composers, each of whom won in the collaboration more fame than independently. The first and most famous was Kurt Weill (1900–50), a pupil of Humperdinck and Busoni with a growing interest in jazz, which he called "an international folk-music." In 1927 Weill set the songs of Brecht that later formed the nucleus for their opera *Mahagonny* (1930). Together meanwhile they adapted the famous *Beggar's Opera* of John Gay (1728) with important borrowings from Chaplin's films, Stravinsky's *Soldier* (1918), and Berg's *Wozzeck* (finished 1923, first performed 1926). *Die Dreigroschenoper* (*The Three-Penny Opera*, 1928) was their first and greatest success, and one of the landmarks of the theater in the 20th century. Brecht's *Dreigroschenbuch* is an enthralling collection of records and commentaries on this work.

Weill gave credit to Brecht for providing him with the necessary occasion to discover his principle of "gestic" music—that is, music evoking bodily gestures. In an essay on this subject (1929) Weill explained that both he and Brecht opposed Wagner's use of music "to create moods, depict situations, underline dramatic accents"; they wanted music for action:

Music can create a sort of basic gesture by means of which it prescribes to the actor a certain attitude, excluding every doubt and every misunderstanding about the action involved. . . Naturally *gestic music is not at all bound to the text*, and if we feel Mozart's music in general, even outside opera, is "dramatic," that is because it never gives up its gestic character.

Weill showed Brecht's melody for a *Mahagonny* song alongside his own setting. He had maintained Brecht's gestic rhythm in an enormously richer harmony, to achieve a fresh (though specially sour) effect. In principle the combination was like Prokofiev's, though the rhythms were different. Finally, Weill's economical and imaginative use of the tawdriest German jazz instrumentation gave his work a perverse elegance.

Brecht decided that *Mahagonny* was too "culinary," that is, too much a product for the entertainment of passive consumers; henceforth he wanted to drive the audience to political action. He invented a new form, *Lehrstück* (didactic piece), of which the first example was *Lindberghflug* (*Lindbergh's Flight*, 1929), set to music jointly by Weill and Hindemith. The finest *Lehrstück* was *Die Massnahme* (*The Measures Taken,* 1930); according to Roger Planchon, Brecht rejected Weill's music for this in favor of a setting by Hanns Eisler.

Weill found a librettist for his biggest work in Brecht's friend and stage designer, Caspar Neher. Their opera, *Die Bürgschaft* (*Bail,* 1932), became a victim of the Nazis. In the judgment of David Drew, who promised a full-length book on Weill, *Die Bürgschaft* was superior in some ways to all his other works, and an important model for study by his would-be successors. Weill's first biographer, Helmut Kotschenreuther, on the contrary accepted the standard Communist judgment that *Die Bürgschaft* was a failure.

In America after 1935, diluting or altogether abandoning Brechtian attitudes, Weill wrote a series of musical shows, successful on Broadway and influential in raising the general level of sophistication there, though not yet so ambitious as the later hit by Leonard Bernstein, *West Side Story* (1957). Weill wrote also one piece for schools, *Down in the Valley* (1948), similarly successful and influential, though inferior to such native products as Douglas Moore's *Headless Horseman* and Copland's *Second Hurricane* (both 1936), which took Brecht's ideas more seriously.

Hanns Eisler (1898–1962) was Brecht's friend from 1928 till he died, and his favorite musician. Eisler, a pupil of Schoenberg whose works were highly praised by Webern in 1929, quickly mastered Weill's melodic technique, without, apparently, caring much about tone color or large forms. He was gratified to have his Brecht songs become favorites at meetings of the Communist Party and its front organizations, and to provide music for the plays. Among Eisler's songs, choruses, and cantatas, republished in Leipzig toward the end of his life, the dozens of Brecht settings were nearly all better than most of the other pieces, so that it was possible to give some credit to the claim of Eric Bentley that the autocratic Brecht corrected the taste of his collaborators. But there were enough exceptions, such as two moving songs to passages from the *Pensées* of Pascal in English translation, to prove Eisler's individuality. Moreover, his biggest work, the opera *Johannes Faustus* (1953), remained unpublished.

During his exile in America (1933–48) Eisler worked successfully in Hollywood, and produced a book on *Composing for Films* (1947) that was the best of its time and not quite superseded by any later one. His miscellaneous occasional writings, including a faithful obituary of Schoenberg and a penetrating study of Brecht, commanded respect and fed curiosity. No younger composer of East Germany had attracted similar attention abroad. Eisler's nearest rival was an older Brecht-collaborator, Paul Dessau (b. 1894).

An American pupil of Schoenberg in Berlin, completely converted by *The Three-Penny Opera,* was Marc Blitzstein (1905–64). On his return home Blitzstein aroused enthusiastic hopes with his Brecht-like opera *The Cradle Will Rock* (1937). His English adaptation of *The Three-Penny Opera* (1952) became an extraordinary hit, starring Weill's widow, Lotte Lenya, who had played in the first German productions. Blitzstein's own efforts kept alive more exalted hopes for American opera than did many temporarily more successful efforts of other men.

An English pupil of John Ireland, Alan Bush (b. 1900), was likewise converted in Berlin around 1930 to the style of Eisler and went home to compose a series of interesting and hopeful works, some of which were highly regarded in East Germany.

——— • • ———

In the Soviet Union during the 1920s, while Shostakovich and a few others learned something from Berg, Weill, Krenek, and Hindemith, a more explicitly proletarian music was envisaged by Aleksandr Aleksandrovich Davidenko (1899–1934) and his associates in the Production Collective and the Russian Association of Proletarian Musicians. Revolting against the traditions of Glazunov, Rachmaninov, and Scriabin, they made their chief form the "mass-song," with political texts and brutally simple march-like melodies and accompaniments, sometimes in choral settings. Just before

Davidenko died, his groups disbanded and their ideas were modified to permit assimilation with ideas that he had opposed; the opera composed jointly by one of his groups, *1905* (1934), was condemned; Davidenko's name was nearly forgotten, but what he stood for persisted and even expanded as one main current in Soviet music.

The chief representative of the popular current within the vague broad stream of "Socialist Realism" was Isaak Osipovich Dunayevsky (1900–55). Though his work was seldom exported, especially beyond the Iron Curtain, its success at home was greater than that of Prokofiev, and far more secure. Dunayevsky was a violinist, pupil of Achron. In the 1920s he distinguished himself by championing jazz as a suitable style for the new Socialist society. Then in the 1930s, in films and operettas, he found a formula for combining patriotism with young love, good clean comedy, and a sufficient number of tunes sufficiently like those of Lehár and Kálmán to make him a favorite of audiences wider than the Party. Foreign students of Soviet music need some acquaintance with Dunayevsky, at least as a background for Khachaturian, Dzerzhinsky, and Khrennikov.

Next to Dunayevsky, as masters of operetta and popular song, were Matvei Isaakovich Blanter (b. 1903), Yurii Sergeievich Miliutin (b. 1903), and Vasilii Pavlovich Soloviov-Sedoi (b. 1907). More distinctive, if not quite so popular, as a composer of songs and choruses, was the folksong collector and choral conductor Vladimir Grigorievich Zakharov (1901–56), who combined modal folk-like melody and folk polyphony with urban rhythms and accordion harmonies, in a blend more tasteful than that of mere arrangers.

The policy of Socialist Realism promoted various efforts to effect a synthesis of the tradition of Tchaikovsky and Rimsky with the more modern popular style. The "formalists" Prokofiev, Miaskovsky, and Shostakovich all tried occasionally to contribute to the field in which Dunayevsky excelled, as well as to include in their symphonies some passages as tuneful as his songs. Ivan Ivanovich Dzerzhinsky (b. 1909), while still a student at the Leningrad conservatory, won favor with a grand opera depending largely on popular songs and on the prestige of its libretto, based on Sholokhov's epic novel, *And Quiet Flows the Don* (1935). Dzerzhinsky and several other composers tried to repeat this success, but the dullness of their results was overwhelming; by 1960 the *Quiet Don* was generally admitted to be inferior to the operas of Prokofiev and Shaporin.

The achievement of Dunayevsky and the ideal of Dzerzhinsky affected developments throughout the Soviet Union. In the capitals of the various Soviet Republics the work begun by Glière and Vassilenko was carried forward by younger Russians, together with an ever growing number of native composers. The most prominent of these were:

Boris Nikolaievich Liatoshinsky (b. 1895) Ukraine
Shalva Mshvelidze (b. 1904) Georgia
Andrei Balanchivadze (b. 1906) Georgia
Alexei Machavariani (b. 1913) Georgia
Otar Taktakishvili (b. 1924) Georgia
Nazib Zhiganov (b. 1911) Tataria
Aleksandr Arutiunian (b. 1920) Armenia
Kara Karaev (b. 1918) Azerbaidzhan
Fikret Amirov (b. 1922) Azerbaidzhan

Especially for their symphonic poems, but also for operas and ballets, Mshvelidze and Karaev were counted among the major figures of the whole Soviet Union, though their works were not yet known abroad. Balanchivadze's music won the approval of the American specialist on Soviet music, Stanley Krebs, but his own brother, the choreographer Balanchine, on a visit in 1961, could not sympathize.

A synthesis of popular and prestigious elements was achieved without any theory of "gestic music" or "realism" by the American George Gershwin (1898–1937). Already in his early twenties Gershwin had amalgamated the two traditions he knew: that of popular song spiked with jazz, which he learned chiefly from Jerome Kern and Irving Berlin, and that of the rhapsody for piano and orchestra, which he learned chiefly from Liszt and Rubinstein, with a tinge of Debussy and Ravel, perhaps filtered through Puccini. The title of his most famous piece, *Rhapsody in Blue* (orchestrated by Ferde Grofé, 1923), indicated the two elements of this amalgam. In later works Gershwin's Lisztian exuberance was restrained by a growing respectful awareness of Stravinsky, Schoenberg, and Berg, a growing appreciation of Beethoven, and an effort to emulate these masters with the help of Joseph Schillinger's methods. His three Preludes for Piano (1936) were the classic achievements of this restrained style; Schoenberg confirmed his stated admiration for Gershwin by orchestrating these preludes. The one big work of his all too short career was the "folk-opera" *Porgy and Bess* (1935). Its tunes were splendid; the merits of the recitatives and of the opera as a whole were disputed. For some listeners, even after its popular success, its incredible characters and pretentious tragic plot made it inferior to Gershwin's best musical comedies, especially *Of Thee I Sing* (1931), which sparkled with unpretentious satire on common American pretensions. But for other listeners the shortcomings of *Porgy* were outweighed by its vitality.

Numerous tunes from Gershwin's shows became "standards" for jazz treatment, alongside the best tunes of Cole Porter (1893–1964) and Vincent

Youmans (1898–1946). The theater bands that introduced such tunes included several musicians who soon made good jazz of them: Ellington, Goodman, Miller, Krupa, Nichols. But none of these men or their forerunners in the jazz tradition had much influence on Gershwin. His amalgam did not reach as far as "real" jazz, just as it did not reach as far as the "real classics," or the "real moderns." Nevertheless, Gershwin's music satisfied a widely felt need better than any other. Its usefulness and influence might well outlast the later hit shows of Frederick Loewe (b. 1904).

Gershwin's Rhapsody helped inspire William Grant Still (b. 1895) to make use of jazz and Negro folksong in his symphonies and operas, although for him these materials were almost as exotic as they were for Dvořák or Milhaud. He had acquired his basic habits as the son of a high-school teacher in Little Rock, Arkansas, playing the violin, clarinet, and other instruments (not piano) and listening with rapture to recordings of Italian opera. His talent and his meager earnings from playing and arranging popular music had won him two years of study at Oberlin, Ohio (1916–18), and after service as a mess-boy in the Navy, four months with Chadwick and two years with Varèse (1923–25). Now, when he began to use folksongs, he quickly achieved renown and respect and enough performances to become a full-time composer. The *Afro-American Symphony* (1933), based on a blues theme, was his best-known work. *Archaic Ritual* (1945) he believed was his most important. In the long perspective of some future history, after the end of racial segregation and the end of a separate tradition of jazz, Still's work would perhaps loom larger than it did in the 1960s, when the struggle for racial equality called for increasing militancy, and jazz was advancing and expanding to include more dissonance and counterpoint than Still's music had room for.

Aaron Copland (b. 1900), came as close as Gershwin or Still to real jazz, and much closer to the real classics and moderns, from Bach to Stravinsky, and ultimately from Machaut to Webern. From this wide range he continually assimilated what he needed to nourish a style more strongly personal than any other American's since MacDowell, steadily changing but unmistakably his in all its phases. Copland's childhood in Brooklyn was similar to Gershwin's, but Copland grew up less precociously and more thoroughly. In the middle 1920s, while Gershwin, already rich and famous, was composing his first purely orchestral work, the tourist's memoir *An American in Paris*, Copland was in Paris too, quietly mastering techniques and forming a catholic taste under the guidance of Boulanger. Then, like Still and Gruenberg, Copland decided that jazz, which he had ignored until he discovered it in Vienna and Paris, might be for him the equivalent of folksong for Mussorgsky or Falla or Villa-Lobos. With his suite, *Music for the Theater* (1925), he at once glorified both the blues and the "snappy" kind of Dixieland jazz, and made his own character unforgettable. Edmund Wilson, reviewing this work, recognized Copland's quality without hesitation: "His vitality is as spontaneous as his culture is genuine. And there is probably more musical drama in his untitled and unannotated *Music for the Theater* than in the whole of Gershwin's opera." Within a few years, like Milhaud, Copland lost interest in jazz, but he held to what he later called, in his lectures on *Music and Imagination*, "this desire of mine to find a musical vernacular, which, as language, would cause no difficulties to my listeners . . . my old interest in making a connection between music and the life about me." Copland found material to help him gratify this desire and this interest now in Latin American popular music, now in cowboy songs, minstrel songs, hymns and dances of the Shaker sect, fanfares and bells. Moreover, what Hall Overton called "Copland's jazz roots" had subtle effects on his later work even in such a tenuous piece as the Violin Sonata or such a refined classical one as the Clarinet Concerto. At the same time, Copland was sensitive to every current of taste among European musicians; he tried twelve-tone technique, for instance, in a *Song* (1927) and developed his own version of it in the Piano Quartet (1950). His solicitude for listeners and "the life about me," he explained, "did not by any means lessen my interest in composing in an idiom that might be accessible only to cultivated listeners." These equal interests might properly be thought of as alternating in dominance. But it was a mistake to think, as many writers did, of one interest excluding the other in any of Copland's works. In a painstaking dissertation, Julia Smith, for example, attempted to define three style-periods in Copland's career, but she noted in nearly every piece some traits that belied her label, and in each "period" several "exceptional" pieces. The whole list of published music was not long, for Copland worked deliberately and withdrew some of his work; also he was active as traveling lecturer, journalist, impresario, and occasional teacher—his four books have values beyond their revelation of his own personality.

The three big works for piano—Variations (1930), Sonata (1939–41), and Fantasy (1952–57)—were commonly classified as "unpopular" Copland, and admired for their motivic ingenuity, their violent dissonance, their hectic syncopations, their avoidance of tunes, and their formal grandeur. But these very pieces, when well known, revealed all the innocent, dreaming lyricism and ironic whimsy of the ballet *Billy the Kid* (1938) or the film score *Red Pony* (1948), something of the patriotic fervor and resolution of the *Lincoln Portrait* (1942), and much of the solemn joyous ecstasy of *Appalachian Spring* (1943–49), whose tunes made them more readily memorable. Conversely, the tune of *Home, Sweet Home,* as Copland disguised and developed it in *Our Town* (1940), took on the individuality and dignity of his most severe music, exactly right for the atmosphere of Thornton Wilder's play. Further, the orchestration in the least pretentious works had variety, delicacy, and brilliance worthy of Mahler or Stravinsky, whose scores Copland had evidently studied well.

No matter what the size of the piece or the size of its prospective audience, Copland's music can be characterized by what David Drew calls "the disproportion between the outward appearance of terseness and economy, and the actual condition of the musical content, which is in fact far from compressed." Without approving this characteristic, Drew admires the intelligence and individuality that it shows. For an American like the present writer, it is lovable as well.

The diverse, memorable achievements of Gershwin and Copland, however they may be measured by the international standards that Copland shares with Piston, Sessions, and Carter, and however ponderous and "square" they may seem by the standards of Armstrong, Ellington, and Parker, are still bright and majestic in the context of most American music. In the wider context of American poetry, fiction, and visual arts, and their world-wide importance, Copland more nearly than any other musician corresponds to an Ezra Pound, a Hemingway, or a Calder.

———•·•———

Hunter Johnson (b. 1906), far less prolific and less famous than Copland, found independently a personal style similar to his in relation to Stravinsky and jazz, distinguishable especially through certain favorite chords and spacings of chords. The pianist Joseph Bloch properly considered Johnson's Sonata (1933–48) next to Carter's, noting that it was more consistent and playable than that of Ives, and "more full-blooded and alive" than that of Harris, which had helped to stimulate it. The ballet for Martha Graham, *Letter to the World* (about Emily Dickinson, 1940), was Johnson's best-known piece. The Trio for flute, oboe, and piano (1958) was still more admirable in its melodic and formal grace.

A long list of younger Americans, together with Johnson, constituted the sort of "American school" that Copland liked to refer to, a worthy counterpart of the American poets and painters of the same generation. During the 1930s some of them showed Copland's influence and many others emphasized their divergence from European traditions. After World War II, like Copland himself, many of them absorbed something from Schoenberg, while further developing their variegated individual qualities.

Born 1906 Paul Creston	1909 Paul Nordoff
1907 Henry Leland Clarke	Elie Siegmeister
Burrill Phillips	1910 Samuel Barber

	Paul Bowles	1916	Ben Weber
1911	Alan Hovhaness	1917	Ulysses Kay
	Robert McBride		Robert Ward
	Gian Carlo Menotti	1918	George Rochberg
1912	Norman Dello Joio	1920	John LaMontaine
	John Edmunds		John Lessard
	Jan Meyerowitz	1921	Seymour Barab
	Jerome Moross	1922	Robert Evett
1913	Gardner Read		Mel Powell
1914	Morton Gould	1923	Ned Rorem
	Alexei Haieff		Lester Trimble
	Gail Kubik		Chou Wen-Chung
	Charles Mills	1926	Carlisle Floyd
1915	David Diamond		William Flanagan

Several of these composers merited the kind of studies that so far only Barber was prominent enough to elicit (from Nathan Broder and Russell Friedewald), while Barber himself surely merited a quality and quantity of criticism more nearly like that accorded to Jackson Pollock or J. D. Salinger.

By contrast, some Americans more readily and regularly than Copland or Gershwin won the attention and approval of performers and audiences at home and abroad without requiring any critical effort. The chief reason for considering representatives of these in a historical survey is to set off the preceding list. Robert Russell Bennett (b. 1894) perfected with the help of Boulanger the skills that had already by 1926 brought him success as an arranger, but even in his six symphonies and other "serious" works he stuck to the taste for Stephen Foster and Norman Rockwell that he shared with millions of his countrymen. Richard Rodgers (b. 1902) prospered beyond the level of Lehár or Kern by composing tunes not too different from theirs for a steady succession of Broadway hits—at least sixteen shows between 1926 and 1965. Bennett and Rodgers were frequent collaborators.

———————

In England William Walton (b. 1902) enlivened the central heritage of Elgar with wise borrowings from Schoenberg, Stravinsky, Satie, Hindemith, and jazz. His most famous work was his first distinctive one: the setting for reciter and chamber orchestra of a series of poems by Edith Sitwell, *Façade*, first performed in 1922, revised several times in the next two decades, and adapted for ballet. Here the poet and the composer, working closely together, achieved, along with a newsworthy scandal, something more readily intelligible than *Pierrot Lunaire* and more durable than the similar products of the *École d'Arcueil*. The poems are fascinating, extremely varied exercises in rhythm, with images irrationally juxtaposed as in a surrealist painting. The music is subservient to the poems, brilliantly matching their variety.

The range of Walton's craft and his character are revealed more fully in his oratorio *Belshazzar's Feast* (1931) and his opera *Troilus and Cressida* (1954). Here satiric wit is still prominent, but soaring passion is allowed a large place, within parentheses. Cressida laments: "What strength have I but love, love deep as death but weak against the world?" Her music is deep and weak, like her love. It claims no staying power.

Two symphonies, three concertos, two quartets, and other imposing works, appearing at wide intervals, maintained Walton's early-won eminence and helped to maintain England's place among up-to-date music-making nations. These pieces, more highly polished than the late symphonies of Vaughan Williams or the large works of Walton's closer contemporaries, Rubbra, Rawsthorne, and Tippett, nevertheless were light in substance when weighed against the rough force and fervor of these other Englishmen. Walton's set of unpretentious piano duets *For Children* (1940) might prove more powerful in the end than his symphonic works.

A less known English composer, Gerald Finzi (1901–56), concentrated on songs and choral music in a style more personal than Walton's, more refined and more conservative, obviously related to Parry, Elgar, Holst, and Vaughan Williams, and not so obviously but nevertheless deeply affected by Byrd, Dowland, and Purcell. Finzi attracted little attention in England and almost none abroad, partly because of this conservatism, partly because he worked slowly and disdained publicity, and more, perhaps, because the personal quality of his style was likely to seem monotonous if performers and listeners did not share his sensitivity to his texts. As he wrote to his friend Howard Ferguson (1936): "I don't think every one realizes the difference between choosing a text and being chosen by one." Finzi was the chosen composer of some of the finest English poetry, including many grim lyrics by Thomas Hardy, the festive *Ode to St. Cecilia* by Edmund Blunden, and the Classic-Romantic *Ode: Intimations of Immortality* by Wordsworth. Finzi's choral music for Wordsworth cleanses, clarifies, and completes the words with "thoughts too deep for tears."

Finzi found his style in his twenties, teaching himself, except for some lessons with the best interpreter of Byrd's counterpoint, R. O. Morris. Vital counterpoint of bass and main melody is fundamental and pervasive in Finzi. His marching bass lines are more varied than those of Elgar or Vaughan Williams, and the underlying harmonic motion is more irregular and expressive. The counterpoint may involve imitation, but there is no routine fugato; often the imitation is at the interval of a third. The counter-point creates dissonance, especially in cross-relations, which occur only as a result of counterpoint. At climactic moments the cross-relations expand to polychords, which likewise occur only when so justified, not merely for decoration. But dissonance arises often too from diatonic passing tones and appoggiaturas, which give every phrase a bittersweet tone.

During World War II Finzi organized and conducted a chamber orchestra, and was inspired to write a few instrumental pieces, such as the Prelude and Fugue for string trio, and the Concerto for Cello, in which his counterpoint is more dramatic than in the vocal music, and the sound equally idiomatic and varied.

The slighter achievements of two older English song-writers were prized by Finzi and by others who knew them: Philip Heseltine, who used the pen-name Peter Warlock (1894–1930), and Ernest John Moeran (1894–1950). Vaughan Williams's pupil, Constant Lambert (1905–51), was more versatile and more famous, especially for his choral setting of Sacheverell Sitwell's jazzy poem *The Rio Grande* (1929), and for his jazzy book of criticism *Music ho!* (1934). While Lambert lived he rivalled Walton and Britten, but Britten's later succession of triumphs made Lambert's work seem merely preparatory. Among many English composers still younger than Britten the excellent critics Wilfrid Mellers (b. 1914), Peter Wishart (b. 1921), and Anthony Milner (b. 1925), together with brilliant, easygoing Malcolm Arnold (b. 1921), solid Francis Burt (b. 1926), modest Christopher Shaw (b. 1924), graceful Thea Musgrave (b. 1928), passionate Kenneth Leighton (b. 1929), and fabulously versatile Malcolm Williamson (b. 1931), helped to preserve a balance in contrast to more esoteric tendencies.

The achievements of Walton and Copland, Finzi and Johnson, and their compatriots were roughly paralleled by contemporary composers of many other nationalities, who deliberately emphasized national traits and addressed national audiences without losing touch with the currents of new international styles. In the new federation of Yugoslavia, for example, three outstanding composers were Jakov Gotovac (b. 1895) at Zagreb (Croatia), Slavko Osterc (1895–1941) at Ljubljana (Slovenia), and Josip Slavenski (1896–1955), first at Zagreb and then at Belgrade (Serbia). A host of younger men carried forward their work, sometimes fusing Webernish techniques into the amalgam, as did Milko Kelemen (b. 1924). In the 1960s Kelemen presided over the world's biggest festival of contemporary music, the Zagreb *Biennale*. In Israel, Paul Ben-Haim (b. 1897), a refugee from Munich, was the most prominent of many nationalists. In Bulgaria two leaders were Petko Staĭnov (b. 1896) and Pantcho Vladigerov (b. 1899).

The Brazilians Oscar Lorenzo Fernández (1897–1948) and Francisco Mignone (b. 1897) and the Mexican Silvestre Revueltas (1899–1940) were the most successful of many comparable Latin Americans in their generation. Among younger men, typical figures were Alejandro García Caturla (1906–40) of Cuba, and Camargo Guarnieri (b. 1907) and Claudio Santoro (b. 1919) of Brazil. In Portugal, a pupil of Koechlin, Fernando Lopes Graça (b. 1906), introduced a classicizing nationalism. None of these men attained the practical success of older nationalists like Kodály or Villa-Lobos, but each of them produced memorable music with a distinctive flavor. Perhaps more important in a world perspective were the popular hits of the Cuban band-leader, Ernesto Lecuona (1896–1963), and his many successors in Latin America.

The group of expatriates who formed the *École de Paris* with Martinů likewise emphasized their various national traits; in a long-range perspective their achievements were similar to those of Walton and Copland too. The Hungarian Tibor Harsányi (1898–1954) was the most brilliant member of the group; a pupil of Kodály, he carried forward the style based on Magyar melodies, absorbing into it some of Bartók's profundity and Stravinsky's finesse. The most facile member of the School was the Pole Alexandre Tansman (b. 1897). The most sober was the Rumanian, Marcel Mihalovici (b. 1898), pupil of d'Indy, admirer of Bartók, and ultimately convert to the twelve-tone technique. The youngest was the Swiss Conrad Beck (b. 1901), pupil of Honegger and others. Together, during the 1930s, these friends represented an international nationalism and a free internationalism that became less conspicuous in music after World War II but remained a potent ideal.

Many young composers, while not attached to Martinů's group, shared in its spirit. Henrik Neugeboren (1901–59), after studies in Budapest, Berlin, and Paris, cultivated a charming style of piano music, along with his interesting paintings, sculptures, and journal writing. Nicolas Nabokov (b. 1903), whose family fled Russia soon after the Revolution, still wrote music recognizable as Russian when he served as director of the world-wide musical activities of UNESCO. The music of another Russian emigré, Igor Markevich (b. 1912), was well remembered after he had ceased composing to become an eminent conductor.

More striking and influential than these men, Mátyás Seiber (1905–60) was essentially faithful to his long studies under Kodály (1919–24) even while he was also a pioneer of jazz in Germany and later of the twelve-tone technique in England. Another Kodály pupil, Sándor Veress (b. 1907), having settled in Switzerland, seemed more nearly than any composer anywhere the heir of Bartók. Another, Pál Kadosa (b. 1903), advanced Bartók's internationalism in Hungary, while another, Endre Szervánsky (b. 1911) was a pioneer in acclimatizing the Webern influence there. And another, Oedoen Partos (b. 1907), was the leading composer of the 1960s in Israel, incorporating twelve-tone technique with Orientalisms in his string quartets.

Among Czech composers younger than Martinů there were many shades of nationalism. Most famous abroad was the most conservative style—that of Jaromir Weinberger (b. 1896). His distinctive achievement was to combine the contrapuntal ingenuities of his teacher, Reger, with tunes like Dvořák's: when the tunes were like the best of Dvořák's, as in the opera *Švanda dudák (Schwanda the Bagpiper,* 1927), Weinberger's success was well deserved. Another conservative, less known abroad but more respected by those who knew him, was Jaroslav Řídký (1897–1956). More popular at home, and more favored by Soviet students of Czech music, was Emil František Burian (b. 1904). More adventurous than Martinů, on the other hand, and at the same time more zealously nationalist, was Eugen Suchoň (b. 1908). The amalgamation of twelve-tone technique with Czech melody, rhythm, and brilliant color was achieved in America by Karel Husa (b. 1921).

In Poland the national-international tradition of Szymanowski was recognizable in the work of many younger composers after the influence of his harmony had waned; the youngest Polish composers attracted most attention abroad, partly because their anti-Russian nationalism led them, after 1955, toward Webern. Among these were:

> Witold Lutosławski (b. 1913)
> Andrzej Panufnik (b. 1914)
> Kazimierz Serocki (b. 1922)
> Stanisław Skrowaczewski (b. 1923)
> Włodzimierz Kotoński (b. 1925)
> Tadeusz Baird (b. 1928)
> Henryk Górecki (b. 1933)
> Krzysztof Penderecki (b. 1933)

The festivals of the "Warsaw Musical Autumns" from 1956 onward provided a unique world center for the stimulation of new syntheses.

In mid-century Germany and Austria a renewal of church music, both Catholic and Protestant, fulfilled the hopes aroused by Schweitzer, Reger, Haas, Kaminski, and others of the older generation. The best composers who took part in this renewal were by no means adequately understood by a hasty comparison with these pioneers or with their own contemporary, Hindemith. Their styles resembled his, to be sure, in the predominance of contrapuntal texture, the frequent resort to fugue and passacaglia, the preference for perfect fourths rather than tritones, and in some cases the addiction to rhythms of pastorale and toccata. But they often surpassed Hindemith as well as Reger in illuminating and interpreting their texts and in genuinely idiomatic writing for voices and for the organ. Moreover, they did not follow Hindemith's whole elaborate theory of harmony, but rather found their own ways of incorporating new dissonance and new modulations into structures essentially more faithful to diatonic tradition than his. Their ties to their churches did not preclude their contributing to the literature of symphony and chamber music, oratorio and sometimes opera, works that were worthy of attention around the world, such as their organ music was beginning to win.

Perhaps the first to chart the direction of this group was Kurt Thomas (b. 1904), pupil of Arnold Mendelssohn and Karl Straube, whose Op. 1 (1925) was an unaccompanied Mass. As choral conductor, ultimately in Bach's post at the Thomaskirche in Leipzig, Thomas exerted a great influence. As composer he was surpassed by at least five of his contemporaries—David, Reutter, Höller, Pepping, and Distler.

Johann Nepomuk David (b. 1895) found the nucleus of his work in chorales. His ten volumes of organ settings (1930–46) were widely used and admired. The range of his style allowed for a novel adaptation of twelve-tone technique in such works as his Second Violin Concerto (1960). Hermann Reutter (b. 1900) excelled especially in songs and folk-like operas; his organ works showed an unfailing melodiousness along with the mastery of a craft equal to Hindemith's. Karl Höller (b. 1907), pupil of Haas, was known chiefly for chamber music, concertos, and orchestral tributes to Frescobaldi (1939) and Sweelinck (1951). His sonatinas for piano had a marvelous vitality and polish.

Ernst Pepping (b. 1901) established his national reputation with a set of orchestral variations (1937) on a song by Ludwig Senfl, *Lust hab ich gehabt zur Musica*, in which cantus firmus and concerto styles were fused in a characteristic new way. At the same time he displayed more concisely the individuality of his harmony and counterpoint in three piano sonatas. These Walter Hamm later analyzed with unusual perception, proposing the notion of "elastic scales" to explain the freely modulating growth of Pepping's long melodic lines, in which two or more motifs developed together; the forms, here on a modest scale, were unconventional, the organic result of melodic development. As early as 1934, in his book *Stilwende der Musik*, Pepping had stated his complex ideal of a style definable only in terms of whole works, not of separable techniques or devices:

Only the specific work leads into the new order . . . a work born of conscious responsibility but not constructed with moralistic compass and ruler, a work that is bound intimately to life, just because it sees only itself, the symbol of things . . . closed in form but open to joy, to the movement of temperament, to delight in music making.

Pepping's setting for chorus and orchestra of the *Te Deum* (1956) truly fulfilled this ideal with a grand rich dancing unity. His many works for organ and for unaccompanied chorus were more widely known; the *St. Matthew Passion* (1950) and the *St. Luke Christmas Story* (1959) were sure to hold a place in choral repertories, and secular works as well, such as the Goethe choruses (1949), were likely to gain such a place.

Hugo Distler (1908–42) was the most strikingly sensitive of all these composers, and the most thoroughly devoted to the ideal of Schütz in both sacred and secular realms. The biggest work of his short career was the moving Passion (1933). Herbert Schmolzi pointed out in this work Distler's characteristic traits: emphatic declamation of the words as the root of all melodies except for the chorales; varied repetition and melodic sequence (not harmonic) in a contrapuntal texture often polyrhythmic; contrast and uncanny unity of ponderous bass-parts with light and mobile soprano parts, in which pentatonic melismas often intensified the key words. Distler's later works, such as the *Geistliche Konzerte* (Sacred Concertos, for high voice and organ, 1937), constitute a marvelous testimony of German religious *Angst* during the Hitler years. His secular choral works, especially the *Mörikeliederbuch*, transcend their time. His Concerto for harpsichord and strings might well transcend both time and place. Among his works for organ the last was much the best: a trio sonata. And his most accessible work for performers was the set of Eleven Little Piano Pieces, also from the final period. According to the account of his friend, the theologian Oskar Söhngen, Distler killed himself at thirty-four rather than serve in the war he knew was unjust. Post-war Germany was deprived of what might well have been its greatest music.

At Lübeck, where Distler's professional career had begun, an archive of his remains was assembled. The first detailed account of his life was written by an American, Larry Palmer; letters and other materials in the archive would eventually supplement this, in all probability to establish Distler's position as a major composer despite his unfulfillment.

The renewal represented by Distler was carried forward by his contemporaries, such as Helmut Bornefeld (b. 1906) and Hans Friedrich Micheelsen (b. 1902), and also by younger men, among whom the most conspicuous were Siegfried Reda (b. 1916), Johannes Driessler (b. 1921), and Anton Heiller (b. 1923).

The movement attracted also the Swiss composer, Willy Burkhard (1900–55). Although his kind of harmony and his ideals of organ sound and choral sound were basically different, closer to those of his teacher Karg-Elert, he resembled Hindemith in his counterpoint, and his continuous concern with chorales was also characteristic. He won international recognition with his vast oratorio *Das Gesicht Jesajas* (*The Face of Isaiah*, 1936). The *a cappella* testament *Die Sintflut* (*The Flood*, 1955) and several pieces of chamber music seemed to the present writer likelier than the oratorio to spread the circle of Burkhard's friends. For until his harmony became familiar enough to make sense on a small scale, his counterpoint and forms seemed awkward. Ernst Mohr, in his monograph on Burkhard, points to the consistently frequent appearance of the tritone, but Mohr does not explain its function. This interval, in the context of a whole phrase, usually suggests a rich dominant chord with minor ninth and altered notes, not unlike the chords of Scriabin. The root progressions of the suggested chords are fairly regular and strong, but obscured by the sparse contrapuntal texture, and organized intuitively rather than in conformity to any obvious tonal plan; the progressions may be overlooked by performers or listeners too much impressed by the hints of modal scales in polytonal combinations. Burkhard and Bartók came to admire each other, as might be expected by anyone who penetrates their harmonic practices. Burkhard's pupils, Armin Schibler (b. 1920) and Klaus Huber (b. 1924), were the most promising of younger Swiss composers.

The secular German musical youth movement, by contrast with the movement in the churches, was too much damaged by its forced coordination and exploitation from 1933 to 1945 in the *Arbeitskreis für Hausmusik* (Working Circle for Domestic Music) and the *Hitlerjugend* to attract fresh talents after the war, although its various organizations were reconstituted to pursue their specialized activities, particularly the study and performance of old music. Some of the representative composers of youth music in the 1930s may be named (omitting many others only a little less successful) to bring out the difference between them and their contemporaries.

> Walter Rein (1893–1955)
> Ernst Lothar von Knorr (b. 1896)
> Hugo Herrmann (b. 1896)
> Karl Marx (b. 1897)
> Fritz Büchtger (b. 1903)

These men, each emphasizing a different aspect of youth music, shared something with Hindemith, Haas, Distler, and Orff, all of whom had also drawn an impetus from the movement in the 1920s. Most of them cultivated canons, fugues, and passacaglias, choruses and amateur fiddlers and recorder players, folksong, and chorale. But the specialists' rhythms and melodies were monotonously simple, and their occasional use of unresolved dissonance was arbitrarily imposed on an impoverished harmonic framework of the primary triads. The violent *Avantgardismus* of Stockhausen and his circle could be viewed sympathetically against this background, and the neglect of Hindemith, Distler, Pepping, and Orff by some of the best German critics could be understood if not excused.

When the International Society for Contemporary Music met for the first time after World War II (London 1946), the most surprising and stirring work on the programs was that of Luigi Dallapiccola (b. 1904). He had been identified before the war as a pianist and piano teacher, whose compositions for the ISCM were as good as Casella's, but not distinctive enough to be much discussed. The new work was different: *Canti di prigionia* (*Songs of Prison*, 1938–41) was a triptych of choruses, with an orchestra of pianos, harps, xylophone, vibraphone, bells, and percussion, on the last words of Mary Stuart, Boethius, and Savonarola, whose relevance to 20th-century anguish and anxiety was clear to every attentive listener. The music was apt for the texts: the central theme was the famous chant, *Dies irae*, and subordinate melodies were not difficult, while the accompaniment, along with its overwhelming novel sound, included enough dissonance and chromaticism to signal a reaction against Casella—yet stopping short of the "atonal" style of Berg, not to mention Schoenberg. It was unmistakably the work of a mature, skillful, sensitive, and sincere composer. It exemplified also, in some passages, according to Dallapiccola himself, a new variant of the twelve-tone technique, and this fact, together with the eloquence of the work, gave it historic importance. Many listeners who had been indifferent to such older converts as Krenek or Riegger were impelled by Dallapiccola to reconsider. Some composers who had hoped to learn from Schoenberg as Frank Martin had done, without adopting the whole technique, found Dallapiccola's example decisive. His importance was confirmed and enhanced when he followed up the *Canti di prigionia,* after several lesser works, with a powerful short opera, *Il Prigioniero* (*The Prisoner*, 1944–48), on the hope of freedom and brotherhood betrayed.

Dallapiccola gave his own account of "The Genesis of the *Canti di prigionia* and *Il Prigioniero*" and of his gradual progress "On the Twelve-Tone Road." These moving documents are helpful for an understanding of his work. Dallapiccola tells of his childhood in Trieste under Austrian rule, of his family's internment at Graz during World War I, and of the profound effect on him of hearing Verdi and Wagner there. He recalls the performance of *Pierrot Lunaire* at Florence (1924) when he, a shy student, watched Puccini go to meet Schoenberg while most of the audience laughed. He describes his arduous search for scores of the Viennese composers and his lonely groping analyses of those he obtained, unaided by Leibowitz or even Krenek. He mentions his love of Debussy and Ravel, and of Renaissance and Baroque music, especially for voices. He gives great emphasis to what he learned not from any music but rather from the writers, Proust and Joyce; his analysis of their structures had encouraged him to proceed with musical techniques that he thought analogous. He dismisses his early unpublished compositions, and points to the one-act opera, *Volo di notte* (*Night Flight*, St. Exupéry, 1937–39), as the turning point of his career, where the subject suggested the juxtaposition of diatonic and twelve-tone passages. Like Schoenberg, he continually subordinates technique and style to idea; like Berg he is desperately eager to convey his idea and his feeling to the public of opera and concert.

His works took a place near *Wozzeck* and *Lulu*, not in any regular repertory, but in the enthusiastic appreciation of a world-wide élite. His later works, advancing in style to incorporate Webern-like rhythm and melodies, were still more demanding, but almost any one of them could be approached by way of its text—Dallapiccola did not presuppose his listeners' familiarity with Webern. Thus English-speaking listeners might well begin with the *Requiescant* (1957–58), with texts from St. Matthew, Oscar Wilde, and Joyce. Pianists might take delight in the *Notebook* for his daughter, Anna Libera (1952–53).

Dallapiccola's combinations of twelve-tone technique with Latin warmth naturally exerted a great influence on younger Italian composers, though no more so than on some young Americans and Germans, Egyptians, Turks, and Israelis. He was easily the strongest attractive force in Italy, though he was rivalled there no less than abroad by the electronic experimenters on the one hand and such populists as Menotti on the other. Among the Italians who cultivated combinations somewhat like Dallapiccola's were

> Riccardo Nielsen (b. 1908)
> Mario Peragallo (b. 1910)
> Riccardo Malipiero (b. 1914)
> Guido Turchi (b. 1916)
> Gino Negri (b. 1919)
> Roman Vlad (b. 1919)
> Aldo Clementi (b. 1925)
> Niccolò Castiglioni (b. 1932).

A pupil of Dallapiccola in America, though a native of Milan, was Luciano Berio (b. 1925).

Syntheses of the twelve-tone technique with other strands of traditional lyricism were achieved independently during the 1930s by two pupils of Busoni, Wladimir Vogel (b. 1896) and Stefan Wolpe (b. 1902). Vogel grew up in Russia and began to compose under the influence of Scriabin, which he never renounced. He soon became interested in Schoenberg's *Sprechstimme* and the speaking choir of Madeleine Renaud in Brussels, which had performed Milhaud's *Choéphores*. He pursued this interest throughout his life, and by 1960 could claim: "I have elevated the speech-choir to the level of a complete, autonomous, and irreplaceable genre of art." The consummation of this development was to be a trilogy of epic oratorios: *Jonah* (in Martin Buber's version), *Moby Dick* (Melville), and *The Old Man and the Sea* (Hemingway). Vogel was credited by Luigi Rognoni with important rhythmic innovations, anticipating Babbitt and Messiaen in the adaptation of the serial idea to durations in his *Variétudes* (1939–40); he had begun to use the twelve-tone technique in 1937 and had elaborated some distinctive rhythmic procedures still earlier. Paul Collaer found the techniques of Vogel's music less remarkable than its warmth, wisdom, grandeur, and sheer beauty. Stefan Wolpe was a Berliner, susceptible to the influences of Weill and Stravinsky; then (1933–38) a participant in the expansion of music in Palestine; then an American "serialist," at once severely intellectual and violently expressive. Erich Itor Kahn (1905–56), a pianist with whom Casals liked to play and a composer ranked by Leibowitz with the great, fled his native Frankfurt in 1933, worked in France until 1940, and then became an American. His music from 1931 on made increasing use of twelve-tone materials and procedures as it became increasingly tragic in tone. This music needed many more performances before Leibowitz's judgment could be widely shared. Paradoxically, the twelve-tone technique, emblem of alienation from the ordinary concert-going public, not to mention any wider group of people, served composers like Dallapiccola and Kahn as a way of attracting more attention than their music had received without this label. After about 1950 the paradox was evident to musicians everywhere, though seldom mentioned; probably some younger composers adopted the technique partly because the label could help them to be heard. But of course the music, not the technique, much less the label, was the communication. And the anxieties and ideals of the age were communicated among composers and listeners by means of all techniques, in spite of all labels.

Francis Poulenc (1899–1963) composed a unique full-length opera, *Dialogues of the Carmelites* (1953–56), for which his whole career could be seen as preparation. Some lines from this work—the words of Georges Bernanos, intended for a film version of the novel by Gertrud von LeFort—may be taken as a clue to Poulenc's character, his achievement, and his true historical position, not generally recognized during his lifetime, despite his considerable fame:

What will become of the epoch in which we live I do not know. I only ask of Holy Providence the modest virtues that are despised by the rich and mighty— good will, patience, the spirit of conciliation. . . For there are several kinds of courage, and that of the great ones of the earth is not that of the little folk, it would not permit them to survive. . . Nothing is so small or unimportant that it does not carry God's signature. . . We are going to fight, each after his fashion, and mine has its risks and perils as does yours. . . Everyone is afraid. Fear is contagious, like a plague. . . Fear is indeed a sickness. . . In times like these dying is nothing. Living is nothing when life is devalued to the point of absurdity. . . Fear does not offend God. I was born in fear. I have lived in it. I still live in it. Everyone scorns fear. So it is fair that I live in scorn too. . . The affliction, my child, is not to be scorned, but only to scorn yourself.

Poulenc, like his heroine Blanche, lived in fear, in fear of everything and of nothingness, of liberty and of constraint. He did not crave the courage of the great. He learned to confess fear freely and to sustain a simple action despite interruptions, in such a way that the interrupting terror could be glimpsed continually through the action. In the final scene of the *Dialogues,* the nuns are guillotined, one after another; as they wait their turns, they sing a hymn, *Salve regina,* and the guillotine interrupts nearly every phrase with its swish and thud, but only for an instant; Blanche is granted the courage to sing the last fragment alone, with a voluptuous serenity. There is no escape, no consolation, no conquest except over scorn of self, by facing the terror. Blanche is no saint. Poulenc is no great one of the earth. But his modest virtues suffice for his own kind of fight. He accepts the scorn of many critics for his unconcealed awe at the works of Debussy and Stravinsky. He loves these "prodigious" composers as he loves Mozart and Chopin, and he imitates them spontaneously, for brief spurts of melody, cut off by his fear. He strives for perfection within his natural limits, such as he envies in Ravel. He also loves Chabrier, Satie, Prokofiev, Strauss, Puccini, Hindemith, Milhaud, Webern, Barber, Britten, and Boulez, as men much like himself, though not all so sensitive to the fear that he feels. He cites as "guides" for the *Carmelites* Monteverdi, Verdi, and Mussorgsky, and tries to follow them in spirit, not in any musical detail. He loves Balinese music, and jazz, and he spontaneously, fragmentarily, imitates them too. He hates mediocrity. No piece of his as a whole resembles any model, while no single phrase is either original or obscure. The mysterious unity of his best smaller compositions, like that of the *Dialogues,* is the amazing result of his accepting his fear, as parallel to his humble loves.

Poulenc grew up in a prosperous Parisian family. At the age of eight, already a promising pianist, he heard Debussy's *Dances* for harp and "awoke to music." At ten he knew by heart poems of Mallarmé. At eleven he began to sing Schubert, to dream of becoming an opera singer, and to compose songs. At fourteen, he was swept away by Stravinsky and temporarily lost his taste for songs. His chief teacher was Ravel's good friend, the pianist Viñes; "I owe him everything," Poulenc told Claude Rostand. Viñes introduced him to Satie in 1916. Satie, who had not yet composed his *Parade* but was already thinking of his *Socrate*, gave Poulenc the courage he needed, almost as the wise old Mother Superior of the Carmelites and the good silly sister Constance were to give courage to Blanche; it was not Satie's music so much as his extraordinary character and his penetrating vision that affected Poulenc. He served a few months in the armed forces, during which time he wrote some tiny gem-like songs and piano pieces, which Stravinsky helped him get published in England. Then, as one of "The Six," he came under the wing of Cocteau, "manager of genius, loyal and exquisite friend." Milhaud introduced him to Koechlin in 1921, and for the next three years Koechlin gave him his only lessons in counterpoint and composition. Needless to say, Poulenc developed no academic habits, but he learned to write well for orchestra, and to pursue a lifelong study of Bach. At twenty-four (1923) he was ready for the great opportunity offered by Cocteau and Diaghilev—a ballet, *Les Biches* (*The House Party*) with décor and costumes by Marie Laurencin and dead-pan choreography by Nijinska. The gay erotic charm of this music was immediately enjoyed and widely admired, without much notice of the moment near the end, where a tragic tone comes to the surface. Yet something self-conscious and ambiguous in the gaiety was felt throughout, so much so that *Les Biches* could never provide comfort or thrills to the naive audience of Gershwin, nor could it command the respect of all admirers of Stravinsky's *Pulcinella*, to which it was evidently indebted. Cocteau himself, to be sure, was acutely aware of the ambiguity, and matched it in his comment: "The beauty and the melancholy of *Les Biches* are not the product of any artifice. I doubt if this music knows it hurts." Enough performers and listeners ignored the ambiguity, or accepted it as *chic* fashion, or tried to interpret it in the light of *Cock and Harlequin* as a revolt against Romanticism and Impressionism, to make a just appreciation of Poulenc very difficult. Even in 1954 (just before the *Carmelites*) the author of the first book on Poulenc, Henri Hell, was overwhelmed by the ambiguity. Poulenc's own charming book on Chabrier, his lively conversations with Rostand and with Stéphane Audel, and a few other writings gave more help—enough, at least, for readers to see vividly several aspects of the composer's personality that entered into his music: his unabashed love for much Romantic music, together with his sure discrimination; his quick, candid, penetrating reactions, based on simple good sense and good humor, together with a vast literary and artistic culture and curiosity; his conscientious concern for every sensuous detail and for the construction of forms as fixing the meanings of details. When Honegger read the *Conversations*

(1954) he began for the first time to understand and love the younger man with whom his name had so long been linked in publicity. After Honegger's death, Poulenc published a letter, with comment, revealing this surprising and beautiful turn of events.

When Poulenc died, Claude Rostand wrote one of the best brief memoirs, trying to sum up provisionally the personality of his friend:

He always placed great value on being regarded as light, charming, frivolous, and flip. He loved risqué jokes and a Rabelaisian way of life. He liked "spicy" stories —especially if they happened to him—and it was a point of honor for him never to appear serious. . . But behind this spontaneity, this easy and ironic cutting up, was hidden much inner turmoil. . . He was basically an anxious man, in life as in his vocation.

Another friend, the American composer Ned Rorem, insisted that the basic "terror" was not really hidden, though it was never dwelt on; rather Poulenc's talk was "always interlocking soul and flesh." The relevance of these comments to Poulenc's music was confirmed by André Schaeffner.

------ • ------

In a complete list of Poulenc's works, the most numerous class would be that of songs with piano accompaniment, over a hundred and fifty of them. Especially after 1934, when he began to play song recitals with the baritone Pierre Bernac, Poulenc steadily devoted himself to composing songs and cycles of songs. His songs made a marvelous anthology of the poetry of Apollinaire, Cocteau, Éluard, Jacob, and Vilmorin, with only a few older texts. (In a beautiful lecture about his songs in 1947, Poulenc said: "I feel musically at ease only with poets I have known," poets whose own voices rang in his ears.) No translation could do justice to these poems. Nor could the perfectly grateful writing for voice and piano convey the depth and strength of the music to anyone insensitive to the poetry. But all who knew the poems agreed that Poulenc's songs were among the best of any time or place.

Another numerous class in his total output was made up of short pieces for piano. Poulenc himself judged these as "neither so good as the virtuosos claim, nor so shoddy as some of your colleagues [critics] have written . . . As soon as the piano becomes accompaniment for songs, then I invent." Any pianist who loves the songs can enjoy the Improvisations and Nocturnes and the one set of variations; for an audience the pianist might better choose to play and recite the story for children about the little elephant, Babar (1940–45).

In his music for two pianos, culminating in the Sonata (1955), and still more in the keyboard concertos—*Concert champêtre* for harpsichord

(1928), *Aubade* (1929), Two-Piano Concerto (1932), and Piano Concerto (1949)—Poulenc achieved works that can delight many unprejudiced listeners, while profoundly moving those who love the songs or the *Carmelites.* The same may be said of the chamber music, especially that in which winds have a part, from the Sonata for trumpet, horn, and trombone (1922) to the Oboe Sonata (1962).

Beginning in 1936 Poulenc wrote also a series of choral works, both long and short, both sacred and secular. Here he showed his greatest originality and density of thought. Like the songs, the choruses with French texts demand poetic sensibility of singers and listeners. Those with Latin texts, like the piano music, demand some appreciation of Poulenc's work as a whole. If these demands are met, the choruses rank far above the instrumental music, next to those of Brahms, Distler, and Pepping. Especially memorable are the cycle of liberation, *Figure humaine* (*The Human Face,* Éluard, 1942), and the *Office for Holy Saturday* (1962).

Poulenc's life as well as his works should take an important place in the history of music. He quietly created a new role for the composer in modern society, parallel to the roles of poet and painter. Changed social institutions had invalidated the heroic role created by Beethoven, exaggerated by Wagner, and played with laughing bravado by Strauss, though many composers still tried it. Poulenc's fame at twenty-five must have tempted him to try this and other roles. The example of Satie must have helped him refuse. But he could not lead Satie's ascetic, eccentric life. When the depression of the 1930s reduced his inherited income, so that it became difficult to maintain his Paris apartment and his 18th-century villa and gardens at Noizay, he did not turn to conducting or writing criticism, or teaching, or composing for films. He declined to trade on the prestige of rarely performed works. Rather he earned his living as a musician, by the pleasure he gave to audiences in playing for Bernac and other singers, including in his programs some of his own oldest and newest songs along with classics, familiar and unfamiliar. Thus he learned much that could benefit him as composer, and more important, he preserved his independence, his freedom to grow in wisdom and to compose the music he wanted to compose, at his own speed, in his own way. He worked hard. He was French through and through, but no nationalist. His work won warmer response in England and America than at home; it was the great Italian publisher Ricordi that commissioned the *Dialogues.* During the German occupation of France Poulenc stayed at home, composing his *Figure humaine* and his short opera on the World War I play of Apollinaire, *Tirésias,* reinforcing its appeal to Frenchmen to make love and make babies.

Georges Auric (b. 1899) was a brilliant rebellious pupil of d'Indy when Viñes introduced him to Poulenc in 1916. Together they explored Schoenberg, were swept away by Stravinsky, were helped by Satie, and "managed" by Cocteau. Auric went on to provide music for many of Cocteau's wonderful films, beginning with *Le Sang d'un poète* (*A Poet's Blood*, 1931)— music composed and recorded independently of the action, and then edited by Cocteau with arbitrary cuts and clever *montage* effects. Auric's most famous success was the waltz theme-song for a lesser film, *Moulin rouge* (*Red Mill*, 1952). The critical strictures of David Drew on Auric and his friend Jean Wiéner (b. 1896) helped to show up the distinction of Poulenc.

Closer than Auric to the modest essence of Poulenc and Satie were some of the works of Henri Sauguet (b. 1901). Lacking the ready wit of Poulenc, however, Sauguet was still closer to Milhaud and Koechlin, his good friends and teachers. Marcel Schneider, in a laudatory brief survey, agreed with Drew that Sauguet's masterpiece was the tragicomic opera, *Les Caprices de Marianne* (Musset, 1954). To the present writer, the later ballet, *La Dame aux camélias*, and some of the chamber music of Sauguet were more appealing, and his electronic study, *Aspect Sentimental*, was more delightfully surprising.

Several other French composers wrote notable works for stage and screen that deserved more international attention than Auric's, if still less than Poulenc's: Marcel Delannoy (1898–1962), Maurice Jaubert (1900–40), Henry Barraud (b. 1900), Manuel Rosenthal (b. 1904), Joseph Kosma (b. 1905, Hungary), and Maurice Thiriet (b. 1906).

Representatives of the younger generation pursuing similar interests were Jacques Chailley (b. 1910), Jean Françaix (b. 1912), Marcel Landowski (b. 1915), Jacques Bondon (b. 1927), and Jean-Michel Damase (b. 1928). Pierre-Octave Ferroud (1900–36) in some ways typified these interests: chief pupil of Schmitt, close friend and ally of Prokofiev, he founded the *Triton* concerts of chamber music (1932) in which old and new, light and heavy works could mingle and enhance each other. He formulated a plausible theory, which contributed to the grace of his own chamber and theater music, that counterpoint was universal, harmony national.

Church music in France was a special field for some composers, and yet not so isolated from main currents as it had been in Debussy's time or Roussel's. Poulenc, Migot, Lesur, Messiaen, and Chailley all helped to draw together once more the strands of sacred and secular tradition as they had been united for Franck and Gounod. Two specialists in vocal liturgical music were Romuald Vandelle (b. 1895) and Maxime Jacob (Brother Clement, b. 1906). The noble tradition of French organ music was carried forward by Maurice Duruflé (b. 1902), Jean Langlais (b. 1907), and Jehan Alain (1911–40). Of all these, Alain showed in his brief life the most profound personal style. His published works, for piano and for organ, are less than half the complete list given by his friend and biographer, Bernard

Gavoty. Arranged in chronological order, these short pieces show ever growing intensity, expanding variety, and steadfast modesty of form. The best-known piece, *Litanies* for organ (1937), represents only one aspect of Alain's style—the vivacity and vitality of his rhythm, incorporating the fluency of Messiaen's without its obscurity. The *Easy Suite for Piano* (1938) shows Alain's melodic grace, and arouses curiosity about the choral works of his last years. None of the piano music is meant for concert performance. In a prefatory note, Alain calls the pieces "a series of impressions," whose aim will be attained "if one of you, readers, suddenly meets himself in one of these lines, if he stops, touched, and then goes on, having received a little of that sweetness that bathes you when your eyes meet a friend's." More than one reader has been touched in just this way.

The period that includes composers like Weill, Copland, Finzi, Distler, Dallapiccola, Poulenc, and Alain would be rich even if it lacked such transcendent figures as Schoenberg, Bartók, and Stravinsky. To illumine this richness, though we must leave it largely unexplored and unexplained, is one of the purposes of the historical patterns we trace. Our pattern should not permit even Stravinsky to cast too deep a shadow over his contemporaries. To be sure, in the light of the rich background such an achievement as Stravinsky's may shine all the brighter, and his youthful vigor in the years after the deaths of Weill, Finzi, Distler, and Alain may seem all the more wonderful. But in calling these younger men and a throng of their contemporaries "successors to Prokofiev" the danger of neglecting their divergences is minimized, and at the same time a generalization is clarified, namely, that the attitude represented by Prokofiev was as vital and productive as the attitudes of Webern and Hindemith in the over-all picture of mid-20th-century music.

An outstanding representative of the generation born in the 1920s, Hans Werner Henze, in one of his *Essays* (1964) indicated the constant renewal of attitudes comparable to Prokofiev's:

A step into unknown territory need not always proceed on a technical foundation, and it need not necessarily be directed "forward." (Who can say which direction is "forward"?) It might even be undertaken with means that seem, in the mist, in the limited visibility of our epoch, obsolete or "useless." . . . The question "where do we stand today?" can be answered only thus: each one stands in another place. On his own feet.

CHAPTER XXVII

Stravinsky
to His Eightieth Birthday

AFTER THE *Rake's Progress*, Stravinsky looked for more English words to set to music, apart from the theater. In the next ten years, he composed six works with English texts, various in their sources, sizes, and shapes, but alike in their religious ideas and, all but one, alike in their excellence: the Cantata on the *Lyke-Wake Dirge* and three other anonymous poems of the late Middle Ages (1951–52); Shakespeare's sonnet, "Music to heare," and two songs from Shakespeare's plays (1952); Dylan Thomas's poem to his father, "Do not go gentle into that good night," in memory of Thomas himself (1954); the *Sermon, Narrative, and Prayer*, from the Bible and Thomas Dekker, in memory of Stravinsky's friend James McLane, Episcopal minister (1960–61); *The Flood*, dance-drama for television, from the Bible and other sources (1961–62); and the anthem "The Dove Descending," from T. S. Eliot's *Four Quartets*, dedicated to Eliot (1962). These works offered an opportunity for English-speaking listeners to become intimately acquainted with Stravinsky and to follow the development of his music through his seventies more closely than any but Russian-speaking listeners could do for his earlier career.

Alongside the English works were two Latin ones: the twenty-minute oratorio, *Canticum sacrum (Sacred Song)* for the city of Venice, in honor of its patron Saint Mark (1955–56), and the forty-minute selection from the Biblical book entitled in the Vulgate *Threni (Dirges, that is, The Lamentations of the Prophet Jeremiah*, 1957–58). The intricacies and moving depths of these works could best be approached after some study of the smaller works that preceded and followed them.

During the same decade Stravinsky added one more masterpiece to his series of ballets: *Agon (Contest*, 1954–57). Balanchine's choreography and the performance of his company in this plotless work made its musical riches of wit, energy, and grace, originality and renewal of tradition, all evident and thrilling to anyone who had ever enjoyed one of the ballets from *Apollo* through *Orpheus*. *Agon* took its place as a favorite in Balanchine's repertory, and the music was recorded more than once.

Besides *Agon* there were two important instrumental pieces: the Septet for three winds, three strings, and piano (1952–53) and the *Movements* for piano and orchestra (1960–61), which might be thought of as successors to the Octet and the concertos. Finally there were the transformations of music by Bach and Gesualdo, comparable to *Pulcinella* and *The Fairy's Kiss*, and some very short pieces in memory of the painter Dufy and the patron Prince Fürstenberg. The *Movements* and the *Monumentum pro Gesualdo* became ballets in turn.

Except for *Agon*, all these new works met with the polite incomprehension or aversion of most audiences and critics. Even some who were beginning to discover the splendors of the *Symphony of Psalms* behind its austerity, or the wisdom of the *Soldier's Tale* behind its grotesquery, were able now only to repeat the old complaints that Stravinsky had exhausted his inspiration, that he had abandoned nature and humane tradition to pursue dry technical problems or to keep up to date with the superficial fashions of the European avant-garde; that in any case, for all his cleverness, he was too cold to be good. Furthermore, without necessarily sharing these complaints, many musicians virtually ignored Stravinsky's new work, forming an opinion of it after a single hearing of a recording or a quick glance at the score; they would do better to ignore it altogether until they could devote real attention to it.

More sympathetic critics were sometimes no more helpful; they rejected the old complaints and praised the composer's vitality, but then they concentrated attention on his surprising *rapprochement* with Schoenberg and Webern. They devoted more ingenuity to interpreting this surprise than to considering the new music itself, or the texts of the vocal works. If they studied the scores, it was chiefly to trace the "serial" technique and the "advance" from one work to the next in the use of this technique. Though Craft, Mason, Keller, Cone, Vlad, and other close students of the scores agreed that the technique was properly subordinate to the ideas, and that Stravinsky was as individual a genius as ever in his latest phase, still they could not forbear to discuss at length the manipulation of the series, and they were rarely able to show the connection between this and the individual harmony and rhythm, or to show convincingly how the series served the form and the idea. Instead, all too often, they relieved the dryness of technical description with sweeping statements about the history of musical "language" rather like those of Krenek and Leibowitz. The unbalanced emphasis of the apologists naturally tended to confirm hostile views. It was easy to invent alternate historical theories, consigning Stravinsky to a blind alley just as his admirers tended to do for Hindemith and Prokofiev, Martin and Poulenc. A history in the service of growing appreciation must proceed differently.

———•—•———

The poems of the Cantata may seem, to a casual reader or to a listener preoccupied with chords and contrapuntal devices, only quaintly charming. An attentive and open-minded listener to Stravinsky's setting, on the contrary, can take the poems seriously, discover connections among them, and feel their relevance to "every night and all." The *Lyke-Wake Dirge* is a litany for the dead, tracing a journey "from hence" to "Whinnymuir," to "Brigg o' Dread," and to "Purgatory fire," always repeating the prayer, "Christe receive thye saule." Stravinsky uses this poem as a tranquil framework for the cantata—a choral prelude, two interludes, and a postlude. On each occasion his pair of phrases is repeated, without variation except for the supplementary instrumental cadence, to advance the journey two lines. At the end, the first line is recapitulated in addition, with a new cadence. Thus the same phrases are heard altogether nine times within half an hour. Their beauty is such that it grows more poignant every time. The chorus is women's voices in two parts, occasionally diverging to three, always together in rhythm. The accompaniment is a band of two flutes, oboe, and English horn, weaving subtle sonorities on the chords of the melody, and a cello providing a simple bass. The chorus has no other part in the cantata. The same instrumental ensemble accompanies throughout, except that the English-horn player changes to second oboe in the central movement. This is a "sacred history," the reply of Christ to the chorus, sung by tenor solo; Stravinsky makes it also a "Ricercar," that is, a contrapuntal elaboration of a single idea.

Tomorrow shall be my dancing day,	Cantus cancrizans
I would my true love did so chance	
to see the legend of my play,	
To call my true love to my dance.	Ritornello
Sing, oh, my love.	Cantus cancrizans
This have I done for my true love.	
Then was I born of a Virgin pure.	
Of her I took fleshly substance.	
Thus was I knit to man's nature,	
to call my true love to my dance.	R
Sing, oh, my love . . .	Cantus cancrizans
In a manger . . .	Canon [A]
to call . . .	R [modified]
Then afterwards baptiz'd . . .	Canon [B]
to call . . .	R

Into the desert I was led . . .	Canon [A modified]
to have me break my true love's dance.	R
The Jews on me they made great suit . . .	Canon [C]
to call my true love to my dance.	R
For thirty pence Judas me sold . . .	Canon [A]
the same is he shall lead the dance.	R
Before Pilate . . .	Canon [D]
judg'd me to die to lead the dance.	R
Then on the cross . . .	Canon [A]
to call my true love to my dance.	R
Then down to Hell . . . and rose . . .	Canon [E]
up to my true love and the dance.	R
Then up to Heav'n . . . that man	Canon [A]
may come unto the gen'ral dance.	R

The opening lines sound like the ornate arioso recitatives of Oedipus or Tom Rakewell-Adonis, but the note "cantus cancrizans" and the brackets provided by Stravinsky in his score call attention to the novel structure of this melody: it is exposing a pattern of pitches, with inversion, retrograde, and retrograde inversion—not a twelve-tone series, but a pattern abstracted from rhythm and so requiring abstract thought before its appearances become perceptible. The same pattern can be recognized embracing every note in the tenor's narrative, though not his "ritornello" or refrain, which is a phrase that might have come from Tom's aria to "Love," again so beautiful that each repetition makes it more so. In the narrative, the oboes and cello weave inconspicuous counterpoint, using the same pattern still more abstractly, with octave substitutions; in these phrases, Stravinsky gives a new vague meaning to the word "canon." His whole "Ricercar" presents a new concentration of musical thought, as different from Schoenberg's kind of concentration as from any previous work of Stravinsky himself, and marvelously apt for the poetic idea of Christ's call to dance. The dance itself is represented in the setting of the famous little love-song, *Westron Wind,* as a joyous duet for the tenor and soprano, with rhythms almost like those of Anne's aria *I go to him,* or of the concluding celebration of victory in *Scènes de ballet.* The bold contrast with the tenor's "Ricercar" would be excessive if the Cantata's unity were not enforced by the instrumentation and by the recurring dirge, and also by the previous introduction of the soprano soloist in a "Ricercar" of her own, "The maidens came . . . After their liff grant them a place eternally to sing," which blends imitative counterpoint with dance-like rhythms, and which contains a little episode of recitative. The Cantata's unity is a more original and meaningful achievement than the novel concentration of the central "Ricercar." This unity interprets and vivifies orthodox truths, just as does that of the *Symphony of Psalms.* Likewise in all the later works, the various novel aspects are means of exemplifying the fundamental principles and attitudes to which Stravinsky is always faithful.

The Shakespeare songs need no such astounding unity, nor such complexity of form. They can be sung by a very limited voice—soprano or alto, since the range is only a tenth up from middle C—and the accompaniment (flute, clarinet, and viola) offers no difficulty in playing. What is difficult is to imagine the right shades of loudness, the right accents, the right ironic tone. When these adjustments elude the performers, listeners have no chance to make sense of the music, for its melodies are not memorable, and its thin sonorities are not appealing. One aspect of the composition has been decoded by David Ward-Steinman more thoroughly than by any other writer: in the sonnet every note except the beginning and end of the accompaniment can be accounted for as belonging to a four-note series; in the second song, after a loosely related introduction, a seven-note series prevails; in the last, a ten-note series is treated somewhat freely. Perhaps these observations will help some singers, but the singer's delight in Stravinsky's minute shadings of the malicious texts will be more help to listeners.

Stravinsky's choice from the poems of Dylan Thomas—one of his best—is a pagan outcry at the approach of death. "Though wise men at their end know dark is right . . . they do not go gentle into that good night . . . Good men . . . rage, rage against the dying of the light . . . And you, my father, . . . curse, bless me now, with your fierce tears." Stravinsky does not go gentle; he too rages. But also he provides the curse and blessing, with an instrumental prelude and postlude of "dirge-canons." The song is for tenor, accompanied by string quartet, sweet and slow except for the four moments of "rage, rage." In the prelude the strings make a subordinate antiphony to a quartet of trombones, like the trio that Mozart had associated with the statue of the good Commendatore in *Don Giovanni,* or like the trombone choirs that Gabrieli and Monteverdi and Schütz had used for their fugal symphonies. In the postlude, the trombones and strings exchange places. Every note of the composition—melody, accompaniment, prelude and postlude—belongs to a series of five notes. In the song itself, the interval between the highest and lowest of these five, bounding each appearance of the series, is a diminished fourth, and the juxtapositions and overlappings of the series make a continuous modulation among minor keys. In the prelude and postlude the bounding interval is reinterpreted as a major third, and the phrases arrive at cadences on major thirds over clear harmonic roots. The fusion of technique, form, and meaning is perfect: the more the technique is studied, the more meaning unfolds. If such a technique were adapted to another form, there could hardly be so much meaning. Both the Cantata and *In memoriam,* and also the Septet, in the decade after their composition, unfolded enough meaning to enough listeners to assume a sure place among the classics of the 20th century. The disconcerting novelty of their "serial" technique had worn off, superseded by the twelve-tone technique, which remained controversial, more difficult to relate to form and meaning.

The cantata, *A Sermon, a Narrative, and a Prayer,* employs mixed chorus and large orchestra, with alto and tenor soloists and a speaker. The text is an amazing compilation. The sermon consists of four cryptic verses from Paul:

We are saved by hope, but hope that is seen is not hope, for what a man sees why does he hope for? (Romans 8:24)

The substance of things hoped for, the evidence of things not seen is faith. (Hebrews 11:1)

And our Lord is a consuming fire. (Heb. 12:29)

If we hope for what we see not, then do we with patience wait for it. (Rom. 8:25)

The two verses from Hebrews are repeated at the end, so that the whole sermon is in two nearly equal parts. Each is introduced by an alto flute solo, with interjections by other solo instruments. The verses from Romans are begun in counterpoint by the choir, and ended by the tenor soloist against a sustained chord for horns. Then the choir begins the answering verse in softly spoken words against *tremolando* strings; it sings "is faith" in a dramatic *forte,* and continues to *fortissimo* for "fire." The chords for "faith" and "fire" are unforgettable.

EXAMPLE XXVII.1   Stravinsky, *A Sermon, a Narrative, and a Prayer,* chords

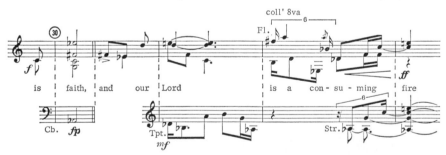

The Narrative is from the Book of Acts, on the trial and death of Stephen, first Christian martyr. It is presented mostly by the speaker, with the alto soloist taking over to sing occasional emphatic phrases; the tenor sings the words of Stephen himself, and also the final words "he fell asleep." Various groups from the orchestra accompany, punctuate, and vividly depict the disputing in the synagogue, the gnashing of teeth, the stoning, and the final sleep.

The Prayer is Thomas Dekker's:

Oh, my God, if it Bee Thy Pleasure to cut me off before night, Yet make me, My Gratious Sheepherd, for one of Thy Lambs to whom Thou Wilt Say, "Come You Blesesd," and cloth me in a white robe of righteousness that I may be one of those singers who shall cry to Thee Alleluia.

Alto solo begins a beautiful melody with soft string accompaniment. Tenor joins in counterpoint, then gradually the chorus joins, accompanied by a quasi-ostinato of bass notes of the harp, piano, and bass viol. The final alleluia is ecstatic, with chorus and strings alternating in chords, while the gongs continue.

EXAMPLE XXVII.2 Stravinsky, *A Sermon, a Narrative, and a Prayer,* end

This music exhibits a twelve-tone set, though obviously it does not conform to Schoenberg's or Webern's rules about harmonic intervals, and its rhythm is pure Stravinsky. The following letters show the forms of the series that appear at the end; throughout the work these are the most frequent, though a few other transpositions are used occasionally, as at measures 31–34.

Eb	E	C	D	Db	Bb	B	F#	G	A	Ab	F
D								F#			
F#								Bb			
E								Ab			
F								A			
Ab								C			
G								B			
C								E			
B								Eb			
A								Db			
Bb								D			
Db	D	Bb	C	B	Ab	A	E	F	G	F#	Eb

It is characteristic of Stravinsky's twelve-tone procedure to prefer the retrograde inversion that begins with the last note of the "original" form, instead of the first. It is characteristic also to detach the six-note groups and combine them arbitrarily, with no concern to avoid doublings and triadic references. A discrepancy may be noted: the viola's A♭ in measure 267 displaces an F♯ that would be required by the series. More important, whether or not it is connected with the series, is the uncanny convergence of the lines to the final chord, and the resolution that this chord provides for the chords of "faith" and "fire" and "sleep," as well as for all of the prayer.

The themes of faith and fire reach a new concentration in the Anthem on Eliot's account of Pentecost:

> The dove descending breaks the air
> With flame of incandescent terror
> Of which the tongues declare
> The one discharge from sin and error.
> The only hope, or else despair
>   Lies in the choice of pyre or pyre—
>   To be redeemed from fire by fire.
>
> Who then devised the torment? Love.
> Love is the unfamiliar Name
> Behind the hands that wove
> The intolerable shirt of flame
> Which human power cannot remove.
>   We only live, only suspire
>   Consumed by either fire or fire.

Stravinsky's setting, for unaccompanied voices, fits the last three lines of each stanza with almost the same music, fervent four-part counterpoint; in the first four lines the counterpoint is only two voices—the upper pair in the first stanza emphasizing the "terror" and "error," the lower pair in the second, rushing to the "flame"—introducing and weaving the twelve-tone series, so that the one long concluding phrase is a climax more powerful than any gongs or trumpets. This anthem is one of Stravinsky's most thoroughly graspable works, a piece worthy to stand beside a Bach chorale or an anthem of Gibbons, yet wholly characteristic of Stravinsky alone.

———— • ————

Once Stravinsky had set to music a sermon and a theological anthem, it was possible, looking back, to see much of his previous work as a kind of preaching. The moral epilogue of the *Rake*, the moral of the *Soldier*, the "dogmatic confessions" of the *Poetics*, and many passages of the *Conversations* fit this description. They preach a consistent gospel. All implicitly demand that we repent, abandon our foolish impossible romantic dreams, and turn to do our duty, the will of God. To seek and to obey God's will for us here and now is the purpose of our freedom. No rule of technique, old or new, and no inspired revelation can relieve us of our freedom. But our freedom cannot be hoarded, any more than it can be evaded. It is meant to be used. Chaos and constraint, madness and damnation end its abuse. Sanity, order, and salvation mean voluntary submission here and now—not once and for all but ever anew in the consuming fire. If we resist this preaching, one of our penalties is to diminish our experience of Stravinsky's work. If we accept the preaching, we can find all his work more and more meaningful.

The *Canticum sacrum* is a sermon within an unusual service of worship. The text is assembled from many Biblical books. The work begins and ends with the chorus chanting in chords, accompanied by brasses, "Go ye and preach . . . and they went and preached everywhere . . ." To prepare for the sermon, there is a celebration, sung by tenor solo with flute obbligato, "*Surge aquilo* . . . Arise, North Wind . . . eat, friends, and drink; be intoxicated, dearest ones." Then the sermon is a triptych of choral exhortations to the theological virtues: faith, hope, and charity; but Stravinsky reverses their order, for the love of God follows naturally from the love of food and drink and friends, while hope is more obscure, and faith is most difficult. Following the sermon is a short dramatic narrative and prayer, mainly by baritone solo, "Lord, I believe; help my unbelief." The music of the sermon is very difficult, severely contrapuntal. The surrounding subordinate parts are immensely attractive—the framing choruses recognizably like the Allegro of the *Symphony of Psalms*, with interludes for organ, slow, contrapuntal, diatonic; the tenor aria a sensuous revision of Webern's wide skips and thin changing sonorities; the narrative and prayer deeply moving, like the English works. The sentences of the sermon are introduced in interludes for organ, presenting the forms of the twelve-tone sets so baldly that there can be little doubt we should learn them as keys to the chromatic choral counterpoint. There can be still less doubt that to hear this music right we must obey the exhortations: love God . . . love our neighbor . . . and pray for help in our unbelief.

Threni is Jeremiah's preaching and prayer. Stravinsky chose verses from the three chapters of the book of Lamentations—elegies I, III, and V—that are sung in services at Matins on Thursday, Friday, and Saturday of Holy Week. Within the Good Friday chapter he chose verses from the three titled sections: complaint, sense of hope, and solace. Within chapters I and III he preserved the Hebrew initials for each verse, in accordance with custom. But the particular verses he chose are only a few of those used in the liturgy, plus a few not used, such as the final verse, "Turn us to thee,

Lord, and renew our days." The setting calls for six solo singers, who must be both extremely able and utterly willing to abjure vocal display. Chorus and instrumental ensemble are subordinate. The present writer is only beginning to discover the beauty of *Threni*, and cannot yet follow more than a phrase or two at a time, but there are enough phrases that approach the perfection of the Anthem to guarantee that his study will continue. Ward-Steinman, who after tracing all the "capricious" treatment of the twelve-tone series, praises the theoretical stylistic unity of the work (Stravinsky's first composition to use the twelve-tone technique throughout), still confesses that the *Canticum sacrum* seems to him "much more logical and convincing."

The Flood is more comprehensive than any sermon. If it contains an implicit sermon within its enormous range of diverse elements, then it resists understanding, indeed, but not in the way that *Threni* does; any listener can find some part of it moving. It is a "dance-drama" for television, framed by a vigorous choral setting of a few lines from the liturgical hymn, *Te Deum* (in Latin), during which the eight dancers represent the cherubim. The two instrumental dance movements, set off distinctly from the rest of the work, occupy only about five minutes out of the half hour. The "drama" is presented chiefly in speech, sometimes with orchestral background, sometimes without. In the course of the drama the main musical passages are deliberately monotonous, anti-dramatic settings of the words of God, for a duet of basses, always preceded by the rapid thumps of a drum. For the text of the drama, Robert Craft compiled fragments from Genesis, from two 16th-century miracle plays, and from unnamed sources; their various literary styles jar with each other. The narrator begins with the story of creation, and continues with the revolt of Satan (tenor), the fall of Adam and Eve, and God's curse. Then, at last, almost halfway through, comes Noah, speaking querulously in reply to God's austere command. The building of the ark is the central dance, with delightful Webernish sounds of hammering and sawing, for large orchestra. Then a "caller" catalogues the animals. Then Noah and his wife play a scene of comedy. Then comes the longest dance, the flood itself. Here, as Stravinsky describes it in his *Expositions and Developments*, the orchestra sounds "full and high, choked, unable to 'breathe,' but not loud," not climactic. God's covenant of the rainbow and a last word by Satan suggest that the Flood is, as Stravinsky says, "the Eternal Catastrophe. *The Flood* is also *The Bomb*." The opening lines of the *Te Deum* return in reverse order and fade away. All these contrasting ideas and feelings may be supposed to constitute a whole in Stravinsky's mind, but no assembly of actors, dancers, and singers can be expected to find that unity and make it perceptible, for the music does not claim to do so, no matter how firmly unified the music itself may be by a single twelve-tone series. The television performance of *The Flood* was an indefensible jumble, described with proper outrage by Richard Franko Goldman. When a preacher consented to such an error, his tone of authority became arrogance; worse, he obscured the preaching of his humblest and most perfect works.

For many prospective hearers of Stravinsky's sermons, it was hard enough to reconcile his irreverent wit and his dancing gusto with sincere piety; if religious associations impelled them to look for an intimate warm feeling of consolation, or a vague mystical sense of transcendence, or a reassuring solidarity with the hallowed forms of organized churches, Stravinsky rebuffed them more sharply than unbelievers. If in addition they saw what seemed to be his cynical attitude toward the production of *The Flood*—or, in the same year, his consent to the use of fragments from the *Soldier* and the Octet as background music for the film version of Jean Genet's play *The Balcony*—they could not be blamed for failing to grasp his true faith, his tough integrity, and his genuine humility before God. But whoever wished to learn from him and to enjoy his work more and more would forget movies and television, and keep trying to comprehend his whole character, which could surely be no less complex than his work.

The testimony of Stravinsky's painter son, Theodore, carried special weight on questions of his character and his faith. When the son's book *The Message of Igor Stravinsky* appeared in 1948, its emphasis on the current slogan of "classicism" overshadowed what was said about religion. After the series of explicitly religious works, it was easier to note and agree with Theodore Stravinsky's insistence that the essence of his father's work would always escape minds for whom religious ideas had become "incomprehensible, or foreign, or chimerical," and that such minds would always distort "the true meaning of his message."

Yet the solemn interpretation of Theodore Stravinsky could do justice to only a part of his father's complex character—an essential part, yes, but inseparable in him from qualities that might be incongruous for anyone else.

———•———

In his several volumes of answers to questions by Robert Craft, Stravinsky reveals more and more of what he calls "an old theater composer's garrulous mind." The autobiography and the *Poetics*, he says, "are much less *like* me, in all my faults, than my conversations." The vast range of thought, the precision of language, the continued mixing of dogmatism and wit, and the lack of any structure beyond the range of a paragraph in these "conversations" offended and confused many readers just as the music did. But persevering students of both words and music could benefit endlessly. The anonymous reviewer of the London *Times* found in Stravinsky's talk "a clarity unique among the verbal declarations of creative artists." Lincoln Kirstein recognized in the talk some of the outstanding elusive qualities of the man, for which he invented apt metaphors:

Surgeons are not necessarily kind men. Their benevolence is questionable, and when they save lives it is secondary. . . The aura of bard, mage, oracle is not of his choosing. His mind is too active, restless, sharp to make comfort for a solid cult. An acetyline torch is bright and cuts steel but it does not glow like a domestic hearth. Stravinsky has never been captured by his myth or his critics. In his life, as in his art, he is a realist—possibly a lyric realist, but with a working intelligence so devoid of self-deception that he repels the benevolent sunset which crowns other mellow careers.

For Kirstein and some others, it was possible to neglect the religious dogma underlying Stravinsky's "realism" and still to relish the cutting intelligence of his personality as well as his work, to delight in the new complexity of harmony and rhythm in his *Movements*, and to trust that whatever at first seemed puzzling or boring would soon prove to be vital. Thus Edmund Wilson testified:

Stravinsky *has* meant a good deal to me—more than any other contemporary artist in any nonliterary art . . . Stravinsky has kept going through his 80's with such tireless pertinacity and vivacity that I feel he has helped *me* to keep going. I'm not in the least religious, but I think it's significant and admirable that Stravinsky should begin every day with a prayer.

In 1962, after celebrating his eightieth birthday in Hamburg with performances of *Agon* and other recent works, Stravinsky visited Moscow and Leningrad—his first trip home since the Revolution. He was accompanied by his wife and by Robert Craft, the American conductor who had lived and worked with him for fifteen years. Craft wrote a revealing diary-like report of the fabulous trip. Rehearsing with a Russian-speaking orchestra for the first time in his life, Stravinsky became "more buoyant than I ever have seen him." At a "Dostoievskian dinner" Stravinsky astonished Craft with a speech that seemed to him extravagantly patriotic:

A man has one birthplace, one fatherland, one country—he *can* have only one country—and the place of his birth is the most important factor in his life. I regret that circumstances separated me from my fatherland, that I did not bring my works to birth there, and above all that I was not there to help the new Soviet Union create its own music. But I did not leave Russia only by my own will, even though I admit that I disliked much in my Russia and in Russia generally—but the right to criticize Russia is mine, because Russia is mine and because I love it. I do not give any foreigner that right.

Craft recovered from his astonishment to become convinced "that to be recognized and acclaimed as a Russian in Russia, and to be performed there, has meant more to him than anything else in the years I have known him." The final event of the trip was a forty-minute conversation with Khrushchev, lively and amicable. Then back to Paris, London, New York, and Hollywood, and to work on the cantata in Hebrew, for Israel, *Abraham and Isaac.*

Craft mentions in this report that Stravinsky's great-grandfather, Ignatievich, lived to be a hundred and eleven, and died as a result of a fall, when he was trying to climb over a fence, because his children had locked him in for safety's sake. Igor Stravinsky could be counted on to take better care—to keep the key in his own pocket.

———— ·•· ————

It could be predicted that if any civilization survived the 20th century, Stravinsky's work would continue to inspire many—not all—younger musicians, in many ways—not one way only. Just as such different composers as Bartók, Varèse, Orff, Messiaen, Shostakovich, Fortner, Carter, Prokofiev, Copland, and Poulenc were all variously related to Stravinsky, so would be some whose careers only began in the last third of the 20th century. And those who achieved something memorable would resemble Stravinsky not so much in any particular style, technique, form, mood, or purpose as in the mysterious power to renew techniques and forms in the service of their own authentic ideas.

In his unfathomable individuality, integrating all his changing experience, Stravinsky represents the barely imaginable unity of all music and the unity of all mankind. He cannot represent Russia, for most of his work does not belong there; yet his Russian birth is "the most important factor in his life," and Russia can never be absent from the unity he represents. He cannot represent America; but here is his "last, longest, happiest, and I should hope final home—though I am still an inveterate voyager in all senses." He cannot represent any other nation, but he participates in the life of nearly every European one—especially France, Germany, and Italy—and he has indirect connections with Africa and Asia. He cannot represent the church, the theater, the concert hall, the school, or any newer institution; yet his relations with institutions are essential parts of himself, and his work contributes to their vitality, so that he represents their possible unity. He cannot represent any traditional genre of music, such as the symphony, opera, song, quartet, or even ballet, which he has most drastically changed; in each genre his works are outstanding exceptions; at the same time all the various traditions of form are relevant to most of his works. He cannot represent the stylistic development of his important contemporaries, yet by his own extreme stylistic range and precision he enriches the very meaning of the notion of style, and affects to some degree the objective relations among the great styles of the past and the future. He does not affect nations, institutions, forms, and styles to such a degree as Debussy did, not to mention Beethoven; he does not found a new category of music, as Schoenberg and jazz did, nor reconcile divisions as Bartók did; yet his achievement is at once as bold and as near perfection as any. For poets, painters, and dancers, Stravinsky's work is the most exciting in music since Debussy's, and not a few of them, like the poet and art critic Herbert Read, consider Stravinsky the most representative artist of the age. Among the multiplying disciplines of science and scholarship, Stravinsky most worthily maintains the place of music as speculative activity, capable of coordination with other disciplines, neither dependent on them nor claiming to replace them. The range, speed, and accuracy of his intelligence enable him to exploit every kind of musical knowledge. But all his knowledge is exploited in his activity; none is pedantically displayed for its own sake. Thus he represents not overweening intellect but man exercising the unprecedented powers that he commands in the 20th century. He represents the whole of music and man because he represents no segregated faction or hypostatized faculty but rather acts in each unique moment with all the resources concentrated in him at that moment.

The philosopher Nicolas Berdyaev, in an essay on "Freedom to Create," eloquently expressed the general ideas that have been exemplified here by Stravinsky.

The true creative act is personal, that is to say, individual, but it is not, in any sense of the word, the result of individualism. . . . Creative activity pre-supposes matter in the world, in nature, in society, and in the soul; it is bound up with them. It cannot, however, be explained by this matter, nor can it be said to arise from necessity. . . Tradition is by no means just another name for the conservative spirit which is actually prejudicial to creative development: it is rather the inner connection with the creation of the past and its cultural values. . . What is most individual and personal is at the same time the most general and universal. Genuine liberty rightly passes beyond the frontiers of all forms of isolated self-sufficiency and knows nothing of our watertight compartments; it overcomes human mediocrity in which man so naturally buries himself. Creative liberty always moves toward the creation of a new life and new values.

Not only Stravinsky but also Schoenberg, Bartók, and many of their contemporaries have created new cultural values, universal in this sense. With such values free individuals can always make "inner connections," continually recreating the tradition of genuine liberty.

Notes on Sources

Most quotations in the text are accompanied by a reference to the source and date, and most articles and monographs referred to will be easily located in the annotated Bibliography that follows. The notes presented here are intended to assist readers who may wish exact page references in locating sources cited in the text. Where no note is given, readers will generally find the Bibliography a sufficient guide for further information.

The notes are keyed to the page and line of the text on which the citation appears, and key words or phrases are given where they would be of assistance. The abbreviations used here are the same as those in the Bibliography.

CHAPTER I

PAGE	LINE	
3	21	Debussy, *Lettres à son éditeur*, Paris, 1927, p. 81.
	28	Gatti-Casazza, interview in *The New York Times*, Mar. 15, 1925, p. x–6.
4	4	[on *Diane*] Léon Vallas, *Claude Debussy et son temps*, Paris, 1932, p. 35.
	23	[to Messager] Debussy, *L'Enfance de Pelléas*, Paris, 1938, p. 74.
	29	*Ibid.*, 37.
	33	Debussy, *Lettres inédites à André Caplet*, Monaco, 1957, p. 57.
5	6	[on opera] Vallas, *The Theories of Claude Debussy*, Oxford, 1929, p. 93.
	25	Debussy, *Lettres à sa femme Emma*, Paris, 1957, p. 103.
13	25	Hellmut Seraphin, *Debussys Kammermusikwerke*, Munich, 1962, p. 81.
14	4	Maurice Emmanuel et al., *Inédits sur Claude Debussy*, Paris, 1942, p. 27; also in Lockspeiser, *Debussy, London*, 1962, I, 204.
	26	[over-precision] Vallas, *Theories*, p. ii.
	33	Debussy, *M. Croche*, Paris, 1927, pp. 21, 19.
16	3	Gustave Samazeuilh, *Musiciens de mon temps*, Paris, 1947, p. 118.
18	6	[chord in a structure] Werner Danckert, *Claude Debussy*, Berlin, 1950, p. 98.
19	8	[to Lenormand] Vallas, *Debussy et son temps*, p. 216.
	19	Louis Laloy, *La Musique retrouvée*, Paris, 1928, p. 115.
	23	Debussy, *M. Croche*, p. 15.
20	38	André Schaeffner, *Debussy et ses rapports avec la musique russe*, in Souvtchinsky, *Un Siècle de la musique russe*, Paris, 1953, I, 123.
22	19	Debussy and Chausson, *Correspondance inédite*, in RM, VII/1 (1925), 118.
	23	Debussy, *Lettres à son éditeur*, p. 124.
	34	Louisa S. Liebich, *An Englishwoman's Memories of Debussy*, in MT, LIX (1918), 250.
	39	Joseph Kerman, *Opera as Drama*, New York, 1956, p. 171.

CHAPTER II

PAGE LINE

25   2   Debussy, *Lettres à son éditeur*, p. 58.
      35   Danckert, *Claude Debussy*, p. 164.
27   4   [Wagner] Vallas, *Theories*, p. 36.
      15   D. J. Grout, *A Short History of Opera*, New York, 1947, p. 425.
29   3   James Ringo, *The Lure of the Orient*, in ACA, 7/2 (1958), 8.
      3   Siegfried Borris, *Einfluss und Einbruch primitiver Musik*, in *Sociologus*, II (1952), 52.
      5   Daniel Chennevière, *Claude Debussy*, Paris, 1913, p. 15.
      34   [to Godet] Debussy, *Lettres à deux amis*, Paris, 1942, p. 130.
30   14   [futurism] Vallas, *Theories*, p. 164.
      32   [Weber] *Ibid.*, 140.
      33   [Berlioz] *Ibid.*, 40.
      37   [Wagner] Debussy, *M. Croche*, p. 143.
31   4   [classical development] Vallas, *Theories*, p. 107.
      6   Debussy, *Lettres à son éditeur*, p. 142.
      12   [Carraud] Vallas, *Debussy et son temps*, p. 131.
      19   [classical ideal] Vallas, *Theories*, p. 60.
      33   [Mozart] René Peter, *Claude Debussy*, Paris, 1944, p. 75.
32   11   Françoise Gervaise, *La Notion d'arabesque chez Debussy*, in RM, 241 (1958), 3.
      12   [workshop] Vallas, *Theories*, p. 12.
      12   [mechanism] Debussy, *Lettres à deux amis*, p. 149.
33   31   Debussy, *Lettres inédites à André Caplet*, p. 38.
36   19   E. J. Dent, *Busoni*, London, 1933, p. 119.
37   7   Schoenberg, *Briefe*, Mainz, 1958, p. 257.
38   27   Stravinsky, *Poétique musicale*, Cambridge, Mass., 1942, p. 140.
      30   [Wagner] *Ibid.*, 62.
      32   [discipline] *Ibid.*, 52, 78.

CHAPTER III

42   5   Boulez, *Debussy*, in *Encyclopédie de la musique Fasquelle*, Paris, 1958, I, 629.
      9   Allen Sapp, review, in MQ, XXXIX (1953), 310.
43   32   Maggie Teyte, *Star on the Door*, London, 1958, pp. 58, 73.
46   24   Debussy, *Lettres à deux amis*, p. 174.
      40   Debussy, *Lettres à son éditeur*, p. 111.

CHAPTER IV

54   15   MacDowell, *Critical and Historical Essays*, Boston, 1912, pp. 185, 202, 251.
      25   Hamlin Garland, *Roadside Meetings*, New York, 1930, p. 323.
55   23   Lawrence Gilman, *Edward MacDowell*, London, 1909, p. 109.
      31   T. P. Currier, *MacDowell as I Knew Him*, in MQ, I (1915), 22.
56   6   O. G. T. Sonneck, *Suum cuique*, New York, 1916, pp. 91, 97.
      17   Upton Sinclair, *MacDowell*, in *Century*, VII (1926), 52.
      25   MacDowell, *Essays*, p. 257.
58   3   Ives, *Essays before a Sonata*, ed. Boatwright, New York, 1961, pp. 75, 86.
      12   [Debussy] *Ibid.*, 82.
      25   [Wagner] *Ibid.*, 72.
60   2   [My God] *Ibid.*, 84.
66   1   Suyeharu Togi, *Music*, in S. Okuma, ed., *Fifty Years of New Japan*, New York, 1909, p. 375.

CHAPTER V

PAGE LINE
67   21   [Sabaneiev] Sergei Bertensson and Jay Leyda, *Sergei Rachmaninoff*, New York, 1956, p. 69.
68   1   [Tolstoy] *Ibid.*, 88.
    24   [interview] *Ibid.*, 369.
71   9   [Scriabin on Bach] Victor Seroff, *Rachmaninoff*, New York, 1950, p. 177.
    33   [Rachmaninov] *Ibid.*, 169.
72   18   [melody-harmony] Lev Danilevich, *Alexander Nikolajewitsch Skrjabin*, Leipzig, 1954, p. 98.
73   2   A. E. Hull, *A Great Russian Tone-Poet, Scriabin*, London, 1918, pp. 99, 215, 268.
74   32   Boris Pasternak, *I Remember*, New York, 1959, pp. 36–44.
76   34   [Rebikov] Boris Asafiev, *Russian Music*, Ann Arbor, 1953, p. 288.
77   14   *Ibid.*, 317.
80   17   [folksongs] Bohumír Štědroň, *Leoš Janáček, Letters and Reminiscences*, Prague, 1955, p. 70.
    19   [melodic curves of speech] *Ibid.*, 90.
    28   [to Mikota] *Ibid.*, 184.
    40   [in *Dalibor*] *Ibid.*, 227.
81   24   [to Zítek] *Ibid.*, 189.
82   24   [advice to young] *Ibid.*, 174.
83   8   Rudolph Quoika, *Kovařovic*, in MGG, VII (1958), 1655.
    31   Stravinsky, excerpt from a letter to A. Rannit, July 19, 1961, in *Lituanus*, VII (1961), 61.

CHAPTER VI

86   13   Bernard Herrmann, in H. A. Chambers, ed., *Edward Elgar*, London, 1957, p. 17.
    32   [on Debussy] P. M. Young, *Elgar*, London, 1955, p. 258.
87   32   Donald Francis Tovey, *Some English Symphonists*, London, 1941, p. 40.
90   15   [C. K. Scott] Philip Heseltine, *Frederick Delius*, ed. by H. Foss, New York, 1952, p. 159.
91   24   Arthur Hutchings, *Delius*, London, 1948, p. 167.
    32   [Debussy] Vallas, *The Theories of Claude Debussy*, p. 155.
99   22   Karl Ekman, *Jean Sibelius*, London, 1936, p. 176.
101   11   [Wagnerian influence] *Ibid.*, 263.
    23   [*Kalevala*] *Ibid.*, 81.
    40   Astra Desmond, *The Songs*, in G. Abraham, ed., *The Music of Sibelius*, New York, 1947, p. 123.
102   16   Ekman, *Sibelius*, p. 119.
    32   Simon Parmet, *The Symphonies of Sibelius*, London, 1959, p. 48.
    39   [Fourth Symphony] Ekman, *Sibelius*, p. 192.
103   1   [Bruckner] *Ibid.*, 193.
    4   [pathos] *Ibid.*, 217.
    6   [professions of faith] *Ibid.*, 239.
    10   Wilfrid Mellers, *Romanticism and the Twentieth Century*, Fairlawn, N.J., 1957, p. 133.
104   10   [Wagner] Torben Meyer and F. S. Petersen, *Carl Nielsen*, Copenhagen, 1947, I, 87.
    17   Nielsen, *Living Music*, London, 1953, p. 45.
    32   [Latin] Meyer and Petersen, *Nielsen*, I, 30.

CHAPTER VII

PAGE LINE

107 7 Egon Wellesz, interview with the present writer, Oxford, March 1962.

108 3 D. J. Grout, *A Short History of Opera*, New York, 1947, p. 438.

109 10 Gianandrea Gavazzeni, *Quaderno del musicista*, Bergamo, 1952, p. 166.

110 36 E. J. Dent, *Busoni*, London, 1933, p. 307.

111 17 [ceremony] Busoni, *Wesen und Einheit der Musik*, Berlin, 1956, p. 16.

112 15 [Frenchmen] *Ibid.*, 81.

     22 [article for *Pan*] *Ibid.*, 75.

113 11 [new beginning] Busoni, *Entwurf einer neuen Aesthetik*, 2d edn., Leipzig, 1910, p. 35.

     13 [super-European music] *Ibid.*, 47.

     17 [up to the gate] *Ibid.*, 48.

     22 [epigraph] *Ibid.*, 4.

     26 [letter to Selden-Goth] Busoni, *Wesen und Einheit*, p. 234.

     35 ["The Essence of Music"] *Ibid.*, 1, 8.

114 4 [miniature models] *Ibid.*, 211.

     10 [Schoenberg] *Ibid.*, 40.

     17 [anarchy] *Ibid.*, 45.

     36 [new classicism] *Ibid.*, 35.

115 1 [letter to son] *Ibid.*, 38.

     10 [on *Soldier's Tale*] Dent, *Busoni*, p. 283.

     13 [Vogel] Busoni, *Wesen und Einheit*, p. 248.

119 37 Gilbert Chase, *The Music of Spain*, 2d edn., New York, 1959, p. 194.

120 6 André Cœuroy, *Dictionnaire critique de la musique*, Paris, 1956, p. 194.

CHAPTER VIII

122 22 [to Walter] Mahler, *Briefe*, Berlin, 1924, p. 417.

     33 [to Göhler] *Ibid.*, 469.

124 13 Wellesz, *Die neue Instrumentation*, Berlin, 1928, II, 151.

     19 *Ibid.*, II, 108.

126 14 [Mahler's walk] Bruno Walter, *Gustav Mahler*, Berlin, 1957, p. 19.

127 35 [*Art of Fugue*] *Ibid.*, 80.

128 3 [to Hammerschlag] Mahler, *Briefe*, p. 407.

129 1 [to Marschalk] *Ibid.*, 191.

130 27 [First Symphony] *Ibid.*, 146.

133 11 George Breazu, *Kiriac*, in MGG, VII (1958), 947.

CHAPTER IX

134 10 [Mozart and Wagner] R. Strauss, *Betrachtungen und Erinnerungen*, 2d edn., Zürich, 1957, p. 175.

137 21 [Johann Strauss] *Ibid.*, 115.

     28 [Brahms] *Ibid.*, 190.

138 1 [Ritter] *Ibid.*, 219.

     11 [Art] *Ibid.*, 11.

     30 [genius and the mass] *Ibid.*, 16.

139 8 Strauss and Rolland, *Correspondance*, Paris, 1951, p. 174.

     11 [to Krauss] Franz Trenner, ed., *Richard Strauss: Dokumente*, Munich, 1954, p. 254.

     24 Strauss and Rolland, *Correspondance*, p. 36.

PAGE LINE

141   17   [Mendelssohn's scherzos] Strauss, *Betrachtungen*, p. 46.
      39   [bitonality] *Ibid.*, 224.
143   7   H. L. Mencken, *Prejudices*, New York, 1926, V, 295.
144   20   Wellesz, *Reger*, in *Cobbett*, II, 278.
      25   [Reger on Bach] Eberhard Otto, *Max Reger*, Wiesbaden, 1957, p. 76.
145   14   *Ibid.*, 76.
      29   [Brahms] *Ibid.*, 53.
146   34   Reger, *Sämtliche Werke*, ed. H. Klotz, Wiesbaden, 1954, XV, xi.
      36   Fritz Stein, *Thematisches Verzeichnis der . . . Werke von Max Reger*, Leipzig, 1953, p. vii.
147   11   Wilfrid Mellers, *Romanticism and the Twentieth Century*, Fairlawn, N.J., 1957, p. 194.
      18   Wellesz, *Analytische Studie über Regers "Romantische Suite,"* in ZfMw, IV (1921), 115.
148   11   Paul Schenk, *Sigfrid Karg-Elert*, Leipzig, 1927, p. 14.
      35   Albert Schweitzer, *Deutsche und französische Orgelbaukunst*, Leipzig, 1906; English transl. in C. R. Joy, *Music in the Life of Albert Schweitzer*, New York, 1951, p. 161.
149   18   Schweitzer, *Kultur und Ethik*, Munich, 1923, p. xvi.

CHAPTER X

151   10   [Debussy review] Vallas, *The Theories of Claude Debussy*, p. 55.
155   12   [Wagner, etc.] Fauré, *Lettres intimes*, Paris, 1951, p. 183.
      23   [*Prometheus*] *Ibid.*, 66.
      25   [Wagnerian] *Ibid.*, 144.
      32   [ardor] *Ibid.*, 147.
158   4   Rollo H. Myers, *Erik Satie*, London, 1948, p. 110.
      24   [to brother] P.-D. Templier, *Erik Satie*, Paris, 1932, p. 32.
160   19   Roger Shattuck, *The Banquet Years*, New York, 1958, p. 131.
162   22   [memoir] Satie, *Satie-ana*, in RM, V (1924), 224; English transl. in Myers, *Satie*, p. 141.
      40   [to brother] Templier, *Satie*, p. 26.
163   2   Jules Écorcheville, *Erik Satie*, in BSIM, VII (1911), 46.
       5   [the good Claude] Templier, *Satie*, p. 33.
      12   Laloy, *La Musique retrouvée*, Paris, 1928, p. 122.
      18   [lecture on Debussy] Templier, *Satie*, p. 19.
165   30   Gabriel Fournier, *Mémoire*, in RM, 214 (1952), 126.
166   5   Cocteau, *Le Rappel à l'ordre*, Paris, 1948, pp. 26, 28, 32–34, 58.
      35   [*Satisme*] Templier, *Satie*, p. 42.
167   3   Cocteau, *Le Rappel à l'ordre*, Paris, 1948, p. 244.
      12   Ravel, *Contemporary Music*, in *Rice Institute Pamphlets*, XV (1928), 138.
      24   David Drew, *Modern French Music*, in H. Hartog, ed., *European Music in the 20th Century*, London, 1957, p. 248.
168   1   Jacques Maritain, *Art and Poetry*, New York, 1943, pp. 94, 101.
171   34   Roland-Manuel, *Maurice Ravel*, Paris, 1938, p. 44.
173   8   Riccardo Viñes, *Fragments*, in RM, XIX (1938), 361.
175   4   Ravel, *Contemporary Music*, p. 131.
      22   Jacques Février, *Les Exigences de Ravel*, in *Revue internationale de musique*, I/5–6 (April 1939), 393.
176   18   [letters of 1917] Victor Seroff, *Maurice Ravel*, New York, 1953, p. 191.
      24   [to Delvincourt] *Ibid.*, 202.
      34   [Sonata] *Ibid.*, 207.

CHAPTER XI

PAGE LINE

180   4   Egon Wellesz, *Arnold Schönberg*, Leipzig, 1921, p. 34.

       6   Bartók, *Über die Bedeutung der Volksmusik*, in B. Szabolcsi, ed., *Béla Bartók, Weg und Werk*, Leipzig, 1956, p. 165.

     14   C. F. Ramuz, *Souvenirs sur Igor Strawinsky*, Lausanne, 1952, p. 121.

183   19   Alan Lomax, *Mr. Jelly Roll*, New York, 1950, pp. 147, 150.

186   13   *Ibid.*, 63.

188   29   *Ibid.*, 62.

     34   [Guy Waterman] Martin Williams, ed., *The Art of Jazz*, New York, 1959, p. 26.

190   2   Lomax, *Mr. Jelly Roll*, p. 63.

192   14   Edmund Wilson, *The Jazz Problem*, in *The New Republic*, XLV (1926), 217.

CHAPTER XII

195   1   [to Rosbaud] Schoenberg, *Briefe*, Mainz, 1958, p. 255.

     25   Erwin Stein, *The Treatment of the Speaking Voice in "Pierrot Lunaire,"* in his *Orpheus in New Guises*, London, 1953, p. 89.

     32   Maggie Teyte, *Star on the Door*, London, 1958, p. 170.

     33   Alois Melichar, *Musik in der Zwangsjacke*, Vienna, 1958, p. 125.

     38   Louis Fleury, *About "Pierrot Lunaire,"* in ML, V (1924), 347.

196   9   Pierre Boulez, *Dire, jouer, chanter*, in *La Musique et ses problèmes*, Paris, 1963, p. 306.

     23   André Schaeffner, *Variations Schoenberg*, in *Contrepoints*, VII (1950), 122.

202   30   Schoenberg, *Harmonielehre*, 3d edn., Vienna, 1922, p. 498.

     38   [to Marya Freund] Schoenberg, *Briefe*, p. 82.

203   14   Schoenberg, *Harmonielehre*, pp. 85–87.

204   1   *Ibid.*, 466, 502, 504.

206   4   *Ibid.*, 464.

207   15   Schoenberg, *Style and Idea*, New York, 1950, p. 47.

     26   ["On revient toujours"] *Ibid.*, 213.

208   10   Schoenberg, *Harmonielehre*, p. 487.

     14   Berg, *Was ist atonal?*, in SMz, LXXXV (1945), 47; English transl. in N. Slonimsky, *Music Since 1900*, New York, 1949, p. 677.

     29   Schoenberg, *Harmonielehre*, p. 184.

209   1   Schoenberg, *Structural Functions of Harmony*, New York, 1954, p. 193.

     11   Schoenberg, *Style and Idea*, p. 107.

211   13   Schoenberg, letter to James Fassett, in program of Schoenberg Festival at Los Angeles County Museum, Jan. 22, 1950.

212   10   H. H. Stuckenschmidt, *Arnold Schönberg*, 2d edn., Zürich, 1957, p. 164.

     22   Wassily Kandinsky, *Die Bilder*, in Berg et al., *Arnold Schönberg*, Munich, 1912, pp. 59, 64.

213   10   T. W. Adorno, *Arnold Schönberg*, in *Die grossen Deutschen*, IV (1957), 508.

214   1   [on *Pelleas*] Schoenberg, *Briefe*, p. 84.

     30   [on Op. 9] Schoenberg, *My Evolution*, in MQ, XXXVIII (1952), 517.

215   8   [to Ferroud] Schoenberg, *Briefe*, p. 77.

     10   [to Klenau] *Ibid.*, 82.

     33   [on Debussy] Schoenberg, *Harmonielehre*, pp. 483, 474.

216   13   [Wagner and Debussy] Schoenberg, *Style and Idea*, p. 104.

     26   Schoenberg, *Nationale Musik*, in Rufer, *Das Werk Arnold Schönbergs*, Kassel, 1959, p. 138.

218   2   Adorno, *Arnold Schoenberg*, in *Die grossen Deutschen*, IV, 512.

     17   [*Klangfarbenmelodie*] Schoenberg, *Harmonielehre*, p. 507.

PAGE LINE

222   5   Berg, *Society for Private Musical Performances in Vienna* (*A Statement of Aims*, in Slonimsky, *Music Since 1900*, New York, 1949, p. 649.

CHAPTER XIII

225   22   [letter to Buşiţia] B. Szabolcsi, ed., *Béla Bartók, Weg und Werk*, Leipzig, 1957, p. 238.
      24   [Kodály] *Ibid.*, 69.
      27   [to Beu] *Ibid.*, 264.
      33   Agatha Fassett, *The Naked Face of Genius*, New York, 1958, p. 6.
226   5   Bartók, *Selbstbiographie*, in Szabolcsi, *Bartók*, 143.
228   27   Bartók, *Über die Bedeutung der Volksmusik, ibid.*, 165.
238   8   [Kodály] *Ibid.*, 55.
      36   Bartók, *Das Problem der neuen Musik*, in *Melos*, I (1920), 107.
242   1   Fassett, *Naked Face*, p. 189.

CHAPTER XIV

244   9   Stravinsky, *An Autobiography*, London, 1936, p. 15.
      14   Stravinsky and Craft, *Conversations*, Garden City, 1959, p. 37.
      28   Stravinsky and Craft, *Memories and Commentaries*, Garden City, 1960, p. 27.
249   11   [Rimsky on Debussy] Stravinsky, *Autobiography*, p. 35.
      14   Stravinsky, *Memories*, p. 124.
      16   [1959 judgment] Stravinsky, *Conversations*, p. 50.
      23   [Debussy's letter] *Avec Stravinsky*, Monaco, 1958, p. 201; another transl. in *Conversations*, p. 54.
250   16   [Scriabin] Stravinsky, *Memories*, p. 63.
      21   [Rachmaninov] Stravinsky, *Conversations*, p. 42.
      34   Marcel Proust, *Remembrance of Things Past*, New York, 1932, II, 544.
251   15   [motivic unity] Stravinsky, *Firebird's First Flight*, in *High Fidelity*, X/6 (June 1960), 34.
      24   S. L. Grigoriev, *The Diaghilev Ballet 1909–1929*, London, 1953, p. 31.
      32   [Debussy on *Petrushka*] *Avec Stravinsky*, p. 199; another transl. in *Conversations*, p. 51.
252   3   Egon Wellesz, *Die neue Instrumentation*, Vienna, 1929, II, 158, 98.
      19   [Diaghilev] E. W. White, *Stravinsky*, London, 1948, p. 48.
      22   [Debussy] *Avec Stravinsky*, p. 199; another transl. in *Conversations*, p. 52.
      27   [pagan rite] Stravinsky, *Autobiography*, p. 55.
      39   André Schaeffner, *Strawinsky*, Paris, 1931, p. 39.
258   41   [jazz] Stravinsky, *Conversations*, p. 131.
259   19   Olivier Messiaen, *Le Rythme chez Igor Strawinsky*, in RM, 191 (1939), 331.
      20   Pierre Boulez, *Propositions*, in *Polyphonie*, II (1948), 65.
      21   Jean Barraqué, *Rythme et développement*, in *Polyphonie*, IX-X (1954), 47.
260   13   Stravinsky, *Poetics of Music*, New York, 1956, pp. 37–41.
263   19   [*Pierrot*] Stravinsky, *Autobiography*, p. 75.
      24   [Schoenberg] Stravinsky, *Conversations*, p. 79.
264   4   [*Pierrot*] Stravinsky and Craft, *Some Composers*, in *Musical America*, LXXXII/6 (June 1962), 6; rev. & abr. version in *Dialogues and a Diary*, Garden City, 1963, p. 54.
      36   [futurists] Stravinsky, *Conversations*, p. 103 ff.
265   36   [translations] *Ibid.*, 36.
266   25   [musical expression] Stravinsky, *Chroniques de ma vie*, Paris, 1935, I, 116.

PAGE LINE

34 Stravinsky and Craft, *Expositions and Developments*, Garden City, 1962, pp. 114, 115, 117.
267 10 [factory tune] Stravinsky, *Memories*, p. 91.
272 13 Stravinsky, *Poetics of Music*, pp. 58, 86.
29 Stravinsky, *Memories*, pp. 104, 121.

CHAPTER XV

287 1 Richard Boyer, *The Hot Bach*, in P. Gammond, ed., *Duke Ellington*, London, 1958, p. 22.

CHAPTER XVI

294 29 Rufer, *Das Werk Arnold Schönbergs*, Kassel, 1959, p. 26.
295 2 Schoenberg, *Style and Idea*, New York, 1950, p. 116.
10 [to Bekker] Schoenberg, *Briefe*, Mainz, 1958, p. 82.
14 [to Kestenberg] *Ibid.*, 224.
27 [1941 lecture] Schoenberg, *Style and Idea*, pp. 102, 107.
300 8 [musical space] *Ibid.*, 109.
33 [purpose of technique] *Ibid.*, 107.
301 6 Rufer, *Das Werk Arnold Schönbergs*, pp. 115, 25.
19 [from lecture] Schoenberg, *Style and Idea*, p. 108.
303 26 Friedrich Wildgans, *J. M. Hauer*, in ÖMz, XIII (1958), 108.
41 Egon Wellesz, *The Origins of Schönberg's Twelve-Tone System*, Washington, D.C., 1958, p. 9.
304 12 Oliver Neighbour, *The Evolution of Twelve-Note Music*, in PRMA, LXXXI (1954), 49.
40 [to Kolisch] Schoenberg, *Briefe*, p. 178.
306 32 Erwin Stein, *Orpheus in New Guises*, London, 1953, p. 95.
307 39 ["true tradition"] Stravinsky and Craft, *Conversations*, Garden City, 1959, p. 79.
40 T. W. Adorno, in *Die grossen Deutschen*, IV, 520.
308 1 [variations] Schoenberg, *Style and Idea*, p. 138.
309 33 Thomas Mann, *Die Entstehung des Doktor Faustus*, Amsterdam, 1949, p. 190; Walter Rubsamen, *Schoenberg in America*, in MQ, XXXVII (1951), 481.
318 5 Chemjo Vinaver, *Anthology of Jewish Music*, New York, 1955, p. 203.

CHAPTER XVII

320 31 Halsey Stevens, *The Life and Music of Béla Bartók*, New York, 1953, p. 191.
321 6 [*Cantata* translation] Bartók, *Levelei*, Budapest, 1948–55, III, 504.
322 4 Serge Moreux, *Béla Bartók*, 2d edn., Paris, 1955, p. 217.
8 Bence Szabolcsi, *Béla Bartók, Weg und Werk*, Leipzig, 1957, p. 37.
35 Jürgen Uhde, *Bartóks Mikrokosmos*, Regensburg, 1954, p. 69.
325 3 Everett Helm, *The Music of Béla Bartók*, in H. Hartog, ed., *European Music in the 20th Century*, London, 1957, p. 31.
14 *Ibid.*, 22, 24.
20 Bernard Wagenaar, *Bartók's Quartets*, in *The New York Times*, Feb. 27, 1949. p. II–x–7.

CHAPTER XVIII

PAGE LINE

331 16 Stravinsky, *Chronological Progress*, in J. F. Cooke, ed., *Great Men*, Philadelphia, 1925, p. 268.

24 Edmund Wilson, *Stravinsky*, in *The New Republic*, XLII (1925), 156.

332 31 Lawrence Morton, *Stravinsky*, in *Encyclopédie de la musique Fasquelle*, Paris, 1961, III, 745.

34 Stravinsky, *Autobiography*, London, 1936, p. 243.

37 Stravinsky and Craft, *Expositions and Developments*, Garden City, 1962, p. 73; the London edn. has still more details.

333 9 Stravinsky and Craft, *Memories and Commentaries*, Garden City, 1960, p. 142.

14 Hans Mersmann, *Strawinsky*, in *Musik der Zeit*, Bonn, 1952, p. 65.

335 23 [*Norwegian Moods*] Stravinsky, *Memories*, p. 93.

336 35 Léon Oleggini, *Connaissance de Strawinsky*, Paris, 1952, p. 113.

337 15 Dagmar Godowsky, *First Person Plural*, New York, 1958, pp. 227, 231, 233, 242.

339 10 Stravinsky, note for recording, Columbia ML 4129, issued c. 1950.

340 19 [slow movement] Stravinsky, *Expositions*, p. 66.

341 6 [new period] Stravinsky, *Memories*, p. 118.

342 6 [origins of *Rake*] *Ibid.*, 144.

344 2 Colin Mason, *Stravinsky's Opera*, in ML, XXXIII (1952), 9.

CHAPTER XIX

345 15 [Stravinsky on Webern] *Die Reihe*, II (1955), 7.

17 Pierre Boulez, *Hommage à Webern*, in *Domaine Musical*, I (1954), 123; also in *Die Reihe*, II (1955), 45.

29 Luigi Dallapiccola, *Gravesano Visit*, in *Gravesaner Blätter*, IV/10 (1958), 3.

346 4 Stravinsky and Craft, *Memories and Commentaries*, Garden City, 1960, p. 97.

27 [letter to Scherchen] *Die Reihe*, II (1955), 25.

349 41 Julien Falk, *Technique de la musique atonale*, Paris, 1959, p. 7.

351 3 Henri Pousseur, *Weberns organische Chromatik*, in *Die Reihe*, II (1955), 56.

16 Walter Kolneder, *Klangtechnik und Motivbildung bei Webern*, in *Annales Universitatis Saraviensis, Philosophische Fakultät*, 9/1 (1960), 44.

18 H. H. Eggebrecht, conversation with the author, May 1962.

24 N. Slonimsky, *The Road to Music*, rev. edn., New York, 1960, pp. 110, vii.

30 [letter to Reich] Webern, *Der Weg zur neuen Musik*, Vienna, 1960, p. 66.

38 Robert Craft, *Anton Webern*, in *The Score*, 13 (1955), 9.

352 20 Webern, *Weg*, p. 52.

354 1 [letter to Berg] *Die Reihe*, II (1955), 22.

9 Hans Moldenhauer, *Rich Webern Legacy*, in *The New York Times*, Sep. 17, 1961, p. x–11.

23 Roberto Gerhard, *Some Lectures by Webern*, in *The Score*, 28 (1961), 25.

28 Friedrich Wildgans, *Anton von Webern*, in ÖMz, XIII (1958), 465.

37 [letter to Berg] *Die Reihe*, II (1955), 23.

355 14 [Nature] Webern, *Weg*, pp. 60, 11.

356 21 Craft, *op. cit.*, 9.

357 14 Pierre Boulez, *Série*, in *Encyclopédie de la musique Fasquelle*, Paris, 1961, III, 696.

366 1 Webern, *Weg*, pp. 37, 38, 41, 42, 47, 56, 58, 60.

368 15 [letter to Reich] Webern, *Weg*, p. 68.

370 8 T. W. Adorno, *Klangfiguren*, Berlin, 1959, p. 173.

18 Simone Weil, *Notebooks*, 2 vols., London, 1956, pp. 605, 628.

CHAPTER XX

PAGE	LINE	
371	22	J. Papaioannou, *Nikos Skalkottas*, in H. Hartog, ed., *European Music in the 20th Century*, London, 1957, p. 320.
372	6	Hans Keller, *Nikos Skalkottas*, in *The Listener*, LII (1954), 1041.
	7	Milein Cosman and Hans Keller, *Stravinsky at Rehearsal*, London, 1962, p. 2.
	12	T. W. Gervais, *Sorabji*, in *Grove*[5], VII, 970.
373	21	Carl Ruggles, letters to John Kirkpatrick, unpublished; excerpts quoted in an article to be published in PNM.
	24	Peter Yates, *Introductory Essay*, in J. Edmunds, *Some 20th-Century American Composers*, New York, 1959, I, 17.
374	4	[Futurists] Edgard Varèse, interview in *The New York Telegraph*, March 1916, cited in J. H. Klarén, *Edgar Varèse*, Boston, 1928, p. 8.
	4	Varèse, *A Communication*, in MQ, XLI (1955), 574.
	10	[list of works] Communicated to the author, April 1962.
377	9	Varèse, *Organized Sound*, in *Commonweal*, XXXIII (1940), 204.
	16	Stravinsky and Craft, *Memories and Commentaries*, Garden City, 1960, p. 96.
	29	[William Grant Still] Madeleine Goss, *Modern Music Makers*, New York, 1952, p. 210.
382	40	[1933] Anton Webern, *Der Weg zur neuen Musik*, Vienna, 1960, p. 16.
383	12	[1951] Pierre Boulez, *Moment de Bach*, in *Contrepoints*, VII (1951), 79.
	18	[1960] Stravinsky, *Memories*, p. 115.
385	15	Vernon Duke, *Passport to Paris*, Boston, 1955, p. 330.
	24	Kathleen Hoover and John Cage, *Virgil Thomson*, New York, 1959, p. 245.
386	15	Virgil Thomson, *Toward Improving the Musical Race*, in *Musical America*, LXXXI/7 (July 1961), 5.
	22	H. H. Stuckenschmidt, *Boris Blacher*, Berlin, 1963, p. 41.
388	6	[*Carmina burana*] Andreas Liess, *Carl Orff, Idee und Werk*, Zürich, 1955, p. 27.
	19	[*Pelléas*] *Ibid.*, 11.
389	25	Ingeborg Kiekert, *Die musikalische Form in den Werken Carl Orffs*, Regensburg, 1957, p. 75.
	38	Winfried Zillig, *Variationen über neue Musik*, Munich, 1959, p. 199.
390	26	[jumble of rainbows] Olivier Messiaen, *The Technique of My Musical Language*, Paris, 1950, p. 52.
391	4	*Ibid.*, 13, 31.
393	15	[mother] Antoine Goléa, *Rencontres avec Olivier Messiaen*, Paris, 1961, p. 19.
	23	[*Pelléas*] *Ibid.*, 27.
394	12	[rhythms] *Ibid.*, 28.
	28	[*personnages rythmiques*] *Ibid.*, 90.
395	11	[bird calls] *Ibid.*, 221, 234.

CHAPTER XXI

396	18	Pierre Boulez, *Tendances de la musique récente*, in RM, 236 (1957), 28.
	29	Hindemith, *A Composer's World*, Cambridge, Mass., 1952, p. 98.
397	4	Hindemith, *The Craft of Musical Composition*, New York, 1942, I, 8 and 10.
	39	Max Rieple, *Musik in Donaueschingen*, Konstanz, 1959, p. 25.
398	5	[Hindemith in *Neue Musikzeitung*] *Ibid.*, p. 33.
	28	[Sekles] Heinz Schröter, *Paul Hindemiths Besuch in Frankfurt*, in *Melos*, XIV (1946), 254.
	40	Winfried Zillig, *Variationen über neue Musik*, Munich, 1959, p. 126.
399	8	Paul Bekker, *Neue Musik*, Stuttgart, 1923, p. 113

PAGE LINE

      12   [war experience] *Paul Hindemith: Zeugnis in Bildern*, Mainz, 1955, p. 38.
401 18   [silly term] Hindemith, *A Composer's World*, p. viii.
      30   *Ibid.*, 214, 217, 219.
405 20   *Ibid.*, 114, 125, 127.

CHAPTER XXII

418 29   [new equilibrium] Marc Pincherle, *Roussel*, Geneva, 1957, p. 58.
      38   [to Laloy] *Ibid.*, 45.
419   9   [1919 on Debussy] *Ibid.*, 51.
      31   [to Boulanger] *Ibid.*, 54.
421 26   [new order] Alfredo Casella, *Music in My Time*, Norman, Okla., 1955.
      39   [Massimo Mila] D'Amico and Gatti, eds., *Alfredo Casella*, Milan, 1958, p. 33.
422 16   [*Faun*] Casella, *Music in My Time*, p. 53.
      28   [style of our own] *Ibid.*, 90.
      37   [duel] *Ibid.*, 105, 110.
423 41   [Roman Vlad] D'Amico and Gatti, eds., *Casella*, p. 135; also Vlad, *Storia della dodecafonia*, Milan, 1958, p. 194.
424   4   Nicolas Slonimsky, *Music Since 1900*, New York, 1949, pp. xxiv, xx.
      38   [Malipiero] G. Scarpa, ed., *L'Opera di G. F. Malipiero*, Bologna, 1952, p. 349.
427   7   Marc Pincherle, *The World of the Virtuoso*, New York, 1963, p. 110.
      16   Federico Sopeña, *Joaquín Turina*, Madrid, 1956, p. 63.
      31   Gilbert Chase, *The Music of Spain*, New York, 1959, pp. 206, 312.
428 33   Cyril Scott, *The Philosophy of Modernism*, London, 1917, pp. 3, 28, 5.
429   1   Scott, *Music: its Secret Influence*, London, 1958, pp. 202, 204.
430 18   Andrew Porter, *Some New British Composers*, in MQ, LI (1965), 12.

CHAPTER XXIII

437 27   Sessions, *Reflections on the Music Life in the United States*, New York, 1956, p. 179.
      34   [friendly argument] *Ibid.*, 13.
438   6   Sessions, *Music in Crisis*, in MM, X/2 (1933), 63.
      24   Sessions, *New Vistas in Musical Education*, in MM, XI (1934), 115.
439 29   Cowell, *Towards Neo-Primitivism*, in MM, X (1933), 149.
      32   Cowell, *New Horizons in Music*, in R. MacIver, ed., *New Horizons in Creative Thinking*, New York, 1954, p. 87.
443   1   Stravinsky and Craft, *Dialogues and a Diary*, Garden City, 1963, p. 48.
      12   Carter, *Shop Talk by an American Composer*, in MQ, XLVI (1960), 189.
444   8   Carter, *Gabriel Fauré*, in *Listen*, VI/1 (May 1945), 8.
      25   Fred Goldbeck, *Willem Pijper*, in *The Chesterian*, 22 (Sep. 1947), 35.
447   1   [on *Karl V*] Conversation with the author, Seattle, May 1962.
      35   Krenek, *The Composer Speaks*, in David Ewen, ed., *The Book of Modern Composers*, New York, 1956, p. 354.
449 11   *Wolfgang Fortner, eine Monographie*, Rodenkirchen, 1960, pp. 132, 137.

CHAPTER XXIV

454 32   Sergei Prokofiev, *Autobiography, Articles, Reminiscences*, transl. by Rose Prokofieva, Moscow, 1959, p. 36.
457   8   [*Giant*] Izrael Nestyev, *Prokofiev*, Stanford, 1960, p. 6.

PAGE   LINE

          15   [*Feast*] *Ibid.*, 13.

          18   [*Maddalena*] *Ibid.*, 59.

          20   [*Gambler*] *Ibid.*, 112.

458   35   [Zhdanov, Khrennikov, Prokofiev] N. Slonimsky, *Music Since 1900*, New York, 1949, pp. 684–709.

461   38   Stravinsky and Craft, *Memories and Commentaries*, Garden City, 1960, p. 64.

462   27   [Diaghilev] Prokofiev, *Autobiography*, p. 42.

463   10   Nicolas Nabokov, *Old Friends and New Music*, Boston, 1951, p. 144.

          30   Prokofiev, *Autobiography*, p. 80.

464   10   Galina Ulanova, *The Author of my Favorite Ballets*, in Prokofiev, *Autobiography*, p. 224.

466   5   D. L. Kinsey, *The Piano Sonatas of Serge Prokofieff*, Columbia Teachers College diss., 1959, p. 170.

          8   Francis Poulenc, *La Musique de piano de Prokofiev*, in P. Souvtchinsky, *Un Siècle de la musique russe*, Paris, 1953, p. 272.

          14   H. C. Schonberg, *The Great Pianists*, New York, 1963, p. 394.

          17   Heinrich Neuhaus, *Prokofiev, Composer and Pianist*, in Prokofiev, *Autobiography*, p. 233.

          30   Vernon Duke, *Passport to Paris*, Boston, 1955, p. 120.

467   6   Prokofiev, *Autobiography*, p. 46.

468   10   Nestyev, *Prokofiev*, p. 435.

CHAPTER XXV

475   1   Honegger, *Ich bin Komponist*, Zürich, 1952, p. 103.

476   4   Koechlin, *Art, liberté, tour d'ivoire*, in *Contrepoints*, VI (1950), 104.

          26   Jeanne Herscher-Clément, *L'Œuvre de Charles Koechlin*, in RM, XVII/169 (1936), 315.

          29   W. H. Mellers, *A Plea for Koechlin*, in MR, II (1942), 190; also in his *Studies in Contemporary Music*, London, 1948, p. 93.

          31   Hélène Jourdan-Morhange, *Mes amis musiciens*, Paris, 1955, p. 201.

          32   Paul Collaer, *La Musique moderne*, Paris, 1955, p. 120.

          35   Pierre Renaudin, *Koechlin*, in MGG, VII (1958), 1316.

477   24   Koechlin, *Le Retour à Bach*, in RM, VIII/1 (1926), 1.

478   7   Milhaud, *Notes without Music*, London, 1952, p. 81.

479   16   David Drew, *Modern French Music*, in H. Hartog, ed., *European Music in the 20th Century*, London, 1957, p. 254.

          33   Milhaud, *Entretiens avec Claude Rostand*, Paris, 1952, p. 12.

480   14   D. J. Grout, *A Short History of Opera*, New York, 1947, p. 527.

481   7   [spell of Debussy] Milhaud, *Entretiens*, p. 46.

          19   Milhaud, *Polytonalité et atonalité*, in RM, IV (1923), 44.

482   20   Milhaud, *Entretiens*, pp. 168, 188.

          29   [Ibert on *Le Chevalier errant*] Gérard Michel, *Ibert*, in MGG, VI (1957), 1035.

483   22   [influence on Messiaen] Antoine Goléa, *Rencontres avec Olivier Messiaen*, Paris, 1961, p. 85.

484   24   Nicolas Slonimsky, ed., *Baker's Biographical Dictionary of Musicians*, New York, 1958, p. 613.

          39   E. M. Maisel, *Charles T. Griffes*, New York, 1943, p. 287.

485   33   [Jewish soul] Marion Bauer, *Ernest Bloch*, in O. Thompson, ed., *International Cyclopedia of Music*, New York, 1949, p. 2271.

488   6   [originality] Hubert Foss, *Ralph Vaughan Williams*, London, 1950, p. 33.

          13   [credo] *Ibid.*, 198–201; Vaughan Williams, *National Music*, London, 1935, p. 17.

489   39   Oliver Neighbour, *Ralph Vaughan Williams*, in *The Score*, 24 (1958), 7.

PAGE LINE

45 Vaughan Williams, *National Music*, p. 75.
490 30 *Ibid.*, 115, 120, 123.
494 14 Pierre Boulez, *Disziplin und Kommunikation*, in *Darmstädter Beiträge zur neuen Musik*, III (1961), 25.
22 [Schoenberg on songs] H. F. Redlich, *Alban Berg*, Vienna, 1957, p. 328.
495 1 [lecture on *Wozzeck*] *Ibid.*, 317.
20 Ernest Ansermet, *An Inner Unity*, in *High Fidelity*, XII/9 (Sep. 1962), 58.
40 Stravinsky and Craft, *Memories and Commentaries*, Garden City, 1960, p. 116.
42 Boulez, *Berg*, in *Encyclopédie de la musique Fasquelle*, Paris, 1958, I, 390.
497 31 Frank Martin, *Literatur und Musik*, in ÖMz, XIV (1959), 403.

CHAPTER XXVI

498 4 Bertolt Brecht, *Betrachtung der Kunst und Kunst der Betrachtung*, in *Sinn und Form*, XIII (1961), 677.
21 Kurt Weill, *Notiz zum Jazz*, in *Anbruch*, XI (1929), 138.
499 6 Weill, *Über den gestischen Charakter der Musik*, in *Die Musik*, XXI (1929), 419.
500 2 Anton Webern, *Brief an Hanns Eisler*, in MuG, VIII (1948), 339.
9 Eric Bentley, ed., *Seven Plays of Bertolt Brecht*, New York, 1961, p. xxiv.
504 9 Copland, *Music and Imagination*, Cambridge, Mass., 1952, p. 109.
505 7 David Drew, *American Chamber Music*, in Alec Robertson, ed., *Chamber Music*, London, 1957, p. 324.
24 Joseph Bloch, *Some American Piano Sonatas*, in *Juilliard Review*, III/3 (1956), 9.
507 30 Howard Ferguson, *Gerald Finzi*, in ML, XXXVIII (1957), 129.
517 25 Poulenc, *Entretiens avec Claude Rostand*, Paris, 1954, p. 29.
518 27 [Cocteau on *Les Biches*] R. H. Myers, *Hommage à Poulenc*, in *Music & Musicians*, XI/7 (Mar. 1963), 8.
519 7 Claude Rostand, *Der heitere und der ernste Poulenc*, in *Melos*, XXX (1963), 125.
14 Ned Rorem, *Poulenc—a Memoir*, in *Tempo*, 64 (1963), 28.
23 [songs] Poulenc, *Mes mélodies et leurs poètes*, in *Les Annales Conferencia*, XXXVI (1947), 507.
31 [piano pieces] Poulenc, *Entretiens*, p. 32.
522 31 H. W. Henze, *Essays*, Mainz, 1964, p. 20.

CHAPTER XXVII

533 34 [*The Flood*] Stravinsky and Craft, *Expositions and Developments*, Garden City, 1962, pp. 142, 144.
534 26 Théodore Stravinsky, *Le Message d'Igor Strawinsky*, Lausanne, 1948, p. 46.
33 [on autobiography and *Poetics*] Stravinsky, *Expositions*, pp. 144, 153.
535 4 Lincoln Kirstein, *Igor Stravinsky*, in *The Nation*, 184 (1957), 530; *Purity Through the Will*, in *The Nation*, 191 (1960), 233.
18 Edmund Wilson, *Every Man his own Eckermann*, in *The New York Review of Books*, I/2 (1963), 4.
29 [trip to Russia] Stravinsky and Craft, *Dialogues and a Diary*, Garden City, 1963, pp. 231, 246.
536 1 *Ibid.*, 247.
537 25 Nicolas Berdyaev, *Towards a New Epoch*, London, 1949, pp. 81–87.

Bibliography

READERS who seek information to supplement what this book contains may use the following list as a guide to the most reliable, most recent, and most interesting sources, with some emphasis on those in English. The present writer has at least scanned every item here (as well as more which have been culled out), and he here comments on many of them, recommending them for their appropriate uses. No doubt some items of value have been rejected or overlooked, and others listed have not yet been thoroughly absorbed— *Ars longa*. However, the list is both extensive and selective enough to help satisfy a widely felt need, always provided that the need to study the music itself is given equal and continual emphasis.

Most of the present list is organized by names of composers and other musicians, in alphabetical order. There are, however, a few subjects that warrant separate treatment. A section of Surveys precedes the composer listing, and at the end there are sections devoted to the subjects of Jazz, Experimental Music (including microtonal, electronic, and other experiments), and Bibliographies; there is also a Miscellaneous section.

LIST OF ABBREVIATIONS USED

ACA	American Composers Alliance, *Bulletin*, New York, 1951– .
AfMw	*Archiv für Musikwissenschaft*, Leipzig, 1918–27; Trossingen, 1952– .
BSIM	*Bulletin de la Société Internationale de Musique* (title varies), Paris, 1908–14.
Cobbett	*Cobbett's Cyclopedic Survey of Chamber Music*, 2d edn., ed. by Colin Mason, 3 vols., London, 1963.
CMJ	*Canadian Music Journal*, Toronto, 1956– .
Grove⁴	*Grove's Dictionary of Music and Musicians*, 4th edn., ed. by H. C. Colles, 5 vols. with supplement, London, 1940.
Grove⁵	*Idem*, 5th edn., ed. by Eric Blom, 9 vols., London, 1954; with *Supplementary Volume*, 1961.
JAMS	*Journal of the American Musicological Society*, Richmond, Va., 1948–
JMT	*Journal of Music Theory*, New Haven, 1957– .
Mf	*Die Musikforschung*, Kassel, 1948– .
MGG	*Die Musik in Geschichte und Gegenwart*, ed. by Friedrich Blume, Kassel, 1949– .
ML	*Music and Letters*, London, 1920– .
MM	*Modern Music*, New York, 1924–47.
MMR	*The Monthly Musical Record*, London, 1871–1960.
MQ	*The Musical Quarterly*, New York, 1915– .
MR	*The Music Review*, Cambridge, 1940– .

MT	*The Musical Times*, London, 1844– .
MuG	*Musik und Gesellschaft*, Berlin, 1951– .
MuK	*Musik und Kirche*, Kassel, 1929– .
NotesMLA	*Notes of the Music Library Association*, Washington, 1943– .
NZfM	*Neue Zeitschrift für Musik* (title varies), Leipzig, 1834– .
ÖMz	*Österreichische Musikzeitschrift*, Vienna, 1946– .
PNM	*Perspectives of New Music*, Princeton, N. J., 1962–
PRMA	*Proceedings of the Royal Musical Association*, London, 1874– .
RM	*La Revue musicale*, Paris, 1920– .
SM	*Sovietskaia Muzyka*, Moscow, 1933– .
SMz	*Schweizerische Musikzeitung*, Zürich, 1861– .
ZfMw	*Zeitschrift für Musikwissenschaft*, Leipzig, 1919–35.

SURVEYS: International and Regional

Abraham, Gerald, *A Hundred Years of Music,* London, 1938; 2d edn., 1949; 3d edn., Chicago, 1964.

Beginning "after Beethoven," this book excels in tracing stylistic development through Wagner and Liszt to the many "nationalists." It is conventional and unsympathetic toward Brahms and most 20th-century music. The 3d edn. includes comments on Boulez and Britten, but does not revise the hasty judgments of late Debussy, Stravinsky, and Webern.

Beckwith, John, and Udo Kasemets, eds., *The Modern Composer and his World. A Report from the International Conference of Composers, Stratford, 1960,* Toronto, 1961.

Blume, Friedrich, *Die Musik von 1830–1914,* in *Musica,* XVI (1962), 283.

Chase, Gilbert, *Creative Trends in Latin American Music,* in *Tempo,* 48 (1958), 28; 50 (1959), 25.

With corrections by Mayer-Serra, in *Tempo,* 51 (1959), 36, this is a good survey.

—— *A Guide to the Music of Latin America,* 2d edn., rev. and enl., Washington, 1962.

Bibliography.

Cohn, Arthur, *The Collector's 20th-Century Music in the Western Hemisphere,* Philadelphia, 1961.

—— *The Collector's 20th-Century Music in Western Europe,* Philadelphia, 1965.

Useful critical discographies, with occasional fresh information on the music itself or the composer, e.g. Villa-Lobos.

Collaer, Paul, *La Musique moderne, 1905–55,* Paris, 1955; 2d rev. edn., 1958; English transl. by Sally Abeles, as *A History of Modern Music,* Cleveland, 1961.

One of the best surveys.

Documents du demi-siècle: tableau chronologique des principales œuvres musicales de 1900 à 1950, établi par genre et par année, special issue of RM, 216 (1952).

Dumesnil, René, *L'Aube du XXe siècle,* Paris, 1958.

—— *La première moitié du XXe siècle,* Paris, 1960.

Issued as continuation volumes of Combarieu's *Histoire de la musique,* these surveys are valuable for information on French composers, especially those least widely known. They seem to supersede earlier books by Dumesnil.

Ewen, David, ed., *The New Book of Modern Composers,* 3d rev. and enl. edn., New York, 1961.

One of the best of Ewen's many compilations, including materials not elsewhere available.

Goléa, Antoine, *L'Aventure de la musique au XXe siècle,* special issue of *Le Point* (Mulhouse), LVIII (1961).

Unusually large, clear photographs of Schoenberg, Messiaen, Boulez, Stockhausen, Henze, et al.

—— *Vingt ans de musique contemporaine,* 2 vols., Paris, 1962.
  Swift and fashionable survey.

Gradenwitz, Peter, *Wege zur Musik der Gegenwart,* Stuttgart, 1963.
  An unusual introduction, designed especially for the non-musician ready to see correspondences between music and literature or painting. Includes many new names from Israel, Greece, and Arabic countries. Ends with tribute to Henze.

Grout, Donald Jay, *A Short History of Opera,* 2 vols., New York, 1947; rev. edn., 1965.

Hartog, Howard, ed., *European Music in the 20th Century,* London, 1957.
  Uneven collection of essays, some excellent.

Hodeir, André, *La Musique étrangère contemporaine,* Paris, 1954.
  Swift survey from Schoenberg to Stockhausen.

—— *Since Debussy: a View of Contemporary Music,* transl. by N. Burch, New York, 1961.
  A polemical view, omitting many composers considered here. Sensibly reviewed by R. Cogan, in PNM, I/2 (1962), 148.

Honolka, Kurt, *Das vielstimmige Jahrhundert: Musik in unserer Zeit,* Stuttgart, 1960.
  An impartial journalistic survey, with pleasant illustrations.

Horton, John, *Scandinavian Music: a Short History,* New York, 1963.
  Well balanced and well written survey, with a chapter comparing Sibelius and Nielsen, and a chapter on 20th-century music in each nation.

Hull, Arthur Eaglefield, *A Dictionary of Modern Music and Musicians,* London, 1924.
  Invaluable in its time, this book remains interesting chiefly because of Bartók's collaboration on a few articles. Alfred Einstein's *Neue Musiklexikon,* Berlin, 1926, was based on Hull.

International Music Council, *Symphonic Music 1880–1954,* London, 1957.
  Useful short catalogue.

Koechlin, Charles, *Évolution de l'harmonie: période contemporaine depuis Bizet et César Franck jusqu'à nos jours,* in *Encyclopédie Lavignac,* Paris, 1923, II¹, 591.
  A book-length article, richly illustrated with musical examples. The best demonstration known to the present author of the gradual stages of development from common-practice harmony toward Stravinsky and Schoenberg.

Lang, Paul Henry, and Nathan Broder, eds., *Contemporary Music in Europe: A Comprehensive Survey,* New York, 1965.
  Essays originally published in the fiftieth anniversary issue of MQ, LI/1 (1965).

Lindlar, Heinrich, ed., *Die Stimme der Komponisten: Aufsätze, Reden, Briefe, 1907–1958,* Rodenkirchen, 1958.
  Well chosen materials, well presented in brief scope. Several pieces are listed separately here.

Machlis, Joseph, *Introduction to Contemporary Music,* New York, 1961.
  Includes useful information on many Americans barely mentioned here.

Maegaard, Jan, *Musikalsk modernisme, 1945–1962,* Copenhagen, 1964.
  Brief survey of conspicuous new trends, beginning with "serialism." Sketches of 50 composers, from Varèse and Eimert to Bo Nilsson and Heinz Holliger.

Martynov, Ivan Ivanovich, *Istoriia zarubezhnoi muzyki pervoi poloviny 20go veka: ocherki,* Moscow, 1963.
  Survey of music outside the USSR in the first half of the 20th century.

Mason, Colin, *European Chamber Music Since 1929,* in *Cobbett,* III, 1.

Mayer, Ludwig K., *Die Musik des 20. Jahrhunderts,* Wels, 1955.
  Lists many German names not elsewhere encountered, and classifies them.

Mellers, Wilfrid H., *Studies in Contemporary Music,* London, 1948.
  Essays written for *Scrutiny* and other journals, on late Debussy, Satie, Koechlin, et al. down to Rubbra and Blitzstein. These helped form the present writer's taste.

—— *Romanticism and the 20th Century* (= *Man and his Music,* Vol. 4), New York, 1959.

Mersmann, Hans, *Musik der Gegenwart,* Berlin, 1923.
  A booklet introducing Mersmann's diagnosis of the exhaustion of romanticism and

the crisis brought on by Schoenberg, and his call for "a new convergence of all powers," towards which Hindemith would be at least one of the leaders. He is especially eloquent here about Bartók and Webern.

—— *Die moderne Musik, seit der Romantik*, Wildpark-Potsdam, 1927.

—— *Die Tonsprache der neuen Musik*, 2d edn., Mainz, 1930.
    Concise, systematic, yet undogmatic treatment of techniques and forms.

—— *Lebensraum der Musik: Aufsätze—Ansprachen*, Rodenkirchen, 1964.
    Includes new brief essays on Stravinsky and Hindemith, along with others on Mozart and general topics relevant to contemporary musical life.

Orrego Salas, Juan, *The Young Generation of Latin American Composers*, in *Inter-American Music Bulletin*, 38 (Nov. 1963), 1.
    Classifies contemporaries of Ginastera.

Prieberg, Fred K., *Musik unterm Strich*, Munich, 1956.
    A lively, sketchy survey of 20th-century music.

—— *Lexikon der neuen Musik*, Freiberg, 1958.
    Biographical dictionary, with many pictures. Appears trustworthy, though not often based on first-hand knowledge.

Proebst, Eugen, ed., *Die neue Musik: Dokumente zu ihrem Verständnis*, Bamberg, 1961.
    Brief collection of short statements, mostly by composers.

Rochas, Milès, *Chroniques musicales*, Neuchâtel, 1958.
    Traces a plausible line of development from Debussy to Messiaen, with critical turning point at Stravinsky's *Soldier*.

Rondi, Brunello, *Prospettiva della musica moderna*, Rome, 1956.
    Brief but thoughtful. Rondi's emphasis on Debussy and Prokofiev, on Debussy's rhythmic "renovation" and Prokofiev's "rhythm as an act of faith," confirmed the present author in outlining this book.

—— *Il cammino della musica d'oggi e l'esperienza elettronica*, Padua, 1959.
    The path now traced by Rondi leads from Debussy to Stravinsky, then via Schoenberg to the various experiments of the 1950s.

Routley, Erik, *Twentieth Century Church Music*, New York, 1964.
    An optimistic survey from Vaughan Williams to Peter Maxwell Davies. Good discussion, with examples, of many English composers. Floundering appreciations of foreigners.

Ruppel, Karl Heinrich, *Musik in unserer Zeit: eine Bilanz von zehn Jahren* [1950–60], Munich, 1960.
    100 brief articles, sympathetic to various new things.

Salazar, Adolfo, *Music in Our Time*, New York, 1946.
    Among the best surveys in English, but hard to use for reference because of its complex organization; occasionally misleading, where Salazar relied on his memories of concerts without consulting specialists.

Salzman, Eric, *New Music of the Americas*, in *The World of Music*, VII (1965), 33.
    Enthusiastic introduction to a host of young composers who consider Carter, Wolpe, and even Schuller as "pioneer" predecessors.

Samuel, Claude, ed., *Panorama de l'art musical contemporain, avec des textes inédits de A. Goléa, A. Hodeir, P. Boulez, I. Xenakis*, Paris, 1962.
    This rich 850-page book, as observed by Claude Baillif, in *Critique*, XIX/193 (1963), 536, offers "a phenomenology of the ideas of the day about the contemporary art of music, rather than a phenomenology of the art of music itself."

Schuh, Willi, *Kritiken und Essays. Band 2: Zeitgenössische Musik*, Zürich, 1947.

—— *Von neuer Musik*, Zürich, 1955.

Slonimsky, Nicolas, *Music since 1900*, New York, 1937; 3d rev. and enl. edn., 1949.
    A compilation of facts in strict order by the calendar, this book was long more useful than some more ambitious ones.

—— *Modern Music: its Styles, its Techniques*, in D. Ewen, ed., *The New Book of Modern Composers*, New York, 1961, p. 3.
    Fresh proof that Slonimsky is ready to discard slogans as fast as he invents them.

Stuckenschmidt, Hans Heinz, *Neue Musik* (= *Zwischen den beiden Kriegen*, Bd. 2), Berlin, 1951.
> Hindemith was Stuckenschmidt's hero at this point. His survey remains interesting.

—— *Schöpfer der neuen Musik: Portraits und Studien*, Frankfurt, 1958.
> Lively biographical sketches, with no claim to completeness.

—— *Die Ordnung der Freiheit: Documenta der neuen Musik*, in *Melos*, XXIX (1962), 261.
> A fresh, swift survey, linking the "great liberators" of the first quarter-century with the young stars of the third.

Wallner, Bo, *Scandinavian Music after the Second World War*, in MQ, LI (1965), 111; also in P. H. Lang and N. Broder, eds., *Contemporary Music in Europe*, New York, 1965, p. 111.
> Survey with many new names.

Wellesz, Egon, *Die neue Instrumentation*, 2 vols., Berlin, 1928.
> Good observations on the orchestration of Strauss, Mahler, Debussy, Stravinsky, Schoenberg, et al.

Westphal, Kurt, *Die moderne Musik*, Leipzig, 1928.
> Brief survey.

Wiora, Walter, *Die vier Weltalter der Musik*, Stuttgart, 1961; English transl. by M. D. Herter Norton, as *The Four Ages of Music*, New York, 1965.
> Lofty survey of universal music history.

—— *Komponist und Mitwelt* (= *Musikalische Zeitfragen*, VI), Kassel, 1964.
> Scholarly discussion of the changing relations between composers and performers, patrons, publics, in broad historical perspective. "There are various ways of adaptation and assimilation, of interaction and coördination, some at high level beside some at low." The principle of non-conformism, too widely prevalent in the 20th century, must be overcome, but not through mere conformity to rule.

Wörner, Karl H., *Musik der Gegenwart: Geschichte der neuen Musik*, Mainz, 1949.

—— *Neue Musik in der Entscheidung*, Mainz, 1954.

—— *Neue Musik 1948–1958: Versuch eines historischen Überblickes*, in *Darmstädter Beiträge zur neuen Musik*, I (1959), 7.
> A good try, but not yet a survey of the whole field.

Zillig, Winfried, *Variationen über neue Musik*, Munich, 1959; new edn. as *Die neue Musik: Linien und Porträts*, 1963.
> A brief, personal survey, not so capricious as the first title suggests.

SURVEYS: National

AUSTRIA

Klein, Rudolf, *Contemporary Music in Austria*, in MQ, LI (1965), 180; also in P. H. Lang and N. Broder, eds., *Contemporary Music in Europe*, New York, 1965, p. 180.
> Sensible classification of about 30 composers, among whom J. N. David is regarded as "probably the most important."

BELGIUM

Leirens, Charles, *Belgian Music*, New York, 1943.

Mueren, Floris van der, *Perspectief van de Vlaamse muziek sedert Benoit*, Hasselt, 1961.
> Scholarly survey of the generations of Gilson and Meulemans.

Vander Linden, Albert, *Belgium from 1914 to 1964*, in MQ, LI (1965), 92; also in P. H. Lang and N. Broder, eds., *Contemporary Music in Europe*, New York, 1965, p. 92.

Wangermée, Robert, *La Musique belge contemporaine*, Brussels, 1959.

CANADA

Beckwith, John, *Composers in Toronto and Montreal*, in *University of Toronto Quarterly*, XXVI (1956), 47.

Clear description of the styles of eight composers, including the leading teacher, John Weinzweig, and his best known pupil, Harry Somers. Most prospective readers would do well to preface this with Beckwith's survey.

—— *Music*, in J. Park, ed., *The Culture of Contemporary Canada*, Ithaca, N.Y., 1957, p. 143. Well-written survey from Healey Willan to Harry Somers.

CHINA

Kagan, Alan L., *Music and the Hundred Flowers Movement*, in MQ, XLIX (1963), 417. An unusual and credible account of recent events in China.

Li Yeh-tao, *Chinese Orchestral Music*, in *Peking Review*, V/26 (June 29, 1962), 14.

Wang, P'ei-lun, *Yin yüeh tz'u tien*, Peking, 1963. Dictionary of European music as regarded in China, including articles on Chinese participants in cultivating European music.

CZECHOSLOVAKIA

Newmarch, Rosa, *The Music of Czechoslovakia*, New York, 1942. For the many worthy composers between Dvořák and Janáček, this book remains an unrivalled source of information in English.

Racek, Jan, and Jiří Vysloužil, *Problems of Style in 20th-Century Czech Music*, in MQ, LI (1965), 191; also in P. H. Lang and N. Broder, eds., *Contemporary Music in Europe*, New York, 1965, p. 191. From Novák and Suk through Janáček, Hába, and Martinů to the generation now middle-aged.

DENMARK

Jacobsen, Ejnar, and Vagn Kappel, *Musikkens Mestre: Danske Komponister*, Copenhagen, 1947. Musical examples, pictures, and bibliography make this thick volume useful even to one who cannot read the text. Besides 33 pages on Nielsen, there are brief sketches of composers down to Niels Viggo Bentzon.

FRANCE

Agence française d'informations musicales, *Documents. Le Courrier musical de France*, 1963– . Concise tables on stiff paper suitable for filing, with biography, discography, and details of publications and performances.

Drew, David, *Modern French Music*, in H. Hartog, ed., *European Music in the 20th Century*, London, 1957, p. 232. Challenging opinions, founded on first-hand knowledge, and stimulating even when wrong.

Favre, Georges, *Musiciens français modernes*, Paris, 1953.

—— *Musiciens français contemporains*, Paris, 1956. Ten composers in each volume, from Saint-Saëns to Messiaen, with musical examples chosen from recorded works. Especially useful for Ropartz, Aubert, Ibert, Loucheur.

Goléa, Antoine, *French Music since 1945*, in MQ, LI (1965), 22; also in P. H. Lang and N. Broder, eds., *Contemporary Music in Europe*, New York, 1965, p. 22.

Koechlin, Charles, *Sur l'évolution de la musique française avant et après Debussy*, in RM, XVI (1935), 264. For other writings of Koechlin, see under his name in the list of composers, and also under Debussy, Fauré, Satie, and Schoenberg.

Machabey, Armand, *Portraits de 30 musiciens français*, Paris, 1949. From Delvincourt and Delannoy to Dutilleux. Based on interviews, 1942–46.

Rohozinski, Ladislas, ed., *Cinquante ans de musique française, de 1874 à 1925*, 2 vols., Paris, 1925. Rich in anecdotes and illustrations.

Rostand, Claude, *La Musique française contemporaine*, Paris, 1952; 2d edn., 1957; English transl. by H. Marx as *French Music Today*, New York, 1958. Perhaps the last book to treat "The Six" as a central group, without losing the tone of a convinced admirer.

Roy, Jean, *Musique française,* Paris, 1963.
> Roy treats 19 composers individually, beginning with Satie and Koechlin, omitting Debussy and Ravel, and proceeding to Boulez and Bondon.

GERMANY

Aus dem Leben und Schaffen unserer Komponisten. . . . Biographien von Komponisten aus der Deutschen Demokratischen Republik, Berlin, 1962.
> Sketches of 23 composers, including Butting, Finke, Eisler, and younger men down to Günter Kochan.

Komponisten und Musikwissenschaftler der DDR. Kurzbiographien und Werkverzeichnisse, Berlin, 1959.
> About 85 composers, among whom Eisler and Dessau are the best known abroad.

Laux, Karl, ed., *Das Musikleben in der Deutschen Demokratischen Republik (1945–1959),* Leipzig, 1963.
> Includes mention of dozens of composers unknown abroad.

Mersmann, Hans, *Deutsche Musik des XX. Jahrhunderts im Spiegel des Weltgeschehens,* Rodenkirchen, 1958.
> Fine brief survey.

Riemer, Otto, *Der Chorkomponist,* in *Musica,* XIV (1960), 638.
> Surveys and classifies many German composers of choral music.

GREAT BRITAIN

Bacharach, A. L., ed., *British Music of our Time,* Harmondsworth, 1946.
> Delius to Britten, appraised for intelligent concertgoers and record collectors, by scholars including J. Westrup.

Drew, David, *The Younger Serial Composers in England,* London, 1960.

Frank, Alan, *Modern British Composers,* London, 1953.
> 21 composers from Vaughan Williams to Fricker. Especially valuable for Moeran, Jacob, Murrill, and Bush.

Howes, Frank, *Music,* in S. Nowell-Smith, ed., *Edwardian England,* London, 1964, p. 413.
> Excellent perspective view of the age of Elgar.

Mason, Colin, *Music in Britain 1951–1962,* London, 1963.
> Good brief survey from Fricker to Davies.

Porter, Andrew, *Some New British Composers,* in MQ, LI (1965), 12; also in P. H. Lang and N. Broder, eds., *Contemporary Music in Europe,* New York, 1965, p. 12.
> Porter identifies a group of 7 young "central" composers.

Schafer, Murray, *British Composers in Interview,* London, 1963.
> 16 composers, from Ireland to Davies. Schafer's well-chosen questions, different for each case, provoked interesting replies.

GREECE

Slonimsky, Nicolas, *New Music in Greece,* in MQ, LI (1965), 225; also in P. H. Lang and N. Broder, eds., *Contemporary Music in Europe,* New York, 1965, p. 225.
> Dismissing Kalomiris as the last of an old style, Slonimsky sets Skalkottas and Xenakis in a context of more than a dozen Greeks unknown abroad.

HUNGARY

Fábián, Imre, *Modern Hungarian Music,* in MQ, LI (1965), 205; also in P. H. Lang and N. Broder, eds., *Contemporary Music in Europe,* New York, 1965, p. 205.

Legány, Deszső, *A magyar zene krónikája: zenei művelődésünk ezer éve dokumentumokban,* Budapest, 1962.

Szabolcsi, Bence, *A Concise History of Hungarian Music,* London, 1965.

ISRAEL

Boskovitch, A. Urijah, *La Musique israélienne contemporaine et les traditions ethniques,* in *Journal of the International Folk Music Council,* XVI (1964), 39.

Gradenwitz, Peter, *Music and Musicians in Israel: a Comprehensive Guide to Modern Israeli Music,* rev. enl. edn., Tel Aviv, 1959.

Ringer, Alexander L., *Musical Composition in Modern Israel*, in MQ, LI (1965), 297; also in
P. H. Lang and N. Broder, eds., *Contemporary Music in Europe*, New York, 1965, p. 297.
Ben-Haim and Partos discussed with respect. Several younger composers introduced
with hopeful enthusiasm.

ITALY

Bortolotto, Mario, *New Music in Italy*, in MQ, LI (1965), 61; also in P. H. Lang and N.
Broder, eds., *Contemporary Music in Europe*, New York, 1965, p. 61.
Admiring yet discriminating comment on works of Nono, Berio, Castiglioni,
Evangelisti, Aldo Clementi, Camillo Togni, Sylvano Bussotti, and Franco Donatoni.

JAPAN

Bekku, Sadao, *The Composer in Japan Today*, in *Music—East and West*, Tokyo, 1961, p. 91.
Survey from Yamada to Bekku's teacher Ikenouchi, leading up to the survey of
younger composers by Hirashima.
Hirashima, Masao, *The Composer in Japan Today*, in *Music—East and West*, Tokyo, 1961,
p. 99.
Survey and classification of composers born since 1900.
Malm, William, P., *Japanese Music and Musical Instruments*, Rutland, Vt., and Tokyo, 1959.
Handsome scholarly survey.
Togi, Suyeharu, *Music*, in Shigenobu Okuma, ed., *Fifty Years of New Japan*, New York,
1909, p. 358.

NETHERLANDS

Reeser, Eduard, ed., *Music in Holland: a Review of Contemporary Music*, Amsterdam, 1959.
—— *Stijlproeven van Nederlandse muziek. Anthologie . . . 1890–1960*, Amsterdam, 1963.
Wouters, Jos, *Dutch Music in the 20th Century*, in MQ, LI (1965), 97; also in P. H. Lang
and N. Broder, eds., *Contemporary Music in Europe*, New York, 1965, p. 97.
—— and André Jurres, eds., *Fifteen Years Donemus, 1947–1962: Conversations with Dutch
Composers: Gespräche mit niederländischen Komponisten*, Amsterdam, 1963.
Like the Donemus journal *Sonorum speculum*, this booklet is bilingual, handsomely
printed and illustrated.

NORWAY

Lange, Kristian, and Arne Østvedt, *Norwegian Music*, London, 1958.

POLAND

Jarociński, Stefan, *Polish Music after World War II*, in MQ, LI (1965), 244; also in P. H.
Lang and N. Broder, eds., *Contemporary Music in Europe*, New York, 1965, p. 244.
A chief source for the present author; the information, however, has been reinter-
preted here.
Music in Poland: a Review, Warsaw, 1964.
Brief articles in French and English.

PORTUGAL

Perkins, Francis D., *Music in Portugal Today*, in MQ, LI (1965), 38; also in P. H. Lang and
N. Broder, eds., *Contemporary Music in Europe*, New York, 1965, p. 38.

RUMANIA

Slonimsky, Nicolas, *Modern Composition in Rumania*, in MQ, LI (1965), 236; also in P. H.
Lang and N. Broder, eds., *Contemporary Music in Europe*, New York, 1965, p. 236.
About 20 composers, from Enescu to Vieru.

RUSSIA and the USSR

Arro, E., et al., eds., *Muzyka sovietskoi Estonii*, Talinin, 1956.
Asafiev, Boris Vladimirovich, *Russian Music from the Beginning of the 19th Century*, transl.
by Alfred Swan, Ann Arbor, Mich., 1953.
Written in 1930, this scholarly survey includes much information not otherwise
available in English. A review by N. Slonimsky, in MQ, XL (1954), 425, provides
illuminating introduction and commentary.

Beliaiev, Viktor Mikhailovich, *Ocherki po istorii muzyki narodov SSSR*, Moscow, 1962.
　　The non-Russian peoples of the Soviet Union, traced down to about 1925, with many short musical examples.

Bernandt, G. B., and A. N. Dolzhansky, *Sovietskie Kompozitory: kratkii biograficheskii spravochnik*, Moscow, 1957.
　　Biographical guide to composers mostly unknown abroad.

Danilevich, Lev Vasilievich, *Kniga o sovietskoi muzyke*, Moscow, 1962.
　　Up-to-date survey, supplementing Poliakova.

Girshman, Ia., *Kompozitory sovietskogo Tatarstan*, Kazan, 1957.

Krebs, Stanley, *Soviet Music Instruction: Service to the State*, in *Journal of Research in Music Education*, IX (1961), 83.
　　Excellent factual material.

—— *Soviet Composers and the Development of Soviet Music*, Univ. of Washington diss., 1963.
　　Critical survey from Ippolitov-Ivanov and Glière to Shchedrin and Volkonsky.

Lebedeva, T. A., ed., *Istoriia russkoi sovietskoi muzyki*, 5 vols., Moscow, 1956–63.
　　Rich in musical examples, documentation, and sympathy.

Olkhovsky, Andrey, *Music under the Soviets: the Agony of an Art*, New York, 1955.

Poliakova, Liudmila Viktorovna, *Soviet Music*, Moscow, 1961.
　　Readable and credible survey.

Raaben, Lev Nikolaievich, *Sovietskaia kamerno-instrumental'naia muzyka*, Leningrad, 1963.
　　Survey of chamber music by Soviet composers.

Sabaneiev, Leonid Leonidovich, *Modern Russian Composers*, transl. by Judah A. Joffe, New York, 1927.
　　After taking part in Soviet musical life, Sabaneiev emigrated, and soon wrote about the composers he had known well, from Taneiev and Scriabin to Shebalin and Shostakovich.

Schwarz, Boris, *Soviet Music Since the Second World War*, in MQ, LI (1965), 259; also in P. H. Lang and N. Broder, eds., *Contemporary Music in Europe*, New York, 1965, p. 259.
　　Unique report, based both on first-hand knowledge from visits to the USSR and on long study of scores and criticisms, both native and foreign. Includes appraisals of late Prokofiev and others from Shebalin to Shchedrin.

Shaverdian, Aleksandr Isakovich, *Izbrannye stati*, Moscow, 1958.
　　Essays.

—— *Ocherki po istorii armianskoi muzyki XIX–XX. vekov*, Moscow, 1959.
　　Outlines for the history of Armenian music.

Souvtchinsky, Pierre, ed., *Un Siècle de la musique russe*, 2 vols., Paris, 1953.
　　Invaluable collection of special studies.

Voprosy ideologicheskoi raboty: Sbornik vazhneishikh reshenii KPSS (1954–1961 gody), Moscow, 1961.
　　Includes (pp. 199–200) official text of the resolution of 1958 correcting errors of 1948.

Zhubanov, A. K., et al., *Ocherki po istorii kazakhskoi sovietskoi muzyki*, Alma-Ata, 1962.
　　Outlines for the history of Kazakh Soviet music.

SPAIN

Chase, Gilbert, *The Music of Spain*, 2d rev. edn., New York, 1959.

Custer, Arthur, *Contemporary Music in Spain*, in MQ, XLVIII (1962), 1; rev. version in MQ, LI (1965), 44; also in P. H. Lang and N. Broder, eds., *Contemporary Music in Europe*, New York, 1965, p. 44.
　　Rare information on developments since 1958. Identifies about 20 composers so far unknown abroad.

Fernandez-Cid, Antonio, *La Musica y los musicos de España en el siglo XX*, Madrid, 1963.
　　Brief supplement to Sopeña, from a cautious viewpoint.

Sopeña, Federico, *La Historia de la música española contemporanea*, Madrid, 1958.
　　Ample scholarly survey from Pedrell through Rodrigo.

Valls Gorina, Manuel, *La Musica española despues Manuel de Falla*, Madrid, 1962.
　　Classifies over 100 composers, among whom the "dominating voice" is that of Joaquín Rodrigo.

Vicente, Eugenio de, *Spanien in den letzten vierzig Jahren,* in *Melos,* XXXII (1965), 225.

SWEDEN

Sweden in Music, special English number of *Musikrevy* (Stockholm), XV/3 (1960).

SWITZERLAND

Reich, Willi, *Swiss Composers of the Present Time,* in MQ, LI (1965), 78; also in P. H. Lang
and N. Broder, *Contemporary Music in Europe,* New York, 1965, p. 78.
> Beginning with Martin, whose statement of 1943 on originality and perfection is
> quoted at length, Reich proceeds to give good accounts of Vogel and 20 younger
> Swiss composers.

Swiss Composers' League, *40 Contemporary Swiss Composers,* Amriswil, 1956.

UNITED STATES

Chase, Gilbert, *America's Music from the Pilgrims to the Present,* New York, 1955.
> Unrivalled survey, coordinating the results of special studies in a new pattern that
> glorifies Ives.

Cowell, Henry, ed., *American Composers on American Music: a Symposium,* New York, 1933;
2d edn., 1962.

Drew, David, *American Chamber Music,* in A. Robertson, ed., *Chamber Music,* London, 1957,
p. 321.

Ewen, David, *The Life and Death of Tin Pan Alley: the Golden Age of American Popular
Music,* New York, 1964.
> A coherent, original narrative of the subject Ewen knows and loves best.

Lang, Paul Henry, ed., *One Hundred Years of Music in America,* New York, 1961.
> Includes a useful brief survey of composers by Nathan Broder, and other good articles.

Machlis, Joseph, *American Composers of Our Time,* New York, 1963.
> 16 composers from MacDowell to Foss. Biographical sketches and pictures.

Mellers, Wilfrid H., *The Avant-Garde in America,* in PRMA, XC (1964), 1.
> Introduction for listeners acquainted with Ives and Ellington, to the music of
> Griffes, Cowell, Varèse, Partch, Ornette Coleman, Cage, Feldman, Mel Powell, Earle
> Brown, and Ralph Shapey.

—— *Music in a New Found Land: Themes and Developments in the History of American
Music,* New York, 1965.
> Meller's first-hand knowledge is amazingly extensive—more so than that of most
> musicians in their native land—yet he disclaims comprehensive coverage. His sym-
> pathy with divergent styles, including jazz, is equally admirable. His point of view,
> however, is that of a composer seeking *the* style for his time and place. Occasional
> mistakes due to haste are outweighed by the unique virtues of this important book.
> See R. F. Goldman, in *The New York Times Book Review,* May 16, 1965, p. 10, and
> V. Thomson, in *The New York Review of Books,* June 3, 1965, p. 3, for excellent
> comments.

Perle, George, *Atonality and the Twelve-Note System in the U.S.,* in *The Score,* 27 (1960), 51.
> Discusses Ruggles et al. as having "anticipated" techniques of Schoenberg or
> Stockhausen.

Reis, Claire [Raphael], *Composers in America,* rev. enl. edn., New York, 1947.
> Over 200 names, from Ives to Foss, with brief biographies and lists of major works.
> Useful chiefly for more obscure names.

Sabin, Robert, *Some Younger American Composers,* in *Tempo,* 64 (1963), 25.
> Cites the estimate of Broadcast Music, Inc., that the U.S. had about 1000 composers
> in 1939, 10,000 in 1963. For 16 of these Sabin proposes a crude classification.

Waters, Edward N., *Music and Musicians,* in R. E. Spiller and E. Larrabee, eds., *American
Perspectives,* Cambridge, Mass., 1961, p. 59.
> Judicious survey of contemporary American composers.

Yates, Peter, *A Collage of American Composers,* in *Arts and Architecture,* LXXV/11 (Nov.
1958), 8; 12 (Dec. 1958), 4; LXXVI/1 (Jan. 1959), 4.

YUGOSLAVIA

Andreis, Josip, ed., *Yugoslav Music,* Belgrade, 1959.
> Scholarly survey.

Helm, Everett, *Music in Jugoslavia,* in MQ, LI (1965), 215; also in P. H. Lang and N. Broder, eds., *Contemporary Music in Europe,* New York, 1965, p. 219.
> Favorable notes on 20 composers, none of whose music is yet enough known abroad to warrant inclusion here.

Kovacević, Krešimir, *Hrvatski kompozitori i njihova djela,* Zagreb, 1960.
> Extensive description of about 380 works by 50 composers, among whom Gotovac is best known abroad. Summaries in English.

———— •◆• ————

COMPOSERS AND OTHER MUSICIANS

ACHRON

Weisser, Albert, *The Modern Renaissance of Jewish Music,* New York, 1954.
> Chief source of information on Achron and his group.

ADLER

Adler, Guido, *Der Stil in der Musik,* Leipzig, 1911.
———— *Style criticism,* in MQ, XX (1934), 172.

ADORNO

Adorno, Theodor Wiesengrund, *Musikalische Wareanalysen,* in *Die neue Rundschau,* 66 (1955), 59.
> Adorno's most distinctive and perhaps most valuable work in music, describing half a dozen pieces of pretentious popular music (*Kitsch*) so as to fix sharply their details and their meanings.

———— *Dissonanzen: Musik in der verwalteten Welt,* Göttingen, 1956.
> Essays on music in relation to bureaucracy.

———— *Quasi una fantasia: musikalische Schriften II,* Frankfurt, 1963.
> Includes studies of Stravinsky, Berg, Zemlinsky, Schreker.

———— *Moments musicaux: neu gedruckte Aufsätze 1928–1962,* Frankfurt, 1964.
> Includes studies of Krenek, Zillig, jazz.

Horkheimer, Max, ed., *Zeugnisse: Theodor W. Adorno zum 60. Geburtstag,* Frankfurt, 1963.
> Contributions by Boulez, Stockhausen, Krenek, Steuermann, many sociologists, poets, and others.

Leibowitz, René, *Der Komponist Theodor W. Adorno,* in Horkheimer, ed., *Zeugnisse: Theodor W. Adorno zum 60. Geburtstag,* Frankfurt, 1963, p. 355.
> Describes chiefly a single song, 1923.

ALAIN

Gavoty, Bernard, *Jehan Alain, musicien français (1911–1940) . . . lettres . . . dessins. . . . ,* Paris, 1945.
> Chief source of information, including list of works.

ALBÉNIZ

Cisteró, José M. Llorens, *Notas inéditas sobre el virtuosismo de Isaac Albéniz y sa producción pianística,* in *Anuario Musical,* XIV (1959), 91.
———— *El "Lied" en la obra musical de Isaac Albéniz,* in *Anuario Musical,* XV (1960), 123.
Laplane, Gabriel, *Albéniz: sa vie, son œuvre* (preface by Francis Poulenc), Paris, 1956.
> Written in 1950, this study supersedes earlier accounts.

ALEKSANDROV

Polianovsky, G. A., *A. V. Aleksandrov,* Moscow, 1959.
> Sketch of the life (1883–1946) of the composer of the Soviet national anthem.

ALFVÉN

Alfvén, Hugo, *I. Första satsen: ungdomsminnen; II. Tempo furioso; III. I dur och moll; IV. Final* (Autobiography, 4 vols.), Stockholm, 1946–52.

Svensson, Sven Erik Emanuel, *Hugo Alfvén, som människa och konstnär*, Uppsala, 1946.

ANTHEIL

Antheil, George, *Bad Boy of Music*, New York, 1945.
    Colorful memoirs.

Pound, Ezra, *Antheil and the Treatise on Harmony*, Chicago, 1927.

APOSTEL

Kaufmann, Harald, *Hans Erich Apostel*, Vienna, 1964.

ARMSTRONG

Armstrong, Louis, *Satchmo: My Life in New Orleans*, New York, 1954.

Goffin, Robert, *Louis Armstrong, le roi du jazz*, Paris, 1947; English transl. as *Horn of Plenty: The Story of Louis Armstrong*, New York, 1947.

McCarthy, Albert J., *Louis Armstrong*, London, 1960.

ASAFIEV

Asafiev, Boris Vladimirovich, *Izbrannye raboty o sovietskoi muzyke. Muzykal'naia forma kak protsess . . ., Tom V, Izbrannye trudy*, Moscow, 1957.
    Collected writings on Soviet music, and the speculative treatise *Musical Form as Process.*

Orlova, Elena Mikhailovna, *B. V. Asafiev: put' issledovatelia i publitsista*, Leningrad, 1964.
    Full-length survey of Asafiev's career as investigator and publicist.

AUBERT

Cadieu, Martine, *Duo avec Louis Aubert*, in *Nouvelles littéraires*, August 24, 1961, p. 1.
    Aubert recalls Debussy and Fauré.

AURIC

Auric, Georges, *Apollinaire et la musique*, in RM, 210 (1952), 147.

Drew, David, *Modern French Music*, in H. Hartog, ed., *European Music in the 20th Century*, London, 1957, p. 232.

Goléa, Antoine, *Georges Auric*, Paris, 1958.

BABBITT

Babbitt, Milton, *Some Aspects of Twelve-Tone Composition*, in *The Score*, 12 (June 1955), 53.
    Babbitt's first public discussion of "combinatoriality."

—— *Who Cares If You Listen?*, in *High Fidelity*, VIII/1 (Jan. 1958), 38.
    Unusual statement of a policy of esotericism, logically argued with no apology.

—— *Twelve-Tone Invariants as Compositional Determinants*, in MQ, XLVI (1960), 246; also in P. H. Lang, ed., *Problems of Modern Music*, New York, 1962, p. 108.

—— *Set Structure as a Compositional Determinant*, in JMT, V (1961), 72.
    Includes detailed references to Schoenberg's late chamber works.

—— *An Introduction to the RCA Synthesizer*, in JMT, VIII (1964), 251.

BACON

Bacon, Ernst, *Words on Music*, Syracuse, 1960.

—— *Notes on the Piano*, Syracuse, 1963.
    Nuggets of wisdom on many musical topics, including American regionalism.

BARBER

Broder, Nathan, *Samuel Barber*, New York, 1954.

Friedewald, Russell E., *A Formal and Stylistic Analysis of the Published Music of Samuel Barber*, State Univ. of Iowa diss., 1957.

BARRAQUÉ

Barraqué, Jean, *Rythme et développement*, in *Polyphonie*, IX–X (1954), 47.
    Analyzes rhythm apart from other elements, in accordance with the theories of

Barraqué's teacher, Messiaen. Helpful on Messiaen's *Cinq rechants,* and interesting on Machaut's Mass, Stravinsky's *Danse sacrale,* and Boulez's Second Sonata.

BARRAUD

Rostand, Claude, *Tendencies and Contrasts in the Music of Henry Barraud,* in *Tempo,* 44 (1957), 31.
    Quotes Barraud: "The composer must always seek to compromise between sensibility and intelligence."

BARTÓK

Abraham, Gerald, *Bartók: String Quartet No. 6,* in MR, III (1942), 72.
—— *The Bartók of the Quartets,* in ML, XXVI (1945), 185.
    A landmark in the appreciation of Bartók.
—— *Bartók and England,* in *New Hungarian Quarterly,* II/4 (1961), 82.
    Includes letters in English.
Austin, William, *Bartók's Concerto for Orchestra,* in MR, XVIII (1957), 21.
Babbitt, Milton, *The String Quartets of Bartók,* in MQ, XXXV (1949), 377.
    "Serialization in Bartók is but one of many integrative methods . . . Never does it create the context."
Bartha, Dénes, *La Musique de Bartók,* in E. Weber, ed., *La Résonance dans les échelles,* Paris, 1963, p. 279.
    Exposition of Lendvai's theories of Bartók's harmonic practice, in relation to ethnomusicological interests, to theories both traditional and novel, and even to jazz.
Bartók, Béla, *Das Problem der neuen Musik,* in *Melos,* I (1920), 107.
—— *A Magyar népdal,* Budapest, 1924; German transl. as *Das ungarische Volkslied,* Berlin, 1925; English transl. as *Hungarian Folk Music,* London, 1931.
—— *Vom Einfluss der Bauernmusik auf die Musik unserer Zeit,* in B. Szabolcsi, ed., *Béla Bartók, Weg und Werk,* Leipzig, 1957, p. 156.
    Three closely connected articles, assembled by Bartók in 1931. Only the first is widely known, under the same or a slightly varying title, from *Melos,* I (1920), 384, and XVI (1949), 145; *The Sackbut,* II/1 (June 1921), 5; *Tempo,* 14 (1949), 16; and *Béla Bartók: A Memorial Review,* New York, 1950, p. 71.
—— *Bartók-breviárium (levelek, írások, dokumentok),* Budapest, 1958.
    Excellent collection of letters, writings, and documents, chosen and edited with copious, reliable notes by J. Ujfalussy.
—— *The Second Piano Concerto,* in *Tempo,* 65 (1963), 5.
    Program note with examples, written 1939.
—— *Selbstbiographie,* in D. Dille, ed., *Documenta Bartókiana,* II (1965), 113.
    This edition collates various versions of 1918, 1921, and 1923, and supplies helpful notes. The article was originally written in German (1918) for a *Musikpädagogische Zeitschrift,* and revised for *Anbruch,* III (1921), 87; also in B. Szabolcsi, ed., *Béla Bartók, Weg und Werk,* Leipzig, 1957, p. 143. The English version in *Tempo,* 13 (1949), 3, and *Béla Bartók: A Memorial Review,* New York, 1950, p. 7, appears to derive from a Hungarian translation.
—— *Vier unbekannte Briefe,* ed. by D. Dille, in ÖMz, XX (1965), 449.
    Important letters, in English and French, to Philip Heseltine, 1920–21, with facts about Bartók's knowledge of Debussy, Schoenberg, Stravinsky, et al., and his judgments of their work.
—— and Albert B. Lord, *Serbo-Croatian Folksongs,* New York, 1951.
Bartók, Béla, Jr., *Mein Vater Béla Bartók—sein Weg für die moderne Musik,* in *Universitas,* XX (1965), 291.
    Touching account of "an exemplary life that can justly be set beside his epoch-making activity as musician."
Bartók, Ditta, *26 September 1945: zum 20. Todestag von Béla Bartók,* in ÖMz, XX (1965), 449.
    The widow's account of Bartók's last days, the funeral, and the burial.
Bator, Victor, *The Béla Bartók Archives: History and Catalogue,* New York, 1963.
Béla Bartók: A Memorial Review, including Articles . . . Reprinted from "Tempo," New York, 1950.

Benary, Peter, *Der zweistimmige Kontrapunkt in Bartóks Mikrokosmos*, in AfMw, XV (1958), 198.

Bónis, Ferenc, *Idézetek Bartók zenéjeben*, in *Magyar Zene*, III (1962), 105.
> Bartók's quotations from Bach, Beethoven, Debussy, Ravel, and Stravinsky, shown by examples for the benefit even of readers ignorant of Hungarian.

—— *Béla Bartóks Leben in Bildern*, Budapest, 1965.

Chapman, Roger, *The Fifth Quartet of Béla Bartók*, in MR, XII (1951), 296.

Citron, Pierre, *Bartók*, Paris, 1963.
> Though lacking documentation, this brief survey is based on thorough knowledge. Citron's independent judgments of strengths and weaknesses in various works, and his placing of Bartók in relation to other composers, make his book valuable to experts as well as appealing and very helpful to beginners. Discography.

Clegg, David, *Bartók's "Kossuth Symphony,"* in MR, XXIII (1962), 215.
> Includes Bartók's own analysis with 9 musical examples.

Demény, János, *The Results and Problems of Bartók Research in Hungary*, in *New Hungarian Quarterly*, II/1 (1961), 9.
> Helpful bibliography with comments.

Dille, Denijs, ed., *Documenta Bartókiana*, Budapest, 1964–   .
> Previously unpublished music, letters, pictures, and articles, in Hungarian and German.

—— *A Bartók-archívum munkájáról*, in *Magyar Zene*, VI (1965), 140.
> On the Budapest Bartók Archive.

Doflein, Erich, *Bartók und die Musikpädagogik*, in *Musik der Zeit*, III (1953), 32.
> Doflein shows how for Bartók "didactic value and artistic value hang together to enhance each other mutually," how the *Mikrokosmos* is related to the rest of Bartók's work as composer, performer, scholar, and teacher, and how his achievement compares with those of Bach and Schumann.

—— *À propos les "44 duos,"* in RM, 224 (1955), 110.
> Doflein asked Bartók to contribute to his violin method, then watched the gradual accumulation of the duos.

—— *Béla Bartóks Kompositionen für die Musikpädagogik*, in *Musik im Unterricht*, XLVI (1955), 284.

—— *Béla Bartók: Lebensweg und Werk*, in *Universitas*, XII (1957), 831.

Downey, John Wilham, *La Musique populaire dans l'œuvre de Béla Bartók*, Univ. of Paris diss., 1956.
> Studies the resemblances of Bartók's melodies to various types of folksong.

Ellsworth, Ray, *The Shadow of Genius: Béla Bartók and Tibor Serly*, in *The American Record Guide*, XXXII (1965), 26.

Fábián, Imre, *Béla Bartók und die Wiener Schule*, in ÖMz, XIX (1964), 255.
> Chiefly concerned with reciprocal influences around 1912.

Fassett, Agatha, *The Naked Face of Genius*, New York, 1958.
> Despite the title and the use of quotation marks for reconstructed talk, this is a credible profile of Bartók in his last years. Mrs. Fassett had studied music in Budapest. In America she was close to Bartók and his wife.

Feng, Chao, *Bartók and Chinese Music Culture*, in *Studia musicologica*, V (1963), 393.

Foldes, Andor, *Béla Bartók*, in *Tempo*, 43 (1957), 22.
> Bartók's pupil describes his playing and teaching.

Forte, Allen, *Bartók's "Serial" Composition*, in MQ, XLVI (1960), 233; also in P. H. Lang, ed., *Problems of Modern Music*, New York, 1962, p. 95.
> On the Fourth Quartet.

Fricsay, Ferenc, *Über Mozart und Bartók*, Copenhagen, 1962.
> Brief but weighty remarks by a fine conductor.

Gerson-Kiwi, Edith, *Béla Bartók—Scholar in Folk Music*, in ML, XXXVIII (1957), 149.
> Good survey of Bartók's scholarly achievement.

Halperson, Maurice, *Béla Bartók Explains Himself*, in *Musical America*, Jan. 21, 1928, p. 9.
> Extensive interview, with references to six musical examples of folksong.

Helm, Everett, *The Music of Béla Bartók*, in H. Hartog, ed., *European Music in the 20th Century*, London, 1957, p. 11.
—— *Bartók on Stage: Fresh Light on a Long Undervalued Dramatic Trilogy*, in *High Fidelity*, XIV/11 (Nov. 1964), 74.
> *Bluebeard, Wooden Prince*, and *Mandarin*, seen in Budapest in 1964, inspire great enthusiasm.
—— *Béla Bartók und die Volksmusik—zur 20. Wiederkehr von Bartóks Todestag*, in NZfM, CXXVI (1965), 330.
> Balanced appreciation of three aspects of the topic: the human significance of folk music in Bartók's composition, its basic effects on his composition, and his scientific studies.
Jakšić, Dura, *Béla Bartók kao društvenopolitički radnik i borac*, in *Zvuk*, 37–38 (1960), 343.
> Bartók as social-political radical and militant.
Kárpáti, János, *Bartók és Schönberg*, in *Magyar Zene*, IV (1963), 563; V (1964), 15, 130.
> Promising by-product of a book in progress on Bartók's quartets.
—— *Béla Bartók and the East (Contribution to the History of the Influence of Eastern Elements on European Music)*, in *Studia musicologica*, VI (1964), 179.
> Exposition of Bartók's borrowings from Arabian and Javanese music, with due credit to the example of Debussy.
Kerényi, Karl, *Über Béla Bartóks "Cantata profana,"* in SMz, LXXXVI (1946), 325.
Kroó, György, *Three Portraits: Bartók's Stage Works*, in *Books from Hungary*, III/3–4 (1961), 7.
—— *Bartók Béla színpadi művei*, Budapest, 1962.
> Discusses *Bluebeard, Wooden Prince*, and *Mandarin*, with many musical examples.
Lendvai, Ernő, *Bartók stílusa a "Szonáta két zongorára és ütőhangszerekre" és a "Zene húros-, ütő- és celestára" tükrében*, Budapest, 1955.
> Bartók's style in the Sonata for Two Pianos and Percussion and the Music for Strings. P. P. Hoffer, in MGG, VIII (1960), 612, says this is Lendvai's most important work.
—— *Einführung in die Formen- und Harmoniewelt Bartóks*, in B. Szabolcsi, ed., *Béla Bartók, Weg und Werk*, Leipzig, 1956, p. 91.
> Chief source of Lendvai's ideas for the present writer.
—— *Bartók und die Zahl*, in *Melos*, XXVII (1960), 327.
> Misleading because only partial sample of Lendvai's ideas: the "golden section" analysis of the Sonata for Two Pianos and Percussion.
—— *A kékszakállú Herceg Vára (Bartók operájának műhelytitkai)*, in *Magyar Zene*, I (1961), 339.
> On *Bluebeard*. First part of a book of analyses, *Bartók dramaturgiája*, Budapest, 1965.
—— *Duality and Synthesis in the Music of Béla Bartók*, in *New Hungarian Quarterly*, III/7 (1962), 91.
> Brief exposition of Lendvai's important ideas.
Liebner, Janos, *Ein wiederentdecktes Werk Béla Bartóks*, in *Beiträge zur Musikwissenschaft*, V (1964), 243.
> A slow movement that Bartók ultimately left out of the Piano Suite, Op. 14.
Lindlar, Heinrich, ed., *Béla Bartók (= Musik der Zeit, III)*, Bonn, 1953.
> Includes Bartók's autobiography with supplement by Dille, and his article on *The Influence of Folkmusic*. Also contributions by Doflein, Mersmann, et al., and a complete list of Bartók's recordings of his own music.
—— *Viermal Bartóks Musik für Saiteninstrumente: Notizen zu einem Interpretationsvergleich*, in S. Borris et al., *Vergleichende Interpretationskunde*, Berlin, 1963, p. 35.
> Detailed comparison of recordings by Karajan, Wand, Solti, and Fricsay.
Mason, Colin, *Bartók's Rhapsodies*, in ML, XXX (1949), 26.
—— *Bartók Through his Quartets*, in MMR, LXXX (1950), 3.
—— *Béla Bartók and Folksong*, in MR, XI (1950), 292.
—— *An Essay in Analysis: Tonality, Symmetry, and Latent Serialism in Bartók's Fourth Quartet*, in MR, XVIII (1957), 189.

—— *Bartók's Early Violin Concerto,* in *Tempo,* 49 (1958), 11.
—— *Bartók's Scherzo for Piano and Orchestra,* in *Tempo,* 65 (1963), 10.
—— *Bartók and Background,* in MT, CVI (1965), 355.
    A book on Bartók by Mason is eagerly anticipated; perhaps the article in *Grove*[5], I, 463, serves as an outline.
Mersmann, Hans, *Der Spätstil Bartóks,* in *Musik der Zeit,* III (1953), 60.
    Mersmann sees the Fifth Quartet and later works as contrasting with the earlier ones and at the same time fulfilling a whole range of tendencies.
Moreux, Serge, *Béla Bartók, sa vie, ses œuvres, son langage,* Paris, 1949; 2d edn., 1955; English transl. by G. S. Fraser and Erik de Mauny, as *Béla Bartók,* London, 1953.
    A first survey, hasty but essentially right.
Nirschy, A., *Varianten zu Bartóks Pantomime "Der wunderbare Mandarin,"* in *Studia musicologica,* II (1962), 189.
Nordwall, Ove, *Béla Bartók och den moderna musiken,* in *Nutida Musik,* VII/2 (1964), 1.
Nüll, Edwin von der, *Béla Bartók,* Halle, 1930.
    First adumbration of Bartók's central significance, and an attempt to explain his "extended tonality."
—— *Moderne Harmonik,* Leipzig, 1932.
    Based on a diss. (Berlin, 1931).
Oláh, Gustav, *Bartók and the Theatre,* in *Béla Bartók: A Memorial Review,* New York, 1950, p. 54.
    Oláh was designer, producer, or adapter of Bartók's stage works on several occasions during his life.
Perle, George, *Symmetrical Formations in the String Quartets of Béla Bartók,* in MR, XVI (1955), 300.
Sacher, Paul, *Béla Bartók zum Gedächtnis,* in SMz, LXXXV (1945), 464.
    Includes brief quotations from letters of Bartók to Sacher.
Sannemüller, Gerd, *Béla Bartóks Suite Opus 14: Stil- und Werkanalyse,* in SMz, CV (1965), 10.
Saygun, A. Adnan, *Bartók in Turkey,* in MQ, XXXVII (1951), 5.
Serly, Tibor, *Story of a Concerto, Bartók's Last Work,* in *The New York Times,* Dec. 11, 1949, p. II–x–7.
    Serly completed the Viola Concerto. His account of his task whets the appetite for more of his recollections, promised in a book on Bartók.
Smith, Robert, *Béla Bartók's Music for Strings, Percussion and Celesta,* in MR, XX (1959), 264.
Stevens, Halsey, *The Life and Music of Béla Bartók,* New York, 1953; 2d edn., 1963.
    The most comprehensive work in English, and, before Ujfalussy, in any language. New edn. has bibliography of recent literature.
Suchoff, Benjamin, *Guide to the "Mikrokosmos" of Béla Bartók,* Silver Spring, Md., 1956.
    Includes Bartók's brief note on each piece, prepared for Ann Chenée, 1944.
—— *History of Béla Bartók's "Mikrokosmos,"* in *Journal of Research in Music Education,* VII (1959), 185.
    From Suchoff's diss. (N.Y. Univ., 1956).
—— *Some Observations on Bartók's Third Piano Concerto,* in *Tempo,* 65 (1963), 8.
Szabolcsi, Bence, *East and West in Béla Bartók's Art,* in *Books from Hungary,* III/3–4 (1961), 2.
—— *Man and Nature in Bartók's World,* in *New Hungarian Quarterly,* II/4 (1961), 90.
——, ed., *Béla Bartók, Weg und Werk,* Leipzig, 1956; French transl. as *Béla Bartók, sa vie et son œuvre,* Budapest, 1956.
    Selected essays and letters of Bartók, some of the best studies of his music, and a list of works superseding all earlier lists.
—— and Ferenc Bónis, *Béla Bartók: his Life in Pictures,* London, 1964.
    Szabolcsi's introductory study, revised from his own volume of 1956, is here combined with an excellent collection of pictures, edited by Bónis.
Thyne, Stuart, *Bartók's "Improvisations": an Essay in Technical Analysis,* in ML, XXXI (1950), 30.

Thyne's observations were extremely helpful to the present author when he was moving from the *Mikrokosmos* to more difficult pieces of Bartók.

Treitler, Leo, *Harmonic Procedures in the Fourth Quartet of Béla Bartók*, in JMT, III (1959), 292.

Twittenhoff, Wilhelm, *Zur Struktur und Thematik des Violinkonzerts von Béla Bartók*, in W. Wiora, ed., *Musikerkenntnis und Musikerziehung, Dankesgaben für Hans Mersmann zu seinem 65. Geburtstage*, Kassel, 1958, p. 143.

Compares Bartók with Beethoven in both formal mastery and dynamic attitude.

Uhde, Jürgen, *Bartóks Mikrokosmos: Spielanweisungen und Erläuterungen: Einführung in das Werk und seine pädagogischen Absichten*, Regensburg, 1954.

Exemplary balance of detail and general interpretation.

—— *Béla Bartók*, Berlin, 1959.

With deep knowledge and love of all Bartók's music, yet also with serious concern for the criticism of the post-Webernites, Uhde presents a beautiful account of Bartók's life and works within 100 pages.

Ujfalussy, József, *Einige inhaltliche Fragen der Brückensymmetrie in Bartóks Werken*, in *Studia musicologica*, V (1963), 541.

——, ed., *Béla Bartóks Kinderjahre: aus den Tagebuchblättern seiner Mutter . . .*, in ÖMz, XX (1965), 461.

—— *Bartók Béla*, 2 vols., Budapest, 1965.

Vinton, John, *The Case of "The Miraculous Mandarin,"* in MQ, L (1964), 1.

Fascinating new details on the history of Bartok's composition, revisions, publication, performance, etc.

—— *New Light on Bartók's Sixth Quartet*, in MR, XXV (1964), 224.

Detailed study of ms. draft and sketches, in the light of all previous work on the subject.

Vitányi, Iván, *Bartók and the Public*, in *New Hungarian Quarterly*, II/2 (1961), 175.

Discusses the reactions of various age-groups, and the changing reactions of Vitányi's own group since Bartók's death.

Volek, J., *Über einige interessante Beziehungen zwischen thematischer Arbeit und Instrumentation in Bartóks Werk: "Concerto für Orchester,"* in *Studia musicologica*, V (1963), 557.

Wagenaar, Bernard, *Bartók's Quartets*, in *The New York Times*, Feb. 27, 1949, p. II–x–7.

First-hand testimony about experiments in string techniques.

Waldbauer, Ivan, *Bartók's "Four Pieces" for Two Pianos*, in *Tempo*, 53–54 (1960), 17.

Based on studies in the N.Y. Bartók Archive.

—— *Bartók's First Piano Concerto: a Publication History*, in MQ, LI (1965), 336.

Close study of mss., editions, and letters leads to an important correction of tempo markings.

Weissmann, John S., *Notes Concerning Bartók's Solo Vocal Music*, in *Tempo*, 36 (1955), 16.

Among many articles on Bartók by Weissmann, this is outstanding because the subject is generally neglected, especially in the writings in English.

—— *Bartokiana*, in *Tempo*, 55-56 (1960), 34.

Critical survey of literature about Bartók, including that in Hungarian, most of which is omitted here.

Wiora, Walter, *Die sogenannten nationalen Schulen der osteuropäischen Musik*, in *Syntagma Friburgense. Historische Studien Hermann Aubin dargebracht zum 70. Geburtstag*, Lindau, 1956, p. 301.

—— *Europäische Volksmusik und abendländische Tonkunst*, Kassel, 1957.

Important scholarly survey of the interrelations between folk music, with its regional varieties and universal allusions, and the dynamic art of Western composers.

BASIE

Horricks, Raymond, *Count Basie and his Orchestra, its Music and its Musicians* (with discography by Alun Morgan), London, 1957.

BAX

Bax, Arnold, *". . . I am a Brazen Romantic"* [Letter to R. Wollstein], in *Musical America*, June 7, 1928, p. 9.

—— *Farewell, my Youth,* London, 1943.
Brief, lively autobiography. "Debussy did not reach England until the spring of 1905, my last year as a student" (p. 22).
Scott-Sutherland, Colin, *The Symphonies of Arnold Bax,* in MR, XXIII (1962), 20.
Enthusiastic, especially about the finale of the Sixth (1934).
—— *Some Unpublished Works of Arnold Bax,* in MR, XXIV (1963), 322.
Shore, Bernard, *Sixteen Symphonies,* London, 1949.
Pp. 341–65 on Bax's Third are uniquely helpful.

BECHET
Bechet, Sidney, *Treat It Gentle,* New York, 1960.
Memoirs of New Orleans, New York, and Paris, presented in a convincing colloquial style. P. 80, on teaching, is especially recommended to teachers and students.

BECK
Mohr, Ernst, *Zum Kompositionsstil von Conrad Beck,* in SMz, CI (1961), 6.

BEIDERBECKE
Wareing, Charles H., and George Garlick, *Bugles for Beiderbecke,* London, 1958.

BENJAMIN
Keller, Hans, *Arthur Benjamin and the Problem of Popularity,* in Tempo, 15 (1950), 4.

BERG
Berg, Alban, *Écrits,* ed. and transl. by Henri Pousseur, Monaco, 1957.
—— *Briefe an seine Frau,* Munich, 1965.
A sample letter of about 1925, published in ÖMz, XX (1965), 110, with the announcement of the collection, arouses great interest.
Blaukopf, Kurt, *New Light on "Wozzeck,"* in Saturday Review, Sep. 26, 1953, p. 62.
Based on over 100 letters to Gottfried Kassowitz, 1913–29.
Brown, Barclay, *Music of Alban Berg: Recordings,* in PNM, I/2 (1963), 170.
Critical comparison of Craft's performances with others.
Downes, Edward, *"Wozzeck,"* in Portfolio, I (1959), 40.
Good introduction, richly illustrated.
Forneberg, Erich, *"Wozzeck" von Alban Berg,* Berlin-Lichterfelde, 1963.
Comprehensive guide and bibliography.
Jouve, Pierre Jean, and Michel Fano, *"Wozzeck" ou le nouvel opéra,* Paris, 1953.
Keller, Hans, *"Lulu,"* in MR, XIV (1953), 302.
"Immeasurably superior to *Wozzeck.*"
Klein, John W., *"Wozzeck"—a Summing Up,* in ML, XLIV (1963), 132.
Criticisms with which the present author agrees, pending some ideal performance that may confirm the more favorable estimates of most authorities.
Krenek, Ernst, [Review of Redlich's *Alban Berg, the Man and his Music*], in MQ, XLIII (1957), 403.
Reveals source of the Carinthian folksong in Berg's Violin Concerto.
Leibowitz, René, *Alban Berg's Five Orchestral Songs after Postcard Texts by Peter Altenberg, Op. 4,* in MQ, XXXIV (1948), 487.
Valuable account, especially detailed for the last song, presented complete in piano score.
Perle, George, *The Music of "Lulu": a New Analysis,* in JAMS, XII (1959), 185.
Drastically different from analyses handed down from the composer's perhaps hasty remarks.
—— *"Lulu": the Formal Design,* in JAMS, XVII (1964), 179.
Helpful with or without the preceding article.
Redlich, Hans Ferdinand, *Alban Berg: Versuch einer Würdigung,* Vienna, 1957.
The most comprehensive study of Berg so far; the English version, *Alban Berg: the Man and his Music,* New York, 1957, is abridged but still valuable.
—— *Unveröffentlichte Briefe Alban Bergs an Arnold Schoenberg,* in A. A. Abert and W. Pfannkuch, eds., *Festschrift Friedrich Blume zum 70. Geburtstag,* Kassel, 1963, p. 272.
6 letters, 1928–33.
Reich, Willi, *Alban Berg . . .,* Vienna, 1937; revised edn., Zürich, 1963; English transl. by

C. Cardew, as *The Life and Works of Alban Berg*, London, 1965.
> The chief value of the slightly expanded 2d edn. is still Reich's first-hand testimony about the man Berg.

—— *Alban Berg, Bildnis im Wort: Selbstzeugnisse und Aussagen der Freunde*, Zürich, 1959.

Rostal, Max, and Hans Keller, *Berg's Violin Concerto: a Revision*, in MT, XCV (1954), 87.
> An improved version of the cadenza in the second movement.

Sabin, Robert, *Alban Berg's "Wozzeck,"* in *Musical America*, Apr. 1951, p. 6.
> Includes a chart of the form, by Fritz Mahler, more convenient than the well-known brochure of Reich.

Smith Brindle, Reginald, *The Symbolism in Berg's "Lyric Suite,"* in *The Score*, 21 (1957), 60.
> Valuable observations, supplementing any other commentary.

Stein, Erwin, *Alban Berg—Anton von Webern*, in *Anbruch*, V (1923), 13; English transl. in *The Chesterian*, 26 (1922), 33.

—— *Berg and Schoenberg*, in *Tempo*, 44 (1957), 4.
> Warns against Redlich's inadequate understanding of Schoenberg in his book on Berg, and discusses Berg's position impartially.

Stravinsky, Igor, [letter to the editor, appealing for the foundation of a Berg Society], in MR, XXVI (1965), 83.

Vlad, Roman, *Storia della dodecafonia*, Milan, 1958.

BERGER

Berger, Arthur, *Stravinsky and the Younger Americans*, in *The Score*, 12 (1955), 38.
> Berger identifies the "Boston group" of which he himself was a leader, together with Irving Fine, Harold Shapero, Louise Talma; also Haieff, Foss, Dahl, Charles Jones, Leo Smit, John Lessard, Paul Des Marais.

BERGSMA

Skulsky, Abraham, *The Music of William Bergsma*, in *Juilliard Review*, III/2 (1956), 12.

BERIO

Prieberg, Fred K., *Imaginäres Gespräch mit Luciano Berio*, in *Melos*, XXXII (1965), 156.

BERKELEY

Dickinson, Peter, *The Music of Lennox Berkeley*, in MT, CIV (1963), 327.
> Calls attention to the intensification and expansion of Berkeley's work in recent years.

—— *Lennox Berkeley*, in *Music & Musicians*, XIII/13 (Aug. 1965), 20.
> Laudatory survey.

BERLIN

Berlin, Irving, and Justus Dickinson, *Words and Music (How They are Written), an Across-The-Table Chat*, in *Green Book*, XIV (July 1915), 98.

BERNSTEIN

Bernstein, Leonard, *The Joy of Music*, New York, 1959.
> Essays and scripts on various topics.

Briggs, John, *Leonard Bernstein, the Man, his Work, and his World*, Cleveland, 1961.

BLACHER

Blacher, Boris, *Über variable Metrik*, in H. Lindlar, ed., *Die Stimme der Komponisten*, Rodenkirchen, 1958, p. 41.
> Famous technical lecture.

—— *Neuland Rhythmus*, in J. Müller-Marein and H. Reinhardt, eds., *Das musikalische Selbstportrait . . .*, Hamburg, 1963, p. 406.
> Charming informal autobiography.

Burt, Francis, *The Teaching and Ideas of Boris Blacher*, in *The Score*, 9 (1954), 12.

Stuckenschmidt, Hans Heinz, *Boris Blacher*, Berlin, 1963.
> Brief but comprehensive survey, chief source of the information presented here.

BLISS

Jefferson, Alan, *Bliss: Composer Royal*, in *Music & Musicians*, XIV/2 (Oct. 1965), 26.
> Sympathetic survey, with list of works.

BLITZSTEIN

Marc Blitzstein, Classified Chronological Catalogue, in *Boletín Interamericano de Musica,* 17 (May 1960), 28.

BLOCH

Bauer, Marion, *Ernest Bloch,* in O. Thompson, ed., *International Cyclopedia of Music and Musicians,* 5th edn., New York, 1949, p. 2271; with addenda by Robert Sabin, in *Ibid.,* 9th edn., New York, 1964, p. 234.
 The best available survey, but in need of supplementing by articles of Cowell, Chapman, and Porter.

Chapman, Ernest, *Ernest Bloch,* in R. Hill, ed., *The Concerto,* London, 1952, p. 315.
 Good analyses of Violin Concerto (1938) and *Concerto Symphonique* (1949).

Cowell, Henry, *Current Chronicle,* in MQ, XL (1954), 235.
 Judicious estimate of Bloch's career.

Engel, Carl, *Bloch and the Library of Congress,* in *Musical America,* Nov. 10, 1928, p. 6.
 Best one of three articles on Bloch in this issue, celebrating his *America.*

Paoli, Rodolfo, *Memoria di Bloch,* in *L'Approdo musicale,* 10 (1960), 109.
 Plea for discriminating attention.

Porter, Andrew, *Ernest Bloch,* in A. Robertson, ed., *Chamber Music,* London, 1957, p. 215.
 Good analyses of the Quartets (1916, 1945, 1951–52) and the Quintet (1923).

BLOMDAHL

Blomdahl, Karl-Birger, *"In the Hall of Mirrors" and "Anabase,"* in R. S. Hines, ed., *The Composer's Point of View,* Norman, Okla., 1963, p. 138.

BORNEFELD

Bornefeld, Helmut, *Selbstbildnis,* in MuK, XVII (1947), 53.

BORRIS

Borris, Siegfried, *Einführung in die moderne Musik,* Halle (Saale), 1949.
 Pupil of Hindemith, sympathetic with a wide range of music, and respectful of Schoenberg without claiming to sympathize, Borris provides an unusually satisfying brief introduction with many examples.

Riemer, Otto, *Ruf des Lebens: zum Schaffen des Komponisten Siegfried Borris,* in *Musica,* IX (1955), 151.

BOSSI

Martinotto, Sergio, *Profilo di Marco Enrico Bossi,* in *Musica d'oggi,* V (1962), 98.
 A reappraisal, with preference for the late works for organ and piano.

Mompellio, Federico, *Marco Enrico Bossi,* Milan, 1952.

BOUGHTON

Hurd, Michael, *Immortal Hour: the Life and Period of Rutland Boughton,* London, 1962.
 Includes wonderful letters from G. B. Shaw, who loyally supported Boughton.

BOULEZ

Boulez, Pierre, *Propositions,* in *Polyphonie,* II (1948), 65.
 "The principal lessons that Messiaen helped us draw from Stravinsky," especially from the *Danse sacrale* in *The Rite of Spring.*

—— *Moment de Bach,* in *Contrepoints,* VII (1951), 71.
 Important essay, full of new ideas, not only on Bach but also on "serialism," chance, and especially Webern. P. 86: "Webern was not predictable; to live usefully after him you won't continue him, you will chop him up."

—— *Schoenberg is dead,* in *The Score,* 6 (1952), 18.
 A manifesto. Taking for granted the necessity of the 12-tone technique, Boulez condemns most of Schoenberg's music except *Pierrot Lunaire,* and indicates Webern as better guide. (Boulez's mature view is more moderate.)

—— *Hommage à Webern,* in *Domaine musical, Bulletin international de musique contemporain,* Paris, 1954, p. 123; English transl. in *Die Reihe* (English edn.), II (1958), 41.
 "The only threshold."

—— *Recherches maintenant,* in *Nouvelle revue française,* II (1954), 898; German transl. as *Einsichten und Aussichten,* in *Melos,* XXII (1955), 161.
> First recommendation of Debussy's late works as guides to form "almost better than Webern."

—— *Expériences, autruches et musique,* in *Nouvelle revue française,* III (1955), 1174.
> Opposed equally to experimentalism and ostrich attitudes.

—— *La Corruption dans les encensoirs,* in *Melos,* XXIII (1956), 276 (French and German texts).
> Proclamation of the role of Debussy as chief "ancestor."

—— *Debussy: "Jeux,"* in *Gravesaner Blätter,* 2/3 (1956), 5.

—— *Aléa,* in *Nouvelle revue française,* V (1957), 839; English transl. by D. Noakes and P. Jacobs, in PNM III/1 (1964), 42.

—— *Tendances de la musique récente,* in RM, 236 (1957), 28.

—— Articles: *Bartók; Berg; Debussy; Schoenberg; Série; Webern,* in *Encyclopédie de la musique Fasquelle,* 3 vols., Paris, 1958.

—— *Son, verbe, synthèse,* in *Revue belge de musicologie,* XIII (1959), 5.

—— *Disziplin und Kommunikation,* in *Darmstädter Beiträge zur neuen Musik,* III (1961), 25.

—— *Wie arbeitet die Avant-garde?,* in *Melos,* XXVIII (1961), 301.

—— *Dire, jouer, chanter,* in *La Musique et ses problèmes,* Paris, 1963, p. 300.
> On Schoenberg's *Pierrot Lunaire* and Boulez's *Marteau sans maître.*

—— *Gespräch "unter zwei Augen,"* in *Melos,* XXX (1963), 185.
> "Freedom can be found only through order."

—— *Poésie—centre et absence—musique,* in *Melos,* XXX (1963), 33.

—— *Nécessité d'une orientation esthétique,* in *Mercure de France,* CCCL (1964), 624; CCCLI (1964), 110; also in M. Horkheimer, ed., *Zeugnisse: Theodor W. Adorno zum 60. Geburtstag,* Frankfurt, 1963, p. 332.

—— *Penser la musique aujourd'hui,* Paris, 1964; German transl. as *Musikdenken heute,* in *Darmstädter Beiträge zur neuen Musik,* VIII (1964).

—— *"Sonate, que me veux-tu?"* in *Médiations,* 7 (1964), 61; English transl. by D. Noakes and P. Jacobs, in PNM, I/2 (1963), 32.
> Mainly concerned with Boulez's Third Sonata and Mallarmé's *Livre.*

—— *Interview with Barrie Hall,* in *Music & Musicians,* XIV/1 (Sep. 1965), 18.
> Perhaps the best introduction in English to the personality and taste of Boulez. Here Bartók is ranked with Stravinsky and the three Viennese.

—— et al., *Wo ist echte Tradition?,* in *Melos,* XXVII (1960), 289.
> A symposium. Boulez says, "I am now in closer relation to Japan than to Europe . . . I make tradition. I have no tradition behind me . . . My position isn't clear."

Bourdet, Denise, *Visages d'aujourd'hui* (preface by François Mauriac), Paris, 1960.
> Vivid glimpses of Stravinsky, Messiaen, Boulez, et al.

Bradshaw, Susan, and Richard Rodney Bennett, *In Search of Boulez,* in *Music & Musicians,* XI/5 (Jan. 1963), 10, and XI/12 (Aug. 1963), 14.
> Best available discussion in English. Includes examples.

Cadieu, Martine, *Duo avec Pierre Boulez,* in *Nouvelles littéraires,* Aug. 16, 1962, p. 11.
> "I stick to one thing and just radiate in several directions at once. I approach the Joyce type. Then too I always think in a big frame."

Goehr, Alexander, *Is There Only One Way?,* in *The Score,* 26 (1960), 63.
> No, despite Eimert. Goehr's teacher Boulez "counters . . . the 'only way.'" Further, "Boulez has created a new kind of sound, by way of an ensemble in which non-sustaining instruments predominate."

Goléa, Antoine, *Rencontres avec Pierre Boulez,* Paris, 1958.

Maw, Nicholas, *Boulez and Tradition,* in MT, CIII (1962), 162.

Philippot, Michel P., *Pierre Boulez aujourd'hui, entre hier et demain,* in *Critique,* XX/210 (1964), 943.
> Review of *Penser la musique.* With many reservations about the aim of the book and the form of its presentation, Philippot judges it nevertheless, because of Boulez's practical achievement, "infallible and definitive."

Souvtchinsky, Pierre, *Le Mot-fantôme,* in *Nouvelle revue française,* IV (1956), 1107.
> On Boulez's *Marteau.*

BRANT

Sankey, Stuart, *Henry Brant's Grand Universal Circus*, in *Julliard Review*, III/3 (1956), 21.

BRECHT

Bentley, Eric, *Brecht und der "Zonk,"* in *Listen*, Mar.–Apr. 1964, p. 8.
>   "Zonk" is Brecht's pronunciation of "Song." Bentley publishes here a typical song of
>   Brecht, and discusses its background.

Brecht, Bertolt, *Dreigroschenbuch: Texte, Materialen, Dokumente*, Frankfurt, 1960.
>   Includes essay "On the Use of Music for an Epic Theater."

—— *Betrachtung der Kunst und Kunst der Betrachtung*, in *Sinn und Form*, XIII (1961), 677.
>   Written in 1939, this essay begins with the consideration of "democratic art."

Hartung, Günter, *Zur epischen Oper Brechts und Weills*, in *Wissenschaftliche Zeitschrift der Martin Luther-Universität Halle-Wittenberg*, VIII (1959), 659.
>   Based on a diss. (Halle).

Parmet, Simon, *Die ursprüngliche Musik zu "Mutter Courage": meine Zusammenarbeit mit Brecht*, in SMz, XCVII (1957), 465.
>   Brecht, caught in Finland in 1941, persuaded the modest conductor Parmet to
>   supply music for his new play in accordance with his ideal derived from Weill and
>   Eisler.

Schumacher, Ernst, *Die dramatischen Versuche B. Brechts, 1918–1933*, Berlin, 1955.
>   A long diss. (Leipzig, 1955) with rich materials on music.

BRIAN

Barsham, Eve, *Havergal Brian's New Cello Concerto*, in *The Strad*, LXXVI/901 (1965), 17.
>   Proposes a festival for Brian's 90th birthday, 1966.

Nettel, Reginald, *Ordeal by Music: the Strange Experience of Havergal Brian*, London, 1945.
>   Much more than a biography, this book treats Brian as symptomatic of musical life
>   in industrial society and throws more light on general questions than most discussions
>   of them do. A summary estimate of Elgar is included.

Simpson, Robert, *The Later Works of Havergal Brian*, in MT, C (1959), 586.

BRIDGE

Howells, Herbert, *Frank Bridge*, in ML, XXII (1941), 208.
Pirie, Peter J., *Frank Bridge*, in *Musical Opinion*, LXXXVIII (1965), 531.
>   Recommends especially the quartets.

Warrack, John, *A Note on Frank Bridge*, in *Tempo*, 66–67 (1963), 27.
Westrup, Jack, *Frank Bridge*, in A. L. Bacharach, ed., *British Music of our Time*, Harmondsworth, 1946, p. 75.

BRITTEN

Benjamin Britten: a Complete Catalogue of his Works, London, 1963.
Britten, Benjamin, *On Receiving the First Aspen Award: a Speech*, London, 1964; also, as *The Artist and Society*, in *Saturday Review*, Aug. 22, 1964, p. 37; and in *Records & Recording*, VIII/2 (Nov. 1964), 14.
>   A precious statement because of its rare good sense.

—— et al., *The Rape of Lucretia: a Symposium*, London, 1948.
Garbutt, J. W., *Music and Motive in "Peter Grimes,"* in ML, XLIV (1963), 334.
>   Unusually discriminating criticism of Britten's most famous opera.

Gishford, Anthony, ed., *Tribute to Benjamin Britten on his 50th Birthday*, London, 1963.
>   27 interesting brief contributions, among which Aaron Copland's is almost uniquely
>   concerned with particular pieces by Britten.

Halsey, Louis, *Britten's Church Music*, in MT, CIII (1962), 686.
>   Surveys an important part of Britten's work, more briefly than Wyton.

Keller, Hans, *Britten as Interpreter*, in *Audio & Record Review*, IV/6 (Feb. 1965), 8.
>   Valuable essay, supplemented by a discography, p. 67.

Mitchell, Donald, *Britten's Revisionary Practice: Practical and Creative*, in *Tempo*, 66–67 (1963), 15.
—— and Hans Keller, eds., *Benjamin Britten: a Commentary on his Works, from a Group of Specialists*, London, 1952.

Robertson, Alec, *More than Music*, London, 1961.
Includes touching comment on Britten's Mass.
—— *Britten's War Requiem*, in MT, CIII (1962), 308.
Among the best of many admiring reports of this work.
Roseberry, Eric, *Britten's Purcell Realizations and Folksong Arrangements*, in *Tempo*, 57 (1961), 7.
Outstanding article among many on Britten in his publisher's magazine.
White, Eric Walter, *Benjamin Britten: a Sketch of his Life and Works*, London, 1949; rev. and enl. edn., 1954.
Whittall, A. M., *Benjamin Britten*, in MR, XXIII (1963), 314.
Interesting over-all appraisal.
Wyton, Alec, *Benjamin Britten and the Church*, in *American Guild of Organists Quarterly*, IX (1964), 3.
Excellent survey, with examples of an important part of Britten's work.

BROONZY

Broonzy, William, and Yannick Bruynoghe, *Big Bill Blues: William Broonzy's Story*, London, 1955.

BRUBECK

Rice, Robert, *The Cleanup Man*, in *The New Yorker*, June 3, 1961, p. 41.
"Profile" of Dave Brubeck.

BURKHARD

Burkhard, Willy, *Briefe an Walter Tappolet*, Zürich, 1964.
Mohr, Ernst, *Willy Burkhard: Leben und Werk*, Zürich, 1957.
Burkhard read most of Mohr's ms., 1945–55, and this book is thus authoritative. Yet the shorter book by Zurlinden is a more attractive introduction.
Zurlinden, Hans, *Willy Burkhard*, Erlenbach, 1956.
Zurlinden was long a close friend of Burkhard. Without attempting technical discussion, he succeeds in revealing something of the spirit of the works.

BUSH

Payne, Anthony, *Alan Bush*, in MT, CV (1964), 263.

BUSONI

Busoni, Ferruccio, *Entwurf einer neuen Aesthetik der Tonkunst*, Trieste, 1907; 2d enlarged edn., Leipzig, 1910; English transl. by Theodore Baker, as *Sketch of a New Esthetic of Music*, New York, 1911; reprinted in *Three Classics in the Aesthetic of Music*, New York, 1962.
—— *Dritteltonmusik*, in *Melos*, III (1922), 198 (with English transl. by H. Leichtentritt).
Supplements Busoni's earlier speculations on microtones, and refers again to Debussy.
—— *Von der Einheit der Musik*, Berlin, 1922; new edn. by J. Herrmann, as *Wesen und Einheit der Musik*, Berlin, 1956; English transl. by Rosamond Ley, as *The Essence of Music, and Other Papers*, London, 1957.
Valuable collection of Busoni's later writings; English translation is unreliable and awkward.
—— *Briefe an seine Frau*, ed. by F. Schnapp, Zürich, 1935; Italian transl. by Luigi Dallapiccola, as *Lettere alla moglie*, Milan, 1955.
—— *Scritti e pensieri sulla musica*, ed. by Luigi Dallapiccola, Milan, 1954.
Busoni, Gerda Sjöstrand, *Erinnerungen an Ferruccio Busoni*, ed. by F. Schnapp, Berlin, 1958.
Booklet by Busoni's wife.
Dent, Edward J., *Ferruccio Busoni, a Biography*, London, 1933.
Chief source of information.
Ferruccio Busoni: Werkverzeichnis, auf Grund der Aufzeichnungen Busonis zusammengestellt u. hrsg. v. seinen Verlegern, Leipzig, 1924.
Guerrini, Guido, *Ferruccio Busoni: la vita, la figura, l'opera*, Florence, 1944.
Jarnach, Philipp, *Das Stilproblem der neuen Klassizität im Werke Busonis*, in *Anbruch*, III (1921), 16.

Busoni's principal disciple here shows clearly what his teacher intended by the slogan "New Classicism," and how it fitted his lifetime's work and thought.

Scherchen, Hermann, *"Neue Klassizität"?*, in *Melos*, I (1920), 242.
> Scherchen quotes most of Busoni's famous letter, and disagrees. His profound critique at this point forecasts his long, varied, fruitful career.

Selden-Goth, Gisella, *Ferruccio Busoni: un profilo*, Florence, 1964.
> Enthusiastic yet concise account of Busoni's whole work.

Stevenson, Ronald, *Ferruccio Busoni*, in MR, XVIII (1957), 234.
> Good survey of literature on Busoni.

Vogel, Wladimir, *Aus der Zeit der Meisterklasse Busoni*, in SMz, CIV (1964), 165.
> Interesting memoir.

BUTTING

Vetter, Walther, *Max Butting als schaffender Musiker der Gegenwart: eine Improvisation zu seinem 75. Geburtstag*, in MuG, XIII (1963), 604.

CAGE

Cage, John, *Goal: New Music, New Dance*, in *Dance Observer*, VI (1939), 296.
> Cage's début.

—— *For More New Sounds*, in MM, XIX (1942), 243.

—— *Grace and Clarity*, in *Dance Observer*, XI (1944), 108.
> "Tomorrow, with electronic music in our ears, we will hear freedom."

—— *Experimental Music*, in *The Score*, 12 (1955), 65.

—— *Unbestimmtheit*, in *Die Reihe*, V (1959), 85; as *Indeterminacy*, in English edn., V (1961), 115.

—— *Silence*, Middletown, Conn., 1961.
> Collected lectures, program notes, etc. Chief source of information.

Hassan, Ihab, *The Dismemberment of Orpheus*, in *The American Scholar*, XXXII (1963), 463.
> Cage considered in relation to Salinger, Burroughs, and other writers.

John Cage, New York, 1962.
> A catalogue; supplements *Silence* with both earlier and later materials.

CAPLET

Marc, Yves, *André Caplet*, in *Le Monde musicale*, XXXV (1924), 269, 297.

CARPENTER

Pierson, Thomas, *The Life and Music of John Alden Carpenter*, Eastman School of Music diss., 1952.

CARRILLO

Carrillo, Julián, *Su vido y su obra*, Mexico City, 1945.

—— *Problems of Music and the Physics of Music*, Mexico City, 1949.

CARTER

Carter, Elliott, *Music as a Liberal Art*, in MM, XXII (1944), 12.

—— *Music in the 20th Century*, in *Encyclopedia Britannica*, 1950 and following editions, Vol. XVI, *s.v.* "Music."

—— [Autobiographical sketch], in *The 25th Anniversary Report of the Harvard Class of 1930*, Cambridge, 1955, p. 165.

—— *The Rhythmic Basis of American Music*, in *The Score*, 12 (1955), 27.
> Suggests a common quality in jazz, Harris, Copland, Sessions, Ives, et al.

—— *Shop Talk by an American Composer*, in MQ, XLVI (1960), 189; also in P. H. Lang, ed., *Problems of Modern Music*, New York, 1962, p. 51.
> Talk at Princeton.

—— *Extending the Classical Syntax*, in *Music—East and West*, Tokyo, 1962, p. 126.

—— *Letter from Europe*, in PNM, I/2 (1963), 195.
> Classification of recent trends.

—— See also articles by Carter listed here under Fauré, Gilbert, Ives, Piston, Sessions.

Goldman, Richard Franko, *Current Chronicle*, in MQ, XXXVII (1951), 83.

—— *The Music of Elliott Carter*, in MQ, XLIII (1957), 151.

Koegler, Horst, *Begegnungen mit Elliott Carter*, in *Melos*, XXVI (1959), 256.
> Vivid portrait by a pupil at Salzburg.

CASELLA

Casella, Alfredo, *Matière et timbre*, in RM, II/6 (1921), 39.

—— *21 + 26*, Rome, 1931.

—— *I Segreti della giara*, Florence, 1941.

—— *Music in My Time: Memoirs*, transl. and ed. by Spencer Norton, Norman, Okla., 1955.
> Based chiefly on *I Segreti della giara*.

—— and Virgilio Mortari, *La Tecnica dell'orchestra contemporanea*, Milan, 1950.

D'Amico, Fedele, and Guido M. Gatti, *Alfredo Casella: con saggi . . . appendice bio-bibliografica*, Milan, 1958.

CASTELNUOVO-TEDESCO

Weber, Roland von, *Castelnuovo-Tedesco*, in D. Ewen, ed., *The New Book of Modern Composers*, New York, 1961, p. 112.

CHAMPAGNE

Archer, Thomas, *Claude Champagne*, in CMJ, II/2 (1958), 3.
> Chief study of the style of the leading French Canadian composer.

CHANLER

Tangeman, Robert, *The Songs of Theodore Chanler*, in MM, XXII/4 (1945), 227.

CHAPLIN

Chaplin, Charles, *Does the Public Know What It Wants?*, in *Ladies' Home Journal*, Oct. 1923, p. 40; also in *Adelphi* (London), I (1924), 702.

—— *Can Art be Popular?*, in *Ladies' Home Journal*, Oct. 1924, p. 34.

Huff, Theodore, *Chaplin as Composer*, in *Films in Review*, I/6 (Sept. 1950), 1; also in Huff, *Chaplin*, New York, 1951, p. 235.
> All too brief a listing of facts.

CHARLES

Woodfin, Henry, *Ray Charles*, in M. Williams, ed., *Jazz Panorama*, New York, 1962, p. 306.

CHÁVEZ

Chávez, Carlos, *Toward a New Music: Music and Electricity*, transl. by H. Weinstock, New York, 1937.

—— *Musical Thought*, Cambridge, Mass., 1961.
> Mellow, modest wisdom concerning many musical matters.

García Morillo, Roberto, *Carlos Chávez: vida y obra*, Mexico City, 1960.

Weinstock, Herbert, *Carlos Chávez*, in MQ, XXII (1936), 425; rev. version in *Composers of the Americas*, III (1957), 60.
> Best available source of information in English until completion of the dissertation by R. L. Johnson (Indiana University).

—— *About Carlos Chávez: Some Notes*, in *Tempo*, 51 (1959), 13.

CHRISTIAN

Ellison, Ralph, *The Charlie Christian Story*, in *Saturday Review*, May 17, 1958, p. 42; also in Ellison, *Shadow and Act*, New York, 1964, p. 233.

CILÉA

D'Amico, Tomasino, *Francesco Ciléa*, Milan, 1960.

ČIURLIONIS

Jakubénas, Vladas, *M. K. Čiurlionis, the Composer*, in *Lituanus*, VII (1961), 62.

Worobiow, Nikolai, *M. K. Čiurlionis, der litauische Maler and Musiker*, Kaunas & Leipzig, 1938.
> Musical contributions by V. Jakubénas. Reproductions of paintings.

CLARKE

Verrall, John, *Henry Leland Clarke*, in ACA, IX/3 (1960), 2.

COLERIDGE-TAYLOR

Berwick Sayers, William Charles, *Samuel Coleridge-Taylor, Musician: his Life and Letters,*
2d rev. edn., London, 1927.

CONE

Cone, Edward T., *Analysis Today,* in MQ, XLVI (1960), 172; also in P. H. Lang, ed.,
Problems of Modern Music, New York, 1962, p. 34.
> Composer, pianist, teacher, and true humanist, Cone practices what he recommends—
> "not description or prescription, but aid to the ear." Examples from Schoenberg and
> Stravinsky.

COPLAND

Aaron Copland: a Complete Catalogue of his Works, London, 1960.
Berger, Arthur, *Aaron Copland,* New York, 1953.
> Sympathetic survey, especially good on the Third Symphony.
—— *Aaron Copland's "Piano Fantasy,"* in *Juilliard Review,* V/1 (1957), 13.
Copland, Aaron, *What to Listen For in Music,* New York, 1938.
> Includes note on Piano Variations.
—— *Our New Music: Leading Composers in Europe and America,* New York, 1941.
> Includes modest autobiography.
—— *Music and Imagination,* Cambridge, Mass., 1952.
—— *America's Young Men of Music,* in *Music & Musicians,* IX/4 (Dec. 1960), 11.
> A talk for the USIS, deliberately superficial but very interesting.
—— *Copland on Music: Essays . . . ,* New York, 1960.
—— *The Composer Speaks . . . A Tape Recorded Interview,* in *Audio & Record Review,*
III/11 (July 1964), 19.
Drew, David, *American Chamber Music,* in A. Robertson, ed., *Chamber Music,* London, 1957,
p. 321.
Evans, Peter, *The Thematic Techniques of Copland's Recent Works,* in *Tempo,* 51 (1959), 2.
—— *Copland on the Serial Road: an Analysis of "Connotations,"* in PNM, II/2 (1964), 141.
Garvie, Peter, *Aaron Copland,* in CMJ, VI/2 (1962), 3.
Goldman, Richard Franko, *Aaron Copland,* in MQ, XLVII (1961), 1.
Kerman, Joseph, [review of Copland's Emily Dickinson Songs and other recent recordings],
in *The Hudson Review,* XIII (1961), 408.
> Uniquely penetrating criticism, justly severe yet framed with sincere affection.
Kirkpatrick, John, *Aaron Copland's Piano Sonata,* in MM, XIX/4 (1942), 246.
Overton, Hall, *Copland's Jazz Roots,* in *Jazz Today,* I (Nov. 1956), 40.
Smith, Julia Frances, *Aaron Copland, his Work and Contribution to American Music,* New
York, 1955.
> Originally a diss. (N.Y. Univ. School of Education, 1952).
Wilson, Edmund, *The Jazz Problem,* in *The New Republic,* XLV (1926), 217.

COWELL

Brant, Henry, *Henry Cowell, Musician and Citizen,* in *The Etude,* LXXV/2 (Feb. 1957), 15;
3 (Mar.), 20; 4 (Apr.), 22.
> The most comprehensive account.
Cowell, Henry, *Impasse of Modern Music,* in *Century,* CXIV (1927), 671.
—— *Hidden Irish Treasure,* in MM, VI/4 (1929), 31.
—— *New Musical Resources,* New York, 1930.
> First written in 1919. Interesting chiefly in relation to Cowell's career.
—— *Towards Neo-Primitivism,* in MM, X (1933), 149.
—— *New Horizons in Music,* in R. MacIver, ed., *New Horizons in Creative Thinking,* New
York, 1954, p. 87.
—— *Oriental Influence on Western Music,* in *Music—East and West,* Tokyo, 1962, p. 71.
Henry Cowell: Catalog, in ACA, III/4 (1953), 6.
Seeger, Charles, *Henry Cowell,* in *Magazine of Art,* XXXIII (1940), 288, 322.

CRESTON

Cowell, Henry, *Paul Creston,* in MQ, XXXIV (1948), 533.
　　Appreciative introduction.
—— *Current Chronicle,* in MQ, XXXVII (1951), 78.
　　Criticism of later works.
Creston, Paul, *Principles of Rhythm,* New York, 1964.
　　Intended to give practical help to students of composition, and confined to measurable
　　rhythms of Western music, ca. 1600–1900. Includes an analysis of Scriabin's First
　　Sonata.

DALLAPICCOLA

Cadieu, Martine, *Duo avec Luigi Dallapiccola,* in *Nouvelles littéraires,* March 1, 1962, p. 9.
　　Vivid display of Dallapiccola's culture and charm.
Dallapiccola, Luigi, *Sulla strada della dodecafonia,* in *Aut Aut,* I (Jan. 1951), 30; English
　　transl. as *On the Twelve-Tone Road,* in *Music Survey,* IV (1951), 318.
　　Includes account of Puccini at performance of *Pierrot Lunaire.*
—— *The Genesis of the "Canti di Prigonia" and "Il Prigioniero": an Autobiographical Frag-
　　ment,* in MQ, XXXIX (1953), 355.
—— *My Choral Music,* in R. S. Hines, ed., *The Composer's Point of View,* Norman, Okla.,
　　1963, p. 151.
—— *Musique et humanité,* in *Journal of the International Folk Music Council,* XVI (1964), 8.
　　"I personally am *for* tradition . . . but I am *against* traditionalism."
D'Amico, Fedele, *Luigi Dallapiccola,* in *Melos,* XX (1953), 69.
　　A rare critical estimate, convincing to the present author.
—— *La Verità di Dallapiccola,* in *I Casi della musica,* Milan, 1962, p. 152.
Drew, David, *Dallapiccola,* in *The New Statesman and Nation,* LVII (1959), 363.
Nathan, Hans, *The Twelve-Tone Compositions of Luigi Dallapiccola,* in MQ, XLIV (1958),
　　289.
　　Valuable survey, to be followed by more extended studies in progress.
Vlad, Roman, *Luigi Dallapiccola,* English transl. by Cynthia Jolly, Milan, 1957.

DAMASE

Cadieu, Martine, *Duo avec Jean-Michel Damase,* in *Nouvelles littéraires,* Dec. 28, 1961, p. 9.
　　Fresh tribute to *Pelléas,* as supreme among lyric forms.

DAVID

Klein, Rudolf, *Johann Nepomuk David und die Reihentechnik,* in ÖMz, XV (1960), 505.
—— *Johann Nepomuk David: eine Studie,* Vienna, 1964.
　　Praises especially David's late works.

DAVIDENKO

Dmitrievskaia, K., *Massovaia pesnia A. Davidenko,* in M. S. Druskin, ed., *Voprosy sovremennoi
　　muzyki,* Leningrad, 1963, p. 5.
　　Davidenko's "mass-songs."
Shekhter, Boris Semenovich, *Iz vospominanii ob A. Davidenko,* in SM, 1959/5, p. 52.
　　Memoirs of Davidenko by his friend and classmate.

DAVIES

Davies, Peter Maxwell, *Problems of a British Composer Today,* in *The Listener,* LXII (1959),
　　563.

DAVIS

Davis, Miles, *Self-Portrait,* in D. Cerulli, ed., *The Jazz World,* New York, 1960, p. 48.
James, Sydney Michael, *Miles Davis,* London, 1961.

DEBUSSY

Ackere, Jules van, *Pelléas et Mélisande, ou le rencontre miraculeuse d'une poésie et d'une
　　musique,* Brussels, 1952.
Almendra, Julia d', *Les Modes grégoriens dans l'œuvre de Claude Debussy,* Paris, 1950.
　　Expanded from a diss. (Gregorian Institute). Debussy's uses of the church modes are

patiently catalogued, and somewhat naively attributed to the influence of Gregorian chant.

Ansermet, Ernest, *An Inner Unity: Conversations with Peter Heyworth, on Debussy*, in *High Fidelity*, XII/9 (Sept. 1962), 56.

Barraqué, Jean, *Debussy*, Paris, 1962.
  Excellent survey from the point of view of a post-Boulez composer; fresh and concise descriptions of the music more than compensate for omissions and slight errors in the biography. Critical discography by Marcel Marnat.

Bathori, Jane, *Sur l'interprétation des mélodies de Claude Debussy*, Paris, 1953.

Bonheur, Raymond, *Souvenirs et impressions d'un compagnon de jeunesse*, in RM, VII (May 1926), 99.
  A valuable primary source. Other authors contributed first-hand reports to the same special issue of RM.

Borris, Siegfried, *Einfluss und Einbruch primitiver Musik in die Musik des Abendlandes*, in *Sociologus*, II (1952), 52.
  Systematic and stimulating, though admittedly incomplete survey. A shorter version was published in *Internationaler Musikkongress Wien 1952 . . . Bericht*, Vienna, 1953, p. 51.

—— *Neue Formen der Mehrstimmigkeit*, in *Musikalische Zeitfragen*, IX (1960), 110.

Brailoiu, Constantin, *Pentatonismes chez Debussy*, in B. Rajeczky and L. Vargyas, eds., *Studia memoriae Belae Bartók sacra*, Budapest, 1957, p. 375; English transl. as *Pentatony in Debussy's Music*, in *Ibid.*, 3d (English) edn., 1959, p. 377.
  Invaluable study.

Caillard, C. François, and José de Bérys, *Le Cas Debussy: une opinion . . . une enquête*, Paris, 1910.

Capellen, Georg, *Exotische Rhythmik, Melodik, und Tonalität als Wegweiser zu einer neuen Kunstentwicklung*, in *Die Musik*, VI (1907), 216.

—— *L'Exotisme et la musique de l'avenir*, in BSIM, VI (1910), 541.
  Rare early recognition of the importance of exoticism, including some reference to Debussy.

Damon, S. Foster, *American Influence on Modern French Music*, in *Dial*, LXV (Aug. 15, 1918), 93.
  Notes use of American popular rhythms by Debussy and Satie.

Danckert, Werner, *Claude Debussy*, Berlin, 1950.
  Penetrating stylistic analysis and judicious assessment of Debussy's historic position.

Debussy, Claude, *Du précurseur*, in BSIM, IX (Mar. 1913), 46.

—— *M. Croche, anti-dilettante*, Paris, 1921; English transl. as *M. Croche, the Dilettante Hater*, New York, 1928; also in *Three Classics in the Aesthetic of Music*, New York, 1962.
  Articles originally published in *La Revue blanche*, 1901, and *Gil Blas*, 1903, slightly revised.

—— [Lettres à M. Vasnier]: see Henry Prunières, *À la Villa Medici*, in RM, VII (1926), 119.

—— *Lettres à son éditeur*, Paris, 1927.
  The most important collection, especially for Debussy's 20th-century works.

—— *L'Enfance de Pelléas: lettres à André Messager*, Paris, 1938.

—— *Lettres à deux amis*, Paris, 1942.
  Letters to R. Godet and G. Jean-Aubry.

—— *Lettres à sa femme Emma*, ed. by P. Vallery-Radot, Paris, 1957.

—— *Lettres inédites à André Caplet (1908–14)*, ed. by E. Lockspeiser, Monaco, 1957.

—— *Lettres inédites à Stravinsky*, in *Avec Stravinsky*, Monaco, 1958, p. 199.

—— *Remarques* (introd. by A. Souris), in *Nouvelle revue française*, XI (1963), 1153.
  Collage of well chosen snippets from the letters and critical writings.

—— *Lettres inédites . . .* , in RM, 258 (1964), 109.

—— and Gabriele d'Annunzio, *Correspondance inédite*, ed. by G. Tosi, Paris, 1948.

—— and Ernest Chausson, *Correspondance inédite*, in RM, VII/1 (1925), 116.
  Important long letters of 1893.

—— and Louis Laloy, *Correspondance*, in *Revue de musicologie*, XLVIII (1962), 3.

—— and Pierre Louÿs, *Correspondance,* ed. by H. Borgeaud, Paris, 1945.
> Borgeaud planned a complete edition of Debussy's letters.

—— and Victor Segalen, *Textes,* ed. by A. Joly-Segalen and A. Schaeffner, Monaco, 1961.

—— and P. J. Toulet, *Correspondance,* Paris, 1929.

Dietschy, Marcel, *The Family and Childhood of Debussy,* in MQ, XLVI (1960), 301.
> Dietschy's new information is also incorporated in the book by Lockspeiser, who translated this article for MQ which contains the best of it.

—— *La Passion de Claude Debussy,* Neuchâtel, 1962.

Dille, Denijs, *Inleiding tot het vormbegrip bij Debussy,* in *Hommage à Charles van den Borren: Mélanges,* Antwerp, 1945, p. 175.
> Unusually accurate analysis of the *Faun.*

Dumesnil, Maurice, *Debussy's Principles in Pianoforte Playing,* in *The Étude,* LVI (1928), 153.

—— *How to Play and Teach Debussy,* New York, 1932.

—— *Debussy's Influence on Piano Writing and Playing,* in *Music Teachers' National Association Proceedings,* XXXIX (1945), 39.

Dupérier, Jean, *Découverte du vieux monde: lettres d'un musicien ambulant à un confrère sédentaire,* Paris, 1957.
> P. 186, Ferdinand Hérold's story of presenting Debussy to Mallarmé.

Durand, Jacques, *Quelques souvenirs d'un éditeur de musique,* 2 vols., Paris, 1924–25.
> Valuable notes on Debussy et al.

Eimert, Herbert, *Debussys "Jeux,"* in *Die Reihe,* V (1959), 5; in English edn., V (1961), 3.

Emmanuel, Maurice, *Pelléas et Mélisande de Claude Debussy: étude historique et critique, analyse musicale,* Paris, 1925.
> The best of many guides to the opera.

—— et al., *Inédits sur Claude Debussy: Collection Comoedia-Charpentier,* Paris, 1942.
> Complete transcription of Emmanuel's notes on Debussy's technical talk with Guiraud, pp. 27–33. Lockspeiser (1962) also translates this document. The collection includes other interesting fragments.

Evans, Edwin, *Debussy for Singers,* in *The Sackbut,* II/5 (1921), 8.
> Excellent suggestions.

Fábián, László, *Debussy und sein Werk, mit besonderer Rücksicht auf den musikalischen Impressionismus,* Munich, 1923.

—— *Debussy élete, kora és művészete,* Budapest, 1957.

Farwell, Arthur, *The Debussy of "St. Sebastian,"* in *Musical America,* Feb. 24, 1912, p. 21.

Frankenstein, Alfred, *Debussy: Orchestral and Vocal Works,* in *High Fidelity,* VIII/1 (Jan. 1958), 79.
> Critical discography, not replaced by Goldsmith and Osborne.

Gatti-Casazza, Giulio, [Interview (mostly continuous quotation) about Debussy, on the occasion of the first *Pelléas* at the "Met"], in *The New York Times,* Mar. 15, 1925, p. x–6.

Gauthier, André, *Debussy: Documents iconographiques,* Geneva, 1952.
> Collection of 205 pictures, unfortunately reproduced too small.

Gervais, Françoise, *La Notion d'arabesque chez Debussy,* in RM, 241 (1958), 3.
> Good discussion of an important notion.

—— *Structures debussystes,* in RM, 258 (1964), 77.
> Presents Debussy's "personal and precise definition" of motivic development, not yet firmly grasped by the present author, but perhaps very important.

—— *Debussy et la tonalité,* in E. Weber, ed., *Debussy et l'évolution,* Paris, 1965, p. 97.

Goldsmith, Harris, and Conrad L. Osborne, *Debussy on Microgroove,* in *High Fidelity,* XII/9 (Sept. 1962), 66.
> Comprehensive critical discography.

Heyer, Hermann, *Claude Debussys musikalische Ästhetik: Versuch einer Analyse,* in *Deutsche Jahrbuch der Musikwissenschaft,* VII (1963), 36.

Jakobik, Albert, *Die assoziative Harmonik in den Klavierwerken C. Debussys,* Würzburg, 1940.
> Diss. (Berlin). Interesting though often mistaken.

—— *Zur Einheit der neuen Musik,* Würzburg, 1957.
> Debussy's contribution is seen as a unifying force, Bartók and Hindemith as Debussy's chief heirs. See K. Dahlhaus in Mf, XII (1959), 236.

Keeton, A. E., *Debussy: his Science and his Music*, in *19th Century*, LXVI/391 (1909), 492.
 Just appraisal, emphasizing *Pelléas* and hoping for a worthy *King Lear*.
Koechlin, Charles, *Debussy*, Paris, 1927.
—— *Souvenirs sur Debussy, la Schola, et la S.M.I.*, in RM, XV (1934), 241.
Kurth, Ernst, *Romantische Harmonik und ihre Krise in Wagners "Tristan,"* 3d edn., Berlin, 1923.
 Influential study in music history and theory, including some discussion of Debussy.
Laloy, Louis, *Claude Debussy*, Paris, 1909; 2d edn., 1944.
 Laloy's generalizations, pp. 83 and 91, serve to help organize the present book as well as to introduce it.
—— *La Musique retrouvée, 1902–1927*, Paris, 1928.
 Memoirs.
Lenormand, René, *Étude sur l'harmonie moderne*, Paris, 1913; English transl. by H. Antcliffe, as *A Study of Modern Harmony*, Boston, 1915.
Lesure, François, *Debussy e Strawinski*, in *Musica d'oggi*, II (1959), 242.
—— *Bibliographie debussyste*, in *Revue de musicologie*, XLVIII (1962), 129.
—— *Debussy et le XVIe siècle*, in W. Brennecke and H. Haase, eds., *Hans Albrecht in Memoriam*, Kassel, 1962, p. 242.
—— *L'Affaire Debussy-Ravel*, in A. A. Abert and W. Pfannkuch, eds., *Festschrift Friedrich Blume zum 70. Geburtstag*, Kassel, 1963, p. 231.
—— *Claude Debussy after his Centenary*, in MQ, XLIX (1963), 277.
 Survey of recent discoveries and re-evaluations.
—— *Debussy et Edgard Varèse*, in E. Weber, ed., *Debussy et l'évolution*, Paris, 1965, p. 333.
——, ed., *Claude Debussy: textes et documents inédites* (special issue of *Revue de musicologie*, XLVIII), Paris, 1962.
Liebich, Louisa Shirley, *An Englishwoman's Memories of Debussy*, in MT, LIX (1918), 250.
 Mrs. Liebich tells of the origins of her book *Claude A. Debussy*, London, 1908, 1925 (not seen by the present author), and then of her hours with Debussy and Laloy. "Especially *Danseuses* and *Des Pas sur la neige* should only be played '*entre quat'z yeux*.'"
Liess, Andreas, *Die Stimme des Orients*, in *Musica*, XIV (1960), 769.
—— *Claude Debussy, der wegweisender Klassiker der modernen Musik*, in *Universitas*, XVII (1962), 1209.
—— *Die okzidentale Gegenwartsmusik und der Einbruch der antiabendländischen Welt: ein Entwurf*, in NZfM, CXXIII (1962), 315.
 These recent articles sum up and revise the conclusions of Liess's earlier books on Debussy and related topics. Beginning with his diss. (Vienna 1928), Liess was a pioneer in attributing central importance to Debussy.
Lockspeiser, Edward, *Debussy*, London, 1936; 3d edn., 1951; 4th edn., 1963.
 The best general book on Debussy in English in its time.
—— *Debussy: his Life and Mind*, 2 vols., London, 1962–65.
 The most thorough biography in any language, with up-to-date documentation.
—— *Debussy et Edgar Poe*, Monaco, 1961.
 Includes sketches of *Usher*.
Long, Marguerite, *Au piano avec Claude Debussy*, Paris, 1960.
Mallarmé, Stéphane, *La Musique et les lettres*, Paris, 1895; English transl. by Bradford Cook in Mallarmé, *Selected Prose Poems, Essays, and Letters*, Baltimore, 1956, p. 43.
Mellers, Wilfrid H., *The Final Works of Claude Debussy, or, Pierrot fâché avec la lune*, in ML, XX (1939), 168; rev. version in Mellers, *Studies in Contemporary Music*, London, 1948, p. 43.
Munro, Thomas, *"The Afternoon of a Faun" and the Interrelation of the Arts*, in *Journal of Aesthetics and Art Criticism*, X (1951), 95; also in Munro, *Toward Science in Aesthetics*, New York, 1956, p. 342.
 A discussion that does equal justice to Mallarmé, Debussy, Monet, and Nijinsky.
Northrup, F. S. C., *The Meeting of East and West: an Inquiry Concerning World Understanding*, New York, 1953.
Palache, John G., *Debussy as Critic*, in MQ, X (1924), 361.

Based mainly on *M. Croche*, but partly also on other materials not available in English.

Perrachio, Luigi, *L'Opera pianistica di Claudio Debussy*, Milan, 1924.

Peter, René, *Claude Debussy*, enl. edn., Paris, 1944.
Includes previously unpublished letters of Debussy.

Pougin, Arthur, *Le Théâtre à l'exposition universelle de 1889: notes et descriptions, histoire et souvenirs*, Paris, 1890.
Detailed account of what Debussy saw and heard, from Annam, Java, Tunis, Algeria.

Raad, Virginia, *Claude Debussy, Anglophile*, in *Musical Courier*, 163 (Mar. 1961), 8.

Reinhard, Kurt, *Exotismen in der abendländischen Gegenwartsmusik*, in *Melos*, XVIII (1951), 129.
Considers Debussy, Messiaen, and, most notably, Hindemith.

Ronga, Luigi, *The Meeting of Poetry and Music*, New York, 1956.
Eloquent praise of *Pelléas*.

Rosen, Charles, *Where Ravel Ends and Debussy Begins*, in *High Fidelity*, IX/5 (May 1959), 42.
A fine pianist's perceptions of similarities and differences.

Rudhyar, Dane [pseud. for Daniel Chennevière], *Claude Debussy et son œuvre*, Paris, 1913.

Samazeuilh, Gustave, *Musiciens de mon temps: chroniques et souvenirs*, Paris, 1947.

Sapp, Allen W., [review of recording of *Pelléas*], in MQ, XXXIX (1953), 310.

Schaeffner, André, *Halifax RG 587*, in *Contrepoints*, V (Dec. 1946), 45.
A long letter to the editor, on Debussy, Ravel and Leibowitz.

—— *Variations Schoenberg*, in *Contrepoints*, VII (1950), 110.
On Debussy's knowledge of Schoenberg and related topics.

—— *Debussy et ses rapports avec la musique russe*, in P. Souvtchinsky, *Un Siècle de la musique russe*, Paris, 1953, I, 95.
Important study presenting fresh information.

—— *Claude Debussy*, in Roland-Manuel, ed., *Histoire de la musique Pléiade*, Paris, 1963, II, 909.
Magisterial summary.

—— *Le Timbre*, in E. Weber, ed., *La Résonance dans les échelles*, Paris, 1963, p. 214.
Fresh perspective on Debussy's exoticism, merely an incidental point in this concise, wise, suggestive essay.

—— *Claude Debussy et ses projets shakespeariens*, in *Revue d'histoire du théâtre*, XVI (1964), 446.

—— *Debussy et ses rapports avec la peinture*, in E. Weber, ed., *Debussy et l'évolution*, Paris, 1965, p. 151.

Schallenberg, E. W., *Cl. Debussys titel musicien français*, in *Mens en melodie*, XX (1965), 108.
"Not only . . . an amalgam of old and new elements . . . but even more of French and foreign."

Schmidt-Garre, Helmut, *Rimbaud—Mallarmé—Debussy: Parallelen zwischen Dichtung und Musik*, in NZfM, CXXV (1964), 290.
Neat compilation of materials.

Schmitz, Elie Robert, *The Piano Works of Claude Debussy*, New York, 1950.

Seraphin, Hellmut, *Debussys Kammermusikwerke der mittleren Schaffenszeit: analytische und historische Untersuchungen im Rahmen des Gesamtschaffens*, Munch, 1962.
Includes, pp. 81–98, valuable fresh study of *Syrinx*. Corrects Vallas's hasty placing of the music in relation to the play; corrects Fleury's alleged changes of Debussy's notation; infers dubious chordal and tonal background.

Seroff, Victor I., *Debussy: Musician of France*, New York, 1956.
Colorful biography.

Souris, André, *Debussy et la nouvelle conception du timbre*, in *Cahiers musicaux*, I/6 (Mar. 1956), 23.

Stanley, May, *Debussy the Man as Maggie Teyte Knew Him*, in *Musical America*, Apr. 13, 1918, p. 5.

Stein, Gertrude, *Paris France*, New York, 1940.
Trenchant comparison of Satie and Debussy, pp. 59–60: "Satie had an extraordinary endowment but he could not work. He [Debussy], being a peasant, believed in work."

Strobel, Heinrich, *Claude Debussy*, Zürich, 1940; 5th edn., 1961.
>   Sound biography, plus one chapter on the music, preferable to many longer discussions.
Teyte, Maggie, *Star on the Door*, London, 1958.
>   Memoirs, valuable for references to Fauré, Ravel, Debussy, and Schoenberg's *Pierrot*.
Tiersot, Julien, *Musiques pittoresques: promenades musicales à l'Exposition de 1889*, Paris, 1889.
>   Scholarly reflections on what Debussy heard, from Java, etc.
Valéry, Paul, et al., *Le Tombeau de Pierre Louÿs*, Paris, 1925.
>   Pp. 26, 94 and elsewhere in this booklet are valuable remarks on Debussy.
Vallas, Léon, *Les idées de Claude Debussy*, Paris, 1927; English transl. by Maire O'Brien, as
>   *The Theories of Claude Debussy*, Oxford, 1929.
>   Superfluous to students in a large French library, this book will long be handy for
>   others, giving access to many ephemeral writings that Debussy left out of *M. Croche*.
>   Vallas's exaggerated patriotism is easily discounted.
—— *Claude Debussy et son temps*, Paris, 1932; new edn., Paris, 1958; English transl. of
>   1932 edn. by Maire and Grace O'Brien, as *Claude Debussy, His Life and Works*, London,
>   1933.
>   The standard biography before completion of Lockspeiser. Cites newspaper reviews
>   of music.
Vincent, John, *The Diatonic Modes in Modern Music*, Berkeley, 1951.
>   "Modern" here means "since about 1600," when the "church modes" were set aside
>   for many purposes, replaced by major and minor. Vincent traces through the 19th
>   century an undercurrent that became important in the 20th. Fresh, scholarly work,
>   if one-sided.
Weber, Edith, ed., *Debussy et l'évolution de la musique au XXᵉ siècle*, Paris, 1965.
>   Papers of the centennial colloquium, 1962, including one by the present author on
>   Schoenberg and Webern.
Wellesz, Egon, *Die letzten Werke Debussys*, in *Melos*, I (1920), 166.
>   Wellesz learned to know Debussy better than his teacher Schoenberg did, and called
>   him "creator of a new classicism."
—— *Der Stil der letzten Werke Debussys*, in *Anbruch*, III (1921), 50.
Wollstein, R. H., *You Know Mr. Dreiser*, in *Musical America*, Feb. 25, 1929, p. 36.
>   Theodore Dreiser testifies that *Pelléas* was "the only operatic performance that com-
>   pletely satisfied me. . . . I remember distinctly that the first time I read Dostoievsky
>   I had the sensation of being carried far ahead of my day. I got the same feeling from
>   Freud. But I haven't gotten it from any composer since Debussy."
Wood, Henry J., *My Life of Music*, London, 1938.
>   Among many detailed memories, those on p. 297 of Debussy (1908, 1909) and
>   p. 335 of Schoenberg (1912) are outstanding.
Woollen, Russell, *Episodic Compositional Techniques in Late Debussy*, in JAMS, XI (1958), 79.

DECAUX

Brelet, Gisèle, *Un "Schoenberg français": Abel Decaux*, in SMz, CI (1961), 33.

DELANNOY

Boll, André, *Marcel Delannoy*, Paris, 1957.

DELIUS

Beecham, Thomas, *Frederick Delius*, London, 1959.
>   First work with access to archival materials, but based rather on Beecham's experience,
>   personal and practical.
Cooke, Deryck, *The Delius Centenary: a Summing-Up*, in *Musical Opinion*, LXXXV (1962),
>   527, 589, 653.
—— *Delius the Unknown*, in PRMA, 89 (1962–63), 17.
Fenby, Eric, *Delius as I Knew Him*, London, 1937.
>   Extraordinary, beautiful book. Fenby served as amanuensis for Delius through his
>   last years. A firm Christian, Fenby was not swayed by Delius's personal beliefs and
>   tastes, but judged him with charity.
Heseltine, Philip, *Frederick Delius*, London, 1923; new edn. with additions, annotations, and
>   comments by Hubert Foss, New York, 1952.

Heseltine thought Delius a Messiah. He changed his mind after this book, and began to compose, as Peter Warlock. Foss's edn. doubles the value of the book.

Hutchings, Arthur, *Delius*, London, 1948.
> The most ample discussion of Delius's music, with interesting critiques and apologies.

Klein, John W., *Delius as a Musical Dramatist*, in MR, XXII (1961), 294.

—— *The Loveliest of Operas*, in MT, CIII (1962), 227.
> Strong arguments for *A Village Romeo*.

Pirie, Peter J., *Epitaph on a Centenary (Fr. Delius, 1862–1962)*, in MR, XXIII (1962), 221.
> Criticizing much of Delius's work and also the famous performances by Beecham, Pirie goes on to praise *Sea Drift, High Hills*, and some other pieces.

Simon, Heinrich, *Frederick Delius*, in Anbruch, V (1923), 1.

Stefan, Paul, *Ein Wort für Delius*, in Anbruch, XIV (1932), 48.
> Stefan emphasizes Delius's debts to "American landscape" and "German schooling," and insists that "he never became French."

DELLO JOIO

Downes, Edward, *The Music of Norman Dello Joio*, in MQ, XLVIII (1962), 149.

DELVINCOURT

Landowski, W.–L., *L'Œuvre de Claude Delvincourt*, Paris, 1948.

DENIJN

Goguet, Jacqueline, *Le Carillon des origines à nos jours*, Paris, 1958.

—— *Le Carillon*, in Roland-Manuel, ed., *Histoire de la musique Pléiade*, Paris, 1963, p. 1471.

Ritchie, Alick P. F., [Sketch of Jef Denijn], in *The Dominant*, II/3 (1929), 27.

DESSAU

Dessau, Paul, *Aus einer autobiographischen Skizze*, in MuG, XIV (1964), 706.
> Written for a program booklet, Berlin, 1953. Republished, with other brief writings by Dessau, list of works, and articles by H. Spieler et al., to celebrate his 60th birthday.

Hennenberg, Fritz, *Dessau—Brecht, musikalische Arbeiten*, Berlin, 1963.
> Ponderous discussion of Dessau's settings of Brecht's words, Brecht's ideas, and later Party interpretations. Perhaps Hennenberg says more about Dessau's music in his shorter volume, *Paul Dessau*, Leipzig, 1964.

Spieler, Heinrich, *Tradition und zeitgenössisches Denken: Paul Dessaus Bach-Variationen*, in MuG, XIV (1964), 714.
> Admiring description, with many examples, of Dessau's most recent orchestral work, which includes a tribute to Schoenberg.

DIEPENBROCK

Diepenbrock, Alphons, *Verzamelde Geschriften*, ed. by E. Reeser with Thea Diepenbrock, Utrecht, 1950.

—— *Brieven en Documenten*, The Hague, 1962.

DIEREN

ApIvor, Denis, *Bernard van Dieren (1887–1936)*, in *Music Survey*, III (1951), 270.

Davenport, John, *Bernard van Dieren*, in MT, XCVI (1955), 188.
> An unusually intimate yet critical picture of this controversial and influential composer and critic.

DISTLER

Bornefeld, Helmut, *Hugo Distler*, in *Musica*, I (1947), 142.
> An introduction for churchmen.

—— *Hugo Distler und sein Werk*, in MuK, XXXIII (1963), 145.
> A valuable supplement.

Distler, Hugo, *Vom Geiste der neuen evangelischen Kirchenmusik*, in NZfM, CII (1935), 1325.

—— *Gedanken zum Problem der Registrierung alter, spez. Bachischer Orgelmusik*, in MuK, XX (1937), 101.

—— *Die Orgel unserer Zeit*, in *Musica*, I (1947), 147.
> A beautiful article, written in 1933.

Grunsnick, Bruno, *Hugo Distler und Hermann Grabner,* in *Musica,* XVIII (1964), 55.
> Describes the Distler-Archiv at Lübeck, and cites correspondence.

Palmer, Larry Garland, *Hugo Distler and his Church Music,* Eastman School of Music diss., 1963.
> Biography based on documents and oral testimony of Distler's widow, friends, pupils, colleagues. Description of the music, programs, photographs.

Rauchhaupt, Ursula von, *Die vokale Kirchenmusik Hugo Distlers,* Gütersloh, 1963.
> Based on a diss. (Hamburg, 1960). Disappointing to the present author, as also to B. Billeter, in SMz, CIV (1964), 130, but welcome nonetheless as the first book on Distler.

Schmolzi, Herbert, *Das Wort-Ton-Verhältnis in Distlers Choralpassion,* in *Musica,* VII (1953), 556.
> Good observations.

Schwinger, Wolfram, *Früh vollendet: Hugo Distler,* in *Fonoforum,* VIII (1963), 50.
> Well-written introduction for non-specialists.

Söhngen, Oskar, *Am Grabe Hugo Distlers,* in *Musica,* III (1949), 81.
> Moving eulogy.

—— *Die Wiedergeburt der Kirchenmusik,* Kassel, 1953.
> Collected essays, 1932–52.

DOHNÁNYI

Dohnányi, Ernst von, *Message to Posterity,* transl. by Ilona von Dohnányi, ed. by Mary F. Parmenter, Jacksonville, Fla., 1960.
> A brief testament, together with list of works.

Podhradszky, I., *The Works of Ernő Dohnányi: a Catalogue,* in *Studia musicologica,* VI (1964), 357.

DOLMETSCH

Donington, Robert, *The Work and Ideas of Arnold Dolmetsch,* Haslemere, 1932.

DORET

Doret, Gustave, *Musique et musiciens,* Lausanne, 1915.

—— *Temps et contretemps,* Fribourg, 1942.
> Memoirs of the Swiss composer and conductor, including fresh comments on Debussy.

Dupérier, Jean, *Gustave Doret,* Lausanne, 1932.

DUKAS

Dukas, Paul, *Écrits sur la musique,* Paris, 1948.

Favre, Georges, *Paul Dukas,* Paris, 1948.
> Together with a special number of RM, XVII (May–June 1936), this book is the chief source of information.

Marcel, Gabriel, *Dukas et le transhumain,* in RM, XVII (1936), 410.

Valéry, Paul, *Paul Dukas,* in RM, XVII (1936), 323.

DUKE

Duke, Vernon, *Passport to Paris,* Boston, 1955.

—— *Listen Here: a Critical Essay on Music Depreciation,* New York, 1963.
> Includes *The Deification of Stravinsky,* also printed in *Listen,* May–June 1964, p. 1.

DUNAEVSKY

Bialik, M., *Dunaevsky segodnia,* in SM, XXIX/9 (Sep. 1965), 34.
> On Dunaevsky's continuing importance today.

Person, D., *Pis'ma I. O. Dunaevskogo,* in *Muzykal'naia Zhizn',* 14 (July 1965), 17.
> Letters of Dunaevsky.

DUNCAN

Dumesnil, Maurice, *Amazing Journey: Isadora Duncan in South America,* New York, 1932.
> Dumesnil was musical director and quasi-manager for the tour, which he describes at length from his diaries. A source neglected by Duncan's chief biographer, Terry, and especially important for its musical point of view.

Duncan, Isadora, *The Art of the Dance*, New York, 1928.
—— *My Life*, New York, 1928.
Terry, Walter, *Isadora Duncan: her Life, her Art, her Legacy*, New York, 1963.
> Good, discriminating account, based on study of documents and on conversations with many people who saw Duncan dance.

DUPRÉ

Delestre, R., *L'Œuvre de Marcel Dupré*, Paris, 1952.
Gehring, Philip Klepfer, *Improvisation in Contemporary Organ Playing*, Syracuse Univ. diss., 1963.
> Chapter IV discusses examples transcribed from recordings by nine organists, including Dupré, Langlais, and Heiller.

DUTILLEUX

Cadieu, Martine, *Duo avec Henri Dutilleux*, in *Nouvelles littéraires*, Mar. 30, 1961, p. 9.
> Unique source for personal comments by Dutilleux.
Dutilleux, Henri, *Diversities in Contemporary French Music*, in J. Beckwith and U. Kasemets, eds., *The Modern Composer and His World*, Toronto, 1961, p. 77.
> This survey, brief but not hasty, has helped confirm the present author's judgments on many topics.
Wayenberg, Daniël, *De Componist Henri Dutilleux*, in *Mens en Melodie*, XX (1965), 77.

DYSON

Dyson, George, *The Texture of Modern Music*, in ML, IV (1923), 107, 203, 293.
—— *The New Music*, London, 1924.
> Thoroughly reasonable conservative view of the main stylistic innovations from Debussy to Hindemith.
—— *Fiddling While Rome Burns: a Musician's Apology*, London, 1954.
Whittall, Arnold, *Dyson the Contemporary*, in ML, XLVI (1965), 35.
> Praises the clarity and contemporary relevance of Dyson's book, *The New Music*, though Whittall hopes that Dyson's cautious attitude is not prerequisite to his kind of clarity.

EGK

Egk, Werner, *Musik, Wort, Bild. Texte und Anmerkungen; Betrachtungen und Gedanken*, Munich, 1960.

EIMERT

Eimert, Herbert, *Atonale Musiklehre*, Leipzig, 1924.
—— *Zum Kapitel: "Atonale Musik,"* in *Die Musik*, XIV (1924), 899.
> First report of Jef Golyscheff's Quartet of 1914, said to be a 12-tone composition.
—— *Kleiner Zwölftonkurs für Anfänger*, in *Das Musikleben*, II (1949), 102.
> Uses a series to make a melody in waltz time, with an octave leap and other features to sweeten the pill. Perhaps helpful to some students in overcoming a prejudice.
—— *Lehrbuch der Zwölftontechnik*, Wiesbaden, 1950; 4th edn., 1958.
> Eimert's technique is not Schoenberg's.

EINEM

Einem, Gottfried von, *Ein Komponist im Turm*, in *Melos*, XXXI (1964), 113.
> Anecdotal memoirs.

EISLER

Brockhaus, Heinz Alfred, *Hanns Eisler*, Leipzig, 1961.
> A useful first book, with no claim to completeness.
Eisler, Hanns, *Composing for the Films*, New York, 1947; in German as *Komposition für den Film*, Berlin, 1949.
—— *Bertolt Brecht und die Musik*, in *Sinn und Form*, IX (1957), 439.
—— *Kurze Selbstbiographie*, in MuG, VIII (1958), 355.
—— *Über die Dummheit in der Musik*, in *Sinn und Form*, X (1958), 442.

Eisler distinguishes between the "stupid" school-music movement and the "bad" (not stupid) popular music.

—— *Eine Auswahl von Reden und Aufsätzen,* Leipzig, 1961.
Includes (p. 112) essay on Schoenberg.

Elsner, Jürgen, *Der Einfluss der Arbeitermusikbewegung auf die Kampfmusik Hanns Eislers,* in *Beiträge zur Musikwissenschaft,* VI (1964), 301.
Detailed study of a narrow range of Eisler's work, with background in the work of predecessors—influence not exaggerated.

Fejes, György, *Hanns Eisler zenéje. Dalai és kantátái tükrében* in *Magyar Zene,* IV (1963), 281.

Kleinig, Karl, *Analysen zu Hanns Eislers Liedern und Chören aus "Die Mutter" von Brecht: ein Beitrag zur Frage des sozialistischen Realismus in der Musik,* in *Wissenschaftliche Zeitschrift der Martin Luther-Univ. Halle-Wittenberg,* VIII (1958), 219.

Klemm, Eberhardt, *Bemerkungen zur Zwölftontechnik bei Eisler und Schönberg,* in *Sinn und Form,* XVI (1964), 771.

Lowenfels, Walter, *Eisler on Schoenberg,* in *Saturday Review,* Aug. 31, 1963, p. 33.
Only part of Eisler's essay, but a fair starting-point for readers ignorant of German.

Nestyev, Izrael V., *Gans Eisler, i ego pesennoe tvorchestvo,* Moscow, 1962.
His songs.

Notowicz, Nathan, *Zum Verzeichnis der Werke Hanns Eislers,* in MuG, VIII (1958), 368.
A list not duplicated elsewhere, including items available through the Internationale Musikleihbibliothek.

—— *Eisler und Schönberg,* in *Deutsches Jahrbuch der Musikwissenschaft,* VIII (1963), 7.
Notowicz sees Eisler's loyal admiration of his teacher only in the light of Communist dogma, but he contributes useful quotations from interviews.

Planchon, Roger, *Hanns Eisler in Lyon,* in *Sinn und Form,* XV (1963), 149.
Planchon reports Brecht's preference for Eisler over Weill.

Webern, Anton, *Brief an Hanns Eisler, 19. iv. 1929,* in MuG, VIII (1958), 339.
Facsimile, with other materials on Eisler.

ELGAR

Chambers, H. A., ed., *Edward Elgar: Centenary Sketches,* London, 1957.
Comments by conductors and others.

Elgar, Edward, *Letters and Other Writings,* ed. by P. M. Young, London, 1956.

Garvie, Peter, *Falstaff and the King: Reflections on Elgar,* in CMJ, II/1 (1957), 26.

Keller, Hans, *Elgar the Progressive,* in MR, XVIII (1957), 294.

Moore, Jerrold N., *Elgar as a University Professor,* in MT, CI (1960), 630, 690.

—— *An Elgar Discography,* in *Recorded Sound,* II/9 (Jan. 1963), 7.
Complete details on all recordings made by Elgar, and a survey of recordings of his music performed by others.

Shaw, George Bernard, *Sir Edward Elgar,* in ML, I (1920), 7.

Tovey, Donald Francis, *Essays in Musical Analysis,* 6 vols., London, 1935–39, II, 114; III, 152, 200; IV, 3, 149; VI, 83.

Whittall, Arnold, *Elgar's Last Judgment,* in MR, XXVI (1965), 23.
Falstaff's banishment by the king is interpreted as a key to Elgar's whole career.

Young, Percy M., *Elgar, O. M., a Study of a Musician,* London, 1955.
The first biography based on documents. Chief basis for the present author's information.

ELLINGTON

Boyer, Richard O., *The Hot Bach,* in *The New Yorker,* June 24, 1944, p. 30; July 1, p. 26; July 8, p. 26; also in P. Gammond, ed., *Duke Ellington,* London, 1958, p. 22 (with "some references brought up to date").

Clar, Mimi, *The Style of Duke Ellington,* in *Jazz Review,* II/3 (Apr. 1959), 6.
Includes musical examples.

Ellington, Mercer, [Studies of his father's music], in *Metronome,* 67 (Aug. 1951), 13.
Duke Ellington sent his son to the Schillinger books. At N.Y. University, he found his own way to grasp more of the music.

Gammond, Peter, ed., *Duke Ellington: his Life and Music,* London, 1958.

Kane, Henry, *How to Write a Song,* New York, 1962.
> Well-organized and well-written series of interviews, beginning with Duke Ellington, whose combination of sound advice, evasion, and candid recounting of his experience has rarely been caught on paper.

Schuller, Gunther, *Early Duke,* in *Jazz Review,* II/11 (Dec. 1959), 6; III/1 (Jan. 1960), 18; III/2 (Feb.), 18; also as *The Ellington Style, its Origins and Early Development,* in N. Hentoff, ed., *Jazz,* New York, 1959, p. 233.

Ulanov, Barry, *Duke Ellington,* New York, 1946.

EMMANUEL

Emmanuel, Maurice, *La Polymodie,* in RM, IX/3 (Jan. 1928), 197.
> Exposition of Emmanuel's chief idea, which was to be further developed by his pupil Messiaen.

Maurice Emmanuel, special issue of RM, 206 (1947).

Stevenson, Ronald, *Maurice Emmanuel: a Belated Apologia,* in ML, XL (1959), 154.

ENESCU

Brailoiu, Constantin, *Enescu,* in MGG, III (1954), 1343.
> Unsurpassed survey (the present author has not seen the thick volume edited by M. Voicana, Bucharest, 1964).

Gavoty, Bernard, *Les Souvenirs de Georges Enesco,* Paris, 1955.

Menuhin, Yehudi, *Georges Enesco,* in *The Score,* 13 (1955), 39.
> Beautiful tribute by Enescu's most famous pupil.

Pincherle, Marc, *The World of the Virtuoso,* transl. by L. H. Brockway, New York, 1963.

Tudor, Andrei, *George Enescu: sein Leben in Bildern,* Bucharest, 1961.

Vancea, Zeno, and Andrei Tudor, *George Enescu,* Vienna, 1957.

ESPLÁ

Iglesias, Antonio, *Oscar Esplá (su obra para piano),* Madrid, 1962.

EUROPE

Europe, James Reese, *A Negro Explains Jazz,* in *Literary Digest,* Apr. 26, 1919, p. 28.
> Important source of information, though fragmentary. Includes discussion of mutes and fluttertongue techniques.

McLaughlin, Irene Castle, *Jim Europe—a Reminiscence,* in *Opportunity, Journal of Negro Life,* VIII (Mar. 1930), 90.

EVETT

Evett, Robert, *Progress in Music,* in R. Richman, ed., *The Arts at Midcentury,* New York, 1954, p. 59.

FALL

Zimmerli, Walther, *Leo Fall, Meister der Wiener Operette,* Zürich, 1957.

FALLA

Arizaga, Rodolfo, *Manuel de Falla,* Buenos Aires, 1961.

Campodonico, Luis, *Falla,* French transl. by Fr. Avila, Paris, 1959.
> Campodonico reports that all previous writing on Falla in Spanish is "mediocre." His brief survey includes a critical discography.

Cœuroy, André, *Dictionnaire critique de la musique ancienne et moderne,* Paris, 1956.
> Latest of many useful books by a leading critic.

Jaenisch, Julio, *Manuel de Falla und die spanische Musik,* Zürich, 1952.
> Chief source of information for the present author.

Mila, Massimo, ed., *Manuel de Falla,* Milan, 1962.
> A "symposium" of articles, all written separately and all sympathetic.

—— *Valori dell' "Atlántida,"* in *Musica d'oggi,* V (1962), 171.
> Outstanding piece in a special issue devoted to Falla, with fine pictures. Here Mila commits himself to more criticism than in the "symposium."

Molina Fajardo, Eduardo, *Manuel de Falla y el "cante jondo,"* Granada, 1962.
> Includes essays on *cante jondo* by Falla and Lorca, pictures, programs, and other fresh information.

Pahissa, Jaime, *Vida y obra de Manuel de Falla,* Buenos Aires, 1947; English transl. by J. Wagstaff, as *Manuel de Falla: his Life and Works,* London, 1954.
>   First-hand account of Falla's last years, and a conventional treatment of the music.
Sopeña, Federico, *Atlántida: introducción a Manuel de Falla,* Madrid, 1962.
>   Includes letters from Falla to A. Barrios and John Trend.
Starkie, Walter, *Don Gypsy: Adventures with a Fiddle in Southern Spain and Barbary,* New York, 1937.
>   One of many delightful books by this English scholar. Includes a good profile of Falla (pp. 343–49). See also Starkie's article on Turina in *Grove*[5], VII, 605, and his booklet on Spanish songs for a recorded concert by Nan Merriman (Angel 35208, 1955).
Viu, Vincente Salas, *The Mystery of Manuel de Falla's "La Atlántida,"* in *Inter-American Music Bulletin,* 33 (Jan. 1963), 1.

FARWELL

Farwell, Arthur, *The Debussy of "St. Sebastian,"* in *Musical America,* Feb. 24, 1912, p. 21.
—— *Pioneering for American Music,* in MM, XII (1935), 116.
>   Memoir of the first decade of the century, by a leading pioneer.

FAURÉ

Carter, Elliott, *Gabriel Fauré,* in *Listen,* VI/1 (May 1945), 8.
Copland, Aaron, *Gabriel Fauré, a Neglected Master,* in MQ, X (1924), 573.
Fauré, Gabriel, *Camille Saint-Saëns,* in RM, III/4 (Feb. 1922), 97.
—— *Souvenirs [de l'école Niedermeyer],* in RM, III/11 (Oct. 1922), 3.
—— *Lettres à une fiancée, août-septembre 1877,* in *Revue des deux mondes,* XCVIII (1928), 911.
>   A rare glimpse of Fauré at this date.
—— *Opinions musicales,* Paris, 1930.
>   Articles for *Le Figaro,* 1903–21.
—— *Lettres intimes,* ed. by Philippe Fauré-Fremiet, Paris, 1951.
>   Mostly to his wife, these letters reveal Fauré's personality and some new facts about his music.
Fauré-Fremiet, Philippe, *Gabriel Fauré,* rev. edn., Paris, 1957.
>   Much expanded from the original of 1929, this is a chief source of information.
Favre, Max, *Gabriel Faurés Kammermusik,* Zürich, 1948.
>   Based on a diss. (Bern), this is a detailed study with emphasis on harmony.
Gervais, Françoise, *Étude parallèle des langages harmoniques de Fauré et de Debussy,* Paris Conservatory diss., 1951.
>   This careful study is summarized by F. Raugel, in *Revue de musicologie,* XXXIV (1952), 61.
Inghelbrecht, Désiré Émile, *Le Chef d'orchestre parle au public,* Paris, 1957.
Koechlin, Charles, *Fauré,* Paris, 1927; English transl. by L. Orrey, London, 1945.
Lockspeiser, Edward, ed., *The Literary Clef: an Anthology of Letters and Writings by French Composers,* London, 1958.
>   Includes important letters of Fauré not otherwise accessible in English.
Long, Marguerite, *Au piano avec Gabriel Fauré,* Paris, 1963.
>   A more interesting story than the volume on Debussy by Mme. Long, but less useful to pianists.
Niedermeyer, Louis Alfred, and J. d'Ortigue, *Traité théorique et pratique d l'accompagnement du plain-chant,* new edn., Paris, 1878.
Noske, Frits, *La Mélodie française de Berlioz à Duparc: essai de critique historique,* Paris, 1954.
>   Accurate and subtle observations of Fauré, especially pp. 231–37.
Servières, Georges, *Gabriel Fauré: étude critique,* Paris, 1930.
>   Valuable dry qualifications to the praises of Koechlin et al.
Vuillermoz, Émile, *Gabriel Fauré,* Paris, 1960.
>   A pretty book; no documentation.

FERROUD

Rostand, Claude, *L'Œuvre de Pierre-Octave Ferroud,* Paris, 1958.

FINZI

Ferguson, Howard, *Gerald Finzi (1901–1956)*, in ML, XXXVIII (1957), 129.

FLANAGAN

Albee, Edward, and Ned Rorem, *William Flanagan and his Music*, in ACA, IX/4 (1961), 12.

FORTNER

Fortner, Wolfgang, *Geistliche Musik heute. Vortrag beim X. Schütz-Fest, Düsseldorf 1956*, in H. Lindlar, *Die Stimme der Komponisten*, Rodenkirchen, 1958, p. 98.
—— *Subtilste Verständigung*, in *Akzente*, IV (1957), 121.
    On his opera, *Blood Wedding*.
—— *Komposition als Unterricht*, in AfMw, XVI (1959), 100.
—— *Die Weltsprache der neuen Musik*, in J. Müller-Marein and H. Reinhardt, eds., *Das musikalische Selbstportrait*, Hamburg, 1963, p. 386.
Wolfgang Fortner: eine Monographie: Werkanalysen, Aufsätze, Reden, Rodenkirchen, 1960.

FOSS

Foss, Lukas, *A Beginning*, in *Juilliard Review*, V/2 (1958), 12.
    On ensemble improvisation.
—— *The Changing Composer-Performer Relationship: a Monologue and a Dialogue*, in PNM, I/2 (1963), 45.

FRANÇAIX

Lanjean, Marc, *Jean Françaix: musicien français*, Paris, 1961.

FRAZZI

Dallapiccola, Luigi, *Vito Frazzi*, in *La Rassegna musicale*, X (1938), 220.
Frazzi, Vito, *Scale alternate*, Florence, 1930.
    Theoretical and historical notes on the two types of 8-note scales alternating whole steps and half steps.

FUMET

Fumet, Stanislas, *La Poésie à travers les arts*, Paris, 1954.
    Includes (pp. 133–41) a memoir on D.-V. Fumet, amplifying the son's article in MGG, IV, 1142.

FURTWÄNGLER

Furtwängler, Wilhelm, *Der Musiker und sein Publikum*, Zürich, 1955.
—— *Briefe*, ed. by Frank Thiess, Wiesbaden, 1964.
Melichar, Alois, *Wilhelm Furtwängler—Sinfoniker in dieser Zeit*, in MuG, XV (1965), 8.
Riess, Curt, *Wilhelm Furtwängler, a Biography*, London, 1955.

GÁL

Waldstein, Wilhelm, *Hans Gál*, Vienna, 1964.

GERHARD

Mason, Colin, *Roberto Gerhard*, in *Music in Britain*, 68 (1965), 10.

GERMAN

Scott, William Herbert, *Edward German: an Intimate Biography*, London, 1932.

GERSHWIN

Bernstein, Leonard, *A Nice Gershwin Tune*, in *The Atlantic Monthly*, CVC/4 (Apr. 1955), 39; also in Bernstein, *The Joy of Music*, New York, 1959, p. 52.
    Ostensibly a flippant dialogue, this essay goes deeper into Gershwin's music than any other study known to the present writer.
Chase, Gilbert, *America's Music*, New York, 1955.
Ewen, David, *A Journey to Greatness: the Life and Music of George Gershwin*, New York, 1956.
    The most ample account, still weak in discussing the music. Most other books on Gershwin, in all languages, depend largely on Ewen.
Keller, Hans, *Gershwin's Genius*, in MT, CIII (1962), 763.
    Acute observations, as usual for Keller, unusual in talk about Gershwin.

GHEDINI

Weissmann, John S., *La Musica di Ghedini e il suo significato europeo*, in *Musica d'oggi*, IV (1961), 201.
　　Recommends as most characteristic the concertos.

GIANNINI

Parris, Robert, *Vittorio Giannini and the Romantic Tradition*, in *Juilliard Review*, IV/2 (1957), 32.

GILBERT

Carter, Elliott, *American Figure with Landscape*, in MM, XX (1943), 219.

GILLESPIE

Boyer, Richard O., *Bop*, in *The New Yorker*, July 3, 1948, p. 28.
　　"Profile" of Dizzy Gillespie.
Gillespie, Dizzy, and Ralph Ginzburg, *Jazz Is Too Good for Americans*, in *Esquire*, XLVII (June 1947), 55.
　　The hostility of the title leads to the conclusion, p. 143, "What I ask is that jazz be taught to school children at all levels of their education."

GINASTERA

Chase, Gilbert, *Alberto Ginastera*, in *Tempo*, 44 (1957), 11.
—— *Alberto Ginastera, Argentine Composer*, in MQ, XLIII (1957), 439.

GLAZUNOV

Glazunov, Alexander Konstantinovich, *Pisma, statti, vospominania: izbrannoe*, Moscow, 1958.
　　Letters, essays, and memoirs, collected and ed. by M. A. Ganina.
Golubovsky, I. V., ed., *Muzykal'noe nasledie Glazunov*, 2 vols., Leningrad, 1959–60.
　　The musical heritage of Glazunov: a collection of scholarly essays.
Yasser, Joseph, *Glazunov's "Heterodox" Compositions*, in MQ, XXVIII (1942), 309.

GLIÈRE

Belza, Igor, *R. M. Glier*, Moscow, 1955; 20th edn., Moscow, 1962.
　　Brief but authoritative study of Glière.
Iagolim, B., *R. M. Glier: notograficheskii spravochnik*, Moscow, 1964.
　　Concise documented catalogue.

GNESIN

Gnesin, Mikhail Fabianovich, *Sbornik statei, vospominanii, materialov*, Moscow, 1961.
　　Collection of essays, memoirs, and documents concerning a leading teacher at Moscow, chief member of the Jewish nationalist group to remain in the USSR.

GODOWSKY

Saxe, Leonard S., *The Published Music of Leopold Godowsky*, in NotesMLA, XIV (1957), 165.

GOEHR

Goehr, Alexander, *Is There Only One Way?*, in *The Score*, 26 (1960), 63.
　　No, despite Eimert. Goehr's teacher Boulez "counters . . . the 'only way.' "

GOODMAN

Connor, Donald Russell, *BG—Off the Record: a Bio-Discography of Benny Goodman*, Fairless Hills, Pa., 1958.

GOOSSENS

Goossens, Eugene, *Overture and Beginners: a Musical Autobiography*, London, 1951.

GRAINGER

Goldman, Richard Franko, *Percy Grainger's "Free Music,"* in *Juilliard Review*, II/3 (1955), 37.

GRANADOS

Fernandez-Cid, Antonio, *Granados*, Madrid, 1956.
　　Chief source of information, with impressive discography. For a perspective view, H. Wirth's article in MGG, V (1956), 677, is useful.

GRIFFES

Maisel, Edward M., *Charles T. Griffes: the Life of an American Composer*, New York, 1943.
Chief source of information, needing no revision despite the bitter critique of Carl
Engel, in MQ, XXIX (1943), 405.

Upton, William Treat, *The Songs of Charles T. Griffes*, in MQ, IX (1923), 314.
With many examples.

HAAS

Haas, Joseph, *Reden und Aufsätze*, Mainz, 1964.

Laux, Karl, *Joseph Haas*, Berlin, 1954.
Shorter versions were published in Mainz, 1931; Hamburg, 1940; and Leipzig, 1958.

HÁBA

Evans, Edwin, *Hába*, in *Cobbett*, I, 502.
Most extensive discussion in English.

Hába, Alois, *Die harmonische Grundlage des Vierteltonsystems*, in *Melos*, III (1922), 201.

—— *Neue Harmonielehre des diatonischen, chromatischen, Viertel-, Drittel-, Sechstel-, und
Zwölftel-Tonsystems*, Leipzig, 1927.

HAHN

Hahn, Reynaldo, *Notes: journal d'un musicien*, Paris, 1933.

—— *Thèmes variés*, Paris, 1946.

—— *Du chant*, Paris, 1957.

Proust, Marcel, *Lettres à Reynaldo Hahn*, Paris, 1956.

HANDY

Handy, William C., *Blues, an Anthology*, New York, 1926.

—— and Abbe Niles, *A Treasury of the Blues*, 2d edn., New York, 1949.

HANSON

Hanson, Howard, *Harmonic Materials of Modern Music: Resources of the Tempered Scale*,
New York, 1960.
A logical survey of "materials," limited by neglect of the music of late Stravinsky,
Schoenberg, and Webern, though not of the 12-tone technique. Hanson's taste links
Bartók with Sibelius and Vaughan Williams.

Tuthill, Burnet C., *Howard Hanson*, in MQ, XXII (1936), 140.

HARRIS

Evett, Robert, *The Harmonic Idiom of Roy Harris*, in MM, XXIII/2 (1946), 103.

Harris, Roy, *The Composer Speaks*, in D. Ewen, ed., *The New Book of Modern Composers*,
New York, 1961, p. 204.

Slonimsky, Nicolas, *Roy Harris*, in MQ, XXXIII (1947), 17.

HARRISON

Yates, Peter, *Lou Harrison*, in ACA, IX/2 (1960), 2.

HAUER

Eschmann, Karl, *Changing Forms in Modern Music*, Boston, 1945.
Among many useful contributions, this book includes the best summary in English
of the ideas of Hauer.

Hauer, Josef Matthias, *Melos und Rhythmus*, in *Melos*, III (1922), 186.

—— *Sphärenmusik*, in *Melos*, III (1922), 132.
Schoenberg left ms. comments on these essays, according to J. Rufer, *Das Werk
Arnold Schönbergs*, Kassel, 1959, p. 172.

—— *Atonale Musik*, in *Die Musik*, XVI (1923), 103.

—— *Zwölftontechnik: die Lehre von den Tropen*, Vienna, 1926.
Hauer's fourth book, emphasizing his new 12-tone notation.

Lichtenfeld, Monika, *Untersuchungen zur Theorie der Zwölftontechnik bei Josef Matthias
Hauer*, Regensburg, 1964.

Diss. (Cologne, 1964), emphasizing Hauer's anticipations of some ideas of Stockhausen.

—— *Schönberg und Hauer,* in *Melos,* XXXII (1965), 118.

Pöstinger, Oswald, *Das Josef-Matthias-Hauer-Studio: eine Pflegestätte echter Geistigkeit,* in *Musik-Erziehung,* XVIII (1965), 168.

Stephan, Rudolph, *Über Josef Matthias Hauer,* in AfMw, XVIII (1961), 265.
Scholarly survey of Hauer's life and works, including catalog of mss.

Szmolyan, Walter, *Josef Matthias Hauer, eine Studie,* Vienna, 1965.
Judicious, sympathetic account of Hauer's life and work.

HAWKINS

McCarthy, Albert J., *Coleman Hawkins,* London, 1963.

HENZE

Cadieu, Martine, *Hans Werner Henze,* in *Nouvelles littéraires,* Oct. 11, 1962, p. 9.

Henze, Hans Werner, *Das neue "Marienleben,"* in *Melos,* XVI (1949), 75.

—— *Gefahren in der neuen Musik,* in H. Lindlar, ed., *Die Stimme der Komponisten,* Rodenkirchen, 1958, p. 51.

—— *Kompositionsunterricht heute,* in ÖMz, XVIII (1963), 366.

—— *Essays,* Mainz, 1964.

—— *In einem einzigen Satz,* in *Melos,* XXXII (1965), 74.
Along with articles by various authors about Henze, this contribution brings up to date his elusive evolution.

Kay, Norman, *Henze, Present-Day Romantic,* in *Music & Musicians,* XIII/5 (Jan. 1965), 201.

La Motte, Diether de, *Hans Werner Henze: Der Prinz von Homburg: ein Versuch über die Komposition und den Komponisten,* Mainz, 1960.

Pauli, Hansjörg, *Hans Werner Henze,* in *Musica,* XIII (1959), 761.

—— *Hans Werner Henze's Italian Music,* in *The Score,* 25 (1959), 26.

HERRMANN

Fett, Armin, ed., *Hugo Herrmann, Leben und Werk; Festschrift zum 60. Geburtstag,* Trossingen, 1956.
Summarized in MGG, VI (1957), 274.

HESELTINE

Cockshott, Gerald, *A Note on Warlock's "Capriol Suite,"* in MMR, LXX (1940), 203.

—— *E. J. Moeran's Recollections of Peter Warlock,* in MT, XCVI (1955), 128.

Copley, Ian A., *Peter Warlock's Vocal Chamber Music,* in ML, XLIV (1963), 358.

—— *Warlock's Cod-Pieces,* in MT, CIV (1963), 410.

—— *Peter Warlock's Choral Music,* in ML, XLV (1964), 318.

—— *The Published Instrumental Music of Peter Warlock,* in MR, XXV (1964), 209.

—— *Warlock in Novels,* in MT, CV (1964), 739.
Promising by-products of a forthcoming book.

Gray, Cecil, *Peter Warlock: a Memoir of Philip Heseltine,* London, 1934.
The most ample source of information until Ian Copley's book appears. Corrected in some details by Kenneth Avery, in ML, XXIX (1948), 398.

Parrott, Ian, *Warlock in Wales,* in MT, CV (1964), 740.
Cites Heseltine's acquaintance with Bartók, and the influence of Bartók's music on *The Curlew.*

HILL

Hill, Edward Burlingame, *Modern French Music,* New York, 1924.

HINDEMITH

Amar, Licco, *Freundschaft mit Paul Hindemith,* in *Melos,* XXII (1955), 314.

Austin, William W., *Hindemith's "Frau Musica": the Versions of 1928 and 1945 compared,* in *Essays on Music in Honor of Archibald Thompson Davison,* Cambridge, Mass., 1957, p. 265.

Bell, M., *Hindemith's "Mathis der Maler,"* in MMR, LXIX (1939), 77.

Boatwright, Howard, *Paul Hindemith as a Teacher*, in MQ, L (1964), 279.
       Excellent survey of Hindemith's career and influence, by one of his best pupils at Yale.

Borris, Siegfried, *Paul Hindemith*, in *Stilporträts der neuen Musik*, Berlin, 1961, p. 65.

Briner, Andreas, *Eine Bekenntnisoper Paul Hindemiths*, in SMz, XCIX (1959), 1, 50.
       On *Die Harmonie der Welt*.

Dallapiccola, Luigi, *Ricordi di Paul Hindemith*, in *Musica d'oggi*, VII (1964), 10.
       Dallapiccola witnessed Hindemith conducting Webern and Bruckner at Florence, 1962.

Gerstenberg, Walter, *Paul Hindemith*, in *Universitas*, XIX (1964), 1243.
       Quotes a letter of 1954 from Hindemith [to Gerstenberg?] on composing vs. concertizing. Surveys the career, and ends with praise for the "subtle, economical music" of the "visionary play, *The Long Christmas Dinner.*"

Henze, Hans Werner, *Das neue "Marienleben,"* in *Melos*, XVI (1949), 75.

Hindemith, Paul, *Mechanische Musik*, in *Musikantengilde*, V (1927), 155.

—— *Unterweisung im Tonsatz*, 2 vols., Mainz, 1937–39; English transl. by Arthur Mendel and Otto Ortmann, as *The Craft of Musical Composition*, New York, 1941–42.
       A landmark in the history of music theory.

—— *Elementary Training for Musicians*, New York, 1946.
       With many later editions, this compact book is perhaps Hindemith's most useful work in theory, though it claims neither originality nor depth.

—— *Über die musikalische Inspiration*, in *Neue Zürcher Zeitung*, Nov. 28, 1951.
       Inaugural lecture at the University of Zürich, cited by W. Reich in *Universitas*, XIX (1964), 137.

—— *A Composer's World: Horizons and Limitations*, Cambridge, Mass., 1952.

Holzmann, Klaus, *Arnold Mendelssohn als Lehrer Paul Hindemiths*, in *Musik im Unterricht*, XLIII (1952), 112.

Jakobik, Albert, *Zur Einheit der neuen Musik*, Würzburg, 1957.
       Despite the unacceptable generalizations of this book, it is valuable for specifying some similarities between Debussy and Hindemith that almost no one else has noticed.

Landau, Victor, *Paul Hindemith, a Case Study in Theory and Practice*, in MR, XXI (1960), 38.

—— *Hindemith the System Builder: a Critique*, in MR, XXII (1961), 136.
       Based on a diss. (N. Y. Univ., 1958), these articles show some surprising facts, sensibly handled.

Lion, Ferdinand, *Cardillac I und II*, in *Akzente*, IV (1957), 126.
       Hindemith's original librettist comments on the composer's revision, with acute criticism.

Louis, Rudolf, *Die deutsche Musik der Gegenwart*, Munich, 1909.

Mason, Colin, *Hindemiths Kammermusik*, in *Melos*, XXIV (1957), 171, 255; English version in *Cobbett*, III, 13.

Mersmann, Hans, *Paul Hindemiths Oper: Cardillac. Uraufführung*, in *Melos*, V (1925), 383.
       See also Mersmann's surveys.

—— *Paul Hindemith*, in *International Music Educator*, 9 (Apr. 1964), 293.
       Text in German, French, and English of a superb summary tribute.

Pannain, Guido, *"Die Harmonie der Welt" e l'ultimo Hindemith*, in *La Rassegna musicale*, XXVII (1957), 193.
       Sympathetic but adverse criticism.

Paul Hindemith: Catalogue of Published Works and Recordings (compiled by Kurt Stone), New York, 1954.

Paul Hindemith: Zeugnis in Bildern, Mainz, 1955; 2d enl. edn., in German and English, 1961.
       Best available introduction to Hindemith.

Redlich, Hans Ferdinand, *Paul Hindemith: a Reassessment*, in MR, XXV (1964), 241.
       Unusually explicit statement of some harsh judgments widely current when Hindemith died, offered with no new evidence. Hindemith's pupil Franz Reizenstein, in *Composer*, 15 (Apr. 1965), 7, brought testimony to vindicate Hindemith against Redlich's worst aspersions.

Reich, Willi, and K. H. Ruppel, *Paul Hindemith und sein Werk für die moderne Musik*, in *Universitas*, XIX (1964), 137.

Reinhard, Kurt, *Exotismen in der abendländischen Gegenwartsmusik*, in *Melos*, XVIII (1951), 129.
> Reinhard suggests that Hindemith often sounds like certain Japanese music.

Rieple, Max, *Musik in Donaueschingen*, Konstanz, 1959.
> Collection of documents, programs, and pictures, with index.

Sauguer, Louis, *"Ludus tonalis" de Paul Hindemith*, in *Contrepoints*, IV (1946), 20.

Schilling, Hans Ludwig, *Paul Hindemiths "Cardillac." Beiträge zu einem Vergleich der beiden Opernfassungen*, Würzburg, 1962.
> A diss., and the best of Schilling's many studies of Hindemith. Not, however, convincing to David Drew, in ML, XLIV (1963), 288.

Schrade, Leo, *Hindemith in der neuen Welt*, in *Melos*, XXII (1955), 315.
> Hindemith's musicological colleague at Yale offers a unique report.

Schröter, Heinz, *Paul Hindemiths Besuch in Frankfurt, und ein Interview*, in *Melos*, XIV (1946), 254.

Seefried, Irmgard, *Meine Wege zu Hindemith und Bartók*, in ÖMz, IX (1954), 113.
> A fine singer's memoir of performances and rehearsals.

Staeps, Hans Ulrich, *Das "Engelkonzert" jenseits der Formenlehre*, in ÖMz, II (1947), 253.
> Searching study of Hindemith's symbolism, independent of his theory.

Stephan, Rudolph, *Hindemith's "Marienleben" (1922–1948): an Assessment of its Two Versions*, in MR, XV (1954), 275.

Strobel, Heinrich, *"Neue Sachlichkeit" in der Musik*, in *Anbruch*, VIII (1926), 254.
> An early application of the literary slogan "new objectivity" to music, especially that of Hindemith, seen as superseding the "expressionism" of Schoenberg.

—— *Paul Hindemith*, Mainz, 1928; 3d edn., 1948.
> Chief source of information in one place, but needing another revision.

—— *Meister seiner Epoche*, in *Melos*, XXXI (1964), 1.
> Here Strobel emphasizes the stylistic unity of Hindemith's whole work.

Thomson, William, *Hindemith's Contribution to Music Theory*, in JMT, IX (1965), 52.
> Positive contribution: the principle that interval precedes triad. Negative: "his proof to us of the ultimate power of rhythm as a determinant of tonal coherence. It is in the failure of his theory that we find this proof."

Westphal, Elisabeth, *Paul Hindemith: eine Bibliographie des In- und Auslandes seit 1922 über ihn und sein Werk*, Cologne, 1957.

HINES

Balliett, Whitney, *Rhythm in my Mind: Earl Hines*, in *The New Yorker*, Jan. 2, 1965, p. 39.

HÖLLER

Wirth, Helmut, *Karl Höller*, in MGG, VI (1957), 516.
> Almost the only source of information (and a good one) on this interesting composer.

HOLBROOKE

Lowe, George, *Josef Holbrooke and his Work*, London, 1920.

Thompson, Kenneth L., *Holbrooke: Some Catalogue Data*, in ML, XLVI (1965), 297.
> Corrections to Lowe, and to *Grove*[5].

HOLST

Dieren, Bernard van, and Richard Cappell, *Stereoscopic View: Gustav Holst*, in *The Dominant*, I/12 (Dec. 1928), 13.

Evans, Edwin, *Holst*, in *The Dominant*, I/6 (Apr. 1928), 24.

Holst, Imogen, *The Music of Gustav Holst*, London, 1951.
> The author's severe judgment of her father's work is a tribute to both of them.

—— *Holst and Stravinsky, a Note*, in *Tempo*, 61–62 (1962), 5.

Rubbra, Edmund, *Gustav Holst*, Paris, 1948.

Vaughan Williams, Ralph, and Gustav Holst, *Heirs and Rebels: Letters Written to Each Other and Occasional Writings on Music*, London, 1959.

HONEGGER

Honegger, Arthur, *Incantation aux fossiles,* Lausanne, 1948.
     Miscellaneous essays.
—— *Je suis compositeur,* Paris, 1951; German transl. as *Ich bin Komponist,* Zürich, 1952.
     Memoirs and mature reflections.
Tappolet, Willy, *Arthur Honegger,* Boudry-Neuchâtel, 1957.
     Last of several works on Honegger by Tappolet, and best by anyone. Large
     bibliography.

HUBER

Oesch, Hans, *Klaus Huber,* in SMz, CI (1961), 12.
Pauli, Hansjörg, *Klaus Huber,* in *Musica,* XVII (1963), 10.

IBERT

Feschotte, Jacques, *Jacques Ibert,* Paris, 1958.
IMBRIE

Boykan, Martin, *Andrew Imbrie: Third Quartet,* in PNM, III/1 (1964), 139.
     Excellent discussion, ending with a contrast between Imbrie and his teacher Sessions,
     which throws a helpful light on both. Compare Imbrie on Sessions, in PNM, I/1
     (1962), 117.

IRELAND

Townshend, Nigel, *The Achievement of John Ireland,* in ML, XXIV (1943), 65.
IVES

Carter, Elliott, *Charles Ives: His Vision and Challenge,* in MM, XXI (1944), 199.
—— *An American Destiny,* in *Listen,* VII (Nov. 1946), 4.
Cohn, Arthur, *Ives,* in *The American Record Guide,* XXX (1964), 761.
     Extended comparative study of five recordings.
Copland, Aaron, *One Hundred and Fourteen Songs,* in MM, XI (1934), 59.
     Review of Ives's volume of songs, beautifully balancing sympathy and criticism. Now
     less valuable as introduction to the subject than as evidence of Copland's finesse and
     range of thought.
Cowell, Henry, and Sidney Cowell, *Charles Ives and his Music,* New York, 1955.
Helms, Hans G., *Der Komponist Charles Ives: Leben, Werk, und Einfluss auf die heutige
Generation,* in NZfM, CXXV (1964), 425.
     Points with appropriate caution to analogies between some procedures of Ives and
     some ideas of Cage, Boulez, Brant, Earle Brown, et al.
Ives, Charles Edward, *Some Quarter-Tone Impressions,* in *Franco-American Music Society
Bulletin,* Mar. 1925, p. 24; also in Ives, *Essays . . . and Other Writings,* ed. by H. Boat-
wright, New York, 1961.
—— *Essays before a Sonata, and Other Writings,* ed. by Howard Boatwright, New York,
1961; *Essays* (unedited) also in *Three Classics in the Aesthetic of Music,* New York, 1962.
Kirkpatrick, John, *A Temporary Mimeographed Catalogue of the Music Mss. and Related
Materials of Charles Edward Ives,* New Haven, 1960.
     Meticulous and monumental study.
—— *What Music Meant to Charles Ives,* in *Cornell University Music Review,* VI (1963), 13.
     Beautiful collage of otherwise unpublished statements by Ives.
Layton, Bentley, *An Introduction to the 114 Songs of Charles Ives,* Harvard Univ. A.B.
thesis, 1963.
     This essay forecasts important new criticism of Ives.
Seeger, Charles, *Charles Ives and Carl Ruggles,* in *Magazine of Art,* XXXII (1939), 396, 435.

JANÁČEK

Brod, Max, *Leoš Janáček: Leben und Werk,* rev. edn., Vienna, 1956.
     Only slightly expanded from the booklet of 1924, a pioneer study by the eminent
     critic and friend of Kafka; still a useful introduction.

Hollander, Hans, *Leoš Janáček: his Life and Work,* transl. by Paul Hamburger, London, 1963.
Best survey in English.

Janáček, Leoš, *O lidové písne a lidové hudbě: dokumenty a studie,* Prague, 1955.

—— *Fejetony z Lidových novin,* ed. by J. Racek, Brno, 1958; German transl. as *Feuilletons aus den "Lidové noviny,"* Leipzig, 1959.
These volumes supplement the 9-volume edition of Janáček's correspondence, edited by A. Rekorys, J. Racek, et al., Prague, 1934–53.

Jiránek, Jaroslav, and Bohumil Karásek, eds., *Leoš Janáček a soudobá hudba: mezinárodní hudebně vědecký kongres, Brno 1958,* Prague, 1963.
60 papers on Janáček and contemporary music, for an international congress. Summaries in Russian and German.

Racek, Jan, *Leoš Janáčeks und Béla Bartóks Bedeutung in der Weltmusik,* in *Studia musicologica,* V (1963), 501.
A summary and a rare perspective view by the foremost specialist in Janáček. This and his article in MGG, VI (1957), 1683, arouse a wish for more to be translated from the Czech.

Shawe-Taylor, Desmond, *The Operas of Leoš Janáček,* in PRMA, 85 (1959), 49.

Štědroň, Bohumír, *Leoš Janáček: Letters and Reminiscences,* transl. by G. Thomsen, Prague, 1955.

—— *The Work of Leoš Janáček,* Prague, 1959.
Best catalogue in English.

—— *Verzeichnis der musikalischen Werke Janáčeks,* in *Beiträge zur Musikwissenschaft,* II (1960), 129; III (1961), 34.

Vogel, Jaroslav, *Leoš Janáček: Leben und Werk,* Prague, 1958; English transl. as *Leoš Janáček: his Life and Works,* London, 1963.
The most ample treatment of Janáček available in English. Some shortcomings are noted by J. Clapham, in MR, XXVI (1965), 70.

JAQUES-DALCROZE

Brunet-Lecomte, Hélène Emma, *Jaques-Dalcroze: sa vie, son œuvre,* Geneva, 1950.
Memoir by the composer's sister.

Jaques-Dalcroze, Émile, *Le Rythme, la musique et l'éducation,* Lausanne, 1920; English transl. by H. F. Rubinstein, New York, 1921.

—— *Souvenirs, notes et critiques,* Geneva, 1942.

—— *Réflexions sur la musique et les musiciens,* in SMz, LXXXV (1945), 311.

Martin, Frank, *Pour les 80 ans de Jaques-Dalcroze,* in SMz, LXXXV (1945), 309.

—— *Eurythmics: the Jaques-Dalcroze Method,* in *Music in Education, Conference . . . Brussels, 29 June to 9 July 1953,* Paris, 1955, p. 225.

JÁRDÁNYI

Járdányi, Pál, *Music and Modern Society,* in *New Hungarian Quarterly,* V/13 (1964), 162.
No nonsense. Calls for the protection of silence, and the educational use of mass media.

JELINEK

Jelinek, Hanns, *Anleitung zur Zwölftonkomposition,* 2 vols., Vienna, 1952.

—— *Die krebsgleichen Allintervallreihen,* in AfMw, XVIII (1961), 115.

Redlich, Hans Ferdinand, *Hanns Jelinek,* in MR, XXI (1960), 66.

JÖDE

Stapelberg, Reinhold, ed., *Fritz Jöde, Leben und Werk; eine Freundesgabe zum 70. Geburtstag,* Trossingen, 1957.

JOHNSON

Bloch, Joseph, *Some American Piano Sonatas,* in *Juilliard Review,* III/3 (1956), 9.

Monaco, Richard, *The Music of Hunter Johnson,* Cornell Univ. diss., 1960.

JOLIVET

Demarquez, Suzanne, *André Jolivet,* Paris, 1958.

Jolivet, André, *Musique et exotisme*, in R. Bezombes, ed., *L'Exotisme dans l'art et la pensée*, Paris, 1953, p. 159.
—— *Paradoxes de la création musicale*, in *L'Age nouveau*, 92 (May 1955), 89.
    Representative samples of many interesting writings by this composer.

KABALEVSKY

Abramovsky, Georgii Konstantinovich, *Cherty stilia D. Kabalevskogo*, in M. S. Druskin, ed., *Voprosy sovremennoi muzyki*, Leningrad, 1963, p. 84.
    Outlines of Kabalevsky's style.
Danilevich, Lev Vasilievich, *Tvorchestvo D. B. Kabalevskogo*, Moscow, 1963.
    Survey of Kabalevsky's works.
Kabalevsky, Dmitri Borisovich, *Izbrannye stati o muzyke*, Moscow, 1963.
    Collection of essays.

KADOSA

Bónis, Ferenc, *Pál Kadosa: Portrait of a Composer*, in *New Hungarian Quarterly*, V/15 (1964), 214.

KAHN

Kahn, Frida, *Generation in Turmoil*, Great Neck, N.Y., 1960.
    Personal memoir by Erich Itor Kahn's wife.
Leibowitz, René, and Konrad Wolff, *Erich Itor Kahn, un grand représentant de la musique contemporaine*, Buchet/Chastel, 1958.
Smith, Russell, *Erich Itor Kahn*, in ACA, IX/2 (1960), 8.

KÁLMÁN

Oesterreicher, Rudolf, *Emmerich Kálmán*, Zürich, 1954.

KAMINSKI

Kaminski, Heinrich, *Einiges über Instrumentation*, in *Melos*, I (1920), 483.
—— *Von der Form in der Musik*, in *Melos*, II (1921), 214.
    Essays indicating Kaminski's concerns at the time Orff was his pupil.
——.*Zu meinem Concerto Grosso*, in *Anbruch*, V (1923), 151.
—— *Über polyphone Musik*, in *Musica*, I (1947), 82.
    Characteristic essay, followed by reminiscences of E. Doflein and a sketch by K. Schleifer.
Samson, Ingrid, *Grundlinien einer Kaminski-Biographie*, in *Musica*, XII (1958), 727.
    Based on Samson's diss. (Frankfurt, 1956), this article supersedes earlier accounts.
Söhngen, Oskar, *Heinrich Kaminski: Gedenkwort bei einer Feier*, in MuK, XVII (1947), 8.
Truscott, Harold, *A Note on Heinrich Kaminski*, in *The Chesterian*, 32 (1958), 75.

KAMINSKY

Kaminsky, Max, with V. E. Hughes, *My Life in Jazz*, New York, 1963.
    Good memoir of the Chicago group.

KARAIEV

Karagicheva, Liudmila Vladimirovna, *Kara Karaiev*, Moscow, 1960.
    Summarized by the authoress in MGG, VII (1958), 678.

KARG-ELERT

Sceats, Godfrey, *The Organ Works of Karg-Elert: a Guide to the Organ and Harmonium Works*, 2d rev. edn., London, 1950.
    Includes selected letters from Karg-Elert to Sceats, and other interesting material.
Schenk, Paul, *Sigrid Karg-Elert: eine monographische Skizze mit vollständigem Werkverzeichnis*, Leipzig, 1925.
    "Complete list" is understated, for Karg-Elert gave Schenk titles of works that were only projected. Despite this and other unsatisfactory features, the book is still needed. Reinhold Sietz, in MGG, VII (1958), 682, after independent study, offers no conclusions.

KAY

Slonimsky, Nicolas, *Ulysses Kay*, in ACA, VII/1 (1957), 3.

KELTERBORN

Kelterborn, Rudolf, *Stilistische Mannigfaltigkeit in der zeitgenössischen Musik*, Amriswil, 1958.
—— *Zum kompositorischen Individualität*— . . . *Selbstporträt*, in SMz, CI (1961), 20.
Mohr, Ernst, *Zur Kompositionstechnik Rudolf Kelterborns*, in Musica, XIV (1960), 278.

KERN

Ewen, David, *The World of Jerome Kern*, New York, 1957.

KERR

Ringer, Alexander L., *Harrison Kerr, Composer and Educator*, in ACA, VIII/2 (1959), 10.

KHACHATURIAN

Khubov, Georgii Nikitich, *A. Khachaturian*, Moscow, 1960.
Shneierson, Grigorii, *Aram Khachaturyan* [in English], Moscow, 1959.

KHRENNIKOV

Kukharsky, Vasilii Fedosievich, *Tikhon Khrennikov: kritiko-biograficheskii ocherk*, Moscow, 1957.
    "Critical-biographical outline" means here a selective favorable treatment.

KILPINEN

Pulkkinen, Maire, *Yrjö Kilpinen*, Helsinki, 1960.
    Booklet in German, including list of works.

KIRCHNER

Ringer, Alexander L., *Leon Kirchner*, in MQ, XLIII (1957), 1.

KLEBE

McCredie, Andrew D., *Giselher Klebe*, in MR, XXVI (1965), 220.

KNAB

Knab, Armin, *Denken und Tun: gesammelte Aufsätze über Musik*, Berlin, 1959.

KNORR

Bauer, Moritz, *Iwan Knorr: ein Gedenkblatt*, Frankfurt, 1916.
    Only a pamphlet but a chief source of information on Knorr, feeding curiosity for more.

KODÁLY

Eősze, László, *Kodály Zoltán élete és művészete*, Budapest, 1956; English transl. as *Zoltán Kodály, his Life and Work*, London, 1962.
    Best source of information in English, though incomplete and uncritical. J. Weissmann, in ML, XLIV (1963), 274, points out shortcomings.
Horusitzky, Zoltán, *Kodály Zoltán szimfóniája*, in Magyar Zene, III (1962), 604.
    Admiring discussion of Kodály's symphony; outstanding article in a special issue of the journal honoring Kodály's 80th birthday.
Kodály, Zoltán, *A magyar népzene*, Budapest, 1956; English transl. as *Folk Music of Hungary*, New York, 1960.
    Kodály provides a new introduction for the English edn. of his book. The first version goes back to 1937.
—— *Confession*, in New Hungarian Quarterly, III/8 (1962), 3.
    A speech from 1933, translated here with articles by colleagues in honor of Kodály's 80th birthday.
Mason, Colin, *Kodály and Chamber Music*, in Studia musicologica, III (1962), 251.
    Outstanding essay in English on Kodály's technique and style.
Richards, Mary Helen, *The Legacy from Kodály*, in Music Educators Journal, June–July 1963, p. 27.

Szabolcsi, Bence, and Dénes Bartha, eds., *Emlékkönyv Kodály Zoltán 70. Születésnapjára,* Budapest, 1953.
> Rich collection of essays about Kodály and his work.

Weissmann, John S., *Kodály's Symphony: a Morphological Study,* in *Tempo,* 60 (1962), 18.

KOECHLIN

Calvocoressi, Michel-Dmitri, *Charles Koechlin's Instrumental Works,* in ML, V (1924), 357.

Herscher-Clément, Jeanne, *L'Œuvre de Charles Koechlin,* in RM, XVII/169 (1936), 315.

Jourdan-Morhange, Hélène, *Mes amis musiciens,* Paris, 1955.
> A violinist's memoirs of Fauré, Roussel, Sauguet, et al.

Koechlin, Charles, *Le Retour à Bach,* in RM, VIII/1 (1926), 1.

—— *Musique et mathématique,* in RM, XII (1931), 424.

—— *Éclipse de la mélancolie: quelques pages sur l'art d'aujourd'hui,* in *Contrepoints,* I (1946), 8.

—— *Art, liberté, tour d'ivoire,* in *Contrepoints,* VI (1950), 104.

Myers, Rollo H., *Koechlin,* in Grove[5], IV, 805.
> Most nearly comprehensive source of information in English.

—— *Charles Koechlin—Some Recollections,* in ML, XLVI (1965), 217.

Renaudin, Pierre, *Charles Koechlin, notice bio-bibliographique,* Paris, 1952.
> A little more ample, and much more readable, than Renaudin's article in MGG, VII (1958), 1316.

KREISLER

Kreisler, Fritz, *Four Weeks in the Trenches: the War Story of a Violinist,* Boston, 1915.

Lochner, Louis P., *Fritz Kreisler,* New York, 1950.
> Unsatisfactory, but so far unsurpassed.

KRENEK

Krenek, Ernst, *Music Here and Now,* transl. by B. Fles, New York, 1939.
> For many Americans, including the present writer, Krenek's book was the first persuasive account of the history of 12-tone technique.

—— *Studies in Counterpoint Based on the Twelve-Tone Technique,* New York, 1940; German edn. as *Zwölfton-Kontrapunkt-Studien,* Mainz, 1952.
> An influential booklet, almost irrelevant to Schoenberg and Webern.

—— *Selbstdarstellung,* Zürich, 1948.

—— *The Composer Speaks,* in D. Ewen, ed., *The Book of Modern Composers,* New York, 1956, p. 354.

—— *Amerikas Einfluss auf eingewanderte Komponisten,* in *Musica,* XIII (1959), 757.
> "If the land of opportunity taught us to pay more attention to reality, it remained for the old continent of limited reality to reawaken our desire for the impossible."

—— *Gedanken unterwegs: Dokumente einer Reise,* Munich, 1959.

—— *Zur Sprache gebracht: Essays über Musik,* Munich, 1959.

—— *Serialism,* in J. Beckwith and U. Kasemets, eds., *The Modern Composer,* Toronto, 1961, p. 65.
> Any reader of *Music Here and Now* would do well to consider this as a supplement.

—— *A Composer's Influences,* in PNM, III/1 (1964), 36.
> The poet Karl Kraus was "most durable." A misreading of the scholar Kurth's "linear counterpoint," 1917, was important.

Saathen, Friedrich, *Ernst Krenek, ein Essay,* Munich, 1959.
> Admiring paraphrase of Krenek's own writings.

Zillig, Winfried, *Variationen über neue Musik,* Munich, 1959.
> Pp. 236–55 constitute one of the best essays on Krenek anywhere.

LAJTHA

Weissmann, John S., *Lajtha and his Symphonies,* in *The Listener,* LXII (1959), 114.
> Along with Weissmann's article on Lajtha in MGG, VIII (1960), 90, this essay is a good introduction.

LAMBELET

Schaefer, Myron, *George Lambelet,* in *Grove*[5], V, 29.
> Chief source of information on this Greek pioneer.

LAMBERT

Lambert, Constant, *Music Ho! A Study of Music in Decline,* New York, 1934.

LANDOWSKA

Landowska, Wanda, *On Music,* ed. and transl. by Denise Restout, assisted by R. Hawkins, New York, 1964.
> Includes a fairly detailed and very touching biographical sketch of Landowska by Mlle. Restout, her closest disciple, a list of Landowska's compositions, and a discography of her performances.

Schaeffner, André, *Wanda Landowska et le retour aux humanités de la musique,* in RM, VIII/3 (1927), 254.

LANDOWSKI

Baignères, Claude, *Marcel Landowski,* Paris, 1959.
> Slightly longer version of the article in MGG, VIII (1960), 171.

LARSSON

Wallner, Bo, Herbert Blomstedt, and Folke Landberg, *Lars-Erik Larsson och hands concertinor,* Stockholm, 1957.

LEES

Cooke, Deryck, *The Music of Benjamin Lees,* in *Tempo,* 51 (1959), 16.
—— *The Recent Music of Benjamin Lees,* in *Tempo,* 64 (1963), 11.

LEEUW

Leeuw, Ton de, *Mensen en muziek in India: Reisdagboekbladen,* in *Mens en melodie,* XVIII (1963), 213, 239.
—— *Muziek van de twintigste eeuw: een onderzoek naar haar elementen & structuur,* Utrecht, 1964.
> After a brief "panorama" of names, dates, and "isms," de Leeuw proceeds to discuss rhythm, melody, harmony, and instrumentation, each topic considered with well-chosen examples from Debussy, Schoenberg, Stravinsky, Bartók, Webern, Hindemith, Messiaen, Boulez, and a few others, neglecting the "swarm of epigones." He praises the variety and vitality of the leaders. He dismisses pessimistic thoughts as reflecting mostly the plight of followers.
—— *Music of the 20th Century,* in *Sonorum speculum,* 20 (1964), 1.
> English and German translation of the introduction to de Leeuw's book.

Paap, Wouter, *De componist Ton de Leeuw,* in *Mens en melodie,* XVIII (1963), 134.
Wouters, Jos, *Ton de Leeuw,* in *Sonorum speculum,* 19 (1964), 1.

LEHÁR

Franz Lehár, Katalog der Bühnenwerke, Vienna, 1955.
Macqueen-Pope, W., and D. L. Murray, *Fortune's Favorite: the Life and Times of Franz Lehár,* London, 1953.
Stein, Fritz, *Fünfzig Jahre die lustige Witwe: eine Studie,* Vienna, 1955.

LIATOSHINSKY

Belza, Igor, *B. M. Liatoshinsky, zasluzhenŭ diîach mistetstv URSR,* Kiev, 1947.

LOEFFLER

Engel, Carl, *Charles Martin Loeffler,* in MQ, XI (1925), 311.

LOPES GRAÇA

Lopes Graça, Fernando, *Musicália,* Salvador, Bahia, 1960.
> Essays written 1936–58.

LUTOSŁAWSKI

Brennecke, Wilfried, *Die "Trauermusik" von Witold Lutosławski,* in A. A. Abert and W. Pfannkuch, eds., *Festschrift Friedrich Blume zum 70. Geburtstag,* Kassel, 1963, p. 60.

Detailed analysis of Lutosławski's most famous piece, based on correspondence with the composer.

Jarociński, Stefan, *Witold Lutosławski,* in *Fonoforum,* VI (June 1961), 10.

LUTYENS

Henderson, Robert, *Elizabeth Lutyens,* in MT, CIV (1963), 551.

Valuable supplement to C. Mason's article in *Grove*⁵, V, 448, especially since Miss Lutyens says, "It has been only in the last ten years or so that I have acquired the technique to enable me to do the things I want to do."

MACDOWELL

Albrecht, Hans, *Impressionismus,* in MGG, VI (1957), 1046.

Brown, Rollo W., *Lonely Americans,* New York, 1929.

Pp. 89–123 on MacDowell, including discussion of his projected opera (p. 115).

Currier, T. P., *MacDowell as I Knew Him,* in MQ, I (1915), 17.

Erskine, John, *MacDowell at Columbia: Some Recollections,* in MQ, XXVIII (1942), 395.

Garland, Hamlin, *Roadside Meetings,* New York, 1930.

Gilman, Lawrence, *Edward MacDowell: a Study,* London, 1909.

The most ample treatment of MacDowell, far from complete.

Hanson, Howard, *Address at the Installation Ceremonies for Edward MacDowell at the Hall of Fame of New York University, October 25, 1964,* in *National Music Council Bulletin,* XXV/2 (1965), 21.

Huneker, James, *Unicorns,* New York, 1917.

Includes a chapter on MacDowell (p. 6).

MacDowell, Edward, *Critical and Historical Essays: Lectures Delivered at Columbia University,* ed. by W. J. Baltzell, Boston, 1912.

MacDowell, Marian, *MacDowell's "Peterboro Idea,"* in MQ, XVIII (1932), 33.

—— *Random Notes on Edward MacDowell and his Music,* Boston, 1950.

Chiefly on the best-known piano pieces.

Peyser, Herbert F., *Twenty Years After: an Estimate of the Anomaly that is MacDowell,* in *Musical America,* Feb. 25, 1929, p. 9.

Best one of four articles on MacDowell in this issue.

Sinclair, Upton, *MacDowell,* in *Century,* VII (1926), 50.

Sonneck, Oscar G. T., *Suum cuique,* New York, 1916.

Collected essays; on pp. 87–103, *MacDowell vs. MacDowell: a Study in First Editions and Revisions.*

MADETOJA

Hillila, Ruth Esther, *The Solo Songs of Toivo Kuula and Leevi Madetoja and their Place in 20th-Century Finnish Art Song,* Boston Univ. diss., 1964.

MAHLER

Adler, Guido, *Gustav Mahler,* Vienna, 1916.

Adorno, Theodor Wiesengrund, *Mahler: eine musikalische Physiognomik,* Frankfurt, 1960.

Beaufils, Marcel, *Le Lied romantique allemand,* Paris, 1956.

The final chapter offers valuable insights on Mahler, Strauss, Reger, and Schoenberg.

Cooke, Deryck, *The Adagio of Mahler's Tenth Symphony,* in MT, CVI (1965), 288.

Duse, Ugo, *Gustav Mahler: introduzione allo studio della vita e delle opere,* Padua, 1962.

—— *Origini popolari del canto mahleriano,* in *L'Approdo musicale,* 16–17 (1963), 85.

Chief fresh study in a special issue devoted to Mahler.

Grange, Henry-Louis de La, *Mahler,* in *Encyclopédie de la musique Fasquelle,* Paris, 1961, III, 132.

Announces a book in press by de la Grange on Mahler, which is likely to provide a wealth of new information and insight.

Gustav Mahler, Verzeichnis der Werke, Vienna, 1959.

Lockspeiser, Edward, *Mahler in France,* in MMR, XC (1960), 52.

Mahler knew Bruneau's *Le Rêve* from 1892, and got to know Bruneau more than any other French composer personally.

Mahler, Gustav, *Briefe, 1897–1911*, ed. by Alma Maria Mahler, Berlin, 1924; later edn. as *Erinnerungen und Briefe*, Amsterdam, 1940; English transl. by B. Creighton, as *Memories and Letters*, New York, 1946.
Mahler-Werfel, Alma, *And the Bridge is Love*, in collaboration with E. B. Ashton, New York, 1958.
> Vivid memoirs of Mahler's wife, with references to Schoenberg, Krenek, and other musicians, as well as to Kokoschka, Gropius, et al.
Mitchell, Donald, *Gustav Mahler: the Early Years*, London, 1958.
> Exceedingly detailed study.
Ratz, Erwin, *Gustav Mahler*, Berlin, 1954.
> As chief editor of an authentic publication of Mahler's works, and as heir, through Schoenberg, of Mahler's spirit, Ratz provides a splendid though provisional survey.
—— *Zum Formproblem bei Gustav Mahler: eine Analyse des I. Satzes der IX. Symphonie*, in Mf, VIII (1955), 169.
—— *Zum Formproblem bei Gustav Mahler: eine Analyse des Finales der VI. Symphonie*, in Mf, IX (1956), 156.
> Here Ratz brings to Mahler the procedures of his *Formenlehre*, elaborated in connection with Bach and Beethoven.
—— *Gustav Mahlers X. Symphonie*, in NZfM, CXXV (1964), 307.
Redlich, Hans Ferdinand, *Bruckner and Mahler*, London, 1955.
—— *Gustav Mahler's Last Symphonic Trilogy*, in W. Brennecke and H. Haase, eds., *Hans Albrecht in Memoriam*, Kassel, 1962, p. 246.
—— *Mahler's Enigmatic "Sixth,"* in W. Gerstenberg et al., eds., *Festschrift Otto Erich Deutsch zum 80. Geburtstag*, Kassel, 1963, p. 250.
Slonimsky, S. M., *"Pesn' o zemle" G. Malera i voprosy orkestrovoi polifonii*, in M. S. Druskin, ed., *Voprosy sovremennoi muzyki*, Leningrad, 1963, p. 179.
> On Mahler's *Song of the Earth.*
Tischler, Hans, *Key Symbolism vs. "Progressive Tonality,"* in *Musicology*, II (1949), 383.
—— *Mahler's "Das Lied von der Erde,"* in MR, X (1949), 111.
—— *Musical Form in Gustav Mahler's Works*, in *Musicology*, II (1949), 231.
—— *Mahler's Impact on the Crisis of Tonality*, in MR, XII (1951), 113.
Truscott, Harold, *Some Aspects of Mahler's Tonality*, in MMR, LXXXVII (1957), 203.
Walter, Bruno, *Gustav Mahler: ein Porträt*, Berlin, 1957; English transl. by Lotte Walter Lindt, as *Gustav Mahler*, New York, 1958.
Wellesz, Egon, *Reminiscences of Mahler*, in *The Score*, 28 (1961), 52.

MALEINGREAU
Borren, Charles van den, *Maleingreau*, in MGG, VIII (1960), 1543.
> A renowned scholar gives serious attention to the work of his compatriot. The only source of information known to the present writer.

MALIPIERO, G. F.
Helm, Everett, *Malipiero*, in *Musical America*, Apr. 1, 1952, p. 8; also in G. Scarpa, ed., *L'Opera di G. F. Malipiero*, Bologna, 1952, p. 167.
> A pupil of Malipiero, Helm provides one of the best introductions to his work as a whole available in any language.
Labroca, Mario, *Malipiero, musicista veneziano*, Venice, 1957.
> Includes a catalogue of works.
Malipiero, Gian Francesco, *Ricordi e pensieri*, in G. Scarpa, ed., *L'Opera di Gian Francesco Malipiero*, Bologna, 1952, p. 285.
—— *Del mio teatro musicale*, in *Musica d'oggi*, IV (1961), 2.
> With appreciative articles by 3 critics.
Santi, Piero, *Il Teatro di Gian Francesco Malipiero*, in *L'Approdo musicale*, III/9 (1960), 19.
> Chief article in a special issue on Malipiero.
Scarpa, Gino, ed., *L'Opera di Gian Francesco Malipiero*, Bologna, 1952.
> Includes a catalogue of works, annotated by the composer.

MALIPIERO, R.
Sartori, Claudio, *Riccardo Malipiero*, transl. by R. Smith Brindle, Milan, 1957.

MARKÉVITCH
Markévitch, Igor, *Point d'orgue: entretiens avec Claude Rostand,* Paris, 1959.
MARTIN
Ansermet, Ernest, *Der Weg Frank Martins,* in ÖMz, XI (1956), 172.
> From his friendship with Martin, dating from 1911, Ansermet cites evidences of the influence of Debussy and Berg. He praises Martin's careful selection and gradual absorption of these and other influences.
Klein, Rudolf, *Frank Martin: sein Leben und Werk,* Vienna, 1960.
—— *Frank Martins jüngste Werke,* in ÖMz, XX (1965), 483.
> Mostly Martin's own program notes on *M. de Pourceaugnac, The Four Elements,* and *Pilate.*
Koelliker, André, *Frank Martin,* Lausanne, 1963.
> Valuable chiefly for the bibliography of articles by and about Martin.
Martin, Frank, *À propos du langage musical contemporain,* in SMz, LXXVII (1937), 501.
> Clear statement of Martin's fundamental stylistic decision, based on a deep and independent study of Schoenberg.
—— *Le Compositeur moderne et les textes sacrés,* in SMz, LXXXVI (1946), 261.
—— *Notes biographiques,* in *Polyphonie,* 2 (1948), 81.
—— *Schoenberg et nous,* in *Polyphonie,* 4 (1949), 68.
—— *À propos de mon concerto de violon,* in RM, 212 (1952), 111.
—— *À propos du "Cornet,"* in *Alte und neue Musik,* Zürich, 1952, p. 166.
—— *"Petite symphonie concertante,"* in *Alte und neue Musik,* Zürich, 1952, p. 170.
—— *Eurythmics: the Jaques-Dalcroze Method,* in *Music in Education, Conference . . . Brussels, 29 June to 9 July 1953,* Paris, 1955, p. 225.
—— *Généralisation de la sensibilité,* in *L'Age nouveau,* 92 (May 1955), 66.
—— *Notwendigkeit einer Gegenwartskunst; Gedanken zum "Vin herbé,"* Amriswil, 1957.
> Two essays, written 1941 and 1943.
—— *Literatur und Musik,* in ÖMz, XIV (1959), 403.
—— *Moderne Musik und Publikum,* in ÖMz, XV (1960), 412.
—— *Golgotha,* in R. S. Hines, ed., *The Composer's Point of View,* Norman, Okla., 1963, p. 196.
—— *Les Sources du rythme musical,* in *Revue musicale de la Suisse Romande,* XVIII/3 (Sep. 1965), 3.
Tupper, Janet Eloise, *Stylistic Analysis of Selected Works by Frank Martin,* Indiana Univ. diss., 1964.
Vlad, Roman, *Modernità e tradizione nella musica contemporanea,* Turin, 1955.
> Essays on various topics and composers, including a good one on Martin.
MARTINO
Martino, Donald, *The Source Set and its Aggregate Functions,* in JMT, V (1961), 224.
MARTINŮ
Clapham, John, *Martinů's Instrumental Style,* in MR, XXIV (1963), 158.
Evans, Peter, *Martinů the Symphonist,* in *Tempo,* 55/56 (1960), 19.
Mihule, Jaroslav, *Symfonie Bohuslava Martinů,* Prague, 1959.
Novák, Stanislav, *O Bohuslavu Martinů,* in Z. Zouhar, ed., *Bohuslav Martinů,* Brno, 1957, p. 43.
Šafránek, Miloš, *Bohuslav Martinů: život a dílo,* Prague, 1961; English transl. by R. Finlayson-Samsourova, as *Bohuslav Martinů: his Life and Works,* London, 1962.
> Šafránek knew Martinů in exile. In 1944, he wrote the standard reference in English on Martinů's personality and style. His new book supersedes the old, with sympathetic treatment of Martinů's whole work.
Zouhar, Zdeněk, ed., *Bohuslav Martinů: sborník vzpomínek a studií,* Brno, 1957.
> Collection of memoirs and essays.
MARX
Marx, Joseph, *Betrachtungen eines romantischen Realisten: gesammelte Aufsätze,* Vienna, 1947.
—— *Weltsprache Musik: Bedeutung und Deutung tausendjähriger Tonkunst,* Vienna, 1964.
> Meandering discussion of technical and esthetic questions, reaffirming Marx's devotion to Debussy, Strauss, Reger, and Scriabin.

Werba, Erik, *Joseph Marx*, Vienna, 1964.

MASON

Mason, Daniel Gregory, *Music in my Time*, New York, 1938.
Tuthill, Burnet C., *Daniel Gregory Mason*, in MQ, XXXIV (1948), 46.

MEDTNER

Boyd, Malcolm, *The Songs of Nicolas Medtner*, in ML, XLVI (1965), 26.
Holt, Richard, ed., *Nicolas Medtner (1879–1951): a Tribute to his Art and Personality*,
    London, 1955.
        Best material in English until Alfred Swan's study is completed.

MELLERS

Henderson, Robert, *The Music of Wilfrid Mellers: Tradition and Necessity*, in MT, CIV
    (1963), 178.

MENNIN

Hendl, Walter, *The Music of Peter Mennin*, in *Juilliard Review*, I/2 (1954), 18.

MENOTTI

D'Amico, Fedele, *Menotti*, in *Encyclopédie de la musique Fasquelle*, Paris, 1961, III, 184.
        Best critique of Menotti known to the present author.
Menotti, Gian Carlo, *Notes on Opera as Basic Theater*, in *Perspectives USA*, 12 (1955), 5.
—— *I Am The Savage*, in *Opera News*, XXVIII/13 (Feb. 8, 1964), 8.
Sargeant, Winthrop, *Orlando in Mount Kisco: Gian Carlo Menotti*, in *The New Yorker*, May
    4, 1963, p. 49.
        Uncritical profile.

MESSIAEN

Bernard-Delapierre, Guy, *Le Cas Messiaen devant la pensée catholique orthodoxe*, in *Conflu-
    ences*, V (1945), 903.
—— *Messiaen*, in *Confluences*, V (1945), 551.
—— *Souvenirs sur Olivier Messiaen*, in *Formes et couleurs*, VII/3–4 (1945) [unpaged].
Boulez, Pierre, Jean Barraqué, Yvonne Loriod, Karlheinz Stockhausen, et al., *Hommage à
    Messiaen*, in *Melos*, XXV (1958), 386.
        Important brief statements about Messiaen's contributions both as composer and as
        teacher.
Drew, David, *Messiaen, a Provisional Study*, in *The Score*, 13 (1955), 59; 14 (1955), 41.
Goléa, Antoine, *Rencontres avec Olivier Messiaen*, Paris, 1961.
        Chief source of information for the present author.
Guth, Paul, *Nébuleuses spirales, stalactites et stalagmites suggèrent des rythmes à Olivier
    Messiaen*, in *Le Figaro littéraire*, Feb. 14, 1953, p. 4.
Messiaen, Olivier, *Technique de mon langage musicale*, 2 vols., Paris, 1944; English transl. as
    The Technique of My Musical Language, Paris, 1950.
—— *Credo musicale: Conférence de Bruxelles prononcée a l'Exposition Universelle de 1958*,
    Paris, 1960.
        Text in French, German, and English. Also printed in *Melos*, XXV (1958), 381,
        and in Goléa, *Rencontres avec Olivier Messiaen*, Paris, 1961.
—— *Liberté*, in ÖMz, XX (1965), 264.
Messiaen, Pierre, *Images*, Paris, 1944.
        Memoir by the composer's father, including (pp. 172 & 339) interesting notes on
        Olivier.
Rostand, Claude, *Olivier Messiaen*, Paris, 1957.
        Valuable as a skeptical counterweight to Goléa.
Tanneguy de Quénetain, *Messiaen, Poet of Nature*, in *Réalités*, 45 (Dec. 1962), 48; also in
    Music & Musicians, XI/9 (May 1963), 8.
        Best survey in English.

MIASKOVSKY

Boganova, Tatiana Vasilievna, *Printsipy polifonii v tvorchestve N. Miaskovskogo*, in S. S.

Skrebkov, ed., *Muzykal'no-teoreticheskie problemy*, Moscow, 1963, p. 88.
> Interesting study of Miaskovsky's principles of polyphony.

Ikonnikov, Alexei A., *Myaskovsky: his Life and Work*, New York, 1946.

—— *Miaskovsky i sovremennost'*, in SM, 1964/3, p. 64.
> Miaskovsky's disciple affirms his contemporary significance.

Livanova, Tamara Nikolaevna, *N. Ia. Miaskovsky: tvorcheskii put*, Moscow, 1953.
> Miaskovsky's creative path, traced by a scholar familiar with his works.

Shlifshtein, S. I., *N. Ia. Miaskovsky: notograficheskii spravochnik*, Moscow, 1962.
> Guide to the works, with details on mss., publications, and first performances. In another volume, 1960, Shlifshtein edited Miaskovsky's essays, letters, and reminiscences.

Vinogradov, Viktor Sergeivich, *Spravochnik-putevoditel' po simfoniam N. Ia. Miaskovskogo*, Moscow, 1954.
> Analytical guide to the symphonies.

MICHEELSEN

Micheelsen, Hans Friedrich, *Selbstbildnis*, in MuK, XVII (1947), 125.

MIGOT

Migot, Georges, *Matériaux et mentions: écrits sur des sujets divers*, Paris, 1932.

—— *Essais commentés*, Paris, 1937.

Pinchard, Max, *Connaissance de Georges Migot, musicien français*, Paris, 1959.

MILHAUD

Beck, Georges, *Darius Milhaud. Étude suivi du catalogue chronologique complet de son ouvrage*, Paris, 1949; *Supplément*, Paris, 1956.

Collaer, Paul, *Darius Milhaud*, Antwerp, 1947.
> A survey, in French, with many musical examples. Brought up to date in MGG, IX (1961), 298.

Drew, David, *Modern French Music*, in H. Hartog, ed., *European Music in the 20th Century*, London, 1957, p. 232.

Mason, Colin, *The Chamber Music of Milhaud*, in MQ, XLIII (1957), 326; also in *Cobbett*, III, 29.

Milhaud, Darius, *La Mélodie*, in *Melos*, III (1922), 195.
> Clear, strong statement of Milhaud's basic ideas.

—— *Polytonalité et atonalité*, in RM, IV (Feb. 1923), 29.
> Famous discussion.

—— *The Jazz Band and Negro Music*, in *Living Age*, CCCXXIII (1924), 169.
> Interesting expression of Milhaud's enthusiasm at the moment of his *Création du monde*.

—— *Notes sans musique*, Paris, 1949; English transl. by D. Evans, as *Notes without Music*, London, 1952; rev. enl. edn. in French, Paris, 1963.
> Includes autobiographical sketch.

—— *Entretiens avec Claude Rostand*, Paris, 1952.
> Chief source of information.

—— *Lettre ouverte à Luigi Dallapiccola*, in *La Rassegna musicale*, XXIII (1953), 41.
> Exposes the 12-tone series in Mozart's *Don Giovanni*, used by Milhaud in *David*.

—— and Paul Claudel, *Correspondance, 1912–1953* (=*Cahiers Paul Claudel*, III), Paris, 1962.

Sert, Misia Godebski, *A "Spectacle-Concert" in Paris*, in *The Chesterian*, 6 (1920), 165.
> Lively account of Cocteau's festive collaborations with Auric, Poulenc, Satie, and especially Milhaud—*Le Boeuf sur le toit*.

MOMPOU

Kastner, Santiago, *Federico Mompou*, Madrid, 1947.

Moreux, Serge, *Federico Mompou: ou le visiteur inattendu*, in *La Revue française*, XXV (Christmas 1950), 96.

MONTEMEZZI

Klein, John W., *Italo Montemezzi*, in MGG, IX (1961), 507.

Though Montemezzi was often called "the Italian Debussy," Klein correctly notes that "the influence of Wagner's *Tristan* was still more potent and more significant than Debussy's."

MORTON

Lomax, Alan, *Mister Jelly Roll: the Fortunes of Jelly Roll Morton, New Orleans Creole and "Inventor of Jazz,"* New York, 1950.
>Important source of facts and of a convincing original interpretation.

NABOKOV

Nabokov, Nicolas, *Old Friends and New Music*, Boston, 1951.

NEUGEBOREN

Henrik Neugeboren, dit Henri Nouveau, 1901–1959, special issue of RM, 246 (1959).

NIELSEN

Balzer, Jürgen, ed., *Carl Nielsen: Centenary Essays*, Copenhagen, 1965.
>8 scholarly studies, well presented.

Meyer, Torben, and Fr. S. Petersen, *Carl Nielsen: kunstneren og mennesket. En biografi*, 2 vols., Copenhagen, 1947–48.
>Comprehensive study.

Nielsen, Carl, *Living Music*, transl. by R. Spink, London, 1953.
>Wise reflections, valuable beyond any concern for Nielsen's own music.

—— *My Childhood*, transl. by R. Spink, London, 1953.
>Beautiful memoir of an extraordinary life.

—— *Breve*, ed. by I. E. Møller and Torben Meyer, Copenhagen, 1954.

Simpson, Robert, *Carl Nielsen, Symphonist, 1865–1931* (biographical appendix by Torben Meyer), London, 1952.

Waterhouse, John C. G., *Nielsen Reconsidered*, in MT, CVI (1965), 425, 514, 593.
>An ample and serious study, interpreting the Fourth and Fifth Symphonies as "flawed stages in a long and complex stylistic upheaval," and recommending the Clarinet Concerto as "most enduringly fascinating and convincing of all his works."

NONO

Cadieu, Martine, *Duo avec Luigi Nono*, in *Nouvelles littéraires*, Apr. 13, 1961, p. 1.

NOVÁK

Lébl, Vladimír, *Vitězslav Novák: život a dílo*, Prague, 1964.
>Thoroughly documented study of Novák's life and works.

NYSTROEM

Christensen, Peter Louis Kai, *The Orchestral Works of Gösta Nystroem: a Critical Study*, Univ. of Washington diss., 1961.
>Chief source of information, much more ample than articles in periodicals and dictionaries.

OBUKHOV

Larronde, Carlos, *Le Livre de vie de Nicolas Obouhow*, Paris, 1940.

Ludwig, Emil, *La Croix sonore*, in RM, XVI (1935), 96.
>A vivid picture of Obukhov.

Orban, Marcel, *Nicolas Obouhow*, in RM, XVI (1935), 100.
>Chief source of information.

Schloezer, Boris de, *Nicolas Oboukhoff*, in RM, III (Nov. 1921), 38.

OPIENSKI

Fornerod, Aloys, *Henryk Opienski*, Lausanne, 1942.

ORFF

Carl Orff, ein Bericht in Wort und Bild, mit Beiträgen von K. H. Ruppel, G. R. Sellner, und W. Thomas, Mainz, 1955; 2d enl. edn., 1960.
>All too brief.

Georgiades, Thrasyboulos, *Zur Antigone-Interpretation von Carl Orff*, in ÖMz, IV (1949), 191.
     A leading scholar of ancient Greek music appraises Orff's work as "an interpretation valid for our here-and-now."
Helm, Everett, *Carl Orff*, in MQ, XLI (1955), 285.
     Cautious introductory survey, unfortunately the best in English even after ten years.
Keller, Wilhelm, *Carl Orff*, in *Stilporträts der neuen Musik*, Berlin, 1961, p. 42.
     Good observations on Orff's techniques, especially in recent works.
Kiekert, Ingeborg, *Die musikalische Form in den Werken Carl Orffs*, Regensburg, 1957.
     Based on a diss. (Munich, 1956), this study presents valuable fresh insights without quite satisfying the hopes aroused by its title.
Krause, Ernst, *Trionfo Carl Orff. Zu seinem 70. Geburtstag*, in MuG, XV (1965), 470.
Liess, Andreas, *Carl Orff, Idee und Werk*, Zürich, 1955.
     Good survey, chief source of information on Orff's early works. Pending a new edn., Liess's survey should be supplemented with Laaff's article in MGG, X (1962), 199, and the special studies of Keller and Kiekert.
—— *Orff and the Theatre*, in *The London Magazine*, V/3 (June 1965), 75.
Lohmüller, Helmut, *Carl Orff über sich selbst*, in *Melos*, XXXII (1965), 194.
     Interview, chief item of a special issue in honor of Orff's 70th birthday.
Orff, Carl, *Gedanken über Musik mit Kindern und Laien*, in *Die Musik*, XXIV (1932), 668; also in H. Lindlar, ed., *Die Stimme der Komponisten*, Rodenkirchen, 1958, p. 56.
     This essay expresses Orff's fundamental beliefs, and is essential for further study.
—— *Das Schulwerk am Mozarteum*, in ÖMz, XVIII (1963), 359.
—— *The Schulwerk: its Origins and Aims*, in *Music Educators Journal*, April-May 1963, p. 69.
—— *Meine Musik zum "Sommernachtstraum,"* in ÖMz, XX (1965), 341.
Stäblein, Bruno, *Schöpferische Tonalität: zum Grossaufbau von Orffs Antigonae*, in *Musica*, VI (1952), 145.

OSTERC
Cvetko, Dragotin, *Pamatce Slavco Osterc*, Prague, 1946.
     A summary transl. and supplement in the *Encyclopédie Fasquelle*, Paris, 1961, III, 364.

OVERTON
Cohen, David, *The Music of Hall Overton*, in ACA, X/4 (Dec. 1962), 8.

PADEREWSKI
Landowska, Wanda, *Recollections of Paderewski*, in *Saturday Review*, June 30, 1951, p. 46.
Opienski, Henryk, *Paderewski*, Lausanne, 1948.
     Originally written in 1910, and revised in 1928, this is the only biography to include much comment on Paderewski's compositions.
Paderewski, Ignaz Jan, and Mary Lawton, *The Paderewski Memoirs*, New York, 1938.

PALMER
Austin, William W., *The Music of Robert Palmer*, in MQ, XLII (1956), 35.

PANUFNIK
Hall, Barrie, *Andrzej Panufnik and his "Sinfonia sacra,"* in *Tempo*, 71 (1964), 14.
Panufnik, Scarlett, *Out of the City of Fear*, London, 1956.
     Memoir by the composer's wife.

PÂQUE
Pâque, Désiré, *L'Atonalité, ou mode chromatique unique*, in RM, 107 (1930), 135.
—— *Notre esthétique*, in RM, XI (1930), 119.
—— *Classicisme*, in RM, XII (1931), 345.
Vander Linden, Albert, *M. J. L. Désiré Pâque*, in MGG, X (1962), 739.
     Unique study of Pâque's work by a scholarly compatriot.

PARKER, C.
Ellison, Ralph, *On Bird, Bird-Watching, and Jazz*, in *Saturday Review*, July 28, 1962, p. 47; also in Ellison, *Shadow and Act*, New York, 1964, p. 221.
     The best single essay on Parker.

Harrison, Max, *Charlie Parker*, London, 1960.
Mehegan, John, *The "Parker Story,"* in *Saturday Review*, Feb. 8, 1958, p. 43.
    Brief, but helpful in clarifying the relation between Parker and Gillespie.
Reisner, Robert George, *Bird: the Legend of Charlie Parker*, New York, 1962.
    Reminiscences of many colleagues. Also many photographs.

PARKER, H.

Chadwick, George Whitefield, *Horatio Parker*, New Haven, 1921.
Parker, Horatio, *Our Taste in Music*, in *The Yale Review*, VII (1918), 777.

PARTCH

Partch, Harry, *A New Instrument*, in *Musical Opinion*, LVIII (1935), 764.
    Announces the "Ptolemy," with 43 tones per octave.
—— *Genesis of a Music: Monophony*, Madison, Wis., 1949.
Yates, Peter, *Genesis*, in *High Fidelity*, XIII/7 (July 1963), 35.
    Fine introduction to the work of Partch.

PEPPING

Adrio, Adam, *Lust hab ich ghabt zur Musica. Zum 60. Geburtstag Ernst Peppings*, in *Musica*,
  XV (1961), 473.
    Along with Adrio's article on Pepping in MGG, X (1962), 1023, this is the chief
    source of information.
Dürr, Alfred, *Gedanken zum Kirchenmusikschaffen Ernst Peppings*, in MuK, XXXI (1961), 145·
    A leading Bach scholar penetrates more deeply into Pepping's techniques of harmony,
    counterpoint, and text-setting than any other student known to the present writer.
Hamm, Walter, *Studien über Ernst Peppings drei Klaviersonaten, 1937*, Würzburg, 1955.
Pepping, Ernst, *Stilwende der Musik*, Mainz, 1934.

PERLE

Perle, George, *Serial Composition and Atonality: an Introduction to the Music of Schoenberg,
  Berg, and Webern*, Berkeley, 1962.
—— *An Approach to Simultaneity in Twelve-Tone Music*, in PNM, III/1 (1964), 91.
    Perle continues to advance his independent ideas, well aware of their relations to
    those of the three masters.

PEROSI

Glinski, Matteo, *Lorenzo Perosi*, Milan, 1953.
Paglialunga, Arcangelo, *Lorenzo Perosi*, Alba, 1952.
    Presents many documents and photographs. Text summarized in MGG, X (1962),
    1076.
Torti, Giancarlo, *Lorenzo Perosi*, Milan, 1959.
    Best of many brief works that, like this one, constitute "a tribute of admiration and
    affection." Torti cites an unpublished biography by Alceo Toni which may upset
    earlier judgments.

PERSICHETTI

Evett, Robert, *The Music of Vincent Persichetti*, in *Juilliard Review*, II/2 (1955), 15.
Persichetti, Vincent, *Twentieth-Century Harmony: Creative Aspects and Practice*, New York,
  1961.
    Examples of Persichetti's eclectic practice in single phrases, with casual references
    to a wide range of music from Debussy to Gunther Schuller, with emphasis on
    Bartók, Stravinsky, Honegger, Copland.
—— *Hymns and Responses*, in R. S. Hines, ed., *The Composer's Point of View*, Norman,
  Okla., 1963, p. 41.
    Excellent article, revealing much about Persichetti's symphonic music and his back-
    ground, as well as many details about his most successful pieces.

PETERSON-BERGER

Carlberg, Bertil, *Peterson-Berger*, Stockholm, 1950.
    Brought up to date by the author's article in MGG, X (1962), 1123.

PETRASSI

Cadieu, Martine, *Duo avec Goffredo Petrassi*, in *Nouvelles littéraires*, Feb. 2, 1961, p. 9.
Weissmann, John S., *Goffredo Petrassi* (in English), Milan, 1957.
—— *Goffredo Petrassi, geb. 16.7.1904*, in *Melos*, XXXI (1964), 227.

PFITZNER

Henderson, Donald Gene, *Hans Pfitzner: the Composer and his Instrumental Works*, Univ. of Michigan diss., 1963.
    Unique discussion in English. "Confirms Pfitzner's nostalgic outlook."
Mann, Thomas, *Tischrede auf Pfitzner*, in his *Gesammelte Werke*, Frankfurt, 1960, X, 417.
—— *Aufruf zur Gründung des Hans Pfitzner-Vereines*, in his *Gesammelte Werke*, Frankfurt, 1960, XI, 744.
Pfitzner, Hans Erich, *Gesammelte Schriften*, 3 vols., Augsburg, 1926.
Rutz, Hans, *Hans Pfitzner: Musik zwischen den Zeiten*, Vienna, 1949.
    Brief study including the first complete list of works.

PIJPER

Dickinson, Peter, *The Instrumental Music of Willem Pijper (1894–1947)*, in MR, XXIV (1963), 327.
Goldbeck, Fred, *Willem Pijper (1894–1947)*, in *The Chesterian*, 22 (Sep. 1947), 35.
Kloppenburg, W. C. M., *Thematisch-bibliografische catalogus van de werken van Willem Pijper (1894–1947)*, Assen, 1960.
    Text in English as well as Dutch.
Mengelberg, Karel, *Willem Pijper*, in R. Myers, ed., *Music Today*, London, 1949, p. 36.
Pijper, Willem, *De quintencirkel: opstellen over muziek*, Amsterdam, 1929.

PINKHAM

Smith, Warren Story, *Daniel Pinkham*, in ACA, X (1961), 9.

PISTON

Austin, William W., *Piston's Fourth Symphony: an Analysis*, in MR, XVI (1955), 120.
Carter, Elliott, *Walter Piston*, in MQ, XXXII (1946), 354.
    Best available survey, despite date.
Daniel, Oliver, et al., *Walter Piston*, New York, 1964.
    70th birthday tribute, with catalogue.
Piston, Walter H., *Principles of Harmonic Analysis*, Boston, 1933.
    Piston's first book is not altogether replaced by his later ones. Its principles, and whenever possible its procedures, are followed by the present author.
—— *Harmony*, New York, 1941; 3d edn., 1962.
—— *Counterpoint*, New York, 1947.
—— *Orchestration*, New York, 1955.
    In these textbooks 20th-century practices are barely touched on, but Piston's experience controls his treatment of traditional disciplines.
—— *More Views on Serialism*, in *The Score*, 23 (1958), 46.
    Concise, cool comment on many controversial topics.
—— *Problems of Intonation in the Performance of Contemporary Music*, in D. Hughes, ed., *Instrumental Music*, Cambridge, Mass., 1959, p. 70.

PIZZETTI

Gatti, Guido Maria, *Ildebrando Pizzetti*, Turin, 1934; English transl. by David Moore, London, 1951; new Italian edn., Milan, 1955.
    The gist of this book may be found in Thompson's *International Cyclopedia*, 9th edn., New York, 1964, p. 1644.
Gavazzeni, Gianandrea, *Tre studi di Pizzetti*, Como, 1937.
—— *Altri studi pizzettiani*, Bergamo, 1956.

PORTER

Boatwright, Howard, *Quincy Porter*, in ACA, VI/3 (1957), 2.

Porter, Quincy, *Modern Harmony*, in R. Hughes, ed., *Music Lover's Encyclopedia*, New York, 1939, p. 758.
> Succinct and eminently sane.

POULENC

Bourdet, Denise, *Pris sur le vif*, Paris, 1957.
> Newspaper interviews, including a good one with Poulenc (p. 225).
Cadieu, Martine, *Duo avec Francis Poulenc*, in *Nouvelles littéraires*, May 4, 1961, p. 1.
Cambon, Elise, *Sacred Music by Francis Poulenc*, in *American Guild of Organists Quarterly*, VIII (1963), 123.
Drew, David, *The Simplicity of Poulenc*, in *The Listener*, Jan. 16, 1958, p. 137.
> Severe critique of the *Carmelites*.
Durey, Louis, *Francis Poulenc*, in *The Chesterian*, 25 (1922), 1.
> Unique early evaluation of Poulenc's music, unaffected by the advertising of Cocteau, and showing the basis for Poulenc's later development.
Hell, Henri, *Francis Poulenc, musicien français*, Paris, 1958; English transl. by E. Lockspeiser, London, 1959.
> See warning above, p. 518.
Hughes, Allen, *Poulenc*, in O. Thompson, ed., *International Cyclopedia of Music and Musicians*, 9th edn., New York, 1964, p. 1665.
> One of the few articles written especially for this edition, and one of the best sources in English on Poulenc's whole work.
Nobel, Felix de, *Herinneringen aan Francis Poulenc*, in *Mens en melodie*, XVIII (1963), 70; English transl. as *Memories of Francis Poulenc*, in *Sonorum speculum*, 15 (1963), 39.
> Outstanding among many memoirs published at Poulenc's death, this one is by a choral conductor whose performances of Poulenc were exemplary.
Poulenc, Francis, *Paris Notes*, in *Fanfare* (London), I (1921), 79, 117.
> Concise, beautiful remarks on new music by Stravinsky, Bartók, Milhaud, Roussel, et al.
—— *Mes mélodies et leurs poètes*, in *Les Annales Conferencia*, XXXVI (1947), 507.
> Important lecture.
—— *Feuilles américaines*, in *Table ronde*, XXX (1950), 66; excerpts transl. in S. Morgenstern, ed., *Composers on Music*, New York, 1956, p. 514.
—— *Entretiens avec Claude Rostand*, Paris, 1954.
—— *Emmanuel Chabrier*, Paris, 1961.
—— *À propos d'une lettre d'Arthur Honegger*, in SMz, CII (1962), 160.
—— *Moi et mes amis. Confidences recueillies par Stéphane Audel*, Paris, 1963.
> Radio interviews, 1953, 1955, 1962. Much duplication from talks with Rostand, but some new details.
—— *Mon ami Honegger*, in *Journal musical français*, Sep. 27, 1963, p. 1.
Rorem, Ned, *Poulenc—a Memoir*, in *Tempo*, 64 (1963), 28.
> Penetrating observation.
Rostand, Claude, *Visages de Poulenc*, in *Revue musicale de la Suisse romande*, 2 (Apr. 1963), 9; German transl. as *Der heitere und der ernste Poulenc*, in *Melos*, XXX (1963), 125.
Roy, Jean, *Francis Poulenc: l'homme et son œuvre*, Paris, 1964.
> First survey of Poulenc's whole work, with proper emphasis on its religious side, but no musical analysis.
Schaeffner, André, *Francis Poulenc, musicien français*, in *Contrepoints*, I (1946), 50.
> Uniquely helpful interpretation when written; still valuable as confirmation of later observations.

POWELL

Cowell, Sidney Robertson, *John Powell*, in *Journal of the International Folk Music Council*, XVI (1964), 112.

PRATELLA

Francesco Balilla Pratella: appunti biografici e bibliografici, Ravenna, 1931.
Marabini, Claudio, *Per una storia del futurismo: Balilla Pratella: musica e futurismo*, in *Nuova antologia*, XCVIII (1963), 67.

Quotes unpublished memoirs and letters of Marinetti.

Nagel, Wilibald, *Musica futuristica*, in *Die Musik*, XIV (1915), 3.

A serious critique of Pratella, considering his music along with the manifesto and the displays of Russolo.

Pratella, Francesco Balilla, *Cronache e critiche dal 1905 al 1917*, Bologna, 1918.

Futurism as an episode in the gradual development of Pratella's nationalism.

PROKOFIEV

Aranovsky, M., *O nekotorykh stilevykh osobennostiakh liricheskoi melodiki S. Prokofieva*, in *Voprosy teorii i estetiki muzyki*, II (1963), 84.

On some stylistic peculiarities of Prokofiev's lyrical melody.

Austin, William W., *Prokofiev's Fifth Symphony*, in MR, XVII (1956), 205.

Berger, Liubov, ed., *Cherty stilia S. Prokofieva: sbornik teoreticheskikh statei*, Moscow, 1962.

The most detailed stylistic studies of Prokofiev anywhere, by authors who know the subject thoroughly and are little hampered by interpretive guidance.

Blok, V., *Ob evoliutsii stilia i o nekotorykh osobennostiakh tvocheskogo metoda S. Prokofieva*, in T. Lebedeva, ed., *Muzyka i sovremennost'*, I (1962), 104.

On Prokofiev's stylistic evolution.

Boganova, Tatiana Vasilievna, *Natsional'no-russkie traditsii v muzyke S. S. Prokofieva*, Moscow, 1961.

Fresh study of an important topic: national Russian traditions in Prokofiev's music.

Brown, Malcolm H., *Prokofiev in America*, in *Listen*, I/1 (Dec. 1963), 2.

—— *Prokofiev's Eighth Piano Sonata*, in *Tempo*, 70 (1964), 9.

First by-products of an important diss. (Indiana, 1964).

Cazden, Norman, *Humor in the Music of Stravinsky and Prokofiev*, in *Science & Society*, XVIII (1954), 52.

Fédorov, Vladimir, *Serge Prokofiev*, in Roland-Manuel, ed., *Histoire de la musique Pléiade*, Paris, 1963, II, 1023.

Superb brief survey.

Gakkel', L., *O fortepiannom stile Prokofieva perioda 1914-1918 godov*, in T. Lebedeva, ed., *Muzyka i sovremennost'*, II (1963), 62.

On Prokofiev's piano style in the years 1914–18.

Hanson, Lawrence and Elisabeth, *Prokofiev, the Prodigal Son: an Introduction to his Life and Work*, London, 1964.

Based largely on Shlifshtein's documents, interpreted with sympathy and admiration for Prokofiev's character, this is a readable and useful biography. On the music, brief comments on pieces are embedded in the narrative; most comments are strangely deprecatory—only *Cinderella* wins the Hansons' warm praise.

Jahn, Renate, *Vom "Spieler" zum "Erzählung vom wahren Menschen,"* in MuG, XI (1961), 232.

Survey of Prokofiev's operas.

Jefferson, Alan, *The Angel of Fire*, in *Music & Musicians*, XIII/13 (Aug. 1965), 32.

Prokofiev's opera introduced with sympathy for the symbolist story on which it is based, and with helpful identification of the chief musical themes.

Khrennikov, Tikhon, *Report at the Composers' Congress*, in *Current Digest of the Soviet Press*, XIV/13 (Apr. 23, 1962), 14.

Cites the resolution of the Central Committee of the Communist Party, May 28, 1958, *On Correcting Errors in the Evaluation of the Operas* . . .

Kinsey, David Leslie, *The Piano Sonatas of Serge Prokofieff: a Critical Analysis of the Elements of Their Style*, Columbia Teachers College diss., 1959.

Kroher, Ekkehart, *Impressionismus in der Musik*, Leipzig, 1957.

Kroher claims Prokofiev and Shostakovich as heirs of impressionism, the last "true epoch" in music. His claim is not likely to meet approval in any quarter, but may be useful as counterweight to various claims for other composers, other labels.

Lyle, Watson, *Serge Prokofiev: an Interview*, in *The Bookman* (London), June 1932, p. 177.

"It is a mistake to say that my rhythm is this or that sort, or my harmony either. They must vary according to my melody."

Nestyev, Izrael V., *Prokofiev*, Moscow, 1957; English transl. by Florence Jonas, Stanford, 1960.
The principal biography.

—— and G. Ia. Edelman, eds., *Sergei Prokofiev 1953–1963: stati i materialy*, Moscow, 1962.
Essays and documents.

Poulenc, Francis, *Works for Solo Piano*, in booklet with Prokofiev's own 1932 recording of his Third Piano Concerto, Angel Records COLH 34 (1958).

Prokofiev, Sergei Sergeievich, *Musical America*, in *Living Age*, 357 (1939), 89.
On jazz, Gershwin, etc.

—— *Aus meinem Leben*, Zürich, 1962.
Compiled by W. Reich from sources in French and English.

—— *K izucheniu nasledia . . . Glavy iz avtobiografie*, in SM, 1963/3, p. 42.
"Toward the study of Prokofiev's heritage. Chapters from the autobiography."
Supplement to Shlifshtein's collection.

—— and V. V. Alpers, *Perepiska, publ. L. M. Kutateladze*, in *Muzykal'noe nasledstvo*, I (1962), 422.
32 letters, previously unpublished, dating from 1926 to 1951.

Rogozhina, Nina Ivanovna, *Muzyka "Alexsandra Nevskogo" Prokofieva v kinofil'me i kantate*, in T. Lebedeva, ed., *Muzyka i souvremennost'*, II (1963), 110.
Prokofiev's music for the film and the cantata *Alexander Nevsky*.

—— *Vokal'no–simfonicheskie proisvedeniia S. Prokofieva*, Moscow, 1964.
On *Alexander Nevsky* and other vocal-orchestral works of Prokofiev.

Sabinina, Marina Dmitrievna, *Sergei Prokofiev*, Moscow, 1956.

—— *Ob opernom stile Prokofieva*, in I. Nestyev and G. Edelman, eds., *Sergei Prokofiev 1953–1963*, Moscow, 1962, p. 53.
On Prokofiev's operatic style.

—— *"Semyon Kotko" i problemy opernoi dramaturgii Prokofieva*, Moscow, 1963.
Intensive study of Prokofiev's first Soviet opera in context of his whole work.

Shlifshtein, S. I., *S. S. Prokofiev: materialy, dokumenty, vospominaniia*, 2d edn., Moscow, 1961; English transl. of 1st edn. by Rose Prokofieva, Moscow, 1960.
Collection of source material for all biographical study, incomplete but invaluable.

—— *S. S. Prokofiev: notograficheskii spravochnik*, Moscow, 1962.
Authoritative catalogue, based on mss.

Skorik, M., *Prokofiev i Shenberg* [Schoenberg], in SM, 1962/1, p. 34.

Slonimsky, Sergei Mikhailovich, *Simfonii Prokofieva: opyt issledovaniia*, Moscow, 1964.
Not only ample program-notes, but a penetrating study of many aspects of the 8 symphonies (including the Symphony-Concertant for cello) in the light of Prokofiev's other works and of symphonies by Shostakovich et al.

Tarakanov, M., *Melodicheskie iavleniia v garmonia S. Prokofieva*, in S. S. Skrebkov, ed., *Muzykal'no-teoreticheskie problemy*, Moscow, 1963, p. 104.
Prokofiev's harmony clarified from the point of view of melody.

Werth, Alexander, *Musical Uproar in Moscow*, London, 1949.
Judicious and also brilliant account of the meetings at which Zhdanov scolded Prokofiev, Shostakovich, et al. Based on documents and interviews in Moscow.

—— *The Real Prokofiev*, in *The Nation*, CLXXVI (1953), 285.
Reports conversations, with some of Prokofiev's opinions not mentioned by Nestyev.

—— *The Kruschchev Phase*, London, 1961.
Music is treated in a chapter, pp. 263–71.

Zemtsovsky, I., *O dvukh tipakh trakovki odnogo tona v proisvedeniakh S. Prokofieva*, in *Voprosy teorii i estetiki muzyki*, II (1963), 111.

PUCCINI

Carner, Mosco, *Puccini: a Critical Biography*, New York, 1959.
Comprehensive study, with original contributions.

Ecclesiis, Gennavo Anthony d', *The Aria Techniques of Giacomo Puccini: a Study in Musico-Dramatic Style*, New York Univ. diss., 1961.

Gavazzeni, Gianandrea, *Quaderno del musicista (1940–1950)*, Bergamo, 1952.
Collected criticism.

Puccini, Giacomo, *Epistolario,* ed. by Giuseppe Adami, Milan, 1928; English transl. as *Letters,* Philadelphia, 1931.
—— *Carteggi pucciniani,* ed. by Eugenio Gara, Milan, 1958.
    Additional letters, plus pictures, bibliography, and discography.
Sartori, Claudio, ed., *Giacomo Puccini . . . saggi . . . catalogo delle opere, discografia, letteratura,* Milan, 1959.
Stuckenschmidt, Hans Heinz, et al., *Was geht uns noch Puccini an?,* in *Opernwelt,* Apr. 1965, p. 21.
Vaughan, Denis, *Puccini's Orchestration,* in PRMA, 87 (1961), 1.

QUILTER

Woodgate, Leslie, *Roger Quilter,* in MT, XCIV (1953), 503.
    Woodgate was secretary to Quilter in 1919. His appreciation has the right degree of warmth under a cool surface.

RACHMANINOV

Apetian, Z., ed., *Vospominaniia o Rachmaninove,* 2d edn., Moscow, 1961.
    Memoirs of Rachmaninov by many associates.
Bertensson, Sergei, and Jay Leyda, *Sergei Rachmaninoff, a Lifetime in Music,* New York, 1956.
Rachmaninov, Sergei, *Pisma,* Moscow, 1955.
    Letters. A large collection, still incomplete.
Seroff, Victor I., *Rachmaninoff,* New York, 1950.
    Vivid biography, less thorough but apparently no less accurate than Bertensson and Leyda.
Swan, Alfred J., *Russian Liturgical Music and its Relation to 20th-Century Ideals,* in ML, XXXIX (1958), 265.
    On Rachmaninov, Grechaninov, et al.
Yasser, Joseph, *Progressive Tendencies in Rachmaninoff's Music,* in *Musicology,* II (1949), 1.
RATHAUS
Schwarz, Boris, *Karol Rathaus,* in MQ, XLI (1955), 481.
RAVEL
Ackere, Jules van, *Maurice Ravel,* Brussels, 1957.
    Summarized in MGG, XI (1964), 58.
Bruyr, José, *Maurice Ravel ou le lyrisme et les sortilèges,* Paris, 1950.
Cocteau, Jean, *Ravel et nous,* in RM, XIX (1938), 396.
—— *Ravel,* in *De la musique encore et toujours: textes inédits de Paul Claudel . . . Stéphane Mallarmé,* Paris, 1946, p. 14.
    A belated apology.
Fargue, Léon-Paul, *Maurice Ravel,* Paris, 1949.
    Memoir of a poet friend.
Février, Jacques, *Les Exigences de Ravel,* in *Revue internationale de musique,* I/5-6 (Apr. 1939), 393.
Jankélévitch, Vladimir, *Ravel,* transl. by M. Crosland, New York, 1959.
    A "profile" with many illustrations.
Jourdan-Morhange, Hélène, *Ravel et nous: l'homme, l'ami, le musicien* (preface by Colette), Geneva, 1945.
Machabey, Armand, *Maurice Ravel,* Paris, 1947.
Maurice Ravel: Catalogue de l'œuvre, Paris, 1954.
Perlemutter, Vlado, and H. Jourdan-Morhange, *Ravel d'après Ravel,* Lausanne, 1953.
Ravel, Maurice, *Contemporary Music,* in *Rice Institute Pamphlets,* XV (1928), 131; English text, with introduction by B. Pilarski, as *Une Conférence de Maurice Ravel à Houston (1928),* in *Revue de musicologie,* L (1964), 208.
    A beautiful lecture, with valuable comments on Schoenberg, Stravinsky, and Milhaud.
—— *Entretien,* in RM, XII (1931), 193.

—— *Esquisse autobiographique,* in RM, XIX (1938), 211; also separately, ed. Jean Poueigh, Liège, 1943.

—— *Letters to Calvocoressi,* in MQ, XXVII (1941), 1.

—— *Ravel au miroir de ses lettres: correspondance,* ed. by M. Gerar and R. Chalupt, Paris, 1956.

Roland-Manuel, Alexis, *Maurice Ravel,* Paris, 1938; English transl. by C. Jolly, London, 1947.
> Chief source of information, but supplemented in many details by Fargue, Machabey, Jourdan-Morhange, et al.

Sannemüller, Gerd, *Ravels Stellung in der französischen Musik,* in W. Brennecke and H. Haase, eds., *Hans Albrecht in Memoriam,* Kassel, 1962, p. 251.
> Based on a diss. (Kiel, 1961), this essay is perhaps the best in German on Ravel.

Seroff, Victor I., *Maurice Ravel,* New York, 1953.

Viñes, Ricardo, *Fragments,* in RM, XIX (1938), 361.
> Marvelous memoir of Ravel by his close friend, the superb pianist Viñes.

RAWSTHORNE

Dickinson, A. E. F., *The Progress of Alan Rawsthorne,* in MR, XII (1951), 87.
> A friendly view, in some contrast to the severe critique by Colin Mason in *Grove*[5], VII, 65.

Myers, Rollo H., *Rawsthorne, Composer of Delicacy,* in *Music & Musicians,* XIII/9 (May 1965), 20.

REBIKOV

Dale, William Henry, *A Study of the Musico-Psychological Dramas of Vladimir Ivanovitch Rebikov,* Univ. of Southern California diss., 1955.

Nabokov, Nicholas, *Old Friends and New Music,* Boston, 1951.
> Pp. 148–50 on Rebikov.

REDA

Reda, Siegfried, *Selbstbildnis,* in MuK, XVI (1947), 81.

REGER

Hasse, Karl, *Max Reger,* Leipzig, 1921.
> Includes Reger's collected essays.

Otto, Eberhard, *Max Reger, Sinnbild einer Epoche,* Wiesbaden, 1957.
> A good brief introduction, in the estimate of H. Wirth, in Mf, XI (1958), 238, as well as the present author.

Reger, Elsa, *Mein Leben mit und für Max Reger,* Leipzig, 1930; 2d rev. edn., 1931.

Reger, Max, *Beiträge zur Modulationslehre,* Leipzig, 1903; 24th edn., 1952.

—— *Briefe eines deutschen Meisters,* ed. by Else von Hase-Koehler, Leipzig, 1928.

—— *Briefwechsel mit Herzog Georg II. von Sachsen-Meiningen,* ed. by H. and E. H. Müller von Asow, Weimar, 1949.

—— *Briefe zwischen der Arbeit,* Bonn, 1956.

Schenker, Heinrich, *Ein Gegenbeispiel: Max Reger, Op. 81,* in Schenker, *Das Meisterwerk in der Musik,* Munich, 1926, II, 171.

Stein, Fritz, *Max Reger,* Potsdam, 1939.

—— *Thematisches Verzeichnis der im Druck erschienenen Werke von Max Reger . . . Bibliographie des Reger-Schrifttums v. J. Bachmair,* Leipzig, 1953.

—— *Max Reger, 1873–1916: sein Leben in Bildern,* 2d edn., Leipzig, 1956.

Stockmann, Bernhard, *Die Kirchenmusik Max Regers und ihr theologischer Hintergrund,* in NZfM, CXXV (1964), 533.
> With factual evidence Stockmann refutes efforts to connect Reger with modern trends in liturgy, organ design, and existential religious thought.

Straube, Karl, *Briefe eines Thomaskantors,* ed. by W. Gurlitt und Hans-Olf Hudemann, Stuttgart, 1952.
> Includes information on Reger, David, et al.

Truscott, Harold, *Reger's "Symphonischer Prolog,"* in MMR, LXXXIX (1959), 214.
> Written in 1909, this symphony "in fact if not in name" is a prologue to a tragedy —that of 1914, says Truscott, who studies the piece in relation to Reger's whole

work and hails it as "the crown of his orchestral music . . . one of the great orchestral pieces of the century."

Waldstein, Wilhelm, *Max Reger*, in ÖMz, XVIII (1963), 115.
> Assigns Reger a "firm place in history" but denies him "living value."

Wellesz, Egon, *Analytische Studie über Regers "Romantische Suite,"* in ZfMw, IV (1921), 106.
> Excellent observations of characteristic traits. See also Wellesz's article on Reger in *Cobbett*, II, 277.

Wirth, Helmut, *Max Reger in his Works*, in MMR, LXXVIII (1948), 143.
> This article, among the most persuasive of any on Reger, is brought up to date in MGG, XI (1963), 119, with a large bibliography.

RESPIGHI

Mila, Massimo, *Probleme di gusto ed arte in Ottorino Respighi*, in *La Rassegna musicale*, VI (1933), 95.

Respighi, Elsa, *Ottorino Respighi: dati biografici ordinati*, Milan, 1954; English transl. as *Ottorino Respighi: his Life Story*, London, 1962.
> Uncritical account by Respighi's wife.

Rinaldi, Mario, *Ottorino Respighi*, in *Musica d'oggi*, IV (1961), 146.
> Affirms a distinctive quality in Respighi's work, operas as well as symphonic music. Two more articles in the same issue support the hope of Respighi's survival.

REUTTER

Lindlar, Heinrich, *Hermann Reutters Liedschaffen—zum 65. Geburtstag des Komponisten*, in NZfM, CXXVI (1965), 238.

Reutter, Hermann, *Wort und Ton in der zeitgenössichen Musik*, in *Musica*, IV (1950), 121; also in H. Lindlar, ed., *Die Stimme der Komponisten*, Rodenkirchen, 1958, p. 74.

—— *Meine Lieder-Zyklen auf Gedichte von Lorca*, in *Melos*, XXX (1963), 283.
> With examples showing Reutter's approach to the 12-tone technique.

—— *Triptychon*, in R. S. Hines, ed., *The Composer's Point of View*, Norman, Okla., 1963, p. 206.

REVUELTAS

Contreras, Guillermo, *Silvestre Revueltas, genio atormentado*, Mexico, 1954.

Mayer-Serra, Oscar, *Silvestre Revueltas*, in MQ, XXVII (1941), 123.

ŘÍDKÝ

Řídký, Jaroslav, [Autobiographical sketch, in Czech], in *Rytmus*, VII (1941–42), 54.

—— *Několik slov k mé činnosti učitelské a skladatelské*, in *Rytmus*, X/4 (1945–46), 11.

RIEGGER

Carter, Elliott, *Wallingford Riegger*, in ACA, II/1 (Feb. 1952), 3.

Cowell, Henry, *A Note on Wallingford Riegger*, in *Juilliard Review*, II/2 (1955), 53.

Goldman, Richard Franko, *The Music of Wallingford Riegger*, in MQ, XXXVI (1950), 39.

Hambraeus, Bengt, *Om Wallingford Riegger och Study in Sonority*, in *Nutida Musik*, VIII/1 (1964), 23.

Schmoll, J. B., *Dedicated Contemporary*, in *Musical America*, May 1955, p. 8.
> By-product of a thesis on Riegger's principal instrumental works (Northwestern Univ., 1954).

RIISAGER

Berg, Sigurd, *Kundåge Riisager*, Copenhagen, 1950.
> Catalogue, discography, and brief biography in English.

RODGERS

Ewen, David, *Richard Rodgers*, New York, 1957.

RODRIGO

Sopeña, Federico, *Joaquín Rodrigo*, Madrid, 1946.

ROGERS

Hanson, Howard, *Bernard Rogers*, in MM, XXII (1945), 170.

ROHWER

Rohwer, Jens, *Tonale Instruktion, und Beiträge zur Kompositionslehre mit einem Beispielbuch,* Wolfenbüttel, 1949.

A special vocabulary and some other hurdles have kept this book from any wide audience, but the present author agrees with Mersmann and Pfrogner that Rohwer offers one of the best contributions to music theory since Hindemith.

—— *Der Sonanzfaktor im Aufbau von Tonsystemen,* in G. Abraham, ed., *Bericht über den Kongress der Internationalen Gesellschaft für Musikwissenschaft, Köln,* Kassel, 1959, p. 230.

More modest and sophisticated than Rohwer's early book, this summary of his diss. (Kiel, 1958) again stirs deep interest. A similar sample of his thought is the article *Intervall, historisch (neuere Zeit) und systematisch,* in MGG, VI (1957), 1347.

—— *Anmerkungen zum "seriellen Denken,"* in Mf, XVII (1964), 245.

Rohwer exempts Webern from his strictures on the "simply false notion of time" introduced by Schoenberg and further developed by Stockhausen.

ROPARTZ

Lamy, Fernand, *J. Guy Ropartz: l'homme et l'œuvre,* Paris, 1948.

Survey in chronological order, with quotations from Ropartz on his style.

ROSENBERG

Pergament, Moses, *Hilding Rosenberg: a Journey in Modern Swedish Music,* in ML, XXVIII (1947), 249.

ROUSSEL

Albert Roussel, catalogue de l'œuvre, Paris, 1947.

Deane, Basil, *Albert Roussel,* London, 1961.

Excellent stylistic study, superseding earlier efforts in both English and French.

Pincherle, Marc, *Albert Roussel,* Geneva, 1957.

Good biography, shunning detailed study of the music.

Rubbra, Edmund, *Albert Roussel,* in MMR, LXII (1932), 217.

RUBBRA

Rubbra, Edmund [and P. and G. Way], *Temple Gongs and Coloured Bubbles,* in *Twentieth Century,* CLXX/1011 (Autumn 1961), 72.

Revealing interview.

RUGGLES

Harrison, Lou, *About Carl Ruggles: Section Four of a Book on Ruggles,* with a note by Henry Cowell, Yonkers, N. Y., 1946.

This rare pamphlet may be regarded as superseded (perhaps temporarily) by the *Score* article listed below.

—— *Carl Ruggles,* in *The Score,* 12 (1955), 15.

Seeger, Charles, *Carl Ruggles,* in MQ, XVIII (1932), 578.

—— *Charles Ives and Carl Ruggles,* in *Magazine of Art,* XXXII (1939), 396, 435.

RUSSOLO

Prieberg, Fred K., *Der musikalische Futurismus,* in *Melos,* XXV (1958), 124.

Ample history of Russolo's career, with admiration for his anticipating Stockhausen et al.

Russolo, Luigi, *L'Arte dei rumori,* Milan, 1916; English transl. by S. Somervell, as *The Art of Noises,* in N. Slonimsky, *Music Since 1900,* New York, 1949, p. 642.

—— *Die Kunst der Geräusche als Fortentwicklung des modernen Orchesters,* in *Melos,* VII (1928), 12.

RUYNEMAN

Hoérée, André, *Daniel Ruyneman,* in RM, 209 (March 1949), 30.

Wouters, Jos, *Daniel Ruyneman,* in *Sonorum speculum,* II (June 1962), 1.

SATIE

Apollinaire, Guillaume, *Selected Writings,* transl. and introd. by Roger Shattuck, New York, 1948.

Austin, William W., *Satie Before and After Cocteau*, in MQ, XLVIII (1962), 216.
> An early version of the treatment of Satie in the present book, but including a complete list of works, and additional quotations from Cocteau.

Cage, John, [Letters on Satie], in *Musical America*, Dec. 15, 1950, p. 12, and Apr. 1, 1951, p. 26.

—— *Erik Satie*, in *Art News Annual*, XXVII (1958), 56.

Cocteau, Jean, *Fragments d'un conférence sur Erik Satie (1920)*, in RM, V (1924), 217; reprinted as *Erik Satie*, Liège, 1957.

—— *Le Rappel à l'ordre. Le Coq et l'arlequin*, Paris, 1926; English transl. by R. H. Myers, as *A Call to Order*, London, 1926.

—— *Ravel et nous*, in RM, XIX (1938), 396.

Collet, Henri, *Un livre de Rimsky et un livre de Cocteau: les Cinq russes, les Six français et Erik Satie*, in *Comoedia*, Jan. 16, 1920, p. 2.

—— *Les Six français*, in *Comoedia*, Jan. 23, 1920, p. 2.
> These articles provided the label that linked friendly acquaintances with each other and with Satie, as if he were their teacher or model.

Cortot, Alfred, *La Musique française de piano*, 3 vols., Paris, 1944; English transl. of Vol. I only, as *French Piano Music*, Oxford, 1932.
> Articles written from 1920 on, about composers from Debussy to Poulenc, by a fine pianist.

Danckert, Werner, *Der Klassizismus Erik Saties*, in ZfMw, XII (1929), 105.
> A rare German tribute for this period.

Debussy, Claude, *Du précurseur*, in BSIM, IX (March 1913), 46.

Drew, David, *Modern French Music*, in H. Hartog, ed., *European Music in the 20th Century*, London, 1957, p. 232.

Écorcheville, Jules, *Erik Satie*, in BSIM, VII (March 1911), 29.
> Basic source of information.

Fournier, Gabriel, *Mémoire*, in RM, 214 (1952), 126.
> Includes Satie's postcard.

Fumet, Stanislas, *La Poésie à travers les arts*, Paris, 1954.
> Includes (pp. 133–141) an essay on Satie.

Hugo, Valentine, *Le Socrate que j'ai connu*, in RM, 214 (1952), 139.
> The most touching of many contributions to the special issue on Satie.

Jungheinrich, Hans-Klaus, *Surrealismus in der Musik*, in *Melos*, XXI (1964), 381.
> In a survey covering several interesting minor figures, Jungheinrich asserts that "Satie is the central figure, if there is such a thing." Pictures from *Relâche*.

Koechlin, Charles, *Erik Satie*, in RM, V (1924), 193.

Leiris, Michael, *L'Humour d'Erik Satie*, in *Nouvelle revue française*, XXVI/50 (1938), 163.

Lockspeiser, Edward, ed., *The Literary Clef: an Anthology of Letters and Writings by French Composers*, London, 1958.
> Includes letters of Satie hardly or not at all accessible otherwise.

Myers, Rollo H., *Erik Satie*, London, 1948.
> Though depending on Cocteau without close first-hand knowledge, Myers's book is valuable as an introduction in English.

Rostand, Claude, *Jean Cocteau et la musique*, in *La Table ronde*, XCIV (1955), 84.

—— *Cocteau—ein Leben mit der Musik*, in *Melos*, XXXI (1964), 48.
> Reports Cocteau's ultimate reconciliation with the spirit of Debussy, 1962. This article is followed by brief obituary tributes from Auric, Milhaud, et al.

Rudhyar, Dane [pseud. for Daniel Chennevière], *Erik Satie and the Music of Irony*, in MQ, V (1919), 469.
> An American introduction, independent of Cocteau but no better. "It cannot be termed music, since music is not intellectual in essence. . . . He has called into being an inchoate form for the sole use of a few musician readers." Timely.

Satie, Erik, *Mémoires d'un amnésiaque*, in BSIM, IV (1911), 69; VII–VIII (1912), 83; XI (1913), 70; reprinted as book, Liège, 1953.

—— *Cahiers d'un mammifère*, in *Esprit nouveau*, I/7 (1921), 833.

——— *Éloges des critiques*, in *Action*, II/8 (1921), 8.

——— *A Composer's Conviction*, in *Vanity Fair*, XIX/6 (Feb. 1923), 39; also in E. Corle, ed., *Igor Stravinsky*, New York, 1949, p. 25.

Satie-ana, in RM, V (1924), 224.

Sert, Misia Godebski, *A "Spectacle-Concert" in Paris*, in *The Chesterian*, 6 (1920), 165.

——— *Misia*, Paris, 1952; English transl. as *Misia and the Muses*, New York, 1953.
> Vivid glimpses of Satie, Stravinsky, et al. Pp. 184–91 of the original are omitted in the English version.

Shattuck, Roger, *The Banquet Years: the Arts in France, 1885–1918: Alfred Jarry, Henri Rousseau, Erik Satie, Guillaume Apollinaire*, New York, 1958.
> Satie in flattering perspective.

Templier, Pierre-Daniel, *Erik Satie*, Paris, 1932.
> Chief source of biographical information and of documents otherwise inaccessible.

SAUGUET

Schneider, Marcel, *Henri Sauguet*, Paris, 1959.

SCHENKER

Forte, Allen, *Schenker's Conception of Musical Structure: a Review and an Appraisal with Reference to Current Problems in Music Theory*, in JMT, III (1959), 1.
> Without being a disciple, Forte has studied all Schenker's works with care. His judgment is thus uniquely convincing.

Kaufmann, Harald, *Fortschritt und Reaktion in der Lehre Heinrich Schenkers*, in NZfM, CXXVI (1965), 5.
> Fresh and challenging view of Schenker's ambivalent relation to contemporary changes of style and technique.

Mitchell, William J., *Elementary Harmony*, New York, 1939; 2d rev. edn., 1948.
> The first and still the best textbook exposition of Schenker's ideas, trimmed of excesses.

Salzer, Felix, *Structural Hearing: Tonal Coherence in Music*, 2 vols., New York, 1952.
> An extension of Schenker's procedures, which Salzer studied in Vienna, 1931–35, to encompass the analysis of Machaut, Stravinsky, et al. With many fine observations, this book stimulated many Americans, including the present author.

Schenker, Heinrich, *Neue musikalische Theorien und Phantasien. I. Bd.: Harmonielehre*, Stuttgart, 1906; English transl. by E. M. Borghese, ed. by O. Jonas, as *Harmony*, Chicago, 1954.
> William J. Mitchell's review of the translation in MQ, XL (1955), 256, should be consulted.

——— . . . *II. Bd., Kontrapunkt*, 2 vols. Stuttgart, 1910.

——— . . . *III. Bd., Der freie Satz*, Vienna, 1935; 2d edn., ed. by O. Jonas, Vienna, 1956.

——— *Der Tonwille: Flugblätter zum Zeugnis unwandelbarer Gesetze der Tonkunst*, 10 issues, Vienna, 1921–24.

——— *Das Meisterwerk in der Musik*, 3 vols., Munich, 1925–30.
> Consideration of all these and more is necessary to arrive at a judgment like Allen Forte's.

SCHILLINGER

Schillinger, Frances, *Joseph Schillinger, a Memoir by his Wife*, New York, 1949.

Schillinger, Joseph, *The Schillinger System of Musical Composition*, New York, 1946.
> Though not in the "mainstream" of music theory, Schillinger's ideas influenced several composers, not only in his lifetime—e.g., Gershwin—but also in the 1960s.

——— *The Mathematical Basis of the Arts*, New York, 1947.

SCHMIDT

Arbeiter, Albert, *Einführung in "Das Buch mit sieben Siegeln,"* Judenberg, 1958.
> Based on a diss. (Vienna, 1954), this is a guide to Franz Schmidt's chief work.

Liess, Andreas, *Franz Schmidt: Leben und Schaffen*, Graz, 1951.

Nemeth, Carl, *Franz Schmidt: ein Meister nach Brahms und Bruckner*, Zürich, 1957.

Comprehensive but not so convincing as Liess, nor so detailed as Arbeiter, Pach, and Waldstein.

Pach, Walter, *Franz Schmidt als Orgelkomponist*, in ÖMz, XIX (1964), 110.

Waldstein, Wilhelm, *Franz Schmidt—1964*, in ÖMz, XIX (1964), 97.
> Sensible up-to-date statement, followed by W. Pach's special study and a survey of literature on Schmidt.

SCHMITT

Hucher, Yves, *Florent Schmitt: l'homme et l'artiste: son époque et son œuvre*, Paris, 1953.

—— *L'Œuvre de Florent Schmitt: Catalogue* [text in English], Paris, 1960.

Marceron, Madeleine, *Florent Schmitt*, Paris, 1959.
> Supplements the longer study by Hucher with a discography.

SCHNABEL

Saerchinger, César, *Artur Schnabel*, New York, 1957.
> Chief source of information; includes list of works.

Schnabel, Artur, *My Life and Music*, New York, 1963.

SCHOECK

Corrodi, Hans, *Othmar Schoeck: Bild eines Schaffens*, 3d rev. and enl. edn., Frauenfeld, 1956.

Othmar Schoeck im Wort: Äusserungen des Komponisten, mit einer Auswahl zeitgenössischer Bekenntnisse, St. Gall, 1957.

Schuh, Willi, *Rückblick auf Othmar Schoeck*, in SMz, CI (1961), 218.
> "Schoeck knew himself to be hidden within the circle of his poets. . . . He needed to live with his favorite poets for years, sometimes decades, for he was always loath merely, as he said, 'to pour music over' a poem." Schuh, in MGG, XII (1965), 7, lists his own book and several other articles about Schoeck, but gives precedence to Corrodi's.

Vogel, Werner, *Wesenszüge von Othmar Schoecks Liedkunst*, Zürich, 1950.

—— *Thematisches Verzeichnis der Werke von Othmar Schoeck*, Zürich, 1956.

SCHOENBERG

Adorno, Theodor Wiesengrund, *Philosophie der neuen Musik*, Tübingen, 1949; new edn., Frankfurt, 1958; French transl. by Hildenbrand and Lindenberg, as *Philosophie de la nouvelle musique*, Paris, 1962.
> Pupil of Schoenberg and eminent sociologist, Adorno argues an influential interpretation of the work of Schoenberg and Stravinsky.

—— *Arnold Schönberg*, in *Die grossen Deutschen*, IV (1957), 508.
> The best of many essays on Schoenberg by Adorno.

—— *Der getreue Korrepetitor: Lehrschriften zur musikalischen Praxis*, Frankfurt, 1963.
> Essays for performers on Schoenberg's Phantasy, Berg's Violin Concerto, and four works of Webern.

Armitage, Merle, ed., *Schoenberg*, New York, 1937.

Arnold Schönberg zum 60. Geburtstag, Vienna, 1934.
> Earlier, more important, *Festschriften* are listed below under their editor, Alban Berg.

Bekker, Paul, *Arnold Schönbergs "Pierrot Lunaire" in Frankfurt*, in Anbruch, IV (1922), 15.
> Describes a performance (1921) by a local group including Hindemith's teacher Rebner.

Berg, Alban, *Arnold Schönberg, Pelleas und Melisande, op. 5: kurze thematische Analyse*, Vienna, 1920.

—— *Arnold Schönberg, Kammersymphonie, op. 9*, Vienna, 1921.

—— *Arnold Schönberg, Gurrelieder-Führer*, Vienna, 1924.

—— *Warum ist Schönbergs Musik so schwer verständlich?*, in Anbruch, VI (1924), 329; English transl. as *Why is Schoenberg's Music So Hard to Understand?*, in MR, XIII (1952), 187.
> Berg analyzes the beginning of Schoenberg's First Quartet, Op. 7, to show that density of thought, more than novelty of technique, is the reason.

—— *Was ist atonal?*, in SMz, LXXXV (1945), 47; English transl. as *What is Atonality?*, in N. Slonimsky, *Music since 1900*, New York, 1949, p. 671.

A radio talk of 1930, first printed, according to Slonimsky, in the magazine *23*, in 1936.

—— et al., *Arnold Schönberg*, Munich, 1912.
Five reproductions of pictures by Schoenberg, and important essays by Webern, Kandinsky, et al.

—— et al., *Arnold Schönberg zum 50. Geburtstag*, in *Anbruch*, VI (Sonderheft, Aug.–Sept. 1924), 269–342.

Calvocoressi, Michel-Dmitri, *The Classicism of Arnold Schoenberg*, in MT, LV (1914), 234.

Capp, Laura Remick, *The Secret of Modernist Music: an Interview with the Foremost of Modern Impressionist Composers, Arnold Schoenberg*, in *The Etude*, LII/10 (1934), 573.
Interesting not only for its title, this article quotes Schoenberg as balancing technical and esthetic considerations more easily than he does in his own writings.

Clapp, Philip Greeley, *Schoenberg: Futurist in Music*, in *Musical News* (London), XLV (1913), 297.

Cooper, Grosvenor W., and Leonard B. Meyer, *The Rhythmic Structure of Music*, Chicago, 1960.
This valuable contribution to the general theory of music includes (pp. 174–77) a good discussion of Schoenberg's *Little Piano Piece*, Op. 19, No. 4.

Dahlhaus, Carl, *Musikalische Prosa*, in NZfM, CXXV (1964), 176.
Schoenberg's George Songs, Op. 15, in the light of Lully, Mozart, Brahms, Mahler, et al.

Dean, Winton, *Moses and Aaron*, in MT, CVI (1965), 612.
Persuasive critique of the London production of Schoenberg's opera.

Del Mar, Norman, *Confusion and Error (II)*, in *The Score*, 22 (1958), 28.
Raises many questions about the published score of Schoenberg's *Kammersymphonie*, Op. 9.

Diether, Jack, *Schoenberg's "Gurrelieder" on LP*, in *Chord & Discord*, II/7 (1954), 62.
Includes testimony about the use of *Sprechstimme* in the part of Klaus-Narr, "necessitated by the sudden illness of the originally scheduled singer."

Ehrenforth, Karl Heinrich, *Ausdruck und Form: Arnold Schoenbergs Durchbruch zur Atonalität in den George-Liedern op. 15*, Bonn, 1963.
Based on a diss. (Hamburg, 1960), this book sensibly discusses delicate and important questions, without proposing any brief answer.

—— *Schoenberg und Webern: das XIV. Lied aus Schoenbergs Georgeliedern op. 15*, in NZfM, CXXVI (1965), 102.
The extreme point in Schoenberg's career where he came closest to Webern.

Eisler, Hanns, *Arnold Schoenberg*, in *Sinn und Form*, VII (1955), 5; also in Eisler, *Eine Auswahl von Reden*, Leipzig, 1961, p. 112.

Fleury, Louis, *About "Pierrot Lunaire": the Impressions Made on Various Audiences by a Novel Work*, in ML, V (1924), 347.

Forte, Allen, *Contemporary Tone-Structures*, New York, 1955.
Includes analysis of Schoenberg's Phantasy.

Francès, Robert, *La Perception de la musique*, Paris, 1958.
A superior contribution to music psychology. Francès's unique experiments tested the recognition of 12-tone series in varying contexts, by musicians of varying experience and taste (some were 12-tone composers).

Friedheim, Philip, *Tonality and Structure in the Early Works of Schoenberg*, N.Y. Univ. diss., 1963.
Fine performance of a difficult task, much needed. With a proper background of understanding the multifarious relations of tonality and structure in music from the 15th century through Schoenberg's last works, Friedheim has studied every note of every available piece of Schoenberg up to and including the Piano Pieces, Op. 11. He presents his findings with many—but not too many—examples, gently and firmly correcting all previous writers on the subject.

Gould, Glenn, *The Dodecaphonist's Dilemma*, in CMJ, I/1 (1956), 20.
Fascinating comments on particular pieces, especially those Gould has played.

——— *Arnold Schoenberg: a Perspective*, Cincinnati, 1964.

   A long lecture, sympathetic in tone, possibly useful as an introduction.

Gradenwitz, Peter, *Reihenkomposition im Orient*, in E. Schenk, ed., *Bericht über den Internationalen Musikwissenschaftlichen Kongress Wien (1956)*, Graz, 1958, p. 238.

   Gradenwitz argues that procedures in ancient Near Eastern music resemble Schoenberg's technique.

——— *Gustav Mahler and Arnold Schoenberg*, in *Leo Baeck Institute Year Book*, V (1960), 262.

   Includes quotations from Schoenberg's drama *Der biblische Weg*.

——— *The Religious Works of Arnold Schoenberg*, in MR, XXI (1960), 19.

Greissle, Felix, *Die formalen Grundlagen des Bläserquintetts von Arnold Schönberg*, in *Anbruch*, VIII (1925), 63.

Hayward, Katherine, *An Interview with Arnold Schoenberg*, in *Southwestern Musician*, XVI (Sep. 1949), 4.

   A rare glimpse of Schoenberg at home, with quotations such as: "I have the aphoristic manner. . . . I like my music to be brave and precise. This is my style."

Hill, Richard S., *Schoenberg's Tone-Rows and the Tonal System of the Future*, in MQ, XXII (1936), 14.

   A suggestive article, especially considering its date.

——— [Review of Schoenberg's Phantasy], in NotesMLA, IX (1952), 647.

   "Almost an epitome of the main principles towards which he has been striving."

Jalowetz, Heinrich, *On the Spontaneity of Schoenberg's Music*, in MQ, XXX (1944), 385.

Kassler, Michael, *The Decision of Arnold Schoenberg's Twelve-Note-Class System and Related Systems*, Princeton, 1961.

   Rigorous mathematical study.

——— *A Sketch of the Use of Formalized Languages for the Assertion of Music*, in PNM, I/2 (1963), 83.

Keller, Hans, *Schönberg and Stravinsky: Schönbergians and Stravinskyans*, in MR, XV (1954), 307.

——— *Strict Serial Technique in Classical Music*, in Tempo, 37 (1955), 12.

——— *Schoenberg's "Moses and Aron [sic],"* in *The Score*, 21 (1957), 30.

——— *Moses, Freud, and Schoenberg*, in MMR, LXXXVIII (1958), 12, 63.

——— *Schoenberg: Erwartung, Von Heute auf Morgen*, in MR, XIX (1958), 319.

——— *Schoenberg's "Moses and Aron [sic],"* in MR, XIX (1958), 52.

Kerman, Joseph, *Wagner: Thoughts in Season*, in *The Score*, 28 (1961), 9.

   A well developed analogy between *Parsifal* and Schoenberg's *Moses*.

Kirchmeyer, Helmut, *Zur Frühgeschichte der Zwölftontechnik: Arnold Schönbergs Serenade Op. 24*, in booklet with recording, Wergo 60,002.

Klemperer, Otto, *Arnold Schoenberg, Teacher, Composer, and Transcriber*, in *The Canon*, III (1949), 102.

   Klemperer recalls his work with Schoenberg, 1935–37. See also Klemperer's *Minor Recollections*, London, 1964.

Koechlin, Charles, *Évolution et tradition: à propos du Pierrot Lunaire de M. Schoenberg*, in *Ménestrel*, LXXXIV (1922), 117.

Langlie, Warren M., *Arnold Schoenberg as a Teacher*, Univ. of California at Los Angeles diss., 1960.

   Based on Langlie's notes during classes and private study with Schoenberg, 1940–50. Several fresh insights turn up, including the notion that invertible counterpoint leads toward 12-tone technique.

Leibowitz, René, *Schoenberg et son école: l'étape contemporaine du langage musical*, Paris, 1947; English transl. as *Schoenberg and his School*, New York, 1949.

   The subtitle states the doctrine of Leibowitz, which exaggerates that of Schoenberg.

——— *Qu'est-ce que la musique de douze sons?*, Liège, 1948.

——— *Introduction à la musique de douze sons*, Paris, 1949.

Lewin, David, *A Theory of Segmental Association in Twelve-Tone Music*, in PNM, I/1 (1962), 89.

   Rigorous mathematics applied to Schoenberg's Violin Concerto.

Lissa, Zofia, *Geschichtliche Vorform der Zwölftontechnik*, in *Acta Musicologica*, VII (1935), 15.

> On "certain far-reaching, though very general analogies between Scriabin and Schoenberg." Professor Lissa recognizes the independence of the two, and the great difference as well as the slight similarity which she defines.

Lück, Rudolf, *Arnold Schönberg und das deutsche Volkslied*, in NZfM, CXXIV (1963), 86.

> Recommends study of Schoenberg's arrangements of so-called folksongs, in order to develop understanding of his procedure of "developing variation."

—— *Die Generalbass-Aussetzungen Arnold Schönbergs*, in *Deutsches Jahrbuch der Musikwissenschaft*, VIII (1964), 26.

Maegaard, Jan, *Some Formal Devices in Expressionistic Works*, in *Dansk Aarbog for Musik Forskning*, I (1961), 69.

> Includes comment on Schoenberg's *Little Piano Piece*, Op. 19, No. 1.

—— *A Study of the Chronology of Op. 23–26 by Arnold Schoenberg*, in *Dansk Aarbog for Musik Forskning*, II (1962), 93.

> Fascinating detailed study, based on work at the Schoenberg Archives.

Melichar, Alois, *Musik in der Zwangsjacke: die deutsche Musik zwischen Orff und Schönberg*, Vienna, 1958.

> Melichar, pupil of Schreker, writes in a shrill tone inspiring no confidence, but his book is full of interesting facts.

—— *Schönberg und die Folgen*, Vienna, 1960.

> Rebuttal to attacks on Melichar's first book.

Milhaud, Darius, *Paris und unser "Pierrot Lunaire,"* in *Anbruch*, IV (1922), 44.

—— *To Arnold Schoenberg on his 70th Birthday: Personal Recollections*, in MQ, XXX (1944), 379.

Nachod, Hans, *The Very First Performance of Schoenberg's "Gurrelieder,"* in *Music Survey*, III (1950), 38.

—— et al., *Involuntary Pilgrimage of Arnold Schoenberg from Vienna to California: a Symposium*, in *The Listener*, XLVII (1952), 105.

Neighbour, Oliver, *The Evolution of Twelve-Note Music*, in PRMA, LXXXI (1954), 49.

> An unusual demonstration of how around 1950 many musicians' interests evolved from Bartók toward Schoenberg.

—— *Moses and Aaron*, in MT, CVI (1965), 422.

> An ideal introduction to Schoenberg's opera, with the plot seen in the perspective of his whole career.

Nelson, Robert U., *Schoenberg's Variation Seminar*, in MQ, L (1964), 141.

> Author of a valuable historical survey of variation forms, and colleague of Schoenberg at UCLA, Nelson presents fascinating new material.

Newlin, Dika, *Bruckner, Mahler, Schönberg*, New York, 1947.

> An important book in its time, to be superseded by Newlin's extensive biography of Schoenberg, now in progress.

Ogdon, Wilbur Lee, *Series and Structure: an Investigation into the Purpose of the 12-Note Row in Selected Works of Schoenberg, Webern, Krenek, and Leibowitz*, Indiana University diss., 1956.

> As pupil of Leibowitz, Ogdon presents a clear contrast between Leibowitz's interpretations of the masters and Krenek's quite different ideas. To the present author this was new and liberating.

Paz, Juan Carlos, *Arnold Schönberg, o, el fin de la era tonal*, Buenos Aires, 1958.

Perle, George, *Schönberg's Late Style*, in MR, XIII (1952), 274.

—— *Serial Composition and Atonality: an Introduction to the Music of Schoenberg, Berg, and Webern*, Berkeley, 1962.

> Based on a diss. (N.Y. Univ., 1956) and on experience as a composer, this book makes a clear distinction between its original ideas and those of the masters.

—— *Pierrot Lunaire*, in G. Reese and R. Brandel, eds., *The Commonwealth of Music*, New York, 1964, p. 307.

> Assembles facts and presents them very neatly, with little comment except that the piece "remains problematical."

Pfannkuch, Wilhelm, *Zu Thematik und Form in Schönbergs Streichsextett*, in A. A. Abert and W. Pfannkuch, eds., *Festschrift Friedrich Blume zum 70. Geburtstag*, Kassel, 1963, p. 258.

Pfrogner, Hermann, *Das Inhalt-Form-Problem im Schaffen Arnold Schönbergs*, in ÖMz, II (1947), 266.

—— *Die Zwölfordnung der Töne*, Zürich, 1953.

　　　Pfrogner contrasts the theory and practice of Schoenberg and Hauer with the manifold scales in which enharmonic changes and ambiguities play an important part. His historical perspective, embracing ancient Chinese theory, helped shape the present author's view.

—— *Zum Tonalitätsbegriff unserer Zeit*, in *Musica*, XVI (1962), 185.

　　　Pfrogner's discussion of this vexed topic is unusually clear and comprehensive. The article can serve as introduction to his far-ranging ideas, more amply stated and defended in *Die Zwölfordnung der Töne*.

Plebe, Armando, ed., *La dodecafonia: documenti e pagine critiche*, Bari, 1962.

　　　Well-chosen anthology of materials by Schoenberg and many other authors.

Redlich, Hans F., *Schoenberg's Religious Testament*, in *Opera*, XVI (1965), 401.

Reich, Willi, *Der "Blaue Reiter" und die Musik*, in SMz, LXXXV (1945), 341.

—— *Versuch einer Geschichte der Zwölftonmusik*, in *Alte und neue Musik*, Zürich, 1952, p. 106.

　　　A pioneer compilation.

—— *Zur Geschichte der Zwölftonmusik*, in H. Federhofer, ed., *Festschrift Alfred Orel zum 70. Geburtstag*, Vienna, 1960, p. 151.

Reti, Rudolph, *The Thematic Process in Music*, New York, 1951.

　　　Controversial "discoveries" of unity among movements in sonatas and symphonies by Beethoven et al. As pupil of Schoenberg, Reti reveals and disseminates some of his thought.

—— *Tonality, Atonality, Pantonality: a Study of Some Trends in 20th-Century Music*, New York, 1958.

　　　Reti proposes special definitions of his terms that are worth learning for the sake of his fairly comprehensive yet critical panorama.

Rubsamen, Walter H., *Schoenberg in America*, in MQ, XXXVII (1951), 469.

Rufer, Josef, *Komposition mit zwölf Töne*, Berlin, 1952; English transl. by H. Searle, as *Composition with Twelve Notes*, London, 1954.

　　　Exposition of Schoenberg's technique, supplemented with brief testimonies from other living composers.

—— *Das Werk Arnold Schönbergs*, Kassel, 1959; English transl. by Dika Newlin, as *The Works of Arnold Schoenberg*, New York, 1963.

　　　Fundamental book for scholarly purposes. The English version includes some additions and corrections.

—— *Schönberg—gestern, heute, und morgen*, in SMz, CV (1965), 190.

Schaeffner, André, *Variations Schoenberg*, in *Contrepoints*, VII (1950), 110.

　　　On the poems of *Pierrot Lunaire*, on Debussy's knowledge of Schoenberg, and related topics.

Scherchen, Hermann, *Arnold Schönberg*, in *Melos*, I (1920), 9.

Schoenberg, Arnold, *Aphorismen*, in *Die Musik*, IX/4 (1910), 159.

—— *Harmonielehre*, Vienna, 1911; 3d rev. edn., 1922; 4th edn., 1956; abridged English transl. by R. D. W. Adams, as *Theory of Harmony*, New York, 1948.

—— *Eine neue Zwölftonschrift*, in *Anbruch*, VII (1925), 1.

　　　Proposes a notation that avoids reference to diatonic scales, and an international society to promote this notation.

—— *Art and the Moving Picture*, in *California Arts and Architecture*, LVII (Apr. 1940), 12.

　　　Schoenberg recalls hearing Wagner's operas 20 to 30 times each.

—— *Models for Beginners in Composition*, New York, 1943.

—— [Notes for recording of *Pelleas und Melisande*], Capitol Records P 8069 (issued c. 1950).

—— *Style and Idea*, New York, 1950.

　　　Collected essays, including *Heart and Brain* and *Composition with Twelve Tones*.

—— *My Evolution*, in MQ, XXXVIII (1952), 512.
—— *Structural Functions of Harmony*, ed. by H. Searle, New York, 1954.
—— [Notes on his quartets], quoted in notes for Columbia Records ML 4735–37 (issued c. 1955).
—— *Briefe*, ed. by E. Stein, Mainz, 1958; English transl. as *Letters*, New York, 1965.
> The English version includes 15 letters not available to Stein; especially interesting are those of 1944 to A. J. Twa, of 1945 to Leibowitz, and of 1950 to Thor Johnson and to Robert Craft.
—— *The Orchestral Variations, Op. 31, A Radio Talk [1931]*, in *The Score*, 27 (1960), 27.
—— *Preliminary Exercises in Counterpoint*, ed. by L. Stein, London, 1963.
—— *Schöpferische Konfessionen*, ed. by Willi Reich, Zürich, 1964.
> Includes some brief articles not readily accessible elsewhere.
Schuller, Gunther, *A Conversation with Steuermann*, in PNM, III/1 (1964), 22.
> Recollections of Schoenberg and Webern by the pianist closest to them.
Somigli, Carlo, *Il Modus operandi di Arnold Schoenberg*, in *Rivista musicale italiana*, XX (1913), 583.
> Based on close study of the scores from Op. 1 to Op. 11, this critique concludes that Schoenberg's *dodecafonia* aptly expresses his rejection of love, and his concern with hitherto unexpressed feelings.
Stein, Erwin, *Einige Bemerkungen zu Schönbergs Zwölftonreihen*, in *Anbruch*, VIII (1926), 251.
—— *Zu Schönbergs neuer Suite Op. 29*, in *Anbruch*, IX (1927), 280.
> Interesting studies not included in *Orpheus in New Guises*.
—— *Orpheus in New Guises*, London, 1953.
> Collected essays. Pp. 55–77 is *New Formal Principles*, from *Anbruch*, 1924, promulgating Schoenberg's 12-tone technique.
Steiner, George, *Schoenberg's "Moses and Aaron,"* in *Encounter*, XXIV/6 (July 1965), 40.
> A literary critic's enthusiasm surpasses that of most musicians.
Steiner, Rudolf, *Der unbekannte Schönberg: aus unveröffentlichten Briefen an Hans Nachod*, in SMz, CIV (1964), 284.
—— and Ena Steiner, *Arnold Schoenberg: an Unknown Correspondence*, in *Saturday Review*, Mar. 27, 1965, p. 47.
> An account of the letters, and also the early music of Schoenberg, acquired by the Steiners from his cousin Hans Nachod.
Stephan, Rudolf, *Zur jüngsten Geschichte des Melodramas*, in AfMw, XVII (1960), 183.
> Survey of *Sprechstimme* from Humperdinck to Fortner and Boulez. Stephan believes Schoenberg heard Humperdinck's *Königskinder* in Vienna in 1897.
Stravinsky, Igor, *Schoenberg Speaks his Mind*, in *The Observer* (London), Oct. 18, 1964, p. 26; as *Schoenberg's Letters*, in *High Fidelity*, XV/5 (May 1965), 136.
Stuckenschmidt, Hans Heinz, *Arnold Schönberg*, Zürich, 1951; 2d enl. edn., 1957; English transl. by E. T. Roberts and H. Searle, New York, 1960.
—— *Stil und Ästhetik Schoenbergs*, in SMz, XCVIII (1958), 97.
—— *Kandinsky und Schönberg*, in *Melos*, XXXI (1964), 209.
—— *Luft von anderen Planeten*, in *Melos*, XXXII (1965), 109.
Tenschert, Roland, *Eine Passacaglia von Arnold Schoenberg: Studie zur modernen Kompositionstechnik*, in *Die Musik*, XVII (1925), 590.
> Analysis of *Nacht* from *Pierrot Lunaire*.
Thomson, Virgil, *How Dead is Schoenberg?*, in *The New York Review of Books*, Apr. 22, 1965, p. 6.
Vinaver, Chemjo, *Anthology of Jewish Music*, New York, 1955.
> Introductory note to Schoenberg's Psalm includes quotations from his letters.
Vlad, Roman, *Storia della dodecafonia*, Milan, 1958.
> Careful comparative study of the music, not misled by slogans, with many musical examples usable by readers ignorant of Italian.
Wadler, Mayo, *An American's Impression of Schoenberg*, in *The Musical Leader*, XLIX (1925), 570.
> Interview. Asked whether he listened to the music of his contemporaries, Schoenberg

replied, "No, but do they really matter?" About art for the people: "Not until the arts ally themselves with some great religious revival."

Walker, Alan, *Schönberg's Classical Background*, in MR, XIX (1958), 283.

> Walker finds "degree-rows" in works of Mozart, K. 387, 491, 516, and Beethoven, Op. 132.

Webern, Anton, *Über Arnold Schönberg*, in *Rheinische Musik- und Theater-Zeitung*, XIII (1912), 99, 118; as *Schönbergs Musik*, in Berg et al., eds., *Arnold Schönberg*, Munich, 1912, p. 22.

> Important essay, with 18 musical examples.

Wellesz, Egon, *Schoenberg et la jeune école viennoise*, in BSIM, VIII/3 (March 1912), 21.

—— *Schoenberg and Beyond*, transl. by Otto Kinkeldey, in MQ, II (1916), 76.

> These early studies are still useful.

—— *Arnold Schönberg*, Leipzig, 1921; English transl. by W. H. Kerridge, London, 1925.

> Pioneer study.

—— *The Origins of Schönberg's Twelve-Tone System*, Washington, D.C., 1958.

> An interesting lecture, crediting Hauer and Webern with influence on Schoenberg. Wellesz's belated testimony, however, refers to a time when he was no longer close to his former teacher.

—— *Schönberg und die Anfänge der Wiener Schule*, in ÖMz, XV (1960), 237.

> Wellesz says that he and Reti conceived the ISCM as an expansion of Schoenberg's *Verein*.

Wörner, Karl H., *Gotteswort und Magie: Die Oper "Moses und Aron" von Arnold Schönberg*, Heidelberg, 1959; English transl. by Paul Hamburger, as *Schoenberg's "Moses and Aaron,"* New York, 1964.

—— *Arnold Schoenberg and the Theater*, in MQ, XLVIII (1962), 444.

> Critical survey, placing *Moses* at the "peak of Schoenberg's creative activity."

—— *"Die glückliche Hand," Arnold Schönbergs Drama mit Musik*, in SMz, CIV (1964), 274.

> Helpful new appraisal.

Yates, Peter, [Notes on Schoenberg's quartets], Alco Records ALP 1002–5 (issued c. 1950).

—— *Moses and Aron by Schoenberg*, in *Arts and Architecture*, LXXV/9 (Sept. 1958), 4 and LXXV/10 (Oct.), 6.

Zillig, Winfried, *Notes on "Die Jakobsleiter,"* in *The Score*, 25 (June 1959), 7.

> Zillig prepared the first performance from Schoenberg's incomplete ms. and sketches. He reports the projected orchestration.

SCHREKER

Neuwirth, Gösta, *Franz Schreker*, Vienna, 1959.

> Summary in MGG, XII (1965), 73, no better than Redlich's article in *Grove*[5], VII, 529. But the emphasis of the book is interesting, e.g.: "his position is unique among German-speaking composers because he . . . chooses the French solution for the problem of tonality but always stays in touch with atonality" (p. 11).

SCHUMAN

Schreiber, Flora Rheta, and Vincent Persichetti, *William Schuman*, New York, 1954.

SCHWEITZER

Joy, Charles R., *Music in the Life of Albert Schweitzer, with Selections from his Writings*, New York, 1951.

Müller-Blattau, Joseph, *Albert Schweitzers Weg zur Bach-Orgel und zu einer neuen Bach-Auffassung*, in H. W. Bähr, ed., *Albert Schweitzer, sein Denken und sein Weg*, Tübingen, 1962, p. 243.

> The most important musical article in a *Festschrift* of distinguished essays; other contributions, by Leo Schrade and Hans Keller, concentrate on Schweitzer's book on Bach.

Quoika, Rudolph, *Albert Schweitzers Begegnung mit der Orgel*, Berlin, 1954.

Schweitzer, Albert, *Deutsche und französische Orgelbaukunst und Orgelkunst*, Leipzig, 1906; English transl., with 1927 epilogue, as *German and French Organ Building and Organ Playing*, in C. Joy, *Music in the Life of Albert Schweitzer*, New York, 1951, p. 138.

SCOTT

Blom, Eric, *Scott,* in *Grove*[5], VII, 665.
> The editor of *Grove*[5] wrote this new article himself. It is the chief source of information on Scott's music.

Hurd, Michael, *Scott,* in MGG, XII (1964), 430.
> Despite the grave weaknesses of Scott's music, Hurd concludes that "his big works by no means deserve the neglect that they have met with."

Scott, Cyril M., *The Philosophy of Modernism (In Its Connection With Music),* London, 1917.

—— *My Years of Indiscretion,* London, 1924.
> Fascinating memoirs of the turn of the century in Frankfurt, London, Paris, etc.

—— *The Influence of Music on History and Morals: a Vindication of Plato,* London, 1928; rev. and ext. edn. as *Music: its Secret Influence Throughout the Ages,* London, 1958.

—— *Die Tragödie Stefan Georges,* Eltville-am-Rhein, 1952.
> Further revelations from the turn of the century.

SCRIABIN

Abraham, Gerald, *Scriabin,* in M. D. Calvocoressi and G. Abraham, *Masters of Russian Music,* New York, 1936, p. 450.
> Fine 48-page biography, collating and criticizing the first-hand reports of Sabaneiev, Schloezer, et al. Abraham's knowledge of the music informs his treatment of the man.

Alschwang, A., *Die Stellung Skrjabins in der Geschichte,* in *Beiträge zur Musikwissenschaft,* VI (1964), 143.
> Sensible account of Scriabin's relations to Liszt, Debussy, Schoenberg, Busoni, Miaskovsky, Shostakovich, Shaporin, et al.

Danilevich, Lev Vasilievich, *Alexander Nikolajewitsch Skrjabin,* transl. by Margarete Hoffmann, Leipzig, 1954.

—— *S Pustia polveka,* in SM, XXIX/4 (1965), 82.
> Renewed concern for Scriabin on the 50th anniversary of his death.

Dickenmann, Paul, *Die Entwicklung der Harmonik bei A. Skrjabin,* Bern, 1935.
> Despite the title, no development is traced, but rather devices used up to Op. 60 are catalogued.

Gleich, Clemens-Christoph von, *Die sinfonischen Werke von Alexander Skrjabin,* Bilthoven, 1963.
> Gleich prints Scriabin's 369-verse *Poem of Ecstasy,* and suggests correspondences between it and the music with the same title. Otherwise he offers no new evidence to support his plea that Scriabin's orchestral music be given more attention than it has yet received. Gleich's article in MGG, XII (1965), 751, is a fine survey.

Hull, Arthur Eaglefield, *A Survey of the Pianoforte Works of Scriabin,* in MQ, II (1916), 601.

—— *A Great Russian Tone-Poet, Scriabin,* London, 1918.

Lissa, Zofia, *Do genezy "akordu prometejskiego" A. N. Skriabina,* in *Muzyka,* IV/2 (1959), 86; German transl. as *Zur Genesis des "Prometheischen Akkords" bei A. N. Skrjabin,* in *Musik des Ostens,* II (1963), 170.
> Tracing a line from Chopin through Scriabin to Szymanowski, Lissa pursues studies that should eventually make a book on Scriabin.

Pasternak, Boris, *I Remember: Sketch for an Autobiography,* New York, 1959.

—— *Ich kannte Skrjabin,* in *Melos,* XXVI (1959), 39.
> Not quite the same material.

Sabaneiev, Leonid Leonidovich, *Prometheus von Skrjabin,* in *Der blaue Reiter,* Munich, 1912, p. 57; also in *Melos,* I (1920), 479.

—— *Skriabin,* Moscow, 1916; 2d edn., 1923.

—— *Vospominaniia o Skriabine,* Moscow, 1925.

—— *Scriabin and the Idea of a Religious Art,* in MT, LXXII (1931), 789.
> Sabaneiev, temporarily in revolt against his teacher Taneiev, became a leading disciple of Scriabin, but later defected.

Schloezer, Boris de, *Scriabin,* in RM, II (1921), 28.

—— *Alexandre Scriabine,* in P. Souvtchinsky, *La Musique russe,* Paris, 1953, II, 229.
> Scriabin's friend gathered his opinions of Debussy, Stravinsky, and Schoenberg.

Scriabin, Alexander Nikolaievich, *Prometheische Phantasien*, transl. and ed. by Oskar Riesemann, Stuttgart, 1924.

SEARLE

Rayment, Malcolm, *Searle, Avant-Garde or Romantic?*, in MT, CV (1964), 430.
> Especially concerned with the four symphonies (1952–62). Supplements Rayment's article in MGG, XII (1965), 440.

Searle, Humphrey, *20th-Century Counterpoint: a Guide for Students*, London, 1954.
> Well-meant but superficial discussion of the practices of Stravinsky, Milhaud, Hindemith, Bartók, Schoenberg, and "some independents."

SEIBER

Ránki, György, *Seiber Mátyás (portré)*, in *Magyar Zene*, I (1960), 431.
Seiber, Mátyás, *Jazz als Erziehungsmittel*, in *Melos*, VII (1928), 281.
—— *Jazz-Instrumente, Jazz-Klang, und neue Musik*, in *Melos*, IX (1930), 122.
Weissmann, John S., *Mátyás Seiber: Style and Technique*, in *The Listener*, XLV (1951), 476.
—— *Die Streichquartette von Mátyás Seiber*, in *Melos*, XXII (1955), 344, and XXIII (1956), 38.
> Along with Weissmann's ample article in MGG, XII (1965), 468, these essays provide a good introduction.

SESSIONS

Boretz, Benjamin, *Current Chronicle*, in MQ, XLVII (1961), 386.
Carter, Elliott, *Current Chronicle*, in MQ, XLV (1959), 375.
Daniel, Oliver, et al., *Roger Sessions*, New York, 1965.
> Unpaged brochure, with pictures and catalogue.

Imbrie, Andrew, *Roger Sessions, in Honor of his 65th Birthday*, in PNM, I/1 (1962), 117.
> Analyzes passages from the Violin Concerto (1935) and the Quintet (1958). Compare M. Boykan on Imbrie, in PNM, III/1 (1964), 139.

Sessions, Roger, *Music in Crisis*, in MM, X/2 (1933), 63.
—— *New Vistas in Musical Education*, in MM, XI (1934), 115.
—— *The Musical Experience of Composer, Performer, Listener*, Princeton, 1950.
—— *Reflections on the Music Life in the United States*, New York, 1956.
> Includes autobiographical bits.

—— *Problems and Issues Facing the Composer Today*, in MQ, XLVI (1960), 159.
> A sample of Sessions's later technical reflections.

SHAPORIN

Grigoriev, S., *Nekotorye cherty stilia i muzykal'nogo iazyka IU. Shaporina*, in S. S. Skrebkov, ed., *Muzykal'no-teoreticheskie problemy*, Moscow, 1963, p. 3.
> Some traits of style and musical language in Shaporin.

Levit, Sofia Iosifosna, *Iurii Aleksandrovich Shaporin: ocherk zhizni i tvorchestva*, Moscow, 1964.
> An unusually handsome and careful book.

SHARP

Fox-Strangways, A. H., and Maud Karpeles, *Cecil Sharp*, London, 1933; 2d edn., 1955.

SHAW, C.

Drew, David, *Christopher Shaw*, in MT, CIV (1963), 479.

SHEPHERD

Loucks, Richard N., *Arthur Shepherd*, Eastman School of Music diss., 1960.
> Includes virtually all of Shepherd's music. Brief summary in MGG, XII (1965), 636.

Newman, William S., *Arthur Shepherd*, in MQ, XXXVI (1950), 159.

SHOSTAKOVICH

Berger, Liubov Grigorievna, ed., *Cherty stilia D. Shostakovicha: sbornik teoreticheskikh statei*, Moscow, 1962.
> Unrivalled collection of studies of Shostakovich's style, packed with interesting observations and hinting at far-ranging questions. Less satisfying than the similar volume on Prokofiev only because of the nature of the case.

Bobrovsky, Viktor Petrovich, *Kamernye instrumental'nye ansambli D. Shostakovicha*, Moscow, 1961.
—— *Pesni i khori D. Shostakovicha*, Moscow, 1962.
    Hasty surveys of Shostakovich's chamber music and vocal music.
—— *Pretvorenie zhanra passacal'i v sonatno-simfonicheskikh tsiklakh D. Shostakovicha*, in T. Lebedeva, ed., *Muzyka i sovremennost'*, Moscow, 1962, p. 149.
    Transformation of the passacaglia type in the sonatas and symphonies of Shostakovich.
Brockhaus, Heinz Alfred, *Dmitri Schostakowitsch*, Leipzig, 1962.
    By-product of a diss. (Berlin, 1962) on Shostakovich's symphonies.
Danilevich, Lev Vasilievich, *D. D. Shostakovich*, Moscow, 1958.
    Uncritical biography, containing some information not elsewhere available.
Dolzhansky, A., *O ladovoi osnove sochinennii Shostakovicha*, in SM, 1947/4, p. 65.
    Based on a diss. (1945), this is the first of many articles analyzing the peculiar scales and interlocked pairs of scales used by Shostakovich.
—— *Iz nabliudenii nad stilem Shostakovicha*, in SM, 1959/10, p. 95.
    Some observations on Shostakovich's style, especially harmony.
Gow, David, *Shostakovich's "War" Symphonies*, in MT, CV (1964), 191.
    Symphonies VII to IX, viewed as a sort of trilogy.
Kay, Norman, *The Art of Shostakovich*, in *Music & Musicians*, XIII/8 (Apr. 1965), 20.
    Calm and sympathetic survey, taking for granted the importance of Shostakovich's best music, and briefly, dispassionately considering his relation to Soviet ideology.
Martynov, Ivan Ivanovich, *Shostakovich, the Man and his Work*, transl. by T. Guralsky, New York, 1947.
    Originally published in Moscow, 1946, this enthusiastic introduction was translated also into French and German. It long provided material for most Western commentary. Superseded by Rabinovich et al.
Mason, Colin, *Form in Shostakovich's Quartets*, in MT, CIII (1962), 531.
Mazel', Lev Abramovich, *O traktovke sonatnoi formy i tsikla v bolshykh simfoniiakh D. Shostakovicha*, in S. S. Skrebkov, ed., *Muzykal'no-teoreticheskie problemy*, Moscow, 1963, p. 60.
    On the treatment of sonata form and of the sonata cycle in Shostakovich's major symphonies. See also Mazel's general works.
Oistrakh, David, *Voploshchenie bol'shogo zamysla (O skripichnom kontserte Shostakovicha)*, in SM, 1956/7, p. 3.
    "The incarnation of a great purpose." Shostakovich's Violin Concerto viewed by the great violinist who first performed it. A translation in *Kunst und Literatur*, IV (1956), has been unavailable to the present writer.
Orlov, Genrikh Aleksandrovich, *Simfonii Shostakovicha*, Leningrad, 1961.
    Extended program-notes for the 12 symphonies.
Ottaway, Hugh, *Shostakovich: Some Later Works*, in *Tempo*, 50 (1959), 2.
    Praise for the Violin Concerto and for the "consistency and stability" shown throughout the 1950s.
Rabinovich, D., *Dmitry Shostakovich, Composer*, Moscow, 1959.
    Brief and uncritical, but up-to-date.
Sabinina, Marina Dmitrievna, *Cheremushki, Moskva*, in SM, 1959/4, p. 41; German transl. in *Kunst und Literatur*, VII (1959), 774.
—— *Simfonizm Shostakovicha*, Moscow, 1965.
Seroff, Victor I., *Dmitri Shostakovich* (in collaboration with Nadejda Galli-Shchat, aunt of the composer), New York, 1943.
Shostakovich, Dmitri Dmitrievich, *My Opera Lady Macbeth of Mtzensk*, in MM, XII (1934), 23; also in U. Weisstein, ed., *The Essence of Opera*, New York, 1964, p. 345.

SIBELIUS
Abraham, Gerald, ed., *The Music of Sibelius*, New York, 1947.
    Collection of scholarly articles.
Borg, Kim, *Zur internationalen Verbreitung der Lieder von Sibelius*, in ÖMz, XX (1965), 153.
    A great singer recommends especially Opp. 34/4 & 6, 37/4, 38/1 & 2, 50/5 (Dehmel), 60/1 (Shakespeare), and 90/1.

Desmond, Astra, *The Songs*, in G. Abraham, ed., *The Music of Sibelius*, New York, 1947, p. 108.

Ekman, Karl, *Jean Sibelius, his Life and Personality*, London, 1936.
  Chief source of biographical information.

Gray, Cecil, *Sibelius*, 2d edn., London, 1934.
  Widely read and admired in England and America, this book is superseded by Ringbom, Johnson, et al., and more specifically corrected by S. M. Collins, *Germ Motives and Guff*, in MR, XXIII (1962), 238.

Jalas, Margareta, ed., *Jean Sibelius*, Helsinki, 1958.
  Booklet of good pictures.

Johnson, Harold E., *Jean Sibelius: the Recorded Music*, Helsinki, 1957.
—— *Jean Sibelius*, New York, 1959.
  Scholarly and critical study of the life and works.

Matter, Jean, *Sibelius et Debussy*, in SMz, CV (1965), 82.
  Points to similarities between Sibelius's Fourth and Debussy's *Nuages* and *La Mer*, and indicates the need for further study.

Mellers, Wilfrid H., *Sibelius and "the Modern Mind,"* in *Music Survey*, 1 (1949), 177.
  An unusual interpretation, taken up again in Mellers's *Romanticism and the 20th Century*.

Parmet, Simon, *Sibelius symfonier: en studie i musikförståelse*, Helsinki, 1955; English transl. by K. A. Hart, as *The Symphonies of Sibelius: a Study in Musical Appreciation*, London, 1959.
  Important book, begun in the 1930s and put aside because some of Parmet's questions made Sibelius "uneasy."
—— *Sibelius und seine Generation*, in ÖMz, XX (1965), 157.
  Parmet discusses the relations between Sibelius and his Finnish contemporaries, then very succinctly the various reactions of two later generations of composers to this group.

Ringbom, Nils-Eric, *Jean Sibelius*, transl. by G. I. C. de Courcy, Norman, Okla., 1954.
  The foremost specialist on Sibelius's style, Ringbom does not claim that his book is definitive. His article in MGG, XII (1965), 652, supplements the book, especially with an immense list of other books and articles.

Rosas, John, *Otryckta kammarmusikverk av Jean Sibelius*, Åbo, 1961.
  Studies 14 unpublished works, 1885–91.

Sibelius, Jean, *Käsikirjoituksia. Manuskript. Manuscripts. From the Archives of Oy R. E. Westerlund, A.B.*, Helsinki, 1945.
  Facsimiles from 12 pieces, 1895–1925, with commentary by Eino Roiha, in Finnish, Swedish, and English.

Tanzberger, Ernst, *Jean Sibelius: eine Monographie*, Wiesbaden, 1962.
  Interesting chiefly as evidence of a new range of interest in Sibelius, though based on an old diss. (Jena, 1942).

Tawaststjerna, Erik, *The Pianoforte Compositions of Sibelius*, Helsinki, 1957; longer version, in Finnish, as *Sibeliuksen pianoteokset*, Helsinki, 1960.
  Tawaststjerna defends pieces that are dismissed abruptly by other students of Sibelius.

Werba, Erik, *Sibelius—ein grosser Europäer*, in ÖMz, XX (1965), 144.

Whittall, Arnold, *Sibelius's Eighth Symphony*, in MR, XXV (1964), 239.
  I.e., *Tapiola*.

SKALKOTTAS

Keller, Hans, *Nikos Skalkottas: an Original Genius*, in *The Listener*, LII (1954), 1041.
  See also Cosman and Keller, *Stravinsky at Rehearsal*, London, 1962.

Papaioannou, John G., *Nikos Skalkottas*, in H. Hartog, ed., *European Music in the 20th Century*, London, 1957, p. 320.
  Chief source of information. Summary in MGG, XII (1965), 744.

SMYTH

St. John, Christopher, *Ethel Smyth: a Biography*, London, 1959.
  Definitive and charming; Kathleen Dale contributes a chapter, *Ethel Smyth's Music: a Critical Study*, with no indulgence.

SOLOVIOV-SEDOI

Kremliev, Iulii Anatolievich, *Vasilii Pavlovich Soloviov-Sedoi: ocherk zhizni i tvorchestva*, Leningrad, 1960.

SONNECK

Engel, Carl, *Oscar G. Sonneck*, in MQ, XXV (1939), 2.
Kinkeldey, Otto, *Oscar George Theodore Sonneck*, in NotesMLA, XI (1954), 25.

SORABJI

Browne, Arthur G., *The Music of Kaikhosru Sorabji*, in ML, XI (1930), 6.
Rubbra, Edmund, *Sorabji's Enigma*, in MMR, LXII (1932), 148.
Sorabji, Kaikhosru, *Oriental Influences in Contemporary Music*, in *The Chesterian*, 3 (1919), 83.
  Sorabji contrasts the superficial Orientalism of Rimsky, Bantock, and Scott with the profound and pervasive influence in the work of Debussy, Ravel, Roussel, et al.

SOWERBY

Tuthill, Burnet C., *Leo Sowerby*, in MQ, XXIV (1938), 249.
  Chief source of information, except for an M.A. diss. by R. M. Huntington (Univ. of Southern California, 1957), cited by Hans Tischler in MGG, XII (1965), 946.

SPENDIAROV

Spendiarova, Marina, *Spendiarov*, Moscow, 1964.

STAĬNOV

Krŭstev, Venelin, *Petko Staĭnov*, Sofia, 1957.
  Includes summary in French.

STENHAMMER

Wallner, Bo, *Wilhelm Stenhammer och kammarmusiken*, in *Svensk Tidskrift för Musikforskning*, XXXIV (1952), 28; XXXV (1953), 5.
—— *Wilhelm Stenhammer's stråkkvartettskisser*, in *Svensk Tidskrift för Musikforskning*, XLIII (1961), 355.

STEPHAN

Holl, Karl, *Das lyrische Schaffen Rudi Stephans*, in *Melos*, II (1921), 157.
—— *Rudi Stephan*, in *Melos*, VII (1928), 121.
—— *Gedenken an Rudi Stephan*, in NZfM, CXXVI (1965), 339.
  Fine brief survey, illustrated with a portrait and facsimile of manuscript.

STILL

Goss, Madeleine Binkley, *Modern Music Makers: Contemporary American Composers*, New York, 1952.
  Biographical material, valuable for several figures like Still.
William Grant Still. Classified Chronological Catalog, in *Composers of the Americas*, V (1958), 85.

STOCKHAUSEN

Cadieu, Martine, *Duo avec Stockhausen*, in *Nouvelles littéraires*, June 15, 1961, p. 9.
  "He reminded me of a sorcerer's apprentice."
Scherchen, Hermann, *Stockhausen and Time*, in *Gravesaner Blätter*, IV/13 (1959), 29.
Schnebel, Dieter, *Karlheinz Stockhausen*, in *Die Reihe*, IV (1958), 119; in English edn., IV (1960), 121.
  Concerned especially with Stockhausen's discontinuity of development, and his continuous fresh efforts "to formulate the historical moment."
Stockhausen, Karlheinz, *Musik in Funktion*, in *Melos*, XXIV (1957), 249; also in H. Lindlar, ed., *Die Stimme der Komponisten*, Rodenkirchen, 1948, p. 146; French transl., as *Musique fonctionelle*, in *Avec Stravinsky*, Monaco, 1958, p. 92.
  A good introduction to Stockhausen's thought.
—— *Musique dans l'espace*, in *Revue belge de musicologie*, XIII (1959), 76.
—— *Musik und Sprache*, in *Die Reihe*, VI (1960), 36; in English edn., VI (1964), 40.
  Copious examples, especially from Boulez's *Marteau*, Nono's *Canto sospeso*, and Stockhausen's *Gesang der Jünglinge*.
—— *The Concept of Unity in Electronic Music*, in PNM, I/1 (1962), 39.

—— *Invention et découverte*, in *La Musique et ses problèmes*, Paris, 1963, p. 147.

> "To establish the equilibrium between the creative and the conservative forces of the spirit will always remain the necessary task. The true Utopia is balance." A volume of collected texts and essays (Cologne, 1964) will presumably enable students to see more clearly Stockhausen's effort toward balance.

Wörner, Karl H., *Karlheinz Stockhausen: Werk und Wollen, 1950–1962*, Rodenkirchen, 1963.

> Much more readable than most of Stockhausen's own writings, and thoroughly fascinating.

STRAUSS, R.

Dahlhaus, Carl, *Richard Strauss und der Opernruhm*, in *Opernwelt*, V/6 (June 1964), 10.

> Centenary summing-up by a scholar not specializing in Strauss but thoroughly informed.

Del Mar, Norman, *Richard Strauss: a Critical Commentary on his Life and Works*, Vol. I, London, 1962.

> Most detailed study in English, still incomplete in many ways.

—— *Some Centenary Reflections*, in *Tempo*, 69 (1964), 2.

> Draft of a concluding appraisal.

Drew, David, *Late Strauss*, in *The New Statesman & Nation*, Feb. 12, 1965, p. 254.

> A sample of Drew's lively journalism. Here he recommends *Intermezzo* above *Arabella* as a perfect realization of Strauss's most distinctive aims.

Fähnrich, Hermann, *Richard Strauss über das Verhältnis von Dichtung und Musik (Wort und Ton) in seinem Opernschaffen*, in Mf, XIV (1961), 22.

Gould, Glenn, *An Argument for Strauss*, in *Records & Recording*, VII/9 (June 1964), 11.

Grasberger, Franz, et al., *Ausstellungskatalog der Wiener Richard Strauss-Ausstellung*, Vienna, 1964.

Kende, Götz Klaus, *Richard Strauss und Clemens Krauss: eine Künstlerfreundschaft und ihre Zusammenarbeit an "Capriccio,"* Munich, 1960.

Lehmann, Lotte, *Five Operas and Richard Strauss*, transl. by E. Pavel, New York, 1964.

> Priceless notes on interpreting the role of the Marschallin in *Rosenkavalier* and interesting reminiscences of other works, padded with plot summaries.

Lorenz, Alfred, *Der formale Schwung in R. Strauss' "Till Eulenspiegel,"* in *Die Musik*, XVII (1925), 658.

Mann, William, *Richard Strauss: a Critical Study of the Operas*, London, 1964.

> Expert, up-to-date, readable as a whole, and useful for reference.

Mueller von Asow, Erich Hermann, *Richard Strauss: thematisches Verzeichnis*, Vienna, 1955– .

> Monumental and meticulous work, modelled on the great Köchel catalogue of Mozart, including discographies; not yet completed.

Ortner, Oswald, *Richard Strauss-Bibliographie, Teil I, 1882–1944*, ed. by Franz Grasberger, Vienna, 1964.

> Classified list of 1763 items.

Richard Strauss Jahrbuch, ed. by W. Schuh, Bonn, 1954– .

Samazeuilh, Gustave, *Richard Strauss as I knew Him*, in *Tempo*, 60 (1964), 14.

Schuh, Willi, *Zur harmonischen Deutung des "Salome"-Schlusses*, in SMz, LXXXVI (1946), 452.

> Sample of Schuh's excellent and voluminous writings on Strauss, of which a recent summary is in MGG, XII (1965), 1474.

Strauss, Richard, *Betrachtungen und Erinnerungen*, ed. by Willi Schuh, Zürich, 1949; English transl. by L. J. Lawrence, as *Recollections and Reflections*, London, 1953; 2d enl. edn. in German, Zürich, 1957.

> Fine collection of scattered brief writings.

—— *Briefe an die Eltern, 1882–1906*, ed. by Willi Schuh, Zürich, 1954.

—— *Über mein Schaffen: eine bisher unveröffentlichte Skizze*, in ÖMz, XIX (1964), 221.

> Dating from 1892, this eloquent discussion of technique vs. inspiration is relevant to Strauss's later music, and indeed to that of most other composers.

—— and Hans von Bülow, *Correspondence*, transl. by A. Gishford, London, 1955.

—— and Josef Gregor, *Briefwechsel 1934–1949*, Salzburg, 1955.

—— and Hugo von Hofmannsthal, *Briefwechsel: Gesamtausgabe*, Zürich, 1952; 3d rev. edn., 1964; English transl. as *A Working Friendship*, New York, 1961.

    The 1964 edition fills in many gaps, especially names, left out in earlier editions.

—— and Romain Rolland, *Correspondance; fragments de journal*, Paris, 1951.

—— and Franz Wüllner, *Briefwechsel*, ed. by D. Kämper, Cologne, 1963.

—— and Stefan Zweig, *Briefwechsel*, Frankfurt, 1957.

Tenschert, Roland, *Versuch einer Typologie der Strauss'schen Melodik*, in ZfMw, XVI (1934), 274.

    85 musical examples with sensible observations about them.

Trenner, Franz, ed., *Richard Strauss: Dokumente seines Lebens und Schaffens*, Munich, 1954. Convenient and reliable.

Wachten, Edmund, *Der einheitliche Grundzug der Strauss'schen Formgestaltung*, in ZfMw, XVI (1934), 257.

    Part of a diss. (Berlin, 1930). Beginning with the treatment of tonality, in which Wachten discerns a systematic procedure, and aiming towards an ineffable appreciation of character, this study is one of the most profound discussions of Strauss's music.

Wellesz, Egon, *Hofmannsthal und die Musik*, in Fiechtner, ed., *Hofmannsthal*, Vienna, 1949, p. 227.

    Wellesz reports comments that supplement the Hofmannsthal-Strauss correspondence, as well as comments on his own collaboration with the poet.

—— *Richard Strauss, 1864–1949*, in MR, XI (1950), 23.

    Extraordinarily acute summing-up, based on much first-hand knowledge and much patient study. Includes report of Schoenberg's amazement at *Salome*.

STRAVINSKY

Ansermet, Ernest, *Igor Stravinsky, the Man and his Work: his First String Quartet*, in *Musical Courier*, LXXI/21 (Nov. 25, 1915), 41.

    The young math professor turned conductor was among Stravinsky's closest friends and best interpreters at this point.

—— *L'Œuvre d'Igor Stravinski*, in RM, V/9 (1921), 1.

    Earliest public statement of several important themes, including (pp. 22–23) the notion of "poles."

—— *Stravinsky's Gift to the West*, in *Dance Index*, VI/10–12 (1947), 235.

—— and J.-Claude Piguet, *Entretiens sur la musique*, Neuchâtel, 1963.

    Includes (pp. 86–99) discussion of Stravinsky—personal recollections from 1912, and detailed comparison of old and new versions of *Petrushka* and *The Rite of Spring*.

Armitage, Merle, ed., *Stravinsky*, New York, 1936.

Asafiev, Boris, *Kniga o Stravinskom*, Leningrad, 1929.

    Especially good on *The Wedding*. English transl. by R. F. French is eagerly awaited.

Avec Stravinsky. Textes d'Igor Stravinsky, R. Craft, P. Boulez, K. Stockhausen; *lettres inédites de C. Debussy, M. Ravel, E. Satie, D. Thomas; photographies d'A. Giacometti*, Monaco, 1958.

    Not completely matched in any English publication.

Babbitt, Milton, *Remarks on the Recent Stravinsky*, in PNM, II/2 (1964), 35.

Babitz, Sol, *Igor Stravinsky's Rhythmic Innovations*, in *International Musician*, XLVII/11 (May 1949), 22, 36.

Balanchine, George, *The Dance Element in Strawinsky's Music*, in *Dance Index*, VI/10–12 (1947), 250.

Beckwith, John, *A Stravinsky Triptych*, in CMJ, VI/4 (1962), 5.

    A good survey of the vocal works in English; a report of Stravinsky's visit to Toronto; a critique of recent books on Stravinsky.

Beliaiev, Viktor Mikhailovich, *Igor Stravinsky's "Les Noces": An Outline*, transl. by S. W. Pring, London, 1928.

—— *Kastalsky and Russian Folk Polyphony*, in ML, X (1929), 378.

    Translated by W. S. Pring, not written by him, as mistakenly indicated in the ML index and elsewhere. Beliaiev makes a tenuous link with Stravinsky's *Wedding*.

Berdyaev, Nicolas, *Towards a New Epoch*, London, 1949.

Blitzstein, Marc, *Towards a New Form*, in MQ, XX (1934), 213.

Boucourechliev, André, *Stravinski maintenant*, in *Preuves*, 140 (Oct. 1962), 70.

—— *"Boulez contre Karajan": deux enregistrements récents du "Sacre du Printemps,"* in *Preuves*, 167 (Jan. 1965), 74.

Boykan, Martin, *"Neoclassicism" and Late Stravinsky*, in PNM, I/2 (1963), 155.
   In *Movements* and *Sermon*, Boykan senses an "implicit tonal dialogue."

Boys, Henry, *Stravinsky: Critical Categories*, in *The Score*, 1 (1949), 3.

—— *Stravinsky: À propos his Aesthetic*, in *The Score*, 2 (1950), 61.

—— *Stravinsky: the Musical Materials*, in *The Score*, 4 (1951), 11.

Casella, Alfredo, *Igor Strawinski*, Rome, 1926; new edn. with added chapter by G. Barblán, Brescia, 1951.

Cingria, Charles-Albert, *"Perséphone" et la critique*, in *Nouvelle revue française*, XXII/43 (1934), 297.
   Good general remarks on Stravinsky, an appreciation of his then-latest work.

Citkowitz, Israel, *Stravinsky and Schoenberg: a Note on Syntax and Sensibility*, in *Juilliard Review*, I/3 (1954), 17.
   Not content with the simple "duel" metaphor of Casella, Citkowitz probes a deeper contrast.

Cocteau, Jean, *Journal d'un inconnu*, Paris, 1953; English transl. by Alec Brown as *The Hand of a Stranger*, London, 1956.

Cone, Edward T., *Stravinsky: The Progress of a Method*, in PNM, I/1 (1962), 18.

—— *The Uses of Convention: Stravinsky and his Models*, in MQ, XLVIII (1962), 287; also in P. H. Lang, ed., *Stravinsky*, New York, 1963, p. 21.

—— *From Sensuous Image to Musical Form*, in *The American Scholar*, XXXIII (1964), 448.

Corle, Edwin, ed., *Igor Stravinsky*, New York, 1949.

Cosman, Milein, and Hans Keller, *Stravinsky at Rehearsal*, London, 1962.
   Pencil sketches and a brief essay.

Craft, Robert, *Working Habits of Stravinsky*, in *Opera & Concert* (San Francisco), XVI (July 1951), 14.

—— *Stravinsky's Revisions*, in *Counterpoint*, 18 (1953), 14.

—— *Reflections on "The Rake's Progress,"* in *The Score*, 9 (1954), 24.

—— *Reihenkompositionen: vom "Septett" zum "Agon,"* in *Musik der Zeit*, I/12 (1955), 43.

—— [Notes for *Stravinsky: Chamber Works, 1911–1954*], Columbia Records ML 5107 (issued c. 1956).

—— *A Concert for St. Mark*, in *The Score*, 18 (1956), 35.

—— *Ein Ballett für 12 Tänzer*, in *Melos*, XXIV (1957), 284.
   Exact dates of Stravinsky's work on the various sections of *Agon*.

—— *The Composer and the Phonograph*, in *High Fidelity*, VII/6 (June 1957), 34.
   Surveys Stravinsky's uses of recordings from 1915 on.

—— *Le Musiche religiose di Igor Strawinsky*, Venice, 1957.

—— *A Note on Gesualdo's "Sacrae Cantiones" and on Gesualdo and Stravinsky*, in *Tempo*, 45 (1957), 5.

—— *Stravinsky, at 75, Is Still the Explorer*, in *The New York Times Magazine*, June 16, 1957, p. 8.

—— *Zwei Widmungen an Debussy*, in *Musik der Zeit*, 2. Folge, I (1958), 68.

Dahlhaus, Carl, *Die Tonalitätsbegriff in der neuen Musik*, in R. Stephan, ed., *Terminologie der neuen Musik*, Berlin, 1965, p. 83.
   Dense, logical, modestly constructive discussion, including helpful fresh observations about Stravinsky's *Canticum Sacrum*.

Dennington, A., *The Three Orchestrations of Stravinsky's "Firebird,"* in *The Chesterian*, 34 (1960), 89.

Drew, David, *Stravinsky's Revisions*, in *The Score*, 20 (1957), 47.

—— *Stravinsky*, in Drew, ed., *The Decca Book of Ballet*, London, 1958, p. 298.
   Especially good on *Jeu de cartes* and *Agon*.

Druckman, Jacob, *Stravinsky's Orchestral Style*, in *Juilliard Review*, 4/2 (1957), 10.
   Detailed observations, uncluttered by esthetic worries.

Dushkin, Samuel, *Working with Stravinsky*, in E. Corle, ed., *Stravinsky*, New York, 1949, p. 179.

The violinist reports on several aspects of Stravinsky in a way unlike anyone else's reports before those of Craft.

Fellerer, Karl, *Probleme neuer Kirchenmusik: Gedanken zu Igor Strawinskys Messe*, in *Begegnung*, VI (1951), 45.
    A rare appreciation, catholic as well as Catholic, by a scholar who writes too seldom on contemporary music.

The Firebird [anonymous review of Stravinsky and Craft, *Memories*, and of Vlad, *Stravinsky*], in *The Times Literary Supplement* (London), Nov. 4, 1960, p. 701.

Fleischer, Herbert, *Strawinsky*, Berlin, 1931.
    Based on a diss. (Berlin, 1928), this non-technical appreciation, with philosophical interpretation, anticipates many later comments.

Fowlie, Wallace, *Petrouchka's Wake*, in *Essays in Honor of A. Feuillerat*, New Haven, Conn., 1943, p. 249.
    Thematic connections in literature, from Mallarmé through Stravinsky to Joyce et al.

Fox, Charles Warren, *Modern Counterpoint: a Phenomenological Approach*, in NotesMLA, VI (1948), 46.

—— [Review of Stravinsky's *Orpheus* and Concerto in D], in NotesMLA, V (1948), 519.
    Important observations on interludes.

Frankenstein, Alfred, *Stravinsky in Beverly Hills*, in MM, XIX (1942), 178.

—— *The Record of a Self-Interpreter*, in *High Fidelity*, VII/6 (June 1957), 42.

—— *Stravinsky—With the Composer's Imprimatur*, in *High Fidelity*, XII/7 (July 1962), 51.

Frederickson, Lawrence, *Stravinsky's Instrumentation: a Study of his Orchestral Techniques*, Univ. of Illinois diss., 1960.

Godowsky, Dagmar, *First Person Plural*, New York, 1958.

Goldman, Richard Franko, *Stravinsky's Mass of 1948*, in *Perspectives USA*, 3 (1953), 110.

—— *Current Chronicle*, in MQ, XLVI (1960), 260.

—— *Current Chronicle*, in MQ, XLVIII (1962), 514.
    Review of *The Flood*.

Goldovsky, Boris, *Mavra, a Lyric Masterpiece*, in *Chrysalis*, IV/11–12 (1951), 3.

Grigoriev, Sergei Leonidovich, *The Diaghilev Ballet 1909–1929*, transl. and ed. by Vera Bowen, London, 1953.
    Detailed and authentic account by the regisseur.

Haggin, B. H., *Composers and Critics*, in *The Hudson Review*, XV (1962), 630.
    Uncommon defense of Stravinsky's polemic against certain critics.

Handschin, Jacques, *Igor Strawinsky: Versuch einer Einführung*, Zürich, 1933.
    Brief but memorable essay by an outstanding speculative scholar.

Hastings, Baird, *Stravinsky and his Choreographers*, in *Chrysalis*, IV/11–12 (1951), 5.

Herzfeld, Friedrich, *Igor Strawinsky*, Berlin, 1961.
    32 photographs, with brief text.

Iarustovsky, Boris Mikhailovich, *Igor Stravinsky: kratkii ocherk zhizni i tvorchestva*, Moscow, 1963.
    "A short outline of his life and work," this first Soviet book on Stravinsky since 1930 includes pictures not elsewhere available.

Igor Strawinsky (zum 70. Geburtstag), London & Bonn, 1952.
    Essays by Auden, Cocteau, Cortot, et al.

Johns, Donald C., *An Early Serial Idea of Stravinsky*, in MR, XXIII (1962), 305.
    On the Sonata for Two Pianos.

Keller, Hans, *Schönberg and Stravinsky: Schönbergians and Stravinskyans*, in MR, XV (1954), 307.

—— *Towards the Psychology of Stravinsky's Genius*, in *The Listener*, LVI (1956), 897.

—— *Stravinsky's Performance of "Agon": a Report*, in *Tempo*, 50 (1959), 22.

—— *No Bridge to Nowhere: an Introduction to Stravinsky's Movements and Schoenberg's Violin Concerto*, in MT, CII (1961), 156.

Kirchmeyer, Helmut, *Igor Stravinsky: Zeitgeschichte im Persönlichkeitsbild: Grundlagen und Voraussetzungen zur modernen Konstructionstechnik*, Regensburg, 1958.
    Based on a diss. (Cologne, 1954), this book cites and classifies hundreds of articles

and reviews in German periodicals, especially from the 1920s. The portentous title does almost as much as the text to give structure to the assemblage.

Kirstein, Lincoln, *Igor Stravinsky*, in *The Nation*, 184 (June 15, 1957), 530.

—— *Purity Through the Will*, in *The Nation*, 191 (Oct. 8, 1960), 233.
> Brilliant reviews.

Laloy, Louis, *Le Sacre du printemps*, in BSIM, X (1914), 45.

Lang, Paul Henry, ed., *Stravinsky: a New Appraisal of his Work*, New York, 1963.
> Articles from MQ by Cone, Mellers, Morton, Nelson, and Schwarz, with bibliography by Wade and introduction by Lang.

Lesure, François, and Nanie Bridgman, *Collection musicale d'André Meyer*, Abbéville, 1961.
> Illustrated catalog of a remarkable private library and museum, including as supplement 10 facsimile pages of an important manuscript of *The Rite of Spring*.

Lindlar, Heinrich, *Igor Strawinskys sakraler Gesang: Geist und Form der Christ-kultischen Kompositionen*, Regensburg, 1957.
> Brief but perceptive.

—— *Strawinsky: Kontakte zur Bildkunst*, in *Musica*, XVII (1963), 99.
> Valuable provisional survey of a vast field: Stravinsky and the visual arts.

Mason, Colin, *Stravinsky's Opera*, in ML, XXXIII (1952), 1.
> On the *Rake*.

—— *Stravinsky's Contribution to Chamber Music*, in *Tempo*, 43 (1957), 6; also in *Musik der Zeit*, I (1958), 72; and in *Cobbett*, III, 123.

—— *Stravinsky's Newest Works*, in *Tempo*, 53/54 (1960), 21.

—— *Stravinsky and Gesualdo*. in *Tempo*, 55/56 (1960), 39.

—— *Stravinsky's New Work*, in *Tempo*, 59 (1961), 5.
> On *A Sermon, A Narrative, and A Prayer*.

—— *Serial Procedure in the Ricercar II of Stravinsky's "Cantata,"* in *Tempo*, 61/62 (1962), 6.

Mayer, Martin, *He Remade the Sound of Music, But Igor Stravinsky Will Not Rest on his Past*, in *The New York Times Magazine*, June 10, 1962, p. 19.
> Unusually good introduction for beginners.

Mellers, Wilfrid H., *Stravinsky's Oedipus as 20th-Century Hero*, in MQ, XLVIII (1962), 300; also in P. H. Lang, ed., *Stravinsky*, New York, 1963, p. 34.

Mersmann, Hans, *Strawinsky*, in *Musik der Zeit*, II (1952), 65.

—— *Feuervogel, Pulcinella, Petruschka, Die Geschichte vom Soldaten, Concerto in Es*, Munich, 1962.

—— *Oedipus Rex, Psalmensymphonie*, Munich, 1962.
> Model notes for educational records.

Messiaen, Olivier, *Le Rythme chez Igor Stravinsky*, in RM, 191 (1939), 331.

Meylan, Pierre, *Une amitié célèbre: C. F. Ramuz—Igor Stravinsky*, Lausanne, 1961.

—— *Au sujet d'Igor Stravinsky et de René Morax*, in SMz, CIV (1964), 170.
> Includes 4 letters and facsimile of Stravinsky's setting of the *Volga Boatmen*.

—— *Igor Stravinsky et Maurice Ravel ont collaboré à Clarens en 1913: d'après des documents et des témoignages inédit*, in *Revue musicale de la Suisse Romande*, XVIII (1965), 5.

Milloss, Aurel von, *Strawinsky und das Ballett: Anmerkungen eines Choreographen*, in ÖMz, XX (1965), 18.

Milner, Anthony, *Melody in Stravinsky's Music*, in MT, XCVIII (1957), 370.
> Good fresh observations, though far from a comprehensive study of the topic.

Morton, Lawrence, *Current Chronicle*, in MQ, XLVIII (1962), 392.
> On *A Sermon, A Narrative, and A Prayer*.

—— *Stravinsky and Tchaikovsky: "Le Baiser de la fée,"* in MQ, XLVIII (1962), 313; also in P. H. Lang, ed., *Stravinsky*, New York, 1963, p. 47.
> A typically thorough, exciting chapter of a book in progress, whose outline, perhaps, can be seen in the article by Morton on Stravinsky in the Fasquelle *Encyclopédie*, Paris, 1961, III, 740.

Nabokov, Nicolas, *Stravinsky Now*, in *The Partisan Review*, XI (1944), 324.

—— *Stravinsky, 1947*, in *Stimmen*, I (1947), 6.

—— *Igor Stravinsky*, in *The Atlantic Monthly*, 184 (1949), 21.

—— *Old Friends and New Music*, Boston, 1951.
Pp. 184–223 of the book include most of the earlier articles.
—— *Christmas 1949 mit Strawinsky*, in *Musik der Zeit*, XII (1955), 5.
—— *Igor Strawinsky*, Berlin, 1964.
The personal testimony of an affectionate, perceptive, witty old friend, reviewing rapidly the whole career of Stravinsky. An excellent introductory survey.
Narodny, Ivan, *High Hats at a Mujik Wedding*, in *Musical America*, May 10, 1929, p. 29.
Review of *The Wedding* as first performed in New York, by a native Russian familiar with Stravinsky's sources. Pictures of Soudekine's set.
Nelson, Robert U., *Stravinsky's Concept of Variation*, in MQ, XLVIII (1962), 327; also in P. H. Lang, ed., *Stravinsky*, New York, 1963, p. 61.
Oleggini, Léon, *Connaissance de Strawinsky*, Paris, 1952.
Onnen, Frank, *De waarheid over "Summermoon,"* in *Mens en melodie*, III (1948), 85.
Account of an attempt to make a pop song of the *Lullaby* from the *Firebird*, foiled by Stravinsky's quick reaction.
—— *Strawinsky*, English transl. by M. M. Kesler-Button, Stockholm, 1949.
Palmer, Ralph, *Stravinsky in Russia*, in *The New Statesman & Nation*, Nov. 2, 1962, p. 613.
First-hand report, confirming and supplementing Craft's diary.
Pauli, Hansjörg, *On Stravinsky's "Threni,"* in *Tempo*, 49 (1958), 16.
Payne, Anthony, *Stravinsky's "The Flood,"* in *Tempo*, 70 (1964), 2.
—— *Stravinsky's "Abraham and Isaac" and "Elegy for JFK,"* in *Tempo*, 73 (1965), 12.
Piston, Walter, *Strawinsky's Rediscoveries*, in *Dance Index*, VI/10–12 (1947), 256.
Ramuz, Charles Ferdinand, *Souvenirs sur Igor Strawinsky*, Paris, 1929; new edn., Lausanne, 1952.
The Swiss poet who worked with Stravinsky on the *Soldier*, etc., provides an irreplaceable account of their friendship, one of the best of all writings about Stravinsky.
Read, Herbert, *Stravinsky and the Muses*, in *Tempo*, 61/62 (1962), 13.
"The most representative artist of our own 20th century."
Reck, Albert von, *Gestaltzusammenhänge im "Canticum sacrum" von Strawinsky: Tonalität und Form*, in SMz, XCVIII (1958), 49.
—— *Möglichkeiten tonaler Audition*, in Mf, XV (1962), 105.
Further comment on the *Canticum Sacrum*.
Satie, Erik, *A Composer's Conviction*, in *Vanity Fair*, XIX/6 (Feb. 1923), 39; also in E. Corle, ed., *Igor Stravinsky*, New York, 1949, p. 25.
Schaeffner, André, *Strawinsky*, Paris, 1931.
Important brief study.
—— *On Stravinsky, Early and Late*, in MM, XII (1934), 3.
A sample of the conclusions reached in Schaeffner's 1931 book.
—— *Critique et thématique*, in RM, 191 (1939), 241.
Postscript to Schaeffner's earlier studies, with rebuttals to criticism, and fresh praise for *Jeu de Cartes*.
—— *Renard et "l'époque russe" de Stravinsky*, in *Cahiers de la Compagnie M. Renaud— J.-L. Barraud*, II/3 (1954), 98.
Scherchen, Hermann, *Konzentration statt Expansion*, in *Gravesaner Blätter*, III/9 (1957), 8.
Program note for Stravinsky's *Soldier*, with 15 musical examples, concise sharp observations. English translation follows original.
Schilling, Hans Ludwig, *Zur Instrumentation in Igor Strawinskys Spätwerke, aufgezeigt an seinem "Septett 1953,"* in AfMw, XXIII (1956), 181.
—— *Igor Strawinskys Erweiterung und Instrumentation der Orgelvariationen "Vom Himmel hoch,"* in MuK, XXVII (1957), 257.
Schwarz, Boris, *Stravinsky in Soviet Russian Criticism*, in MQ, XLVIII (1962), 340; also in P. H. Lang, ed., *Stravinsky*, New York, 1963, p. 74.
Shattuck, Roger, *Making Time: a Study of Stravinsky, Proust, and Sartre*, in *The Kenyon Review*, XXV (1963), 248.
Good non-technical appreciation of Stravinsky's late works.

Siohan, Robert, *Stravinsky*, Bourges, 1959; German transl. as *Igor Strawinsky in Selbstzeug-nissen und Bilddokumenten*, Hamburg, 1960.
> Brief, tendentious text, combined in the German edn. with a fair selection of pictures.

Souvtchinsky, Pierre, *La Notion du temps et la musique (Réflexions sur la typologie de la création musicale)*, in RM, 191 (1939), 310.
> Important article, cited by Stravinsky in his *Poetics*. Epigraphs from Sartre.

—— *Zeit und Musik*, in *Musik der Zeit*, I (1958), 12.
> Revision of the above, transl. with the author's guidance by B. Nottmeyer.

Spies, Claudio, *Notes on Stravinsky's "Abraham and Isaac,"* in PNM, III/2 (1965), 104.
> Equal emphasis on poetic and technical aspects. Spies is likelier than most students to find the "hidden correlation."

Spingel, Hans Otto, *Hamburg: Uraufführung von Strawinskys Sintflut in der Staatsoper*, in *Fonoforum*, VI (1963), 205.
> Stravinsky is said to have preferred the Hamburg staging to the TV production. See also K. Wagner, in *Melos*, XXX (1963), 201.

Stein, Erwin, *Strawinsky's Septet (1953) . . . An Analysis*, in *Tempo*, 31 (1954), 7.

Steinitz, Paul, *On Rehearsing a Choir for the "Canticum sacrum,"* in *The Score*, 19 (1957), 56.
> "As soon as the notes and rhythm of any section were grasped, the fitness of the music began to become self-evident."

Stempowski, G., *Auf Igor Strawinskys Spuren in Wolhynien*, transl. by Magda H. Larsen, in *Du* (Zürich), 12 (1950), 33.
> Pictures taken in 1939 of Stravinsky's home in Ustilag, and report of peasant music in the neighborhood.

Sternfeld, Fred W., *Some Russian Folksongs in Stravinsky's Petrushka*, in NotesMLA, II (1945), 95.

Stravinsky, Igor, *Chronological Progress in Musical Art*, in J. F. Cooke, ed., *Great Men and Famous Musicians on the Art of Music*, Philadelphia, 1925, p. 266; also in *The Etude*, XLIV (1926), 559.

—— *Avertissement*, in *The Dominant*, I/2 (Dec. 1927), 13.
> Warning on neo-Classicism. French and English texts.

—— *Chroniques de ma vie*, Paris, 1935; English transl. as *An Autobiography*, New York, 1936.

—— *Poétique musicale*, Cambridge, Mass., 1942; English transl. by Arthur Knodel and Ingolf Dahl, as *Poetics of Music*, Cambridge, Mass., 1947; with preface by Darius Milhaud, New York, 1956; rev. edn. in French, Paris, 1952. (1961), 61.

—— *JFK, Ultimate Sacrilege, & Stravinsky*, in *The New York Times*, Dec. 6, 1964, p. x–15.
> An interview, mainly on the *Elegy for J. F. Kennedy*. A comment on it is applicable to *The Rake's Progress*: "Auden is almost too skillful. Able to anticipate the uses of music, both for better and for worse, he is also prepared to subordinate himself to it, which means that he has to be circumvented to be kept far enough upstage."

—— *Schoenberg Speaks his Mind*, in *The Observer* (London), Oct. 18, 1964, p. 26; also, as *Schoenberg's Letters*, in *High Fidelity*, XV/5 (May 1965), 136.
> Stravinsky now sees Schoenberg as "centripetal," though of course "other developments were and are possible." In the American reprint he mentions some letters to him from Schoenberg, 1919.

—— *An Interview*, in *The New York Review of Books*, June 3, 1965, p. 4.
> Includes shocking slurs at Casals, Kodály, American culture-boosting, and reviewers. Also glimpses of the next composition, Variations.

—— [Letter to the editor, announcing formation of a committee for the foundation of a Berg Society], in MR, XXVI (1965), 83.

—— and Robert Craft, *Conversations*, Garden City, N.Y., 1959.

——— *Memories and Commentaries*, Garden City, N.Y., 1960.

——— *Expositions and Developments*, Garden City, N.Y., 1962.

——— *Dialogues and a Diary*, Garden City, N.Y., 1963.

Stravinsky, Théodore, *Le Message d'Igor Strawinsky*, Lausanne, 1948; English transl. by R. Craft and A. Marion, as *The Message of Igor Stravinsky*, London, 1953.

Stravinsky: a Complete Catalogue of his Published Works, London, 1957.

Stravinsky and the Dance (introduction by Herbert Read), New York, 1962.
> Catalogue of a 1962 exhibition, with a detailed and reliable survey of ballet productions, by Selma Jeanne Cohen.

Stravinsky as Seen by Giacometti—Giacometti as Seen by Stravinsky, in *Vogue*, Aug. 15, 1958, p. 82.

Strawinsky in Amerika: das kompositorische Werk von 1939 bis 1955, London & Bonn, 1955.

Strawinsky in the Theater, special issue of *Dance Index*, VI/10–12 (1947); rev. edn. as book, New York, 1949.

Strawinsky unter uns, in *Melos*, XXIX (1962), 180.
> Brief contributions by 15 leaders of culture including Martin Heidegger, Walter Gropius, Henry Moore, Jean Renoir.

Strobel, Heinrich, *Stravinsky: Classic Humanist*, New York, 1955; in German as *Igor Strawinsky*, Zürich, 1956.

—— *Igor Strawinsky und seine Kunstauffassung*, in *Universitas*, XX (1965), 131.
> Strobel reprints a chapter of his book with very slight change; "classic" still fits, he thinks.

Stuart, Charles, *Stravinsky: the Dialectics of Dislike*, in *Music Survey*, II (1950), 142.
> Logical refutation of various common adverse criticisms of Stravinsky.

Stuckenschmidt, Hans Heinz, *Strawinsky und sein Jahrhundert*, Berlin, 1957.
> Brief text with handsome illustrations.

Tachezi, Herbert, *Igor Strawinsky*, in *Musik-Erziehung*, XVI (1962), 75.
> Good summary biography and some thoughts on the use of Stravinsky's music in schools.

Tansman, Alexandre, *Igor Strawinsky*, Paris, 1948; English transl. by T. and C. Bleefeld, New York, 1949.
> One-sided and obsolete interpretation of the music, but irreplaceable vignettes of the composer.

Taper, Bernard, *Balanchine*, New York, 1963.
> Includes valuable material on Stravinsky.

Tomek, Otto, ed., *Igor Strawinsky; eine Sendereihe des Westdeutschen Rundfunks zum 80. Geburtstag*, Cologne, 1963.
> Includes lively conversation by Boulez, Sacher, and Schuh.

Travis, Roy, *Toward a New Concept of Tonality?*, in JMT, III (1959), 257.
> Includes a persuasive analysis of the beginning of *The Rite of Spring*.

Valéry, Paul, *The Art of Poetry*, transl. by Denise Folloit (=his *Collected Works*, VII), New York, 1956.

Vlad, Roman, *Strawinsky*, Turin, 1958; English transl. by F. and A. Fuller, London, 1960.
> The most comprehensive study up to its time, but too short to supersede many earlier writings, and too partisan and literary to be recommended as introduction.

—— *"The Rake's Progress" di Stravinsky, l'ultima opera classica*, in *La Rassegna musicale*, XXXII (1962), 248.
> Reconsideration of Stravinsky's entire operatic career, based on comparative study of the *Conversations*, etc., with new ideas on *Nightingale, Wedding, Renard, Soldier, Mavra, Oedipus, Persephone*, and *Flood*, as well as *The Rake's Progress*.

Wade, Carroll D., *A Selected Bibliography of Igor Stravinsky*, in P. H. Lang, ed., *Stravinsky*, New York, 1963, p. 97.
> Comprehensive list of books by and about Stravinsky. Good selection of articles and reviews, though it lacks some items listed here.

Ward-Steinman, David, *Serial Techniques in the Recent Music of Igor Stravinsky*, Univ. of Illinois, D.M.A. diss., 1961.
> Admirable study.

Weissmann, Adolf, *Strawinsky spielt sein Klavierkonzert*, in *Anbruch*, VI (1924), 407.
> Interesting evidence of Viennese bafflement at Stravinsky's new style.

White, Eric Walter, *Stravinsky's Sacrifice to Apollo*, London, 1930.

—— *Stravinsky, a Critical Survey*, New York, 1948.

—— *Stravinsky and Debussy*, in *Tempo*, 61/62 (1962), 2.

—— First Performances [Variations and Introit], in Tempo, 74 (1965), 18.

Wilson, Edmund, Stravinsky, in The New Republic, XLII (1925), 156.

—— Every Man his own Eckermann, in The New York Review of Books, I/2 (1963), 1.

SUCHOŇ

Clapham, John, The Whirlpool: a Slovak Opera, in MR, XIX (1958), 47.
> On Suchoň's Krútňava (1941–49).

Kresánek, Jozef, Národný umelec Eugen Suchoň, Bratislava, 1961.

SUTER

Merian, Wilhelm, Hermann Suter: ein Lebensbild als Beitrag zur schweizerischen Musik-geschichte, Basel, 1936.

SVIRIDOV

Poliakova, Liudmila, Nekotorye voprosy tvorcheskogo stilia G. Sviridova, in T. Lebedeva, ed., Muzyka i sovremennost', Moscow, 1962, p. 183.
> Some questions about the creative style of Sviridov.

SZYMANOWSKI

Chominski, Jósef Michal, ed., Z życia i twórczości Karola Szymanowskiego: studia i materialy, Cracow, 1960.
> Documents for the continuing study of Szymanowski, life and works.

Klemm, Eberhard, Wissenschaftlicher Szymanowski-Kongress in Warschau, in Beiträge zur Musikwissenschaft, IV (1963), 309.
> Surveys a wealth of material in Polish that needs translation.

Łobaczewska, Stefania, Karol Szymanowski: zycie i twórczość, Cracow, 1950.
> Basic biography, with 158 brief musical examples and nearly 50 photographs.

Robertson, Alec, Karol Szymanowski, in R. Hill, ed., The Concerto, London, 1952, p. 357.

Szymanowski, Karol, Z Pism, Warsaw, 1962.
> Letters.

TAGORE

Baké, Arnold A., Tagore, the Musician, in East and West (Rome), XII/2–3 (1961), 172.

Roy, Trina, Outlines of Tagore's Music, in D. Weise, ed., Festschrift Joseph Schmidt-Görg zum 60. Geburtstag, Bonn, 1957, p. 235.

Tagore, Rabindranath, My Reminiscences, London, 1917.

TCHEREPNIN

Reich, Willi, Alexander Tscherepnin, Bonn, 1961; in French as Alexandre Tchérepnine, special issue of RM, 252 (1962).
> Survey of an interesting life and work, with a catalog completed by Tcherepnin himself.

TEAGARDEN

Smith, Jay D., and Len Guttridge, Jack Teagarden, the Story of a Jazz Maverick, London, 1960.
> An extensive study, in contrast to most of the Cassell series of booklets.

THIRIET

Solar, Jean, Maurice Thiriet, Paris, 1957.

THOMPSON

Forbes, Elliot, The Music of Randall Thompson, in MQ, XXXV (1949), 1.

THOMSON

Hoover, Kathleen, and John Cage, Virgil Thomson: his Life and Music, New York, 1959.
> Chief source of information, not yet assimilated by most people who know Thomson's name.

Thomson, Virgil, The State of Music, New York, 1939; new edn., with preface and postlude, New York, 1962.

—— Ending the Great Tradition: a Modest Proposal, in Encounter, XII/1 (Jan. 1959), 64.

—— Looking Back on a Decade, in Encounter, XV/5 (Nov. 1960), 47.

—— America's Musical Maturity: a 20th-Century Story, in The Yale Review, LI/1 (1961), 60.

—— *A Survey of the State of Music in Europe Today,* in *Musical America,* LXXXI/1 (Jan. 1961), 11.

—— *Toward Improving the Musical Race,* in *Musical America,* LXXXI/7 (July 1961), 5.

On the mutual need of East and West, and the risks of hybrids.

TIESSEN

Tiessen, Heinz, *Zur Geschichte der jüngsten Musik, 1913–1928: Probleme und Entwicklungen,* Mainz, 1928.

Includes valuable first-hand reports, especially on the provocative role of the conductor Scherchen.

—— *Selbstzeugnis des Künstlers,* in *Musica,* II (1948), 12.

Includes list of works.

—— *Die neue Musik, die IGNM und ihre deutsche Sektion vor 1933,* in *Neue Musik in der Bundesrepublik,* Mainz, 1959, p. 7.

Fascinating history of Berlin's avant-garde, 1912–22. Tiessen's book, *Wege eines Komponisten,* Berlin, 1962, may supersede some of these articles.

TIPPETT

Atkinson, Neville, *Michael Tippett's Debt to the Past,* in MR, XXIII (1962), 195.

Almost a survey of the history of music, from a unique perspective.

Goodwin, Noël, *Tippett, the Explorer,* in *Music & Musicians,* XIII/6 (Feb. 1965), 20.

Kemp, Ian, ed., *Michael Tippett: a Symposium on his 60th Birthday,* London, 1965.

Brief tributes by friends and admirers, valuable to any admirer of Tippett, but not enough to change the view of such a critic as Scott Goddard, in MT, CVI (1965), 111.

Mason, Colin, *Michael Tippett,* in MT, LXXXVII (1946), 137.

Penetrating discussion of Tippett's style. "Hindemith appeals to him (as his own antithesis) . . . Tippett is least acquainted with the music of Bartók, yet in general feeling is closest to him."

Milner, Anthony, *Rhythmic Techniques in the Music of Michael Tippett,* in MT, XCV (1954), 468.

—— *The Music of Michael Tippett,* in MQ, L (1964), 423.

Tippett, Michael, *Moving into Aquarius,* London, 1959.

Appealing essays, affording an unusually intimate view of a composer's concerns.

—— *"A Child of Our Time,"* in R. S. Hines, ed., *The Composer's Point of View,* Norman, Okla., 1963, p. 111.

Both a fascinating history of Tippett's most famous piece and a sample of his wise reflections on general issues.

TOCH

Pisk, Paul. *Ernst Toch,* in MQ, XXIV (1938), 438.

Rutz, Hans, *Ernst Toch,* in *Melos,* XIX (1952), 139.

Includes list of published works.

TOMMASINI

Rinaldi, Mario, *Vincenzo Tommasini,* in *Rivista musicale italiana,* LIII (1951), 323.

Comprehensive study, correcting errors in most accounts of Tommasini.

TOSCANINI

Corte, Andrea della, *Toscanini, visto da un critico,* Turin, 1958.

Detailed critical account of Toscanini's life and work, with references to many other books on Toscanini.

TOVEY

Dent, Edward J., *Donald Tovey,* in MR, III (1942), 1.

Grierson, Mary, *Donald Francis Tovey: a Biography Based on Letters,* London, 1952.

No comment on Tovey's compositions, and little material of general interest beyond what is included in Dent's lively article.

TURINA

Sopeña, Federico, *Joaquín Turina,* 2d rev. and enl. edn., Madrid, 1956.

VALEN

Gurvin, Olav, *Fartein Valen, en banebryter: i nyere norsk musikk,* Drammen and Oslo, 1962.
    Includes thematic catalog, usable and interesting to those without knowledge of
    Norwegian.
Kortsen, Bjarne, *Studies of Form in Fartein Valen's Music,* Oslo, 1962.

VAN BAAREN

Wouters, Jos, *Kees van Baaren,* in *Sonorum speculum,* 16 (Sep. 1963), 1.

VARÈSE

Anhalt, István, *Varèse,* in CMJ, V/2 (1961), 34.
    Compares recordings by Craft and Boulez.
Cowell, Henry, *The Music of Edgard Varèse,* in MM, V/2 (1928), 9; also in Cowell, *American
    Composers,* New York, 1933, p. 43.
—— *Current Chronicle,* in MQ, XLI (1955), 370.
Klarén, J. H., *Edgar Varèse, Pioneer of New Music in America,* Boston, 1928.
    Compilation of early newspaper interviews and critiques.
Le Corbusier [pseud. for Charles-Édouard Jeanneret-Gris], *Le Poème électronique,* Paris, 1958.
    Includes (pp. 186–198) a statement by Varèse; also discussions by Xenakis and
    copious illustrations.
—— et al., *The Philips Pavilion and the Electronic Poem,* in *Arts & Architecture,* Nov. 11,
    1958, p. 23.
Lesure, François, *Debussy et Edgard Varèse,* in E. Weber, ed., *Debussy et l'évolution,* Paris,
    1965, p. 333.
Schuller, Gunther, *Conversation with Varèse,* in PNM, III/2 (1965), 32.
Tenney, James, *Meta (+) Hodos: a Phenomenology of 20th-Century Musical Materials and
    an Approach to the Study of Form,* New Orleans, 1964.
    An elaborate vocabulary for describing works by Ives, Ruggles, Varèse, Schoenberg,
    and Webern, probably relevant to Varèse and perhaps to some younger composers.
Varèse, Edgard, *Organized Sound for the Sound Film,* in *Commonweal,* XXXIII (1940), 204.
—— *Answers,* in *Possibilities,* Winter 1947–48, p. 96.
—— *Musik auf neuen Wegen,* in *Stimmen,* XV (1949), 401.
—— *A Communication,* in MQ, XLI (1955), 574.
—— *Les Instruments de musique et la machine électronique,* in *L'Age nouveau,* 92 (May
    1955), 28.
—— *Erinnerungen und Gedanken,* in *Darmstädter Beiträge zur neuen Musik,* II (1960), 65.
Vivier, Odile, *Innovation instrumentale d'Edgar Varèse,* in RM, 226 (1955), 188.
    Compare Mlle. Vivier's article on Varèse in the Ricordi *Enciclopedia della musica,*
    ed. by C. Sartori, Milan, 1964, IV, 464.
Wilkinson, Marc, *An Introduction to the Music of Edgard Varèse,* in *The Score,* 19 (1957), 5.
    Analyzes the flute solo, *Density 21.5.*

VASILENKO

Polanovsky, Georgii Aleksandrovich, *Sergei Nikiforovich Vasilenko: zhizn' i tvorchestvo,*
    Moscow, 1964.

VAUGHAN WILLIAMS

Bergsagel, John D., *The National Aspects of the Music of Ralph Vaughan Williams,* Cornell
    Univ. diss., 1957.
Dickinson, A. E. F., *The Vaughan Williams Manuscripts,* in MR, XXIII (1962), 177.
—— *Vaughan Williams,* London, 1963.
    Survey of life and works.
Foss, Hubert, *Ralph Vaughan Williams: a Study,* London, 1950.
Garvie, Peter, *Ralph Vaughan Williams, 1872–1958,* in CMJ, III/2 (1959), 36.
    Excellent introductory essay.
Kennedy, Michael, *The Works of Ralph Vaughan Williams,* London, 1964.
    Authorized guide, supplementing Mrs. Vaughan Williams's biography.

Kimmel, William, *Vaughan Williams's Choice of Words*, in ML, XIX (1938), 132.
—— *Vaughan Williams's Melodic Style*, in MQ, XXVII (1941), 491.
Murrill, Herbert, *Vaughan Williams's Pilgrim*, in ML, XXXII (1951), 324.
    Compares Vaughan Williams's humility with that of Debussy's *Pelléas*.
Neighbour, Oliver, *Ralph Vaughan Williams, 1872–1958*, in *The Score*, 24 (1958), 7; also in
    D. Ewen, ed., *The New Book of Modern Composers*, New York, 1961, p. 423.
    Uniquely penetrating study of style.
Pakenham, Simona, *Ralph Vaughan Williams*, New York, 1957.
    Extraordinary account of an amateur's deepening devotion, through systematic listen-
    ing to recordings, radio, and concert performance.
Payne, Elsie, *Vaughan Williams and Folk-Song*, in MR, XV (1954), 103.
    Based on a diss. (Liverpool, 1953). Shows variants of the two tunes, *The Captain's
    Apprentice* and *Bushes and Briars*, with many of their derivatives, in Vaughan
    Williams's works.
*Ralph Vaughan Williams: a Comprehensive List Giving Full Details of All Works Now
    Available, together with a complete Discography*, London, 1961.
Schwartz, Elliott S., *The Symphonies of Ralph Vaughan Williams*, Amherst, Mass., 1964.
    Based on a diss. (Columbia, 1962), this exposition and critique lacks the perspective
    of Kennedy or Neighbour, but may still be useful to some listeners.
Vaughan Williams, Ralph, *National Music*, London, 1935.
    Lectures at Bryn Mawr, 1932.
—— *Some Thoughts on Beethoven's Choral Symphony, with Writings on Other Musical
    Subjects*, London, 1953.
    Includes (p. 132) autobiographical sketch.
—— *The Making of Music*, Ithaca, New York, 1955.
—— *National Music and Other Essays*, London, 1963.
    This volume includes all three earlier ones.
—— and Gustav Holst, *Heirs and Rebels: Letters Written to Each Other and Occasional
    Writings on Music*, London, 1959.
Vaughan Williams, Ursula, *R. V. W., a Biography*, London, 1964.
    The composer's widow, a poet, gives the fullest available account of his life.

VERESS

Doflein, Erich, *Sándor Veress*, in *Melos*, XXI (1954), 74.

VERRALL

Beale, James, *The Music of John Verrall*, in ACA, VII/4 (1958), 10.

VIANNA DA MOTTA

Lopes Graça, Fernando, *Viana da Motta: subsídios para uma biografia incluindo 22 cartas ao
    autor*, Lisbon, 1949.

VIERNE

Gavoty, Bernard, *Louis Vierne: la vie et l'œuvre*, Paris, 1943.

VILLA-LOBOS

Helm, Everett, *The Many-Sided Villa*, in *High Fidelity*, XII/7 (July 1962), 39.
    Excellent introductory essay.
Mariz, Vasco, *Heitor Villa-Lobos*, Rio de Janeiro, 1950; abr. English transl., Gainesville, Fla.,
    1963.
—— *A canção brasileira (erudita, folclórica e popular)*, Rio de Janeiro, 1959.
    Includes (pp. 55–65) excellent comments on the songs of Villa-Lobos.
Maul, Carlos, *A glória escandalosa de Heitor Vila-Lôbos*, Rio de Janeiro, 1960.
Muricy, Andrade, *Villa-Lobos—una interpretação*, Rio de Janeiro, 1960.
    Includes list of works in English and Portuguese; cites (p. 87) a 309-page typescript
    by Marcel Beaufils which is likely to be an important contribution.
Peppercorn, Lisa M., *Some Aspects of Villa-Lobos's Principles of Composition*, in MR, IV
    (1943), 28.
    Severe critique.

Smith, Carleton Sprague, *Heitor Villa-Lobos*, in *Composers of the Americas*, III (1957), 1.
> Good introduction, followed by a list of 727 works.

Villa-Lobos, Heitor, *O ensino popular da música no Brasil*, Rio de Janeiro, 1937.

VOGEL

Oesch, Hans, *Wladimir Vogels Werke für Klavier*, in SMz, XCVII (1957), 51.

Rognoni, Luigi, *Porträt Wladimir Vogel*, in *Melos*, XXII (1955), 165.

Vogel, Wladimir, *Il coro parlato*, in *Musica d'oggi*, III (1960), 354.

—— *Zu meiner Modigliani-Kantate*, in SMz, CII (1962), 78.

VYCPÁLEK

Smolka, Jaroslav, *Ladislav Vycpálek: tvůrčí vývoj*, Prague, 1960.

WALLER

Fox, Charles, *Fats Waller*, London, 1960.

WALTON

Howes, Frank, *The Music of William Walton*, London, 1965.
> Revised and expanded from two earlier publications. S. Walsh, in *Tempo*, 74 (1965), 29, defines the book's shortcomings.

Pirie, Peter J., *Scapino: the Development of William Walton*, in MT, CV (1964), 258.
> Good critical account of recent works in the light of Walton's whole career.

Sitwell, Osbert, *Laughter in the Next Room*, Boston, 1948.
> Memoirs, including (pp. 191–226) intimate glimpses of Elgar, Berg, Gershwin, and especially Walton.

WARLOCK: *see* HESELTINE

WEBERN

Adorno, Theodor Wiesengrund, *Anton Webern, zur Aufführung der Fünf Orchesterstücke in Zürich*, in *Anbruch*, VIII (1926), 280.

—— *Klangfiguren*, Berlin, 1959.
> Collected essays on contemporary musical thought; a fine new one on Webern.

Anton Webern, special issue of *Die Reihe*, II (German edn., 1955; English edn., 1958).
> First extensive publication of material on Webern.

Anton Webern zum 50. Geburtstag, special issue of *"23" eine Wiener Musikzeitschift*, 14 (1934).

Beale, James, *Weberns musikalischer Nachlass*, in *Melos*, XXI (1964), 297.
> Some detailed information about the works preceding Op. 1.

Bresgen, Cesar, *Anton Webern in Mittersill*, in ÖMz, XVI (1961), 226.
> Bresgen testifies to Webern's persistent interest in Debussy, among other things. Further recollections in a manuscript by Bresgen are cited by Kolneder, *Anton Webern*, p. 172.

Chamfray, Claude, *Variations pour piano (op. 27) de Webern*, in RM, XIX/184 (1938), 386.
> Rare early appreciation.

Craft, Robert, and Kurt Stone, *Anton Webern*, in *The Score*, 13 (1955), 9.
> Includes the text of the booklet for Craft's recording of the complete works of Webern (Columbia Records K4L–232), supplemented by important notes on ranges and on Debussy.

Dallapiccola, Luigi, *Gravesano Visit*, in *Gravesaner Blätter*, IV/10 (1958), 3.
> Report of conversation with Webern, 1942.

—— *Begegnung mit Anton Webern*, in *Melos*, XXXII (1965), 115.
> The same report, in a context of Dallapiccola's acquaintance with Webern's music, 1935–45.

Dimov, Boschidar, *Webern und die Tradition*, in ÖMz, XX (1965), 411.
> An assemblage of quotations aiming to expedite the recognition of Webern's "real ethical mission."

Döhl, Friedhelm, *Weberns opus 27*, in *Melos*, XXX (1963), 400.

—— *Die Welt der Dichtung in Weberns Musik,* in *Melos,* XXXI (1964), 88.

Dorian, Frederick Deutsch, *Webern als Lehrer,* in *Melos,* XXVII (1960), 101.
> Includes description of Webern's singing, playing, and conducting, and his fondness for such works as *Fidelio* and *Zar und Zimmermann.*

Falk, Julian, *Technique de la musique atonale,* Paris, 1959.
> Concise rules and exercises, well calculated to produce something like Webern's music.

Fant, Göran, *Mest om Anton Weberns kantater,* in *Nutida Musik,* VIII/1 (1964), 25.
> Analytical notes on several works of Webern, plus a complete list of works (compiled by Ove Nordwall) and a discography, both useful to readers ignorant of Swedish.

Fiore, Mary Emma, *The Formation and Structural Use of Vertical Constructs in Selected Serial Compositions,* Indiana Univ. diss., 1963.
> Schoenberg's *Moses* and *Phantasy,* Berg's *Lyric Suite* and Violin Concerto, and Webern's Opp. 20, 27, 29, 30, studied to confirm the impression that each composer has his own preference or habit with respect to chords.

Forte, Allen, *A Theory of Set-Complexes for Music,* in *JMT,* VIII (1964), 136.
> Basic mathematical treatment of unordered sets of from 2 to 12 notes or intervals. Use of the theory for analysis is shown with Webern's Op. 5, No. 4.

Fortner, Wolfgang, *Anton Webern und unsere Zeit,* in *Melos,* XXVII (1960), 325.

Goebel, Walter F., *Anton Weberns Sinfonie,* in *Melos,* XXVIII (1961), 359.

Irvine, Demar, ed., *Anton Webern: Perspectives,* in preparation.
> Papers of the 1st Webern Festival, 1962, including a report by James Beale on the unpublished music.

Karkoschka, Erhard, *Der missverstandene Webern,* in *Melos,* XXIX (1962), 13.
> Author of a diss. on Webern (Tübingen, 1959), Karkoschka offers acute criticism of Kolneder's book.

Kolneder, Walter, *Klangtechnik und Motivbildung bei Webern,* in *Festgabe für Joseph Müller-Blattau zum 65. Geburtstag (Annales Universitatis Saraviensis, Philosophische Fakultät, 9/1),* Saarbrücken, 1960, p. 27.

—— *Anton Webern: Einführung in Werk und Stil,* Rodenkirchen, 1961.
> First comprehensive survey, correcting the exaggerations of Stockhausen et al.

—— *Klang in Punkt und Linie: Anton Weberns Variationen op. 27,* in S. Borris et al., *Vergleichende Interpretationskunde,* Berlin, 1963, p. 49.
> Comparison of 5 recorded performances.

Leibowitz, René, *Anton Webern,* in *L'Arche,* II/11 (Nov. 1945), 130.

—— *The Tragic Art of Anton Webern,* in *Horizon,* XV/88 (1947), 282.

—— *Introduction à la musique de douze sons,* Paris, 1949.
> Includes discussion of Webern's Concerto.

Lewin, David., *A Metrical Problem in Webern's Op. 27,* in *JMT,* VI (1962), 125.
> Excellent study of the first six measures from the second movement of the Piano Variations.

Lippman, Edward Arthur, [review of Craft's recording of the works of Webern], in *MQ,* XLIV (1958), 416.
> Scholarly esthetician, Lippman pays tribute to "the most representative musical product of our times."

McKenzie, Wallace Chessley, *The Music of Anton Webern,* N. Texas State College diss., 1960.
> Demonstrates in detail that "each new complexity of relationship is counter-balanced by a significant simplification at another structural level."

Maegaard, Jan, *Some Formal Devices in Expressionistic Works,* in *Dansk Aarbog for Musik Forskning,* I (1961), 69.
> Fresh observations on Webern's Bagatelle, Op. 9, No. 4.

Mason, Colin, *Webern's Later Chamber Music,* in *ML,* XXXVIII (1957), 232; also in *Cobbett,* III, 6.

Moldenhauer, Hans, *The Death of Anton Webern: a Drama in Documents,* New York, 1961.

—— *Rich Webern Legacy. . . ,* in *The New York Times,* Sept. 17, 1961, p. x–11.

—— *Wealth of Webern Manuscripts Now at University of Washington,* in *Music of the West,* XVII/3 (Nov. 1961), 11.

Ogdon, Wilbur, *A Webern Analysis*, in JMT, VI (1962), 133.
> On the second movement of the Piano Variations, Op. 27.

Pisk, Paul A., *Anton Webern, Profile of a Composer*, in *Texas Quarterly*, V/4 (1962), 114.

Pousseur, Henri, *Weberns organische Chromatik*, in *Die Reihe*, II (1955), 56; in English edn., II (1958), 51.

Powell, Mel, *A Note on Webern*, in *Juilliard Review*, IV/3 (1957), 3.

—— *Webern's Influence on our Young Composers*, in *The New York Times*, May 3, 1959, p. x–11.

Reich, Willi, ed., *Anton Webern: Weg und Gestalt. Selbstzeugnisse und Worte der Freunde*, Zürich, 1961.
> Concise and attractive presentation of materials already published elsewhere.

—— *Anton Webern über Alban Berg*, in NZfM, CXXIV (1963), 143.
> Facsimile of a letter of 1930.

Ringger, Rolf Urs, *Zur Wort-Ton-Beziehung beim frühen Anton Webern: Analyse von Op. 3, Nr. 1*, in SMz, CIII (1963), 330.

—— *Zur Formstruktur in Anton Weberns späten Klavierliedern: Analyse von Op. 23/II*, in SMz, CV (1965), 20.
> By-products of a dissertation (Zürich, 1964).

Rochberg, George, *Webern's Search for Harmonic Identity*, in JMT, VI (1962), 109.
> On the first movement of Cantata I, Op. 29.

Schmidt-Garre, Helmut, *Webern als Angry Young Man: aus alten Zeitungkritiken*, in NZfM, CXXV (1964), 132.

Searle, Humphrey, *Conversations with Webern*, in MT, LXXXI (1940), 405.

—— *Webern's Last Works*, in MMR, LXXVI (1946), 231.

—— *Studying with Webern*, in *Royal College of Music Magazine*, LIV (1958), 39.

Spinner, Leopold, *A Short Introduction to the Technique of Twelve-Tone Composition*, London, 1960.
> Rules and exercises for imitating Webern.

—— *Anton Weberns Kantate Nr. 2, Opus 31*, in SMz, CI (1961), 303.
> Emphasizes the formal function of the main melody and the accompaniment function of the canons.

Spitzmüller, Alexandre de, *Le Triomphe de la sensibilité*, in *Contrepoints*, II (Feb. 1946), 71.
> Lament for Webern, important in its time and place.

Stadlen, Peter, *Serialism Reconsidered*, in *The Score*, 22 (1958), 12.
> Describes Webern's own performance of his Piano Variations, Op. 27, then proceeds to criticize and speculate in a way that provoked controversy.

Stein, Erwin, *Alban Berg—Anton von Webern*, in *The Chesterian*, 26 (1922), 33; German version in *Anbruch*, V (1923), 13.

—— *The Art of Anton Webern*, in *The Christian Science Monitor*, June 22, 1929, p. 5.
> "In the matter of content, Webern's music . . . is far less difficult than Schoenberg's. But in its sonority it constitutes a problem for most people."

Stephan, Rudolph, *Über einige geistliche Kompositionen Anton von Weberns*, in MuK, XXIV (1954), 152.

—— *Anton von Webern*, in *Deutsche Universitätszeitung*, XI/13–14 (July 19, 1956), 26.
> The second article is expanded from the first. Both present an unusual and interesting appraisal.

Stockhausen, Karlheinz, *Weberns Konzert für 9 Instrumente Op. 24: Analyse des I. Satzes*, in *Melos*, XX (1953), 343.
> Influential one-sided view.

—— *Struktur und Erlebniszeit*, in *Die Reihe*, II (1955), 69; as *Structure and Experiential Time* in English edn., II (1958), 64.
> Characteristically novel and elaborate analysis of Webern's Quartet, Op. 28, second movement.

Teitelbaum, Richard, *Intervallic Relations in Atonal Music*, in JMT, IX (1965), 72.
> Using an IBM 709 computer at Yale, Teitelbaum studied 19 pieces of Webern and Schoenberg, written 1908–23, and confirmed an "astonishing consistency in Webern's

preference for" 3-note groups with the intervals (or mostly, in fact, their inversions) minor second, major and minor third. Teitelbaum's procedure interests him as much as the results of this first effort.

Vlad, Roman, *Storia della dodecafonia*, Milan, 1958.

Webern, Anton, *Über Arnold Schönberg*, in *Rheinische Musik- und Theater-Zeitung*, XIII (1912), 99, 118; as *Schönbergs Musik*, in Berg et al., *Arnold Schönberg*, Munich, 1912, p. 22.

—— *Brief an H. Eisler 19. iv. 1929*, in MuG, VIII (1958), 339.
    Facsimile.

—— *Was ist Musik?*, in *Melos*, XXV (1958), 305.

—— *Briefe an Hildegard Jone und Josef Humplik*, ed. by J. Polnauer, Vienna, 1959.
    Selections only, but very valuable as rare material for an authentic picture of Webern's personality.

—— *Der Weg zur neuen Musik*, ed. by Willi Reich, Vienna, 1960; English transl. by L. Black as *The Path to the New Music*, Bryn Mawr, Pa., 1963.
    Notes on Webern's informal lectures, with an epilogue including letters from Webern to Reich.

—— *Towards a New Music*, in *The Score*, 28 (1961), 29.
    Excerpts from *Der Weg*.

—— and Arnold Schoenberg, *Letters to Roberto Gerhard*, in *The Score*, 24 (1958), 36.

Webern Archive of the Moldenhauer Collection at the University of Washington, Seattle, 1963.

Wellesz, Egon, *Anton von Webern: Lieder Opus 12, 13, 14*, in *Melos*, II (1921), 38.

—— *E. J. Dent and the ISCM*, in MR, VII (1946), 205.
    Refers to Webern's "nervous breakdown" at Barcelona in 1936.

—— *Reminiscences of Mahler*, in *The Score*, 28 (1961), 52.
    Wellesz recalls Webern's shock on hearing the march in Mahler's Third Symphony, 1904.

Westergaard, Peter, *Some Problems in Rhythmic Theory and Analysis*, in PNM, I/1 (1962). 180.
    On the third movement of Webern's Piano Variations, Op. 27.

—— *Webern and "Total Organization": an Analysis of the Second Movement of Piano Variations Op. 27*, in PNM, I/2 (1963), 107.

Wildgans, Friedrich, *Anton von Webern, zu seinem 75. Geburtstag*, in ÖMz, XIII (1958), 456.
    First-hand testimony about Webern's "eminently practical" attitude.

—— *Gustav Mahler und Anton von Webern*, in ÖMz, XV (1960), 302.
    Quotes manuscript material not elsewhere available.

WEILL

Drew, David, *Brecht versus Opera: Some Comments*, in *The Score*, 23 (1958), 7.

—— *Topicality and the Universal: the Strange Case of Weill's "Die Bürgschaft,"* in ML, XXXIX (1958), 242.

Kotschenreuther, Hellmut, *Kurt Weill*, Berlin, 1962.
    Brief and biased, but useful.

Leydi, Roberto, *Precisioni su "Mahagonny" e altre questioni a proposito di Kurt Weill*, in *La Rassegna musicale*, XXXII (1962), 195.

Weill, Kurt, *Zeitoper*, in *Melos*, VII (1928), 106.

—— *Notiz zum Jazz*, in *Anbruch*, XI (1929), 138.

—— *Über den gestischen Charakter der Musik*, in *Die Musik*, XXI (1929), 419.

WEINBERGER

Weinberger, Jaromír, *Was mir blieb*, in *Musik der Zeit*, VIII (1954), 37.
    Memoir, with catalogue.

WEINER

Gál, György Sándor, *Weiner Leo életmüve*, Budapest, 1959.

WEISS

Weiss, Adolph, *Autobiographical Notes*, in ACA, VII/3 (1958), 2.

WELLESZ

Fiechtner, Helmuth A., *Egon Wellesz*, in ÖMz, XVI (1961), 284.

Nettel, Reginald, *According to Damon: an Essay in Special Pleading,* in MR, XII (1951), 212.
Warm appreciation of Egon Wellesz.
Reti, Rudolph, *Egon Wellesz, Musician and Scholar,* in MQ, XLII (1956), 1.
Balanced account of a unique career.
Schollum, Robert, *Egon Wellesz: eine Studie,* Vienna, 1964.
A booklet on Wellesz primarily as composer.
Wellesz, Egon, *Essays on Opera,* London, 1950.
Valuable material on Wellesz's own works, as well as on 18th-century operas, Debussy, and Weill.

WHITHORNE

Howard, John Tasker, *Emerson Whithorne,* New York, 1929.

WILLIAMS

Slonimsky, Nicolas, *Alberto Williams: Father of Argentine Music,* in *Musical America,* Jan. 1942, p. 11.

WOLF-FERRARI

Grisson, Alexandra Carola, *Ermanno Wolf-Ferrari,* 2d edn., Zürich, 1958.
Chief source of information, pending a publication by W. Pfannkuch, who points out some of Grisson's mistakes in Mf, XIII (1960), 94, on the basis of his own diss. (Kiel, 1953).
Ringo, James, *Ermanno Wolf-Ferrari: an Appreciation of his Work,* in *Rivista musicale italiana,* XLIX (1949), 224.

WORDSWORTH

Goddard, Scott, *William Wordsworth,* in MT, CV (1964), 732.

XENAKIS

Xenakis, Yannis, *In Search of a Stochastic Music,* in *Gravesaner Blätter,* IV/11–12 (1958), 98.
—— *Elements of Stochastic Music,* in *Gravesaner Blätter,* V/18 (1960), 61, and VI/21 (1961), 102.
—— *Musiques formelles: nouveaux principes formels de composition musicale,* special issue of RM, 253/254 (1963).
—— *Free Stochastic Music from the Computer,* in *Gravesaner Blätter,* 26 (1965), 79.
Similar to Chapter IV of *Musiques formelles,* a good introduction to Xenakis's thought.

YVAIN

Yvain, Maurice, *Ma belle opérette,* Paris, 1962.
Informal memoir.

ZAKHAROV

Livanova, Tamara Nikolaievna, *Vladimir Grigor'evich Zakharov: tvorcheskii put',* Moscow, 1954.
—— *V. G. Zakharov: kratkii ocherk zhizni i tvorchestva,* Moscow, 1962.
The earlier book, on Zakharov's creative path, is the more ample one.

ZEMLINSKY

Adler, Felix, *Zemlinsky,* in *Anbruch,* V (1923), 144.
Chief source of information on Schoenberg's teacher.

ZILLIG

Zillig, Winfried, *Variationen über neue Musik,* Munich, 1959.
—— *Ein kleines Selbstporträt,* in *Musica,* XVIII (1964), 319.
Taped interview with W.-E. von Lewinski. Zillig emphasizes the current collective synthesis of the achievements of Schoenberg and Stravinsky.

JAZZ
(not including items devoted to a single individual)

Balliett, Whitney, *The Sound of Surprise: 46 Pieces on Jazz*, New York, 1959.
—— *Dinosaurs in the Morning: 41 Pieces on Jazz*, Philadelphia, 1962.
  Reviews from *The New Yorker*, distinguished by Balliett's fresh metaphors for
  sonorities. See also William Youngren's comment on Balliett in *The Partisan Review*,
  XXXII (1965), 92.
Berendt, Joachim-Ernst, *Der Jazz: eine zeitkritische Studie*, Stuttgart, 1950.
  First of many books by a leading German specialist on the subject, offering a serious
  interpretation. Berendt's more recent books, available in English and Italian as well
  as German, include well-organized comprehensive information, but little new thought.
—— *The New Jazz Book: a History and Guide*, transl. by D. Morgenstern, New York, 1962.
Blesh, Rudi, *Shining Trumpets, a History of Jazz*, New York, 1946; 4th enl. edn., London,
  1958.
  Pioneer research on the legendary New Orleans bandsmen and their background, full
  of information and insight, though one-sided. N. Waterman, in NotesMLA, XVI
  (1959), 254, points out that the new edn. exaggerates the bias of the first.
—— and Harriet Janis, *They All Played Ragtime: the True Story of American Music*, New
  York, 1950.
  More fresh information again presented with unfortunate polemics.
Broyard, Anatole, *A Portrait of the Hipster*, in *The Partisan Review*, XV (1948), 721.
—— *Keep Cool, Man: the Negro Rejection of Jazz*, in *Commentary*, XI (1951), 359.
  Well written essays, of a type that is mostly badly written.
Brubeck, Dave, and Daniel G. Hoffman, *Two Views of Jazz*, in *Perspectives USA*, 15
  (1956), 21.
Brunn, H. O., *The Story of the Original Dixieland Jazz Band*, Baton Rouge, 1960.
  First fruits of the Archive of New Orleans Jazz at Tulane University. Lacking in
  perspective but valuable for detailed facts.
Burlin, Natalie Curtis, *Negro Music at Birth*, in MQ, V (1919), 86.
—— *Black Singers and Players*, in MQ, V (1919), 499.
Carl Gregor, Herzog zu Mecklenburg, and Waldemar Scheck, *Die Theorie des Blues im
  modernen Jazz*, Strasbourg, 1963.
  Brief study, including (pp. 86–88) an unusually good account of jazz syncopation.
Carter, Elliott, *Once Again Swing*, in MM, XVI (1939), 99.
—— *The Rhythmic Basis of American Music*, in *The Score*, 12 (1955), 27.
  Carter discerns an underlying common element in jazz, Ives, Sessions, Harris,
  Copland, et al.
Cerulli, Dom, Burt Korall, and Mort Nasatir, *The Jazz Word*, New York, 1960.
  Uneven collection of short pieces, including a "self-portrait" by Miles Davis (p. 48)
  and a tribute to Charlie Parker by Jack Kerouac (p. 126).
Charters, A. R. Danberg, *Negro Folk Elements in Classic Ragtime*, in *Ethnomusicology*,
  V (1961), 174.
Charters, Samuel B., *Jazz: New Orleans 1885–1957. An Index to the Negro Musicians of New
  Orleans*, Belleville, N.J., 1958.
  Brief and factual.
—— *The Country Blues*, New York, 1959.
  Valuable survey, including fresh information and sensible comparisons.
—— and Leonard Kunstadt, *Jazz: a History of the New York Scene*, New York, 1962.
  First attempt at a hard task.
Cœuroy, André, and André Schaeffner, *Le Jazz*, Paris, 1926.
  First book-length criticism.
Coker, Jerry C., *Improvising Jazz*, Englewood Cliffs, 1964.
  A book of systematic instructions for capable players. Forewords by Stan Kenton
  and Gunther Schuller.

Condon, Eddie, and Richard Gehman, *Treasury of Jazz*, New York, 1956.
> Anthology of first-hand testimony, lacking documentation.

Cook, Will Marion, *"Spirituals" and "Jazz,"* in *The New York Times*, Dec. 26, 1926, p. vii–8–2.
> On the long history of the Charleston.

Dauer, Alfons M., *Der Jazz: seine Ursprünge und seine Entwicklung*, Eisenach, 1958.
> Nearly 100 pages of musical examples transcribed by the author from recordings of early jazz and African music make this book uniquely valuable, even to readers ignorant of German. A. Schaeffner, in *Revue de musicologie*, XLV (1960), 116, and H. Reinecke, in Mf, XIII (1960), 105, cogently criticize Dauer's interpretation of his material.

—— *Jazz: die magische Musik: ein Leitfaden durch den Jazz*, Bremen, 1961.
> A survey, more interesting than most, though often arguable.

Davin, Tom, *Conversations with James P. Johnson*, in *Jazz Review*, II/5 (June 1959), 15, and II/6 (July), 10.
> Uniquely valuable memoirs of music in Jersey City and New York before World War I.

Ellison, Ralph, *As the Spirit Moves Mahalia*, in *The Saturday Review*, Sept. 27, 1958, p. 41; also in Ellison, *Shadow and Act*, New York, 1964, p. 213.
> Superb evocation of religious jazz, in particular the singing of Mahalia Jackson.

Feather, Leonard G., *The Encyclopedia of Jazz*, new edn., New York, 1960.
> Chiefly a biographical dictionary, but supplemented with interesting general material. The best of many similar efforts, and best of many books on jazz by Feather.

Ferstl, Erich, *Die Schule des Jazz*, Munich, 1963.
> Unique well-written guide for a musically literate reader who wants to play jazz. Almost no proper names, no concern with stylistic subdivisions, but packed with suggestions for an alert critic or historian as well as amateur.

Finkelstein, Sidney, *Jazz: a People's Music*, New York, 1948.
> Excellent survey up to the beginnings of "bop," organized by a Marxist interpretation and informed by genuine love and understanding of many kinds of music.

—— *What Jazz Means to Me*, in *Studies in Ethnomusicology*, I (1961), 23.
> Finkelstein's summing-up: "A thin stream of beautiful, creative music within a mass of music that because of its methods of plagiarism and robbery, its mechanical production, its heartlessness doused with sentimentality, is the worst music in the history of the world."

Fletcher, Tom, *100 Years of the Negro in Show Business*, New York, 1954.
> Includes rare detailed information, especially for the years 1890–1910 when the author was active himself.

Fox, Charles, Peter Gammond, and Alun Morgan, *Jazz on Record: a Critical Guide*, London, 1960.
> Alphabetical list of performers, with biography and discography. More comprehensive and reliable than other books of similar size (352 pp.) and similar aims.

Frank, Waldo D., *Jazz and Folk Art*, in *The New Republic*, XLIX (1926), 42.
> A poet's insight, too little noted: "Jazz is not so much a folk music—like the spirituals—as a folk accent in music. It expresses well a mass response to our world of . . . mechanized laws. The response is of the folk and passive . . . a personal maladjustment to this world, righted by sheer and shrewd compliance."

Frankenstein, Alfred, *Syncopating Saxophones*, Chicago, 1925.
> Essays by a clarinetist, admirer of Paul Whiteman, later to become an outstanding critic of serious music.

Gleason, Ralph J., ed., *Jam Session: an Anthology of Jazz*, New York, 1958.
> Well chosen essays on major figures.

Gombosi, Otto, *The Pedigree of the Blues*, in *Music Teachers' National Association: Proceedings*, XL (1946), 382.

Green, Benny, *The Reluctant Art: Five Studies in the Growth of Jazz*, London, 1962.
> Fresh interpretations of Beiderbecke, Goodman, Lester Young, Billie Holiday, and Charlie Parker.

Grossman, William L., and Jack W. Farrell, *The Heart of Jazz*, New York, 1956.
> Information on the Dixieland jazz of the 1940s, with an appeal for amateur maintenance of "the tradition."

Haenschen, Merle, *"He who Hesitates . . .,"* in *Musical America*, Oct. 27, 1928, p. 15.
> Interview with (or perhaps, in view of the author's unusual name, a direct statement by) Merle Johnston, saxophonist, who "has made a thorough study of microphone technique," and prepares his pupils for jobs in radio and recording.

Hanson, Chadwick Clarke, *Social Influences on Jazz Style: Chicago 1920–30*, in *American Quarterly*, XII (1960), 493.
> Based on part of an interesting diss. (Minnesota, 1956), this article contributes new facts and sensible interpretations.

Hentoff, Nat, *The Jazz Life*, New York, 1962.

Hodeir, André, *Introduction à la musique du jazz*, Paris, 1948.
> Superseded, at least for English readers, by Hodeir's *Jazz, its Evolution and Essence*, but memorable to the present writer as changing his orientation in the field.

—— *Jazz: its Evolution and Essence*, transl. by Warren D. Noakes, New York, 1956.

—— *Toward Jazz*, transl. by N. Burch, New York, 1962.
> Collected essays.

Jones, LeRoi, *Blues People: Negro Music in White America*, New York, 1963.
> Survey from slave songs to the latest jazz by a young poet-dramatist whose main motive is to challenge American society by exalting the "Negro psyche." A more sustained effort, but less penetrating than those of James Baldwin and Ralph Ellison. See Ellison's review of Jones in *Shadow and Act*, New York, 1964, p. 247.

Kurath, Gertrude P., and Nadia Chilkovsky, *Jazz Choreology*, in A. F. C. Wallace, ed., *Men and Cultures: Selected Papers of the Vth International Congress of Anthropological and Ethnological Sciences, 1956*, Philadelphia, 1960, p. 152.
> Specifies 13 characteristics of bodily movement associated with jazz.

Longstreet, Stephen, *The Real Jazz, Old and New*, Baton Rouge, 1956.

Lucas, John, *The Fine Art Jive of Stuart Davis*, in *Arts*, XXXI/10 (Sept. 1957), 32.
> With reference also to Matisse, Léger, Dubuffet, and other painters, Lucas shows the development of Davis's continuing deep concern with jazz.

Malson, Lucien, *Histoire du jazz moderne*, Paris, 1961.
> Independent, incisive criticism, worth attention in America.

—— *Maîtres du jazz*, Paris, 1958; 4th edn., 1962.

Mehegan, John F., *Jazz Improvisation: Tonal and Rhythmic Principles* (preface by Leonard Bernstein), New York, 1959.
> A textbook for patient learners.

Merriam, Alan P., *Music in American Culture*, in *American Anthropologist*, LVII (1955), 1173.
> Good summary of musical acculturation, with some emphasis on jazz.

—— *The Jazz Community*, in *Social Forces*, XXXVIII (1960), 211.
> Scholarly and sympathetic description of a state of affairs usually discussed in supercilious tones.

Morgan, Alun, and Raymond Horricks, *Modern Jazz: a Survey of Developments Since 1939*, London, 1956.
> Comprehensive and open-minded, but concluding that Ellington ranks first.

Newton, Francis, *The Jazz Scene*, New York, 1960.
> The best comprehensive book since Finkelstein's, by a native of Vienna long resident in England. Useful as an introduction, and useful also as critique for more expert readers.

Ostransky, Leroy, *The Anatomy of Jazz*, Seattle, 1960.

Panassié, Hugues, *Le Jazz hot*, Paris, 1934; English transl. as *Hot Jazz*, New York, 1936.
> First of many influential books on jazz by Panassié. Original in combining precise discography with enthusiastic literary interpretation.

—— *The Real Jazz*, rev. enl. edn., New York, 1960.
> Mostly uncomprehending criticism of developments since 1940.

Pyke, Launcelot Allen, II, *Jazz, 1920 to 1927: an Analytical Study*, Univ. of Iowa diss., 1962.
> Includes transcriptions of 10 scores, from records available on Folkways label.

Discussion of these pieces is uniquely detailed. Though no new insight results, this study is a good beginning.

Ramsey, Frederic, *Been Here and Gone*, New Brunswick, N.J., 1960.
Pioneer scholar of American Negro music, including jazz, Ramsey presents here a beautiful distillation of his findings on the place of many kinds of music in Negro life. A Folkways recording matches the book.

—— and C. E. Smith, *Jazzmen*, New York, 1939; new edn., London, 1957.
Well written studies of 15 leading musicians, not superseded by later events.

Rogers, M. Robert, *Jazz Influence in French Music*, in MQ, XXI (1935), 53.
Examples from Debussy, Satie, Milhaud, and Stravinsky.

Roth, Russell, *On the Instrumental Origins of Jazz*, in American Quarterly, IV (1952), 305.
Reports fresh study of "skiffle bands," and claims exaggerated importance for them.

Sargeant, Winthrop, *Jazz: Hot and Hybrid*, New York, 1938; new enl. edn., 1946.

Schuller, Gunther, *The Future of Form in Jazz*, in Saturday Review, Jan. 12, 1957, p. 62.
Schuller surveys recent jazz in the light of Schoenberg and Webern. Compare Schuller's articles on Ellington.

Shapiro, Elliott, *"Ragtime" USA*, in NotesMLA, VIII (1951), 457.

Shapiro, Nat, and Nat Hentoff, eds., *Hear Me Talkin' to Ya: the Story of Jazz by the Men Who Made It*, New York, 1955.
Fascinating material, lacking documentation.

—— *The Jazz Makers*, New York, 1957.
21 profile sketches.

Shaw, Arnold, *Popular Music from Minstrel Songs to Rock 'n' Roll*, in P. H. Lang, ed. *One Hundred Years of Music in America*, New York, 1961, p. 140.

Stearns, Marshall Winslow, *The Story of Jazz*, New York, 1956; new edn., with expanded bibliography, 1958.
A Chaucer scholar and devoted admirer of jazz, Stearns provides a uniquely impartial and documented survey, lacking however in musical precision.

—— *Main Trends in Jazz Today*, in Musical America, Jan. 1961, p. 22.
Four-fold classification.

Ulanov, Barry, *A History of Jazz in America*, New York, 1955.

—— *A Handbook of Jazz*, New York, 1957.

Waterman, Guy, *Ragtime*, in M. Williams, ed., *The Art of Jazz*, New York, 1959, p. 11.
Excellent study of style and forms.

Williams, Martin T., ed., *The Art of Jazz: Essays on the Nature and Development of Jazz*, New York, 1959.
Unusually sober collection of studies.

—— *Jazz Panorama, from the Pages of the Jazz Review*, New York, 1962.

Wilson, John S., *Forty Years in the Groove: the Vital Role of Records in the Growth of Jazz*, in High Fidelity, VII (Feb. 1957), 45.

Work, John W., *Changing Patterns in Negro Folk Songs*, in Journal of American Folklore, LXII (1949), 136.
Valuable source of information on instrumental music in the Holiness Church and on the gospel songs of Thomas A. Dorsey.

EXPERIMENTAL MUSIC
(microtones, electronic music, *musique concrète*, etc.)

Barbour, J. Murray, *Tuning and Temperament: a Historical Survey*, East Lansing, Mich., 1951.
Based on a diss. (Cornell, 1935), this survey is valuable but not definitive.

Bender, G., *Interview d'un apôtre du futurisme musical*, in Guide du concert, III (1912), 321.

Cahill, Thaddeus, *The Generating and Distributing of Music by Means of Alternators*, in *Electrical World*, XLVII (1906), 519.

Source for Roy Stannard Baker's illustrated article, *New Music for an Old World*, in *McClure's Magazine*, XXVII (1906), 291, which came to the attention of Busoni.

Cavallini, Edoardo, *Il pluricromatismo nell'evoluzione musicale*, in *Rivista musicale italiana*, XLVIII (1946), 130.

—— *Per un'intesa sull'unificazione dei segni pluricromatici*, in *Rivista musicale italiana*, XLVIII (1946), 516.

—— *Dodecafonia e pluricromatismo*, in *Rivista musicale italiana*, LII (1950), 263.

Clark, Melville, Jr., *Proposed Keyboard Musical Instrument*, in *Journal of the Acoustical Society of America*, XXXI (1959), 403.

> A keyboard sensitive to both speed and distance of depression would control a tone generator with specified attack and decay transients characteristic of familiar instruments. Choral effects and variable room resonance simulated. This design should be realized.

Daniélou, Alain, *Traité de musicologie comparée*, Paris, 1959.

> Concerned almost exclusively with scales, Daniélou presents a maximum of differentiations of pitch.

Döhl, Friedhelm, *Wege der neuen Musik: zur Entwicklung der seriellen, elektronischen und experimentellen Musik*, in NZfM, CXXVI (1965), 105; also in *Das Orchester*, XIII (1965), 124.

> Clear, concise account of one brightly lighted path in the 1950s and early 1960s.

Drudi Gambillo, Maria, and Teresa Fiori, *Archivi del futurismo*, 2 vols., Rome, 1958.

> Complete manifestos and other documents.

Écorcheville, Jules, *Le Futurisme ou le bruit dans la musique*, in BSIM, IX/2 (Dec. 1913), 1.

Fabbro, Beniamino dal, *Esperienze musicali di Jean Dubuffet*, Venice, 1962.

> A booklet, with text in Italian and French, to introduce the painter Dubuffet's six discs recording his experiments in sound.

Fickénscher, Arthur, *The "Polytone" and the Potentialities of a Purer Intonation*, in MQ, XXVII (1941), 356.

Fokker, Adriaan Daniel, et al., *Recherches musicales, théoriques et pratiques*, The Hague, 1951.

—— *Equal Temperament and the 31-Keyed Organ*, in *Scientific Monthly*, 81 (1955), 161.

Hiller, Lejaren A., Jr., *Informationstheorie und Computermusik*, Mainz, 1964.

> Interesting account of work at Hiller's studio in Illinois, both in composition and analysis. Includes study of Webern's Symphony, first movement.

—— and Robert A. Baker, *Computer Cantata: a Study in Compositional Method*, in PNM, III/1 (1964), 62.

—— *Automated Music Printing*, in JMT, IX (1965), 129.

—— and Leonard M. Isaacson, *Experimental Music: Composition with an Electronic Computer*, New York, 1959.

> Includes score of the *Iliac Suite* for string quartet (1956).

—— *Computer Music*, in *Scientific American*, CCI/6 (Dec. 1959), 109.

Johnston, Ben, *Scalar Order as a Compositional Resource*, in PNM, II/2 (1964), 56.

> Logical argument for anticipating a non-tempered microtonal scale. "Serial technique is only an interim solution."

Judd, Frederick C., *Electronic Music and Musique Concrète*, London, 1961.

> A short introduction, especially for amateur composers ready to learn a bit of engineering.

Klein, Sigmund, *Quarter-Tone Data*, in *Franco-American Musical Society Bulletin*, Mar. 1925, p. 21.

Kornerup, Thorvald Otto, *Musical Acoustics*, Copenhagen, 1922.

Kraehenbuehl, David, and Christopher Schmidt, *On the Development of Musical Systems*, in JMT, VI (1962), 32.

Labroca, Mario, et al., *Un problema aperto*, in *La Biennale*, XI/44–45 (Dec. 1961), 3.

> Questionnaire on "experimental music," with replies by Berio and other composers, mostly rejecting the label. Summaries in French, German, English, and handsome pictures.

Le Caine, Hugh, *Synthetic Means*, in J. Beckwith and U. Kasemets, eds., *The Modern Composer and his World*, Toronto, 1961, p. 109.

Mandelbaum, Mayer Joel, *Multiple Division of the Octave and the Tonal Resources of 19–Tone Temperament*, Indiana Univ. diss., 1961.

> Excellent systematic survey of previous efforts, unbiased by the decision in favor of 19 tones per octave, which is supported rather by short compositions in diverse styles.

Marie, Jean-Étienne, *Musique électronique, expérimentale et concrète*, in Roland-Manuel, ed., *Histoire de la musique Pléiade*, Paris, 1963, II, 1418.

Marks, Robert, *Theremin Plans Electrical Orchestra*, in *Musical America*, Sept. 15, 1928, 25.

Mathews, Max V., *An Acoustic Compiler for Music and Psychological Stimuli*, in *Bell System Technical Journal*, XL (1961), 677.

Moellendorf, Willi von, *Musik mit Vierteltönen*, Leipzig, 1917.

Moles, Abraham A., *Perspectives de l'instrumentation électronique*, in *Revue belge de musicologie*, XIII (1959), 11.

—— *Les Musiques expérimentales: revue d'une tendance importante de la musique contemporaine*, Paris, 1960.

> Translated [from English?] by D. Charles, this is one of the best surveys of the field, by an expert in technology with an admirable literary style and sensible political-philosophical point of view, enabling him to avoid all worries about the relation of the new "tendency" to musical traditions. Moreover, the book is unusually handsome.

Noé, Günther von, *Terminologie der seriellen Musik—über Herkunft und Bedeutung neuer musikalischer Begriffe*, in NZfM, CXXV (1964), 422.

> Sensible, concise exposition of such fashionable terms as "parameter," "permutation," and "aleatory."

Olson, H. F., and H. Belar, and J. Timmens, *Electronic Music Synthesis*, in *Journal of the Acoustical Society of America*, XXXII (1960), 311.

Paik, Nam June, et al., *Die Fluxus-Leute*, in *Magnum* (Cologne), 47 (Apr. 1963), 32.

> Part of a richly illustrated special issue on experimentalism in cultural life generally.

Prieberg, Fred K., *Musik des technischen Zeitalters*, Zürich, 1956.

—— *Musica ex machina: über das Verhaltnis von Musik und Technik*, Berlin, 1960.

> Quick sweep from futurism to the latest electronic manifestations, with pictures.

Schaeffer, Pierre, *A la recherche d'une musique concrète*, Paris, 1952.

> Charming, unpretentious, diary-like account of the origins of *musique concrète*.

—— *Vers une musique expérimentale*, special issue of RM, 236 (1957).

—— ed., *Expériences musicales, musiques concrète, électronique, exotique*, special issue of RM, 244 (1959).

—— *Musique concrète et connaissance de l'objet musical*, in *Revue belge de musicologie*, XIII (1959), 62.

Shackford, Charles R., *Some Aspects of Perception*, in JMT, V (1961), 162, and VI (1962), 66.

> Rigorous work on the frontier of knowledge about hearing.

Stein, Richard H., *Vierteltonmusik*, in *Die Musik*, XV (1923), 510, 741.

> Reports congress at Stein's home, 1922, attended by Hába, Vyshnegradsky, Mager, Moellendorff, Baglioni and Lourié.

Tanaka, Shohé, *Studien im Gebiete der reinen Stimmung*, in *Vierteljahrschrift für Musikwissenschaft*, VI (1890), 23.

Tipple, Esther Watson, and R. M. Frye, *A Graphic Introduction to the Harmon*, Boston, 1942.

> On the invention of James Paul White, providing 53 tones per octave.

Ussachevsky, Vladimir, *The Processes of Experimental Music*, in *Journal of the Audio Engineering Society*, VI (1958), 202.

—— *Columbia-Princeton Electronic Music Center*, in *Revue belge de musicologie*, XIII (1959), 129.

Vyshnegradsky, Ivan, *Manuel d'harmonie à quarts de ton*, Paris, 1933.

—— *L'Énigme de la musique moderne*, in *Revue d'esthétique*, II (1949), 67 and 181.

—— *Problèmes d'ultrachromatisme*, in *Polyphonie*, IX/X (1954), 129.

Winckel, Fritz, *Limites de la musique électronique*, in *Revue belge de musicologie*, XIII (1959), 26.

—— *Berliner Electronik*, in *Melos*, XXX (1963), 279.

> Good account of the Tonstudio der Technischen Universität, where Winckel collaborated with Blacher and Manfred Krause.

Würmschmidt, Joseph, *Viertel- und Sechsteltonmusik: eine kritische Studie,* in *Neue Musikzeitung,* XLII (1921), 183.

—— *Die 19-stufige Skala: eine natürliche Erweiterung unseres Tonsystems,* in *Neue Musikzeitung,* XLII (1921), 215.

Yasser, Joseph, *A Theory of Evolving Tonality,* New York, 1932.

    The most ample discussion before Mandelbaum of microtones in the context of recent Western music, with a genuine new theory, not widely known.

—— *The Future of Tonality,* in MM, supplement to issue of Nov.–Dec. 1930.

    Same as pp. 329–352 of *A Theory of Evolving Tonality.*

BIBLIOGRAPHIES

Andreis, Josip, *Tragom suvremene muzičke bibliografie,* in *Zvuk,* 37–38 (1960), 348.

    Summary in French. Selective bibliography of contemporary music, drawn from Andreis's card file of 7000 items.

Basart, Ann Phillips, *Serial Music: a Classified Bibliography on 12-Tone and Electronic Music,* Berkeley, 1961.

Bull, Storm, *Index to Biographies of Contemporary Composers,* New York, 1964.

    About 6000 names of composers born since 1900 or living since 1949, with reference to some 60 books such as music dictionaries. Occasionally useful.

Deliège, Célestin, *Bibliographie [de la musique atonale et sérielle . . . textes parus depuis la publication des ouvrages de Leibowitz],* in *Revue belge de musicologie,* XIII (1959), 132.

Edmunds, John, *Some 20th-Century American Composers: a Selective Bibliography* (Introductions by P. Yates and N. Slonimsky), 2 vols., New York, 1959–60.

    Valuable lists for 32 composers.

Merriam, Alan P., *A Short Bibliography of Jazz,* in NotesMLA, X (1953), 202.

    163 items selected from 3000, with Merriam's notes. A similar or still shorter list brought up-to-date would be valuable.

Mitchell, Donald, *"The Emancipation of the Dissonance." A Selected Bibliography,* in *Hinrichsen's Music Book,* VII (1952), 141.

Reisner, Robert George, *The Literature of Jazz: a Selective Bibliography,* 2d edn., New York, 1959.

    Supplements Merriam's list, but without comments.

MISCELLANEOUS

Adrio, Adam, *Die Komposition des Ordinarium Missae in der evangelischen Kirchenmusik der Gegenwart—ein Überblick,* in A. A. Abert and W. Pfannkuch, eds., *Festschrift Friedrich Blume zum 70. Geburtstag,* Kassel, 1963, p. 22.

Alaleona, Domenico, *I moderni orizzonti della tecnica musicale,* in *Rivista musicale italiana,* XVIII (1911), 382.

—— *L'armonia modernissima: le tonalità neutre e l'arte di stupore,* in *Rivista musicale italiana,* XVIII (1911), 769.

    After an abstract explanation of the "neutral" character of the whole-tone scale and of *dodecafonia* (his neologism), Alaleona presents an interesting series of examples, from Verdi to his own works, showing "the art of stunning."

Alberti, Luciano, *L'opera del novecento e le molte vie della sua messinscena,* in *La Rassegna musicale,* XXXII (1962), 296.
> Longest article in a special issue devoted to 20th-century opera, with fine illustrations.

Alte und neue Musik. Das Basler [Kammerchor und] Kammerorchester unter Leitung von Paul Sacher, 1926–1951, Zürich, 1952.
> Program notes, including contributions by and about composers commissioned for the Basel orchestra—Bartók, Stravinsky, Martin, et al.

Ansermet, Ernest, *Les Fondements de la musique dans la conscience humaine,* 2 vols., Neuchâtel, 1961.
> Intricate argument, ranging from acoustics to theology, and including many pages on Debussy, Stravinsky, Schoenberg, et al.

Armstrong, Thomas, *The Frankfort Group,* in PRMA, 85 (1959), 1.
> Cyril Scott, Percy Grainger, Balfour Gardiner, Roger Quilter, and Norman O'Neill, all pupils of Ivan Knorr around 1900.

Auden, Wystan Hugh, *Some Reflections on Music and Opera,* in *The Partisan Review,* XIX (1952), 10; also in U. Weisstein, ed., *The Essence of Opera,* New York, 1964, p. 354.
> Wise, witty, wide-ranging remarks by the most eminent librettist of the 20th century.

Bachman, Fritz, *Lied, Schlager, Schnulze: einige Möglichkeiten und Ergebnisse der Melodie-Analyse der "Alltagsmusik,"* Leipzig, 1960.
> Thousands of examples of phrases, contrasting the debilitating character of most popular melodies with the true simplicity of folksong. An extraordinary study, useful even without knowledge of German.

Beaufils, Marcel, *Musique du son—musique du verbe,* Paris, 1954.
> Survey of styles of declamation, especially valuable on Fauré and Debussy.

Beck, Georges, *Compositeurs contemporains,* Paris, 1960.
> A booklet presenting 27 little-known composers whose music is published by Heugel, with biographical sketches. A few are American, most French; all born since 1898, most since 1920.

Bekker, Paul, *Klang und Eros* (his *Gesammelte Schriften,* II), Stuttgart, 1923.
> Includes valuable critiques of early Hindemith, Rottenberg, and Stephan.

—— *Neue Musik* (his *Gesammelte Schriften,* III), Stuttgart, 1923.
> More here on Rottenberg.

—— *Organische und mechanische Musik,* Stuttgart, 1928.

—— *Briefe an zeitgenössische Musiker,* Berlin, 1932.

Berger, Karlhanns, *Die Funktionsbestimmung der Musik in der Sowjetideologie,* Berlin, 1963.
> Excellent assemblage of documents, presented with critical sympathy. Concerned mainly with the period 1948–58, and with ideas more than with particular pieces of music.

Borris, Siegfried, *Über Wesen und Werden der neuen Musik in Deutschland: vom Expressionismus zum Vitalismus* (his *Beiträge zu einer neuen Musikkunde,* II), Berlin, 1948.

—— et al., *Vergleichende Interpretationskunde. 7 Beiträge,* Berlin, 1963.

Briggs, Asa, *Mass Entertainment: the Origins of a Modern Industry,* Adelaide, 1960.
> A distinguished economist's brilliant lecture, packed with detail that is hard to find elsewhere.

Bruyr, José, *L'Operette,* Paris, 1962.
> Brief, up-to-date survey, with emphasis on France but some account of other nations.

Burkhart, Charles, *Anthology for Musical Analysis,* New York, 1964.
> Bartók and Webern are represented by 3 short pieces each; Schoenberg, Stravinsky and Hindemith by 2; Debussy, Ives, Dallapiccola and Babbitt by 1. Brief introductory notes and references to readings are well chosen.

Butor, Michel, *La Musique, art réaliste,* in *Esprit,* XXVIII/1 (Jan. 1960), 138.
> In a special issue devoted to modern music, all contributions of composers and music critics are surpassed by this long essay by the novelist.

Calvocoressi, Michel-Dmitri, *Musician's Gallery: Music and Ballet in Paris and London: Recollections,* London, 1933.

Ravel's close friend knew also Satie, Stravinsky, Vaughan Williams, et al. His memoirs of them are lively.

Carpitella, Diego, *Convergenze fra indagine etnomusicologica e ricerche espressive contemporanee*, in *Rassegna musicale*, XXXI (1961), 390.

Charles, Daniel, *Entr'acte: "Formal" or "Informal" Music?*, in MQ, LI (1965), 144; also in P. H. Lang and N. Broder, eds., *Contemporary Music in Europe*, New York, 1965, p. 144.
Boulez and Xenakis contrasted with each other, and both with Cage, in terms of their philosophical programs.

Chasins, Abram, *Speaking of Pianists*, New York, 1957; 2d edn., with suppl., 1961.
Vivid accounts of the playing of Rachmaninov, Schnabel, Godowsky, Tovey, Gershwin, Prokofiev, et al., by a pianist-composer with rare skill at description.

Chemodanov, Sergei Mikhailovich, *Istoria muzyki v sviazi s istoriei obshchestvennogo razvitia: oput marksistskogo postroenia istorii muzyki*, Kiev, 1927.

—— *An Economic Approach to Music*, in MM, X (1933), 175.

Colpi, Henri, *Défense et illustration de la musique dans le film*, Lyon, 1963.
Conscientious and thoughtful study, including discussion of Jaubert (pp. 116–22), and of Chaplin (pp. 153–55).

Costère, Edmond, *Mort ou transfiguration de l'harmonie*, Paris, 1962.
Based on a diss. (Paris, 1958), this book presents fresh ideas on the harmonic details of music from Debussy through Webern. Stimulating but not convincing.

Crosland, Margaret, *Jean Cocteau*, London, 1955.
Sympathetic and discriminating survey, with much attention to music.

D'Amico, Fedele, *I Casi della musica*, Milan, 1962.
Superior critical journalism, 1954–61.

Dent, Edward J., *Looking Backward*, in R. H. Myers, ed., *Music Today*, London, 1949, p. 6.
Recollections of Donaueschingen and the founding of the ISCM.

Draper, Muriel, *Music at Midnight*, New York, 1929.
Recollections of a musical household in London, 1909–14, where Szymanowski, Casals, and other friends were often "at home."

Druskin, M. S., et al., eds., *Voprosy sovremennoi muzyki*, Leningrad, 1963.
Questions of contemporary music; interesting essays on techniques.

Edlund, Lars, *Modus novus: Lärobok i fritonal melodiläsning; Studies in Reading Atonal Melodies*, Stockholm, 1963.
Unique practical contribution to the "theory" of 20th-century music. Working at the exercises and selections from music that Edlund has arranged systematically helps a student develop the ability to make his own analyses. Ability to read swiftly and accurately in older styles is presupposed.

Ellison, Ralph, *Shadow and Act*, New York, 1964.
Essays and reviews, 1942–64, including 7 fine pieces on music.

Erpf, Hermann, *Entwicklungszüge in der zeitgenössischen Musik*, Karlsruhe, 1922.
One of the first attempts by a scholar to treat the work of Schoenberg, Stravinsky, and Bartók at length.

—— *Studien zur Harmonie- und Klangtechnik der neueren Musik*, Leipzig, 1927.
Erpf's concept of extended (*erweiterte*) tonality works well for Bartók.

—— *Vom Wesen der neuen Musik*, Stuttgart, 1949.
Erpf's contribution to the catching-up process of younger German musicians.

—— *Tagesfragen des Musiklebens, 1950–1957: Rundfunkreferate, Aufsätze, Ansprachen*, Stuttgart, 1957.

—— *Wie soll es weitergehen?*, Rodenkirchen, 1958.
"We are still in a transition."

—— *Lehrbuch der Instrumentation und Instrumentenkunde*, Mainz, 1959.
Includes examples from Webern, Messiaen, Boulez, et al., and a final consideration of the relations between instrumental medium and form.

Fischer, Kurt von, *Die Begegnung der abendländischen Tonkunst mit der aussereuropäischen Musik*, in *Europa und der Kolonialismus*, Zürich, 1962, p. 267.
Excellent survey, defining Debussy's absorption of exotic elements, in a perspective including plainsong and synagogue chant, Messiaen and Boulez.

Flesch, Carl, *The Memoirs*, transl. by H. Keller, London, 1957.
> Detailed recollections of a fine violinist and teacher, who knew many composers well.

Fleury, Louis, *Souvenirs d'un flutiste*, in *Le monde musical*, XXXV (1924), 44, 89, 139, 218; XXXVI (1925), 10.

—— *Chamber Music for Wind Instruments*, in *The Chesterian*, 36 (1924), 111, and 37 (1924), 144.

Flothuis, Marius, *Vocal Compositions by Dutch Composers Based on English Texts*, in *Musical Opinion*, LXXXVIII (1965), 471.

Forte, Allen, *Contemporary Tone-Structures*, New York, 1955.
> Careful analysis of short pieces by Stravinsky, Milhaud, Sessions, Copland, Bartók, Hindemith, and longer pieces by Schoenberg, Stravinsky and Bartók. Method of analysis varies with style of music.

Fünf und zwanzig Jahre neue Musik; Jahrbuch 1926 der Universal-Edition, Vienna, 1926.

Gollancz, Victor, *Journey Towards Music: a Memoir*, London, 1964.
> Rich memoirs and lively expression of opinions by a modest connoisseur.

Hacquard, Georges, *La Musique et le cinéma*, Paris, 1959.
> Good brief survey.

Hadow, William Henry, *Some Aspects of Modern Music*, in MQ, I (1915), 57.
> The great Victorian scholar was more perceptive than many of his juniors in recognizing Schoenberg and Stravinsky as leaders, and in defining some of the differences between them.

—— *Diatonic and Chromatic*, in *The Dominant*, I/1 (Nov. 1927), 9.
> An up-to-date survey, with a graceful recantation on Gesualdo, and an expression of open-mindedness toward Schoenberg.

Harrison, Frank Ll., and Joan Rimmer, *European Musical Instruments*, New York, 1965.
> Essay by an excellent scholar addressing the common reader with freshly organized material, illustrated by 248 splendid pictures. A salutary perspective on the 20th century.

Herzfeld, Friedrich, *Der Reiz des Krebses*, in NZfM, XI (1955), 71.
> Assembles examples of retrograde motion from various composers, and comments briefly.

Hines, Robert Stephen, ed., *The Composer's Point of View: Essays on 20th-Century Choral Music by Those Who Wrote It*, Norman, Oklahoma, 1963.
> 18 contributors, including Martin, Dallapiccola, Tippett, Fricker and Persichetti, each writing on a particular piece or group of pieces.

Hughes, Gervase, *Composers of Operettas*, London, 1962.
> Unique among books on this subject in first-hand observations of the music, rather than personal anecdotes or sociological speculations.

Iankovsky, Moisei Osipovich, *Sovietskii teatr operetty*, Leningrad, 1962.
> Crowded survey of operetta, foreign and native, as produced in the USSR.

Internationaler Musikkongress Wien 1952 . . . Bericht, ed. by Dr. Fritz Racek, Vienna, 1953.

Iz arkhivov russkikh muzykantov, Moscow, 1962.
> Includes previously unpublished letters by Taneiev, Rachmaninov, Prokofiev, et al.

Jöde, Fritz, *Vom Wesen und Werden der Jugendmusik*, Mainz, 1954.
> Booklet presenting an authoritative survey, by the most eminent leader of the movement. Together with Richard Schall's article on *Jugendmusik*, in MGG, VII (1958), 286, this book seems a sufficient sampling.

Johns, Donald C., *The Protestant Chorale in Contemporary German Organ Music*, in *The American Music Teacher*, XIII/4 (Mar.-Apr. 1964), 14.
> Guide to works by David, Pepping, Distler, and especially younger men.

Keller, Hans, *The Audibility of Serial Technique*, in MMR, LXXXV (1955), 231.
> Unusually sustained concentration on questions often touched on but hastily dismissed. Keller's answers differ from the present writer's, and help induce him to regard these as tentative.

—— *Principles of Composition*, in *The Score*, 26 (Jan. 1960), 35; 27 (July 1960), 9.
> Systematic though concise discussion of "precomposition, purity and consistency of

style, audibility, rhythm, form, contemporaneity; writing for, against, and beyond the instruments; and the teaching of composition."

Kerman, Joseph, *Opera as Drama*, New York, 1956.
> First-rate criticism of selected works from Monteverdi's *Orfeo* to Stravinsky's *Rake*, including praise for *Pelléas* and *Wozzeck*, blame for the continuing presence in this company of *Tosca* and *Rosenkavalier*.

Klein, Fritz Heinrich, *Die Grenze der Halbtonwelt*, in *Die Musik*, XVII (1925), 281.
> An early instance of speculations arising out of Schoenberg's 12-tone technique. Klein's *Mutterakkord*, containing all 12 tones and all 6 intervals, fascinated Nicolas Slonimsky and anticipated a few of the concerns of Milton Babbitt.

Klein, Rudolf, *Anbruch unseres Jahrhunderts: von der literarischen zur optischen Epoche*, in ÖMz, XIX (1964), 202.
> Good presentation of an appealing generalization—that music has moved away from poetry toward painting. The opposite thesis, equally valid in the present author's view, would be less timely in the season of "optical art."

Klemperer, Otto, *Minor Recollections*, London, 1964.
> Memoirs of Mahler, Strauss, Schoenberg, Stravinsky, Hindemith, et al.

Kogranov, Tomas Iosifovich, and Ivan Dmitrievich Frolov, *Kino i muzyka: muzyka v dramaturgii fil'ma*, Moscow, 1964.
> Systematic discussion of the role of music in films, based chiefly on Soviet films, but including some mention of foreign films also.

Kremliev, Iulii Anatolievich, *Esteticheskie problemy sovietskoi muzyki*, Leningrad, 1959.
> Essays on esthetic (often political) problems of Soviet music, by a scholar who adapts slogans to the facts rather than facts to slogans.

Lebedeva, T. A., ed., *Muzyka i sovremennost': sbornik statei*, 2 vols., Moscow, 1962–63.
> Music and contemporaneity: collection of essays on Hindemith, Honegger, Orff, and Soviet composers.

Levit, Sofia Iosifovna, *Sovietskaia muzyka v borbe za mir*, Moscow, 1957.
> Chronicle of musical events connected with world peace conferences, 1947–53.

Lindlar, Heinrich, *77 Premieren. Ein Opern-Journal. Kritisches und Ketzerisches aus 7 Jahren*, Rodenkirchen, 1965.

——, ed., *Die Stimme der Komponisten: Aufsätze, Reden, Briefe, 1907–1958*, Rodenkirchen, 1958.
> Good selection of materials, well presented in brief scope. Several of the essays are listed separately here.

McCarty, Clifford, *Film Composers in America: a Checklist of their Work* (foreword by Lawrence Morton), Glendale, Calif., 1953.

Manvell, Roger, and John Huntley, *The Technique of Film Music*, London, 1957.

May, Elizabeth, *The Influence of the Meiji Period on Japanese Children's Music*, Berkeley, 1963.

Mazel', Lev Abramovich, *O melodii*, Moscow, 1952.
> Remarkable original study of melodic types, valuable especially for Rachmaninov and Shostakovich.

—— *K diskussii o sovremennoi garmonii*, in SM, 1962/5, p. 52.
> Contribution to the discussion of contemporary harmony.

—— *Zwei wichtige Prinzipien der künstlerischen Wirkung*, in *Kunst und Literatur*, XII (1964), 870.
> Part of a book in progress that aims toward a synthesis of theory and esthetics. Two principles: 1) usually several means work to one goal, and 2) each essential means serves several goals.

Mellers, Wilfrid H., *Music for 20th-Century Children*, in MT, CV (1964), 342, 421, 500.
> An outstanding fresh contribution, including sound criticisms of Orff, Kodály, Copland, Britten, Cage, and several younger composers.

Mellott, George Kenneth, *A Survey of Contemporary Flute Solo Literature with Analyses of Representative Compositions*, State Univ. of Iowa diss., 1964.
> Analyses of sonatas, etc., by Prokofiev, Hindemith, Varèse, Martin, Poulenc, Ibert, Dutilleux, Dahl, Boulez and Berio.

Mersmann, Hans, *Zur Methodik der Werkanalyse neuer Musik*, in *Musik im Unterricht*, LIII/7–8 (1962), 3.
—— *Leo Kestenberg (1882–1962)*, in Mf, XV (1962), 209.
    Memoir of a great reformer of music education.
Mitchell, William J., *The Study of Chromaticism*, in JMT, VI (1962), 2.
    Novel but not eccentric treatment of an idea that pervades thinking on 20th-century music. Mitchell's rigor and finesse could help any reader worried by this idea to get past his worries.
Müller-Marein, Josef, and Hannes Reinhardt, *Das musikalische Selbstportrait von Komponisten, Dirigenten, Instrumentalisten, Sängerinnen und Sängern unserer Zeit*, Hamburg, 1963.
Music—East and West. Report on 1961 Tokyo East-West Music Encounter Conference, Tokyo, 1962.
    Contributions by Bekku, Cowell, Hirashima, Thomson, et al.
La Musique et ses problèmes contemporains 1953–1963, Paris, 1963.
    Reprint of the 1954 issue of *Cahiers de la compagnie Madeleine Renaud—Jean-Louis Barrault*, in honor of the inauguration of Boulez's concert series "Domaine musicale," followed by a larger collection of new articles for the 10th anniversary.
Neumann, Friedrich, *Synthetische Harmonielehre*, Leipzig, 1951.
—— *Tonalität und Atonalität: Versuch einer Klärung*, Landsberg am Lech, 1955.
—— *Die Zeitgestalt: eine Lehre vom musikalischen Rhythmus*, 2 vols., Vienna, 1959.
    Includes examples from Bartók, Stravinsky, Hindemith, Orff, and J. N. David.
—— *Grundlagen des theoretischen Unterrichts*, in ÖMz, XVIII (1963), 356.
Norman, Gertrude, and Miriam L. Schrifte, eds., *Letters of Composers: an Anthology*, New York, 1946.
    Includes many contemporaries, down to David Diamond. Especially interesting are single letters of Varèse and Piston.
Ogolevets, Aleksei S., *Vvedenie v sovremennoe muzykal'noe myshlenie*, Moscow, 1946.
    Introduction to contemporary musical thought by a veteran theorist, with no effort to cover ground completely, and with little concern for ideology.
Parrott, Ian, *A Guide to Musical Thought*, London, 1955.
    Unique book, intended for beginning composers who admire Bartók and Vaughan Williams. Readers unable to write the exercises and readers disagreeing with Parrott's taste might still gain much from his insights.
Peeters, Flor, *The Organ in the Soviet Union*, in *Diapason*, LXVI/662 (Jan. 1965), 38.
    Specifications of chief instruments, and list of sample works by 15 composers.
Pierce, J. A., *Symbols, Signals, and Noise: the Nature and Process of Communication*, New York, 1961.
    Good survey of information theory, with a chapter on music (p. 250) for which Milton Babbitt provided some advice.
Pohlmann, Peter, *Harmonische Gesetzmässigkeiten im atonalen Bereich*, in Mf, XIII (1960), 257.
    Based on a diss. (Hamburg, 1956), this article proposes an ingenious new way of analyzing chords.
Polignac, Winnaretta Singer, Princess Edmond de, *Memoirs*, in *Horizon*, XII (1945), 110.
    Friend of Fauré, Chabrier, acquaintance of Debussy, Ravel, Hahn, and patroness of Falla, Stravinsky, Satie, and also some painters, the princess chats about them pleasantly.
Pope John XXIII, *Epistola ad Rev.mum P.D. Hyginam Angles Pamies . . .*, in *Acta apostolicae sedis*, LIII (1961), 811.
—— *Allocutio iis qui interfuerunt Coetui e variis nationibus Romae habito a consilio v. "Conseille international de la musique de l'UNESCO,"* in *Acta apostolicae sedis*, LIV (1962), 721.
Pope Pius X, *Motu proprio: Inter pastoralis officii*, in *Acta sanctae sedis*, XXXVI (1904), 329 (Ital. text) & 387 (Latin); Engl. transl. in Slonimsky, *Music since 1900*, New York, 1949, p. 629.

Pope Pius XI, *Constitutio apostolica: Divini cultus sanctitatem,* in *Acta apostolicae sedis,* XXI (1929), 33.

Pope Pius XII, *Litterae encyclicae: "Mediator Dei,"* in *Acta apostolicae sedis,* XXXIX (1947), 521.

—— *Litterae encyclicae: "Musicae sacrae disciplinae semper,"* in *Acta apostolicae sedis,* XLVIII (1956), 5.

—— *Sacra congregatio ritum. "Instructio de musica sacra,"* in *Acta apostolicae sedis,* L (1958), 630.

 The most explicit interpretation of church policy.

Rimmer, Frederick, *Mutation and Symmetry in 20th-Century Melody,* in MR, XXVI (1965), 28, 85.

 Discusses phrase-long examples of tonal curve and rhythmic succession. 3 or 4 examples from each composer: Stravinsky, Bartók, Vaughan Williams, Hindemith, Britten, Schoenberg, Webern, and Boulez.

Ringo, James, *The Lure of the Orient,* in ACA, 7/2 (1958), 8.

 Sketchy survey of influences, from Holst to Hovhaness.

Rösler, Walter, *Zeitkritik in der Musik des Kabaretts (1901–1933),* in *Beiträge zur Musikwissenschaft,* VII (1965), 3.

Rognoni, Luigi, *Espressionismo e dodecafonia,* Milan, 1954.

 Rognoni makes the ideas of Adorno and Leibowitz appealing by connecting them with a rich background of German literature and painting.

—— *Alienazione e intenzionalità musicale,* in *Aut Aut,* 79–80 (1964), 7.

 Leading article in a special issue on problems of contemporary music, treated *à la* Husserl.

Rosenfeld, Paul, *An Hour with American Music,* Philadelphia, 1929.

 Deliberately impressionistic critiques.

Skrebkov, S. S., ed., *Muzykal'no-teoreticheskie problemy sovietskoi muzyki,* Moscow, 1963.

 Collection of essays by advanced students on "music-theoretical problems," i.e., technical rather than esthetic or ideological topics, in Soviet music, particularly that of Prokofiev, Shostakovich, Miaskovsky and Shaporin.

Slonimsky, Nicolas, *The Road to Music,* rev. edn., New York, 1960.

 Articles for children from *The Christian Science Monitor.*

Smither, Howard E., *The Rhythmic Analysis of 20th-Century Music,* in JMT, VIII (1964), 54.

 Based on a diss. (Cornell, 1960), Smither's article is outstanding for its caution and penetration.

Steinberg, Michael, *Some Observations on the Harpsichord in 20th-Century Music,* in PNM, 1/2 (1963), 189.

Stephan, Rudolph, ed., *Terminologie der neuen Musik,* Berlin, 1965.

 9 papers read at Darmstadt, 1964, by 8 scholars; one of the two by Dahlhaus refers to Stravinsky.

Stilporträts der neuen Musik: sieben Beiträge (Veröffentlichungen des Instituts für Neue Musik und Musikerziehung, Darmstadt, Bd. 2), Berlin, 1961.

 Articles by S. Borris, W. Keller, H. Lindlar, W. Kolneder and W. Zillig.

Szigeti, Joseph, *With Strings Attached: Reminiscences and Reflections,* New York, 1947.

 The memoirs of a fine and adventurous violinist, with pages on Stravinsky, Bartók, Hindemith, et al.

Teatr i muzyka: dokumenty i materialy, Moscow, 1963.

 Theater and music: documents and materials. Includes letters to A. V. Ossovsky from Stravinsky, Miaskovsky, Glazunov, et al.

Thomas, Hans Alex., *Die deutsche Tonfilmmusik von den Anfängen bis 1956,* Gütersloh, 1962.

 Condensed from a diss. (Marpurg, 1957).

Tovey, Donald Francis, *Essays in Musical Analysis,* 6 vols., London, 1935–39.

 Exemplary program notes, mostly on classic works, but also on Elgar, Vaughan Williams, Somervell, and Walton. These are available separately in *Some English Symphonists: a Selection,* London, 1941.

Várnai, Péter, *Hungarian String Quartets,* in *New Hungarian Quarterly,* IV/9 (1963), 224.

Dates and brief, authoritative appraisals of the Waldbauer, Léner, Budapest, Roth, Hungarian, Végh, and Tátrai Quartets.

Weisstein, Ulrich, ed., *The Essence of Opera*, New York, 1964.
Useful anthology of writings by composers and librettists, including Debussy, Cocteau, Ramuz, Puccini, Strauss, Berg, Claudel, Weill, Brecht, Shostakovich and Auden. Several items are not available readily elsewhere, or not at all in English.

Westermann, Gerhart von, *Drei baltische Musiker*, in *Baltische Hefte*, VI (1960), 153.

—— *Musikleben in Riga Anfang des 20. Jahrhunderts*, in *Baltische Hefte*, VIII (1962), 200.

Winckel, Fritz, *Von den Wandlungen des Klangstils: über das Farbspektrum der Musik*, in *Melos*, XIX (1952), 135.
Winckel points out that electronic means can achieve a goal long aimed toward: continuous gradation of all colors throughout the audible range of pitch.

—— *Phänomene des musikalischen Hörens: aesthetisch-naturwissenschaftliche Betrachtungen; Hinweise zur Aufführungspraxis in Konzert und Rundfunk*, Berlin, 1960.
Excellent survey of recent findings in acoustics, psychology, physiology, and information theory. Summary in MGG, X (1962), 1716. A translation is in preparation.

—— *Die informationstheoretische Analyse musikalischer Strukturen*, in Mf, XVI (1964), 1.
Authoritative, modest, and readable treatment of a fashionable topic.

Wolpert, F. A., *Neue Harmonik. Die Lehre von den Akkordtypen (Kurz-Ausgabe)*, Regensburg, 1951.
After classifying all possible chords in his own way, Wolpert proceeds to an unusually good discussion (pp. 22–26) of the "principles and obstacles of chord-connection," and then swiftly to vaguer topics.

Wulf, Joseph, *Musik im dritten Reich: eine Dokumentation*, Gütersloh, 1963.
With minimum comment, Wulf presents a large collection of letters, newspaper clippings, and other documents to show how the Nazis affected music. The selection and organization of material is criticized by F. Prieberg in *Melos*, XXXI (1964), 126.

Yates, Peter, *An Amateur at the Keyboard*, New York, 1964.
Includes a chapter on 20th-century piano music, in the context of extraordinary devotion and critical thought ranging from the 16th century onward.

Index

- In alphabetization of titles, articles are disregarded.
- Readers checking the inter-relations of two composers should consult both, since these entries do not duplicate each other.
- Compositions with distinctive titles are listed both by title and under their composers; works with generic titles—i.e. symphonies and concertos—are indexed only under their composers. However, single references have been omitted under the composer when these merely duplicate the entry for the composer.
- For all references to a country, consult its principal city as well as the nation itself.
- Asterisks indicate the presence of music examples.